T0394586

BURIAL AND MEMORIAL IN LATE ANTIQUITY

BURIAL AND MEMORIAL IN LATE ANTIQUITY

VOL. 2: REGIONAL PERSPECTIVES

EDITED BY

ALEXANDRA DOLEA
LUKE LAVAN

BRILL

LEIDEN | BOSTON

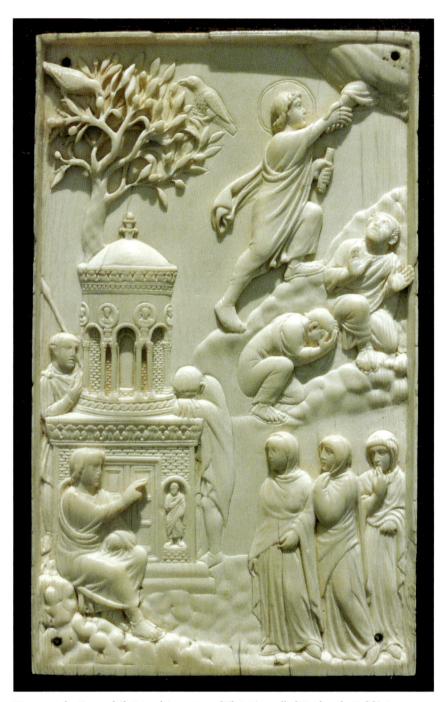

Women at the Grave of Christ and Ascension of Christ (so-called 'Reidersche Tafel'); Ivory; Milan or Rome, c. 400 AD.

Library of Congress Cataloging-in-Publication Data

Names: Lavan, Luke, editor.
Title: Burial and memorial in late antiquity set / managing editor, Luke
   Lavan.
Description: Leiden ; Boston : Brill, 2024. | Series: Late antique
   archaeology, 1570-6893 ; vol. 13 | Includes bibliographical references
   and index. | Contents: v. 1. Thematic perspectives—v. 2. Regional
   perspectives. | Summary: "Burial and Memorial explores funerary and
   commemorative archaeology, A.D. 284-650, across the late antique world,
   from Catalonia to Cappadocia. The first volume includes an overview of
   research, and papers exploring bioarchaeology, mortuary rituals,
   mausolea, and funerary landscapes. It considers the sacralisation of
   tombs, movements of relics, and the political significance of
   cemeteries. The fate of statue monuments is explored, as memorials for
   individuals. Authors also compare the spoliation or preservation of
   tombs to other buildings, and, finally, how the city itself, with its
   monuments, served as a place of collective memory, where meanings were
   long maintained. The second volume includes papers exploring all aspects
   of funerary archaeology, from scientific samples in graves, to grave
   goods and tomb robbing and a bibliographic essay. It brings into focus
   neglected regions not usually considered by funerary archaeologists in
   NW Europe, such as the Levant, where burial archaeology is rich in grave
   good, to Sicily and Sardinia, where post-mortem offerings and burial
   manipulations are well-attested. We also hear from excavations in
   Britain, from Canterbury and London, and see astonishing fruits from the
   application of science to graves recently excavated in Trier"—Provided
   by publisher.
Identifiers: LCCN 2023059384 (print) | LCCN 2023059385 (ebook) | ISBN
   9789004687950 (v. 1 ; cloth) | ISBN 9789004687967 (v. 2 ; hardback) |
   ISBN 9789004688162 (hardback) | ISBN 9789004687981 (v. 1 ; ebook) | ISBN
   9789004687974 (v. 2 ; ebook)
Subjects: LCSH: Funeral rites and ceremonies, Ancient. | Burial. |
   Excavations (Archaeology)
Classification: LCC GT3170 .B86 2024 (print) | LCC GT3170 (ebook) | DDC
   393/.930936—dc23/eng/20240202
LC record available at https://lccn.loc.gov/2023059384
LC ebook record available at https://lccn.loc.gov/2023059385

Typeface for the Latin, Greek, and Cyrillic scripts: "Brill". See and download: brill.com/brill-typeface.

ISSN 1570-6893
ISBN 978-90-04-68795-0 (hardback, volume 1)
ISBN 978-90-04-68796-7 (hardback, volume 2)
ISBN 978-90-04-68816-2 (hardback, set)
ISBN 978-90-04-68798-1 (e-book, volume 1)
ISBN 978-90-04-68797-4 (e-book, volume 2)
DOI 10.1163/9789004687974

Contents

Funerary Landscapes

Other Memorials: Statue Monuments

Tombs and Spolia in City Walls

Spolia and Civic Memory

Acknowledgements

The conference which inspired this volume met at Birkbeck College, London in November 2017 under the title "Fieldwork in Late Antique Archaeology: Burial and Funerary Practice". The conference was convened by Luke Lavan, Rebecca Darley, assisted by Michael Mulryan. It would not have been possible without the collaboration at Birkbeck provided by Rebecca Darley. Financial support came from the School of European Culture and Languages (University of Kent), the Virtual Centre for Late Antiquity, Birkbeck, and Museum Selection. Our thanks also go out to the many people with whom we have discussed different aspects of this project for their advice and encouragement, and to the referees who read the articles contained here and offered many helpful comments. Finally, we are grateful to Dirk Bakker and Marcella Mulder at Brill for their help in overseeing the submission and page-setting of this book. We must apologise to all involved in the book, for delays in the editing, which Peter Crawford did much to minimise, caused by COVID and changes in editing personnel. This has been a frustrating experience for our authors. However, we believe the quality of papers in the volume to be high and range to be good, for what is the first overview of burial in Late Antiquity to cover a wide range of regions across the Mediterranean. It is to be hoped that the book will not only serve specialists but also bring a rich area of archaeology to the attention of mainstream late antique historians, who might better appreciate phenomena such as the cult of relics from studying mid to late antique funerary practices more widely.

Luke Lavan

List of Contributors

Jens Amendt
Ph.D. (2003), and Associated Professor (2021), is a researcher and lecturer in Forensic and Medical Entomology at the University of Frankfurt/Main. He is (co)author of more than 100 scientific papers on forensic biology and entomology and co-editor of *Current Concepts of Forensic Entomology*.

Ádám Bollók
Ph.D. (2012), is a Senior Research Fellow of the Institute of Archaeology, Research Centre for the Humanities, Eötvös Loránd Research Network (Budapest). His main field of expertise includes the mortuary archaeology of the late antique Eastern Mediterranean and the Carpathian Basin.

Paul Booth
(BA FSA, MCIfA) is a former Senior Project Manager at Oxford Archaeology. He is currently working principally on the publication of excavations at Dorchester-on-Thames and has recently taken over as editor of *Britannia Monographs for the Society for the Promotion of Roman Studies*.

Valentina Caminneci
is archaeologist of the Archaeological and Landscape Park of the Valley of the Temples of Agrigento. Her scientific interests and research projects focus especially on ancient Akragas/Agrigentum: houses, agora, baths. She has also undertaken new investigations into the late antique necropolis, harbour, and viability. She has directed projects of landscape archeology on small settlements along the Western Sicilian coast and the exploitation of gypsum.

Martin Carver
is Professor Emeritus at the University of York. He is the author of *Formative Britain*, *The Sutton Hoo Story* and *Archaeological Investigation* and was PI of the ERC project Sicily in Transition.

Alexandra Chavarría Arnau
is Full Professor of Medieval Archaeology at the University of Padua (Italy) has developed research and published in different subjects related to the period between the end of the Roman World and the Late Middle Ages such as rural settlement, cemeteries and churches.

Lukas Clemens
is Professor of Medieval History at the University of Trier. Previously, he was curator at the Rheinisches Landesmuseum Trier and head of the City Archaeology Department. His research focuses on the afterlife of Roman remains in the Middle Ages and he leads two research projects on St. Maximin in Trier and a Medieval bishop's seat in Apulia.

Sam Cleymans
Ph.D. (1991), is Visiting Assistant Professor in Classical Archaeology at KU Leuven (Belgium) and works as Exhibition Development Officer at the Gallo-Roman Museum (Belgium). His research focuses mostly on the funerary practices in Hellenistic, Roman and Byzantine Sagalassos and Asia Minor.

Ciprian Crețu

Ph.D. (2021), is a Postdoctoral Fellow at the "1 Decembrie 1918" University in Alba Iulia, and Research Assistant at the Institute of Anthropology of the Romanian Academy in Bucharest. He is currently working on a project about the bioarchaeology of children in Late Roman and Early Byzantine Scythia.

Rainer Drewello

Ph.D. (1998), is Vice President of the Trimberg Research Academy of the University of Bamberg as Emeritus of Excellence. He was Professor of Restoration and Conservation Sciences at the University of Bamberg (2000–2021) and is (co-)author of approx. 60 publications and scientific papers with interest in microbial and anthropogenic changes of cultural-historical objects.

Ursula Drewello

is a biologist and managing director of the Labor Drewello & Weißmann GmbH in Bamberg. The focus of her scientific investigations is on material science issues in the fields of monument conservation, archaeology and museum conservation using methods such as light and electron microscopy, IR micro-spectroscopy, ionic chromatography, and thermogravimetric techniques.

Elizabeth Duffy

is an Instructor and PhD Candidate in Archaeology at Canterbury Christ Church University.

Adrian Gollop

is a Project Officer with Canterbury Archaeological Trust. He led the excavations at the former Hallet's Garage, Canterbury.

Carl Heron

is Director of Scientific Research at the British Museum. Prior to this, he was Professor of Archaeological Sciences at the University of Bradford with interests in molecular and isotopic investigation of archaeological materials.

Solinda Kamani

Ph.D. (2015), is an Honorary Research Associate at the University of Kent and author of *Neglected Architectural Decoration from the Late Antique City.*

Hiltrud Merten

Ph.D. (1983), is an archaeologist and historian specialising in the Roman and Late Roman to Early Medieval periods in the city of Trier. She has researched the cult of Mars in Gaul and worked on epitaphs and small finds in the Early Christian cathedral at Trier.

Elisabeth O'Connell

Ph.D. (2007), is Byzantine World Curator at the British Museum. Her most recent edited volumes are *Egypt and Empire: Religious Identity after Rome* and *The Hay Archive of Coptic Spells on Leather: A Multi-disciplinary Approach to the Materiality of Magical Practice* (both 2022).

Mauro Puddu

Ph.D. (2017), is a Marie Skłodowska-Curie Fellow at Ca' Foscari University of Venice working on the archaeology of identities and social relationships in the Roman Empire through the lens of postcolonial, feminist, and semiotic theories.

Nicole Reifarth

is Professor of Conservation Science and Textile Archaeology at the University of Applied Science in Cologne. Her research focuses on multidisciplinary investigations of textile traces in terms of taphonomic alterations and indications for ancient preparation techniques on textiles.

Victoria Ridgeway

(MLitt; FSA) is a Director and Head of Post-Excavation at Pre-Construct Archaeology. She is series editor and manages production of PCA's monograph series and other in-house publications.

Joseph F. Rife

is Associate Professor of Classical and Mediterranean Studies at Vanderbilt University. He is the author of *Isthmia IX: The Roman and Byzantine Graves and Human Remains.* He directs excavations at Kenchreai, Greece, and Caesarea Maritima, Israel.

Maria Serena Rizzo

is an archaeologist in the Archaeological and Landscape Park of the Valley of Temples of Agrigento. She is currently working on a research project related to late antique and Early Medieval urban landscape of Agrigento.

Kaja Stemberger Flegar

Ph.D. (2018) is an archaeologist specialising in Roman mortuary archaeology. She is currently employed in the private sector but has remained academically active since her Ph.D. studies at King's College London, regularly presenting her research on archaeological theory, small finds, and mortuary archaeology at conferences and in print.

Andrei D. Soficaru

Ph.D. (2009), is a Senior Researcher at the Institute of Anthropology of the Romanian Academy in Bucharest. With more than 20 years of expertise in the field of bioarchaeology, his latest research focuses on migration and mobility in the Lower Danube region during the Roman and Post-Roman periods.

Peter Talloen

Ph.D. (2003), is Visiting Professor of Practice at the University of Leuven (Belgium) and Assistant Professor of Archaeology at Bilkent University (Türkiye). He is director of the excavations at the ancient city of Sagalassos in Türkiye and author of *Cult in Pisidia.*

Wolf-Rüdiger Teegen

Ph.D. (1996), Habilitation (2006) is Professor of Archaeology and Anthropology at the University of Munich (LMU). He specialised in the palaeopathological study of human remains and is research associate in several projects, e.g., the German Pergamon excavation and the Trier-St. Maximin project.

Ina Vanden Berghe

is head of the Textile Research Laboratory at Royal Institute for Cultural Heritage in Brussels (KIK/IRPA). She specialised in the material-technical study of art and heritage textiles with chromatographic, spectroscopic, and microscopic techniques.

Sadie Watson

Ph.D. (2015), is a Research Fellow at MOLA. She has excavated and published extensively on Roman cemetery sites across the City of London.

Jake Weekes

is Research Officer for Canterbury Archaeological Trust. He is author of 'Cemeteries and funerary practice' in the *Oxford Handbook of Roman Britain,* and co-editor of *Death as Process: The Archaeology of the Roman Funeral.*

Julian Wiethold

is head of the Archaeobotanical Laboratory at the Institut National de Recherches Archéologiques Préventives (Inrap) in Metz. His research focuses are ancient agriculture, food and food processing, and the role of plants in funeral contexts.

Burial in Late Antiquity: a Bibliographic Essay
Part 1: Thematic and Regional Studies

Solinda Kamani and Luke Lavan

General Syntheses

So far, we lack a general archaeological synthesis on late antique burial. The foremost text available comes from the pen of Rebillard, a historian drawing extensively on epigraphy, whose belief in the development of Christian burial is not without controversy. There are, however, article-length treatments of the subject by a mixture of historians and archaeologists, with the latter perhaps preferring to synthesise the evidence rather than thematic topics. There are, nonetheless, syntheses and interpretative essays which focus on the West and, in one case, the East, which draw on excavated cemeteries, complemented now by a series of conference volumes, appearing during the editing of this book. These provide the kind of overview of late antique funerary practice that students and researchers have long lacked. To these can be added a series of earlier burial conferences focused on the early imperial period. However, the very rich nature of burial evidence and the professional frameworks of the archaeologists who produce it, often connected to civic and national professional archaeology, have perhaps hindered the emergence of literature examining burial practice across the late antique world, despite the clear presence of common trends.

General syntheses (Late Antique): Rebillard É. (2009) *The Care of the Dead in Late Antiquity* (Ithaca 2009); Rebillard É. (1999) "Les formes de l'assistance funéraire dans l'empire romain et leur évolution dans l'Antiquité tardive", *Antiquité Tardive* 7 (1999) 269–82; Bollok A. (2018) "Mortuary display, associated artefacts, and the resurrection of the body in early Christian thought: Some considerations for archaeologists", *Antaeus* 35–36 (2018) 245–70; Bond S. E. (2013) "Mortuary workers, the Church, and the funeral trade in Late Antiquity", *Journal of Late Antiquity* 6/1 (2013) 135–51; Maes N. (2006) "Caring for body and soul in the early Christian Mediterranean: eastern and western perspectives", *Byzantion* 76 (2006) 571–79; Brandenburg H. (1994) "Coemeterium. Der Wandel des Bestattungswesens als Zeichen des Kulturumbruchs der Spätantike", *Laverna* 5 (1994) 206–33; Duval Y. and Picard J.-Ch. (1986) *L'inhumation privilégiée du IVᵉ au VIIIᵉ siècle en Occident: actes du colloque tenu à Créteil les 16–18 mars 1984* (Paris 1986); Sodini J.-P. (1986) "Les 'tombes privilégiées' dans l'Orient chrétien (à la exception du diocèse d'Egypte)", in *L'Inhumation privilégiée du IVᵉ au VIIIᵉ siècle en Occident*, edd. Y. Duval and J.-C. Picard (Paris 1986) 233–43.

The West: Schrumpf S. (2006) *Bestattung und Bestattungswesen im Römischen Reich: Ablauf, soziale Dimension und ökonomische Bedeutung der Totenfürsorge im lateinischen Westen* (Göttingen 2006); Cooke N. (1998) *The Definition and Interpretation of Late Roman Burial Sites in the Western Empire* (PhD Thesis, University of London 1998); Cleary Esmonde S. (2013) "Breakdown and barbarians", in *The Roman West AD 200–500: An Archaeological Survey*, S. Esmonde Cleary (Cambridge 2013) 338–394; Harries J. (1992) "Death and the dead in the late Roman west", in *Death in Towns. Urban Responses to the Dying and the Dead, 100–1600*, ed. S. Bassett (Leicester 1992) 56–67.

The East: Fox S. C. and Tritsaroli P. (2019) "Burials and human remains of the Eastern Mediterranean in Early Christian context", in *The Oxford Handbook of Early Christian Archaeology*, edd. D. K. Pettegrew, W. R. Caraher and T. W. Davis (Oxford 2019) (2019; online edn, Oxford Academic, 8 Jan. 2019), https://doi.org/10.1093/oxfordhb/9780199369041.013.7, accessed 22 Oct. 2023; Samellas A. (2002) *Death in the Eastern Mediterranean (50–600 AD). The Christianization of the East: An Interpretation* (Tübingen 2002).

Collective volumes (Late Antique): Granier G., Boyer C. and Anstett E. (2023) edd. *Death and the Societies of Late Antiquity. Les sociétés de l'Antiquité tardive face à la mort: nouvelles méthodes, nouvelles questions* (Aix Marseille 2023); Ardeleanu S. and Cubas Diaz J. C. (2023) edd. *Funerary Landscapes of the Late Antique Oecumene: Contextualizing Epigraphic and Archaeological Evidence of Mortuary Practices: Proceedings of an International Conference in Heidelberg, May 30–June 1, 2019*, edd. S. Ardeleanu and J. C. Cubas Diaz (Heidelberg 2023). It is also worth mentioning the following volume as providing an overview, despite its stated concentration

© KONINKLIJKE BRILL BV, LEIDEN, 2024 | DOI:10.1163/9789004687974_002
Alexandra Dolea and Luke Lavan (eds) *Burial and Memorial in Late Antiquity* (Late Antique Archaeology 13) (Leiden 2024), pp. 539–563

on high-status burial: Vingo P., Marano Y. A. and Pinar Gil J. (2021) edd. *Sepolture di prestigio nel bacino mediterraneo (secoli IV–IX). Definizione, immagini, utilizzo 1. Saggi 2. Poster Atti del convegno, Pella (NO), 28–30 giugno 2017* (Turin 2021).

Collective volumes (Roman): Scheid J. and Rüpke J. (2010) edd. *Bestattungsrituale und Totenkult in der römischen Kaiserzeit* (Stuttgart 2010); Brink L. and Green D. (2008) edd. *Commemorating the Dead: Texts and Artefacts in Context. Studies of Roman, Jewish, and Christian Burials* (Berlin 2008); Beck L. (1995) ed. *Regional Approaches to Mortuary Analysis* (New York and London 1995); Reece R. (1977) ed. *Burial in the Roman World* (CBA Research Report 22) (London 1977).

Existing Bibliographies: Pearce J. (2020) *Death and Burial in the Roman Age* (Oxford Bibliographies Online) (Oxford 2020). http://10.1093/OBO/9780195389661-0356

Regional Syntheses

In contrast, we are particularly well-served with regional syntheses. This seems to be the greatest level of aspiration for most archaeological writers, who have first-hand experience of producing the data, allowing text-based historians to muscle in and write eye-catching general narratives, which is a pity. Britain is well-served, its Roman period burial archaeology being the most-intensively studied of any part of the Roman Empire, though with some syntheses seeing a unity in the subject across he first four centuries AD and a break in the 5th c., leading to two different, if not entirely separated burial traditions, one late antique, the other Germanic. Spain seems to have surprisingly few overviews, despite a rich literature on specialised topics. The same is true in Gaul with few scholars risking their pen to provide an overview of use to the non-specialist, although many write thematic regional works and rural burials are well-synthesised, as we will see later. Italy and Greece are bit better served. For all these regions funerary epigraphy forms a big part of the study of the dead, as it is in the East, and is presented in large-scale corpuses and monographs, as will be discussed later. Such evidence is dominant in Asia Minor, where the very rich funerary archaeology is somewhat neglected in excavation strategies.

Britain: *Late Roman*: Gerrard J. G. (2015) "Synthesis, chronology, and "Late Roman" cemeteries in Britain", *AJA* 119 (2015) 565–72; Rahtz P. A. (1977) "Late Roman cemeteries and beyond", in *Burial in the Roman World*, ed. R. Reece (York 1977) 53–64; Lorans E. (2016) "Funerary patterns in towns in France and England between the fourth and tenth centuries: a comparative approach", in *Making Christian Landscapes in Atlantic Europe: Conversion and Consolidation in the Early Middle Ages*, ed. T. ò Carragain (Newcastle 2016) 303–23. *Roman*: Moore A. (2016) "The life course", in *The Oxford Handbook of Roman Britain*, edd. M. Millett, L. Revell and A. Moore (Oxford 2016) 321–40; Pearce J. (2013) *Contextual Archaeology of Burial Practice. Case Studies from Roman Britain* (BAR Brit. Ser. 588) (Oxford 2013); Philpott R. (1991) *Burial Practices in Roman Britain. A Survey of Grave Treatment and Furnishing AD 43–410* (BAR Brit. Ser. 219) (Oxford 1991). *Post Roman*: Petts D. (2004) "Burial in western Britain AD 400–800: Late antique or Early Medieval?", in *Debating Late Antiquity in Britain AD 300–700* (BAR Brit Ser. 365), edd. R. Collins and J. Gerrard (Oxford 2004) 77–87; Sparey-Green C. (2003) "Where are the Christians? Late Roman cemeteries in Britain", in *The Cross goes North, Processes of Conversion in Northern Europe, AD 300–1300*, ed. M. Carver (York 2003) 93–107. *Anglo-Saxon*: Lucy S. (2000) *The Anglo-Saxon Way of Death* (Gloucester 2000), one essential work, amongst very many.

Hispania: Chavarría A. (2015) "Tumbas e iglesias en la Hispania Tardoantigua", *Arqueologia Medieval. Els Espais Sagrats* 7, edd. F. Sabaté i Curull and J. Brufal Sucarrat (2015) 13–45; Ripoll G. and Molist N. (2014) "Cura mortuorum en el nordeste de la Península Ibérica", *Territorio, Sociedad y Poder* 9 (2014) 5–66; Molist N. and Ripoll G. (2012) *Arqueologia funerària al nord-est peninsular (segles VI–XII)* (Barcelona 2012); Palol P. (1967) *Arqueología cristiana de la España Romana, siglos IV al VI* (Madrid-Valladolid 1967); Vaquerizo G. D. (2002) ed. *Espacios y usos funerarios en el occidente romano* (Córdoba 2002).

Gaul: *General*: Raynaud C. (2006) "Le monde des morts", *Gallia* 63 (2006) 137–70; Effros B. (2002) *Caring for Body and Soul: Burial and the Afterlife in the Merovingian World* (Pennsylvania 2002); van Andringa W. (2012) *Nécropoles et sociétés: cinq ensembles funéraires des provinces de Gaule (Ier–Ve siècle apr. J.-C.) Gallia* 69.1 (2012) 1–346. *Sub-regions*: Achard-Corompt N., Kasrpzyk M. and Fort B. (2016) edd. *L'Antiquité tardive dans l'est de la Gaule II. Sépultures, nécropoles et pratiques funéraires en Gaule de l'est. Actualité de la recherche, actes du colloque ATEG (Châlons-en-Champagne, 16–17 septembre 2010)* (RAE suppl. 41) (Dijon 2016). Merten H. (2010) "Reiche Bestattungen des frühen Mittelalters", in *Einblicke wahrnehmen*, ed. M. Groß-Morgen (Trier 2010) 72–3; Prien R. (2023) "Shifting burial rites – shifting identities? Late antique burial practices on the Rhine frontier", in *Funerary Landscapes of the Late Antique Oecumene: Contextualizing Epigraphic and Archaeological Evidence of Mortuary Practices: Proceedings of an International Conference in Heidelberg*, May 30–June 1, 2019, edd. S. Ardeleanu and J. C. Cubas Diaz (Heidelberg 2023) 459–82. Colardelle M. (1983) *Sépulture et traditions funéraires du Vᵉ au XIIIᵉ siècle ap. J.-C. dans les campagnes des Alpes françaises du nord* (Société alpine de documentation et de recherche en archéologie historique) (Grenoble 1983).

Italy: Chavarría Arnau A. (in this volume) "Funerary patterns in late Roman cities (3rd to 7th c.): Reviewing archaeological data in Northern Italy"; Barbiera I. (2012) *Memorie sepolte. Tombe e identità nell'alto medioevo (secoli V–VIII)* (Rome 2012); Brogiolo G. P. and Cantino Wataghin G. (1998) edd. *Sepolture tra IV e VIII secolo* (Documenti di Archeologia 13) (Mantua 1998); Cantino Wataghin G. and Lambert C. (1998) "Sepolture e città. L'Italia settentrionale tra IV e VIII secolo", in *Sepolture tra IV e VIII secolo*, edd. G. P. Brogiolo and G. Cantino Wataghin (Documenti di Archeologia 13) (Mantua 1998) 89–114. For two older works synthesising the Germanic evidence, see: AAVV *La civiltà dei Longobardi in Europa. Atti del Convegno Internazionale (Roma – Cividale del Friuli, 24–28 maggio 1971)* (Rome 1974); Bierbrauer V. (1975) *Die ostgotischen Grab- und Schatzfunde in Italien* (Biblioteca degli Studi medievali 7) (Spoleto 1975).

Pannonia: Migotti B., Kos M. S. and Radman-Livaja I. (2018) *Roman Funerary Monuments of South-Western Pannonia in their Material, Social, and Religious Context* (Oxford 2018). Mócsy A. (1962) "Pannonia", in *Paulys Realenzyklopädie der klassischen Altertumswissenschaft* (Suppl. IX), ed. G. Wissowa (Stuttgart 1962) cols. 515–775; Brunšmid J. (1895) "Arheološke bilješke iz Dalmacije i Panonije [Archaeological notes on Dalmatia and Pannonia]", *Vjesnik Hrvatskoga Arheološkog Društva* n.s. 1 (1895) 148–83; Lanyi V. (1972) "Die spätantiken Gräberfelder von Pannonien", *ActaArchHung* 24 (1972) 52–312.

Africa: Stone D. L. and Stirling L. (2007) *Mortuary Landscapes of North Africa* (London 2007); Trousset P. (1995) ed. *L'Afrique du nord antique et médiévale: Monuments funéraires: institutions autochtones: VIᵉ colloque international sur l'histoire et l'archéologie de l'Afrique du Nord* (Paris 1995); Duval N. (1995) "Les nécropoles chrétiennes d'Afrique du Nord", in *L'Afrique du nord antique et médiévale: Monuments funéraires: institutions autochtones: VIᵉ colloque international sur l'histoire et l'archéologie de l'Afrique du Nord*, ed. P. Trousset (Paris 1995) 187–206; Kleemann J. (2002) "Quelques réflexions sur l'interprétation ethnique des sépultures habillées considérées

comme vandales", *Antiquite Tardive* 10 (2002) 123–29; Gatto M. C., Mattingly D. J., Ray N. and Martin S. (2019) edd. *Burials, Migration and Identity in the Ancient Sahara and Beyond* (Cambridge 2019).

Thrace: Crețu C. and Soficaru A. D. (in this volume) "Death at the edge of empire: Burial practices in the province of Scythia (4th–7th c. AD)"; Soficaru A. D. and Sofaer J. (2021) "Regional patterns in mortuary practice in the Lower Danube region in the 4th–6th centuries", *Archäologisches Korrespondenzblatt* 51/2 (2021) 263–85.

Macedonia: Rife J. L. (in this volume) "Burial and society in the Greek world during Late Antiquity"; Rife J. L. (2012) *Isthmia Volume IX. The Roman and Byzantine Graves and Human Remains* (Princeton 2012); Laskaris N. (1996) "Παλαιοχριστιανικὰ καὶ Βυζαντινὰ ταφικὰ μνημεῖα τῆς Ἑλλάδος", *Byzantiaka* 16 (1996) 295–350; Laskaris N. (2000) *Monuments funéraires paléochrétiens (et byzantins) de Grèce* (Athens 2000); Marki E. (2002) "Τα χριστιανικά κοιμητήρια στην Ελλάδα. Οργάνωση, τυπολογία, ταφική ζωγραφική, μαρτύρια, κοιμητηριακές βασιλικές", *Deltion* (2002) 163–76. See also Flämig C. (2007) *Grabarchitektur der römischen Kaiserzeit in Griechenland* (Rahden 2007).

Asia: Brandt J. R., Hagelberg E., Bjørnstad G. and Ahrens S. (2017) edd. *Life & Death in Asia Minor in Hellenistic, Roman, and Byzantine times: Studies in Archaeology and Bioarchaeology* (Oxford 2017) 306–17; Cormack S. H. (2004) *The Space of Death in Roman Asia Minor* (Vienna 2004). See also extensive epigraphic corpora.

Oriens: Eger C. and Mackensen M. (2018) edd. *Death and Burial in the Near East from Roman to Islamic Times: Research in Syria, Lebanon, Jordan and Egypt* (Münchner Beiträge zur provinzialrömischen Archäologie 7) (Wiesbaden 2018); de Jong L. (2017) *The Archaeology of Death in Roman Syria. Burial, Commemoration, and Empire* (Cambridge 2017); Sartre-Fauriat A. (2001) *Des tombeaux et des morts. Monuments funéraires, société et culture en Syrie du Sud du Iᵉʳ s. av. J.-C. au VIIᵉ apr. J.-C.* (Bibliothèque Archéologique et Historique 158) (Beirut 2001); Hachlili R. (2005) *Jewish Funerary Customs, Practices and Rites in the Second Temple Period* (Leiden 2005); Gwiazda M. (2022) "Burial practices in early Byzantine Syro-Palestine (4th–7th centuries CE) – review article", *Polish Archaeology in the Mediterranean* 31/2 (2022) 285–331.

Egypt: O'Connell E. R. (in this volume) "The archaeology of death, burial and commemoration in late antique Egypt"; Denzey Lewis N. (2013) "Death on the Nile: Egyptian codices, gnosticism, and early Christian books of the dead", in *Practicing Gnosis. Ritual, Magic, Theurgy and Liturgy in Nag*

Hammadi, Manichaean and other Ancient Literature. Essays in Honor of Briger A. Pearson, edd. A. DeConick, G. Shae and J. D. Turner (Leiden 2013) 161–80; O'Connell E. R. (2018) "Egypt; dead, disposal of, Egypt", in *Oxford Dictionary of Late Antiquity*, ed. O. Nicholson (Oxford 2018). Selected papers in Buzi P., Camplani A. and Contardi F. (2016) edd. *Coptic Society, Literature and Religion from Late Antiquity to Modern Times. Proceedings of the Tenth International Congress of Coptic Studies, Rome, September 17th–22nd, 2012, and Plenary Reports of the Ninth International Congress of Coptic Studies, Cairo, September 15th–19th, 2008* (Orientalia Lovaniensia Analecta 247) (Leuven 2016); selected papers in Fluck C., Helmecke G. and O'Connell E. R (2015) edd. *Egypt: Faith after the Pharaohs* (London 2015).

Theory and Method

The number of theoretical texts produced about burial in late antiquity is not great. Few continental researchers are enamoured by the British-led theoretical turn and few theoretically-literate Brits have dug cemeteries in the heartlands of the late antique world. Therefore, there is space for a great deal more such writing, if one should be so inclined. There are some texts of general application that are worth mentioning, but their focus is mainly elsewhere, especially the Neolithic/Bronze Age or Anglo-Saxon periods in Britain, where funerary archaeology is particularly rich. Nonetheless, there are a few works that could be explicitly recognised as theoretical.

Theory: *General works*: Tarlow S. and Nilsson Stutz L. (2013) *Handbook on the Archaeology of Death and Burial* (Oxford 2013); Parker Pearson M. (1999) *The Archaeology of Death and Burial* (2003 ed.) (Stroud 1999); Rakita G., Buikstra J., Beck L. and Williams S. (2005) edd. *Interacting with the Dead: Perspectives on Mortuary Archaeology for the New Millenium* (Gainesville 2005); Davies J. (1999) *Death, Burial, and Rebirth in the Religions of Antiquity* (London and New York 1999). *Specific studies*: Härke H. (1993) "Intentionale und funktionale Daten. Ein Beitrag zur Theorie und Methodik der Gräberarchäologie", *Archäologisches Korrespondenzblatt* 23 (1993) 141–46; Clarke G. (1975) "Popular movements and late Roman cemeteries', *World Archaeology* 7/1 (1975) 46–56. http://www.jstor.org/stable/124108; Weekes J. (2002) "Acculturation and the

temporal features of ritual action", in *TRAC 2001: Proceedings of the Eleventh Annual Theoretical Roman Archaeology Conference, Glasgow 2001*, edd. M. Carruthers, C. van Driel-Murray, A. Gardner, J. Lucas, L. Revel and E. Swift (Oxford 2002) 73–82; Puddu M. (2019) "An archaeology of the subalterns' disaggregated history: interpreting burial manipulations of Roman-period Sardinia through Gramsci's Theory", *Theoretical Roman Archaeology Journal* 2 (2019). doi: https://doi.org/10.16995/traj.373.

Methodology: *General works*: Pearce J. and Weekes J. (2017) edd. *Death as a Process. The Archaeology of the Roman Funeral* (Oxford 2017); Pearce J. (2013) "Beyond the grave. Excavating the dead in the Late Roman provinces", in *Field Methods and Post Excavation Technique in Late Antique Archaeology* (Late Antique Archaeology 9) (Leiden-Boston 2013) 441–82; Duffy E., Gollop A. and Weekes J. (in this volume) "New cemetery evidence from late Roman Canterbury: the Former Hallet's Garage site in context"; Härke H. (1993) "Intentionale und funktionale Daten. Ein Beitrag zur Theorie und Methodik der Gräberarchäologie", *Archäologisches Korrespondenzblatt* 23 (1993) 141–46; Bonnet C. (2016) "Le céramologue au service des problématiques funéraires: approche d'une méthode globale", *SFECAG, Actes du Congrès d'Autun* (2016) 13–26. *Specific studies*: Hill D. J. A., Lieng Andreadakis L. T. and Ahrens S. (2016) "The north-east necropolis survey 2007–2011: methods, preliminary results and representivity", in *Hierapolis Di Frigia VIII (1): Le attivita delle campagne di scavo restauro 2007–2011*, edd. F. D'Andria, M. Pierra Caggia and T. Ismaelli (Istanbul 2016) 109–20; Poulou-Papadimitrio N., Tzavella E. and Ott J. (2012) "Burial practices in Byzantine Greece: Archaeological evidence and methodological problems for its interpretation", in *Rome, Constantinople and Newly-Converted Europe. Archaeological and Historical Evidence*, edd. M. Salamon, M. Wołoszyn, A. Musin, P. Špehar, M. Hardt, M. P. Kryk and A. Sulikowska-Gąska (Kraków 2012) 377–428; Jones R. F. J. (1977) "A quantitative approach to Roman burial", in *Burial in the Roman world* (CBA Res. Rep. 22), ed. R. Reece (London 1977) 20–5.

Textual Sources

It is regretful in some ways that the material record of burial is so rich. As deliberately buried assemblages, funerary contexts are perhaps the best-preserved in archaeology, and surface-level memorial contexts are now being recognised as full of meaningful artefacts that can be used to write the history of funerary practice. But despite this there are many aspects of burial ritual that would have held a great deal of meaning to participants, which are still not detected by archaeology. This makes a knowledge of pertinent late antique texts still critical to understanding the social and religious significance of what archaeologists find. Here follow a few key texts to which must be added dispersed references in hagiographic and other literature, accessible from articles listed later under funerary rituals.

Laws: *General*: MacCoull L. S. B. (2009) *Coptic Legal Documents: Law as Vernacular Text and Experience in Late Antique Egypt* (Medieval & Renaissance Texts & Studies 377) (Arizona Studies in the Middle Ages and the Renaissance 32) (Tempe 2009); Bérard R. M. (2021) "Le droit à la sépulture dans la Méditerranée antique : regards croisés", in *Il diritto alla sepoltura nel Mediterraneo antico*, ed. R. M. Bérard (Rome 2021) 1–15; Lafferty S. D. W. (2014) "*Ad sanctitatem mortuorum*: tomb raiders, body snatchers and relic hunters in late antiquity", *EME* 22.3 (2014) 249–79; Engels J. (1998) *Funerum sepulcrorumque magnificentia: Begräbnis- und Grabluxusgesetze in der griechisch-römischen Welt mit einigen Ausblicken auf Einschränkungen des funeralen und sepulkralen Luxus im Mittelalter und in der Neuzeit* (Hermes Einselschriften 78) (Stuttgart 1998); Emmanouelides N. E. (1989) *Τὸ δίκαιο τῆς ταφῆς στὸ Βυζάντιο* (Athens 1989); Robinson O. (1973) "The Roman law on burials and burial ground", *Irish Jurist* 10.1 (1973) 175–86; De Visscher F. (1963) *Le droit des tombeaux romains* (Milan 1963). *Specific*: Cod Theod 9.17 = T. Mommsen, Meyer P., *et al.* (1905) edd. *Theodosiani Libri XVI cum Constitutionibus Sirmondianis*, 2 vols. (Berlin 1905); Pharr C. transl. (1952) *The Theodosian Code and Novels: and the Sirmondian Constitutions* (Princeton 1952); Just. *Nov* 53 = Schoell R. and Kroll W. (1895) edd. *Justinian. Novellae* (Berlin 1895); Bloom E. transl. (2014) *Justinian's Novels* 2nd edn. http://www.uwyo.edu/lawlib/blume-justinian/ajc-edition -2/books/ (last accessed March 2014). http://www.uwyo.edu /lawlib/blume-justinian/ajc-edition-2/novels/index.html.

Liturgies: Schmidt A. (1994) *Kanon der Entschlafenen. Das Begräbnisrituale der Armenier. Der altarmenische Bastattungsritus für die Laien* (Orientalia Biblica et Christiana 5) (Wiesbaden 1994).

Rabbinic texts: Neusner J. (2000) "Death and afterlife in the later rabbinic sources: the two Talmuds and associated Midrash-compilations", in *Death, Life-After-Death,*

Resurrection and the World-to-Come in Judaisms of Antiquity, edd. A. J. Avery-Peck and J. Neusner (Leiden, Boston, Köln 2000).

Funerary Inscriptions by Region

The following catalogue, and subsequent thematic sections, running through into the next article, should be regarded as a series of initial pointers. They are compiled by two non-specialists, working mainly from the bibliography submitted for these volumes, with uneven support of regional specialists, provided more comprehensively for the East than for the West. This means there will be holes, especially given the intensity of work in NW Europe. Therefore, the following two bibliographies are to be considered as simply better than anything currently available, not much more. I thank Joseph Rife, Mariusz Gwiazda, Alexandra Chavarría, Hiltrud Merten, and Christopher Sparey-Green in particular for offering help, and Dirk Bakker at Brill for his patience. Gaps are perhaps visible for Asia Minor, where we had a contributor pull out, though the diocese of Pontus there are simply no sites excavated as far as we know. The reader should also be aware that my desire to fit the literature into the late antique diocesan organisation has not been entirely successful. The literature on burial is typically conceived by authors as a series of national archaeological practices, often with a sharp linguistic boundary. Thus, sometimes the regional organisation has had to make concessions to the frontiers of modern countries, whilst it is sometimes grouped by ancient regional names like 'Palestine' or 'Arabia' that do not actually equate with late antique provinces. This is far from ideal but does not prevent the lists being used.

General works: Carletti C. (2008) *Epigrafia dei cristiani in occidente dal III al VII secolo: ideologia e prassi* (Bari 2008b); Dresken-Weiland J., Angerstorfer A. and Merkt A. (2012) edd. *Himmel, Paradies, Schalom: Tod und Jenseits in christlichen und jüdischen Grabinschriften der Antike* (Regensburg 2012); Trout D. (2009) "Inscribing identity: The Latin epigraphic habit in Late Antiquity", in *A Companion to Late Antiquity*, ed. P. Rousseau (Chichester 2009) 170–86; Jalabert L. and Mouterde R. (1926) "Inscriptions grecques chrétiennes", *DACL* 7 (1926) columns 623–94.

Spain: Santiago Fernández J. (2011) "Memoria de la vida y publicidad de la muerte en la Hispania tardorromana y visigoda. Las inscripciones funerarias", in *IX Jornadas científicas sobre Documentación: La muerte y sus testimonios escritos* (Jornadas Científicas de Paleografía, Diplomática, Epigrafía y Numismática 11), edd. J. Galende Díaz and J. Santiago Fernández (Madrid 2011) 365–40.

Gaul: Handley M. (2003) *Death, Society and Culture: Inscriptions and Epitaphs in Gaul and Spain, AD 300–750* (Oxford 2003); Epp V. (2015) "Frühmittelalterliche Grabinschriften als 'Statussymbole'", in *Rank and Order: The Formation of Aristocratic Elites in Western and Central Europe, 500–1500* (Ostfildern 2015) 59–84; Osnabrügge J. (2023) "Transformation und Verschwinden. Inschriften in der Funerärkultur an Oberrhein und südlichem Mittelrhein in Spätantike und Frühmittelalter", in *Funerary Landscapes of the Late Antique Oecumene: Contextualizing Epigraphic and Archaeological Evidence of Mortuary Practices: Proceedings of an International Conference in Heidelberg, May 30–June 1, 2019*, edd. S. Ardeleanu and J. C. Cubas Diaz (Heidelberg 2023) 483–506; Uberti M. (2023) "Les épitaphes en leur milieu Remarques à partir du matériel épigraphique de l'Aquitaine tardo-antique et alto-médiévale", in *Funerary Landscapes of the Late Antique Oecumene: Contextualizing Epigraphic and Archaeological Evidence of Mortuary Practices: Proceedings of an International Conference in Heidelberg, May 30–June 1, 2019*, edd. S. Ardeleanu and J. C. Cubas Diaz (Heidelberg 2023) 529–64; Descombes F. (1985) *Recueil des inscriptions chrétiennes de la Gaule antérieures à la Renaissance carolingienne XV: Viennoise du Nord* (Paris 1985).

Italy: Mainardis F. (2023) "Luoghi, monumenti, epigraphic habit. Note sulle necropoli tardoantiche della parte orientale della Venetia et Histria", in *Funerary Landscapes of the Late Antique Oecumene: Contextualizing Epigraphic and Archaeological Evidence of Mortuary Practices: Proceedings of an International Conference in Heidelberg, May 30–June 1, 2019*, edd. S. Ardeleanu and J. C. Cubas Diaz (Heidelberg 2023) 429–58; Nuzzo D. (2023) "Le iscrizioni sepolcrali della provincia Apulia et Calabria in età tardoantica (IV–VII s. d. C.)", in *Funerary Landscapes of the Late Antique Oecumene: Contextualizing Epigraphic and Archaeological Evidence of Mortuary Practices: Proceedings of an International Conference in Heidelberg, May 30–June 1, 2019*, edd. S. Ardeleanu and J. C. Cubas Diaz (Heidelberg 2023) 365–82; Corda A. M. (1999) *Le iscrizioni cristiane della Sardegna anteriori al VII secolo* (Vatican City 1999).

Africa: Ardeleanu S. (2023) "Materializing death in late antique North Africa. Epitaphs, burial types and rituals in changing funerary landscapes", in *Funerary Landscapes of the Late Antique Oecumene: Contextualizing Epigraphic and Archaeological Evidence of Mortuary Practices: Proceedings of an International Conference in Heidelberg, May 30–June 1, 2019*, edd. S. Ardeleanu and J. C. Cubas Diaz (Heidelberg 2023) 107–57.

Macedonia: Feissel D. (1983) *Recueil des inscriptions chrétiennes de Macédoine du IIIe et VIe siècle* (BCH suppl. 8) (Paris 1983); Sironen E. (1997) *The Late Roman and Early Byzantine Inscriptions of Athens and Attica: An Edition with Appendices on Scripts, Sepulchral Formulae, and Occupations* (Helsinki 1997); Bayet C. (1878) *De tituli atticae Christianis antiquissimis* (Paris 1878); Sironen E. (2018) "Early Christian inscriptions from the Corinthian and the Peloponnese," in *Authority and Identity in the Christianities of Asia Minor and Greece*, edd. C. Breytenbach and J. Ogereau (Ancient Judaism and Early Christianity 103) (Leiden and Boston 2018) 201–16; Bees N. ([1941] 1978) ed. *Inscriptiones graecae Christianae veteres et byzantinae 1: Peloponnesus, Isthmos, Korinthos* (Athens 1941; Chicago repr. 1978); Guarducci M. (1978) *Epigrafia greca 4: Epigrafi sacre pagane e cristiane* (Rome 1978); Bandy A. (1970) *The Greek Christian Inscriptions from Crete* (Athens 1970).

Asia: Destephen S. (2023) "The funerary epigraphic landscape of late antique Asia Minor", in *Funerary Landscapes of the Late Antique Oecumene: Contextualizing Epigraphic and Archaeological Evidence of Mortuary Practices: Proceedings of an International Conference in Heidelberg, May 30–June 1, 2019*, edd. S. Ardeleanu and J. C. Cubas Diaz (Heidelberg 2023) 233–48; Mitchell S. (2017) "The Christian epigraphy of Asia Minor in Late Antiquity", in *The Epigraphic Cultures of Late Antiquity*, edd. K. Bolle, C. Machado and Ch. Witschel (HABES 60) (Stuttgart 2017) 271–86.

Oriens: Gatier P.-L. (2023) "L'épigraphie et les pratiques funéraires dans la province protobyzantine d'Arabie (IVe–VIIe s. apr. J.-C.)", in *Funerary Landscapes of the Late Antique Oecumene: Contextualizing Epigraphic and Archaeological Evidence of Mortuary Practices: Proceedings of an International Conference in Heidelberg, May 30–June 1, 2019*, edd. S. Ardeleanu and J. C. Cubas Diaz (Heidelberg 2023) 199–232; Ameling W., Cotton H. M., Eck W., Isaac B., Kushnir-Stein A., Misgav H., Price J. and Yardeni A. (2014) *Corpus Inscriptionum Iudaeae/Palaestinae. A multi-lingual corpus of the inscriptions from Alexander to Muhammad* (Berlin and Boston 2014).

Egypt: Nauerth C. (2023) "Traditionelle Elemente in der christlichen Grabkultur Ägyptens", in *Funerary Landscapes of the Late Antique Oecumene: Contextualizing Epigraphic and Archaeological Evidence of Mortuary Practices: Proceedings of an International Conference in Heidelberg, May 30–June 1, 2019*, edd. S. Ardeleanu and J. C. Cubas Diaz (Heidelberg 2023), 159–76; Tudor B. (2011) *Christian Funerary Stelae of the Byzantine and Arab Periods from Egypt* (Marburg 2011).

Funerary Inscriptions, by Site

Gaul: *Arles*: Heijmans M. (2000) "Épigraphie païenne ou épigraphie chrétienne, ILN ou RICG? Réflexions à propos des inscriptions d'Arles", *Revue archéologique de Narbonnaise* 33.1 (2000) 87–95. *Trier*: 1. Overviews: Merten H. (2015) "Frühchristliche Grabinschriften in Trier. Stand der Bearbeitung", in *Frühchristliche Grabinschriften im Westen des Römischen Reiches. Beiträge zur Internationalen Konferenz "Frühchristliche Grabinschriften im Westen des Römischen Reiches", Trier, 13.–15. Juni 2013*, edd. L. Clemens, H. Merten and C. Schäfer (Interdiziplinärer Dialog zwischen Archäologie und Geschichte 3) (Trier 2015) 29–36; Merten H. (2011) "Christliche Epigraphik und Archäologie in Trier seit ihren Anfängen", *RömQSchr* 106 (2011) 5–26; Krämer K. (1974) *Die frühchristlichen Grabinschriften Triers* (Trierer Grabungen und Forschungen 8) (Mainz 1974); Gose E. (1958) *Katalog der frühchristlichen Inschriften in Trier* (Trierer Grabungen und Forschungen 3) (Berlin 1958). 2. St Matthias: Newel N. (1995) "Die Cyrillus-Inschrift von St. Matthias in Trier (Gauthier, RICG I 19). Neue Quellen zu ihrer Überlieferungsgeschichte, Auswertung ihres Formulars", *TrZ* 58 (1995) 211–265. 3. St Maximin: Merten H. (2018) "Die frühchristlichen Grabinschriften aus St. Maximin in Trier", in *Die Abtei Trier-St. Maximin von der späten Antike bis zur frühen Neuzeit*, edd. M. Embach and B. Simon (Quellen und Abhandlungen zur mittelrheinischen Kirchengeschichte 142) (Mainz 2018) 101–8; Merten H. (2023) "Christliche Bestattungskultur in Spätantike und Frühmittelalter am Beispiel von St. Maximin in Trier", in *Funerary Landscapes of the Late Antique Oecumene: Contextualizing Epigraphic and Archaeological Evidence of Mortuary Practices: Proceedings of an International Conference in Heidelberg, May 30–June 1, 2019*, edd. S. Ardeleanu and J. C. Cubas Diaz (Heidelberg 2023) 507–28; Neyses A. (1999) "Lage und Gestaltung von Grabinschriften im Spätantiken Coemeterial-Grossbau von St. Maximin in Trier", *Jahrbuch des Römische-Germanischen Zentralmuseums Mainz* 46 (Mainz 1999) 413–46. 4. Other: Schwinden L. (1999) "Zur Herkunft des Formulars der frühchristlichen Inschriften von Trier. Neue Sarkophage als missing links", in *Atti, Congresso internazionale di epigrafia greca e latina* 11, *Roma, 18–24 settembre 1997*,

2 (Rome 1999) 729–38; Schwinden L. (1984) "Grabinschrift für Hariulf" in *Trier – Kaiserresidenz und Bischofssitz. Ausstellungskatalog, Rheinisches Landesmuseum Trier* (Mainz 1984) 349–50 cat. 186. *Elsewhere*: Matijević K. (2015) "Frühchristliche Grabinschriften von der Untermosel: Kobern-Gondorf und Umgebung", in *Frühchristliche Grabinschriften im Westen des Römischen Reiches. Beiträge zur Internationalen Konferenz "Frühchristliche Grabinschriften im Westen des Römischen Reiches", Trier, 13.–15. Juni 2013*, edd. L. Clemens, H. Merten and C. Schäfer (Interdiziplinärer Dialog zwischen Archäologie und Geschichte 3) (Trier 2015) 125–35.

Italy: *Canosa*: De Santis P. and Polito V. (2020) "Tituli picti. Testimonianze epigrafiche dipinte dal complesso cimiteriale di Lamapopoli a Canosa di Puglia alla luce di recenti acquisizioni (ipogei F e G)", *Vetera Christianorum* 57 (2020) 107–29. *Karales*: Floris P. (2005) *Le iscrizioni funerarie pagane di Karales* (Bari 2005).

Rome: Felle A. E. (2023) "Paesaggi epigrafici nelle necropoli della Roma tardoantica. Alcuni casi esemplari per una 'epigrafia archeologica'", in *Funerary Landscapes of the Late Antique Oecumene: Contextualizing Epigraphic and Archaeological Evidence of Mortuary Practices: Proceedings of an International Conference in Heidelberg, May 30–June 1, 2019*, edd. S. Ardeleanu and J. C. Cubas Diaz (Heidelberg 2023) 407–28; Felle A. E. (2012) "Alle origini del fenomeno devozionale cristiano in Occidente. Le inscriptiones parietariae ad memoriam Apostolorum", in *Martiri, santi, patroni: per una archeologia della devozione. Atti X Congresso Nazionale di Archeologia Cristiana*, edd. A. Coscarella and P. De Santis (Arcavacata di Rende (Cs) 2012) 477–502. Guyon J. (1974) "La vente des tombes à travers l'épigraphie de la Rome chrétienne (IIIe, VIIe siècles): le rôle des fossores, mansionarii, praepositi et prêtres", *MEFRA* 86/1 (1974) 549–96.

Pannonia: *Salona*: Gauthier N. (2015) "Les inscriptions funéraires tardo-antiques de Salone", in *Frühchristliche Grabinschriften im Westen des Römischen Reiches: Beiträge zur Internationalen Konferenz "Frühchristliche Grabinschriften im Westen des Römischen Reiches", Trier, 13.–15. Juni 2013*, edd. L. Clemens, H. Merten and C. Schäfer (Trier 2015) 209–16; Gauthier N., Marin E. and Prévot D. (2010) edd. *Salona IV: inscriptions de Salone chrétienne, IVe–VIIe siècles* (Rome-Split 2010).

Africa: *Tipasa*: Ardeleanu S. (2018) "Directing the faithful, structuring the sacred space: funerary epigraphy in its archaeological context in late-antique Tipasa", *JRA* 31 (2018) 475–500.

Macedonia: *Corinth*; Sironen E. (1999) "Formulae in early Christian epitaphs of Corinthia", in *XI Congresso Internazionale di*

Epigrafia Greca e Latina. Roma, 18–24 settembre 1997: Preatti (Rome 1999) 741–45; Sironen E. (2008) ed. *Inscriptiones graecae II/III2: Inscriptiones Atticae aetatis quae est inter Herulorum incursionem et Imp. Mauricii tempora* (Berlin 2008); Creaghan J. and Raubitschek A. (1947) "Early Christian epitaphs from Athens", *Hesperia* 16 (1947) 1–54; Kent J. (1966) *Corinth VIII.3: The Inscriptions 1926–1950* (Princeton 1966); Pallas D. and Dandis S. (1979) "Ἐπιγραφὲς ἀπὸ τὴν Κορίνθο", *ArchEph* 1977 (1979) 61–83; Rife J. (2022) "Inscriptions", *in On the Edge of a Roman Port: The Excavations at Koutsongila, Kenchreai, 2007–2014*, edd. E. Korka and J. Rife (Hesperia suppl. 52) (Princeton 2022) 1195–1214; Robert L. (1960) "Épitaphes et acclamations byzantines à Corinthe", *Hellenica* 11/12 (Paris 1960) 21–52; Sironen E. (2016) ed. *Inscriptiones graecae IV 3: Inscriptiones Corinthiae saeculorum IV, V, VI* (Berlin 2016); Sironen E. (2018) "Early Christian inscriptions from the Corinthian and the Peloponnese," in *Authority and Identity in the Christianities of Asia Minor and Greece*, edd. C. Breytenbach and J. Ogereau (Ancient Judaism and Early Christianity 103) (Leiden and Boston 2018) 201–16; Walbank M. E. H. and Walbank M. (2006) "The Grave of Maria, wife of Euplous: A Christian epitaph reconsidered", *Hesperia* 75 (2006) 267–88.

<u>Oriens</u>: <u>*el-Huweinat*</u>: Dahari U. and Di Segni L. (2009) "More early Christian inscribed tombstones from el-Huweinat in northern Sinai", in *Man Near a Roman Arch. Studies Presented to Prof. Yoram Tsafrir*, edd. L. Di Segni, Y. Hirschfeld, J. Patrich and R. Talgam (Jerusalem 2009) 125–41. <u>*Feinan*</u>: Knauf E. A. (1986) "Three new tombstones from Feinan", *Newsletter of the Institute of Archaeology and Anthropology* (Yarmouk University 2) (1986) 16–17. <u>*Khirbet es-Samra*</u>: Bader N. *et al.* (2017) "New Greek inscriptions from Ḥirbet es-Samrā cemetery in north Jordan", *ZDMG* 133 (2017) 176–85; Desreumaux A. (1998) "Les inscriptions funéraires araméennes de Samra", in *Khirbet es-Samra en Jordanie 1: La voie romaine, le cimitière, les documents épigraphiques*, edd. J.-B. Humbert and A. Desreumaux (Bibliothèque de l'Antiquité Tardive 1) (Turnhout 1998) 435–509; Desreumaux A. and Couson D. (1998) "Catalogue des stèles funéraires", in *Khirbet es-Samra en Jordanie 1: La voie romaine, le cimitière, les documents épigraphiques*, edd. J.-B. Humbert and A. Desreumaux (Bibliothèque de l'Antiquité Tardive 1) (Turnhout 1998) 281–316; Gatier P.-L. (1998) "Les inscriptions grecques et latines de Samra et de Rihab", in *Khirbet es-Samra en Jordanie 1: La voie romaine, le cimitière, les documents épigraphiques*, edd. J.-B. Humbert and A. Desreumaux (Bibliothèque de l'Antiquité Tardive 1) (Turnhout 1998) 359–431; Nabulsi A. and Macdonald M. C. A. (2014) "Epigraphic diversity in the cemetery at Khirbet es-Samrā', Jordan", *PEQ* 146 (2014) 149–61. <u>*Korykos*</u>: F. R. "Korykos in Cilicia Trachis. The economy of a small coastal city in late antiquity, saec. V–VI. A précis," *Ancient History Bulletin* (1987) 16–23. <u>*Zoora*</u>: Meimaris Y. and Kritikakou-Nikolaropoulou K. I. (2005) *Inscriptions from Palaestina Tertia vol. 1a. The Greek inscriptions from Ghor es-Safi (Byzantine Zoora)* (Athens 2005).

<u>Egypt</u>: van der Vliet J. (2020) "Coptic epitaphs from Abydos", *Journal of Coptic Studies* 22 (2020) 205–28; Grenier J. C. (1983) "La stèle funéraire du dernier taureau Bouchis (Caire JE 31901=Stèle Bucheum 20): Ermant – 4 novembre 340", *Bulletin de l'Institut Français d'Archéologie Orientale* 83 (1983) 197–208; Krastel L. (2017) "Die koptischen Stelen des Deir Anba Hadra im Koptischen Museum: Die Arbeiten des Jahres 2017", iDAI.publications (2017) 35–38 (https://www.topoi.org/project/b-4-6-1/ [accessed 08/09/2018]).

Mortuary Space

<u>General studies</u>: Fiocchi Nicolai V. (2003) "Elementi di trasformazione dello spazio funerario tra tarda antichità e altomedioevo", in *Uomo e spazio nell'alto medioevo. Settimane di Studio del Centro Italiano di Studi sull'Alto Medioevo (Spoleto, 4–8 aprile 2002)* (Spoleto 2003) 921–69; Fiocchi Nicolai V. (2006) "Gli spazi delle sepolture cristiane tra il III e il V secolo: Genesi edinamica di una scelta insediativa", in *La comunità cristiana de Roma: La sua vita e la sua cultura dalle origini all'alto medioevo*, edd. L. Pani Ermini and P. Siniscalco (Vatican City 2006) 341–69; Rebillard É. (1993) "Koimetérion et Coemeterium: tombe, tombe sainte, nécropole", *MEFRA* 105.2 (1993) 975–1001. See also Ewald B. C. (2015) "Funerary monuments", in *The Oxford Handbook of Roman Sculpture*. edd. E. A. Friedland and M. G. Sobocinski (Oxford 2015) 390–406.

<u>Cemetery location</u>: <u>*Rural Sites*</u>: Smith A., Allen M., Brindle T., Fulford M., Lodwick L. and Rohnbognor A. (2018) *Life and Death in the Countryside of Roman Britain* (London 2018). <u>*Villas*</u>: Dodd J. (2021) "Transitional burials in late antique villas in the North-Western Provinces: Assessing distributions and characteristics", *European Journal of Archaeology* 24.1 (2021) 68–88; Graen D. (2008) *Sepultus in villa – die Grabbauten römischer Villenbesitzer. Studien zu Ursprung und Entwicklung von den Anfängen bis zum Ende des 4. Jahrhunderts nach Christus* (Schriftenreihe Antiquitates 46) (Hamburg 2008). <u>*Cities*</u>: Cantino Wataghin G. (1999) "The ideology of urban burials", in *The Idea and Ideal of the Town between Late Antiquity and the*

Early Middle Ages, edd. G. P. Brogiolo and B. Ward-Perkins (The Transformation of the Roman World 4) (Leiden 1999) 147–80; Henry O. (2013) ed. *2ᵉᵐᵉˢ Rencontres d'archéologie de l'ɪꜰᴇᴀ: Le Mort dans la ville. Pratiques, contextes et impacts des inhumations intra-muros en Anatolie, du début de l'Age du Bronze à l'époque romaine, Nov 2011, Istanbul, Turkey* (Istanbul 2013);

Cemetery design: *Tomb Orientation*: Rahtz Ph. (1978) "Grave orientation", *The Archaeological Journal* 135.1 (1978) 1–14; López A. (1999) "Orientaciones de tumbas y sol naciente. Astronomía cultural en la Antigüedad Tardía", in *XXIV Congreso Nacional de Arqueología (Cartagena, 1997)* (Murcia 1999) 593–610. *Mass Graves*: McCormick M. (2015) "Tracking mass death during the fall of Rome's empire (I)", *JRA* 28 (2015) 325–57; McCormick M. (2016) "Tracking mass death during the fall of Rome's empire (II): a first inventory of mass graves", *JRA* 29 (2016) 1004–1046. *Ad Sanctos Burial*: Eastman D. L. (2019) "Martyria", in *The Oxford Handbook of Early Christian Archaeology*, edd. D. K. Pettegrew, W. R. Caraher and T. W. Davis (Oxford 2019) (2019; online edn, Oxford Academic, 8 Jan. 2019), https://doi.org/10.1093/oxfordhb/9780199369041.013.6, accessed 22 Oct. 2023; Rizos E. (in this volume) "Burying the saints next to the common dead: the burial habits of the Christian elite in the 4th c. and the first translations of relics"; Wiśniewski R. (2019) *The Beginnings of the Cult of Relics* (Oxford 2019); Yasin A-M. (2009) *Saints and Church Spaces in the Late Antique Mediterranean: Architecture, Cult, and Community* (Cambridge 2009); Duval Y. (1988) *Auprès des saints corps et âme: l'inhumation "ad sanctos" dans la chrétienté d'Orient et d'Occident du IIIᵉ au VIIᵉ siècle* (Paris 1988). This bibliography does not treat the post-funerary cult of relics except for the location of burials *ad sanctos*.

Stelae: See above for funerary epigraphy.

Burial Caves: Kogan-Zehavi E. (2006) "A burial cave of the Byzantine period in the Naḥalat Aḥim Quarter, Jerusalem", *'Atiqot* 54 (2006) 61*–86*, 160–161 (Hebrew with English summary); Stern E. J. (1997) "Burial caves at Kisra", *'Atiqot* 33 (1997) 103–135, 17 (in Hebrew, with English summary); Sellers O. R. and Baramki D. C. (1953) "A Roman-Byzantine burial cave in Northern Palestine", *BASOR* (Supplementary Studies 15/16) (1953) 1–55; Rudin T. *et al.* (2018) "Two burial caves at Kefar Shemaryahu: More on Samaritan and Christian interactions in the Byzantine-period Central Coastal Plain", *Liber Annuus* 68 (2018) 269–302.

Hypogea/Rock-cut burials: *Italy (Sardinia)*: Serra P. B. (2007) "Documenti di età altomedievale: la tomba a camera in muratura voltata a botte in località San Costantino", in *Villa dei Greci. Una Villagreca inedita fra storia, archeologia e arte*, edd. N. Rossi and S. Meloni (Dolianova 2007) 65–73; Serra P. B. (1990) "Tombe a camera in muratura con volta a botte nei cimiteri altomedievali della Sardegna", *in Le sepolture in Sardegna dal IV al VII secolo, IV Convegno sull'archeologia tardoromana e medievale* (Oristano 1990) 133–60. *Oriens*: Krug H. P. (1998) "Comparative Roman-Byzantine tombs in Transjordan", in *The Necropolis of Hesban: A Typology of Tombs*, ed. D. Waterhouse (Hesban 10) (Michigan 1998) 133–71; Huster Y. and Sion O. (2006) "Late Roman and byzantine vaulted tombs in the southern coastal plain", *Jerusalem and Eretz Israel* 3 (2006) 49–67 (in Hebrew); Johnson K. L. (2004) "Sa'ad tomb types", in *Sa'ad: A Late Roman/Byzantine Site in Northern Jordan*, edd. J. C. Rose and D. L. Burke (Irbid 2004) 109–11; Makhouly N. (1939) "Rock-cut tombs at el Jīsh", *QDAP* 8 (1939) 45–50; Richmond E. T. (1932) "A rock-cut tomb at Nazareth", *QDAP* 1 (1932) 53–4; Iliffe J. H. (1934) "Rock-cut tomb at Tarshīḥā", *QDAP* 3 (1934) 9–16.

Catacombs: *Syntheses*: Fiocchi Nicolai V. (2019) "The catacombs", in *The Oxford Handbook of Early Christian Archaeology*, edd. W. R. Caraher, T. W. Davis and D. K Pettegrew (New York 2019) 67–88; Pergola P. (1997) *Le catacombe Romane. Storia e topografia* (Rome 1997); Pergola P. (1998) ed. *Le catacombe Romane: storia e topografia* (Rome 1998); Fiocchi Nicolai V. (2014) "Le catacombe Romane", in *Lezioni di archeologia cristiana*, edd. F. Bisconti and O. Brandt (Vatican 2014) 273–360. *Thematic Studies*: Rutgers L. V. (2009) "Neue Recherchen in den jüdischen und frühchristlichen Katakomben Roms: Methode, Deutungsprobleme und historische Implikationen einer Datierung mittels Radiokarbon", *Mitteilungen zur Christlichen Archäologie* 15 (2009) 9–24; Fiocchi Nicolai V. (2018) "Padre Umberto M. Fasola studioso degli antichi cimiteri cristiani. A proposito delle origini delle catacombe e dei loro caratteri identitari", *Rivista di Archeologia Cristiana* 94 (2018) 99–137; Bisconti F. (2017) *Le catacombe per i bambini* (Todi 2017). *Sites, Rome*: Fasola U. M. (1980) "Indagini nel sopratterra della catacomba di S. Callisto", *RACrist* 56 (1980) 221–78; Guyon J. (1987) *Le cimetière aux deux lauriers: recherches sur les catacombes romaines* (Rome 1987); Martorelli R. (2011) "Le catacombe di Sant'Antioco", in *S. Antioco da primo evangelizzatore di Sulci a glorioso Protomartire "Patrono della Sardegna*, edd. R. Lai and M. Massa (Sant'Antioco 2011) 59–76; Rossi D. and Di Mento M. (2013) edd. *La catacomba ebraica di Monteverde: vecchi dati e nuove scoperte* (Rome 2013); Dunn G. D. (2015) "Life in the cemetery: Boniface I and the catacomb of Maximus", *Augustinianum* 55.1 (2015) 137–57; Zimmermann N. (2023) "Die

römischen Katakomben Überlegungen zu Besitzverhältnissen, zur räumlichen Nutzung und zur Grabtypologie anhand
der Katakomben Domitilla, ss. Marcellinoe Pietro und Randanin", in *Funerary Landscapes of the Late Antique Oecumene:
Contextualizing Epigraphic and Archaeological Evidence of
Mortuary Practices: Proceedings of an International Conference in Heidelberg, May 30–June 1, 2019*, edd. S. Ardeleanu
and J. C. Cubas Diaz (Heidelberg 2023) 383–406. *Sites, Malta*:
Buhagiar M. (1986) *Later Roman and Byzantine Catacombs
and Related Burial Places in the Maltese Islands* (Oxford 1986);
Buhagiar M. (2007) *The Christianisation of Malta – Catacombs,
Cult Centres and Churches in Malta to 1530* (Oxford 2007).
Sites, Melos: Lampakis G. (1907) "Περὶ τῶν ἐν Μήλῳ χριστιανικῶν κατακομβῶν, τοῦ ἐν αὐτῇ βαπτιστηρίου καὶ ἑτέρων χριστιανικῶν ἀρχαιοτήτων", *Deltion tes Christianikes Archaiologikes
Hetaireias* 1.7 (1907) 29–37; Soteriou G. (1928) "Ἡ χριστιανικὴ
κατακόμβη τῆς νήσου Μήλου", *PraktAktAth* (1928) 33–46.

Mausolea/Funerary Buildings: *General*: *Hortus Artium Medievalium* 18.2 (2012) (Mausolées & Églises, IVᵉ–VIIIᵉ siècle); von
Hesberg H. (1992) *Römische Grabbauten* (Darmstadt 1992).
Imperial mausolea: Coarelli F. (2016) "Mausolei imperiali tardoantichi: le origini di un tipo architettonico", in *Costantino
e i costantinidi – l'innovazione costantiniana, le sue radici e i
suoi sviluppi: Acta XVI Congressus Internationalis Archaeologiae Christianae, Romae (22–28.9.2013)*, edd. O. Brandt, G. Castiglia and V. Fiocchi Nicolai (Vatican 2016) 493–508; Johnson
M. J. (2009) *The Roman Imperial Mausoleum in Late Antiquity*
(Cambridge 2009); Johnson M. J. (1991) "On the burial places
of the Theodosian dynasty", *Byzantion* 61.2 (1991) 330–39.
Imperial mausolea, examples: Rasch J. J. (1993) *Das Mausoleum
bei Tor de' Schiavi in Rom* (Mainz 1993); Rasch J. J. (1984) *Das
Maxentius-Mausoleum an der Via Appia in Rom* (Mainz 1984);
Rasch J. J. and Arbeiter A. (2007) *Das Mausoleum der Constan-
tina in Rom* (Mainz 2007); Oosten D. (2016) "The mausoleum
of Helena and the adjoining basilica Ad Duas Lauros: con-
struction, evolution and reception", in *Monuments & Memory
Christian Cult Buildings and Constructions of the Past. Essays in
Honour of Sible de Blaauw*, edd. M. Verhoeven, L. Bosman and
H. van Asperen (Turnhout 2016) 131–43; Vendittelli L. (2011) *Il
mausoleo di Sant'Elena. Gli scavi* (Milan 2011); Rasch J. J. (1998)
*Das Mausoleum der Kaiserin Helena in Rom und der "Tempio
della Tosse" in Tivoli* (Mainz 1998); Deliyannis D. M. (2010)
"The Mausoleum of Theoderic and the seven wonders of the
world", *Journal of Late Antiquity* 3 (2010) 365–85.

Mausolea, Regional Syntheses: Celdrán J. M. N. and Javier
Arce J. (in this volume) "Late Roman "mausolea" in Hispania";
Sparey-Green C. (in this volume) "Mausolea in North-West
Europe: The transition from the Roman to late antique periods"; Chavarría A. (2007) "Splendida sepulcra ut posteri
audiant. Aristocrazie, mausolei e chiese funerarie nelle campagne tardoantiche", in *Archeologia e società tra tardo antico
e alto Medioevo, XII Seminario sul tardoantico e l'altomedioevo
(Padova, 29 settembre–1 ottobre 2005)*, edd. G. P. Brogiolo and
A. Chavarría (Mantua 2007) 127–46; Magyar Z. (in this volume) "Late Roman mausolea in Pannonia"; Nikolaus J. (in this
volume) "Changing funerary landscapes in Late Antiquity:
mausolea in North Africa"; Laporte J-P. (2009) "Une contribution méconnue du monde amazigh à l'architecture mondiale:
Les grands mausolées d'Afrique du Nord", in *Haut Commissar-
iat de l'Amazighité (Ed.), L'apport des amazighs à la civilisation
universelle* (Alger 2009) 137–54.

Mausolea, Sites: *Pannonia*: Brukner O. (1995) "Mauzolej – oktogonalna građevina [Mausoleum – an octagonal tomb]", in *Arheološka istraživanja duž autoputa kroz Srem*, ed. Z. Vapa (Novi
Sad 1995) 175–80; Fülep F. and Bachman Z. (1990) *Pécs frühchristliches Mausoleum* (Budapest 1990); Burger A. Sz. (1987)
"The Roman villa and mausoleum at Kővágószőlős, near Pécs
(Sopianae). Excavations 1977–1982", *A Janus Pannonius Múzeum
Évkönyve* 30–31 (1985–1986) (1987) 65–228; Fülep F. (1987) "A
pécsi későrómai-ókeresztény mauzóleum feltárásáról [The
excavation of the Late Roman-Early Christian Mausoleum in
Pécs]", *A Janus Pannonius Múzeum Évkönyve* 32 (1987) 31–44;
Fülep F. (1977) "A pécsi ókeresztény mauzóleum ásatása [Exca-
vations of the Early Christian mausoleum of Pécs]", *ArchÉrt*
104 (1977) 246–57; Dyggve E. (1935) "Das Mausoleum in Pécs
(Ein christliches Heroon aus Pannonia Inferior)", *Pannonia* 1
(1935) 62–77; Foerk E. (1923) "Újabb leletek a Viktoria telkén
[New finds from the Victoria estate]", *Budapest Régiségei* 10
(1923) 74–80; Petrović M. (1995) "Mauzolej – arhitektonska
analiza i rekonstrukcija [The mausoleum – architectonic
analysis and reconstruction]", in *Arheološka istraživanja
duž autoputa kroz Srem*, ed. Z. Vapa (Novi Sad 1995) 181–84;
Euzennat M. and Hallier G. (1992) "Le mausolea de Taksebt
(Algérie)", *CRAI* 136.1 (1992) 235–48. *Africa*: Ferchiou N. (1986)
"The anonymous mausoleum of Thuburnica", *MEFRA* 98
(1986) 665–705; Gsell S. (1898) "Le mausolée de Blad-Guitoun
(fouilles de M. Viré)", *Comptes rendus des séances de l'Académie
des Inscriptions et Belles-Lettres* 42 (1898) 481–99; Laporte J-P.

(2013) "Le mausolée de Blad Guitoun", *Ikosim* 2 (2013) 91–108. *Oriens*: Charpentier G. (2003–2004) "La construction du mausolée pyramidal de Sergilla: une étude de cas", *Tempora* 14–15 (2003–2004) 123–32; Huguenot C. (2018) "Étude d'une tombe monumentale de Resafa", *Zeitschrift für Orient-Archäologie* 11 (2018) 302–53.

Reuse: Williams H. (1997) "Ancient landscapes and the dead: the reuse of prehistoric and Roman monuments as early Anglo-Saxon burial sites", *Medieval Archaeology* 41 (1997) 1–32; Smith R. W. (1992) "Secondary use of the necropoleis of the Decapolis", *Aram* 4 (1992) 215–28; Zissu B. and Klein E. (2014) "On the use and reuse of rock-cut tombs and a ritual bath at Tell en-Naṣbeh: new perspectives on the Roman and Byzantine necropoleis", in *"As for Me, I Will Dwell at Mizpah ...": The Tell en-Naṣbeh Excavations after 85 Years*, edd. J. R. Zorn and A. J. Brody (Georgias Studies in the Ancient Near East 9) (Piscataway 2014) 199–224.

Spoliation of tomb monuments: *General*: Lavan L. (in this volume) "Memorial and oblivion in Late Antiquity: the testimony of spolia in city walls"; Underwood D. (in this volume) "The destruction, preservation, and adaptive reuse of funerary monuments within urban fortifications in Late Antiquity: the West"; Mishkovsky N. (in this volume) "The destruction, preservation, and adaptive reuse of funerary monuments in urban fortifications in Late Antiquity: the East. *Selected regional highlights* (See more in appendices of works in this volume): Baccrabère G. and Badie A. (1996) "L'enceinte du Bas-Empire à Toulouse", *Aquitania* 14 (1996) 125–29; Theocharaki A. M. (2011) "The ancient circuit wall of Athens: its changing course and the phases of construction", *Hesperia* 80 (2011) 71–156; Frey J. M. (2016) *Spolia in Fortifications and the Common Builder in Late Antiquity* (Boston 2016), which relates to three sites in Greece, if not especially to tomb spolia (Aegina, Isthmia, Sparta); Castrianni L., Giacomo G. D. and Ditaranto I. (2010) "La cinta muraria di Hierapolis di Frigia: Il geodatabase dei materiali di reimpiego come strumento di ricerca e conoscenza del monumento e della città", *Archeologia e Calcolatori* 21 (2010) 93–126; De Staebler P. (2008) "The City Wall and the Making of a Late Antique Provincial Capital," in C. Ratté and R. R. R. Smith (eds.) *Aphrodisias Papers 4: New Research on the City and its Monuments* (Journal of Roman Archaeology Supplementary Series 70: Portsmouth, RI, 2008) 284–318; Juchniewicz K., Ascad K. and al Hariri K. (2010) "The defence wall in Palmyra after recent Syrian excavations", *Studia Palmyreńskie* 9 (2010) 55–73.

Funerary Art

Thematic works: Braconi M. (2018) "'Il cielo in una stanza'. I sistemi decorativi delle cupole dei mausolei imperiali e le formule emulative della committenza privata nei monumenti funerari tardoantichi", in *Entre terre et ciel. Les édifices à coupole et leur décor entre l'Antiquité tardive et le haut Moyen Âge*, edd. C. Croci and V. Ivanovici (Études de Lettres no. 307) (Laussane 2018) 17–41; Braconi M. (2016) "I mausolei, le cupole, le decorazioni: tra committenza imperiali ed emulazione privata", in *Acta XVI Congressus internationalis archaeologiae Christianae (Roma 22–28.9.2013)* (Vatican City 2016) 987–1008; Bisconti F. and Braconi M. (2015) "Rotte figurative cristiane della tarda antichità: la rete dei movimenti iconografici tra isole e terraferm", in *Isole e terraferma nel primo cristianesimo. Identità locale ed interscambi culturali, religiosi e produttivi. Atti XI Congresso Nazionale di Archeologia Cristiana*, edd. R. Martorelli, A. Piras and P. G. Spanu (Cagliari 2015) 535–55; Bisconti F. and Braconi M. (2013) *Incisioni figurate nella tarda antichità* (Vatican City 2013); Michaeli T. (2007) *Circulación de temas y sistemas decorativos en la pintura mural antigua Actas del IX Congreso Internacional de la Association Internationale pour la Peinture Murale Antique* [*AIPMA*], ed. C. Guiral Pelegrín (Gobierno de Aragon 2007); Grabar A. (1981) *Christian Iconography, a Study of its Origins* (Princeton 1981).

By type of monument: Feraudi-Gruénais F. (2015) "The decoration of Roman tombs", in *The Blackwell Companion to Roman Art*, ed. B. E. Borg (Chichester 2015) 429–51; Koortbojian M. (2015) "Roman sarcophagi", in *The Blackwell Companion to Roman Art*, ed. B. E. Borg (Chichester 2015) 286–300; Bisconti F. and Brandenburg H. (2004) edd. *Sarcofagi tardoantichi, paleochristiani e altomedievali* (Vatican City 2004); Zimmermann N. (2015) "Catacombs and the beginnings of Christian tomb decoration", in *The Blackwell Companion to Roman Art*, ed. B. E. Borg (Malden 2015) 452–70; Tortorella S. (2010) "Mausolei imperiali tardo-antichi: le decorazioni pittoriche e musive delle cupole", in *Monumenta. I mausolei Romani, tra commemorazione funebre e propaganda celebrativa*, ed. M. Valenti (Rome 2010) 131–46; Mackie G. (2003) *Early Christian Chapels in the West. Decoration, Function, and Patronage* (Toronto 2003); Valeva J. (2001) "La peinture funéraire dans les provinces orientales de l'empire romain dans l'Antiquité Tardive", *Hortus Artium Medievalium* 7 (2001) 167–208; Duval N. (1976) *La mosaique funéraire dans l'art paléochrétien* (Ravenna 1976).

Funerary Art, by Region

Britain: Sparey-Green C. J. (1993) "The mausolea painted plaster", in *Excavations at Poundbury 1966–80, Vol. II, The Cemeteries*, edd. D. E. Farwell and T. I. Molleson (Dorset Natural History and Archaeological Society Monograph 11) (Dorchester 1993) 135–40.

Rome: Nuzzo D. (2022) "Un nuovo cubicolo dipinto nella catacomba di S. Ippolito sulla via Tiburtina", *Rivista di archeologia cristiana* XCVIII (2022) 241–66; Bisconti F. (2019) "The art of the catacombs", in *The Oxford Handbook of Early Christian Archaeology*, edd. W. R. Caraher, T. W. Davis and D. K. Pettegrew (New York 2019) 209–20; Braconi M. (2016) "Forme e codici dell'autorappresentazione dei defunti nell'immaginario figurativo della pittura catacombale", *Rivista di Archeologia Cristiana* 92 (2016) 35–83; Zimmermann N. (2015) "Catacombs and the beginnings of Christian tomb decoration", in *The Blackwell Companion to Roman Art*, ed. B. E. Borg (Malden 2015) 452–70; Bisconti F. (2011) *Le pitture delle catacombe Romane. Restauri e interpretazioni* (Todi 2011).

Pannonia: Popović I. (2011) "Wall painting of late antique tombs in Sirmium and its vicinity", *Starinar* 61 (2011) 223–49; Hudák K. (2009) "The iconographical program of the wall paintings in the Saint Peter and Baul Burial Chamber of Sopianae (Pécs)", *Mitteilungen zur Christlichen Archäologie* 15 (2009) 47–76; Hudák K. (2009) "The chronology of the paintings in the Saint Peter and Paul Burial Chamber of Sopianae", in *Ex officina ... Studia in honorem Dénes Gabler*, ed. Sz. Bíró (Győr 2009) 225–38; Fülep F. and Duma Gy. (1972) "Examinations of the wall paintings in the Cella Trichora of Pécs", *FolArch* 23 (1972) 195–213; Gerke F. (1952) "Die Wandmalereien der neugefundenen Grabkammer in Pécs (Sopianae). Ihre Stellung in der spätrömischen Kunstgeschichte", in *Neue Beiträge zur Kunstgeschichte des 1. Jahrtausends, 1. Halbband: Spätantike und Byzanz* (Forschungen zur Kunstgeschichte und christliche Archäologie 1) (Baden-Baden 1952) 115–37; Rossi de G. B. (1874) "Fünfkirchen in Ungheria camera sepolcrale sotterranea dipinta", *Bulletiono di Archeologia Cristiana* Ser. II. 5 (1874) 150–52.

Thrace/Dacia: Valeva J. (2023) "Architecture and decoration of late antique tombs in the diocese of Thracia and Eastern Illyricum", in *Funerary Landscapes of the Late Antique Oecumene: Contextualizing Epigraphic and Archaeological Evidence of Mortuary Practices: Proceedings of an International Conference in Heidelberg, May 30–June 1, 2019*, edd. S. Ardeleanu and J. C. Cubas Diaz (Heidelberg 2023) 325–64.

Macedonia (i.e. Greece): Marki E. (2006) *Η Νεκρόπολη της Θεσσαλονίκης στους Υστερορωμαϊκούς και Παλαιοχριστιανικούς Χρόνους (μέσα του 3ου έως μέσα του 8ου αι. μ.Χ.)* (Athens 2006).

Cherson: Zubar V. M. and Pillinger R. (2000–2001) "New tombs with early Christian murals from the necropolis of Tauric Chersonesus (preliminary note)", *Talanta* 32–33 (2000–2001) 123–30.

Oriens: Michaeli T. (1996) "Family burial in late antique and early Christian paintings in Eretz-Israel", *ASSAPH 1996* (Studies in Art History, B, 2) (1996) 27–48; Michaeli T. (2008) "A painted tomb in the east cemetery", in *The Necropolis of Bet Guvrin-Eleutheropolis* (=IAA Reports 36), edd. G. Avni, U. Dahari and A. Kloner (Jerusalem 2008) 187–99; Moulton W. J. (1921–1922) "A painted Christian tomb at Beit Jibrin", *AASOR* 2–3 (1921–1922) 95–102; Michaeli T. (2013) "Wall paintings from the late Roman or early Byzantine period in cave 4 at Ben Shemen", *Atiqot* 73 (2013) (in Hebrew with English summary) 45–50; Olszewski M. T. (2011) "The Orpheus funerary mosaic from Jerusalem in the Archaeological Museum at Istanbul", in *Mosaics of Turkey and Parallel Developments in the Rest of the Ancient and Medieval World: Questions of Iconography, Style and Technique from the Beginnings of Mosaic until the Late Byzantine Era (11th International Colloquium on Ancient Mosaics October 16th–20th, 2009, Bursa)*, ed. M. Şahin (Istanbul 2011) 655–64; Jakubiak K. (2014–2015) "Painted decorations in the Jiyeh tombs", *Archaeology & History in Lebanon* 40–41 (2014–2015) 146–53.

Egypt: Picton J., Quirke S. and Roberts P. C. (2007) edd. *Living Images: Egyptian Funerary Portraits in the Petrie Museum* (London 2007); Heinen H. (2002) "Dipinti aus der West-Necropole Alexandrias Gabbari", in *Nécropolis II*, edd. J.-Y. Empereur and M.-D. Nenna (Études Alexandrines 7) (Cairo 2002) 639–52; Subías Pascual E. (2003) *La corona immarcescible: Pintures de l'antiguitat tardana de la Necròpolis Alta d'Oxirinc (Mínia, Egipte)* (Institut Català d'Arqueologia Clàssica 1) (Barcelona 2003); Innemee K. (2015) "Funerary aspects in the paintings from the Apollo Monastery at Bawit", in *Christianity and Monasticism in Middle Egypt. Al-Minya and Asyut*, edd. G. Gabra and H. N. Takla (Cairo-New York 2015) 241–53.

Burial Forms

Cremation: Weekes J. (2017) "Afterword – process and polysemy: an appreciation of a cremation burial", in *Death as a Process: The Archaeology of the Roman Funeral* (Studies in Funerary

Archaeology 12), edd. J. Pearce and J. Weekes (Oxford 2017) 287–300; McKinley J. I. (2017) "How did it go?" Putting the process back into cremation", in *Death as a Process: The Archaeology of the Roman Funeral* (Studies in Funerary Archaeology 12), edd. J. Pearce and J. Weekes (Oxford 2017) 257–86.

Inhumation: Keegan S. L. (2002) *Inhumation Rites in Late Roman Britain. The Treatment of the Engendered Body* (Brit. Archaeol. Rep. 333) (Oxford 2002); Sparey Green C. J. (1977) "The significance of plaster burials for the recognition of Christian cemeteries", in *Burial in the Roman World*, ed. R. Reece (Council for British Archaeology, Research Report 22) (London 1977) 46–53.

Mummification: Spindler K., Wilfing H., Rastbichler-Zissernig E., zur Nedden D. and Nothdurfter H. (1996) edd. *Human Mummies: a Global Study of their Status and the Techniques of Conservation* (Man in the Ice 3) (Vienna 1996); Chioffi L. (1998) *Mummificazione e imbalsamazione a Roma ed in altri luoghi del mondo romano* (Rome 1998).

Amphora Burial: *General*: Stevens S. T. (2013) "Stages of infancy in Roman amphora burial", in *The Oxford Handbook of Childhood and Education in the Classical World*, edd J. E. Grubbs and T. Parkin (Oxford 2013) 625–39. *Gaul*: Richarte C. and Raynaud F. (2019) "Mise en bière, mise en boîte ou mise en pot? Amphores et terres cuites recyclées en milieu funéraire à travers quelques exemples méridionaux (IVᵉ–VIIIᵉ s.)", in *Archéologie et histoire en territoire arlésien. Mélanges offerts à Jean Piton*, edd. D. Djaoui and M. Heijmans (Lafage 2019) 551–69; Bonifay M. and Roth Congès A. (2009) "Les sépultures en amphores du cimetière de Saint-Victor", in *Saint-Victor de Marseille. Études archéologiques et historiques, Actes du colloque de Saint-Victor, Marseille, 18–20 novembre 2004*, edd. M. Fixot and J. P. Pelletier (Turnhout 2009) 17–24. *Italy*: Caminneci V. (2012) "Animam sepulcro condimus"; sepolcreto tardoantico in anfore presso l'Emporion di Agrigento (Sicilia, Italia)", in *Rei Cretariae Romanae Fautorum Acta, 27th Congress of the Rei Cretariae Romanae Fautores, Belgrade 19–26 September 2010* (Bonn 2012) 259–66; Caminneci V. (2012) "Enchytrismos. Seppellire in vaso nell'antica Agrigento", in *Parce sepulto. Il rito e la morte tra passato e presente*, ed. V. Caminneci (Palermo 2012) 111–32; Caminneci V. and Di Giuseppe Z. (2019) "Sepoltura in anfora di infans dall'Emporion di Agrigento", in *Una favola breve. Archeologia e antropologia per la storia dell'infanzia*, ed. C. Lambrugo (Florence 2019) 109–15.

Sarcophagi: See above entries on Funerary Art. Koch G. (2000) *Frühchristliche Skarophage* (Munich 2000); Deckers J. G. and Koch G. (2018) edd. *Konstantinopel*

Kleinasien – Thracia – Syria – Palaestina – Arabia (*Repertorium der christlich antiken Sarkophage*) (Wiesbaden 2018); Dresken-Weiland J. G. (2003) *Sarkophagbestattungen des 4.–6. Jhs. im Westen des römischen Reiches* (Rome 2003); *Antiquité Tardive 1* (1993) *Les sarcophages d'Aquitaine*; Studer-Karlen M. (2013) "Les représentations des défunts sur les sarcophages chrétiens: sarcophages païens et chrétiens en comparaison", in *Iconographie funéraire romaine et société: corpus antique, approches nouvelles?*, edd. M. Gallinier and F. Baratte (Perpignan 2013) 233–45; Studer-Karlen M. (2008) "Quelques réflexions sur les sarcophages d'enfants (fin 3ᵉ siècle–début 5ᵉ siècle)", in *Nasciturus, Infans, Puerulus, Vobis Mater Terra*, edd. F. Gusi, S. Muriel and C. Olària (Castello 2008) 551–74; Konstantinidis P. (1881) "Σαρκοφάγος Κληματίου ἐπισκόπου Ἀθηνῶν", *Parnassios* 5 (1881) 822–25.

Funerary Rituals

Funerary rituals general: Latham J. A. (2022) "Bring out yer dead: A funerary ritual koine and its Christian dialects from little tradition to a great tradition", in *Death and Rebirth in Late Antiquity: Essays in Honor of Robin M. Jensen*, ed. L. M. Jefferson (Lanham 2022) 159–96; Nenna M.-D., Huber S. and van Andringa W. (2018) edd. *Constituer la tombe, honorer les défunts en Méditerranée antique* (Alexandria 2018); Pearce J. (2013) "Beyond the grave: excavating the dead in the late Roman provinces", in *Field Methods and Post-Excavation Techniques* (Late Antique Archaeology 9), edd. L. Lavan and M. Mulryan (Leiden 2013) 441–82. Lavan L A. (in this volume) "Funerary processions in Late Antiquity"; Burman J. (2004) "Christianising the celebrations of death in Late Antiquity. Funerals and society", in *Games and Festivals in Classical Antiquity. Proceedings of the Conference Held in Edinburgh 10–12 July 2000*, edd. S. Bell and G. Davies (Oxford 2004) 137–42; Weekes J. (2002) "Acculturation and the temporal features of ritual action", in *TRAC 2001: Proceedings of the Eleventh Annual Theoretical Roman Archaeology Conference, Glasgow 2001*, edd. M. Carruthers, C. van Driel-Murray, A. Gardner, J. Lucas, L. Revel and E. Swift (Oxford 2002) 73–82;

Funerary rituals (regional): *Britain*: Brettell R., Schotsmans E., Martin W. Stern B. and Heron C. (2018) "The final masquerade: resinous substances and Roman mortuary rites", in *The Bioarchaeology of Ritual and Religion*, edd. A. Livarda, R. Madgwick and S. R. Mora (Oxford 2018) 44–57; Pearce J. (2015) "Urban exits: commercial archaeology and the study of

death rituals and the dead in the towns of Roman Britain",
in *The Towns of Roman Britain. The Contribution of Commercial Archaeology since 1990*, edd M. Fulford and N. Holbrook (London 2015) 138–66. Devièse T. (2008) *Elucidating Funeral Rituals in Burials from the End of the Roman Empire: Development of a Multi-Analytical Approach* (Ph.D thesis, Univ. of Pisa 2008); Quensel-von-Kalben L. (2000) "Putting Late Roman burial practice (from Britain) in context", in *Burial, Society and Context in the Roman World*, edd. J. Pearce, M. Millett and M. Struck (Oxford 2000) 217–30; Thomas C. (1999) "Laid to rest on pillow of bay leaves", *British Archaeology* 50 (1999) http://www.archaeologyuk.org; Black E. W. (1986) "Romano-British burial customs and religious beliefs in south-east England", *Archaeology* 143 (1986) 201–39. Gaul: Prien R. (2023) "Shifting burial rites – shifting identities? Late antique burial practices on the Rhine frontier", in *Funerary Landscapes of the Late Antique Oecumene: Contextualizing Epigraphic and Archaeological Evidence of Mortuary Practices: Proceedings of an International Conference in Heidelberg, May 30–June 1, 2019*, edd. S. Ardeleanu and J. C. Cubas Diaz (Heidelberg 2023) 459–82; Murail P. and Girard L. (2000) "Biology and burial practices from the end of the first century AD to the beginning of the fifth century AD: the rural necropolis of Chantambre (essonne, France)", in *Burial, Society and Context in the Roman World*, edd. J. Pearce, M. Millett and M. Struck (Oxford 2000) 105–11. Italy: 1. General: Giuntella A. M. (1998) "Note su alcuni aspetti della ritualità funeraria nell'alto medioevo. Consuetudini e innovazioni", *in Sepolture tra IV e VIII secolo. 7° Seminario sul Tardo Antico e l'Alto Medioevo*, edd. G. P. Brogiolo and G. Cantino Wataghin (Mantua 1998) 61–75; Giuntella A. M. and Amante Simoni C. (1992) "L'uso degli spazi, sepolture, e riti funerari", in *La civitas cristiana. Urbanistica delle città' italiane tra trarda antichità' e altomedioevo, Atti del I seminario di studio. Mediterraneo tardoantico e medievale*, edd. P. Demeglio and C. Lambert (Turin 1992) 127–43; Giuntella A. M. (1990) "Sepoltura e rito: consuetudini e innovazioni", in *Le Sepolture in Sardegna dal IV al VII secolo: IV Convegno sull'Archeologia TardoRomana e Medievale (Cuglieri, 27–28 giugno 1987)* (Oristano 1990) 215–29. 2. Northern Italy: Giostra C. (2007) "Luoghi e segni della morte in età longobarda: tradizione e transizione nelle pratiche dell'aristocrazia", *Archeologia e società tra tardo antico e altomedievale (V–IX secolo)*, edd. G. P. Brogiolo and A. Chavarría Arnau (Mantua 2007) 311–44; La Rocca C. (2005) "Rituali di famiglia. Pratiche funerarie nell'Italia longobarda", in *Sauver son âme et se perpétuer. Transmission du patrimoine et mémoire au haut Moyen Âge*, edd. F. Bougard, C. La Rocca and R. Le Jan (Rome 2005) 431–75; Grossi W., Knobloch R. and Lumacone A. (2008) "I rituali funerari", in *Bollettino di Archeologia On-Line. International Congress of Classical Archaeology (Rome 1982)* 29–37; La Rocca C. (1997) "Segni di distinzione. Dai corredi funerari alle donazioni "post obitum" nel regno longobardo", in *L'Italia centrosettentrionale in età longobarda. Atti del Convegno (Ascoli Piceno, 1995)*, ed. L. Paroli (Florence 1997) 31–54; Vuga D. (1980) "A study of burying methods in the period of the Great Migration (5th to 6th centuries) in the south-eastern Alpine and Cisalpine world", *Balcanoslavica* 9 (1980) 17–25. 3. Sardegna: De Santis P. (2015) "Riti pratiche funerarie nel processo di costruzione di una memoria identitaria: esempi da Sardegna e Sicilia", in *Isole e terraferma nel primo Cristianesimo. Identità locale ed interscambi culturali, religiosi e produttivi (Atti XI Congressi Nazionale di Archeologia Cristiana)*, edd. R. Martorelli, A. Piras and P. G. Spanu (Cagliari 2015) 203–20; Martorelli R. (2011) "Usi e consuetudini funerarie nella Sardegna centro-occidentale fra tarda antichità e altro medioevo", in *Oristano e il suo Territorio*, edd. P. G. Spanu and R. Zucca (Rome 2011) 700–59. Pannonia: Leleković T. (2012) "Cemeteries", in *The Archaeology of Roman Southern Pannonia: The State of Research and Selected Problems in the Croatian Part of the Roman Province of Pannonia*, ed. B. Migotti (Oxford 2012) 313–57. Macedonia: Tritsaroli P. (2006) *Pratiques funéraires en Grèce centrale à la période byzantine: Analyse à partir des données archéologiques et biologiques* (Ph.D. diss., Muséum national d'histoire naturelle, Paris 2006). Oriens: Bollók A. (in this volume) "The archaeology of late antique mortuary practices in the Near East"; Bollók Á. (2020) "The Christianisation of the mortuary realm in the late antique Levant as seen through the written and the archaeological record", *ARAM* 32 (2020) 471–99; Eger C. and Hamoud M. (2011) "Spätrömisch-frühbyzantinischer Grabbrauch in Syrien. Die Nekropole von Darayya bei Damaskus", *Antike Welt* 42 (2011) 70–6; de Jong L. (2010) "Performing death in Tyre: the life and afterlife of a Roman cemetery in the Province of Syria", *AJA* 114 (2010) 597–630. Egypt: Dunand F. (2007) "Between tradition and innovation: Egyptian funerary practices in Late Antiquity", in *Egypt in the Byzantine World, 300–700*, ed. R. S. Bagnall (Cambridge 2007) 163–84.

Christian Funerary Rituals: *General*: Rebillard É. (2003) "Conversion and burial in the Late Roman Empire", in *Conversion in Late Antiquity and Early Middle Ages: Seeing and Believing*, edd. K. Mills and A. Grafton (Rochester 2003) 61–83; Rebillard É. (2003) *Religion et Sépulture: L'église, les vivants et* les morts dans l'antiquité tardive (Paris 2003); Volp U. (2002) Tod und Ritual in den christlichen Gemeinden der Antike (Supplements to VigChr 65) (Leiden and Boston 2002); Davies J. (1999) Death, Burial, and Rebirth in the Religions of Antiquity (London 1999); Paxton F. S. (1990) Christianizing Death. The Creation of a Ritual Process in Early Medieval Europe (Ithaca 1990); Février P.-A. (1987) "La mort chrétienne", in Segni e riti nella chiesa altomedievale occidentale: 11–17 aprile 1985 (Settimane di studio del Centro italiano di studi sull'alto Medioevo 33) (Spoleto 1987) 881–952; Kyriakakis J. (1974) "Byzantine burial customs: care of the deceased from death to the prosthesis", Greek Orthodox Theological Review 19 (1974) 37–72; Rush A. (1941) Death and Burial in Christian Antiquity (Washington D.C. 1941). Regional: 1. Italy: Stasolla F. R. (2013) "Vescovi e rituali funerari: quadro normativo e realtà archeologica", in Episcopus, civitas, territorium. Atti del XV Congresso Internazionale di Archeologia Cristiana (Toledo, 8–12 settembre 2008), edd. S. Cresci, J. Lopez Quiroga, O. Brandt and C. Pappalardo (Vatican City 2013) 349–55. 2. Oriens: Bear C. (2017) Christian Funeral Practices in Late Fouth-Century Antioch (PhD Thesis, Berkley University 2017). 3: Egypt: Toralles Tovar S. (2013) "Egyptian burial practices in Late Antiquity: The case of Christian mummy labels", in Cultures in Contact: Transfer of Knowledge in the Mediterranean Context, edd. S. Torallas Tovar and J. P. Monferrer (Córdoba 2013) 13–24; Krause M. (1983) "Das Weiterleben ägyptischer Vorstellungen und Bräuche im koptischen Totenwesen", in Das römisch-byzantinische Ägypten: Akten des internationalen Symposions 26.–30. September 1978 in Trier, edd. G. Grimm, H. Heinen and E. Winter (Mainz am Rhein 1983) 85–92. Sites (by region): Bowen G. E. (2003) "Some observations on Christian burial practices at Kellis", in The Oasis Papers 3: Proceedings of the Third International Conference of the Dakhleh Oasis, edd. G. E. Bowen and C. A. Hope (Dakhleh Oasis Project 14) (Oxford 2003) 167–79; Voytenko A. (2012) "Preliminary report on Coptic burial customs at the necropolis of Deir el-Banat", in Achievements and Problems of Modern Egyptology: Proceedings of the International Conference Held in Moscow on September 29–October 2, 2009, edd. G. A. Belova and S. V. Ivanov (Moscow 2012) 402–11; Cipriano G. (2016) "Ritual equipments in the cemetery of el-Bagawat (Kharga Oasis): Some remarks", in Coptic Society, Literature and Religion from Late Antiquity to Modern Times. Proceedings of the Tenth International Congress of Coptic Studies, Rome, September 17th–22nd, 2012, and Plenary Reports of the Ninth International Congress of Coptic Studies, Cairo, September 15th–19th, 2008, edd.

P. Buzi, A. Camplani, and F. Contardi (Orientalia Lovaniensia Analecta 247) (Leuven 2016) 1447–62.

Pagan-Christian funerary rituals: Johnson M. J. (1997) "Pagan-Christian burial practices of the fourth century: shared tombs?", Journal of Early Christian Studies 5 (1997) 37–59; Sodini J.-P. (1977) "Témoignages archéologiques sur la persistance à l'époque paléochrétienne et byzantine de rites funéraires païens", in La Mort au Moyen Âge: Colloque de l'Association des historiens médiévistes français réunis à Strasbourg (Strasbourg 1977) 11–21.

Jewish rituals: Rizzone V. (2014) "Ebrei e non ebrei in Sicilia e a Malta nella tarda antichità: il punto di vista delle necropoli", in Coesistenza e cooperazione nel medioevo. IV Congresso Europeo di Studi Medievali. In memoriam L. E. Boyle (Palermo, 23–27 giugno 2009), P. Spallino, A. Panzavecchia, I. Panzeca, D. Parisi, L. Parisoli, M. Pavon Ramirez, R. Pereta Rives et al. (Palermo 2014) 1259–77; Misgav H. (2002) "Development of Jewish memorial customs in the Roman-Byzantine period based on burial inscriptions", Judea and Samaria Research Studies 11 (2002) 123–136 (in Hebrew with English summary).

Samaritan rituals: Tal O. and Taxel I. (2014) "Samaritan burial customs outside Samaria. Evidence from Latte Roman and Byzantine cemeteries in the Southern Sharon Plain", Zeitschrift des Deutschen Palästina-Vereins 130.2 (2014) 55–80.

Apotropaic Rituals: Bollók Á. (2013) "Apotropaion and burial in early Byzantium: some preliminary considerations", in Byzanz und das Abendland: Begegnungen zwischen Ost und West, ed. E. Juhász (Budapest 2013) 227–41; Bollók Á. (2016) "The "phylactery of the cross" and late antique/early Medieval mortuary practices in the eastern Mediterranean and on its fringes", in GrenzÜbergänge: Spätrömisch, frühchristlich, frühbyzantinisch als Kategorien der historisch-archäologischen Forschung an der mittleren Donau, edd. I. Bugarski, O. Heinrich-Tamáska, V. Ivanišević and D. Syrbe (Forschungen zu Spätantike und Mittelalter 4) (Remshalden 2016) 215–30; Quast D. (2010) "Christliche Amulette' Bemerkungen zu Glöckchen aus merowingerzeitlichen Gräbern", Bayerische Vorgeschichtsblätter 75 (2010) 169–78; Nuzzo D. (2000) "Amulet and grave in Late Antiquity: some examples from Roman cemeteries", in Burial, Society and Context in the Roman World, edd. J. Pearce, M. Millett and M. Struck (Oxford 2000) 249–55; Marchetta I. (2016) "Gli oggetti in tomba e il loro significato simbolico alcuni esempi da necropoli lucane di V–VII secolo", in Territorio, insediamenti e necropoli fra tarda antichità e alto medioevo. Atti del Convegno internazionale di studi.

Cimitile-Santa Maria Capua Vetere, 19–20 giugno 2014, edd. C. Ebanista and M. Rotili (Napoli 2016) 387–411.

Magic: Leglay M. (1987) "La magie et la mort", in *La mort les morts et l'au-delà dans le monde romain*, ed. F. Hinard (Caen 1987) 245–48; Engemann J. (2007) "Magie", in *Konstantin der Große: Imperator Caesar Flavius Constantinus*, edd. A. Demandt and J. Engemann (Ausstellungskatalog Trier) (Mainz 2007) 295–301. *In funerary rituals*: Alfayé S. (2009) "*Sit tibi terra gravis*: Magical-religious practices against restless dead in the ancient world", in *Formae mortis: el tránsito de la vida a la muerte en las sociedades antiguas*, edd. F. M. Simón, F. Pina Polo and J. Remesal Rodríguez (Barcelona 2009) 181–216. Meyer M. and Smith R. (1994) *Ancient Christian Magic: Coptic Texts of Ritual Power* (San Francisco 1994); Quast D. (2010) "Christliche Amulette' Bemerkungen zu Glöckchen aus merowingerzeitlichen Gräbern", *Bayerische Vorgeschichtsblätter* 75 (2010) 169–78. *By site*: Leontsini M. and Panopoulou A. (2013) "'Μαγικά' και αποτροπαϊκά τεκμήρια από τη βυζαντινή Κόρινθο: Συμβολικές χρήσεις και συλλογικές συμπεριφορές", in *Αντικήνσωρ. Τιμητικός τόμος Σπύρου Ν. Τρωιάνου για τα ογδοήκοστα γενέθλια του/Antecessor: Festschrift für Spyros N. Troianos zum 80. Geburtstag 1*, edd. V. Leontaritou, K. Bourdara and E. Papagianni (Athens 2013) 855–80.

Funerary meals: *General*: Février P. A. (1977) "A propos du repas funéraire : culte et sociabilité", *Cahiers Archéologiques* 26 (1977) 29–45. *Regional*: Wilson R. J. A (2017) "Dining with the dead in early Byzantine Sicily" (Eleventh Babesch Byvanck Lecture; http://www.babesch.org/downloads/BABESCH_Byvanck_Lecture_2017_Wilson.pdf); Wilson R. J. A. (2011) "Funerary feasting in Early Byzantine Sicily: New evidence from Kaukana", *AJA* 115 (2011) 263–302; Rizzone V. (2016) "La cristianizzazione dell'arcipelago maltese alla luce delle indagini sulle pratiche funerarie", in *Quis est qui ligno pugnat ? Missionaries and Evangelization in Late Antique and Medieval Europe (4th–13th centuries)*, ed. E. Piazza (Verona 2016) 7–25.

Human sacrifice: Dan R. J. (2007) "Changing patterns of violence at Qustul and Ballana in the post-Meroitic period. Part One: The Humans", *MittSAG* 18 (2007) 189–200.

Animal sacrifices (by site): Osypińska M. (2011) "Animal remains in post-Meroitic burials in Sudan", *Polish Archaeology in the Mediterranean* 20 (2011) 541–48; Haimovici S. (2005) "O problemă incomplet rezolvată – studiul resturilor animaliere depuse ca ofrandă în necropole aparţinând culturii Sântana de Mureş-Cerneahov", *Arheologia Moldovei* 28 (2005) 327–34; Stanc S. and Bejenaru L. (2004) "Animal offerings found in necropoleis belonging to Sântana of Mureş Cerniahov culture from the east and the south extra-Carpatian Zones of Romania", in *Behaviour Behind Bones: The Zooarchaeology of Ritual, Religion, Status and Identity*, edd. S. J. O'Day, W. Van Neer and A. Ervynck (Oxford 2004) 14–9.

Libations: Spalla E. (2005) "Strutture per libagioni nella ritualità funeraria Romana: i dati archeologici", in *La Signora del sarcofago. Una sepoltura di rango nella necropoli dell'Università Cattolica*, edd M. P. Rossignani, M. Sannazaro and G. Le Grottaglie (Milan 2005) 47–54.

Object smashing: Grinsell L. (1961) "The breaking of objects as a funerary rite", *Folklore* 72 (1961) 475–91.

Ceramics in Rituals: *General*: Stasolla F. M. and Marchetti M. I. (2010) "Ceramiche dai contesti funerari tardoantichi ed altomedievali: aspetti simbolici e formali", in LRCW3 *Late Roman Coarse Wares, Cooking Wares and Amphorae in the Mediterranean. Archaeology and Archaeometry. Comparison between Western and Eastern Mediterranean* (British Archaeological Reports Int. Ser. 2185) (Oxford 2010) 131–38; *Regional*: Mamedow M. (2017) "Die Rekonstruktion ritueller Handlungen: Funktionale Analyse und Kontextualisierung von Keramik aus einem ptolemäisch-römischen Gräberfeld in Mittelägypten", in *Burial and Mortuary Practices in Late Period and Graeco-Roman Egypt: Proceedings of the International Conference held at Museum of Fine Arts, Budapest, 17–19 July 2014*, ed. K. A. Kóthay (Budapest 2017) 61–70.

Coins in Rituals: *General*: Burström N. M. and Ingvardson G. T. (2018) edd. *Divina Moneta: Coins in Religion and Ritual* (London – New York 2018); Perassi C. (2011/2012) "Monete romane forate. Qualche riflessione su « un grand thème européen » (J.-P. Callu)", *Aevum* 85 (2011/2012) 257–315; Stevens S. T. (1991) "Charon's Obol and other coins in ancient funerary practice", *Phoenix* 45.3 (1991) 215–29. *Regional*: Duchemin J.-P. (2012) "Numismatique et archéologie du rituel : réflexion sur le rite dit de l'« obole à Charon » à partir de l'exemple de la nécropole tardo-antique de Nempont-Saint-Firmin (Pas-de-Calais, France)", *Journal of Archaeological Numismatics* 2 (2012) 127–98; Perassi C. (2001) "Le monete della necropoli: osservazioni sul rituale funerario", in *Ricerche archeologiche nei cortili dell'Università Cattolica. La necropoli tardoantica,* ed. M. Sannazaro (Milan 2001) 101–14; Amante Simoni C. (1990) "Sepoltura e moneta: obolo viatico-obolo offerta", in *Le sepolture in Sardegna dal IV al VII secolo. IV Convegno sull'archeologia tardoromana e medievale* (Oristano 1990) 231–42; Găzdac C. and Cosma C. (2014) "Social memory and statute. Roman coins in medieval graves from the Necropolis Noşlac, Romania", *The Journal of Archaeological Numismatics* 4 (2014) 182–92.

Dress: Reifarth N. (2013) *Zur Ausstattung spätantiker Elite-gräber aus St. Maximin in Trier: Purpur, Seide, Gold und Harze* (Internationale Archäologie 124) (Westfalen 2013); Mitschke S. and Paetz gen. Schieck A. (2012) "Dressing the dead in the city of Rome: burial custom according to textiles", in *Dressing the Dead in Classical Antiquity*, edd. M. Caroll and J. P. Wild (Stroud 2012) 115–33; Martorelli R. (2000) "Clothing in burial practice in Italy in the early Christian period", in *Burial, Society and Context in the Roman World*, edd. J. Pearce, M. Millett and M. Struck (Oxford 2000) 244–48; Pleşa A. D. (2017) "Religious belief in burial: Funerary dress and practice in the late antique and early Islamic cemeteries at Matmar and Mostagedda, Egypt (late fourth-early ninth century CE)", *Ars Orientalis* 47 (2017) 18–42.

Colour: Hermann A. (1969) "Farbe", in *Reallexikon für Antike und Christentum* 7, edd. T. Klauser *et al.* (Stuttgart 1969) 358–447; Clark C. (in this volume) "The colour of death: Colour symbolism and burial in Roman Britain".

Eulogia: Bollók Á. (2018) "Portable sanctity brought to the after-life. Pilgrim eulogia as grave good in the late antique Eastern Mediterranean", in *Across the Mediterranean – Along the Nile. Studies in Egyptology, Nubiology and Late Antiquity dedicated to László Török on the Occasion of His 75th Birthday*, edd. T. A. Bács, Á. Bollók and T. Vida (Budapest 2018) 763–803.

Grave goods (regional): Pearce J. (2015) "A "civilized" death? The interpretation of provincial Roman grave good assemblages", in *Death and Changing Rituals: Function and Meaning in Ancient Funerary Practices*, edd. J. Rasmus Brandt, H. Roland and M. Prusac (Oxford 2015) 223–48; Swift E. (2010) "Identi-fying migrant communities: A contextual analysis of grave assemblages from continental late Roman cemeteries", *Britannia* 41 (2010) 237–82; Philpott R. (1991) *Burial practices in Roman Britain. A Survey of Grave Treatment and Furnishing AD 43–410* (BAR Brit. Ser. 219) (Oxford 1991); Härke H. (2014) "Grave goods in early medieval burials: messages and mean-ings", *Mortality* 19.1 (2014) 41–60.

Funerary rituals (by site): *Britain*: Thompson T. J. U., Szigeti J., Gowland R. L. and Witcher R. E. (2016) "Death on the frontier: Military cremation practices in the north of Roman Britain", *Journal of Archaeological Science: Reports* 10 (2016) 828–36; Weekes J. (2008) "Classification and analysis of archaeolog-ical contexts for the reconstruction of early Romano-British cremation funerals", *Britannia* 39 (2008) 145–60; Boylston A., Knüsel C. J., Roberts C. and Dawson M. (2000) "Investigation of a Romano-British rural ritual in Bedford", *Journal of Archaeol. Science* 27 (2000) 241–54; Harman M., Molleson T. I. and Price D. L. (1981) "Burials, bodies and beheadings in Romano-British and Anglo-Saxon cemeteries", *Bulletin of the British Museum (Natural History). Geology* 35 (1981) 145–89; Crerar B. (2016) "Deviancy in late Romano-British burial", in *The Oxford Handbook of Roman Britain*, edd. M. Millett, L. Revell and A. Moore (Oxford 2016) 381–405. *Hispania*: Ciurana J. (2011) *Pràctiques i rituals funeraris a Tarraco i el seu ager (segles II aC–III/IV dC)* (PhD. Diss., Univ. of Tarragona 2011). *Gaul*: Blaizot F. (2018) "Tradition and innovation: burials during Late Antiquity in eastern central Gaul", in *Constituer la tombe, honorer les défunts en Méditerranée antique*, edd. M.-D. Nenna, S. Huber and W. van Andringa (Alexandria 2018) 487–542; Blaizot F. (2009) ed. *Pratiques et espaces funéraires dans le centre et sud-est de la Gaule durant l'Antiquité* (*Gallia* 66.1) (2009). *Italy*: De Santis P. (2020) "Riti della commemorazione presso le tombe nel complesso cimiteriale di Lamapopoli a Canosa di Puglia", in *Taccuino per Anna Maria Giuntella. Piccoli scritti di archeologia cristiana e medievale*, edd. F. Bisconti and G. Ferri (Todi 2020) 141–50; Pazienza A. M. (2014) "Iden-tity, funerary practices and memory in Lombard Tuscia (6th to 8th centuries)", *Zeitschrift für Archäologie des Mittelalters* 42, edd. S. Brather, U. Müller and H. Steuer Jahrgang (Bonn 2014) 1–32. Ferreri D. (2009) "Sepolture e riti funerari a Classe: una lunga prospettiva diacronica", in *V Congresso Nazionale Arche-ologia medievale, Foggia-Manfredonia 2009*, edd. G. Volpe and P. Favia (Florence 2009) 459–64; Spera L. (2005) "Riti funerari e "culto dei morti" nella tarda antichità: un quadro archeo-logico dai cimiteri paleocristiani di Roma", *Augustinianum* 45 (2005) 5–34; Deiana M. I. (1997) "Incinerazione e inumazione: il caso della Sardegna", *Ann. Fac. Lettere e Filos. Univ. Cagliari* 15, 1996–1997 (1997) 17–66; Barbiera I. and Ferreri D. (2007) "Plac-ing bodies and constructing memory at San Severo", *Annual of Medieval Studies* 13 (2007) 187–96; Caminneci V. (2015) "'Carnem suam quisque naturaliter diligit' (August. de cura pro mortuis, 7,9). La cura dei corpi in una necropoli tardo antica dell'Emporion di Agrigento", in *VII Congresso Nazi-onale di Archeologia Medievale, Lecce 2015*, edd. P. Arthur and M. Leo Imperiale (Florence 2015) 50–4. *Macedonia*: Walbank M. E. H. (2005) "Unquiet graves: Burial practices of the Roman Corinthians," in *Urban Religion in Roman Corinth: Interdisciplinary Approaches*, edd. D. Schowalter and S. Friesen (Harvard Theological Studies 53) (Cambridge, Mass. 2005) 249–80; Marki E. (1987) "Ἀνίχνευση παλαιοτέρων ἐπιδράσεων στὴν παλαιοχριστιανικὴ ταφικὴ ἀρχιτεκτονικὴ καὶ τὴ νεκρικὴ λατρεία", in *Ἡ Καθημερινὴ Ζωὴ στὸ Βυζάντιο. Τομὲς καὶ Συνέχειες στὴν Ἑλληνιστικὴ καὶ Ῥωμαϊκὴ Παράδοση. Πρακτικὰ τοῦ Α´ Διεθνοῦς Συμποσίου, 15–17 σεπτεμβρίου 1988*, edd. C. Angelidi and C. Malte-zou (Athens 1987) 89–104. *Asia*: Cleymans S. and Talloen P. (in this volume) "From necropoleis to koimētēria: Burial practices in late antique (late 3rd–7th c. AD) Sagalassos, South-West Turkey".

Grave Goods

Regional: _Britain_: Härke H. (2014) "Grave goods in early medieval burials: messages and meanings", _Mortality_ 19.1 (2014) 41–60; Williams H. (2004) "Artefacts in early medieval graves – a new perspective", in _Debating Late Antiquity in Britain AD300–700_ (BAR Brit. Ser. 365), edd. R. Collins and J. Gerrard (Oxford 2004) 89–102; Philpott R. (1991) _Burial Practices in Roman Britain. A Survey of Grave Treatment and Furnishing AD 43–410_ (BAR Brit. Ser. 219) (Oxford 1991); Clarke G. (1979) _Pre-Roman and Roman Winchester – Part II. The Roman Cemetery at Lankhills_ (New York 1979). _Italy_: Schneider-Schnekenburger G. (1979) "Raetia I vom 4. bis 8. Jahrhundert auf Grund der Grabfunde", in _Von der Spätantike zum frühen Mittelalter. Aktuelle Probleme in historisches und archäologischer Sicht_, edd. J. Werner and E. Ewig (Vorträge und Forschungen 25) (Sigmaringen 1979) 179–91; Amante Simoni C. and Martorelli R. (1986) "Cultura, materiali e fasi storiche del complesso archeologico di Cornus: primi risultati di una ricerca. I corredi funerari e la suppellettile metallica", in _Cuglieri I. L'archeologia Romana e altomedievale nell'Oristanese. Atti del I Convegno. Mediteranno tardoantico e medievale. Scavi e ricerche 3_, ed. A. M. Giuntella (Taranto 1986) 161–89. _Pannonia_: Bitenc P. and Knific T. (2001) _Od Rimljanov do Slovanov. Predmeti_ (Ljubljana 2001); Rendić-Miočević D. (1954) "Neue Funde in der altchristlichen Nekropole Manastirine in Salona", _Archaeologia Iugoslavica_ 1 (1954) 53–70. _Macedonia_: Pazaras T. (2009) ed. Ανασκαφικές έρευνες στην περιοχή Επανομής Θεσσαλονίκης. Το Νεκροταφείο στο Λιμόρι και η Βασιλική στο Μπγιαδούδι (Thessalonica 2009); Zeiss H. (1940) "Avarenfunde aus Korinth", in _Serta Hoffileriana: Commentationes gratulatorias Victori Hoffiler sexagenario_ (Zagreb 1940) 95–99; Soteriou G. (1956) "Ἀνασκαφαὶ ἐν Νέᾳ Ἀγχιάλῳ", _Prakt_ (1956) 110–18; Davidson G. (1952) _Corinth XII: The Minor Objects_ (Princeton 1952). _Oriens_: Rudin T. _et al._ (2018) "Two burial caves at Kefar Shemaryahu: More on Samaritan and Christian interactions in the Byzantine-period Central Coastal Plain", _Liber Annuus_ 68 (2018) 269–302; Nabulsi A., Husan A. and Schönrock-Nabulsi P. (2013) "The 2012 seasons of excavations in the ancient Khirbat as-Samrā cemetery", _ADAJ_ 57 (2013) 551–57; Nabulsi A. _et al._ (2011) "The ancient cemetery of Khirbat as-Samrā: 2010 excavations at site A2",

ADAJ 5 (2011) 25–31; Nabulsi A. _et al._ (2009) "Khirbat as-Samrā ancient cemetery: preliminary discussion of Site C", _ADAJ_ 53 (2009) 167–72; Nabulsi A. _et al._ (2008) "The 2007 season of excavations at Khirbat as-Samrā ancient cemetery", _ADAJ_ 52 (2008) 203–7; Nabulsi A. _et al._ (2007) "The ancient cemetery in Khirbat as-Samrā after the sixth season of excavation (2006)", _ADAJ_ 51 (2007) 273–81; Nabulsi A. (1998) "The Byzantine cemetery in Samra", in _Khirbet es-Samra en Jordanie 1: La voie romaine, le cimitière, les documents épigraphiques_, edd. J.-B. Humbert and A. Desreumaux (Bibliothèque de l'Antiquité Tardive 1) (Turnhout 1998) 271–9; Sakal F. (2010) "Graves and grave goods of the late Roman and medieval cemeteries", in _Emar after the Enclosure of the Tabqa Dam: The Syrian-German Excavations 1996–2002, vol. 1: Late Roman and Medieval Cemeteries and Environmental Studies_, edd. U. Finkbeiner and F. Sakal (Subartu 25) (Turnhout 2010) 3–52; Rose J. C. _et al._ (2004) "Cemeteries and contents", in _Sa'ad: A Late Roman/Byzantine Site in Northern Jordan_, edd. J. C. Rose and D. L. Burke (Irbid 2004) 43–98; Tatcher A., Nagar Y. and Avshalom-Gorni D. (2002) "Excavations at Khirbet el-Shubeika: The burial caves", in _Eretz Zafon: Studies in Galilean Archaeology_, ed. Z. Gal (Jerusalem 2002) 263–88 (in Hebrew, with English Summary); Nabulsi A. _et al._ (2010) "Excavation at the Blakhiya Byzantine cemetery in Gaza, 1996", _RBibl_ 117 (2010) 602–13; Godlewski W. (1986) _Deir el-Bahari V: Le monastère de St. Phoibammon_ (Warsaw 1986). _Egypt_: Pleşa A. D. (2017) "The late antique and early Islamic necropolises at Matmar and Mostagedda, Middle Egypt: A reassessment of the excavation and present state of the collection", in _Excavating, Analysing, Reconstructing: Textiles of the 1st Millennium AD from Egypt and Neighbouring Countries. Proceedings of the 9th Conference of the Research Group 'Textiles from the Nile Valley', Antwerp, 27–29 November 2015_, edd. A. De Moor, C. Fluck, and P. Linscheid (Tielt 2017) 72–87; Gessler-Löhr B. (2010) "Two child mummies and some grave goods of the Byzantine period from the Egyptian collection at Heidelberg University, Germany", in _Mummies of the World_, edd. A. Wieczorek and W. Rosendahl (Munich 2010) 310–15.

Lamps: Rife J. (2022) "Lamps", in _On the Edge of a Roman Port: The Excavations at Koutsongila, Kenchreai, 2007–2014_, edd. E. Korka and J. Rife (Hesperia Suppl. 52) (Princeton 2022) 749–904; Gerousi E. (2014) Sepulkralkultur auf der Insel Thera (Santorin): _Der spätantike Friedhof in Perissa und seine Ausgrabungsfunde unter besonderer Berücksichtigung der Tonlampen_ (Marburg 2014).

Metal finds: Panelas G. (2022) "The metal finds," in *On the Edge of a Roman Port: The Excavations at Koutsongila, Kenchreai, 2007–2014*, edd. E. Korka and J. Rife (Hesperia Suppl. 52) (Princeton 2022) 1051–14; Nikolsky V. et al. (2004) "Metal objects", in *Ḥorvat Karkur ʿIllit: A Byzantine Cemetery Church in the Northern Negev* (*Final Report of the Excavations 1989–1995*), ed. P. Figueras (Beer-Sheva Archaeological Monographs 1) (Beer-Sheva 2004) 237–64.

Bone and leather: Figueras P., Areal Guerra R. and Metz V. (2004) "Bone, leather and other materials mostly found in tombs", in *Ḥorvat Karkur ʿIllit: A Byzantine Cemetery Church in the Northern Negev* (*Final Report of the Excavations 1989–1995*), ed. P. Figueras (Beer-Sheva Archaeological Monographs 1) (Beer-Sheva 2004) 232–6.

Basket: South K. (2017) "The use of basket-weave linen in burials of the necropolis of Fag el-Gamus, Egypt", in *Excavating, Analysing, Reconstructing: Textiles of the 1st Millennium AD from Egypt and Neighbouring Countries. Proceedings of the 9th Conference of the Research Group 'Textiles from the Nile Valley', Antwerp, 27–29 November 2015*, edd. A. De Moor, C. Fluck and P. Linscheid (Tielt 2017) 88–107.

Textiles (General): Schrenk S. (2004) *Textilien des Mittelmeerraumes aus spätantiker bis frühislamischer Zeit* (Abegg-Stiftung. Textilsammlung der Abegg-Stiftung 4) (Riggisberg 2004).

Textiles (Regional): *Gaul*: Rast-Eicher A., Nowik W. and Garnier N. (2017) "Textiles from two Late Roman graves found in a mausoleum in Jaunay-Clan near Poitiers, France", in *Archaeological Textiles – Links Between Past and Present. NESAT XIII – North European Symposium for Archaeological Textiles*, edd. M. Bravermanová, H. Březinová and J. Malcolm-Davies (Prague 2017) 73–80. *Trier*: De Jonghe D. and Tavernier M. (1977–78) "Die spätantiken Köper-4-Damaste aus dem Sarg des Bischofs Paulinus in der Krypa der Paulinus-Kirche zu Trier", *TrZ* 40/41 (1977–78) 145–74; Desrosiers S. (2000) "Textiles découverts dans les deux tombes du Bas Empire à Naintré (Vienne)", in *Archéologie des textiles des origines au Vᵉ siècle: actes du colloque de Lattes*, edd. D. Cardon and M. Feugère (Monographies Instrumentum 14) (Montagnac 2000) 195–207; Kajitani N. (2006) "Textiles and their context in the third to fourth century CE cemetery of al-Bagawat, Khargah Oasis, Egypt, from the 1907–1931 excavations by The Metropolitan Museum of Art", in *Textiles in Situ: Their Find Spots in Egypt and Neighbouring Countries in the First Millennium CE*, ed. S. Schrenk (Riggisberger Berichte 13) (Riggisberg 2006) 95–115; Dreyspring B. and Schrenk S. (2007) "Seidenfragmente mit Spuren einer Stickerei aus dem Paulinusgrab", in *Konstantin der Große: Imperator Caesar Flavius Constantinus*, edd. A. Demandt and J. Engemann (Ausstellungskatalog Trier) (Mainz 2007) Kat. 11.4.34 (on CD-ROM or www.dreyspring-textilrestaurierung.de/paulinusgrab.htm, accessed 07.07.2018); Reifarth N. (2013) "Rätselhafte Goldgewebestreifen in spätantiken Sarkophagen aus St. Maximin in Trier", in *Die Macht der Toga. Dresscode im Römischen Weltreich*, edd. M. Tellenbach, R. Schulz and A. Wieczoreck (Publikation der Reiss-Engelhorn-Museen in Kooperation mit dem Roemer- und Pelizaeus-Museum 56) (Regensburg 2013) 242–7; Reifarth N. (2013) *Zur Ausstattung spätantiker Elitegräber aus St. Maximin in Trier: Purpur, Seide, Gold und Harze* (Internationale Archäologie 124) (Westfalen 2013). *Egypt*: Forrer R. (1891) *Römische und byzantinische Seiden-textilien aus dem Gräber-felde von Achmim-Panopolis* (Strassburg 1891); Letellier-Willemin F. (2012) "Contribution of textiles as archaeological artefacts to the study of the Christian cemetery of el-Deir", in *The Oasis Papers 6: Proceedings of the Sixth International Conference of the Dakhleh Oasis Project*, edd. R. S. Bagnall et al. (Dakhleh Oasis Project 15) (Oxford-Oakville 2012) 491–99; Letellier-Willemin F. (2013) "The embroidered tunic of Dush: A new approach", in *Drawing the Threads Together: Textiles and Footwear of the 1st Millennium AD from Egypt. Proceedings of the 7th Conference of the Research Group 'Textiles from the Nile Valley', Antwerp 7–9 October 2011*, edd. A. De Moor, C. Fluck and P. Linscheid (Tielt 2013) 22–33; South K. and Muhlestein K. M. (2013) "Regarding ribbons: The spread and use of narrow purpose-woven bands in Late Roman Egyptian burials", in *Drawing the Threads Together: Textiles and Footwear of the 1st Millennium AD from Egypt. Proceedings of the 7th Conference of the Research Group 'Textiles from the Nile Valley', Antwerp 7–9 October 2011*, edd. A. De Moor, C. Fluck and P. Linscheid (Tielt 2013) 56–73; Pritchard F. (2017) "Textiles from Wadi Sarga, a 6th to 8th-century monastic site in Middle Egypt excavated in 1913/1914", in *Excavating, Analysing, Reconstructing: Textiles of the 1st Millennium AD from Egypt and Neighbouring Countries. Proceedings of the 9th Conference of the Research Group 'Textiles from the Nile Valley', Antwerp, 27–29 November 2015*, edd. A. De Moor, C. Fluck and P. Linscheid (Tielt 2017) 60–71; Tatz S. (2017) "The textile finds from the monastery of Deir el-Bachît/Paulos monastery (6th–10th century) in Western Thebes", in *Excavating, Analysing, Reconstructing: Textiles of the 1st Millennium AD from Egypt and Neighbouring Countries. Proceedings of the 9th Conference of the Research Group 'Textiles from the Nile Valley', Antwerp, 27–29 November 2015*, edd. A. De Moor, C. Fluck and

P. Linscheid (Tielt 2017) 108–24; Tolmacheva E. (2017) "Archae-
ological textiles at the Deir el-Banat site (Fayyum): Parallels,
study, conservation and general description", in *Excavating,
Analysing, Reconstructing: Textiles of the 1st Millennium AD
from Egypt and Neighbouring Countries. Proceedings of the 9th
Conference of the Research Group 'Textiles from the Nile Valley',
Antwerp, 27–29 November 2015*, edd. A. De Moor, C. Fluck and
P. Linscheid (Tielt 2017) 32–59.

Dress Ornaments: *General*: Pröttel P.-M. (1999) "Zur Chronologie
der Zwiebelknopffibeln", *JRGZM* 35 (1999) 347–72; Werner W.
(1955) "Byzantinische Gürtelschnallen des 6. und 7. Jahrhunderts aus der Sammlung Diergardt," *KölnJb* 1 (1955) 36–48.
Regional: Pogačnik M. (2007) *Poznorimske pasne spone v grobnih kontekstih na področju Norika in Panonije* (Unpublished
PhD thesis, University of Ljubljana 2007); Soupault V. (2003)
*Les éléments métalliques du costume masculin dans les prov-
inces romaines de la mer Noire: IIIᵉ–Vᵉ s. ap. J.-C.* (Oxford 2003).
By Site: Tomažinčič Š. (2018) "Belt types, identity and social
status in late antiquity: the belt set in Emona's grave 18", *JRA*
31 (2018) 426–44; Čaval S. (2013) "Poznoantične okrasne igle
vrste stilus v Sloveniji / Late Antique decorative pins of the
stylus type in Slovenia", *Arheološki vestnik / Acta archaeologica*
64 (2013) 197–248; Vuga D. (1985) "Moški grob z vrta Narodnega muzeja v Ljubljani. Poznorimske in barbarske ledvičaste
pasne spone z ovalnim okovom", *Arheološki vestnik / Acta
archaeologica* 36 (1985) 237–54.

Glass: Antonaras A. (2003) "The use of glass in Byzantine jewellery – the evidence from Northern Greece (fourth-sixteenth
centuries)", *Annales du 16ᵉ Congrès AIHV* (2003) 331–35; Eger
C., Nabulsi A. and Ahrens A. (2011) "Ein spätrömisches Grab
mit einem Glasbecher E. 216 und einem Skarabäus aus Jordan – Khirbet es-Shamra, Grab 310", *KölnJb* 44 (2011) 215–31.

Mummy Labels: Wilfong T. G. (1995) "Mummy labels from the
Oriental Institute's excavations at Medinet Habu", *Bulletin of
the American Society of Papyrologists* 32 (1995) 157–81.

Coins: Makropoulou D. (2001) "Ταφικά ευρήματα, νομίσματα και
νομισματικοί θησαυροί στα παλαιοχριστιανικά κοιμητήρια της
Θεσσαλονίκης", in *Αφιέρωμα στη μνήμη του Σωτήρη Κίσσα*, edd.
A. Kalamartzi-Katsarou and S. Tampaki (Thessaloniki 2001)
263–72.

Ceramics: *Regional*: Salvi D. (2010) "La Campidanese. Ceramica comune da mensa della Sardegna meridionale nei
contesti chiusi di eta' tardoantica della necropoli di Pill'e
Matta, Quartucciu (Cagliari – Sardegna – Italia)", in *LRCW3
Late Roman Coarse Wares and Amphorae in the Mediterranean (BAR International Series 2185) (1)*, edd. S. Menchelli,

S. Santoro, M. Pasquinucci and G. Guiducci. (Oxford 2010)
235–43; Giuntella A. M. (1985) "Materiali ceramici", in *Mensea e riti funerari in Sardegna. La testimonianza di Cornus.
Mediterraneo tardoantico e medievale. Scavi e ricerche*, edd.
A. M. Giuntella, G. Borghetti, and D. Stiaffini (Taranto 1985)
69–116; Plesničar Gec L. (1977) *Keramika emonskih nekropol*
(Ljubljana 1977); Kormazopoulou L. and Chatzilazarou D.
(2010) "Τα αγγεία του σπηλαιοβαράθρου Ανδρίτσας Αργολίδας:
Προκαταρκτική παρουσιάση ενός κλειστού συνόλου του τέλους
της ύστερης αρχαιότητας και κάποιες απόπειρες ερμηνείας", in
*Κεραμική της υστέρης αρχαιότητας από τον Ελλαδικό χώρο (3ος–7ος αι.
μ.Χ.). Επιστημονική συνάντηση*, edd. D. Papanikola-Bakirtzi and
D. Kousoulakou (Thessaloniki 2010) 169–84; Tzavella E. (2010)
"Κεραμική από αθηναϊκούς τάφους του τέλους της αρχαιότητας
και οι μαρτυρίες της για τον 7ο αι. στην Αττική", in *Κεραμική της
υστέρης αρχαιότητας από τον Ελλαδικό χώρο (3ος–7ος αι. μ.Χ.). Επιστημονική συνάντηση*, edd. D. Papanikola-Bakirtzi and D. Kousoulakou (Thessaloniki 2010) 649–70.

Science

Methods: Killgrove K. (2018) "Using skeletal remains as a proxy
for Roman lifestyles: The potential and problems with osteological reconstructions of health, diet, and stature", in *The
Routledge Handbook of Diet and Nutrition in the Roman World*,
edd. C. Holleran and P. Erdkamp (London 2018) 245–58;
Redfern R. C. and DeWitte S. N. (2011) "A new approach to the
study of Romanization in Britain: a regional perspective of cul-
tural change in late Iron Age and Roman Dorset using the Siler
and Gompertz – Makeham models of mortality", *American
Journal of Physical Anthropology* 144 (2011) 269–85; Devièse Th.,
Ribechini E., Castex D., Stuart B., Regert M. and Colombini M. P.
(2017) "A multi-analytical approach using FTIR, GC/MS and
Py-GC/MS revealed early evidence of embalming practices in
Roman catacombs", *Microchemical Journal* 133 (2017) 49–59;
Fuller B. T., Molleson T. I., Harris D. A., Gilmour L. T., and
Hedges R. E. M. (2006) "Isotopic evidence for breastfeeding
and possible adult dietary differences from late/sub Roman
Britain", *American Journal Physical Anthropology* 129 (2006)
45–54; Jordana X., Malgosa A., Casté B. *et al.* (2019) "Lost in
transition: the dietary shifts from Late Antiquity to the Early
Middle Ages in the North Eastern Iberian Peninsula", *Archaeo-
logical and Anthropological Science* 11 (2019) 3751–63.

Isotopes (Regional): *Britain*: Cummings C. (2008) *Food and Society in Late Roman Britain: Determining Dietary Patterns Using*

Stable Isotope Analysis (Unpublished Doctoral Thesis, University of Oxford 2008); Eckardt H., Müldner G. and Lewis M. (2014) "People on the move in Roman Britain", *World Archaeology* 46 (2014) 534–50; Müldner G., Chenery C. and Eckardt H. (2011) "The 'Headless Romans': multi-isotope investigations of an unusual burial ground from Roman Britain", *Journal of Archaeological Science* 38 (2011) 280–90; Müldner G. (2013) "Stable isotopes and diet: their contribution to Romano-British research", *Antiquity* 87 (2013) 137–49. <u>Macedonia</u>: Bourbou C., Fuller B., Garvie-Lok S. and Richards M. (2011) "Reconstructing the diets of Greek Byzantine populations (6th–15th centuries AD) using carbon and nitrogen stable isotope ratios", *American Journal of Physical Anthropology* 146 (2011) 569–81.

Isotopes (By site): <u>Britain</u>: Eckardt H. *et al* (2009) "Oxygen and strontium isotope evidence for mobility in Roman Winchester", *Journal of Archaeological Science* 36 (2009) 2816–25; Cummings C. and Hedges R. (2010) "Carbon and nitrogen stable isotope analyses", in *The Late Roman Cemetery at Lankhills, Winchester, Excavations 2000–2005*, P. Booth, A. Simmonds, A. Boyle, S. Clough, H. E. M. Cool and D. Poore (Oxford Archaeology Monograph 10) (Oxford 2010) 411–21; Chenery C. and Evans J. (2012) "Results of oxygen, strontium, carbon and nitrogen isotope analysis for the 'Kingsholm Goth'", *Trans Bristol and Gloucestershire Archaeol Society* 130 (2012) 89–98; Cheung C., Schroeder H. and Hedges R. E. M. (2012) "Diet, social differentiation and cultural change in Roman Britain: new isotopic evidence from Gloucestershire", *Archaeological and Anthropological Science* 4 (2012) 61–73; Eckardt H., Muldner G. and Speed G. (2015) "The late Roman field army in northern Britain? Mobility, material culture, and multi-isotope analysis at Scorton (N Yorks)", *Britannia* 46 (2015) 191–223; Shaw H., Montgomery J., Redfern R., Gowland R. L. and Evans J. (2016) "Identifying migrants in Roman London using lead and strontium stable isotopes", *Journal Archaeol Science* 66 (2016) 57–68; Redfern R., Gowland R., Millard A., Powell L. and Gröcke D. (2018) "'From the mouths of babes': A subadult dietary stable isotope perspective on Roman London (Londinium)", *Journal of Archaeological Science: Reports* 19 (2018) 1030–40. <u>Asia</u>: Wong, M., Rasmus Brandt J., Ahrens S., Jaouen K., Bjørnstad G., Naumann E., Wenn C. C., Kiesewetter H., Laforest C., Hagelberg E., Lam V. C. and Richards M. (2018) "Pursuing pilgrims: Isotopic investigations of Roman and Byzantine mobility at Hierapolis, Turkey", *Journal of Archaeological Science: Reports* 17 (2018) 520–28. <u>Oriens</u>: Gregoricka L. A. and Sheridan S. G. (2012) "Food for thought. Isotopic evidence for dietary and weaning practices in a Byzantine urban

monastery in Jerusalem", in *Bioarchaeology and behavior. The people of the ancient Near East*, ed. M. A. Perry (Gainesville 2012) 138–64; Perry M. A., Coleman D. S., and Dettman D. L. (2012) "Condemned to metallum? Illuminating life at the Byzantine mining camp at Phaeno in Jordan", in *Bioarchaeology and behavior. The people of the ancient Near East*, ed. M. A. Perry (Gainesville 2012) 115–37. <u>Egypt</u>: Dupras T., Schwarcz H. P., and Fairgrieve S. I. (2008) "Dining in the Dakhla Oasis: Determining diet from stable isotopes", in *The Oasis Papers 2: Proceedings of the Second International Conference of the Dakhleh Oasis Project*, ed. M. F. Wiseman (Dakhleh Oasis Project 12) (Oxford-Oakville 2008) 119–27.

DNA: Geary P. (2019) "The use of Ancient DNA to analyse population movements between Pannonia and Italy in the sixth century", in *Le migrazioni nell'Alto Medioevo, Atti della LXVI Settimana del Centro di Studi sull'Alto Medioevo (Spoleto 2018)*, (Spoleto 2019) 45–62 (Italian version published as: "Tracciare la migrazione longobarda attraverso il DNA nucleare", in *Migrazioni, Clan, Culture. Archeologia, Genetica, Isotopi Stabili*, ed. Giostra C. (Archeologia Barbarica 3) (Mantua 2019) 35–49); Harbeck M., Seifert L., Hänsch S., Wagner D. M., Birdsell D., Parise K. L., Wiechmann I., Grupe G., Thomas A., Keim P., Zöller L., Bramanti b., Riehm J. M. and Scholz H. C. (2013) "Yersinia pestis DNA from skeletal remains from the 6th century AD reveals insights into Justinianic plague", *Plos Pathogens* 9.5: e1003349 (2013).

Resinous materials: <u>General</u>: Brettell R., Schotsmans E., Martin W. Stern B. and Heron C. (2018) "The final masquerade: resinous substances and Roman mortuary rites", in *The Bioarchaeology of Ritual and Religion*, edd. A. Livarda, R. Madgwick and S. R. Mora (Oxford 2018) 44–57. <u>Britain</u>: Brettell R. (2016) *The Final Masquerade: a Molecular-Based Approach to the Identification of Resinous Plant Exudates in Roman Mortuary Contexts in Britain and Evaluation of their Significance* (Ph.D thesis, Univ. of Bradford 2016); Brettell R., Schotsmans E. M. J., Walton Rogers P., Reifarth N., Redfern R. C., Stern B., and Heron C. P. (2015) "'Choicest unguents': molecular evidence for the use of resinous plant exudates in late Roman mortuary rites in Britain", *Journal of Archaeological Science* 53 (2015) 639–48; Brettell R., Stern B., and Heron C. P. (2015) "Mersea Island barrow: molecular evidence for frankincense", *Essex Society for Archaeology and History* 4 (2015) 81–7; Brettell R., Stern B., Reifarth N. and Heron C. (2014) "The 'semblance of immortality'? Resinous materials and mortuary rites in Roman Britain", *Archaeometry* 56 (2014) 444–59. <u>Gaul</u>: Devièse T. Ribechini P., Baraldi B., Farago-Szekeres H. and Duday M. (2011) "First chemical evidence of royal purple as a material used for funeral treatment discovered in a Gallo Roman burial, Naintré, France, third century AD", *Analytical and Bioanalytical Chemistry* 401 (2011) 1739–48. *Italy*: Bruni S. and Guglielmi V. (2005) "Le analisi chimiche", in *La signora del sarcofago: una sepoltura di rango nella necropoli dell'Università Cattolica*, edd. M. P. Rossignani, M. Sannazaro and G. Legrottaglie (Milan 2005) 131–6.

Anthropology (Regional): *Britain*: Moore A. (2016) "The life course", in *The Oxford Handbook of Roman Britain*, edd. M. Millett, L. Revell and A. Moore (Oxford 2016) 321–40. *Italy*: Di Salvo R. (2016) "La necropoli paleocristiana di San Miceli: aspetti antropologici e paleopatologici", *Sicilia Archeologica* 108 (2016) 235–40; Fabbri P. F. and Farina L. (2010) "Note antropologiche su alcune sepolture tardoantiche (SAS 3&4) 2007–08", *Annali della Scuola Normale Superiore di Pisa* 5.2/2 (2010) 21–5; Ronco D. (1995) "Studio antropologico del materiale scheletrico", in *La necropoli paleocristiana sub divo di Agrigento*, ed. R. M. Bonacasa Carra (Rome 1995) 328–56. *Pannonia*: Leben-Seljak P. (2018) "Antropološka analiza skeletov", in *Miren. Grobišče iz časa preseljevanja ljudstev*, edd. V. Tratnik and Š. Karo (Ljubljana 2018) 58–70; Leben-Seljak P. (2003) "Antropološka analiza poznoantičnega grobišča na Vrajku v Gornjem Mokronogu", *Arheološki vestnik / Acta archaeologica* 54 (2003) 397–420; Leben-Seljak P. (1996) *Antropološka analiza poznoantičnih in srednjeveških grobišč Bleda in okolice / Anthropological analysis of late antiquity and medieval necropolises at Bled and surroundings* (Unpublished PhD., Univ. of Ljubljana 1996); Miriţoiu N. and Soficaru A. D. (2003) "Studiu antropologic al osemintelor descoperite în cripta basilicii de la Murighiol (anticul Halmyris)", *Peuce* 14 (2003) 531–80. *Oriens*: Nagar Y. and Sonntag F. (2008) "Byzantine period burials in the Negev: anthropological descriptions and summary", *IEJ* 58 (2008) 79–93; Grossschmidt K. and Tutschek H. (2005) "Anthropologische Aussagen und ein mikroradiographischer Nachweis von Brandspuren", in *Emmaus-Nicopolis: Ausgrabungen 2001–2005*, edd. K. H. Fleckenstein and L. Fleckenstein (Neckenmarkt 2005) 404–35. *Egypt*: Kaczmarek M. (2012) "Anthropological studies on juvenile skeletal remains from the necropolis at Marina el-Alamein, Egypt", in *L'enfant et la mort dans l'Antiquité II: Types de tombes et traitement du corps des enfants dans l'Antiquité gréco-romaine. Actes de la table ronde internationale organisée à Alexandrie, Centre d'Études Alexandrines, 12–14 novembre 2009*, ed. M.-D. Nenna (Études Alexandrines 26) (Alexandria 2012) 293–313.

Osteology: *Britain*: Rohnbogner A. (2017) "Listening to the kids: the value of childhood palaeopathology for the study of rural Roman Britain", *Britannia* 48 (2017) 221–52; Gowland R. L. (2016) "That "tattered coat upon a stick" the ageing body: evidence for elder abuse and marginalisation in Roman Britain", in *Care in the Past: Archaeological and Inter-Disciplinary Perspectives*, edd. L. Powell, W. Southwell-Wright and R. L. Gowland (Oxford 2016) 71–92; Lewis M. E. (2010) "Life and death in a civitas capital: Metabolic disease and trauma in the children from late Roman Dorchester, Dorset", *American Journal of Physical Anthropology* 142 (2010) 405–16; Redfern R. and Roberts C. A. (2005) "Health in Romano-British urban communities: reflections from the cemeteries", in *Fertile Ground: Papers in Honour of Susan Limbrey. Symposia of the Association for Environmental Archaeology*, edd. D. N. Smith, M. B. Brickley and W. Smith (Oxford 2005) 115–29; Mays S. (2003) "Comment on 'A Bayesian approach to ageing perinatal skeletal material from archaeological sites: implications for the evidence for infanticide in Roman Britain' by R. L. Gowland and A. T. Chamberlain", *Journal of Archaeological Science* 30 (2003) 1695–700; Gowland R. L. and Chamberlain A. T. (2002) "A Bayesian approach to ageing perinatal skeletal material from archaeological sites: implications for the evidence for infanticide in Roman Britain", *Journal of Archaeological Science* 29 (2002) 677–85. *Pannonia*: Šlaus M., Novak M., Bedić Ž. and Strinović D. (2012) "Bone fractures as indicators of intentional violence in the eastern Adriatic from the antique to the late medieval period (2nd–16th century AD)", *American Journal of Physical Anthropology* 149 (2012) 26–38; Novak M. and Šlaus M. (2010) "Bone traumas in late antique populations from Croatia", *Collegium anthropologicum* 34 (2010) 1239–48. *Thrace*: Miriţoiu N. and Soficaru A. D. (2007) "Osteobiographical study of the human remains discovered in the crypt of Murighiol (antique Halmyris) basilica", *Il Mar Nero* 5 (2007) 169–90. *Oriens*: Nagar Y. (2011) "Human osteological database at the Israel antiquities authority: Overview and some examples of use", *Bioarchaeology of the Near East* 5 (2011) 1–18; Zias J. and Spigelman M. (2004) "Report on burials and osteoarchaeological analysis", in *Ḥorvat Karkur 'Illit: A Byzantine Cemetery Church in the Northhusseiern Negev (Final Report of the Excavations 1989–1995)*, ed. P. Figueras (Beer-Sheva Archaeological Monographs 1) (Beer-Sheva 2004) 307–15; Smith P. and Kahila G. (1992) "Identification of infanticide in archaeological sites: a case study from the late Roman and Byzantine periods at Ashkelon, Israel", *JAS* 19 (1992) 667–75. *Egypt*: Lösch S., Hower-Tilmann E., and Zink A. (2012) "Mummies and skeletons from the Coptic monastery complex Deir el-Bachit in Thebes-West, Egypt", *Anthropologischer Anzeiger* 70 (2012) 27–41

Bioarchaeology: *General*: Gowland R. L. (2015) "Entangled lives: Implications of the developmental origins of health and disease hypothesis for bioarchaeology and the life course", *American Journal of Physical Anthropology* 158 (2015) 530–40; Stathakopoulos D. (2012) "Death in the countryside: some thoughts on the effects of famine and epidemics", *Antiquité Tardive* 20 (2012) 105–14. *Britain*: Gowland R. L. (2017) "Embodied identities in Roman Britain: a bioarchaeological approach", *Britannia* 48 (2017) 177–94; Redfern R., DeWitte S. N., Pearce J., Hamlin C. and Dinwiddy, K. E. (2015) "Urban – rural differences in Roman Dorset, England: A bioarchaeological perspective on Roman settlements," *American Journal of Physical Anthropology* 157 (2015) 107–20; Pitts M. and Griffin R. (2012) "Exploring health and social well-being in Late Roman Britain: an intercemetery approach", *American Journal of Archaeology* 116.2 (2012) 253–76; Redfern R. and Roberts C. A. (2005) "Health in Romano-British urban communities: reflections from the cemeteries", in *Fertile Ground: Papers in Honour of Susan Limbrey. Symposia of the Association for Environmental Archaeology*, edd. D. N. Smith, M. B. Brickley, and W. Smith (Oxford 2005) 115–29; Gowland R. L. (2004) "The social identity of health in late Roman Britain", *Theoretical Roman Archaeology Journal* (2004) 135–46. *Gaul* (Rhaetia): Depaermentier M., Kempf M., Spichtig N., Krause-Kyora B. *et al.* (2023) "Bioarchaeological analyses reveal long-lasting continuity at the periphery of the Late Antique Roman Empire", *iScience* 26 (2023). DO – 10.1016/j.isci.2023.107034. *Macedonia*: Tritsaroli P. and Kardima C. (2017) "The people of early byzantine Maroneia", *Bioarchaeology of the Near East* 11 (2017) 29–62; Tritsaroli P. (2017) "Life and death at early byzantine Akraiphnio, Greece: A biocultural approach", *Anthropologie* 55 (2017) 243–63; Bourbou C. (2004) *The People of Early Byzantine Eleftherna and Messene (6th–7th Centuries AD): A Bioarchaeological Approach* (Athens 2004); Bourbou C. (2016) *Health and Disease in Byzantine Crete (7th–12th Centuries AD)* (Abingdon 2016). *Asia*: Paine R. R., Vargium R., Coppa A., Morselli, C. and Schneider E. E. (2007) "A health assessment of high status Christian burials recovered from the Roman-Byzantine archeological site of Elaiussa Sebaste, Turkey", *Homo* 58 (2007) 173–90. *Egypt*: Dupras T. L., Williams L. J., Wheeler S. M., and Sheldrick P. G. (2016) "Life and death in the desert: A bioarchaeological study of human remains from the Dakhleh Oasis, Egypt", in *Mummies, Magic and Medicine in Ancient Egypt: Multidisciplinary Essays for Rosalie David,* edd. C. Price, R. Forshaw, A. Chamberlain and P. Nicholson (Manchester 2016) 286–304; Tritsaroli P. (2006) *Pratiques funéraires en Grèce centrale à la période byzantine: Analyse à partir des données archéologiques et biologiques* (Ph.D. diss., Muséum national d'histoire naturelle, Paris 2006). *Plague*: Gelabert P. (2020) "Past diseases: present questions and future perspectives from an archaeogenetic approach", *European Journal of Post-Classical Archaeologies* 10 (2020) 35–56; Eisenberg M. and Mordechai L. (2019) "The Justinianic Plague: an interdisciplinary review", *Byzantine and Modern Greek Studies* 43.2 (2019) 156–80; Keller M., Spyrou M. A., Scheib C. L., Neumann G. U., Kröpelin A., Haas-Gebhard B., Päffgen B., Haberstroh J., Ribera A., Raynaud C., Cessford C., Durand R., Stadler P., Nägele K., Bates J. S., Trautmann B., Inskip S. A., Peters J., Robb J. E., Kivisild T., Castex D., McCormick M., Bos K. I., Harbeck M., Herbig A. and Krause J. (2018) "Ancient Yersinia pestis genomes from across Western Europe reveal early diversification during the First Pandemic (541–750)", *PNAS* 116.25 (2019) 12363–72; Mordechai l. and Eisenberg M. (2019) "Rejecting catastrophe: The case of the Justinianic plague", *Past and Present* 244.1 (2019) 3–50; Little L. K. (2007) ed. *Plague and the End of Antiquity: The Pandemic of 541–750* (Cambridge 2007); Stathakopoulos D. (2000) "The Justinianic plague revisited", *Byzantine and Modern Greek Studies* 24 (2000) 256–76; Birabem J.-N. (1989) "Rapport: la peste du VIe siècle dans l'empire byzantin", in *Hommes et richesses dans l'Empire byzantin. Tome 1. IVe–VIIe siècle*, ed. Abadie-Reynal (Paris 1989) 120–5; Durliat J. (1989) "La peste du VIe siècle. Pour un nouvel examen des sources byzantines", in *Hommes et richesses dans l'Empire byzantin. Tome 1. IVe–VIIe siècle*, ed. Abadie-Reynal (Paris 1989) 107–19. *Children*: Gowland R. L. and Redfern R. (2010) "Childhood health in the Roman world: perspectives from the centre and margin of the empire", *Childhood in the Past* 3 (2010) 15–42; Lewis M. E. (2007) *The Bioarchaeology of Children: Perspectives from Biological and Forensic Anthropology* (Cambridge 2007); Gowland R. L. (2016a) "Ideas of childhood in Roman Britain: the biological and material evidence", in *The Oxford Handbook of Roman Britain*, edd. M. Millett, L. Revell, and A. Moore (Oxford 2016) 303–20; Mays S. and Eyers J. (2011) "Perinatal infant death at the Roman villa site at Hambleden, Buckinghamshire, England", *Journal of Archaeological Science* 38 (2011) 1931–8.

Social Data

General: Selected papers in Struck M. (1993) ed. *Romerzeitliche Graber als Quellen zu Religion, Bevolkerungsstruktur und Sozialgeschichte, Archaeologische Schriften des Institute fur*

Vor- und Fruhgeschichte der Johannes Gutenburg-Universitat Mainz (Mainz 1993); Morris I. (1992) *Death Ritual and Social Structure in Classical Antiquity* (Cambridge 1992).

Age: Gowland R. (2006) "Ageing the past: examining age identity from funerary evidence", in *Social Archaeology of Funerary Remains*, edd. R. Gowland and Ch. Knüsel (Oxford 2006) 143–54. *Britain*: Moore A. (2010) "Age and identity in funerary contexts: The elderly in southern Roman Britain", *Theoretical Roman Archaeology Journal* 105. 10.16995/TRAC2009 (2010) 105–19; Gowland R. L. (2007) "Age, ageism and osteological bias: the evidence from late Roman Britain", *JRA* Suppl. Ser. 65 (2007) 153–69; Gowland R. L. (2002) *Examining Age as an Aspect of Social Identity in Fourth to Sixth Century England Through the Analysis of Mortuary Evidence* (Unpublished Ph.D. thesis, University of Durham 2002); Gowland R. L. (2001) "Playing dead: implications of mortuary evidence for the social construction of childhood in Roman Britain", in *Tenth Annual Theoretical Roman Archaeology Conference*, edd. G. Davies, A. Gardner and K. Lockyear (Oxford 2001) 152–68. *Gaul*: Schwinden L. (1986) "Kinderleben und Kindersterblichkeit nach antiken Denkmälern aus Trier", *Funde und Ausgrabungen im Bezirk Trier* 18 = *Kurtrierisches Jahrbuch* 26 (1986) 30–37. *Thrace*: Achim I. (2012) "Early Roman and late Roman child graves in Dobrudja (Romania). Preliminary considerations", in H*omines, Funera, Astra: Proceedings of the International Symposium on Funerary Anthropology: 5–8 June 2011 '1 Decembrie 1918' University* (*Alba Iulia, Romania*), edd. R. Kogălniceanu *et al.* (BAR Int. Ser. 2410) (Oxford: 2012) 183–96.

Gender: *General*: Mogen S. M. (2012) *Women and Death Rituals in Late Antiquity: Forming the Christian Identity* (Lambert Academic Publishing 2012); Šterbenc Erker S. (2011) "Gender and Roman funeral ritual", in *Memory and Mourning. Studies on Roman Death*, edd. V. M. Hope and J. Huskinson (Oxford 2011) 40–60). *Britain*: Hamlin C. (2007) *The Material Expression of Social Change: The Mortuary Correlates of Gender and Age in Late Pre-Roman Iron Age and Roman Dorset* (Wisconsin 2007); Redfern R. (2003) "Sex and the city: A biocultural investigation into female health in Roman Britain", in *TRAC 2002: Proceedings of the Twelfth Annual Theoretical Roman Archaeology Conference*, edd. G. Carr, E. Swift and J. Weekes (Kent 2002) 147–70; Watts D. J. (2001) "The silent minority: women in Romano-British cemeteries", *Archaeological Journal* 158 (2001) 332–47; Davison C. (2000) "Gender imbalances in Romano-British cemetery populations: a re-evaluation of the evidence", in *Burial, Society and Context in the Roman World*, edd. J. Pearce, M. Millett and M. Struck

(Oxford 2000) 231–7; Stoodley N. (1999) *The Spindle and the Spear; A Critical Enquiry into the Construction and Meaning of Gender in the Early Anglo-Saxon Burial Rite* (BAR 288) (Oxford 1999). *Pannonia*: Gilmour R. J., Gowland R., Roberts C., Bernert Z., Kiss K. K. and Lassányi G. (2015) "Gendered differences in accidental trauma to upper and lower limb bones at Aquincum, Roman Hungary", *International Journal of Paleopathology* 11 (2015) 75–91; Stemberger K. (2020) "A study of female-associated burials from Roman-period Slovenia", in *Un-Roman Sex: Gender, Sexuality, and Lovemaking in the Roman Provinces and Frontiers,* edd. T. Ivleva and R. Collins (London 2020) 210–37; Stemberger K. (2014) "Identity of females buried at Colonia Iulia Emona / Rekonstruiranje identitet žensk z emonskih nekropol", *Arheo* 31 (2014) 69–81; Knific T. (2005) "Gospe iz mesta Karnija", *Kranjski zbornik* (2005) 331–43.

Infants: *General*: Vitale L. (2015) "Lo spazio degli infanti nei cimiteri tardoantichi: organizzazione e distribuzione spaziale fra ritualità e consuetudini sociali", in *Isole e terraferma nel primo cristianesimo. Identità locale ed interscambi culturali, religiosi e produttivi, Atti XI Congresso Nazionale di Archeologia Cristiana, Cagliari, 23–27 settembre 2014*, edd R. Martorelli, A. Piras and P. G. Spanu (Cagliari 2015) 197–202; Scott E. (2001) "Unpicking a myth: the infanticide of female and disabled infants in antiquity", in *Tenth Annual Theoretical Roman Archaeology Conference*, edd. G. Davies, A. Gardner and K. Lockyear (Oxford 2001) 143–51; Martin-Kilcher S. (2000) "Mors immatura in the Roman world – a mirror of society and tradition", in *Burial, Society and Context in the Roman World*, edd. J. Pearce and M. Millett (Oxford 2000) 63–77; Scott E. (1999) *The Archaeology of Infancy and Infant Death* (Oxford 1999). *Britain*: Gowland R. L., Chamberlain A. T., and Redfern R. C. (2014) "On the brink of being: re-evaluating infanticide and infant burial in Roman Britain", in *Infant health and death in Roman Italy and beyond* (*JRA* Suppl. Ser. 96), edd. P. M. Carroll and E-J. Graham (Ann Arbor 2014) 69–88; Watts D. J. (1989) "Infant burials and Romano-British Christianity", *Archaeological Journal* 146.1 (1989) 372–83.

Social Status/Social Identity: Volp U. (2016–2017) "Sacra privata, family duties, and the dead: insights from the fathers and cultural anthropology", *ArchRel* 18–19 (2016–2017) 171–85; Yasin A. M. (2005) "Funerary monuments and collective identity: From Roman family to Christian community", *The Art Bulletin* 87 (2005) 433–57; Pearce J. (2016) "Status and burial", in *The Oxford Handbook of Roman Britain*, edd. M. Millett, L. Revell and A. Moore (Oxford 2016) 341–62; Swift E. (2003) "Late-Roman bead necklaces and bracelets", *JRA* 16 (2003)

336–49; Bollók Á. (forthcoming) "Mortuary display and the burial of the rich in the late antique eastern Mediterranean" (forthcoming).

Ethnicity: Hakenbeck S. E. (2009) ""Hunnic" modified skulls: Physical appearance, identity and the transformative nature of migrations", in *Mortuary Practices and Social Identities in the Middle Ages: Essays in Honour of Heinrich Härke*, edd. H. Williams and D. Sayer (Exeter 2009) 64–80. *Africa:* Kleemann J. (2002) "Quelques réflexions sur l'interprétation ethnique des sépultures habillées considérées comme vandales", *Antiquite Tardive* 10 (2002) 123–29. *Pannonia*: Knific T. and Lux J. (2010) "Otroci iz mesta Karnija", *Kranjski zbornik* (2010) 26–36; Theuws F. (2009) "Grave goods, ethnicity, and the rhetoric of burial rites in late antique Northern Gaul", in *Ethnic Constructs in Antiquity: The Role of Power and Tradition*, edd. T. Derks and N. Roymans (Amsterdam 2009) 283–19.

Burial in Late Antiquity: A Bibliographic Essay

Part 2: Key Sites

Solinda Kamani

Britain

Northern England: *Brougham*: Cool H. E. (2004) *The Roman Cemetery at Brougham, Cumbria; Excavations 1966–67* (Society for the promotion of Roman Studies) (Britannia Monograph Series 21) (London 2004). *York*: Ramm H. G. (1971) "The end of Roman York", in *Soldier and Civilian in Roman Yorkshire*, ed. R. M. Butler (Leicester 1971) 179–99; Leach S., Ekhardt H., Chenery C., Muldner G., and Lewis M. (2009) "A lady of York: migration, ethnicity and identity in Roman Britain", *Antiquity* 84 (2009) 131–45; Leach S., Lewis M., Chenery C., Muldner G., and Eckhardt H. (2010) "Migration and diversity in Roman Britain: a multidisciplinary approach to the identification of immigrants in Roman York, England", *American Journal of Physical Anthropology* 140 (2010) 546–61.

Midlands: *Bingham*: Simmonds A., Allen M., McIntyre L., Simmonds A., and Champness C. (2023) "Agriculture and population: occupation and burials in the extramural area of Margidunum on the Fosse Way in Nottinghamshire", *Britannia* 54 (2023) 1–38. *Lincoln*: Gilmour B. (2007) "Sub-Roman or Saxon, Pagan or Christian: who was buried in the early cemetery at St Paul in the Bail, Lincoln?", in *Pagans and Christians-From Antiquity to the Middle Ages, Papers in Honour of Martin Henig, Presented on the Occasion of his 65th Birthday*, ed. L. Gilmour (BAR Int. Ser. 1610) (Oxford 2007) 229–56. *Wasperton*: Montgomery J., Evans J., and Chenery C. (2009) "Oxygen and strontium isotopes", in *Wasperton. A Roman, British and Anglo-Saxon Community in Central England*, edd. M. Carver, C. Hills and J. Scheschkewitz (Woodbridge 2009) 48–9.

East Anglia: *Blestsoe*: Dawson M. (1994) *A Late Roman Cemetery at Bletsoe, Bedfordshire* (Bedfordshire Archaeology Monograph 1) (Newcastle 1994). *Colchester*: Crummy N., Crummy P., and Crossan C. (1993) *Excavations of Roman and Later Cemeteries, Churches and Monastic Sites in Colchester, 1971–88* (Colchester Archaeol. Rep. 9) (Colchester 1993) 4–163; Millett M. (1995) "An early Christian community at Colchester?", *Archaeological Journal* 152 (1995) 451–54. *Godmanchester*: Jones A. (2003) ed. *Settlement, Burial and Industry in Roman Godmanchester* (BAR Brit. Ser. 346) (Oxford 2003).

London: *Overview*: Ridgeway V. and Watson S. (in this volume) "Burial in Late Antiquity: evidence from Londinium"; Redfern R. C., Marshall M., Eaton K., and Poinar H. N. (2017) ""Written in bone": New discoveries about the lives and burials of four Roman Londoners", *Britannia* 48 (2017) 253–77; Hall J. (1996) "The cemeteries of Roman London: a review", in *Interpreting Roman London: Papers in Memory of Hugh Chapman*, edd. J. Bird, M. Hassall and H. Sheldon (Oxford 1996) 57–84. *Draper's Gardens*: Butler J. and Ridgeway V. (2009) edd. *Secrets of the Gardens: Archaeologists Unearth the Lives of Roman Londoners at Drapers' Gardens* (London 2009). *Eastern Cemetery*: Barber B. and Bowsher D. (2000) *The Eastern Cemetery of Roman London, Excavations 1983–90* (MoLAS Monograph 4) (London 2000). *Spitalfields*: Killock D., Gerrard J., and Langthorne J. (forthcoming) *Excavations at 28–30 Trinity Street* (Pre-Construct Archaeology Monograph); McKenzie M., Thomas C., Powers N. and Wardle A. (2021) *In the Northern Cemetery of Roman London: Excavations at Spitalfields Market, London E1, 1991–2007* (MOLA Monograph 58) (London 2021); Museum of London (1999) *The Spitalfields Roman* (London 1999). *Walbrook*: Ranieri S. and Telfer A., with Walker D., and Yendell V. (2017) *Outside Roman London: Roadside Burials by the Walbrook Stream* (Crossrail Archaeology Series 9) (London 2017); Harward C., Powers N., and Watson S. (2015) *The Upper Walbrook Roman Cemetery: Excavations at Finsbury Circus* (MOLA Monograph Series 69) (London 2015). *Southwark*: Killock D., Shepherd J., Gerrard J., Hayward K., Rielly K., and Ridgeway V. (2015) *Temples and Suburbs: Excavations at Tabard Square, Southwark* (PCA Monograph 18) (London 2015); Melikian M. and Sayer K. (2007) "Recent excavations in the 'Southern Cemetery' of Roman Southwark", in *Proceedings of the Seventh Annual Conference of the British Association for Biological Anthropology and Osteoarchaeology* (BAR Int. Ser. 1712), edd. S. R. Zakrzewski and W. White (Oxford 2007) 14–23; Butler J. (2006) *Reclaiming the Marsh: Archaeological Excavations at Moor House, City of London* (Pre-Construct Archaeology Limited, Monograph 6) (London 2006); Mackinder A. (2000) *A Romano-British Cemetery on Watling Street: Excavations at 165 Great Dover Street,*

© KONINKLIJKE BRILL BV, LEIDEN, 2024 | DOI:10.1163/9789004687974_003
Alexandra Dolea and Luke Lavan (eds) *Burial and Memorial in Late Antiquity*
(Late Antique Archaeology 13) (Leiden 2024), pp. 564–594

Southwark, London (MoLAS Studies Series 4) (London 2000); Beard D. and Cowan C. (1988) "Excavations at 15–23 Southwark Street", *London Archaeologist* 5 (1988) 375–81; Dean M. (1981) "Evidence for more Roman burials in Southwark", *London Archaeologist* 4.2 (1981) 52–3. *Other*: McKinley J. I. (2009) "Inhumation burial in a ditch", in *Living and Working in Roman and Later London* (Wessex Archaeology Report 25), edd. V. Birbeck and J. Schuster (Maidstone 2009) 13–14; Swift D. (2003) *Roman Burials, Medieval Tenements and Suburban Growth: 201 Bishopsgate, City of London* (MoLAS Archaeology Studies 10) (London 2003); Bentley D. and Pritchard F. (1982) "The Roman cemetery at St Bartholomew's Hospital, London", *Trans Middlesex Archaeol Soc* 33 (1982) 134–72; Langton B. (1990) *Excavations and Watching Brief at 1–4 Giltspur Street, 24–30 West Smithfield and 18–20 Cock Lane, EC4 (WES89)* (unpublished MoLAS report) (1990).

South East England: *Canterbury*: Duffy E., Gollop A., and Weekes J. (in this volume) "New cemetery evidence from late Roman Canterbury: the Former Hallet's Garage site in context"; Weekes J. (2017) "Funerary archaeology at St Dunstan's Terrace, Canterbury", in *Death as a Process. The Archaeology of the Roman Funeral*, edd. J. Pearce and J. Weekes (Oxford 2017) 83–122; Weekes J. (2011) "A review of Canterbury's Romano-British cemeteries", *Archaeologia Cantiana* 131 (2011) 23–42; Casa-Hatton R. and Wall W. (2006) "A late Roman cemetery at Durobrivae, Chesterton", *Proceedings of the Cambridge Antiquarian Society* 95 (2006) 5–24. *Dorchester on Thames*: Booth P. (2014) "A late Roman military burial from the Dyke Hills, Dorchester on Thames, Oxfordshire", *Britannia* 45 (2014) 243–73; Chambers R. A. (1987) "The late- and sub-Roman cemetery at Queenford Farm, Dorchester-on-Thames, Oxon", *Oxoniensia* 52 (1987) 35–69. *Oxfordshire*: Booth P. (2001) "Late Roman cemeteries in Oxfordshire: a review", *Oxoniensia* 66 (2001) 13–42; Boylston A., Knüsel C. J., Roberts C., and Dawson M. (2000) "Investigation of a Romano-British rural ritual in Bedford", *Journal of Archaeological Science* 27 (2000) 241–54. *Purton*: Chandler C. J. (1994) *Excavations at the Romano-British Walled Cemetery, Northview Hospital, Purton* (Site monograph, second draft, WILT MC890036, Purton 806, Swindon Museum and Art Gallery 1994). *Winchester*: Ottaway P. J., Qualmann K. E., Rees H., and Scobie G. D. (2012) *The Roman Cemeteries and Suburbs of Winchester: Excavations 1971–86* (Winchester 2012); Booth P., Simmonds A., Boyle A., Clough S., Cool H. E. M., and Poore D. (2010) *The Late Roman Cemetery at Lankhills, Winchester, excavations 2000–2005* (Oxford Archaeology Monograph 10) (Oxford 2010); Cummings C. and Hedges R. (2010) "Carbon and nitrogen stable isotope analyses", in *The late Roman cemetery at Lankhills, Winchester, excavations 2000–2005* (Oxford Archaeology Monograph 10), P. Booth, A. Simmonds, A. Boyle, S. Clough, H. E. M. Cool and D. Poore (Oxford 2010) 411–21; Clough S. and Boyle A. (2010) "Inhumations and disarticulated human bone", in *The Late Roman Cemetery at Lankhills, Winchester, Excavations 2000–2005* (Oxford Archaeology Monograph 10), P. Booth, A. Simmonds, A. Boyle, S. Clough, H. E. M. Cool and D. Poore (Oxford 2010) 339–404; Clarke G. (1979) *Pre-Roman and Roman Winchester – Part II. The Roman Cemetery at Lankhills* (New York 1979).

South-West England: *Cirencester*: McWhirr A., Viner L., and Wells C. (1982) *Roman-British Cemeteries at Cirencester, Cirencester Excavations II* (Cirencester 1982); Holbrook N., Wright J., McSloy E. R., and Geber J. (2017) *The Western Cemetery of Roman Cirencester. Excavations at the Former Bridges Garage, Tetbury Road, Cirencester, 2011–2015, Cirencester Excavations VII* (Cirencester 2017). *Dorchester*: Lewis M. E. (2010) "Life and death in a civitas capital: Metabolic disease and trauma in the children from late Roman Dorchester, Dorset", *American Journal of Physical Anthropology* 142 (2010) 405–16; Davies S. M., Bellamy P. S., Heaton M. J., and Woodward P. J. (2002) *Excavations at Alington Avenue, Fordington, Dorchester, Dorset, 1984–87* (Dorset Natural History and Archaeological Society Monograph 15) (2002); Egging Dinwiddy K. (2009) "A late Roman cemetery at Little Keep, Dorchester, Dorset", http://www.wessexarch.co.uk/projects/dorset/dorchester/little-keep; McKinley J. I. and Egging Dinwiddy K. (2009) "'Deviant' burials from a late Romano-British cemetery at Little Keep, Dorchester", *Proceedings Dorset Natural History & Archaeological Society* 130 (2009) 1–19; Green C. J. S. (1982) "The cemetery of a Romano-British Christian community at Poundbury, Dorchester, Dorset", in *The Early Church in Western Britain and Ireland*, ed. S. M. Pearce (BAR Brit. Ser. 102) (Oxford 1982) 61–76; Farwell D. E. and Molleson T. L. (1993) *Excavations at Poundbury 1966–80, Vol. II, The Cemeteries* (Dorset Natural History and Archaeological Society Monograph 11) (Dorchester 1993); Sparey-Green C. (2004) "Living amongst the dead- From Roman cemetery to post-Roman monastic settlement at Poundbury", in *Debating Late Antiquity in Britain AD 300–700* (BAR Brit. Ser. 365), edd. R. Collins and J. Gerrard (Oxford 2004) 103–11. *Gloucester*: Heighway C. (2012) "Goths and Saxons? The late Roman cemetery at Kingsholm, Gloucester", *Trans Bristol and Gloucestershire Archaeological Society* 130 (2012) 63–88; Chenery C. and Evans J. (2012) "Results of oxygen, strontium, carbon and nitrogen isotope analysis for the 'Kingsholm Goth'", *Trans Bristol and Gloucestershire Archaeological Society* 130 (2012) 89–98; Cullen K., Holbrook N., Watts M., Caffell A., and Holst M. (2006) "A post-Roman cemetery at Hewlett Packard, Filton, South Gloucestershire: excavations in 2005", in *Two Cemeteries from Bristol's Northern Suburbs* (Bristol and Gloucestershire Archaeological Report 4), ed. M. Watts (Circencester 2006) 51–96. *Kempsford*: Booth P. (2017) "The Roman and post-Roman cemeteries [Discussion]", in *Horcott Quarry, Fairford and Arkell's Land, Kempsford: Prehistoric, Roman and Anglo-Saxon Settlement and Burial in the Upper Thames Valley in Gloucestershire*, C. Hayden, R. Early, E. Biddulph, P. Booth, A. Dodd, A. Smith, G. Laws and K. Welsh (Oxford Archaeology Thames Valley Landscapes Monograph 40) (Oxford 2017) 411–22; Hayden C., Early R., Biddulph E., Booth P., Dodd A., Smith A., Laws G., and Welsh K. (2017) edd. *Horcott Quarry, Fairford and Arkell's Land, Kempsford: Prehistoric, Roman and Anglo-Saxon Settlement and Burial in the Upper Thames Valley in Gloucestershire* (Oxford Archaeology Thames Valley Landscapes Monograph 40) (Oxford 2017). *Other*: Redfern R. (2008) "A bioarchaeological investigation of cultural change in Dorset, England (Mid-to-late fourth century B.C. to the end of the fourth century AD", *Britannia* 39 (2008) 161–91; Redfern R. C. and DeWitte S. N. (2011) "A new approach to the study of Romanization in Britain: a regional perspective of cultural change in late Iron Age and Roman Dorset using the Siler and Gompertz – Makeham models of mortality", *American Journal of Physical Anthropology* 144 (2011) 269–85; Redfern R. C. (2006) *A Gendered Analysis of Health From the Iron Age to the End of the Romano-British Period in Dorset, England* (*Mid to Late 8th century BC to the End of the 4th Century AD*) (Ph.D. diss., Univ. of Birmingham 2006); Cheung C., Schroeder H., and Hedges R. E. M. (2012) "Diet, social differentiation and cultural change in Roman Britain: new isotopic evidence from Gloucestershire", *Archaeological and Anthropological Science* 4 (2012) 61–73.

Hispania

Hispania (North-West): Galicia: *Lanzada*: Lopez-Costas O. (2015) "Taphonomy and burial context of the Roman/post-Roman funerary areas (2nd to 6th Centuries AD) of a Lanzada, NW Spain", *Estudos do Quaternário / Quaternary Studies* 12 (2015) 55–67. *Olmeda*: Abásolo J. A., Cortes J., and Pérez Rodríguez-Aragón F. (1997) *La necrópolis norte de la Olmeda* (*Pedrosa de la Vega, Palencia*) (Valencia 1997). Castile and León: *Salamanca*: Mergelina C. (1948) "El sepúlcro de La Alberca", in *Crónica del III Congreso Arqueológico del Sudeste Español* (*Murcia, 1947*) (Murcia 1948) 283–93. *Segovia*: Izquierdo J. M. "Mausoleo de época paleocristiana en Las Vegas de Pedraza (Segovia)", in *Segovia. Symposium de arqueología Romana,* edd. D. J. Perez Villanueva, W. Grunhagen, A. Beltran Martinez and J. M. Gomez-Tabanera (Barcelona 1977) 213–21.

Hispania (North-East): Catalonia: *Overview*: Bolós J. (2012) "L'estudi de les necròpolis medievals catalanes, entre l'arqueologia i la història", in *Arqueologia funerària al nord-est peninsular* (*segles VI–XII*), edd. N. Molist and G. Ripoll (Barcelona 2012) 71–85. *Barcelona*: Roig J. and Coll J. M. (2012) "El món funerari dels territoria de Barcino i Egara entre l'Antiguitat Tardana i l'època altmedieval (segles V al XII)", in *Arqueologia funerària al nord-est peninsular (segles VI–XII)*, edd. N. Molist and G. Ripoll (Barcelona 2012) 373–401; Roig J. (2015) "Necròpolis, aixovars i dipòsits humans anòmals en estructures no funeràries als territoria de Barcino (Barcelona) i Egara (Terrassa) entre el Baix Imperi romà i l'època visigòtica", in *Necropolis and Funerary World in Rural Areas* (Studies in the Rural World for the Roman Period 9), ed. J. Tremoleda (Banyoles 2015) 33–8; López A. (2012) "El suburbi funerari de Barcino a l'Antiguitat Tardana", in *Arqueologia funerària al nord-est peninsular* (*segles VI–XII*), edd. N. Molist and G. Ripoll (Barcelona 2012) 431–56; Travesset M. (1993) "Una necròpolis paleocristiana a la Barcelona de l'època del bisbe Sant Pacià (segle IV d.C.)", *Finestrelles* 5 (1993) 71–140; Burch J. and Nolla J. M. (2005) "Can Bel (Pineda de Mar, el Maresme)", in *In suo fundo. Els cementiris rurals de les antigues civitates d'Emporiae, Gerunda i Aquae Calidae* (Estudi General 25), edd. J. M. Nolla, J. Casas and P. Santamaria (Girona 2005) 107–15. *Centcelles*: Godoy Fernández C. and Muñoz Melgar A. (2022) edd. *El monument tardoromà de Centcelles. Dades, context, propostes. Actes del congrés Tarragona – Contantí, 28–30 de juny de 2022* (Studia Archaeologiae Christianae 5) (Barcelona 2022); Arce J. (2002) ed. *Centcelles. El monumento tardoromano. Iconografía y arquitectura* (Rome 2002); Hauschild T. and Schlunk H. (1986) *La villa Romana i el mausoleu constantinià de Centcelles* (Tarragona 1986); Hauschild T. and Schlunk H. (1962) *Informe preliminar sobre los trabajos realizados en Centcelles* (EAE 18) (Madrid 1962); Hauschild T. and Schlunk H. (1961) "Vorbericht über die Untersuchungen in Centcelles", *MM* 2 (1961) 66–77; Schlunk H. (1959) "Untersuchungen im frühchristlichen Mausoleum von Centcelles", in *Neue deutsche Ausgrabungen im Mittelmeergebiet und im Vorderen Orient* (Berlin 1959) 344–65; Hauschild T. (2002) "Centcelles: exploraciones en la sala de la cúpula", in *Centcelles. El monumento tardoromano. Iconografía y arquitectura*, ed. J. Arce (Rome 2002) 51–7; Warland R. (2002) "Die Kuppelmosaiken von Centcelles. Als Bildprogramm spätantiker Privatrepräsentation", in *Centcelles. El monumento tardoromano. Iconografía y arquitectura*, ed. J. Arce (Rome 2002) 21–35; Schlunk H. (1988) *Die Mosaikkuppel von Centcelles* (Madrider Beiträge 13) (Mainz 1988); Recio A. (1998) "Il mausoleo di Centcelles (Tarragona) del 350–355 ca.: Lettura ed interpretazione iconografica di alcune scene musive del registro B della cupola", in *Domum tuam dilexi. Miscellanea in onore di Aldo Nestori* (Rome 1998) 709–37; Engemann J. (1989) "Die Mosaikdarstellungen des Kuppelsaals in Centcelles. Anlässlich der Publikation von Helmut Schlunk", *JbAC* 32 (1989) 127–38; Arbeiter A. and Korol D. (1988–1989) "El mosaico de la cúpula de Centcelles y el derrocamiento de Constante por Magnencio", *BATarr* 11–12 (1988–1989) 193–244. *Girona*: Nolla J. M. and Sureda M. (1999) "El món funerari antic, tardoantic i altomedieval a la ciutat de Girona. Un estat de la qüestió", *Annals de l'Institut d'Estudis Gironins* 40 (1999) 13–66; Pera J. and Guitart J. M. (2010) "Necròpolis tardanes a la ciutat Romana de Iesso. Un problema a resoldre", in *Arqueologia funerària al nord-est peninsular (segles VI–XII)*, edd. N. Molist and G. Ripoll (Barcelona 2012) 161–73; Tremoleda J., Castanyer P., and Santos M. (2012) "Les necròpolis tardoantigues i altmedievals d'Empúries (l'Escala, Alt Empordà)", in *Arqueologia funerària al nord-est peninsular (segles VI–XII)*, edd. N. Molist and G. Ripoll (Barcelona 2012) 331–57; Nolla J. M. and Sagrera J. (1995) *Civitatis Impuritanae coementeria. Les necròpolis tardanes de la Neàpoli* (Estudi General 15) (Girona 1995); Nolla J. M. (1997) "Roses a l'antiguitat tardana. El cementiri de Santa Maria", *Annals de l'Institut d'Estudis Empordanesos* 30 (1997) 107–46. *Tarragona*: Ciurana J. (2011) *Pràctiques i rituals funeraris a Tarraco i el seu ager (segles II aC–III/IV dC)* (PhD. Diss., Univ. of Tarragona 2011); Del Amo M. D. (1979) *Estudio crítico de la necrópolis paleocristiana de Tarragona* (Tarragona 1979); TED'A (1987) *Els enterraments del Parc de la Ciutat i la problemàtica funerària de Tàrraco* (Tarragona 1987); Serra J. (1929) *Excavaciones en la necrópolis romano-cristiana de Tarragona* (Madrid 1929); Menchón J. J. (2012) "Necròpolis de l'antiguitat tardana i alta edat mitjana a les comarques del Camp de Tarragona, Conca de Barberà i Priorat", in *Arqueologia funerària al nord-est peninsular (segles VI–XII)*, edd. N. Molist and G. Ripoll (Barcelona 2012) 125–54; López J. and Piñol Ll. (1993) "El món funerari en època tardana al Camp de Tarragona", *Butlletí de la Reial Societat Arqueològica Tarraconense* 17 (1993) 65–121; Bea D. and Vilaseca A. (2000) "Dues necròpolis del segle V d. n. E. a Tarragona: excavacions al carrer de Prat de la Riba i al Mas Rimbau", in *Tàrraco 99. Arqueologia d'una capital provincial Romana*, ed. J. Ruiz de Arbulo (Tarragona 2000) 155–64; Garcia M., Macias J. M., and Teixell I. (1999) "Necròpoli de la villa dels Munts", in *Del romà al romànic, història, art i cultura de la Tarraconense mediterrània entre els segles IV i X*, edd. P. Palol and A. Pladevall (Barcelona 1999) 278–79; Macias J. M. and Remolà, J. A. (1995) "L'àrea funerària baix-imperial i tardo-romana de Mas Rimbau (Tarragona)", *Citerior. Revista d'Arqueologia i Ciències de l'Antiguitat* 1 (1995) 189–201; Del Amo M. D. (1971–1972) "La necrópolis de Pere Martell", *Butlletí Arqueològic de la Reial Societat Arqueològica Tarraconense* (1971–1972) 103–71.

Hispania (East): Valencia: González R. (2001) *El mundo funerario Romano en el País Valenciano. Monumentos funerarios y sepulturas entre los siglos I a. de C.–VII d. de C.* (Madrid-Alicante 2001); Alapont L. and Ribera A. (2006) "Los cementerios tardoantiguos de Valentia: arqueologia y antropologia. Espacios y usos funerarios en la ciudad histórica", *Anales de Arqueologia Cordobesa* 17 (2006) 161–94; Ribera A. and Soriano R. (1987) "Enterramientos de la antigüedad tardía en Valentia", *Lucentum* 6 (1987) 139–64; Martínez M. A. (2015) "Monumentos funerarios romanos en la Comunidad Valenciana. Tipos y ejemplos más destacados", *ArqueoWeb* 16 (2015) 102–23; Alapont L. (2009) "El mundo funerario en el limes visigodo-bizantino: el territorio valenciano", in *Contextos funeraris a la Mediterrània nordoccidental (segles VVIII)*, edd. J.Pinar Gil and T. Juarez Villena (Gausac 2009) 145–58; Ribera A. and Soriano R. (1996) "Los cementerios de época visigoda", *Saetabi* 46 (1996) 195–230; Ribera A. and Alapont Martín L. (2023) "Justinian plague mass grave found in Valentia's episcopal cemetery", in *Death and the Societies of Late Antiquity*, edd. G. Granier, C. Boyer and E. Anstett (Aix Marseille 2023) 167–75. *Castellón La Plana*: Arasa F. (1999) "Noves propostes d'interpretació sobre el conjunt monumental de La Muntanyeta dels Estanys d'Almenara (La Plana Baixa, Castelló)", *ArchPrehistLev* 23 (1999) 301–58. *Orriols*: Martínez M. A. (2016) "La necròpolis de Orriols (Valencia): ejemplos de ritual funerario en época romana (siglos II–IV d.C.)", *Lucentum* 35 (2016) 171–91; Martínez Pérez M. A. (2016) "La necròpolis de Orriols (Valencia): ejemplos de ritual funerario en época Romana (siglos II–IV d.C.)", *Lucentum* XXXV (2016) 171–91.

Hispania (South-East): Castilla La-Mancha: Albacete: Sarabia J., Bolivar Sanz H., and Ureña I. (2022) "Who was buried there and what did they eat? Dietary study of the Balazote late Roman villa (Albacete, Spain)", *Post-Classical Archaeologies* 12 (2022) 135–62. *Toledo*: Vidal S. (2016) "Análisis arqueométricos del sarcófago de Pueblanueva (Toledo) y estudio de cinco fragmentos de sarcófago procedentes de Pueblanueva en las colecciones del Museo Arqueológico Nacional", *Boletín del Museo Arqueológico Nacional* 34 (2016) 195–210; De la Llave S. and Escobar A. (2017) "Redescubriendo el mausoleo tardoromano de Las Vegas (La Pueblanueva, Toledo)", *Urbs Regia*

2 (2017) 26–45; Hauschild T. (1969) "Das Mausoluem bei Las Vegas de Puebla Nueva", *MM* 10 (1969) 293–316. Mursia: *Cartagena*: San Martín P. A. and de Palol P. (1972) "Necrópolis paleocristiana de Cartagena", in *VII Congreso Internacional de Arqueología Cristiana* (Barcelona 1972) 447–58; Berrocal M. and Laiz M. D. (1995) "Tipología de enterramientos en la necrópolis de San Antón en Cartagena", in *IV Reunió d'Arqueologia cristiana hispànica* (*Lisboa, 28 sept.–2 oct. 1992*) (Barcelona 1995) 173–85. *El Casón:* Noguera J. M. (2004) *El Casón de Jumilla. Arqueología de un mausoleo tardorRomano* (Murcia 2004). *Molineta*: Iniesta Á. and Martínez M. (2000) "Nuevas excavaciones en la necrópolis tardorRomana de la La Molineta (Puerto de Mazarrón, Murcia)", *AnMurcia* 16 (2000) 199–224; García L. A. and Amante M. (1993) "La necrópolis de La Molineta. Puerto de Mazarrón, Murcia", *MemAMurcia* 4 (1993) 245–60; Amante M. and López M. (1991) "La necrópolis de La Molineta: aproximación a la historia social y económica en el Puerto de Mazarrón (Murcia) durante la Antigüedad Tardía", in *Arte, sociedad, economía y religión durante el Bajo Imperio y la Antigüedad Tardía* (Antigüedad y Cristianismo 8), edd. A. G. Blanco, F. J. Fernández Nieto and J. Remesal Rodríguez (Murcia 1991) 475–81.Hispania (South): Andalusia: *Almeria*: García J. L. and Cara L. (1987) "Excavación arqueológica efectuada en el mausoleo tardorRomano de El Daimuz (El Ejido-Almería)", *AnAAnd* 3 (1987) 29–36; Cara L. (1986) "El mausoleo tardoromano de El Daymun (El Ejido, Almería)", *Historia de la Baja Alpujarra* (Almería 1986) 67–79. *Cordoba*: Ortega Ruíz R., Gutiérrez Durán C., and Izquierdo C. (2023) "The change of funerary rituals during the Late Antiquity through the Cortijo Nuevo and Cortijo Coracho sites, Lucena, Córdoba", in *Death and the Societies of Late Antiquity*, edd. G. Granier, C. Boyer and E. Anstett (Aix Marseille 2023) 43–57; Rodero Pérez S. and Asensi Yacer M. J. (2008) "Nuevos datos sobre la necrópolis tardoantigua de "el Ochavillo" (Hornachuelos, Córdoba). Campañ de excavaión 2007", *Romula* 7 (2008) 271–98. *Granada*: Román Punzón J. M. (2004) *El mundo funerario rural en la provincia de Granada durante la Antigüedad Tardía* (Granada 2004). *Huelva*: Teba J. A. (1989) "Mausoleo de la Punta del Moral (Ayamonte, Huelva)", *Anuario Arqueológico de Andalucía, III, Actividades de Urgencia. 1987* (Seville 1989) 317–22. *Seville*: Barragán M. (2010) *La necrópolis tardoantigua de Carretera de Carmona (Hispalis), Sevilla* (Scripta 2) (Seville 2010); Barragán M. (2009) "La necrópolis tardoantigua de Carretera de Carmona, Hispalis", *Rómula* 8 (2009) 227–56; Eger Ch. (2009) "Spätantike Gräner in Munigua. Zu Grabformen, Bestattungsweise und Beigabensitte einer südspanischen Kleinstadt vom 3./4.–7. Jahrhundert", in *Dunkle Jahrhunderte in Mitteleuropa? Tagungs- beiträge der Arbeitsgemeinschaft Spätantike und Frühmittelalter. 1: Rituale und Moden (Xanten, 8. Juni 2006); 2: Möglichkeiten und Probleme archäologischnaturwissenschaftlicher Zusammen arbeit (Schleswig, 9.10. Oktober 2007)* (Stud. Spätant. u. Früh-mittelalter 1), edd. O. Heinrich-Tamaska, N. Krohn and S. Ristow (Hamburg 2009) 11–26.

Hispania (South-West): Extremadura: *Badajoz*: Serra J. de C. (1949) "La capilla funeraria de la dehesa de La Cocosa", *Revista de Estudios Extremeños* 1–2 (1949) 105–16. *Merida*: Mateos P. ànd Sastre I. (2009) "Mérida and its funerary spaces during the Late Antiquity", in *Morir en el Mediterráneo Medieval*, edd. J. López Quiroga and A. M. Martínez Tejera (Oxford 2009) 185–202.

Hispania (West): *Portugal*: Graen D. (2004) "'Sepultus in villa'. Bestattet in der Villa. Drei Zentralbauten in Portugal zeugen vom Grabbprunk der Spätantike", *Antike Welt* 35.3 (2004) 65–74; Graen D. (2005) "Two Roman mausoleums at Quinta de Marim (Olhão). Preliminary results of the excavations in 2002 and 2003", *Revista portuguesa de arqueología* 8.1 (2005) 257–78.

Gaul & Germany

Gaul: *Overview* in mausolea: *Hortus Artium Medievalium* 18.2 (2012) (Mausolées & Églises, IVe–VIIIe siècle): https://www.brepols.net/products/ON-M1-F1-04010343-1.

Gaul (North): Selected sites: *Vireux-Molhain*: Vrielynck O. (2010) *Le cimetière mérovingien de Vieuxville (ve–viies.). Catalogue des salles permanentes du Musée de Logne* (Vieuxville 2010); Lemant J.-P. (1985) *Le cimetière et la fortification du Bas-Empire de Vireux-Molhain, dép. Ardennes* (Monographien Römisch-Germanisches Zentralmuseum 7) (Mainz 1985). *Bouc-Bel-air*: Rigeade C., Parmentier S., and Lang-Desvignes S. (2023) "Évolution des pratiques funéraires durant l'antiquité tardive en Provence: l'exemple de la nécropole de Bouc-Bel-air (Bouches-du-Rhône)", in *Death and the Societies of Late Antiquity*, edd. G. Granier, C. Boyer and E. Anstett (Aix Marseille 2023) 325–34. *Cadarache*: Pouyé B., Allouis M.-F., Bonifay M., Bouville C., Calvet A., Lopez A., and Lopez C. (1994) "Une nécropole de l'antiquité tardive à Cadarache (Saint-Paul-lès-Durance, Bouches-du-Rhône)", *Archéologie médiévale* XXIV (1994) 51–135. *Chantambre*: Murail P. and Girard L. (2000) "Biology and burial practices from the end of the first century AD to the beginning of the fifth century AD: the rurla necropolis of Chantambre (Essonne, France)", in *Burial, Society and Context in the Roman World*, edd. J. Pearce, M. Millett and M. Struck (Oxford 2000) 105–11. *Les Ruelles*: Blaizot F. (2014) "From the skeleton to the funerary architecture: a logic of the plausible", *Anthropologie* 52 (2014) 263–84. *Nempont-Saint-Firmin*: Duchemin J.-P. (2012) "Numismatique et archéologie du rituel : réflexion sur le rite dit de "l'obole à Charon" à partir de l'exemple de la nécropole tardo-antique de Nempont-Saint-Firmin (Pas-de-Calais, France)", *Journal of Archaeological Numismatics* 2 (2012) 127–98. *Namur*: Dasnoy A. (1998) "Incinérations funéraires des ive et ve siècles dans la région namuroise", *Annales de la Société archéologique de Namur* 65 (1998) 391–406; Dasnoy A. (1997) "Les cimetières d'Eprave et Han-sur-Lesse: la "Croix-Rouge" et "Sur-le-Mont"", *Annales de la Société archéologique de Namur* 71(1997) 3–82. *Other*: Brulet R. (1995) *La Sépulture du roi Childéric à Tournai et le site funéraire* (Louvain-la-Neuve 1995); Hanut, F., Destexhe G., Laforest C., Polet C., and Goffette Q. (2023) "Les crémations de l'Antiquité tardive (270–450 de n. è.) dans la cité des Tongres (Germanie seconde): entre continuités et nouveaux apports", in *Death and the Societies of Late Antiquity*, edd. G. Granier, C. Boyer and E. Anstett (Aix Marseille 2023) 71–83.

Gaul (North-East): *Aube*: Thiol S. (2015) *Ramerupt (Aube) "Cour Première" occupations néolithiques, enclos funéraires protohistoriques et nécropole tardo-antique* (Metz 2015); Choquenet C. (2015) *Continuité d'un espace funéraire: des enclos de l'âge du Fer aux tombes Bas-Empire: Prunay-Belleville (Aube), "le Bas d'Avon": Canalisation de transport de gaz dite "Arc de Dierrey"* (Metz 2015); Paresys C. (2011) *Nécropole du Bas-Empire: Arcis-sur-Aube, Aube, 40 route de Troyes, RFO* (Metz 2011); Ahü-Delor A., Aurore Louis A., and Paresys C. (2023) "Des mobiliers usagés, réformés, réparés pour les morts. Exemples aubois au cours de l'antiquité tardive", in *Death and the Societies of Late Antiquity*, edd. G. Granier, C. Boyer and E. Anstett (Aix Marseille 2023) 145–53; Ahü-Delor A. and Louis A. (2016) "Complémentarité et fonction des assemblages de vaisselle en verre et en céramique dans les tombes du iiie et ive siècles: exemples dans l'Aube", in *Société française d'étude de la céramique antique en Gaule: Actes du congrès d'autun* (Marseille 2016) 227–34. *Reims*: Sindonino S., Cavé M., Thiol S., Marthelat P., Brunet M., and Rollet P. (2016) "Les sépultures tardo-antiques de la fouille du tramway à Reims (Marne)", in *L'antiquité tardive dans l'est de la Gaule II. Sépultures, nécropoles et pratiques funéraires en Gaule de l'est – Actualité de la recherche,* edd. N. Achard-Corompt, M. Kasprzyk and

B. Fort (Dijon 2016) 45–60; Cave M., Herrscher E., Mathelart P., Mendisco F., Pruvost M., Rollet P., and Thiol S. (2023) "Regards croisés sur une pratique funéraire marginale à Reims aux iiie–ive s. ap. J.-C.: études archéo-anthropologique, isotopique et paléogénomique", in *Death and the Societies of Late Antiquity*, edd. G. Granier, C. Boyer and E. Anstett (Aix Marseille 2023) 229–54. *Other*: Cartier-Mamie E. and Putelat O. (2023) "Ittenheim "Lotissement du Stade" (Bas-Rhin): une nécropole du Bas-Empire (350–450 après J.-C.) et ses dépôts funéraires d'origine animale", in *Death and the Societies of Late Antiquity*, edd. G. Granier, C. Boyer and E. Anstett (Aix-Marseille 2023) 201–23.

Gaul (Central): *Bourges*: Durand R. (2023) "Des élites dans la nécropole: expression et influence dans l'organisation de l'espace funéraire. L'exemple de Saint-Martin-des-Champs à Avaricum (Bourges, France)", in *Death and the Societies of Late Antiquity*, edd. G. Granier, C. Boyer and E. Anstett (Aix Marseille 2023) 155–65; Fossurier C. and Burgevin A. (2023) "Les nécropoles péri-urbaines de l'antiquité tardive en Bourgogne. Pratiques funéraires et topographie", in *Death and the Societies of Late Antiquity,* edd. G. Granier, C. Boyer and E. Anstett (Aix Marseille 2023) 381–97; Grose R. (2023) "Inscribing moral communities in late-antique Burgundy: old values, multivalent meanings, and new avenues of research", in *Death and the Societies of Late Antiquity*, edd. G. Granier, C. Boyer and E. Anstett (Aix Marseille 2023) 59–70; Handley M. (2000) "Epitaphs, models, and texts: A Carolingian collection of late antique inscriptions from Burgundy", *Bulletin of the Institute of Classical Studies* (Supplement) (2000) 47–56. *Corsica*: Corbara A.-G. (2022) "Les ensembles funéraires tardo-antiques et médiévaux (v^e–xve s.): bilan des données récentes et perspectives", in *Archéologie de la Corse, vingt années de recherche,* Actes du colloque d'Ajaccio novembre 2017 (Paris 2022) 199–208; Duperron G. and Istria D. (2022) "L'agglomération tardo-antique de Sagone (ive–première moitié du ve siècle): un *hub* régional sur le littoral corse ?", *MEFRA* 134–2 (2022) 317–31; Corbara A.-G., Duperron G., and Istria D. (2023) "Pratiques et espaces funéraires en Corse durant l'antiquité tardive. L'exemple du site de Sant'Appianu de Sagone (Vico, Corse-du-sud)", in *Death and the Societies of Late Antiquity,* edd. G. Granier, C. Boyer and E. Anstett (Aix Marseille 2023) 369–80; Istria D. (2022) "Le mausolée de Sagone (Vico, Corse-du-Sud)", *MEFRA* 134–1 (2022) 1–20

Gaul (East): *Marne*: Rabasté Y. (2018) *Un petit groupe funéraire du milieu du iiie siècle de n. è.: tome II: secteur ouest: Isles-sur-Suippe, Marne, Sohettes et Val des Bois, Tr5b, secteurs est et ouest, Grand*

Est (Inrap GE) (Metz 2018); Achard-Corompt N. (2016) "Deux nécropoles du Bas-Empire à Bezannes "sites K et L" (Marne)", in *L'antiquité tardive dans l'est de la Gaule II. Sépultures, nécropoles et pratiques funéraires en Gaule de l'est. Actualité de la recherche, actes du colloque ATEG (Châlons-en-Champagne, 16–17 septembre 2010)* (41ᵉ suppl. à la RAE) (Dijon 2016) 69–77; Achard-Corompt N., Ahü-Delor A., and Le Goff I. (2023) "Compertrix 'Saint-Pierre': un exemple d'évolution des marqueurs statutaires funéraires durant l'antiquité", in *Death and the Societies of Late Antiquity*, edd. G. Granier, C. Boyer and E. Anstett (Aix Marseille 2023) 31–42. *Other*: Granier G., Helly B., Bizot B., and Signoli M. (2011) "La population du site de la place de l'Égalité à Sainte-Colombe (Rhône): un cas archéologique de *Collegia* à vocation funéraire de l'antiquité tardive?", *Bulletins et Mémoires de la Société D'Anthropologie de Paris* 23 (2011) 152–75.

Gaul (South-East): *Lyon*: Reynaud J. (1998) *Lugdunum Christianum: Lyon du ivᵉ au viiᵉ s.: topographie, nécropoles et édifices religieux* (Paris 1998); Soulet M-H. (1990) "L'image de l'amour conjugal et de l'épouse dans l'épigraphie chrétienne lyonnaise aux viᵉ et viiᵉ siècles", in *La femme au moyen âge. Actes du colloque de Maubeuge, 6–9 octobre 1988,* edd. M. Rouche and J. Heuclin (Maubeuge 1990) 139–46; Reynaud J. F. (1986) *Lyon aux premiers' temps chrétiens: basiliques et necropolis* (Paris 1986). *Nice*: Civetta A., Chevaux B., Jossier B., and Mercurin R. (2023) "Nikaia et Cemenelum (Nice, Alpes-Maritimes): deux cités voisines, deux espaces culturels différents ?", in *Death and the Societies of Late Antiquity*, edd. G. Granier, C. Boyer and E. Anstett (Aix Marseille 2023) 85–96. *Vienne*: Granier G., Helly B., and Signoli S. (2016) "Évolution de la topographie et de la nature des lieux funéraires de la ville de *Vienna* durant l'antiquité tardive", *Revue Archéologique de l'Est* (Supplément "L'antiquité tardive dans l'est de la Gaule II: archéologie funéraire") (2016) 239–54; Prisset J.-L. and Brissaud L. (2015) *Saint-Romain-en-Gal aux temps de Ferréol, Mamert et Adon. L'aire funéraire des thermes des Lutteurs (IVᵉ–Xᵉ siècles)* (Collection Bibliothèque de l'Antiquité tardive 28) (Turnhout 2015); Granier G. (2014) "Espaces, pratiques funéraires et populations à Vienne du Iᵉʳ au VIᵉ siècle", in *Carte archéologique de la Gaule. 38/2: Vienne,* F. Adjadj, R. Lauxerois and A. Helly (Paris 2014) 171–80; Helly B., Granier G., Paturet A., Ancel M. J., Baradat-Joly A., Clément B., Frascone D., and Gisclon J.-L. (2023) "The transformation of funerary areas in *Vienna* (Vienne, France) at the end of the 3rd and in the 4th century CE: location and nature of burials within public monuments and abandoned buildings", in *Death and the Societies of Late Antiquity*, edd. G. Granier, C. Boyer

and E. Anstett (Aix Marseille 2023) 203–27; Granier G. (2017) "Évolution de la conception de la mort et de la gestion des morts dans l'espace urbain et peri-urbain durant l'antiquité: l'exemple des nécropoles tardives de Vienne et Arles", in *Rencontre autour de nouvelles approches de l'archéologie funéraire. Actes de la 6ᵉ rencontre du groupe d'anthropologie et d'archéologie funéraire(4–5 avril 2014, INHA, Paris)* (Tours 2017) 285–90. *Other*: Bosc-Zanardo B., Gandia D., and Vanhove C. (2023) "Ollioules "Quartier Quiez 2": une nécropole tardo-antique avec vue sur la mer", in *Death and the Societies of Late Antiquity*, edd. G. Granier, C. Boyer and E. Anstett (Aix Marseille 2023) 179–87; Colardelle R. (2008) *La ville et la mort. Saint-Laurent de Grenoble, 2000 ans de tradition funéraire* (Turnhout 2008); Carru D., Boccacino C., Borgard P., Bouillot J., Buchet L., Buisson-Catil J., and Vatteoni S. (1991) *Une nécropole de l'antiquité tardive à Vaison-la-Romaine* (Document d'Archéologie Vauclusienne 2) (Avignon 1991); Lattard A., Huguet C., Mocci F., Thuaudet O., Foy D., Dedonder Y., Magniez P., and Isoardi D. (2023) "Les sociétés alpines de l'antiquité tardive face à la mort en montagne: au cœur de la civitas d'*Eturamina*, le site de Saint-Pierre 2 à Thorame-Basse (Alpes-de-Haute-Provence, 04)", in *Death and the Societies of Late Antiquity*, edd. G. Granier, C. Boyer and E. Anstett (Aix Marseille 2023) 353–76.

Gaul (South): *Hérault*: Raynaud C. (2010) *Les nécropoles de Lunel-Viel (Hérault) de l'antiquité au moyen âge* (Revue Archéologique de Narbonnaise Suppl. 40) (Montpellier 2010); Blaizot F., Raux S., Bonnet C., Henry E., Forest V., Ecard P., Jorda C., and Macabeo G. (2008) "L'ensemble funéraire rural de Malbosc (Montpellier, Hérault); pratiques funéraires de l'Antiquité tardive", *Revue archéologique de Narbonnaise* 4 (2008) 53–99. *Marseille*: Richarté C., Richier A., and Barra C. (2016) "Notes sur le cimetière marseillais du promontoire du Pharo: un faciès caractéristique de l'extrême fin de l'Antiquité", in *Historiographie et nouvelles perspectives. Histoires Matérielles: terre cuite, bois, … : Mélanges offerts à Lucien RIVET.* (Archéologie et Histoire Romaine 33), ed. D. Djaoui (2016) 283–301; Boyer R. (1987) *Vie et mort à Marseille à la fin de l'antiquité. Inhumations habillées des Vᵉ et VIᵉ siècles et sarcophage reliquaire trouvés à l'abbaye de Saint-Victor* (Marseille 1987); Bonifay M. and Roth Congès A. (2009) "Les sépultures en amphores du cimetière de Saint-Victor", in *Saint-Victor de Marseille. Études archéologiques et historiques, Actes du colloque de Saint-Victor, Marseille, 18–20 novembre 2004,* edd. M. Fixot and J. P. Pelletier (Turnhout 2009) 17–24. *Saint-Mitre-les-Remparts*: Valenciano M. (2023) "L'aire funéraire rupestre de l'agglomération secondaire d'Ugium

(Saint-Blaise, Saint-Mitre-les-Remparts, 13920, France), état des lieux de la recherche", in *Death and the Societies of Late Antiquity,* edd. G. Granier, C. Boyer and E. Anstett (Aix Marseille 2023) 189–201. *Valensole*: Richier A., Barbier S., Borgard P., Hernandez J., Lang-Desvignes S., Lefevre-Gonzalez L., and Mezzoud A. (2009) *La Baisse de Sainte-anne: une nécropole de l'antiquité tardive et du haut moyen âge à Valensole (Alpes-de-Haute-Provence)* (Inrap Méditerranée) (2009) 2 vols. *Other*: Ardagna Y., Rigeade C., Forest V., Seguin M., and Vidal L. (2023) "Un dispositif singulier de l'antiquité tardive à la chapelle Saint-Jean-de-Todon (Laudun-l'Ardoise, Gard, France)", in *Death and the Societies of Late Antiquity,* edd. G. Granier, C. Boyer and E. Anstett (Aix Marseille 2023) 129–43; Granier G., Sperandio E., and Duperron G. (2023) "The funerary area of the 5th and 6th c. CE of Saint-Martin-le-Bas at Gruissan (Aude, France). New elements of reflection on the occupation of the Narbonne coast during Late Antiquity", in *Death and the Societies of Late Antiquity*, edd. G. Granier, C. Boyer and E. Anstett (Aix Marseille 2023) 335–52.

Gaul (West): *Poitiers*: Rast-Eicher A., Nowik W., and Garnier N. (2017) "Textiles from two late Roman graves found in a mausoleum in Jaunay-Clan near Poitiers, France", in *Archaeological Textiles – Links Between Past and Present. NESAT XIII – North European Symposium for Archaeological Textiles*, edd. M. Bravermanová, H. Březinová and J. Malcolm-Davies (Prague 2017) 73–80; Treffort C. and Uberti M. (2010) "Identité des défunts et statut du groupe dans les inscriptions funéraires des anciens diocèses de Poitiers, Saintes et Angoulême entre le IVe et le Xe siècle", in *Wisigoths et francs autour de la bataille de Vouillé (507). Recherches récentes sur le haut moyen âge dans le centre-ouest de la France, Actes des XXVIIIe journées internationales d'archéologie mérovingienne Vouillé et Poitiers* (Vienne 2010) 193–214.

Gaul (South-West): *Limoges*: Lhermite X. (2017) "La mausolée du 1, rue de la Courtine á Limoges", *Association pour L'Antiquité Tardive Bulletin* 26 (2017) 80–7; Lhermite X. (2013) "Limoges. Découvert d'un mausolée de l'antiquite tardive au seins de la nécropole de Saint-Martial, 1, rue de la Courtine", *Bulletine Monumentale* 171.2 (2013) 160–2.

Germany: North Rhine-Westphalia: *Nijmegen*: Steures D. C. (2013) *The Late Roman Cemeteries of Nijmegen: Stray Finds and Excavations 1947–1983* (Nijmegen 2013). *Bonn*: Keller C. (2003) "From a late Roman cemetery to the Basilica Sanctorum Cassii et Florentii in Bonn, Germany", in *The Cross goes North, Processes of Conversion in Northern Europe, AD 300–1300*, ed. M. Carver (York 2003) 415–27; Prien R. (2002–2003) "Ein Massengrab aus der Mitte des 4. Jahrhunderts n. Ch. im Bonner Legionslager", *Bonner Jahrbücher* 202–203 (2002–2003) 171–98. *Other*: Pirling R. (1966–) *Das Römisch-fränkische Gräberfeld von Krefeld-Gellep (Germanische Denkmäler der Völkerwanderungzeit)* (Wiesbaden 1966–); Schulze-Dörrlamm M. (1990) *Die spätrömischen und frühmittelalterlichen Gräberfelder von Gondorf, Gem. Kobern-Gondorf, Kr. Mayen-Koblenz*, 2 vols (Germanische Denkmäler der Völkerwanderungzeit B.14) (Stuttgart 1990).

Trier: Reifarth, N., Merten, H., Teegen W.-R., Amendt J., Vanden Berghe I., Heron C., Wiethold J., Drewello U., Drewello R., and Clemens L. (in this volume) *"Levis aesto terra* – early Christian elite burials from St. Maximin, Trier (Germany)"; Merten H. (2023) "Christliche Bestattungskultur in Spätantike und Frühmittelalter am Beispiel von St. Maximin in Trier", in *Funerary Landscapes of the Late Antique Oecumene: Contextualizing Epigraphic and Archaeological Evidence of Mortuary Practices: Proceedings of an International Conference in Heidelberg, May 30–June 1, 2019*, edd. S. Ardeleanu and J. C. Cubas Diaz (Heidelberg 2023) 507–28; Merten H. (2018) "Die frühchristlichen Grabinschriften aus St. Maximin in Trier", in *Die Abtei Trier-St. Maximin von der späten Antike bis zur frühen Neuzeit*, edd. M. Embach and B. Simon (Quellen und Abhandlungen zur mittelrheinischen Kirchengeschichte 142) (Mainz 2018) 101–8; Reifarth N. (2013) *Zur Ausstattung spätantiker Elitegräber aus St. Maximin in Trier: Purpur, Seide, Gold und Harze* (Internationale Archäologie 124) (Rahden/Westf 2013); Reifarth N., Teegen W. R., Boenke N., and Wiethold J. (2006) "Das spätantike Grab 279 aus St. Maximin in Trier. Technologische, anthropologische und archäobotanische Untersuchungen", *Funde und Ausgrabungen im Bezirk Trier* 38 (2006) 58–70; Schwinden L. (2001) "Sankt Maximin: Antiker Bestattungsplatz und frühchristliche Verehrungsstätte im Norden Triers", in *Das römische Trier*, ed. H.-P. Kuhnen (Führer zu archäologischen Denkmälern in Deutschland 40) (Stuttgart 2001) 188–201; Siedow M. (2016) *Der Baukomplex auf dem Friedhof zu St. Matthias in Trier: Überlegungen zur Genese spätantiker Coemeterialbauten* (Ph.D. diss., Univ. of Trier 2016); Clemens L. and Wilhelm J. C. (2001) "Sankt Matthias und das südliche Gräberfeld", in *Das römische Trier*, ed. H.-P. Kuhnen (Führer zu archäologischen Denkmälern in Deutschland 40) (Stuttgart 2001) 175–87; Merten H. (2015) "Frühchristliche Grabinschriften in Trier. Stand der Bearbeitung", in *Frühchristliche Grabinschriften im Westen des Römischen Reiches. Beiträge zur Internationalen Konferenz "Frühchristliche Grabinschriften im Westen des Römischen Reiches", Trier, 13.–15. Juni 2013,* edd. L. Clemens, H. Merten and C. Schäfer (Interdisziplinärer Dialog zwischen Archäologie und Geschichte 3) (Trier 2015) 29–36; Merten H. (2011) "Christliche Epigraphik und Archäologie in Trier seit ihren Anfängen", *RömQSchr* 106 (2011) 5–26; Teegen W.-R. (2006) "Zur saisonalen Sterblichkeit im spätantiken und frühmittelalterlichen Trier", *Funde und Ausgrabungen im Bezirk Trier* 38 (2006) 52–7.

Italy

Italy (North): *General*: Chavarría Arnau A. (2019) "The topography of early medieval burials: some reflections on the archaeological evidence from northern Italy (fifth-eight centuries)", in *Polity and Neighbourhood in Early Medieval Europe*, edd. J. Escalona, O. Vesteisson and S. Brookes (Turnhout 2019) 83–120; Chavarría Arnau A. and Marinato M. (2015) "Frammentazione e complessità nelle pratiche funerarie altomedievali in Italia settentrionale", in *VI congresso degli archeologi medievisti italiani, Lecce settembre 2015*, ed. P. Arthur (Florence 2015) 61–8. Vuga D. (1980) "A study of burying methods in the period of the Great Migration (5th to 6th centuries) in the south-eastern Alpine and Cisalpine world", *Balcanoslavica* 9 (1980) 17–25; Lambert C. (2003) "Spazi abitativi e sepolture nei contesti urbani", in *Abitare in città. La Cisalpina tra impero e medioevo* (Palilia 12), edd. J. Ortalli and M. Heinzelmann (Wiesbaden 2003) 229–39. *Trento*: Cavada E. (1998) "Cimiteri e sepolture isolate nella città di Trento (secoli V–VIII)", in *Sepolture tra VI e VIII secolo* (Documenti di Archeologia 13), edd. G. P. Brogiolo and G. Cantino Wataghin (Mantua 1998) 127–37; Gaio S. (2004) "'Quid sint suggrundaria'. La sepoltura infantile ad *enchytrismòs* di Loppio s. Andrea (TN)", *Ann. Mus. Civ. Rovereto* 20 (2004) 53–90.

Rhaetia: *General*: Castella D. (2016) "Monuments funéraires et lieux de culte privés en pays helvète", in Mausolées et grands domains ruraux à l'époque romaine dans le nord-est de la Gaule, edd. J-N. Castorio and Y. Maligorne (Scripta Antiqua 90) (Bordeaux 2016) 105–22. *Chur*: Sulser W. and Classen H. (1978) Sankt Stephan in Chur. Frühchristliche Grabkammer und Friedhofskirche (Zürich 1978).

Lombardia: *Brescia*: Brogiolo G. P. (1997) "Le sepolture a Brescia tra tarda antichità e prima età longobarda (ex IV–VII secolo)", in *L'Italia centro-settentrionale in età longobarda*, ed. L. Paroli (Florence 1997) 413–24. *Milan*: Sannazaro M. (2001) ed. *Ricerche archeologiche nei cortili dell'Università Cattolica. La necropoli tardoantica* (Milan 2001); Lusuardi S. and Giostra C.

(2012) edd. *Archeologia medievale a Trezzo sull'Adda. Il sepolcreto longobardo e l'oratorio di San Martino. Le chiese di S. Stefano e San Michele in Sallianense* (Milan 2012); Rossignani M. P., Sannazaro M., and Legrottaglie G. (2005) *La Signora del sarcofago. Una sepoltura di rango nella necropoli dell'Università Cattolica. Ricerche archeologiche nei cortili dell'Universita Cattolica* (Milan 2005); Spalla E. (2005) "Strutture per libagioni nella ritualità funeraria Romana: i dati archeologici", in *La Signora del sarcofago. Una sepoltura di rango nella necropoli dell'Università Cattolica. Ricerche archeologiche nei cortili dell'Universita Cattolica*, edd M. P. Rossignani, M. Sannazaro and G. Le Grottaglie (Milan 2005) 47–54; Perassi C. (2001) "Le monete della necropoli: osservazioni sul rituale funerario", in *Ricerche archeologiche nei cortili dell'Università Cattolica. La necropoli tardoantica*, ed. M. Sannazaro (Milan 2001) 101–14.

Emilia Romagna: Belcastro M. G. and Ortalli J. (2010) edd. *Sepolture anomale. Indagini archeologiche e antropologiche dall'epoca classica al medioevo in Emilia Romagna. Giornata di studi (Castelfranco Emilia, 19 dicembre 2009)* (Florence 2010). *Ravenna*: Ferreri D. (2014) "La città dei vivi e la città dei morti. La ridefinizione degli spazi urbani e le pratiche funerarie a Ravenna e nel territorio circostante tra la tarda antichità e l'alto medioevo", *Hortus Artium Medievalium* 20 (2014) 112–22; Ferreri D. (2009) "Sepolture e riti funerari a Classe: una lunga prospettiva diacronica", in *V congresso nazionale archeologia medievale, Foggia-Manfredonia 2009*, edd. G. Volpe and P. Favia (Florence 2009) 459–64; Deliyannis D. M. (2010) "The mausoleum of Theoderic and the seven wonders of the world," *Journal of Late Antiquity* 3 (2010) 365–85

Veneto: *Aquileia*: Giovannini A. (2012–2013) "Aquileia e l'archeologia funeraria tardoantica. Censimento dei dati, tracce di usi e costumi", *Aquileia Nostra* LXXXIII–LXXXIV (2012–2013) 217–47. *Padua*: Canci A., Marinato M., and Zago M. (2017) "Le aree cimiteriali: studio bioarcheologico", in *Ricerche sul complesso episcopale di Padova (Scavi 2011–2012)*, ed. A. Chavarría Arnau (Mantua 2017) 131–49; Marinato M. (2017) "Analisi tafonomica e antropologica delle sepolture longobarde e della chiesa di Santa Giustina", in *Monselice. Archeologia e architetture tra longobardi e carraresi*, edd. G. P. Brogiolo and A. Chavarría Arnau (Mantua 2017) 83–94. *Venice*: Mainardis F. (2023) "Luoghi, monumenti, *epigraphic habit*. Note sulle necropoli tardoantiche della parte orientale della *Venetia* et *Histria*", in *Funerary Landscapes of the Late Antique Oecumene: Contextualizing Epigraphic and Archaeological Evidence of Mortuary Practices: Proceedings of an International Conference in Heidelberg, May 30–June 1, 2019*, edd. S. Ardeleanu and J. C. Cubas Diaz

(Heidelberg 2023) 429–58; Bolla M. (2015) "Sepoltura non perpetua: la riapertura delle tombe e il caso concordiense", in *Le necropoli della media e tarda età imperiale (III–IV sec. d.C.) a Iulia Concordia e nell'arco altoadriatico. Atti del Convegno di Concordia Sagittaria (giugno 2014)*, edd. F. Rinaldi and A. Vigoni (Rubano – Padua 2015) 357–77. <u>Verona</u>: Cavalieri Manasse G., Meloni F., and Piazza Corrubio (2012) "Piazza Corrubio. Lo scavo dell'area cimiteriale 2009–2011", *Quaderni di Archeologia del Veneto* 27 (2012) 79–81.

<u>Tuscania</u>: Costantini A. (2014) "Sepolture tardoantiche in Toscana (III–VI d.C.): i corredi e le epigrafi", *SCO* 60 (2014) 99–161; Costantini A. (2013) "Il reimpiego delle anfore tardoantiche considerazioni sulle sepolture ad enchytrismòs in Toscana", *Archeologia Classica* 64 (2013) 657–75. <u>Siena</u>: Braconi M., Facchin G., Ferri G., Bernardi M., and Sperduti A. (2023) "New researches at the catacomb of Santa Mustiola. Funerary rituals and biosocial composition of the early Christian community of Chiusi (Siena, Italy)", in *Death and the Societies of Late Antiquity*, edd. G. Granier, C. Boyer and E. Anstett (Aix Marseille 2023) 283–97; Braconi M., Sperduti A., Fattore L., Interlando S., and Cavazzuti C. (2021) "Un caso di deformazione cranica artificiale dalla catacomba di Santa Mustiola a Chiusi (Si). Lo scavo, il contesto e lo studio antropologico", *RAC* 97/1 (2021) 53–98; Cipollone V. (2000) *Le catacombe di Chiusi* (Catacombe di Roma e d'Italia 6) (Vatican City 2000); Cipollone V. (1998) "Nuove ricerche sulla catacomba di Santa Mustiola a Chiusi", *RAC* 74/1 (1998) 3–147.

<u>Italy</u> (Central): Lambert C. (1997) "Le sepolture in urbe nella norma e nella prassi (tarda antichità-alto medioevo)", in *L'Italia centro-settentrionale in età longobarda*, ed. L. Paroli (Florence 1997) 285–93; Staffa A. R. (1998) "Sepolture urbane in Abbruzzo (secc. VI–VII)", in *Sepolture tra IV e VIII secolo. Settimo seminario sul tardoantico e l'alto medioevo in Italia centro-settentrionale (Gardone Riviera 24–26 Ottobre 1996)*, edd. G. P. Brogiolo and G. Cantino Wataghin (Mantua 1998) 161–78; *Umbria longobarda. La necropoli di Nocera Umbra nel centenario della scoperta (Catalogo della mostra)*, AA.VV. (Rome 1997); Pazienza A. M. (2014) "Identity, funerary practices and memory in Lombard Tuscia (6th to 8th centuries)", *Zeitschrift für Archäologie des Mittelalters* 42, edd. S. Brather, U. Müller and H. Steuer Jahrgang (Bonn 2014) 1–32. <u>Selected sites</u>: <u>Priverno</u>: Miguelez A., Caserta E., Alfonso J., Colaiacomo F., Martín L. A., and Cancellieri M. (2023) "Burying on Roman ruins: the late-Roman necropolis of Priverno, Italy", in *Death and the Societies of Late Antiquity*, edd. G. Granier, C. Boyer and E. Anstett (Aix Marseille 2023) 315–24. <u>Sabina Hills</u>: Fiocchi

Nicolai V. (2009) *I cimiteri paleocristiani del Lazio II. Sabina* (Monumenti di Antichità Cristiana pubblicati a cura del Pontificio Istituto di Archeologia Cristiana, serie II, XX) (Vatican City 2009). <u>Teverina</u>: Montagnetti R., Pickel D., Wilson J., Rizzo F., and Soren D. (2020) "New research in the Roman villa and late Roman infant and child cemetery at Poggio Gramignano (Lugnano in Teverina, Umbria, Italy)", *European Journal of Classical Archaeologies* 10 (2020) 279–302; Soren D. and Soren N. (1999) edd. *A Roman Villa and a Late-Roman Infant Cemetery: Excavations at Poggio Gramignano, Lugnano in Teverina* (Rome 1999). <u>Tolentino</u>: Nestori A. (1996) *Il mausoleo e il sarcofago di Flavius Iulius Catervius a Tolentino* (Vatican City 1996).

<u>Campania</u>: Ebanista C. and Amodio M. (2008) "Aree funerarie e luoghi di culto in rupe: le cavità artificiali campane tra tarda antichità e medioevo", in *"Opera Ipogea", 1–2, Atti del VI Convegno Nazionale di Speleologia in Cavità Artificiali (Napoli, 30 maggio–2 giugno 2008)* (2008) 117–44; Ebanista C. (2006) *La tomba di S. Felice nel santuario di Cimitile a cinquant'anni dalla scoperta (Coemeterium 4)* (Marigliano 2006). <u>Other</u>: Marchetta I. (2016) "Gli oggetti in tomba e il loro significato simbolico alcuni esempi da necropoli lucane di V–VII secolo", in *Territorio, insediamenti e necropoli fra tarda antichità e alto medioevo. Atti del convegno internazionale di studi. Cimitile-Santa Maria Capua Vetere, 19–20 giugno 2014*, edd. C. Ebanista and M. Rotili (Napoli 2016) 387–411.

<u>Apulia</u>: D'Angela C. and Volpe G. (1991) "Insediamenti e cimiteri rurali tra tardoantico e alto medioevo nella Puglia centro settentrionale: alcuni esempi", *MEFRA* 103/2 (1991) 785–826; Adriani F., Armenise F., and Sublimi Saponetti S. (2021) "Signs of interpersonal violence and war: study of paleotraumatology in Apulia during the Late Antiquity and the Middle Ages", *PCA European Journal of Postclassical Archaeologies* 11 (2021) 189–252; Rizzone V. (2014) "Ebrei e non ebrei in Sicilia e a Malta nella tarda antichità: il punto di vista delle necropoli", in *Coesistenza e cooperazione nel medioevo. IV congresso europeo di studi medievali. In memoriam L.E. Boyle (Palermo, 23–27 giugno 2009)*, P. Spallino, A. Panzavecchia, I. Panzeca, D. Parisi, L. Parisoli, M. Pavon Ramirez, R. Pereta Rives *et al.* (Palermo 2014) 1259–77. <u>Selected sites</u>: <u>Canosa</u>: De Santis P., Ginevra Panzarino G., and Sperduti A. (2023) "Analyse intégrative d'un espace funéraire complexe: le cas du cimetière de l'antiquité tardive de Canusium (Lieu-dit Lamapopoli, Canosa, Pouilles)", in *Death and the Societies of Late Antiquity*, edd. G. Granier, C. Boyer and E. Anstett (Aix Marseille 2023) 99–117; De Santis P. and De Felice G. (2021) "Strumenti e

tecniche digitali per la ricostruzione di un contesto catacombale. Gli ipogei H e F del cimitero in loc. Lamapopoli a Canosa di Puglia", *Rivista di Archeologia Cristiana* 97/2 (2021) 291–316; De Santis P. (2020) "Riti della commemorazione presso le tombe nel complesso cimiteriale di Lamapopoli a Canosa di Puglia", in *Taccuino per Anna Maria Giuntella. Piccoli scritti di archeologia cristiana e medievale*, edd. F. Bisconti and G. Ferri (Todi 2020) 141–50; De Santis P. (2020) "L'ipogeo H nel complesso catacombale di Canosa di Puglia alla luce delle recenti indagini (2018–2019). Dati preliminari", *RAC* 96 (2020) 91–115; De Santis P. (2017) "Il complesso catacombale di *Canusium* tardoantica. Nuovi dati dagli ipogei F e G (indagini 2016–17)", *RAC* 93 (2017) 97–134; Carletti C., Nuzzo D., and De Santis P. (2006–2007) "Il complesso cimiteriale di Ponte della Lama (Canosa): nuove acquisizioni dagli scavi delle catacombe e dell'area subdiale", *RPAA* 79 (2006–2007) 205–90. *Herdonia*: Piepoli L. (2008) "Sepolture urbane nell'Apulia tardo antica e altomedievale. Il caso di Herdonia", in *Ordona XI. Ricerche archeologiche a Herdonia*, edd. G. Volpe and D. Leone (Bari 2008) 579–94. *San Severo*: Barbiera I. and Ferreri D. (2007) "Placing bodies and constructing memory at San Severo", *Annual of Medieval Studies* 13 (2007) 187–96.

Calabria: Papparella F. C. (2009) *Calabria e Basilicata: L'archeologia funeraria dal IV al VII secolo* (Reggio 2009); Nuzzo D. (2023) "Le iscrizioni sepolcrali della provincia Apulia et Calabria in età tardoantica (IV–VII s. d. C.)", in *Funerary Landscapes of the Late Antique Oecumene: Contextualizing Epigraphic and Archaeological Evidence of Mortuary Practices: Proceedings of an International Conference in Heidelberg, May 30–June 1, 2019*, edd. S. Ardeleanu and J. C. Cubas Diaz (Heidelberg 2023) 365–82.

Sicily: Caminneci V., Rizzo M. S., and Carver M. (in this volume) "Burial rites in Byzantine Sicily – new approaches and discoveries"; Carra Bonacasa R. M., Falzone G., Schirò G., Vitale E., and Sanna E. (2015) "Le aree funerarie fra isole e terraferma: esempii dalla Sicilia e dalla Sardegna", in *Isole e terraferma nel primo cristianesimo. Identità locale ed interscambi culturali, religiosi e produttivi* (*Atti XI congressi nazionale di archeologia cristiana*), edd. R. Martorelli, A. Piras and P. G. Spanu (Cagliari 2015) 135–80; Wilson R. J. A. (2017) "Dining with the dead in early Byzantine Sicily" (Eleventh Babesch Byvanck Lecture; http://www.babesch.org/downloads/BABESCH_Byvanck_Lecture_2017_Wilson.pdf). Selected sites: *Agrigento*: Caminneci V. (2020) "Sepolture tardoantiche e bizantine nell'Emporion di Agrigento", in *From Polis to Madina, La trasformazione delle città siciliane tra tardoantico*

e alto medioevo, edd. L. Arcifa and M. R. Sgarlata (Bari 2020) 285–95; Carra R. M. and Ardizzone F. (2007) edd. *Agrigento dal tardoantico al medioevo. Campagne di scavo nell'area della necropoli paleocristiana. Anni 1986–1999* (Todi 2007); Carra Bonacasa R. M. (1995) *La necropoli paleocristiana sub divo di Agrigento* (Roma 1995); Caminneci V. and Di Giuseppe Z. (2019) "Sepoltura in anfora di infans dall'Emporion di Agrigento", in *Una favola breve. Archeologia e antropologia per la storia dell'infanzia*, ed. C. Lambrugo (Florence 2019) 109–15; Caminneci V. (2015) "'Carnem suam quisque naturaliter diligit' (August. de cura pro mortuis, 7,9). La cura dei corpi in una necropoli tardo antica dell'Emporion di Agrigento", in *VII congresso nazionale di archeologia medievale, Lecce 2015*, edd. P. Arthur and M. Leo Imperiale (Florence 2015) 50–4; Caminneci V. (2012) "Animam sepulcro condimus"; sepolcreto tardoantico in anfore presso l'Emporion di Agrigento (Sicilia, Italia)", in *Rei Cretariae Romanae Fautorum Acta, 27th Congress of the Rei Cretariae Romanae Fautores, Belgrade 19–26 September 2010* (Bonn 2012) 259–66; Caminneci V. (2012) "Enchytrismos. Seppellire in vaso nell'antica Agrigento", in *Parce sepulto. Il rito e la morte tra passato e presente*, ed. V. Caminneci (Palermo 2012) 111–32; Ronco D. (1995) "Studio antropologico del materiale scheletrico", in *La necropoli paleocristiana sub divo di Agrigento*, ed. R. M. Bonacasa Carra (Rome 1995) 328–56. *Lilibeo*: Giglio R. (2016) "La necropoli di Lilibeo alla luce delle ultime scoperte", in *Se cerchi la tua strada verso Itaca … Omaggio a Lina Di Stefano*, edd. E. Lattanzi and R. Spadea (Rome 2016) 101–14; Giglio R. and Canzonieri E. (2009) "Nuovi dati dalle necropoli ellenistiche e tardo antiche di Lilibeo", in *Immagine e immagini della Sicilia e di altre isole del Mediterraneo antico* vol II, ed. C. Ampolo (Pisa 2009) 573–80. *Palermo*: Bonacasa Carra R. M. (1989) "Le necropoli paleocristiane di Palermo: aspetti, problemi e ipotesi di ricerca", *Quaeritur inventus colitur. Studi di antichità cristiana* XL (Vatican City 1989) 53–69; Bonacasa Carra R. M., Cipriano G., Schirò G., and Vitale E. (2008) "I cubicoli VIII.19 e X.10 nella catacomba di Villagrazia di Carini (Palermo)", *RACr* LXXXIV (2008) 81–150. *Other*: Fabbri P. F. and Farina L. (2010) "Note antropologiche su alcune sepolture tardoantiche (SAS 3&4) 2007–08", *Annali della Scuola Normale Superiore di Pisa* 5.2/2 (2010) 21–5; Wilson R. J. A. (2011) "Funerary feasting in early Byzantine Sicily: New evidence from Kaukana", *AJA* 115 (2011) 263–302; Rizzone V. (2008) "Catacombe degli Iblei: un primo approccio sociologico", in *Malta negli Iblei, gli Iblei a Malta (Catania – Sliema, 30 settembre e 10 novembre 2006)*, edd. A. Bonanno and P. Militello (Palermo 2008) 195–208; Bonacasa Carra R. M.

(1993) "Recenti scoperte nell'area delle catacombe di Marsala", in *1983–1993: Dieci anni di archeologia cristiana in Italia. Atti del VII congresso nazionale di archeologia cristiana (Cassino, 20–24 settembre 1993)*, ed. E. Russo (Cassino 1993) 821–27; Greco C., Mammina G., and Di Salvo R. (1991) "Necropoli tardoromana in Contrada S. Agata (Piana degli Albanesi)", in *Di terra in terra: nuove scoperte archeologiche nella provincia di Palermo,* ed. C. A Di Stefano (Palermo 1991) 161–88.

Malta (part of Sicily): Rizzone V. (2016) "La cristianizzazione dell'arcipelago maltese alla luce delle indagini sulle pratiche funerarie", in *Quis Est Qui Ligno Pugnat? Missionaries and Evangelization in Late Antique and Medieval Europe (4th–13th Centuries)*, ed. E. Piazza (Verona 2016) 7–25; Rizzone V. (2014) "Ebrei e non ebrei in Sicilia e a Malta nella tarda antichità: il punto di vista delle necropoli", in *Coesistenza e cooperazione nel medioevo. IV congresso europeo di studi medievali. In memoriam L.E. Boyle (Palermo, 23–27 giugno 2009)*, P. Spallino, A. Panzavecchia, I. Panzeca, D. Parisi, L. Parisoli, M. Pavon Ramirez, R. Pereta Rives *et al.* (Palermo 2014) 1259–77; Buhagiar M. (2007) *The Christianisation of Malta – Catacombs, Cult Centres and Churches in Mata to 1530* (Oxford 2007); Buhagiar M. (1986) *Later Roman and Byzantine Catacombs and Related Burial Places in the Maltese Islands* (Oxford 1986).

Sardegna: Puddu M. (in this volume) "Funerary practices in late antique Sardinia: overview and potential"; De Santis P. (2015) "Riti pratiche funerarie nel processo di costruzione di una memoria identitaria: esempi da Sardegna e Sicilia", in *Isole e terraferma nel primo cristianesimo. Identità locale ed interscambi culturali, religiosi e produttivi (Atti XI congressi nazionale di archeologia cristiana),* edd. R. Martorelli, A. Piras and P. G. Spanu (Cagliari 2015) 203–20; Fiocchi Nicolai V. and Spera R. (2015) "Sviluppi monumentali e insediativi dei santuari dei martiri in Sardegna", in *Isole e terraferma nel primo cristianesimo. Identità locale ed interscambi culturali, religiosi e produttivi. Atti dell'XI congresso nazionale di archeologia cristiana,* edd. R. Martorelli, A. Piras, and P. G. Spanu (Cagliari 2015). https://www.academia.edu/22465499; Martorelli R. (2011) "Usi e consuetudini funerarie nella Sardegna centro-occidentale fra tarda antichità e altro medioevo", in *Oristano e il suo territorio,* edd. P. G. Spanu and R. Zucca (Rome 2011) 700–59; Deiana M. I. (1997) "Incinerazione e inumazione: il caso della Sardegna", *Ann.Fac. Lettere e Filos. Univ. Cagliari* 15, 1996–1997 (1997) 17–66; Giuntella A. M. and Amante Simoni C. (1992) "L'uso degli spazi, sepolture, e riti funerari", in *La civitas cristiana. Urbanistica delle citta' italiane tra trarda antichita' e altomedioevo. Atti del I seminario di studio mediterraneo tardoantico e medievale,* edd. P. Demeglio and C. Lambert (Turin 1992) 127–43. *Cagliari*: Giuntella A. M. (1998) "Note su alcuni aspetti della ritualità funeraria nell'alto medioevo. Consuetudini e innovazioni", in *Sepolture tra IV e VIII secolo. 7° seminario sul tardo antico e l'alto medioevo,* edd. G. P. Brogiolo and G. Cantino Wataghin (1998) 61–75; Mureddu D. (1990) "Alcuni contesti funerari cagliaritani attraverso le cronache del seicento", in *Le Sepolture in Sardegna dal 4° al 7° secolo. Convegno sull'archeologia tardoromana e medievale* (Cuglieri 1987) 179–206; Salvi D. and Fonzo O. (2016) "La tomba bizantina di San Sebastiano a Monastir, con novità e considerazioni sulle tombe impogee altomedievali e note di antropologia sulle sepolture collettive di bivio Monte Pranu, Tratalias, e T4, Sett. I di San Saturnino, Cagliari", *Quaderni della soprintendenza archeologica di Cagliari e Oristano* (2016) 447–80; Locci C. (2012) "Tipologie funerarie nella necropoli romana dell'ex albergo "La Scala di Ferro" – Cagliari", *Quaderni della soprintendenza archeologica di Cagliari e Oristano* 23 (Cagliari 2012) 108–33; Salvi D. (2002) "Cagliari: l'area cimiteriale di San Saturnino", in *Insulae christi. Il cristianesimo primitivo in Sardegna, Corsica e Baleari.* ed. P. G. Spanu (Oristano 2002) 215–24; Serra P. B. (1990) "Complesso sepolcrale bizantino nel Mastio del Nuraghe Su Nuraxi di Siurgus Donigala – Cagliari", in *Le sepolture in Sardegna dal IV al VII secolo* (AA.VV.) (Cagliari 1990) 107–31. *Cornus*: Giuntella A. M. (2002) "Brevi note sull'area cimiteriale orientale di Cornus (Cuglieri provincia di Oristano)", in *Insuale christi. Il cristianesimi primitivo in Sardegna, Corsica e Baleari*, ed. P. G. Spanu (Oristano 2002) 245–52; Giuntella A. M. (1999) *Cornus I, I. L'area cimiteriale orientale* (Mediterraneo tardoantico e medievale. Scavi e ricerche 13) (Oristano 1999); Amante Simoni C., and Martorelli R. (1986) "Cultura, materiali e fasi storiche del complesso archeologico di Cornus: primi risultati di una ricerca. I corredi funerari e la suppellettile metallica", in *Cuglieri I. L'archeologia romana e altomedievale nell'Oristanese. Atti del I convegno* (Mediteranno tardoantico e medievale. Scavi e ricerche 3), ed. A. M. Giuntella (Taranto 1986) 161–89. *Cuglieri*: Amante Simoni C. (1990) "Sepoltura e moneta: obolo viatico-obolo offerta", in *Cuglieri IV. Le sepolture in Sardegna dal IV al VII secolo* (Oristano 1990) 231–42; Giuntella A. M. (1990) "Sepoltura e rito: consuetudini e innovazioni", in *Cuglieri IV. Le sepolture in Sardegna dal IV al VII secolo* (Oristano 1990) 215–29. *Nora*: La Fragola A. (2003) "La necropoli romana", in *Ricerche su Nora II (1990–1998)*, ed. C. Tronchetti (Elmas 2003) 99–115. *Other*: Casagrande M. (2015) "Tomba ipogeica di Decimoputzu, loc. San Giorgio", in *Isole e terraferma nel primo cristianesimo. Identità locale ed interscambi culturali, religiosi e produttivi. Atti XI congresso nazionale di archeologia cristiana*, edd. R. Martorelli, A. Piras and P. G. Spanu (Cagliari 2015) 807–14; Salvi D. (2015) "La tomba 100 di Pill'e Matta e altri Militaria nella necropoli tardoantica di Quartucciu (CA)", *Quaderni friulani di archeologia* XXV (2015) 195–206; Martorelli R. (2011) "Le catacombe di Sant'Antioco", in *S. Antioco da primo evangelizzatore di Sulci a glorioso Protomartire "Patrono della Sardegna*, edd. R. Lai and M. Massa (Sant'Antioco 2011) 59–76; Manos A. and Floris R. (2005) "La necropoli di Mitza Salida – Masullas – Oristano (OR)", *Rendiconti seminarion facolta di scienze universita di Cagliari* 75 (Cagliari 2005) 65–73; Salvi D. (2002) "Quartucciu, località Pill'e Matta: la necropoli tardo-romana", in *Insulae christi: il cristianesimo primitivo in Sardegna, Corsica e Baleari*, ed. P. G. Spanu (Oristano 2002) 473–74.

Rome

General: Borg B. (2018) "Roman cemeteries and tombs", in *A Companion to the City of Rome*, edd. C. Holleran and A. Claridge (Malden 2018) 403–24; Borg B. E. (2013) *Crisis and Ambition: Tombs and Burial Customs in Third-Century AD Rome* (Oxford 2013).

Selected sites: Marcelli M., Alapont Martín L., Evans S. F. and Cicone C. (2023) "The Via Ostiensis necropolis in Rome: Endurance, change, and a complex transition to the paleochristian funerary world", in *Death and the Societies of Late Antiquity*, edd. G. Granier, C. Boyer and E. Anstett (Aix Marseille 2023) 301–14; Giuliani R., Ricciardi M., and Castex D. (2023) "Late burials near the martyrs' sanctuary discovered in the Roman catacomb of ss. Marcellinus and Peter (4th–7th c)", in *Death and the Societies of Late Antiquity*, edd. G. Granier, C. Boyer and E. Anstett (Aix Marseille 2023) 257–82; Liverani P., Spinola G., and Zander P. (2010) *The Vatican Necropoles. Rome's City of the Dead* (Turnhout 2010); Augenti A. (1998) "Iacere in Palatio. Le sepolture altomedievali nel Palatino", in *Sepolture tra IV ed VIII secolo. Struttura, topografia, processi di acculturazione, VII Seminario sul tardoantico e l'alto medioevo in Italia centrosettentrionale, Gardone Riviera 1996*, edd. G. P. Brogiolo and G. Wataghin Cantino (Mantua 1998) 115–21; Rizzo G., Villedieu F., and Vitale M. (1999) "Mobilier de tombes des VIᵉ–VIIᵉ siècles mises au jour sur le Palatin (Rome, Vigna Barberini)", *MEFRA* 111.1 (1999) 351–403; Luschi L. (1984) "Un edificio funerario della via Prenestina nei disegni degli Uffizi", *Prospettive* 39 (1984) 30–7.

Burial topography and landscape: *Urban burials*: Cohen S. (2018) "Liberius and the cemetery as space of exile in late antique Rome", in *Mobility and Exile at the End of Antiquity*, edd. D. Rohmann, J. Ulrich and M. Vallejo Girvés (Frankfurt 2018) 141–60; Meneghini R. and Santangeli Valenzani R. (2000) "Intra-mural burials at Rome between the fifth and seventh centuries AD", in *Burial, Society and Context in the Roman World*, edd. J. Pearce, M. Millett and M. Struck (Oxford 2000) 263–69; Meneghini R. and Santangeli Valenzani R. (1995) "Sepolture intramuranee a Roma tra V e VII sec.d.C. Aggiornamenti e considerazioni", *Archeologia Medievale* 22 (1995) 283–90; Osborne J. (1984) "Death and burial in sixth-century Rome", *Echos du Monde Classique: Classical Views* 28/3 (1984) 291–99. *Suburban burials:* Cohen S. (in this volume) "Topography and ideology: Contested episcopal elections and suburban cemeteries in late antique Rome"; Vella A. (2016) "Le sepulture dei 'non cristiani' nel suburbio di Roma", in *Costantino e i costantinidi – l'innovazione costantiniana, le sue radici e i suoi sviluppi: Acta XVI congressus internationalis archaeologiae christianae, Romae (22–28.9.2013)*, edd. O. Brandt, G. Castiglia and V. Fiocchi Nicolai (Vatican City 2016) 681–709; Lehmann T. (2003) "'Circus Basilicas', 'coemeteria subteglata' and church buildings in the suburbium of Rome", *ActaAArtHist* 17 (2003) 57–77; Spera L. (1999) *Il paesaggio suburbano di Roma dall'antichità al medioevo: il comprensorio tra le vie Latina e Ardeatina dalle Mura Aureliane al III miglio* (Rome 1999). *Villa burials*: Di Gennaro F. and Griesbach J. (2003) "Le sepolture all'interno delle ville con particolare referimento al territorio di Roma", in *Suburbium. Il suburbio di Roma dalla crisi del sistema delle ville a Gregorio Magno*, edd. P. Pergola, R. Santangeli Valenzani and R. Volpe (Rome 2003) 123–66.

Christian burials (general): De Rossi G. B. (1864–1877) *La Roma sotterranea cristiana* 3 vols. (1864–1877); Fiocchi Nicolai V. (2001) *Strutture funerarie ed edifici di culto paleocristiani di Roma dal IV al VI secolo* (Vatican City 2001); Fiocchi Nicolai V. (2006) "Gli spazi delle sepolture cristiane tra il III e il V secolo: genesi e dinamica di una scelta insediativa", in *La comunità cristiana de Roma. La sua vita e la sua cultura dalle origini all'alto medioevo*, edd. L. Pani Ermini and P. Siniscalco (Vatican City 2006) 341–69; Rebillard E. (1997) "L'Église de Rome et le développement des catacombes. À propos de l'origine des cimetières chrétiens", *MEFRA* 109 (1997) 741–63; Goodson C. (2008) "Building for bodies: the architecture of saint veneration in early medieval Rome", in *Felix Roma: The Production, Experience and Reflection of Medieval Rome*, edd. É. Ó Carragain and C. Neuman de Vegvar (London 2008) 51–80; Costambeys M.

(2001) "Burial topography and the power of the church in fifth- and sixth-century Rome", *PBSR* 69 (2001) 169–89.

Christian burials (selected sites): Fiocchi Nicolai V. and Vella A. (2016–17) "Nuove ricerche nella basilica di Papa Marco sulla via Ardeatina: la tomba "dei gioielli" e il riuso di un acquedotto Romano", *RendPontAcc* 89 (2016–17) 299–366; Hellström M. (2015) "On the form and function of Constantine's cruciform funerary basilicas in Rome", in *Pagans and Christians in Late Antique Rome: Conflict, Competition, and Coexistence in the Fourth Century*, edd. M. R. Salzman, M. Sághy and R. Lizzi Testa (Cambridge 2015) 273–90; Johnson M. J. (2015) "La chiesa di Santa Maria de Mesumundu a Siligo e gli edifici rotondi nei cimiteri cristiani della tarda antichità: datazione e funzione", in *Itinerando. Senza confini dalla preistoria ad oggi. Studi in ricordo di Roberto Coroneo*, ed. R. Martorelli (Perugia 2015) 425–40; Nieddu A. M. (2009) *La Basilica Apostolorum sulla Via Appia e l'area cimiteriale circostante* (Vatican City 2009); Spera L. (2004) *Il complesso di pretestato sulla Via Appia: storia topografica e monumentale di un insediamento funerario paleocristiano nel suburbio di Roma* (Vatican City 2004); Windfeld-Hansen H. (2003) "Le cimetière de Prétextat. Edifice funéraire à plan cruciforme de l'area sub divo", in *Suburbium. Il suburbio di Roma dalla crisi del sistema delle ville a Gregorio*, edd. P. Pergola, R. Santangeli Valenzani and R. Volpe (Rome 2003a) 727–34; Windfeld-Hansen H. (1969) "L'hexaconque funéraire de l'area sub divo du cimetrière de Prétextat à Rome", *ActaAArtHist* 4 (1969) 61–93; Fiocchi Nicolai V. (2002) "Basilica Marci, coemeterium Marci, basilica coemeterii Balbinae. A proposito della nuova basilica circiforme della via Ardeatina e della funzione funeraria delle chiese 'a deambulatorio' del suburbio Romana", in *Ecclesiae urbis*, vol. 2, edd. F. Guidobaldi and A. G. Guidobaldi (Vatican City 2002) 1175–201; Rasch J. J. (1990) "Zur Rekonstruktion der Andreasrotunde an Alt-St.Peter", *RömQSchr* 85 (1990) 1–18; Gai S. (1986) "La "Berretta del prete" sulla Via Appia antica. Indagini preliminari sull'insediamento medievale 1984", *Archeologia medievale* 13 (1986) 365–404; Pagliardi N. (1985) "Sepolcro c.d. Berretta del prete (circ. XI)", *BullCom* 90 (1985) 100–1; Paolucci L. (2008) "La tomba dell'imperatrice Maria e altre sepulture di rango di età tardoantica a San Pietro", *Temporis signa. Archeologia della tarda antichità e del medioevo* 3 (2008) 225–52.

Catacombs (General): Fiocchi Nicolai V. (2014) "Le catacombe romane", in *Lezioni di archeologia cristiana*, edd. F. Bisconti and O. Brandt (Vatican City 2014) 273–360; Guyon J. (2005) "À propos d'un ouvrage récent: retour sur "les dossiers" des origines des catacombes chrétiennes de Rome", *Rivista di Archeologia Cristiana* 81 (2005) 235–53; Fiocchi Nicolai V., Bisconti F., and Mazzoleni D. (1999) *The Christian Catacombs of Rome: History, Decoration, Inscriptions* (Regensburg 1999); Testini P. (1966) *Le catacombe e gli antichi cimiteri cristiani di Roma* (Rome 1966); Zimmermann N. (2023) "Die römischen Katakomben Überlegungen zu Besitzverhältnissen, zur räumlichen Nutzung und zur Grabtypologie anhand der Katakomben Domitilla, ss. Marcellino e Pietro und Randanin", in *Funerary Landscapes of the Late Antique Oecumene: Contextualizing Epigraphic and Archaeological Evidence of Mortuary Practices: Proceedings of an International Conference in Heidelberg, May 30–June 1, 2019*, edd. S. Ardeleanu and J. C. Cubas Diaz (Heidelberg 2023) 383–406; De Santis P. (2000) "Glass vessels as grave goods and grave ornaments in the catacombs of Rome", in *Burial, Society and Context in the Roman World*, edd. J. Pearce, M. Millett and M. Struck (Oxford 2000) 238–43.

Catacombs (Selected sites): Ingle G. (2019) "A fourth century tomb of the followers of mithras from the catacomb of Ss. Peter and Parcellinus in Rome", *Studies in ancient art and civilisation* 23 (2019) 227–39; Nuzzo D. (2017) "Osservazioni sulla topografia cimiteriale del primo piano della catacomba di San Sebastiano (scavi 1995–1996)", *Rivista di archeologia cristiana* 93 (2017) 71–95; Carletti C. (2008) "Nuovi graffiti devozionali nell'area cimiteriale di S. Sebastiano a Roma", in *Unexpected Voices: The Graffiti in the Cryptoporticus of the Horti Sallustiani and Papers from a Conference on Graffiti at the Swedish Institute in Rome, 7 March 2003*, ed. O. Brandt (Stockholm 2008) 137–47; Bisconti F. and Braconi M. (2015) edd. *Le catacombe di San Callisto. Storia, contesti, scavi, restauri, scoperte. A proposito del cubicolo di Orfeo e del Museo della Torretta* (Todi 2015); Fasola U. M. (1980) "Indagini nel sopratterra della catacomba di S. Callisto", *RACrist* 56 (1980) 221–78; Rossi D. and Di Mento M. (2013) edd. *La catacomba ebraica di Monteverde: vecchi dati e nuove scoperte* (Rome 2013); Bartolazzi Casti G. (2010) "Gli Anici e il mausoleo di famiglia presso la basilica vaticana", *Palladio* 23/45 (2010) 15–30; Nuzzo D. (2000) *Tipologia sepolcrale delle catacombe romane: i cimiteri ipogei delle vie Ostiense, Ardeatina e Appia* (Oxford 2000); Ferrua A. (1960) "Il cimitero sopra la catacomba di Domitilla", *RACrist* 36 (1960) 173–210.

Pagan burials: Couzin R. (2019) "Where did all the pagans go" The non-Christian sarcophagi of fourth-century Rome", *PBSR* 87 (2019) 145–75; Lewis N. D. (2016) "Reinterpreting "pagans" and "Christians" from Rome's late antique mortuary evidence", in *Pagans and Christians in Late Antique Rome.*

Conflict, Competition, and Coexistence in the Fourth Century, edd. M. R. Salzman, M. Sághy and R. L. Testa (Cambridge 2016) 273–90.

Mausolea (Selected sites): Borg B. E. (2022) "Peter and Paul ad catacumbas: A pozzolana mine reconsidered", in *The Economy of Death: New Research on Collective Burial Spaces in Rome from the Late Republican to the Late Roman Period. Proceedings of the 19th International Congress of Classical Archaeology, Cologne/Bonn 2018,* edd. T. Fröhlich and N. Zimmermann (Heidelberg 2022) 45–58; Oosten D. (2016) "The mausoleum of Helena and the adjoining basilica ad duas lauros: Construction, evolution and reception", in *Monuments & Memory Christian Cult Buildings and Constructions of the Past. Essays in Honour of Sible de Blaauw,* edd. M. Verhoeven, L. Bosman and H. van Asperen (Turnhout 2016) 131–43; Rasch J. J. (1998) *Das Mausoleum der Kaiserin Helena in Rom und der "Tempio della Tosse" in Tivoli* (Mainz 1998); Blanco A., Nepi D., and Vella A. (2013) "Il mausoleo e la basilica circiforme della cd. Villa dei Gordiani sulla via Prenestina: tecnica e strategia die rilievo", *BullCom* 114 (2013) 285–94; Vendittelli L. (2011) *Il mausoleo di Sant'Elena. Gli scavi* (Milan 2011); Rasch J. J. (1993) *Das Mausoleum bei Tor de' Schiavi in Rom* (Mainz 1993); Rasch J. J. (1984) *Das Maxentius-Mausoleum an der Via Appia in Rom* (Mainz 1984).

Collective burials: Bodel J. (2008) "From columbaria to catacombs: Collective burials in pagan and Christian Rome", in *Commemorating the Dead: Texts and Artefacts in Context: Studies of Roman, Jewish, and Christian Burials,* edd. L. Brink and D. Green (Berlin 2008) 177–242; Blanchard P., Castex D., Coquerelle M., Giuliani R., and Ricciardi M. (2007) "A mass grave from the catacomb of Saints Peter and Marcellinus in Rome, second-third century AD", *Antiquity* 81 (2007) 989–99; Rasch J. J. and Arbeiter A. (2007) *Das Mausoleum der Constantina in Rom* (Mainz 2007).

Funerary epigraphy: Felle A. E. (2023) "Paesaggi epigrafici nelle necropoli della Roma tardoantica. Alcuni casi esemplari per una 'epigrafia archeologica'", in *Funerary Landscapes of the Late Antique Oecumene: Contextualizing Epigraphic and Archaeological Evidence of Mortuary Practices: Proceedings of an International Conference in Heidelberg, May 30–June 1, 2019,* edd. S. Ardeleanu and J. C. Cubas Diaz (Heidelberg 2023) 407–28.

Funerary rituals: Spera L. (2009) "Forme di autodefinizione identitaria nel mondo funerario: cristiani e non cristiani a Roma nella tarda antichità", in *Miscellanea in onore di Roberto Pretagostini,* edd. E. Dettori, C. Braidotti (Roma 2009) 769–803;

Spera L. (2005) "Riti funerari e "culto dei morti" nella tarda antichità: un quadro archeologico dai cimiteri paleocristiani di Roma", *Augustinianum* 45 (2005) 5–34.

Bioarchaeology: Emmerson A. L. (2020) "Re-examining Roman death pollution", *JRS* 110 (2020) 5–27; André J. -M. (1980) "La notion de Pestilentia à Rome: du tabu religieux à l'interprétation préscientifique", *Latomus* 39(1) (1980) 3–16.

Pannonia

Croatia: Migotti B. (1994) "The archaeological material of the early Christian period in continental Croatia", in *From the Invincible Sun to the Sun of Justice. Early Christianity in Continental Croatia,* ed. Ž. Demo (Zagreb 1994) 187–209. Selected sites: *Salona*: Gauthier N. (2015) "Les inscriptions funéraires tardo-antiques de Salone", in *Frühchristliche Grabinschriften im Westen des Römischen Reiches: Beiträge zur Internationalen Konferenz „Frühchristliche Grabinschriften im Westen des Römischen Reiches", Trier, 13.–15. Juni 2013,* edd. L. Clemens, H. Merten and C. Schäfer (Trier 2015) 209–16; Gauthier N., Marin E., and Prévot D. (2010) edd. *Salona IV: inscriptions de Salone chrétienne, IVe–VIIe siècles* (Rome-Split 2010); Rendić-Miočević D. (1954) "Neue Funde in der altchristlichen Nekropole Manastirine in Salona", *Archaeologia Iugoslavica* 1 (1954) 53–70; Dyggve E. and Egger R. (1939) *Forschungen in Salona III: der altchristliche Friedhof Marusinac* (Vienna 1939). *Vinkovci*: Dimitrijević S. (1979) "Archäologische Topographie und Auswahl archäologischer Funde vom Vinkovcer Boden", in *Corolla memoriae Iosepho Brunšmid dicata,* ed. Ž. Rapanić (Vinkovci 1979) 201–82.

Slovenia: *Overview*: Stemberger K. (in this volume) "Late Roman burials in Slovenia"; Pavletič K. (2020) "Kratek pregled razvoja teoretskih pristopov v arheologiji grobišč pozne antike in zgodnjega srednjega veka (A short overview of theoretical approaches in the archaeological research of late antique and early medieval cemeteries)", *Arheo* 37 (2020) 25–45; Pleterski A. (2001) "O nekaterih možnostih interpretiranja zgodnjesrednjeveških grobišč", *Arheo* 21 (2001) 69–71; Mikl Curk, I. (1997) "Iz materialne kulture k vprašanjem verstva in premožnosti na slovenskem ozemlju ob koncu 4. st. / Von der materiellen Kultur zur Frage von Religion und Vermögenverhältnissen im heutigen Slowenien am Ende des 4. Jhs.", *Arheološki vestnik / Acta archaeologica* 48 (1997) 179–89. *Dress accessories*: Čaval S. (2013) "Poznoantične okrasne igle vrste stilus v Sloveniji / Late antique decorative pins of the stylus type in Slovenia", *Arheološki vestnik / Acta archaeologica* 64 (2013) 197–248. *Social data*: *Gender*: Stemberger K. (2020) "A study of female-associated burials from Roman-period Slovenia", in *Un-Roman Sex: Gender, Sexuality, and Lovemaking in the Roman Provinces and Frontiers,* edd. T. Ivleva and R. Collins (London 2020) 210–37. *Identity*: Čaval S. (2013) "Poznoantične okrasne igle vrste stilus v Sloveniji / Late antique decorative pins of the stylus type in Slovenia", *Arheološki vestnik / Acta archaeologica* 64 (2013) 197–248.

Slovenia (Selected sites): *Bled*: Kastelic J. (1960) *Slovanska nekropola na Bledu.* (Dela 1. reda SAZU / Opera Instituti Archaeologici Sloveniae 13) (Ljubljana 1960); Leben-Seljak P. (1996) *Antropološka analiza poznoantičnih in srednjeveških grobišč Bleda in okolice / Anthropological Analysis of Late Antique and Medieval Necropolises at Bled and Surroundings* (Unpublished PhD., Univ. of Ljubljana 1996). *Emona*: Petru S. (1972) *Emonske nekropole. Odkrite med leti 1635–1960* (Katalogi in monografije / Catalogi et monographiae 7) (Ljubljana 1972); Županek B. (2018) "Pokrajine umrlih: struktura in dinamika severnega grobišča Emone", in *Nova odkritja med Alpami in Črnim morjem. Rezultati raziskav rimskodobnih najdišč v obdobju med leti 2005 in 2015. Zbornik 1. mednarodnega arheološkega simpozija, Ptuj, 8. in 9. oktober 2015: Zavod za varstvo kulturne dediščine Slovenije,* edd. M. Janežič, B. Nadbath, T. Mulh and I. Žižek (Ljubljana 2018) 253–80; Plesničar Gec L. (1972) *Severno emonsko grobišče / The Northern Necropolis of Emona* (Katalogi in monografije / Catalogi et monographiae 8) (Ljubljana 1972); Plesničar Gec L. (1977) *Keramika emonskih nekropol* (Ljubljana 1977); Tomažinčič Š. (2018) "Belt types, identity and social status in late antiquity: the belt set in Emona's grave 18", *JRA* 31 (2018) 426–44; Stemberger K. (2014) "Identity of females buried at Colonia Iulia Emona / Rekonstruiranje identitet žensk z emonskih nekropol", *Arheo* 31 (2014) 69–81; Miškec A., Županek B., Karo Š., and Tica G. (2020) *Severno emonsko grobišče – raziskave na najdišču Kozolec* (Situla 45) (Ljubljana 2020). *Karnija*: Knific T. and Lux J. (2010) "Otroci iz mesta Karnija", *Kranjski zbornik* (2010) 26–36; Knific T. (1995) "Vojščaki iz mesta Karnija", *Kranjski zbornik* (1995) 23–40; Knific T. (2005) "Gospe iz mesta Karnija", *Kranjski zbornik* (2005) 331–43. *Kranj*: Sagadin M. (1987) *Kranj – križišče Iskra. Nekropola iz časa preseljevanja ljudstev in staroslvanskega obdobja / Kranj – Iskra Crossroads. A Cemetery from the Migration Period and the Early Slavic Period.* (Katalogi in Monografije / Catalogi et monographiae 24) (Ljubljana 1987); Stare V. (1980) *Kranj. Nekropola iz časa preseljevanja ljudstev / Kranj. Necropolis from the Time of the Migration of Peoples* (Katalogi in

monografije / Catalogi et monographiae 18) (Ljubljana 1980). *Ljubljana*: Mulh T. (2008) *Poročilo o zaščitnih arheoloških izkopavanjih na lokaciji Potniški center Ljubljana 2007/2008* (poročilo št. 1/2003 – BV TM). (Ljubljana 2008); Plesničar Gec L. (1967) "Obeležje in kronologija antičnih grobov na Prešernovi in Celovški cesti v Ljubljani / Caractère et chronologie des tombes antiques sur la Prešernova et la Celovška cesta à Ljubljana", *Arheološki vestnik / Acta archaeologica* 18 (1967) 137–51; Vuga D. (1985) "Moški grob z vrta Narodnega muzeja v Ljubljani. Poznorimske in barbarske ledvičaste pasne spone z ovalnim okovom", *Arheološki vestnik / Acta archaeologica* 36 (1985) 237–54. *Ptuj*: Korošec P. (1999) *Nekropola na Ptujskem gradu, Turnirski prostor* (Ptuj 2010); Tušek I. (1997) "Skupina poznorimskih grobov iz območja izkopa za stanovanjski blok B-2 v Rabelčji vasi – zahod na Ptuju", *Arheološki vestnik* 48 (1997) 289–300; Jevremov B., Tomanič Jevremov M., and Ciglenečki S. (1993) "Poznorimsko grobišče na Ptujskem gradu / Spätrömisches Gräberfeld auf dem Ptujski grad", *Arheološki vestnik / Acta archaeologica* 44 (1993) 223–34; Istenič J. (1999) *Poetovio, zahodna grobišča 1. Grobne celote iz Deželnega muzeja Joanneuma v Gradcu / Poetovio, the Western Cemeteries 1: Grave-groups in the Landesmuseum Joanneum, Graz* (Katalogi in monografije / Catalogi et monographiae 32) (Ljubljana 1999); Curk I. (1966) "Poznoantično grobišče na Zgornjem Bregu v Ptuju", *Časopis za zgodovino in narodopisje* 2 (1966) 46–62. *Rifnik*: Bolta L. (1981) *Rifnik pri Šentjurju. Poznoantična naselbina in grobišče. / spätantike Siedlung und Gräberfeld* (Katalogi in monografije / Catalogi et monographiae 19) (Ljubljana (1981); Vičič B. (1990) "Horizontalna stratigrafija poznoantičnega grobišča na Rifniku", *Arheološki vestnik / Acta archaeologica* 41 (1990) 439–54; Bolta L. (1970–1971) "Poznoantično grobišče pri Rifniku pri Šentjurju / Spätantikes Gräberfeld auf Rifnik bei Šentjur", *Arheološki vestnik / Acta archaeologica* 21–22 (1970–1971) 127–40. *Vrajk*: Bavec U. (2003) "Predhodno poročilo o poznoantičnem grobišču na Vrajku v Gorenjem Mokronogu / Preliminary report on the late Roman cemetery at Vrajk in Gorenji Mokronog", *Arheološki vestnik / Acta archaeologica* 54 (2003) 325–30; Leben-Seljak P. (2003) "Antropološka analiza poznoatičnega grobišča na Vrajku v Gornjem Mokronogu", *Arheološki vestnik / Acta archaeologica* 54 (2003) 397–420. *Other*: Štular B. (2007) "Posamezniki, skupnost in obred v zgodnjem srednjem veku. Primer grobiščnih podatkov z Malega gradu v Sloveniji / The individuals, the community, and the ritual in the Early Middle Ages", *Studia Mythologica Slavica* 10 (2007) 23–50; Pleterski A. (2008) *Zgodnjesrednjeveška naselbina na Blejski Pristavi. Najdbe.*

(Dela 1. reda SAZU / Opera Instituti Archaeologici Sloveniae 14) (Ljubljana 2008); Pleterski A. (2002) "Od deklice do starke. Od doma do moža", *Arheo* 22 (2002) 53–8; Pahič S. (1969) *Antični in staroslovanski grobovi v Brezju nad Zrečami. Razprave 1. razreda* SAZU 6. (Ljubljana 1969) 217–308; Zavrtanik J. (1984) "Poznoantično grobišče pri Kosovelih", *Goriški letnik* 11 (1984) 85–94; Leben-Seljak, P. (2018) "Antropološka analiza skeletov", in *Miren. Grobišče iz časa preseljevanja ljudstev,* edd. V. Tratnik and Š. Karo (Ljubljana 2018) 58–70; Bitenc P. and Knific T. (2001) *Od Rimljanov do Slovanov. Predmeti* (Ljubljana 2001); Peterski A. and Beljak M. (2002) "Grobovi s Puščave nad Starim trgom pri Slovenj Gradcu / Die Gräber von Puščava oberhalb von Stari trg bei Slovenj Gradec", *Arheološki vestnik / Acta archaeologica* 53 (2002) 233–300; Orožen-Adamič, A., Zorc M., and Zupanc D. (1975) "Antropološka obdelava izkopanega gradiva", in *Vranje pri Sevnici. Starokrščanske cerkve na Ajdovskem gradcu / frühchristliche Kirchenanlagen auf dem Ajdovski Gradec* (Katalogi in monografije / Catalogi et monographiae 12), edd. P. Petru and Th. Ulbert (Ljubljana 1975) 117–22.

Pannonia (Hungary): Gáspár D (2002) *Christianity in Roman Pannonia. An Evaluation of Early Christian Finds and Sites in Hungary* (BAR Int. Ser. 1010) (Oxford 2002); Deichmann F. (1970) "Märtyrerbasilika, Martyrion, Memoria und Altargrab", *RömMitt* 77 (1970) 144–69.

Pannonia (Selected sites): *Alsóhetén*: Tóth E. (1988) "Az alsóhetényi 4. századi erőd és temető kutatása, 1981–1986: eredmények és vitás kérdések [The research of the 4th century fortress and cemetery in Alsóhetény, 1981–1986: results and questions for discussion]", *ArchErt* 114–115 (1987–1988) 22–61; Tóth E. (1987–1988) "Vorbericht über die Ausgrabung der Festung und des Gräberfeldes von Alsóhetény 1981–1986. Ergebnisse und umstrittere Fragen", *AÉrt* 114–115 (1987–1988) 22–62. *Kővágószőlős*: Burger A. Sz. (1987) "The Roman villa and mausoleum at Kővágószőlős, near Pécs (Sopianae). Excavations 1977–1982", *A Janus Pannonius Múzeum Évkönyve* 30–31 (1985–1986) 65–228; Burger A. Sz. (1986–1987) "The Roman villa and mausoleum at Kővágószőlős, near Pécs (Sopianae): excavations, 1977–1982", *A Janus Pannonius Museum Évkönyve* 30–31 (1986–1987) 65–228. *Ságvár*: Schmidt W. (2000) "Spätantike Gräberfelder in den Nordprovinzen des römischen Reiches und das Aufkommen christlichen Bestattungsbrauchtums: Tricciana (Ságvár) in der Provinz Valeria", *Saalburg-Jahrbuch* 50 (2000) 213–441; Burger A. Sz. (1966) "The Late Roman cemetery at Ságvár", *ActaArchHung* 18 (1966) 99–234. *Other*: Masek Z. (2016) "The transformation of late antique comb types on the frontier of the Roman and Germanic world – Early medieval antler combs from Rákóczifalva (County Jász-Nagykun-Szolnok, Hungary)", *Antaeus* 34 (2016) 105–72; Ilon G. (2015) ed. *The Early and Late Roman Rural Cemetery at Nemesbőd (Vas County, Hungary)* (Archaeopress Roman Archaeology 5) (Oxforrd 2015); Eke I. and Horváth L. (2006) "Late Roman cemeteries at Nagykanizsa", *Régészeti Kutatások Magyarországon* (2005) 73–86; Sági K. (1960) "Die spätrömische Bevölkerung der Umgebung von Keszthely", *ActaArchHung* 12 (1960) 187–256; Nagy L. (1931) *Az óbudai ókeresztény cella trichora a Raktár-utcában (Az Aquincumi Múzeum 1930. évi ásatása* (Budapest 1931).

Sopiane: Fülep F., Bachman Z., and Pintér A. (1988) *Sopianae-Pécs ókeresztény emlékei* [The Early Christian remains of Sopianae-Pécs] (Budapest 1988); Fülep F. (1984) *Sopianae. The History of Pécs During the Roman Era and the Problem of Continuity of the Late Roman Population* (Budapest 1984); Fülep F. (1977) *Roman Cemeteries on the Territory of Pécs (Sopianae)* (Budapest 1977); Fülep F. (1962) "Újabb kutatások a pécsi későrómai temetőben [New investigations in the Late Roman cemetery of Pécs]", *ArchErt* 89 (1962) 23–46; Gábor O. (2016) *Sopianae késő antik temetői épületei* [The late antique cemetery buildings of Sopianae] (Kaposvár – Pécs 2016); Gábor O. (2013) "Sopianae ókeresztény temetőjének épületei [The buildings of the early Christian cemetery of Sopianae]", in *Pécs története* I., ed. Zs. Visy (Pécs 2013) 195–222; Nagy L. (2013) "Túlvilági elképzelések és értelmezési problémák a pécsi késő rómao-ókeresztény temetőben [Beliefs of the afterlife and the problems of interpretation on the late Roman-early Christian cemetery of Pécs]", *Műemlékvédelem* 57 (2013) 1–12; Hudák K. and Nagy L. (2009) *A Fine and Private Place: Discovering the Early Christian Cemetery of Sopianae/Pécs*, 2nd edition (Pécs 2009); Visy Zs. (2007) "Recent data on the structure of the early Christian burial buildings in Pécs", *Acta Classica Debreceniensis* 43 (2007) 137–55; Magyar Zs. (2007) "Sopianae: a study of cultural influences in fourth century southern Pannonia", *Buletinul cerculior ştiinţifice studenţeşti: Arheologie-istorie-muzeologie* 13 (2007) 41–58; Gábor O. (2007) "Ókeresztény jellegek a pécsi késő antik temetőben [Early Christian characteristics in the late antique cemetery of Pécs]", in *FiRKáK I.: fiatal római koros kutatók I. konferenciakötete: Xantus János Múzeum, Győr 2006. március 8–10.*, ed. Sz. Bíró (Győr 2007) 367–77; Kraft J. (2006) *A pécsi ókeresztény temető geológiája és felszínének fejlődése* (Örökségi Füzetek 5) (Pécs 2006); Tóth E. (2006) "A pogány és keresztény Sopianae: a császárkultusz-központ

Pannonia Inferiorban, valamint a pogány és keresztény temetkezések elkülönítésének lehetőségéről, a 11. sírkamra [The pagan and Christian Sopianae: the center of the imperial cult in Pannonia Inferior and the possibility to separate the Christian and pagan burials, Burial Chamber 11]", *Specimina Nova* 20 (2006) 49–102; Gosztonyi Gy. (1943) *A pécsi ókeresztény* (Pécs 1943); Tóth Zs., Buzás G., and Neményi R. (2020) "Előzetes beszámoló a pécsi székesegyház altemplomában végzett 2019. évi régészeti kutatásról [Preliminary report on the archaeological excavation in the crypt of the cathedral of Pécs in 2019]", in *Pécsi Tudományegyetem Bölcsész Akadémia 4.*, edd. G. Bőhm, D. Czeferner and T. Fedeles (Pécs 2020) 9–70; Visy Zs. (2006) "Cella Septichora. Előzetes beszámoló a Szent István téren az ókeresztény temető területén folytatott régészeti kutatásokról [Cella Septichora. Preliminary report on the archaeological investigations on the area of the early Christian cemetery in the Szent István Square]", *Pécsi Szemle* 9/2 (2006) 3–13; Fülep F. and Bachman Z. (1990) *Pécs frühchristliches Mausoleum* (Budapest 1990); Kárpáti G. (2002) "A pécsi v. számú sírkamra [Burial Chamber number 5 of Pécs]", *Műemlékvédelem* 44 (2002) 142–44; Fülep F. (1987) "A pécsi későrómai-ókeresztény mauzóleum feltárásáról [The excavation of the late Roman-early Christian mausoleum in Pécs]", *A Janus Pannonius Múzeum Évkönyve* 32 (1987) 31–44; Fülep F. (1977) "A pécsi ókeresztény mauzóleum ásatása [Excavations of the early Christian mausoleum of Pécs]", *ArchErt* 104 (1977) 246–57; Fülep F. and Fetter A. (1971) "Neuere Forschungen in der ausgemalten, frühchristlichen Grabkammer Nr. 11 von Pécs", *A Janus Pannonius Múzeum Évkönyve* 16 (1971) 91–103; Fülep F. (1969) "Scavi archeologici a Sopiane", *Corso di cultura sull'arte ravennate e bizantina* 16 (1969) 151–63; Fülep F. (1959) "Újabb ásatások a pécsi cella trichorában [Recent excavations in the cella trichora of Pécs]", *A Janus Pannonius Múzeum Évkönyve* 4 (1959) 75–91; Fülep F. (1959a) "Neuere Ausgrabungen in der Cella Trichora von Pécs (Fünfkirchen)", *ActaArchHung* 11 (1959) 399–417; Gosztonyi Gy. (1942) "A pécsi 11. számú ókeresztény festett sírkamra és sírkápolna [The early Christian painted burial chamber no. 2. and chapel from Pécs]", *ArchErt* 69 (1942) 196–206; Gosztonyi Gy. (1940) "A pécsi hétkaréjos ókeresztény temetői épület [The early Christian cemetery building with seven apses from Pécs]", *ArchErt* 67 (1940) 56–61; Dyggve E. (1935) "Das Mausoleum in Pécs (Ein christliches Heroon aus Pannonia Inferior)", *Pannonia* 1 (1935) 62–77.

Pannonia (Serbia, Vojvodina): Đorđević M. (2007) *Arheološka nalazišta rimskog perioda u Vojvodini – Archaeological Sites from the Roman Period in Vojvodina* (Belgrade 2007).

Selected sites: *Sirmium*: Popović I. (2012) "La nécropole de la basilique urbaine à Sirmium", *Starinar* 62 (2012) 113–35; Milošević P. (2001) *Arheoloija i istorija Sirmijuma* (Novi Sad 2001); Jeremić M. (2005) "Adolf Hytrek et les premieres fouilles archeologiques a Sirmium", *Starinar* 55 (2005) 115–30; Milošević P. (1976) *Kompleks rimskih nekropola u Sirmijumu (nastanak, geneza i kraj)* (Ph. D. diss., Univ. of Belgrade 1976). *Other*: Brukner O. (1995) "Mauzolej – oktogonalna građevina [Mausoleum – an octagonal tomb]", in *Arheološka istraživanja duž autoputa kroz Srem*, ed. Z. Vapa (Novi Sad 1995) 175–80; Petrović M. (1995) "Mauzolej – arhitektonska analiza i rekonstrukcija [The mausoleum – architectonic analysis and reconstruction]", in *Arheološka istraživanja duž autoputa kroz Srem*, ed. Z. Vapa (Novi Sad 1995) 181–84; Brukner O. (1995) "Rimska naselja i vile rustike [Roman settlements and a villae rusticae]", in *Arheološka istraživanja duž autoputa kroz Srem,* ed. Z. Vapa (Novi Sad 1995) 137–74; Brukner O. (1987) "Sremska Mitrovica/Livade villa rustica", *Arheološki Pregled* 28 (1987) 113–18; Hytrek A. (1894) "Starikršćansko grobište sv. Sinerota u Sremu [The early Christian cemetery of St Syneros in Srem]", in *Ephemeris Salonitana* (Zadar 1894) 5–10.

Africa

North Africa: *Overview*: Stone D. L. and Stirling L. M. (2007) "Funerary monuments and mortuary practices in the landscapes of North Africa", in *Mortuary Landscapes of North Africa*, edd. D. L. Stone and L. M Stirling (Toronto 2007) 3–31. Christian burials: Camps G. (1986) "Funerary monuments with attached chapels from the northern Sahara", *The African Archaeological Review* 4 (1986) 151–64.

Numidia/Mauretania (Algeria): Selected sites: *Blad-Guitoun*: Laporte J-P. (2013) "Le mausolée de Blad Guitoun", *Ikosim* 2 (2013) 91–108; Gsell S. (1898) "Le mausolée de Blad-Guitoun (fouilles de M. Viré)", *Comptes rendus des séances de l'Académie des Inscriptions et Belles-Lettres* 42 (1898) 481–99. *Fenda*: Kadra F. (1983) *Les Djedars. Monuments funéraires Berbères de la région de Frenda* (Algiers 1983). *Taksebt*: Euzennat M. and Hallier G. (1992) "Le mausolea de Taksebt (Algérie)", *CRAI* 136/1 (1992) 235–48. *Tiaret*: Laporte J-P. (2005) "Les djedars, monuments funéraires berbères de la region de Frenda et Tiaret", in *Identités et culture dans l'Algérie antique*, ed. C. Briand-Ponsart (Rouen 2005) 321–406. *Tipasa*: Ardeleanu S. (2018) "Directing the faithful, structuring the sacred space: funerary epigraphy in its archaeological context in late-antique Tipasa", *JRA* 31

(2018) 475–500; Albertini E. and Leschi L. (1932) "Le cimetière de Sainte-Salsa, à Tipasa", *CRAI* (1932) 77–88.

Africa Proconsularis/Byzacena (Tunisia): Duval N. (1986) "L'inhumation privilegiee en Tunisie et en Tripolitaine", in *L'inhumation privilégiée du IVᵉ au VIIIᵉ siècle en Occident. Actes du colloque tenu à Créteil les 16–18 mars 1984*, edd. Y. Duval and J.- C. Picard (Paris 1986) 25–34. Selected sites: *Bulla Regia*: Chaouali M., Fenwick C., and Booms D. (2018) "Bulla Regia I: A new church and Christian cemetery", *Libyan Studies* 49 (2018) 187–97. *Carthage*: Potthof S. E. (2017) *The Afterlife in Early Christian Carthage. Near-Death Experience, Ancestor Cult, and the Archaeology of Paradise* (London, New York 2017); Stevens S. T. (2008) "Commemorating the dead in the communal cemeteries of Carthage", in *Commemorating the Dead: Texts and Artefacts in Context. Studies of Roman, Jewish, and Christian Burials*, edd. L. Brink and D. Green (Berlin 2008) 79–106; Leone A. (2002) "L'inumazione in "spazio urbano" a Cartagine tra V e VII secolo D.C.", *Antiquite Tardive* 10 (2002) 233–48; Stevens S. T. (1995) "Sépultures tardives *intra muros à* Carthage", in *L'Afrique du nord antique et mediévale: monuments funéraires, institutions autochtones*, ed. P. Trousset (Paris 1995) 207–18; Stevens S. (1995) "A late-Roman urban population in a cemetery of Vandalic date at Carthage", *JRA* 8 (1995) 263–70; Norman N. (2003) "Death and burial of Roman children: the case of the Yasmina cemetery at Carthage II: The archaeological evidence", *Mortality* 8 (2003) 36–47; Norman N. and Haeckl A. (1993) "The Yasmina necropolis at Carthage, 1992", *JRA* 6 (1993) 238–50; Duval N. and Lézine A. (1959) "La chapelle funéraire souterraine dite d'Astérius a Carthage", *MEFRA* 71 (1959) 339–57. *Maktar*: Laporte J-P. (1980) "Un mausolée du IVᵉ siècle: La Ghorfa des ouled Selama, pres d'Auzia", *Bulletin d'Archéologie Algérienne* 7 (1980) 55–9. *Pupput*: Ben Abed A. and Griesheimer M. (2001) "Fouilles de la nécropole romaine de Pupput (Tunisie)", *Comptes rendus des séances de l'Académie des Inscriptions et Belles-Lettres, 145ᵉ année* 1 (2001) 553–92. *Thuburnica*: Ferchiou N. (1986) "The anonymous mausoleum of Thuburnica", *MEFRA* 98 (1986) 665–705.

Tripolitania: Selected sites: *Ghadames*: Mattingly D. J. and Sterry M. (2010) *Ghadames Archaeological Survey, Phase 1* (Unpublished Desktop Report) (Leicester 2010). *Ghirza*: Brogan O. and Smith D. J. (1984) *Ghirza. A Libyan Settlement in the Roman Period* (Libyan Antiquities Series 1) (Tripoli 1984). *Khoms*: Matoug J. M. (1998) "Wadi al-Fani (Khoms): mausoleum with subterranean tomb", *Libya Antiqua* (New Series 4) (1998) 274–76. *Leptis Magna*: Fontana S. (2001) "Leptis Magna. The Romanization of a major African city through burial evidence", in *Italy and the West: Comparative Issues in Romanization*, edd. S. Keay and N. Terrenato (Oxford 2001) 161–72; Fontana S. (1996) "Le necropoli di Leptis Magna. Introduzione", *Libya Antiqua* (New Series 2) (1996) 79–84. *Sabratha*: Rizzo M. A. (2015) "L'area sacro-funeraria di Sidret el-Balik e le tombe dipinte", in A*rcheologia ed epigrafia a Macerata: cinquant'anni di ricerche in Ateneo*, ed S. Cingolani (Macerata 2015) 86–7; Di Vita A. (1980–1981) "L'area sacro-funeraria di Sidret el-Balik a Sabratha", *Rendiconti della Pontificia Accademia Romana di Archeologia* 53–54 (1980–1981) 273–82.

Dacia

Northern Illyricum: Ivanišević V. and Bugarski I. (2018) "Transformation of burial space in the cities of Northern Illyricum during the late antiquity", *Antaeus* 35–36 (2018) 91–118.

Serbia: Selected sites: *Jagodin Mala*: Popović S. (2014) ed. *Late Antique Necropolis Jagodin Mala* (Nis 2014). *Romuliana*: Srejović D. and Vasić Č. (1994) "Emperor Galerius's buildings in Romuliana (Gamzigrad, Eastern Serbia)", *Antiquité Tardive* 2 (1994) 123–41. *Other*: Špeha P., Miladinović-Radmilović N., and Stamenković S. (2013) "Late antique necropolis in Davidovac-Crkvište", *Starinar* LXIII (2013) (in Serbian) 269–86; Mladonović D. (2009) "Astral path to soul salvation in late antiquity? The orientation of two late Roman imperial mausolea from Eastern Serbia", *AJA* 113.1 (2009) 81–98; Bachran W. (1975) "Das Gräberfeld (Grobišče)", in *Vranje pri Sevnici. Starokrščanske cerkve na Ajdovskem gradcu / Frühchristliche Kirchenanlagen auf dem Ajdovski Grdec* (Katalogi in monografije / Catalogi et monographiae 12), edd. P. Petru and Th. Ulbert (Ljubljana 1975) 99–115.

Kosovo: Milošević P. (1995) "Rimska nekropola na izlaznici mitrovačke petlje [Roman necropolis at Mitrovica at the exit of the motorway]", in *Arheološka istraživanja duž autoputa kroz Srem*, ed. Z. Vapa (Novi Sad 1995) 195–218.

Macedonia

Eastern Illyricum: Snively C. (1984) "Cemetery churches of the early Byzantine period in Eastern Illyricum: location and martyrs," *Greek Orthodox Theological Review* 29 (1984) 117–24.

Albania: Selected sites: *Butrint*: Beatrice, J., Fenton T. W., Isaac C. V., Jenny L., Wankmiller J., Mutolo M., Rauzi C., and Foran D. (2020) "The human skeletons from the Triconch

Palace and the Merchant's House", in *Butrint 5: Life and Death at a Mediterranean Port: The Non-Ceramic Finds from the Triconch Palace*, ed. W. Bowden (Butrint Archaeological Monographs, Volume 5.2) (Oxford 2020) 42–67; Soler A., Isaac C., Beatrice J. and Fenton T. W. (2019) "The human skeletons from the Vrina Plain", in *Butrint 6: Excavations on the Vrina Plain Volume 2: The Finds*, ed. S. Greenslade (Butrint Archaeological Monographs, Volume 6.2) (Oxford 2019) 59–76. Dyrrachium: Shkodra-Rrugia B. (2018) "Hapësirat funerale dhe qyteti në Dyrrachium gjatë periudhës romake të vonë deri në mesjetën e hershme (Funerary spaces and the city at Dyrrachium from late Roman to early Medieval period)", *Iliria* XLI (2018) 289–304.

Greece (Overview): Tritsaroli P. (2006) *Pratiques funéraires en Grèce centrale à la période Byzantine: Analyse à partir des données archéologiques et biologiques* (Ph.D. diss., Muséum national d'histoire naturelle, Paris 2006). Diet: Bourbou C., Fuller B., Garvie-Lok S., and Richards M. (2011) "Reconstructing the diets of Greek Byzantine populations (6th–15th centuries AD) using carbon and nitrogen stable isotope ratios," *American Journal of Physical Anthropology* 146 (2011) 569–81. Infants: Tritsaroli P. and Valentin F. (2008) "Byzantine burials practices for children: Case studies based on a bioarchaeological approach to cemeteries from Greece", in *Nasciturus, infans, puerulus vobis mater terra: la muerte en la infancia*, edd. F. Gusi Jener, S. Muriel and C. Olària (SIAP) (2008) 93–113.

North Greece: Central Macedonia: Selected sites: *Thessaloniki*: Pazaras T. (2009) ed. *Ανασκαφικές έρευνες στην περιοχή Επανομής Θεσσαλονίκης. Το Νεκροταφείο στο Λιμόρι και η Βασιλική στο Μπγιαδούδι* (Thessaloniki 2009); Makropoulou D. (2007) *Τάφοι και ταφές από το Δυτικό Νεκροταφείο της Θεσσαλονίκης (β΄ μισó 3ου αι.–6ος αι. μ. X.)* (Ph.D. diss., Univ. of Athens 2007); Marki E. (2006) *Η Νεκρόπολη της Θεσσαλονίκης στους Υστερορωμαϊκούς και Παλαιοχριστιανικούς Χρόνους (μέσα του 3ου έως μέσα του 8ου αι. μ.X.)* (Athens 2006).

North-East Greece: Eastern Macedonia and Thrace: Selected sites: *Samothrace*: Dusenbery, E. (1998) *Samothrace* 11: *The Nekropoleis and Catalogues of Burials* (Princeton 1998). Maroneia: Tritsaroli P. and Kardima C. (2017) "The people of early Byzantine Maroneia," *Bioarchaeology of the Near East* 11 (2017) 29–62.

Crete: Bourbou C. (2016) *Health and Disease in Byzantine Crete (7th–12th Centuries AD)* (Abingdon 2016); Bandy A. (1970) *The Greek Christian Inscriptions from Crete* (Athens 1970). Selected sites: *Eleftherna*: Yangaki A. (2004) "Οι τάφοι", in *Πρωτοβυζαντινή Ελεύθερνα. Τομέας I* 1, ed. P. Themelis (Rethymno 2004)

115–86. Gortyn: Di Vita A. (1988) ed. *Gortina* I (Rome 1988). Knossos: Sweetman R. and Becker M. (2005) "Knossos medical faculty site: Late antique graves and other remains", *BSA* 100 (2005) 331–86; Catling H., Smyth D., Musgrave J., and Jones G. (1976) "An early Christian osteotheke at Knossos", *BSA* 71 (1976) 25–47; Frend W. and Johnston D. (1962) "The Byzantine Basilica Church at Knossos", *BSA* 57 (1962) 186–238.

Central Greece: Attica: Selected sites: *Athens*: Tzavella E. (2008) "Burial and urbanism in Athens (4th–9th c. AD)," *JRA* 21 (2008) 353–68; Rife J. (2004–2009) "An early Christian epitaph from the Panathenaic Stadium in context", *Horos* 17–21 (2004–2009) 267–78; Sironen E. (1997) *The Late Roman and Early Byzantine Inscriptions of Athens and Attica: An Edition with Appendices on Scripts, Sepulchral Formulae, and Occupations* (Helsinki 1997); Creaghan J. and Raubitschek A. (1947) "Early Christian epitaphs from Athens", *Hesperia* 16 (1947) 1–54; Stikas E. (1955) "Συνέχισις της ανασκαφής της παρά την Βραυρώνα παλαιοχριστιανικής βασιλικής", *Prakt* 1952 (1955) 53–76; Soteriou G. (1919) "Παλαιά χριστιανική βασιλική Ἰλίσου", *ArchEph* (1919) 1–31. Boetia: *Akraiphnio*: Tritsaroli P. (2017) "Life and death at early Byzantine Akraiphnio, Greece: A biocultural approach," *Anthropologie* 55 (2017) 243–63; Dilesi: Hamilaki K. (2009) "Το νεκροταφείο στο λόφο Αγριλέζα στο Δήλεσι Βοιωτίας", in *Αρχαιολογικό έργο Θεσσαλίας και Στερεάς Ελλάδας 2006: Πρακτικά επιστημονικής συνάντησης, Βόλος 16.3–19.3.2006 2: Στερεά Ελλάδα*, ed. A. Ainian (Volos 2009) 1167–86. *Thebes*: Soteriou G. (1929) "Αἱ χριστιανικαὶ Θῆβαι τῆς Θεσσαλίας", *ArchEph* (1929) 1–158; Keramopoullos A. (1929) "Παλαιαὶ χριστιανικαὶ καὶ βυζαντιναὶ ταφαὶ ἐν Θήβαις", *ArchDelt* 10 (1929) 124–36; Keramopoullos A. (1917) "Θηβαϊκά, Α΄ μέρος—ἀνασκαφαὶ ἐν Θήβαις", *ArchDelt* 3 (1917) 2–252.

South Greece: Peloponnese: Bees N. ([1941] 1978) ed. *Inscriptiones graecae Christianae veteres et byzantinae 1: Peloponnesus, Isthmos, Korinthos* (Athens 1941; Chicago repr. 1978). Selected sites: *Argos*: Oikonomou-Laniado A. (2003) *Argos paléochrétienne: Contribution à l'étude du Péloponnèse byzantin* (BAR Int. Ser. 1173) (Oxford 2003); Oikonomou-Laniado A. (1998) "Les cimetières paléochrétiens d'Argos", in *Recherches franco-hélleniques 3: Argos et l'Argolide, topographie et urbanisme*, edd. A. Pariente and G. Touchais (Athens and Paris 1998) 405–16. *Corinth*: Ott J. (2023) "Burying at Corinth in late antiquity. Evidence from the late 5th to the early 7th century", in *Funerary Landscapes of the Late Antique Oecumene: Contextualizing Epigraphic and Archaeological Evidence of Mortuary Practices: Proceedings of an International Conference in Heidelberg, May 30–June 1, 2019*, edd. S. Ardeleanu and J. C. Cubas

Diaz (Heidelberg 2023) 283–324; Rife J. (2022) "Catalogue of burials", in *On the Edge of a Roman Port: The Excavations at Koutsongila, Kenchreai, 2007–2014*, edd. E. Korka and J. Rife (Hesperia Suppl. 52) (Princeton 2022) 359–494; Rife J. L. and Morison Moore M. (2017) "Space, object, and process in the Koutsongila Cemetery at Roman Kenchreai, Greece", in *Death as a Process: The Archaeology of the Roman Funeral*, edd J. Pearce and J. Weekes (Oxford 2017) 27–59; Slane K. (2017) *Corinth XXI: Tombs, Burials, and Commemoration in Corinth's Northern Cemetery* (Princeton 2017); Meleti P. (2013) "Παλαιοχριστιανικό νεκροταφείο στην Αρχαία Κόρινθου", in *The Corinthia and the Northeast Peloponnese: Topography and History from Prehistoric Times until the End of Antiquity. Proceedings of the International Conference Organized by the Directorate of Prehistoric and Classical Antiquities, the ΛΖ' Ephorate of Prehistoric and Classical Antiquities, and the German Archaeological Institute, Athens, Held at Koutraki, March 26–29, 2009*, edd. K. Kissas and W.-D. Niemeier (Athenaia 4) (Munich 2013) 161–68; Walbank M. (2010) "Where have all the names gone? The Christian community in Corinth in the late Roman and early Byzantine eras", in *Corinth in Context: Comparative Studies on Religion and Society*, edd. S. Friesen, D. Schowalter and J. Walters (Leiden 2010) 257–323; Ivison E. (1996) "Burial and urbanism at late antique and early Byzantine Corinth (c. AD 400–700)", in *Towns in Transition: Urban Evolution in Late Antiquity and the Early Middle Ages*, edd. N. Christie and S. Loseby (Brookfield 1996) 99–125; Sanders G. (2005) "Archaeological evidence for early Christianity and the end of Hellenic religion at Corinth", in *Urban Religion in Roman Corinth: Interdisciplinary Approaches*, edd. D. Schowalter and S. Friesen (Harvard Theological Studies 53) (Cambridge, Mass. 2005) 419–44; Walbank M. E. H. (2005) "Unquiet graves: Burial practices of the Roman Corinthians", in *Urban Religion in Roman Corinth: Interdisciplinary Approaches*, edd. D. Schowalter and S. Friesen (Harvard Theological Studies 53) (Cambridge, Mass. 2005) 249–80; Rife J. (2012) *The Roman and Byzantine Graves and Human Remains* (Isthmia 9) (Princeton 2012); Walbank M. E. H. and Walbank M. (2015) "A Roman Corinthian family tomb and its afterlife", *Hesperia* 84 (2015) 149–206; Bookidis N. and Stroud R. (1997) *Corinth XVIII.3: The Sanctuary of Demeter and Kore: Topography and Architecture* (Princeton 1997); Rife J., Morison M., Barbet A., Dunn R., Ubelaker D., and Monier F. (2007) "Life and death at a port in Roman Greece: The Kenchreai Cemetery Project 2002–2006", *Hesperia* 76 (2007) 143–81; Davidson Weinberg G. (1974) "A wandering soldier's grave at Corinth", *Hesperia* 43 (1974) 512–21; Gejvall N.-G. and Henschen F. (1968) "Two late Roman skeletons with malformation and close family relationship from ancient Corinth", *OpAth* 8 (1968) 179–201; Stikas E. (1964) "Κοιμητηριακή Βασιλική Παλαιάς Κορίνθου", *Prakt* 1961 (1964) 129–36; Davidson G. (1952) *Corinth XII: The Minor Objects* (Princeton 1952); Scranton R. (1951) *Corinth I.3: Monuments in the Lower Agora and North of the Archaic Temple* (Princeton 1951); Roebuck C. (1951) *Corinth XIV: The Asklepieion and Lerna* (Princeton 1951); Shelley J. (1943) "The Christian basilica near the Cenchrean Gate at Corinth", *Hesperia* 12 (1943) 166–89. <u>Mani</u>: Drandakis N. and Gioles N. (1980) "Ἀνασκαφὴ στὸ Τηγάνι τῆς Μάνης", *Prakt* (1980) 247–58. <u>Messene</u>: Bourbou C. (2004) *The People of Early Byzantine Eleftherna and Messene (6th–7th Centuries AD): A Bioarchaeological Approach* (Athens 2004). <u>Olympia</u>: Völling T. (2018) *Olympia in frühbyzantinischer Zeit. Siedlung – Landwirtschaftliches Gerät – Grabfunde – Spolienmauer* (OlForsch 34) (Berlin 2018); Vida T. and Völling T. (2000) *Das slawische Brandgräberfeld von Olympia* (Archäologie in Eurasien 9) (Rahden 2000). <u>Porto Heli</u>: Rudolph W. (1979) "Excavations at Porto Cheli and vicinity, preliminary report V: The early Byzantine remains", *Hesperia* 48 (1979) 294–320.

<u>South Aegean</u>: <u>Selected sites</u>: <u>Aliki</u>: Buchet J.-L. and Sodini J.-P. (1984) "Les tombes", in *Aliki II: La basilique double*, edd. J.-P. Sodini and K. Kolokotsas (Études thasiennes 10) (Athens and Paris 1984) 211–42. <u>Milos</u>: Bayet C. (1878) "La nécropole chrétienne de Milo", *BCH* 2 (1878) 347–59; Soteriou G. (1928) "Η χριστιανικὴ κατακόμβη τῆς νήσου Μήλου", *PraktAktAth* (1928) 33–46; Diamandis N. (2004) "Το παλαιοχριστιανικό νεκροταφείο της Κισάμου", in *Creta romana e protobizantina. Atti del congresso internazionale (Iraklion, 23–30 settembre 2000)* 2, edd. M. Livadiotti and I. Simiakaki (Padua 2004) 383–96. <u>Sifnos</u>: Brock J. and Mackworth Young G. (1949) "Excavations in Siphnos", *BSA* 44 (1949) 1–92. <u>Thera</u>: Gerousi E. (2014) *Sepulkralkultur auf der Insel Thera (Santorin): Der spätantike Friedhof in Perissa und seine Ausgrabungsfunde unter besonderer Berücksichtigung der Tonlampen* (Marburg 2014). <u>Vronti Karpathos</u>: Geraskli E. (2004) "Παλαιοχριστιανικό νεκροταφείο στη Βροντή Καρπάθου: Πρώτη παρουσίαση", in *Χάρις Χαίρε: Μελέτες στη Μνήμη της Χάρης Κάντζια*, ed. D. Damaskos (Athens 2004) 389–402.

Thrace

<u>Bulgaria</u>: <u>Selected sites</u>: <u>Lozenetz</u>: Boyadjiev S. (2006) "L'architecture du mausolée de Lozenetz et sa correlation avec ceux de la

Moesie et de la Thrace", in *Early Christian Martyrs and Relics and Their Veneration in East and West*, ed. A. Minchev (Acta Musei Vernaensis 4) (Varna 2006) 129–40. *Silistra*: Atanasov G. (2007) "Late antique tomb in Durostorum-Silistra and its master", *Pontica* 40 (2007) 447–68.

Romania (Selected sites): *Callatis*: Preda C. (1980) *Callatis. Necropola romana-bizantină* (Bucharest 1980); Soficaru AD (2009) "Un studi de bioarcheologie asupra necropolei romano-buzantine de la Callatis", *Pontica* 42 (2009) 562–84; Ungureanu M. and Radu L. (2006) "Cercetări arheologice în necropola romano-bizantină de la Callatis", *Pontica* 39 (2006) 259–78; Ionescu M., Alexandru N., and Constantin R. (2002–2003) "Noi cercetări în necropola paleocreștină callatiană", *Pontica* 35–36 (2002–2003) 225–77. *Halmyris*: Zahariade M. (2009) "The episcopal basilica from Halmyris and the crypt of Epictetus and Astion", *Thraco-Dacica* 24 (2009) 131–50; Zahariade M. (2001–2003) "The Halmyris Episcopal Basilica and the Martyrs' Crypt", *Il Mar Nero* 5 (2001–2003) 143–68; Mirițoiu N. and Soficaru A. D. (2007) "Osteobiographical study of the human remains discovered in the crypt of Murighiol (antique Halmyris) basilica", *Il Mar Nero* 5 (2007) 169–90; Mirițoiu N. and Soficaru A. D. (2003) "Studiu antropologic al osemintelor descoperite în cripta basilicii de la Murighiol (anticul Halmyris)", *Peuce* 14 (2003) 531–80. *Histria*: Crețu C. (2022) *Practici funerare în mormintele de epocă romană de la Histria (secolele II–VII p. Chr.)* (Cluj-Napoca 2022); Crețu C., Dabîca M., and Soficaru A. (2020) "Digging up the archives: a reassessment of burial practices in the cemeteries from the extra muros Basilica sector at Histria", *Materiși cercetări arheologice* 16 (2020) 139–80; Crețu C. (2018) "Despre moartea infantilă și practicile funerare din lumea Romană. Studiu de caz: mormintele de copii de la Histria", *Buletinul Cercurilor Științifice Studențești* 24(1) (2018) 55–66; Hamparțumian N. (1971) "Contribuții la topografia cetății Histria în epoca romano-bizantină. Considerații generale asupra necropolei din sectorul Bazilicii extra muros", *Studii și Cercetări de Istorie Veche* 22(2) (1971) 199–215; Condurach E. (1962) "Șantierul Histria", *Material și cercetări arheologice* 8 (1962) 382–437; Condurachi E. (1960) "Șantierul arheologic Histria", *Material și cercetări arheologice* 7 (1960) 227–72; Condurachi E. (1957) "Șantierul arheologic Histria", *Material și cercetări arheologice* 4 (1957) 9–102. *Ibida*: Soficaru A. D., Radu C., and Tica C. I. (2019) "A mass grave outside the walls. The commingled assemblage from Ibida", in *Bioarchaeology of Frontiers and Borderlands*, edd. C. I. Tica and D. L. Martin (Gainesville 2019) 187–211; Aparaschivei D., Iacob M., Soficaru A. D., and Paraschiv D. (2012) "Aspects of everyday life in Scythia Minor reflected in some funerary discoveries from Ibida (Slava Rusă, Tulcea County)", in *Homines, Funera, Astra: Proceedings of the International Symposium on Funerary Anthropology 5–8 June 2011, "1 Decembrie 1918" University, Alba Iulia, Romania*, edd. R. Kogălniceanu, R. -G. Curcă, M. Gligor and S. Stratton (Oxford 2012) 169–82; Mirițoiu N. and Soficaru A. D. (2003) "Studiul antropologic al osemintelor din cavoul Romano-bizantin „Tudorka" de la Slava Rusă (antica Ibida)", *Peuce* 14 (2003) 511–30. *Tomis*: Bucovală M. (1993) "Cavou din secolul IV d. Chr. Descoperit în necropola de vest a Tomisului", *Pontica* 26 (1993) 207–14; Bucovală M. and Pașca C. (1988–1989) "Descoperiri recente în necropolele de epocă romană și romano-bizantină la Tomis", *Pontica* 21–22 (1988–1989) 123–61; Barbu V. (1971) "Din necropolele Tomisului I. Tipuri de morminte din epoca Romană", *Studii și cercetări de istorie veche* 22(1) (1971) 47–68; Cheluță-Georgescu N. (1974) "Complexe funerare din secolul VI e.n. la Tomis", *Pontica* 7 (1974) 363–76; Barbet A. and Bucovală M. (1996) "L'hypogée paléochrétien des Orants à Costanța (Roumanie), l'ancienne Tomis", *MEFRA* 108/1 (1996) 105–58; Lungu V. and Chera-Mărgineanu C. (1982) "Contribuții la cunoaștrea unei necropole creștine a Tomisului (I)", *Pontica* 15 (1982) 175–99; Barbu V. (1961) "Considérations chronologiques basées sur les données fournies par les inventaires funéraires des nécropoles tomitaines", *Studii Clasice* 3 (1961) 203–25. *Tropaeum Traiani (Adamklissi)*: Soficaru A. D. (2006–2007) "Human remains discovered in the Basilica D from Tropaeum Traiani", *Annuaire Roumain d'Anthropologie* 43–44 (2006–2007) 3–8; Barnea I. (1978) "Bazilica „simplă" (A) de la Tropaeum Traiani", *Pontica* 11 (1978) 181–87; Mirițoiu N. and Nicolăescu-Plopșor D. (1978) "Analiza antropologică a osemintelor descoperite în cripta basilicii "simple" (A) de la Tropaeum Traiani", *Pontica* 11 (1978) 189–207. *Other*: Baumann V. H. (2015) *Sângele martirilor* (Tulcea 2015); Baumann V. H. (2006) "Isaccea – Noviodunum, Sector cariera de lut – necropola", *Cronica cercetărilor arheologice din România. Campania 2005* (2006) 185–86; Soficaru (2014) "Anthropological data about the funeral discoveries from Slava Rusă, Tulcea County, Romania", *Peuce* 12 (2014) 307–40; Găzdac C. and Cosma C. (2014) "Social memory and statute. Roman coins in medieval graves from the Necropolis Noșlac, Romania", *The Journal of Archaeological Numismatics* 4 (2014) 180–90.

Romania (Unspecified sites) *Dobrudja*: Ailincăi S., Constantinescu M., Curta F., and Soficaru A. (2014) "An early seventh-century female grave From Dobruja", *Archaeologia Bulgarica* 18(1) (2014) 65–84; Achim I. (2012) "Early Roman and late Roman child graves in Dobrudja (Romania).

Preliminary considerations", in *Homines, Funera, Astra: Proceedings of the International Symposium on Funerary Anthropology: 5–8 June 2011 '1 Decembrie 1918' University Alba Iulia, Romania* (BAR Int. Ser. 2410)), edd. R. Kogălniceanu *et al.* (Oxford 2012) 183–96.

Moldova (Selected sites): *Tigheci*: Simalksik A. and Vornic Vl. (2019) "Necropola de tip Sântana de Mureş-Cerneahov de la Tigheci (campania 2017). Date paleoantropologice", *Acta Musei Tutovensis* XV (2019) 175–83. *Brăviceni*: Vornic Vl. (2016) "Cronologia necropolei de tip Sântana de Mureş-Cerneahov de la Brăviceni, r. Orhei", *Acta Musei Tutovensis* XII/2 (2016) 183–200. *Lipoveni*: Matveev S. and Vornic Vl. (2016) "Vase ceramice descoperite în necropola de tip Sântana de Mureş- Cerneahov de la Lipoveni", in *Istorie, cultura, cercetare*, vol. I, edd. D.-C. Rogojanu and Gh. Boda (Deva 2016) 39–55. *Other*: Haimovici S. (2005) "O problemă incomplet rezolvată – studiul resturilor animaliere depuse ca ofrandă în necropole aparţinând culturii Sântana de Mureş-Cerneahov", *Arheologia moldovei* 28 (2005) 327–34.

Constantinople

Themes: Rizos E. (in this volume) "Burying the saints next to the common dead: the burial habits of the Christian elite in the 4th c. and the first translations of relics"

Specific sites: Foletti I. and Monney G. (2013) "Of holes and a holy man: New discoveries in the Silivri-Kapi mausoleum in Istanbul", *Kunstchronik* 66 (2013) 178–82; Deckers J. and Serdaroğlu Ü. (1993) "Das Hypogäum beim Silivri-Kapı in Istanbul", *JAC* 36 (1993) 140–63; Mango C. (1990) "Constantine's mausoleum and the translation of relics", *ByzZeit* 83 (1990) 51–61; Fıratlı N. (1966) "Notes sur quelques hypogées paléo-chrétiens de Constantinople", in *Tortulae. Studien zu altchristlichen und byzantinischen Monumenten*, ed. W. N. Schumacher (Freiburg 1966) 131–39.

Asia

Overview: Ivison E. A. (2017) "Funerary archaeology", in *The Archaeology of Byzantine Anatolia: From the End of Late Antiquity until the Coming of the Turks*, ed. Ph. Niewohner (Oxford 2017) 160–75.

Asia Minor (Northwest): Selected sites: *Ilıpınar* and *Barcın*: Roodenberg J. J. (2009) "The Byzantine graveyards from Ilıpınar and Barcın in Northwest Anatolia", in *Archaeology of the Countryside in Medieval Anatolia*, edd. T. Vorderstrasse and J. J. Roodenberg (Leiden 2009) 154–67. *Samsun*: Hnila P. (2015) "Rural necropoleis and settlement dynamics. Thoughts on Roman and Byzantine graves at Oymaağaç Höyük, Samsun province", in *Landscape Dynamics and Settlement Patterns in Northern Anatolia During the Roman and Byzantine Period* edd. K. Winther-Jacobsen and L. Summerer (Stuttgart 2015) 147–64.

Asia Minor (South): Cilicia: *Eastern Rough Cilicia*: Cubas Diaz J. C. (2023) "Burying between *Lamos* and *Kalykadnos*. The many faces of the late antique lunerary landscapes of Eastern Rough Cilicia", in *Funerary Landscapes of the Late Antique Oecumene: Contextualizing Epigraphic and Archaeological Evidence of Mortuary Practices: Proceedings of an International Conference in Heidelberg, May 30–June 1, 2019*, edd. S. Ardeleanu and J. C. Cubas Diaz (Heidelberg 2023) 249–82. *Elaiussa Sebaste*: Paine R. R, Vargiu R., Coppa A., Morselli C., and Schneider E. E. (2007) "A health assessment of high status Christian burials recovered from the Roman-Byzantine archeological site of Elaiussa Sebaste, Turkey", *Homo* 58/2 (2007) 173–90.

Asia Minor (South-West): Pisidia: Selected sites: *Sagalassos*: Cleymans S. and Beaujean B. (1022) "Where to put them? Burial location in Middle Hellenistic to late Roman (second century BC–fifth century AD) Sagalassos, southwest Anatolia", *AnSt* 72 (1022) 1–28; Cleymans S., Van de Vijver K., and Matsuo H. (forthcoming) "Who did the Moriai favour most? Life expectancy at Roman and middle Byzantine Sagalassos", *Population* (forthcoming); Cleymans S., Claeys J., Van de Vijver K., and Poblome J. (2021) "Burial terraces in the eastern necropolis. The excavations of site F at Sagalassos (SW Anatolia)", *Anatolica* 47 (2021) 147–98; Claeys J. and Poblome J. (2014) "Alan PQ1: Naiskos Mezarı", in *Sagalassos'ta 2012 yili kazı ve restorasyon çalışmaları* (*KST* 35.2), edd M. Waelkens, R. Rens, J. Richard *et al.* (2014) 249; Claeys J. and Poblome J. (2013) "Sagalassos' un Güneyi: Çatal Oluk 2 Bizans Kilise Alanının Kazı Çalışmaları", in *Sagalassos 2011 kazı ve restorasyon sezonu* (*KST* 34.3), edd. M. Waelkens *et al.* (2013) 146. Kommagene: Ergeç R. (2003) *Nekropolen und Gräber in der südlichen Kommagene* (Asia Minor Studien 47) (Bonn 2003).

Asia Minor (West): *Ephesus*: Steskal M. (2013) "Wandering cemeteries: Roman and late Roman burials in the capital of the province of Asia", in *Le mort dans la ville. Pratiques, contextes et impacts des inhumations* intra-muros *en Anatolie, du début de l'Age du Bronze à l'époque romaine*, ed. O. Henry (Istanbul 2013) 243–58; Miltner F. (1937) *Forschungen in Ephesos* IV.2: *Das*

Cömeterium der sieben Schläfer (Vienna 1937). <u>Phrygia</u>: *Amorium*: Demirel F. A. (2017) "Infant and child skeletons from the Lower City Church at Byzantine Amorium", in *Life and Death in Asia Minor in Hellenistic, Roman, and Byzantine times: Studies in Archaeology and Bioarchaeology*, edd. J. R. Brandt, E. Hagelberg, G. Bjørnstad and S. Ahrens (Oxford 2017) 306–17. *Hierapolis*: Wong M., Rasmus Brandt J., Ahrens S., Jaouen K., Bjørnstad G., Naumann E., Wenn C. C, Kiesewetter H., Laforest C., Hagelberg E., Lam V. C., and Richards M. (2018) "Pursuing pilgrims: Isotopic investigations of Roman and Byzantine mobility at Hierapolis, Turkey", *Journal of Archaeological Science: Reports* 17 (2018) 520–28; Hill D. J. A., Lieng Andreadakis L. T., and Ahrens S. (2016) "The north-east necropolis survey 2007–2011: methods, preliminary results and representivity", in *Hierapolis Di Frigia VIII (1): Le Attivita delle Campagne di scavo sestauro 2007–2011*, edd. F. D'Andria, M. Pierra Caggia and T. Ismaelli (Istanbul 2016) 109–20.

Oriens

Syria (in general): Séiquer G. M. and Carrillo J. G. (1998) "Urbanismo: ciudades y necrópolis", in *Romanización y christianismo en la Síria mesopotamica*, edd. G. M. Séiquer and J. G. Carrillo (Antigüedad y Christianismo 15) (Murcia 1998) 247–98.

Syria (North-West): <u>Selected sites</u>: *Gabala*: Badawi M. (2010) "La tombe protobyzantine d'al-Thawra dans l'arrière-pays de Gabala (Jablé, Syrie)", *Syria* 87 (2010) 265–75. *Serǧilla*: Charpentier G. (2013) "L'architecture funéraire", in *Serǧilla. Village d'Apamène 1: Une architecture de pierre*, 3 vols, G. Tate *et al.* (BAHBeyrouth 203) (Beirut and Damascus 2013) 451–73; Charpentier G. (2003–2004) "La construction du mausolée pyramidal de Sergilla: une étude de cas", *Tempora* 14–15 (2003–2004) 123–32.

Syria (North): <u>Overview</u>: Greisheimer M. (1997) "Cimetières et tombeaux des villages de la Syrie du nord", *Syria* 74 (1997) 165–211. <u>Selected sites</u>: *Frikya*: Altheeb D. (2015) "Funerary sculptures in the tomb of Abedrapsas at Frikya", *Zeitschrift für Orient-Archäologie* 8 (2015) 236–49.

Syria (North-East): <u>Selected sites</u>: *Emar*: Sakal F. (2010) "Graves and grave goods of the late Roman and medieval cemeteries", in *Emar after the Enclosure of the Tabqa Dam: The Syrian-German Excavations 1996–2002, vol. 1: Late Roman and Medieval Cemeteries and Environmental Studies*, edd. U. Finkbeiner and F. Sakal (Subartu 25) (Turnhout 2010) 3–52. *Halabya*:

Blétry S. (2012) "Les nécropoles e Halabiya-Zénobia. Premier résultats (2009 et 2010)", *Syria* 89 (2012) 305–30. *Tall as-Sin*: Martínez L. M., Estebaranz-Sánchez F. *et al.* (2019) "Human remains from Tell es-Sin, Syria, 2006–2007", *Bioarchaeology of the Near East* 13 (2019) 60–77; Montero Fenollós J. L. and al-Shbib S. (2008) edd. *La necrópolis bizantina de Tall as-Sin (Deir ez-Zor, Siria)* (Memorias del Proyecto Arqueológico Medio Éufrates Syirio 1) (Madrid 2008).

Syria (Central): <u>Selected sites</u>: *Palmyra*: Gawlikowski M. (1970) *Monumets funéraires de Palmyre* (Travaux du Centre d'Archéologie Méditerranéenne de l'Académie Polonaise des Sciences 9) (Warsaw 1970). <u>Syria</u> (East): <u>In general</u>: Egea Vivancos A. (2004) "Costumbres funerarias en el Alto Éufrates sirio durante época romana y bizantina", *HuelvaArq* 20 (2004) 89–114. Selected sites: *Resafa*: Huguenot C. (2018) "Étude d'une tombe monumentale de Resafa", *Zeitschrift für Orient-Archäologie* 11 (2018) 302–53.

Syria (South): <u>Overview</u>: Sartre-Fauriat A. (2001) *Des tombeaux et des morts: monuments funéraires, société et culture en Syrie du Sud du Ier s. av. J.-C. au VIIe s. apr. J.-C*, 2 vols. (BAHBeyrouth 158) (Beirut 2001). Selected sites: *Hauran*: Fischer T. and Oenbrink W. (2010) "Spätantik-byzantinische Grabfunde aus al-Qrayya im Hauran/Südsyrien", *KölnJb* 43 (2010) 197–243; Fisher T. (2010) "Zu spätantik-frühbyzantinischen Grabbeigaben aus Qrayya/Hauran", in *Hauran V: la Syrie du sud du néolithique à l'antiquité tardive*, edd. M. al-Maqdissi, F. Braemer, and J.-M. Denzter (BAHBeyrouth 191) (Beirut 2010) 497–504.

Syria (South-West): <u>Selected sites</u>: *Damascus*: Eger C. and Hamoud M. (2011) "Spätrömisch-frühbyzantinischer Grabbrauch in Syrien. Die Nekropole von Darayya bei Damaskus", *Antike Welt* 42 (2011) 70–6. *Doumar*: Al-Maqdissi M. and Hussami S. (1990) "Deux hypogées de l'époque Byzantine (IVe–Ve s. après J.-C.) dans la region de Doumar", *Syria* 67 (1990) 465–66.

Lebanon: <u>Selected sites</u>: *Tyre*: de Jong L. (2010) "Performing death in Tyre: the life and afterlife of a Roman cemetery in the Province of Syria", *AJA* 114 (2010) 597–630; Chéhab M. (1986) "Fouille de Tyr, la nécropole IV: description des fouilles", *BMusBeyr* 36 (1986); Chéhab M. (1985) "Fouille de Tyr, la nécropole III: description des fouilles, deuxième part: au nord de la route: complexe XXIII–XL", *BMusBeyr* 35 (1985); Chéhab M. (1984) "Fouille de Tyr. La nécropole II: description des fouilles, premiére part: au sud de la route: complexes I–XXII", *BMusBeyr* 34 (1984). *Other*: Schmauder M. (2020) *Das Mausoleum von Dair Solaib (Dayr Salib/Deil al-Salib), Contextus. Festschrift fur Sabine Schrenk*, edd. S. de Blaauw, E. Enss, P. Linscheid (Jahrbuch fur Antike und Christentum, Erganzungsband 41)

(Munster 2020); Sołtysiak A. and Waliszewski T. (2021) "Human remains from Chhîm, Lebanon, 1998–2009", *Bioarchaeology of the Near East* 15 (2021) 104–10.

Palestine (General): Goldfus H. (1997) *Tombs and Burials in Churches and Monasteries of Byzantine Palestine (324–628 AD)* (Ph.D. Diss., Princeton Univ. 1997); Ameling W., Cotton H. M., Eck W., Isaac B., Kushnir-Stein A., Misgav H., Price J., and Yardeni A. (2014) *Corpus Inscriptionum Iudaeae/Palaestinae. A multi-lingual corpus of the inscriptions from Alexander to Muhammad* (Berlin and Boston 2014); Kraemer D. (2000) "Jewish death-practices in Early Byzantine Palestine: the Yerushalmi and Aggadic Midrashim", in *The Meanings of Death in Rabbinic Judaism,* D. Kraemer (London 2000) 72–94

Palestine (Themes): *Funerary Epigraphy*: Rugers L. V. (2000) "Death and afterlife: the inscriptional evidence", in *Death, Life-After-Death, Resurrection and the World-to-Come in Judaisms of Antiquity*, edd. A. J. Avery-Peck and J. Neusner (Leiden, Boston, Köln 2000) 293–310. *Funerary textual sources*: Rugers L. V. (2000) "Death and afterlife: the inscriptional evidence", in *Death, Life-After-Death, Resurrection and the World-to-Come in Judaisms of Antiquity*, edd. A. J. Avery-Peck and J. Neusner (Leiden, Boston, Köln 2000) 293–310. *Osteology*: Nagar Y. (2011) "Human osteological database at the Israel antiquities authority: Overview and some examples of use", *Bioarchaeology of the Near East* 5 (2011) 1–18. *Funerary Art*: Michaeli T. (1996) "Family burial in late antique and early Christian paintings in Eretz-Israel", *ASSAPH 1996* (Studies in Art History, B, 2) (1996) 27–48. *Funerary Furnishing*: Rahmani L. Y. (1999) *A Catalogue of Roman and Byzantine Lead Coffins from Israel* (Jerusalem 1999).

Palestine (North): Selected sites: *Beth She'an*: Fleck V. (n.d.) "The late antique tombs of the Northern Cemetery at Beth Shean", https://static1.squarespace.com/static/534849e8e4b0dd67a1620643/t/5370f2cfe4b020808025ebc3/1399911119974/Northern+Cemetery+fleck.pdf; Avshalom-Gorni D. (2000) "A burial cave of the Byzantine period at Bet She'an", *'Atiqot* 39 (2000) 49–60, 198*–200* (in Hebrew with English summary). *Beth She'arim*: Weiss Z. (1992) "Social aspects of burial in Beth She'arim", in *The Galilee in Late Antiquity*, ed. L. Levine (New York 1992) 357–72; Avigad N. (1976) *Beth She'arim, vol. 3: Catacombs 12–23* (Jerusalem 1976); Mazar B. (1973) *Beth She'arim, vol. 1: Catacombs 1–4* (Jerusalem 1973). *Galilee*: Russo J. D. (2015) "Tomb tracking: A new burial survey of Roman Galilee (1st-6th cent. CE)", *The Ancient Near East Today: Current News About the Ancient Past* 3 (2015) 1–6. *Ḥorbat Zikhrin*: Haddad E. (2007) "A burial cave from the first–second centuries CE and

double-arcosolia tombs from the fourth–fifth centuries CE on the fringes of Ḥorbat Zikhrin", *'Atiqot* 56 (2007) 25–57, 74*–75* (in Hebrew with English summary). *Jīsh*: Makhouly N. (1939) "Rock-cut tombs at el Jīsh", *QDAP* 8 (1939) 45–50. *Kefar 'Ara*: Sussman V. (1976) "A burial cave at Kefar 'Ara", *'Atiqot* 11 (1976) 92–101. *Kisra*: Stern E. J. (1997) "Burial caves at Kisra", *'Atiqot* 33 (1997) 103–35, 17* (in Hebrew, with English summary). *Nazareth*: Richmond E. T. (1932) "A rock-cut tomb at Nazareth", *QDAP* 1 (1932) 53–4. *Sajur*: Braun E., Dauphin C., and Hadas G. (1994) "A rock-cut tomb at Sajur", *'Atiqot* 24 (1994) 103–15. *Tarshīḥā*: Iliffe J. H. (1934) "Rock-cut tomb at Tarshīḥā", *QDAP* 3 (1934) 9–16.

Palestine (Central): Selected sites: *Apollonia*: Tal O. (1995) "Roman-Byzantine cemeteries and tombs around Apollonia", *Tel Aviv* 22 (1995) 107–20. *Atara*: Taha H. (2003) "A Byzantine tomb at Atara", in *One Land – Many Cultures: Archaeological Studies in Honour of Stanislao Loffreda OFM*, edd. G. C. Bottini, L. Di Segni, and L. D. Chrupcała (Studium Biblicum Franciscanum, Collectio Maior 41) (Jerusalem 2003) 87–110. *Beit Fajjār*: Husseini S. A. (1935) "A fourth-century AD tomb at Beit Fajjār", *QDAP* 4 (1935) 175–77. *Samaria*: Hartal M. *et al.* (2009) "The northern cemeteries", in *Panias IV: The Aqueduct and the Northern Suburbs*, ed. M. Hartal (Israel Antiquities Authority Reports 40) (Jerusalem 2009) 111–42. *Tell Keila*: Blétry S. (2023) "La question de l'occupation des tombes sur le "temps long" à partir de l'exemple des nécropoles de Tell Keila (Territoires Palestiniens)", in *Death and the Societies of Late Antiquity*, edd. G. Granier, C. Boyer and E. Anstett (Aix Marseille 2023) 399–415. *Other*: Sellers O. R., Baramki D. C., and Albright W. A. (1953) "A Roman-Byzantine burial cave in Northern Palestine", *BASOR* (Suppl. Studies 15–16) (1953) 1–55.

Palestine (South): Huster Y. and Sion O. (2006) "Late Roman and Byzantine vaulted tombs in the southern coastal plain", *Jerusalem and Eretz Israel* 3 (2006) 49–67 (in Hebrew). Selected sites: *Ascalon*: Kol-Ya'akov S. and Farhi Y. (2012) "Asqelon (al-Nabi Ḥussein): evidence for the burial of Jews, Christians and pagans in a late Roman-period burial ground", *Atiqot* 70 (2012) 87–111 (in Hebrew with English); Smith P. and Kahila G. (1992) "Identification of infanticide in archaeological sites: a case study from the late Roman and Byzantine periods at Ashkelon, Israel", *JAS* 19 (1992) 667–75. *Bet Guvrin – Eleutheropolis*: Avni G., Dahari U., and Kloner A. (2008b) *The Necropolis of Bet Guvrin – Eleutheropolis* (Israel Antiquities Authority Reports 36) (Jerusalem 2008). *Emmaus-Nicopolis*: Grossschmidt K. and Tutschek H. (2005) "Anthropologische Aussagen und ein mikroradiographischer Nachweis von

Brandspuren", in *Emmaus-Nicopolis: Ausgrabungen 2001–2005*, K. H. Fleckenstein and L. Fleckenstein (Neckenmarkt 2005) 404–35. *Gaza*: Nabulsi A. *et al.* (2010) "Excavation at the Blakhiya Byzantine cemetery in Gaza, 1996", *RBibl* 117 (2010) 602–13. *Saffa*: Al-Houdalieh S. H. (2014) "Vandalised and looted, rock-cut tombs of the Roman and Byzantine periods: a case study from Saffa village, Ramallah province", *PEQ* 146 (2014) 224–40. *Jerusalem*: Winter T. (2015) "Late Roman funerary customs in light of the grave goods from the cemetery on Ṣallaḥ ed-Din street, Jerusalem", *'Atiqot* 80 (2015) 81–123; Avni G. (2010) "The Persian conquest of Jerusalem (614 c.e.). An archaeological assessment", *BASOR* 357 (2010) 35–48; Kogan-Zehavi E. (2006) "A burial cave of the Byzantine period in the Naḥalat Aḥim Quarter, Jerusalem", *'Atiqot* 54 (2006) 61–86, 160*–61* (Hebrew with English summary); Gregoricka L. A. and Sheridan S. G. (2012)" Food for thought. Isotopic evidence for dietary and weaning practices in a Byzantine urban monastery in Jerualem", in *Bioarchaeology and Behavior. The People of the Ancient Near East*, ed. M. A. Perry (Gainesville 2012) 138–64; Gibson Sh. and Taylor J. E. (1994) *Beneath the Church of the Holy Sepulchre Jerusalem. The archaeology and early history of traditional Golgotha* (London 1994). *Khirbat Tabaliya*: Kogan-Zehavi E. (1998) "The tomb and memorial of a chain-wearing anchorite at Kh. Tabaliya, near Jerusalem", *'Atiqot* 35 (1998) 135–49. *Negev*: Nagar Y. and Sonntag F. (2008) "Byzantine period burials in the Negev: anthropological descriptions and summary", *IEJ* 58 (2008) 79–93; Figueras P. (2004) ed. *Ḥorvat Karkur 'Illit: A Byzantine Cemetery Church in the Northern Negev* (*Final Report of the Excavations 1989–1995*) (*Beer-Sheva Archaeological Monographs* 1) (Beer-Sheva 2004); Zias J. and Spigelman M. (2004) "Report on burials and osteoarchaeological analysis", in *Ḥorvat Karkur 'Illit: A Byzantine Cemetery Church in the Northhusseiern Negev* (*Final Report of the Excavations 1989–1995*), ed. P. Figueras (Beer-Sheva Archaeological Monographs 1) (Beer-Sheva 2004) 307–15. *Neshar – Ramla*: Kol-Ya'akov S. (2010) "The cemetery", in *Salvage Excavations at Neshar – Ramla Query* 1, ed. S. Kol-Ya'akov (Haifa 2010) 103–19. *Samaria*: Tal O. and Taxel I. (2015) *Samaritan Cemeteries and Tombs in the Central Coastal Plain. Archaeology and History of the Samaritan Settlement outside Samaria (ca. 300–700 CE)* (Munster 2015). *Tell en-Naṣbeh*: Zissu B. and Klein E. (2014) "On the use and reuse of rock-cut tombs and a ritual bath at Tell en-Naṣbeh: new perspectives on the Roman and Byzantine necropoleis", in *"As for Me, I Will Dwell at Mizpah …": The Tell en-Naṣbeh Excavations after 85 Years*, edd. J. R. Zorn and A. J. Brody (*Georgias Studies in the Ancient Near East* 9) (Piscataway 2014) 199–224.

Arabia (North): Selected sites: *Gadara*: Weber T. (1992) "Ein frühchristliches Grab mit Glockenketten zu Gadara in der syrischen Dekapolis", *Jahrbuch der Österreichischen Byzantinistik* 42 (1992) 249–85; Künzl E. and Weber T. M. (1991) "Das spätantike Grab eines Zahnarztes zu Gadar in der Dekapolis", *DamMitt* 5 (1991) 81–118. *Khirbat as-Samrā*: Bader N. *et al.* (2017) "New Greek inscriptions from Ḥirbet es-Samra cemetery in north Jordan", *ZDMG* 133 (2017) 176–85; Nabulsi A. and Macdonald M. C. A. (2014) "Epigraphic diversity in the cemetery at Khirbet es-Samrā', Jordan", *PEQ* 146 (2014) 149–61; Nabulsi A., Husan A., and Schönrock-Nabulsi P. (2013) "The 2012 seasons of excavations in the ancient Khirbat as-Samrā cemetery", *ADAJ* 57 (2013) 551–57; Nabulsi A. *et al.* (2011) "The ancient cemetery of Khirbat as-Samrā: 2010 excavations at site A2", *ADAJ* 5 (2011) 25–31; Nabulsi A. (2010) "Khirbat as-Samrā cemetery: Site E, season 2009", *ADAJ* 54 (2010) 217–19; Nabulsi A. *et al.* (2009) "Khirbat as-Samrā ancient cemetery: preliminary discussion of Site C", *ADAJ* 53 (2009) 167–72; Nabulsi A. *et al.* (2008) "The 2007 season of excavations at Khirbat as-Samrā ancient cemetery", *ADAJ* 52 (2008) 203–7; Nabulsi A. *et al.* (2007) "The ancient cemetery in Khirbat as-Samrā after the sixth season of excavation (2006)", *ADAJ* 51 (2007) 273–81; Humbert J.-B. (1998) "Le cimitière de Samra. Présentation historique et archéologique", in *Khirbet es-Samra en Jordanie 1: La voie romaine, le cimitière, les documents épigraphiques*, edd. J.-B. Humbert and A. Desreumaux (Bibliothèque de l'Antiquité Tardive 1) (Turnhout 1998) 259–70; Nabulsi A. (1998) "The Byzantine cemetery in Samra", in *Khirbet es-Samra en Jordanie 1: La voie romaine, le cimitière, les documents épigraphiques*, edd. J.-B. Humbert and A. Desreumaux (Bibliothèque de l'Antiquité Tardive 1) (Turnhout 1998) 271–79; Desreumaux A. and Couson D. (1998) "Catalogue des stèles funéraires", in *Khirbet es-Samra en Jordanie 1: La voie romaine, le cimitière, les documents épigraphiques*, edd. J.-B. Humbert and A. Desreumaux (Bibliothèque de l'Antiquité Tardive 1) (Turnhout 1998) 281–316; Desreumaux A. (1998) "Les inscriptions funéraires araméennes de Samra", in *Khirbet es-Samra en Jordanie 1: La voie romaine, le cimitière, les documents épigraphiques*, edd. J.-B. Humbert and A. Desreumaux (Bibliothèque de l'Antiquité Tardive 1) (Turnhout 1998) 435–509. *Sa'ad*: Rose J. C., Burke D. L., and Johnson K. L. (2004) "Tombs", in *Sa'ad: A Late Roman/Byzantine Site in Northern Jordan*, edd. J. C. Rose and D. L. Burke (Irbid 2004) 99–108; Johnson K. L. (2004) "Sa'ad tomb types", in *Sa'ad: A Late*

Roman/Byzantine Site in Northern Jordan, edd. J. C. Rose and D. L. Burke (Irbid 2004) 109–11; Rose J. C., *et al.* (2004) "Cemeteries and contents", in *Sa'ad: A Late Roman/Byzantine Site in Northern Jordan*, edd. J. C. Rose and D. L. Burke (Irbid 2004) 43–98. *Yasileh:* Al-Muheisen Z. (2008) "Archaeological excavations at the Yasileh site in Northern Jordan: the necropolis", *Syria* 85 (2008) 315–37; Al-Muheisen Z. and El-Najjar M. (1994) "An anthropological study of the human remains from Yasileh: a classical site in Northern Jordan", *Mu'tah: Journal for Research and Studies* 9 (1994) 5–27.

Arabia (Central): Selected sites: *Hesban:* Waterhouse D. (1998) *The Necropolis of Hesban: A Typology of Tombs* (Hesban 10) (Michigan 1998); Waterhouse D. (1994) "Tomb types in the Roman and Byzantine cemeteries of Hesban", in *Hesban: After 25 Year*s, edd. D. Merling and L. T. Geraty (Michigan 1994) 283–99. *Khirbet Edh-Dharih:* Lenoble P., *et al.* (2001) "Fouilles de Khirbet Edh-Dharih (Jordanie), I: le cimetière au sud du Wadi Sharheh", *Syria* 78 (2001) 89–151. *Ma'in:* Barag D. (1985) "Finds from a tomb of the Byzantine period at Ma'in", *Liber Annuus* 35 (1985) 367–74.

Arabia (South): Selected sites: *Feinan:* Findlater G. *et al.* (1998) "The Wadi Faynan project: the south cemetery excavation, Jordan, 1996: a preliminary report", *Levant* 30 (1998) 69–83; Knauf E. A. (1986) "Three new tombstones from Feinan", *Newsletter of the Institute of Archaeology and Anthropology, Yarmouk University* 2 (1986) 16–7. *Ghor es-Safi:* Meimaris Y. and Kritikakou-Nikolaropoulou K. I. (2005) *Inscriptions from Palaestina Tertia vol. 1a. The Greek inscriptions from Ghor es-Safi* (Byzantine Zoora) (Athens 2005). *Humayma:* Shumka L., Olsen J. P., and Ramsay J. (2013) "Tomb groups", in *Humayma Excavation Project, Vol. 2: Nabatean Campground and Necropolis, Byzantine Churches, and Early Islamic Domestic Structures* (AASOR 18), edd. J. P. Olsen and R. Schick (Boston 2013) 381–401. *M'uta:* Al-Samadi T. (2001) "Findings of the archaeological salvage excavations at Byzantine M'uta graveyard", *Newsletter of the Institute of Archaeology and Anthropology, Yarmouk University* 23 (2001) 24–6. *Phaeno:* Perry M. A., Coleman D. S., and Dettman D. L. (2012) "Condemned to metallum? Illuminating life at the Byzantine mining camp at Phaeno in Jordan", in *Bioarchaeology and Behavior. The People of the Ancient Near Eas*t, ed. M. A. Perry (Gainesville 2012) 115–37. *Wadi Mudayfa'at and Wadi Abu Khasharif:* Al-Salameen Z. and Falahat H. (2009) "Burials from Wadi Mudayfa'at and Wadi Abu Khasharif, Southern Jordan – Results of a survey and salvage excavations", *Mediterranean Archaeology and Archaeometry* 9 (2009) 85–108.

Arabia (West): Selected sites: *Amman:* Ibrahim M. M. and Gordon R. L. (1987) *A Cemetery at Queen Alia International Airport* (Yarmouk University Publications, Institute of Archaeology and Anthropology Series 1) (Wiesbaden 1987); Harding G. L. (1950) "A Roman family vault on Jebel Jofeh, 'Amman", *QDAP* 14 (1950) 81–94.

Egypt

Egypt: *Overview:* Yohe R. M. *et al.* (2012) "The evolution of Byzantine burial practices between the third and seventh centuries CE in Middle Egypt", *Coptica* 11 (2012) 59–87; Fletcher A., Antoine D., and Hill J. D. (2014) edd. *Regarding the Dead: Human Remains in the British Museum* (Research Publication 197) (London 2014); Grossmann P. (2002) *Christliche Architektur in Ägypten* (Handbuch der Orientalistik 62) (Leiden-Boston-Cologne 2002) 315–47; Derda T. (1992) "Necropolis workers in Graeco-Roman Egypt in the light of Greek papyri", *Journal of Juristic Papyrology* 21 (1992) 13–36. Funerary Rituals: Förster H. (2008) "Mumifizierung von Christen in Ägypten – Eine religionsgeschichtliche Anfrage", *Journal of Coptic Studies* 10 (2008) 167–82; Krause M. (1983) "Das Weiterleben ägyptischer Vorstellungen und Bräuche im koptischen Totenwesen", in *Das römisch-byzantinische Ägypten: Akten des internationalen Symposions 26.–30. September 1978 in Trier*, edd. G. Grimm, H. Heinen, and E. Winter (Mainz am Rhein 1983) 85–92. Coptic Mummies: Horak U. (1995) "Kopische Mumien. Die koptische Tote in Grabungsberichten, Funden und literarischen Nachrichten", *Biblos* 44 (1995) 39–71; Gessler-Löhr B. *et al.* (2007) "Ausklang: Eine koptische Mumie aus christlicher Zeit", in *Ägyptische Mumien: Unsterblichkeit im Land der Pharaonen* (Mainz am Rhein 2007) 255–77; Castel G. (1979) "Étude d'une momie copte", in *Hommages à la mémoire de Serge Sauneron, 1927–1976* (Bibliothêque d'Étude 81) (Cairo 1979) 121–43. Funerary Textiles: selected papers in De Moor A., Fluck C., and Linscheid P. (edd.) (2017) *Excavating, Analysing, Reconstructing: Textiles of the 1st Millennium AD from Egypt and Neighbouring Countries. Proceedings of the 9th Conference of the Research Group 'Textiles from the Nile Valley', Antwerp, 27–29 November 2015* (Tielt 2017); selected papers in De Moor A., Fluck C., and Linscheid P. (edd.) (2013) *Drawing the Threads Together: Textiles and Footwear of the 1st Millennium AD from Egypt. Proceedings of the 7th Conference of the Research Group 'Textiles from the Nile Valley', Antwerp 7–9 October 2011* (Tielt 2013); selected papers in De Moor A. and Fluck C. (edd.) (2011) *Dress*

Accessories of the 1st Millenium AD from Egypt: Proceedings of the 6th Conference of the Research Group 'Textiles from the Nile Valley', Antwerp, 2–3 October 2009 (Tielt 2011).

Cyrenaica: *Cyrene*: Cherstich L., Menozzi O., Antonelli S., and Cherstich I. (2018) "A 'living' necropolis: change and reuse in the cemeteries of Cyrene", *Libyan Studies* 49 (2018) 121–52.

Egypt (Lower): Selected sites: *Abu Mina*: Grossmann P. (1989) *Abū Mīnā 1: Die Gruftkirche und die Gruft (Archäologische Veröffentlichungen 44)* (Mainz am Rhein 1989). *Alexandria*: Empereur J.-Y. and Nenna M.-D. (2001–2003) edd. *Nécropolis* (Etudes alexandrines 5, 7) (Cairo 2001–2003); Alix G., Boës É., Georges P., and Nenna M.-D. (2012) "Les enfants dans la nécropole gréco-romaine du Pont de Gabbari à Alexandrie: Problématiques et études de cas", in *L'enfant et la mort dans l'antiquité II: Types de tombes et traitement du corps des enfants dans l'antiquité gréco-romaine. Actes de la table ronde internationale organisée à Alexandrie, Centre d'Études Alexandrines, 12–14 novembre 2009*, ed. M.-D. Nenna (Études Alexandrines 26) (Alexandria 2012) 79–137; Blaizot F. (2012) "Le loculus A1 de la salle B28.3, nécropole du Pont de Gabbari, Alexandrie: Une sépulture collective réservée aux très jeunes enfants", in *L'enfant et la mort dans l'antiquité II: Types de tombes et traitement du corps des enfants dans l'antiquité gréco-romaine. Actes de la table ronde internationale organisée à Alexandrie, Centre d'Études Alexandrines, 12–14 novembre 2009*, ed. M.-D. Nenna (Études Alexandrines 26) (Alexandria 2012) 151–208; Heinen H. (2002) "Dipinti aus der West-Necropole Alexandrias Gabbari", in *Nécropolis II*, edd. J.-Y. Empereur and M.-D. Nenna (Études Alexandrines 7) (Cairo 2002) 639–52; Sabah A. (2012) "Burials of the Kahlil el-Khayat site, Kafr Abdou District, East Alexandria", in *L'enfant et la mort dans l'antiquité II: Types de tombes et traitement du corps des enfants dans l'antiquité gré-co-romaine. Actes de la table ronde internationale organisée à Alexandrie, Centre d'Études Alexandrines, 12–14 novembre 2009*, ed. M.-D. Nenna (Études Alexandrines 26) (Alexandria 2012) 253–74. *Dahshur*: Cortés E. (2009) "Long-term preservation of Ptolemaic to late antique period burials at The Metropolitan Museum of Art Excavation in Dahshur, Egypt", in *Conservation of Three-Dimensional Textiles: 7th North American Textile Conservation Conference Pre-prints* (Québec City 2009) 219–38. *Marina el-Alamein*: Kaczmarek M. (2012) "Anthropological studies on juvenile skeletal remains from the necropolis at Marina el-Alamein, Egypt", in *L'enfant et la mort dans l'antiquité II: Types de tombes et traitement du corps des enfants dans l'antiquité gréco-romaine. Actes de la table ronde internationale organisée à Alexandrie, Centre d'Études Alexandrines, 12–14 novembre 2009*, ed. M.-D. Nenna (Études Alexandrines 26) (Alexandria 2012) 293–313; Daszewski W. A. and Zych I. (2012) "Child burials of the Roman period in the necropolis of Marina El-Alamein, Egypt", in *L'enfant et la mort dans l'antiquité II: Types de tombes et traitement du corps des enfants dans l'antiquité Gréco-Romaine. Actes de la table ronde internationale organisée à Alexandrie, Centre d'Études Alexandrines, 12–14 Novembre 2009*, ed. M.-D. Nenna (Études Alexandrines 26) (Alexandria 2012) 283–92. *Saqqara*: Jeffreys D. G. and Strouhal E. (1982) "North Saqqara 1978–9: The Coptic cemetery site at the Sacred Animal Necropolis. Preliminary report", *Journal of Egyptian Archaeology* 66 (1980) 28–35; Quibell J. E. and Thompson H. S. (1912) *Excavations at Saqqara (1908–9, 1909–10): The Monastery of Apa Jeremias* (Cairo 1912); Quibell J. E., Thompson H. S., and Spiegelberg W. (1909) *Excavations at Saqqara (1907–1908)* (Cairo 1909). *Philoxenite/Marea*: Gwiazda M., Derda T., and Baranski T. (2022.)"Philoxenite/Marea: From Roman industrial centre to early Islamic town (Field seasons in 2020–2021)", *Polish Archaeology in the Mediterranean* 31 (20220) 333–73; Martin G. T. (1974) "Excavations in the Sacred Animal Necropolis at North Saqqara, 1972–3: Preliminary report", *Journal of Egyptian Archaeology* 60 (1974) 15–29; Smith H. S., Davies S., and Frazer K. J. (2005) *The Sacred Animal Necropolis at North Saqqara.* (Egypt Exploration Society Excavation Memoir 75) (London 2005).

Egypt (Middle): Selected sites: *Amarna*: Stevens A. (2018) "Death and the city: The cemeteries of Amarna and their urban context", *Cambridge Archaeological Journal* 28 (2018) 103–26. *Bawit*: Innemee K. (2015) "Funerary aspects in the paintings from the Apollo Monastery at Bawit", in *Christianity and Monasticism in Middle Egypt. Al-Minya and Asyut*, edd. G. Gabra and H. N. Takla (Cairo-New York 2015) 241–54; Clédat J. *et al.* (1904–99) *Le monastère et la nécropole de Baouît*, 3 vols. (Cairo 1904–99). *El Hibeh*: Nauerth C. (1996) *Karara und El-Hibe: Die spätantiken ('koptischen') Funde aus den badischen Grabungen 1913–1914* (Heidelberg 1996); Ranke H. (1926) *Koptische Friedhöfe bei Karâra und der Amontempel Scheschonks I bei el Hibe: Bericht über die badischen Grabungen in Ägypten in den Wintern 1913 und 1914* (Berlin-Leipzig 1926). *Kom el-Ahmar*: Huber B. (2004) "Die Grabkirche von Kom el-Ahmar/Šaruna (Mittelägypten): Archäologie und Baugeschichte", in *Coptic Studies on the Threshold of a New Millennium: Proceedings of the Seventh International Congress of Coptic Studies, Leyden 2000*, edd. M. Immerzeel and J. van der Vliet (Orientalia Lovaniensia Analecta 133) (Leuven 2004) 1081–103; Huber B. (2009) "The funerary beds from the monastic cemetery at el-Ghalida (el-Kom el-Ah. mar/Šaruna)", in *Clothing the House. Furnishing Textiles of the 1st Millennium AD from Egypt and Neighbouring Countries*, edd. A. De Moor and C. Fluck (Tielt 2009) 57–72. <u>Matmar</u>: Pleșa A. D. (2017) "The late antique and early Islamic necropolises at Matmar and Mostagedda, Middle Egypt: A reassessment of the excavation and present state of the collection", in *Excavating, Analysing, Reconstructing: Textiles of the 1st Millennium AD from Egypt and Neighbouring Countries. Proceedings of the 9th Conference of the Research Group 'Textiles from the Nile Valley', Antwerp, 27–29 November 2015*, edd. A. De Moor, C. Fluck, and P. Linscheid (Tielt 2017) 72–87. <u>Oxyrynchos</u>: Subías Pascual E. (2008) *La maison funéraire de la nécropole haute à Oxyrynchos (el Minyâ, Êgypte): Du tombeau à la diaconie* (Barcelona 2008); Codina Reina D. (2016) "Le monde funéraire byzantin du Vᵉ au VIIᵉ siècles sur le site d'Oxyrhinchus, el-Bahnasa, Égypte", in *Coptic Society, Literature and Religion from Late Antiquity to Modern Times. Proceedings of the Tenth International Congress of Coptic Studies, Rome, September 17th–22nd, 2012, and Plenary Reports of the Ninth International Congress of Coptic Studies, Cairo, September 15th–19th, 2008*, edd. P. Buzi, A. Camplani and F. Contardi (Orientalia Lovaniensia Analecta 247) (Leuven 2016) 1397–412; Petrie W. M. F. (1925) *Tombs of the Courtiers and Oxyrhynkhos* (British School of Archaeology in Egypt 37) (London 1925). <u>Qarara</u>: Huber B. and Nauerth C. (2018) "Coptic coffins from Qarara: The Pfauensarg – the peacock coffin – in context", in *Ancient Egyptian Coffins: Craft Traditions and Functionality*, edd. J. H. Taylor and M. Vandenbeusch (British Museum Publications on Egypt and Sudan 4) (Leuven 2018) 435–69. <u>Wadi Sarga</u>: Pritchard F. (2017) "Textiles from Wadi Sarga, a 6th to 8th-century monastic site in Middle Egypt excavated in 1913/1914", in *Excavating, Analysing, Reconstructing: Textiles of the 1st Millennium AD from Egypt and Neighbouring Countries. Proceedings of the 9th Conference of the Research Group 'Textiles from the Nile Valley', Antwerp, 27–29 November 2015*, edd. A. De Moor, C. Fluck, and P. Linscheid (Tielt 2017) 60–71.

Egypt (Upper): <u>Selected sites</u>: <u>Abydos</u>: Peet T. E. (1914) *The cemeteries of Abydos* 2 (Memoirs of the Egypt Exploration Fund 34) (London 1914); Gabr A. M. (2011) "A new archaic period cemetery at Abydos: Osteological report", in *Egypt at its Origins 3: Proceedings of the Third International Conference, Origin of the State. Predynastic and Early Dynastic Egypt, London, 27th July–1st August 2008*, edd. R. F. Friedman and P. N. Fiske (Orientalia Lovaniensia Analecta 205) (Leuven 2011) 281–91; van der Vliet J. (2020) "Coptic epitaphs from Abydos",

Journal of Coptic Studies 22 (2020) 205–28; Gosner L. R and Bestock L. (2020) "Living with the dead: three examples of Christian reuse in the Abydos north cemetery", in *Abydos in the First Millennium AD*, ed. E. R. O'Connell (Leuven, Paris, Bristol 2020) 149–75. <u>Antinoe</u>: Pintaudi R. (2014) ed. *Antinoupolis II* (Scavi e materiali 3) (Florence 2014); Pintaudi R. (2008) ed. *Antinoupolis I* (Scavi e materiali 1) (Florence 2008); Fluck C. (2015) "Children's burials from Antinoopolis: Discoveries from recent excavations", in *Christianity and Monasticism in Middle Egypt: Al-Minya and Asyut*, edd. G. Gabra and H. N. Takla (Cairo 2015) 215–27; Castrizio D. (2010) *Le monete della necropoli nord di Antinoupolis (1937–2007)* (Florence 2010); Grilleto R. (1981) "I copti e la mummificazione, note agliscavi della necropolis di Antinoe", *Corso di cultura sull'arte ravennate e bizantina* (Ravenna 1981) 119–23. <u>Armant</u>: Mond R. and Myers O. H. (1937) *Cemeteries of Armant 1–2* (Egypt Exploration Society Memoirs 42) (London 1937). <u>Deir el-Banat</u>: Voytenko A. (2016) "Grave 249/2 at Deir el-Banat: A typical example of Coptic ordinary burial custom", in *Coptic Society, Literature and Religion from Late Antiquity to Modern Times: Proceedings of the Tenth International Congress of Coptic Studies, Rome, September 17th–22nd, 2012, and Plenary Reports of the Ninth International Congress of Coptic Studies, Cairo, September 15th–19th, 2008*, edd. P. Buzi, A. Camplani and F. Contardi (Orientalia Lovaniensia Analecta 247) (Leuven 2016) 1421–32; Voytenko A. (2012) "Preliminary report on Coptic burial customs at the necropolis of Deir el-Banat", in *Achievements and Problems of Modern Egyptology: Proceedings of the International Conference Held in Moscow on September 29–October 2, 2009*, edd. G. A. Belova and S. V. Ivanov (Moscow 2012) 402–11. <u>Fayum</u>: Griggs C. W. (2005) "Early Christian burials in the Fayoum", in *Christianity and Monasticism in the Fayoum Oasis*, ed. G. Gabra (Cairo-New York 2005) 185–95. <u>Hawara</u>: Uytterhoeven (2009) *Hawara in the Graeco-Roman Period: Life and Death in A Fayum Village* (Orientalia Lovaniensia Analecta 174) (Leuven 2009). <u>Naqlun</u>: Dzierzbicka D. and Ożarek M. (2012) "Two burials from cemetery A in Naqlun: Archaeological and anthropological remarks", *Polish Archaeology in the Mediterranean* 21 (2012) 233–43 <u>Qau and Badari</u>: Brunton G. (1927–30) *Qau and Badari*, 3 vols. (British School of Archaeology in Egypt and Egyptian Research Account 45, 46, 50) (London 1927–30). <u>Sohag</u>: Bolman E. S. *et al.* (2014) "The tomb of St. Shenoute at the White Monastery: Final conservation and documentation", *Bulletin of the American Research Center in Egypt* 204 (2014) 21–4; Bolman E. S., Davis S. J., and Pyke G. (2010) "Shenoute and a recently discovered tomb chapel at the White Monastery", *Journal of Early Christian Studies* 18 (2010) 453–62. *Tebtunis*: Gallazzi C. and Hadji-Minaglou G. (2012) "Sépultures de nouveau-nés et d'enfants dans une nécropole de la fin du VIIIᵉ et du IXᵉ siècles apr. J.-C. à Umm-el-Breigât, Tebtynis", in *L'enfant et la mort dans l'Antiquité II: Types de tombes et traitement du corps des enfants dans l'Antiquité gréco-romain. Actes de la table ronde internationale organisée à Alexandrie, Centre d'Études Alexandrines, 12–14 novembre 2009,* ed. M.-D. Nenna (Alexandria 2012) (Études Alexandrines 26) 389–406; Gessler-Löhr B. (2010) "Two child mummies and some grave goods of the Byzantine period from the Egyptian collection at Heidelberg University, Germany", in *Mummies of the World,* edd. A. Wieczorek and W. Rosendahl (Munich 2010) 310–15. *Thebes*: Tatz S. (2017) "The textile finds from the monastery of Deir cl-Bachît/Paulos monastery (6th–10th century) in Western Thebes", in *Excavating, Analysing, Reconstructing: Textiles of the 1st Millennium AD from Egypt and Neighbouring Countries. Proceedings of the 9th Conference of the Research Group 'Textiles from the Nile Valley', Antwerp, 27–29 November 2015,* edd. A. De Moor, C. Fluck and P. Linscheid (Tielt 2017) 108–24; Lösch S., Hower-Tilmann E., and Zink A. (2012) "Mummies and skeletons from the Coptic monastery complex Deir el-Bachit in Thebes-West, Egypt", *Anthropologischer Anzeiger* 70 (2012) 27–41; Macke A. (2012) "Une nécropole copto-Byzantine découverte sur le bas-côté nord (BCN) du Ramesseum", *Memnonia* 23 (2012) 165–79; Lecuyot G. (2000) "Le Ramesseum à l'époque copte: A propos des traces chrétiennes au Ramesseum", in *Études coptes VI: Huitième journée d'études, Colmar 29–31 mai 1997,* ed. A. Boud'hors (Cahiers de la Bibliothèque Copte 11) (Paris-Louvain 2000) 121–34; Bács T. A. (2009) "The late antique period on Sheikh abd el-Gurna: The Monastery of Cyriacus", in *Hungarian Excavations in the Theban Necropolis: A Celebration of 102 Years of Fieldwork in Egypt. Catalogue for the Temporary Exhibition in the Egyptian Museum, Cairo, November 6, 2009–January 15, 2010,* edd. T. A. Bács *et al.* (Budapest 2009) 147–49; Winlock H. E. and Crum W. E. (1926) *The Monastery of Epiphanius at Thebes I* (Publications of the Metropolitan Museum of Art Egyptian Expedition 3) (New York 1926); el-Bialy M. A. (1992) "Découverte d'une nécropole tardive aux environs de Gurnet Murrai", *Memnonia* 3 (1992) 83–7.

Sinai: Dahari U. and Di Segni L. (2009) "More early Christian inscribed tombstones from el-Huweinat in northern Sinai", in *Man Near a Roman Arch. Studies Presented to Prof. Yoram Tsafrir,* edd. L. Di Segni, Y. Hirschfeld, J. Patrich and R. Talgam (Jerusalem 2009) 125–141.

Eastern Desert: *Berenike*: Sidebotham S. E. (2014) "Religion and burial at the Ptolemaic-Roman Red Sea emporium of Berenike, Egypt", *African Archaeological Review* 31.4 (2014) 599–635.

Western Desert: *Dakhla*: Bleuze M. M, Wheeler S. M, Williams L. J, and Dupras T. L. (2014) "Ontogenetic changes in intralimb proportions in a Romano-Christian period sample from the Dakhleh Oasis, Egypt", *American Journal of Human Biology* 26 (2014) 221–28; Dupras T., Schwarcz H. P., and Fairgrieve S. I. (2008) "Dining in the Dakhla Oasis: Determining diet from stable isotopes", in *The Oasis Papers 2: Proceedings of the Second International Conference of the Dakhleh Oasis Project,* ed. M. F. Wiseman (Dakhleh Oasis Project 12) (Oxford-Oakville 2008) 119–27. *El-Bagawat (Kharga Oasis)*: Cipriano G. (2016) "Ritual equipments in the cemetery of el-Bagawat (Kharga Oasis): Some remarks", in *Coptic Society, Literature and Religion from Late Antiquity to Modern Times. Proceedings of the Tenth International Congress of Coptic Studies, Rome, September 17th–22nd, 2012, and Plenary Reports of the Ninth International Congress of Coptic Studies, Cairo, September 15th–19th, 2008,* edd. P. Buzi, A. Camplani and F. Contardi (Orientalia Lovaniensia Analecta 247) (Leuven 2016) 1447–62; Fakhry A. (1951) *The Necropolis of el-Bagawat in Kharga Oasis* (Cairo 1951). *El Deir (Kharga Oasis)*: Dunand F., Heim J.-L., and Lichtenberg R. (2010–2015) *El-Deir nécropoles,* 3 vols (Paris 2010–2015); Coudert M. (2012) "The Christian necropolis of el-Deir in the north of Kharga Oasis", in *The Oasis Papers 6: Proceedings of the Sixth International Conference of the Dakhleh Oasis,* edd. R. S. Bagnall *et al.* (Dakhleh Oasis Project 15) (Oxford 2012) 451–58; Letellier-Willemin F. (2012) "Contribution of textiles as archaeological artefacts to the study of the Christian cemetery of el-Deir", in *The Oasis Papers 6: Proceedings of the Sixth International Conference of the Dakhleh Oasis Project,* edd. R. S. Bagnall *et al.* (Dakhleh Oasis Project 15) (Oxford-Oakville 2012) 491–99. *Kharga Oasis*: Dunand F. and Lichtenberg R. (2012) "L'inhumation des enfants dans les nécropoles de l'oasis de Kharga, désert libyque", in *L'enfant et la mort dans l'antiquité II: Types de tombes et traitement du corps des enfants dans l'antiquité gréco-romaine: Actes de la table ronde internationale organisée à Alexandrie, Centre d'Études Alexandrines, 12–14 novembre 2009,* ed. M.-D. Nenna (Études Alexandrines 26) (Alexandria 2012) 331–49. *Kellis*: Bowen G. E. (2012) "Child, infant and foetal burials of the late Roman period at Ismant el-Kharab, ancient Kellis, Dakhleh Oasis", in *L'enfant et la mort dans l'antiquité II: Types de tombes et traitement du corps des*

Aspects of Late Roman Burial Practice in Southern Britain

Paul Booth

Abstract

This summary attempts an overview of the main characteristics of Late Roman burial practice in central and southern Britain, with an emphasis on results of recent excavations and analyses. These include a few urban examples but the main focus is on evidence for burial in rural contexts, including the so-called 'small towns'. This ranges from individual burials to cemeteries of varying size, organisation, and orientation. The principal rite was extended inhumation but variants on this, other forms of burial, and the variety of grave construction and provision of grave goods are reviewed. The importance of osteological evidence both for understanding the buried individual and wider questions of origins and health of communities is emphasised. Regional variation in practice is seen to be important and at least in part related to socio-economic factors. Interfaces with Early Anglo-Saxon practice and the influence of Christianity in Late and 'post-Roman' burials are also considered.

Introduction

The aim of this contribution is to summarise the main characteristics of Late Roman burial practice in central and southern Britain based on recent work in this field. The evidence is examined both in its own terms and also to provide some wider background and context for the selected site-specific urban studies from south-eastern Britain presented elsewhere in this volume (for which reason references to Canterbury and London are strictly limited here). After setting out the general trends briefly, the main focus of discussion will be on work in rural contexts but many characteristics of Late Roman burial in Britain are common to both rural and urban settings and will have general relevance. As far as possible, recent evidence will be used to exemplify the range of topics chosen for discussion, although in some cases this may involve relatively recent publication of sites excavated some time ago; inevitably, recent work does not illuminate every aspect of Late Roman burial practice in Britain.

The particular circumstances of the administrative separation of Britain from the Western Roman Empire in the early 5th c. mean that the study of burial in Britain across the full chronological range conventionally assigned to Late Antiquity (i.e. from *ca.* AD 300–700) falls within several distinctly different traditions. Traditional Romano-British burial studies do not generally extend beyond the first few decades of the 5th c., at most, while the study of Anglo-Saxon cemeteries, mainly dating from the middle of the 5th c. onwards, is a very different discipline developed out of a long historical tradition of very detailed analysis of a bewildering variety of categories of grave goods.[1] This dichotomy of tradition, however, is only relevant to eastern and central England. In the west, the influence of 'Anglo-Saxon' burial practices was not felt for some considerable time (and never in the far south-west of England, for example). In the west, therefore, 5th, 6th, and 7th c. burial practice showed aspects of continuity with what had gone before (although practice was not, of course, immutable), and so it has to be considered here.[2] The present review does not engage at length with classic 'Anglo-Saxon' burial practice as seen in eastern England but it will refer to a number of sites where there appears to be particularly interesting evidence of chronological or spatial interfaces between 'Romano-British' and 'Anglo-Saxon' burial practices.[3] It will also be argued that in parts of central England, for example, the contrast between the practices of these two periods is perhaps less stark than traditional views would suggest.

As far as the study of Romano-British burial practice is concerned, the obvious starting point is the work of Philpott (1991), the first (and only) attempt at a systematic review of the evidence for the whole period, with a focus on the grave and its furnishing. Thereafter, selected aspects of burial in Roman Britain were addressed in papers in edited volumes by Metzler *et al.* (1995) and Pearce *et al.* (2000) and in a variety of other papers subsequently. These studies were complemented by publications of key excavations at sites of various types and with various settlement associations but with the larger monographs inevitably focused mainly on urban cemeteries of Late Roman date. Lankhills, Winchester,[4] Cirencester,[5] Poundbury, Dorchester,[6] and

---

1 E.g. Lucy (2000); Bayliss *et al.* (2013).
2 Petts (2004); see also Gerrard (2015a).
3 For example, at Mucking, Essex; Hirst and Clarke (2009); Lucy and Evans (2016).
4 Clarke (1979).
5 McWhirr *et al.* (1982).
6 Farwell and Molleson (1993).

© KONINKLIJKE BRILL BV, LEIDEN, 2024 | DOI:10.1163/9789004687974_004
Alexandra Dolea and Luke Lavan (eds) *Burial and Memorial in Late Antiquity*
(Late Antique Archaeology 13) (Leiden 2024), pp. 597–629

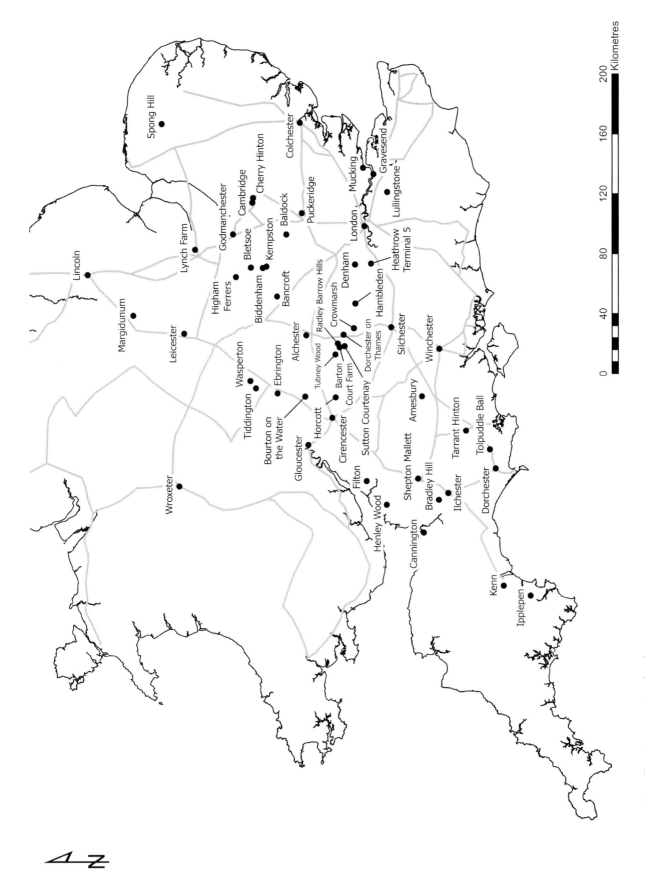

FIGURE 1   Map of locations mentioned in the paper.

Butt Road, Colchester[7] formed the basis of a number of subsequent analyses, such as a study of gender with a specifically Late Roman focus by Keegan (2002). These reports were joined later by that for the east London cemetery.[8] Cannington, Somerset[9] was the major rural exception to the urban focus of substantial cemetery reports. Regionally based summary reviews[10] have been relatively uncommon. A wide-ranging review covering the whole of our period was presented by O'Brien (1999), based on a 1996 doctoral thesis but its principal emphasis was on Anglo-Saxon cemetery evidence.

Subsequently, extensive treatment of aspects of burial in Roman Britain, with a specific contextual focus and based on selected case studies, has been presented by Pearce (2013a), who also produced an important review of urban cemetery evidence.[11] These and other studies include the substantial Late Roman evidence but are not confined to this period, while a further review with a specifically late antique emphasis has a British focus within a wider geographical range.[12] Most recently, the evidence for burial practice in rural Roman Britain has been extensively examined[13] and aspects of this important study are discussed further below. Overall, the volume of data now available for Romano-British burial in this period is such that the following summary is inevitably superficial and partial, using a small number of selected examples to underline particular points, although it is hoped that all the main trends followed by recent work have at least been identified and their potential indicated.

Two key trends are evident in recent work on burials of this and other periods. One is an emphasis on the individual body and the great range of information that it can provide on origins, health, demography, and other aspects of the human population. The second, partly driven by the realisation of the first, is the development of theoretical frameworks within which the evidence can be viewed. Some of the complexities of a variety of theoretical positions in a Romano-British context are set out by Pearce (2013a).[14] In his view, burial practices are socially constructed, although the significance of what they represent may be open to a wide range of interpretation;[15] "the funerary context is not a straight-

forward index of either status or afterlife beliefs".[16] The importance of the social background of the burial is emphasised by consideration of the processes that relate to death and burial.[17] This identifies significant stages of activity that both precede and succeed the act of interment or cremation,[18] the latter usually the only part of the process that is revealed by archaeological evidence. These trends have informed this review, although it does not follow the sequence of Weekes' outline closely. Important questions concern the expression of social identities in burial rites. To what extent does variation in practice, sometimes at a level of fine detail, tell us about individuality, whether innate or imposed by the burying community? Consequently, should our narratives homogenise practice or emphasise diversity in practice? In a review at this level the former is unavoidable but that this treatment conceals substantial variation, the significance of which may be unclear, must be acknowledged.

General Trends

The Early Roman period in southern Britain saw a wide range of burial practice. A long-lived view saw cremation as totally dominant,[19] but this is far from being the case. Both cremation and inhumation traditions were present and comprehended considerable variety, with regional variation, including, in some areas, an almost total absence of evidence for burial, notable.[20] From the 2nd c., inhumation traditions increased in importance, a trajectory comparable to that seen in Italy,[21] although the extent to which these trends were correlated, if at all, is uncertain. The broad characteristics of Late Roman burial in southern Britain can be summarised very briefly. By the beginning of the 4th c., the dominant burial practice in central and south-eastern Britain in both urban and rural contexts was extended inhumation in a supine position – this situation prevailed throughout the century and beyond. Even now, however, inhumation was not universal – small numbers of cremation burials are also found. Overall, there was apparently less regional variation in burial practice than was seen in the Early Roman period but there was considerable variation from site to site in terms of cemetery size, organisation, grave orientation, the extent of use of coffins (mostly of

7   Crummy and Crossan (1993).
8   Barber and Bowsher (2000).
9   Rahtz *et al.* (2000).
10 E.g. Booth (2001).
11 Pearce (2015).
12 Pearce (2013b).
13 Smith *et al.* (2018).
14 Pearce (2013a) 1–11.
15 E.g. Brandt (2015) xvi.

16 Weekes (2016) 440.
17 Pearce (2017).
18 Weekes (2016) 425 provides a concise summary.
19 E.g. Collingwood and Richmond (1969) 166.
20 Booth (2017a).
21 E.g. Graham (2015) 44–46.

wood), body position, the incidence of 'non-normative' practices such as decapitation and prone burial, provision of grave goods, and other characteristics. While ditches, and probably other boundary features, defining single graves or small groups of graves were not uncommon, there is very little good evidence for the use of formal tomb structures or mausolea (i.e. above-ground monuments) in this period. Pearce (2011) reviews these in relation to setting but almost all predate our period.

The well-known temple-mausoleum at Lullingstone, Kent, is a very rare 4th c. example associated with a villa.[22] Another temple-mausoleum, at Bancroft, Milton Keynes, probably built in the later 2nd c., was demolished in the 4th c.,[23] but the nature of active use and commemoration there in the 3rd c. is unknown. A probable tower-tomb at Colchester, containing remains of 6 cremation burials, is likely to have been at least of the later 3rd c.[24] The monuments at Poundbury, Dorchester, Dorset remain exceptional. Inscribed grave markers are effectively unknown (again exceptional, and again from Dorset, is a fragment of a tomb structure from Tarrant Hinton with a consular date of AD 258[25]) apart from late examples in western Britain. These appear to have an ancestry distinct from mainstream early Romano-British practice, although this is debated.[26] More broadly, burials, whether individual, in small groups, or forming larger cemeteries, were often aligned in relation to boundary features which could be either existing landscape divisions or enclosure features in some cases laid to define spaces specifically intended for burial. A final general point to make is that recent evidence comes entirely from work carried out by archaeologists working in the commercial sector in a development-led context. Philpott's dataset,[27] while substantial, completely predated the expansion of commercial 'rescue' archaeology which followed from changes in planning legislation in 1990 (the introduction of PPG16, Planning and Archaeology) and has resulted in the excavation of a large number of burials and cemeteries of varying size, many of them in rural contexts. This evidence forms the basis of the Smith *et al.* (2018) study mentioned above. With one partial exception the writer is not aware of any significant recent or current research excavations on cemeteries in southern Britain (and in that instance the burial evidence, although important, is not the primary driver of the project).

The Data Set

The body of data for Late Roman burial in southern Britain is thus substantial, even if there is much uncertainty about chronology at the level of both individual burials and some cemetery groups (see further below) which appear to be of broad Late Roman character. This uncertainty is in part a result of the increasing recognition of inhumation burials and cemeteries of Early Roman date in some regions, with the result that in those areas undated inhumations cannot automatically be assigned to the Late Roman period, as might once have been the case; routine radiocarbon dating of such burials is desirable. It remains true, however, that in some regions Early Roman burial practices are not readily recognised at all in the archaeological record (perhaps reflecting continuation of pre-Roman traditions that did not involve conventional interment, whether of inhumed or cremated remains), and in such regions the majority of identified burials are inevitably of Later Roman date, at least in broad terms. The large urban cemeteries mentioned above, with the partial exception of the East London cemetery, are dominated by burials of 4th c. date and on their own provide a significant data set. Pearce calculated that more than 4,000 burials had then been excavated at Roman towns in Britain since 1990;[28] while there is no precise chronological breakdown, a majority are of Later Roman date.[29]

There is no exactly comparable data for rural burials but order of magnitude figures are provided by the database compiled for the recently completed Roman Rural Settlement project.[30] This gives totals of burials recorded for the approximately 2,500 sites (not all of which have burials) in this database, excavated to very differing extents but many examined since 1990.[31] A consequence of the nature of post-PPG16 archaeology is that a significant number of sites are only recorded in 'grey' literature rather than being formally published but the RRS project dataset incorporates these reports – making it a particularly important summary of unpublished as well as published literature. The RRS data was assembled on a regional basis: depending on the region the compilation of evidence was completed

22   Meates (1979) 122–32.

23   Williams and Zeepvat (1994) 99–101.

24   Brooks (2006).

25   RIB III, 3045.

26   Charles-Edwards (2013) 116 and 168 provides a very concise
       summary.

27   Philpott (1991).

28   Pearce (2015) 138.

29   Pearce (2015) 143.

30   Hereafter abbreviated to RRS; Smith *et al.* (2016); for the burial
       evidence, Smith (2018).

31   http://dx.doi.org/10.5284/1030449.

between 2012 and 2013. In total, some 15,579 burials were recorded from 1,162 excavated sites,[32] although analysis was based on some 11,760 'complete' records,[33] which include records for almost 5,000 burials from 153 sites specifically of 'Late Roman' (3rd–4th c.) date, comprising 256 cremation burials and 4,714 inhumations from sites in midland and southern England and the whole of Wales (i.e. excluding the northern regions which are not covered here). The present review draws very heavily on this resource but also takes some account of even more recent fieldwork.

Some Urban Cemeteries

The term 'urban' is here reserved for the major towns of Roman Britain – the so-called 'small towns' have many characteristics which are broadly rural (although the organisation of burial is not necessarily one of these) and they will generally be considered with other rural sites. All the major towns, of course, had extensive cemeteries, although in no instance can these be considered well-known in relation to the numbers of burials that must once have been present around these towns[34] – a generalisation that includes the specific case studies presented elsewhere in this volume. In some cases, they remain hardly known at all – for example at Wroxeter and at Silchester, although recent extensive geophysical survey at the latter has identified some of the likely cemetery areas.[35] The (diachronic) urban evidence has been very well reviewed recently by Pearce.[36] The most recent additions to that picture do not in any way alter his main conclusions but add further to the picture of widely varying use of space in extramural cemeteries.

This variety is seen for example at Leicester, where recently-reported burials forming part of a larger cemetery at Newarke Street[37] were lain out in relation to ditched rectilinear plot boundaries aligned on the main road leading SSE from the walled town. Four burials were on this alignment and 17 on the perpendicular WSW-ENE orientation. Slight deviations from the latter to a more strictly west-east alignment, included the only burial with grave goods (rings and a comb), for which a late 4th c. date is likely. By contrast, at Western Road, beside the Fosse Way a little to the south-west of the town, some 83 burials excavated from 2010–2015 (again

forming only part of a larger cemetery) were less clearly organised, although a roughly north-west/south-east alignment, perpendicular to the road, can be recognised in some cases. Arrangement of graves in rows, at least partly evident at Newarke Street, was absent here, as was, apparently, clear evidence for land division within the cemetery. These burials included 12 in a prone position, of which half were in marginal locations; a relatively large proportion (almost 25%) of non-adults (mostly 1–12 years), and a high incidence of trauma (almost a quarter have one or more broken bones), including one violent decapitation (although it is not clear if this was a peri-mortem or slightly later feature). Roughly half of the burials were in wooden coffins and at least a quarter had nailed footwear. Grave goods were preferentially associated with some of the subadults, the principal exception being the occurrence of a fine (but poorly-preserved) belt set with a buckle of Hawkes (1961) type IVA in a grave at the southern end of the excavated area;[38] such finds, presumably indicating an individual with some sort of official status, are still very rare in Late Romano-British cemeteries.

These summaries encapsulate many of the aspects of Late Roman cemeteries that will be returned to below. Comparable listing of each characteristic for all the sites mentioned is, of course, not possible but further consideration of spatial aspects of some urban cemeteries is worthwhile. A relative lack of systematic layout of the graves is characteristic of a number of recently excavated or reported sites and has no obvious explanation. At Gloucester, cemeteries with contrasting locations – at Brunswick Road (153 inhumations and 4 cremations) just outside the south-east gate[39] and well to the north-east at London Road, Wotton[40] – both show this characteristic and an uncertain relationship with, or possible lack of, linear boundaries (although this may be a function of the size of excavated areas, with boundaries lying beyond their limits). In both cases, some clustering of burials is evident. The significance of such groups at Brunswick Road is uncertain, although an obvious possibility is that they form family groups, since some cemetery areas here do not show particularly intensive use – there was not obviously a huge amount of competition for burial space. At London Road, by contrast, it is notable that a group of inhumation burials of several phases was positioned, probably not coincidentally, above a mass grave of later 2nd c. date.[41] The Late Roman Kingsholm

32   Smith (2018) 206.
33   Smith (2018) 208.
34   E.g. Jones (1977) 20.
35   Creighton and Fry (2016) 369–87.
36   Pearce (2015).
37   Thomas (2017).

38   Chapman et al. (2016) 322, fig. 21.
39   Chapman et al. (2015) 340–41; Cotswold Archaeology unpublished draft report (Joyce et al. (forthcoming)).
40   Simmonds et al. (2008); Ellis and King (2014).
41   Simmonds et al. (2008) fig. 2.3.

cemetery, north of Gloucester, is also characterised as being not strictly ordered, although replanning of part of it in the late 4th c. involved the introduction of "east-west burials and more orderly rows".[42]

Part of the western cemetery of Cirencester, at Tetbury Road, has been examined recently.[43] Here, the majority of the 118 inhumation and 8 cremation burials (of all phases but with a majority of Later Roman date) related to the north-east/south-west alignment of the adjacent road (the Fosse Way again) and broadly coaxial boundaries. These burials almost certainly reflected developing use of the rearward part of the roadside burial zone, the area closest to the road having been initially occupied mainly by cremation burials, some of which were recorded in difficult conditions in the 1960s. The overall density of burials is difficult to judge owing to the presence of extensive areas of modern truncation but density clearly reduced with distance from the road frontage, although it is not certain that the furthest distant burials, lying beyond a ditched boundary parallel to the road, were necessarily the latest in the sequence, which in any case might not have extended much beyond the middle of the 4th c.[44]

This variability in apparent density of burials (although truncation, a factor at most of the sites already mentioned, makes reliable assessment uncertain), and in orientation and extent of organisation of grave layout, can be broadly contrasted with the picture from some other towns with 'managed' Late Roman cemeteries,[45] Dorchester (Poundbury) and Colchester (Butt Road) being obvious examples. Winchester Lankhills is another striking example, particularly with the addition of more recent work[46] to the results of the earlier excavations.[47] On present evidence, the cemetery was not established before the beginning of the 4th c., and it probably continued in use at least into the early decades of the 5th. Like the other cemeteries already discussed, its overall layout is dependent upon the alignments of a road and associated ditched enclosures but the differences between the patterns of burial density and organisation seen in such sites and in some other (sometimes contemporary) cemeteries, such as the Bath Gate cemetery at Cirencester[48] do appear to be real, if not always very marked. They might suggest a contrast between the organic (although not necessarily

unorganised) growth of cemeteries with 1st–2nd c. origins and the more systematic layout of some new foundations, such as Lankhills. Nevertheless, the superficial orderliness of such cemeteries can conceal variations in grave alignment and orientation reflecting chronological development. Whether the establishment of new cemeteries simply represented the requirement for extra accommodation for the growing population of the dead or was associated with particular communities within the wider population, is a question for further consideration. The case of Winchester offers interesting possibilities here, although in the publication of older excavations Ottaway and Rees[49] suggest a practical explanation for the appearance of cemeteries significantly closer to the town walls than Lankhills, based on ownership of particular parcels of land. Lankhills was over 500 m distant from the walls, which although exceptional in the case of Winchester was by no means unusual when compared with other Late Roman urban cemeteries in Britain.

Some 'Small Town' and Rural Cemeteries

An obvious contrast between the cemeteries just mentioned and those associated with a variety of non-urban settlements is that many of the latter are complete in plan. While we cannot know if they contained all the population of the associated settlement(s) there is at least reasonable confidence (subject to issues of truncation and other aspects of preservation) that as cemetery populations they are complete. Some of the larger nucleated settlements or 'small towns' had associated cemeteries of greatly variable size but including some substantial ones with characteristics (such as, sometimes, only partial excavation) more akin to those of urban sites mentioned above. A well-known example (although in this case not based on recent work) is Ilchester, Somerset, a site often considered to have become a civitas centre in the Late Roman period (and hence grouped with 'potential cities' by Burnham and Wacher[50]). In extramural areas in the southern part of the settlement, inhumation burials both west and east of the main road (the Fosse Way) were aligned in relation to existing boundaries (a pattern found in both urban and rural contexts) in turn aligned on the road. To the west, the 42 burials[51] assigned to period V (late 4th c. and later) were confined almost entirely to the rear parts of roadside plots (rather than plots further west again, further from the road) and

42   Heighway (2012) 81.
43   Holbrook et al. (2017).
44   Holbrook et al. (2017) 127.
45   A term first used by Thomas (1981) 232.
46   Booth et al. (2010).
47   Clarke (1979).
48   McWhirr et al. (1982) 69–109.
49   Ottaway and Rees (2012) 367.
50   Burnham and Wacher (1990) 62–70.
51   Leach (1982) 86 table 1.

were aligned NNE-SSW and WNW-ESE but it seems likely that they were contemporary with late structures closer to the road frontage in the same plots.[52] The smaller number of burials recorded east of the road were of similar character and clearly formed part of a larger cemetery.[53] The western group included only 2 small children, whilst 19 males and 16 females were identified amongst the adults. A majority of the burials were in wooden coffins. Four were decapitated (all coffined); 2 of the 4 prone burials were also within coffins but none of the 3 recorded as flexed. Nailed footwear was present in about a third of the graves. Grave goods were slightly less common but notable associations included a pot containing chicken bones in one case, and a dog buried with a mature adult female.[54]

Just north of the town, a rather different but contemporary arrangement was apparent.[55] Here, evaluation of a previously known cemetery revealed some 122 graves, although only a very few of these were excavated. Contained within and aligned upon ditched boundaries laid out approximately perpendicular to the line of the Roman road but again probably lying behind buildings fronting on to the west side of the road, giving a prevailing grave alignment of WNW-ESE, this was clearly a 'managed' cemetery with a fairly organised layout. An overall cemetery population perhaps in excess of 1,500 graves is estimated.[56] Notable characteristics include the presence of stone coffins, 3 with lead inner coffins and 1 other, and 2 other lead coffins, with a further 2 stone coffins and 3 lead ones known from antiquarian finds. Proximity to good sources of stone and lead might perhaps be a factor in the relative frequency of coffins using these materials at Ilchester but this need not necessarily follow.[57] This major cemetery has potential parallels with sites such as Poundbury but at present its exact character, chronology, and development sequence remain uncertain.

Dorchester-on-Thames, Oxfordshire is another 'small town' with a group of unusually large cemeteries of 'managed' appearance.[58] It has parallels with Ilchester in that one of these cemeteries, with a well-defined and associated features confirmed by recent geophysical survey (unpublished), is barely known from excavation,

and like the Ilchester northern cemetery is very substantial and separated from the town by a river but without the immediate road link seen at Ilchester. It is particularly unfortunate that the excavation of one of the clearest examples of a 'small town' cemetery of this type, at Ashton (Northants), remains unpublished,[59] as do a number of the Late Roman cemeteries at Baldock, Hertfordshire.[60]

Elsewhere, patterns of burial at small towns can be strikingly similar to those seen in strictly rural contexts. Examples include the scattering of inhumations in small groups[61] at Higham Ferrers, Northants[62] and in part also at Shepton Mallet, Somerset, where burial continued into the post-Roman period.[63] A striking example of a rural burial pattern has been revealed recently close to Margidunum, Nottinghamshire, where some 65 inhumation burials were mostly closely aligned in relation to the rear ditched boundaries of a linear arrangement of plots examined over a distance of *ca.* 350 m extending on both sides of the Fosse Way south-west of the small town: Cooke and Mudd[64] report 14 burials from 13 graves west of the road, while excavations by Oxford Archaeology east of the road have revealed a further 54 burials in 52 graves, plus a single individual suffering from leprosy placed in the top of a Roman well and dated to the Early Anglo-Saxon period.[65] Similarly, at The Parks, Godmanchester, Cambridgeshire, some 62 burials probably mainly of 4th c. date appear to have constituted a largely complete cemetery group at the margin of the 'small town'. Two dominant grave alignments, approximately north-west/south-east and (particularly) south-west/north-east, were broadly related to earlier ditched boundaries but the cemetery layout contrasted markedly with that at Margidunum, the graves being widely spaced, so it is difficult to see how their basic alignment was maintained, except perhaps by relating graves to features which have left no archaeological trace. There were 5 decapitated burials (and 3 further possible examples) and 5 prone burials. Thirteen of the burials (just 20%) were in coffins, and grave goods were relatively scarce.[66] This cemetery provides a classic set of characteristic 'rural' burial features.

52   Leach (1982) 62, fig. 35, 84.
53   Leach (1982) 102.
54   Leach (1982) 86 table 1.
55   Leach (1994) 91–102.
56   Leach (1994) 97.
57   See e.g. Pearce (2016) 348.
58   Harman *et al.* (1978); Chambers (1987); much more recently parts of another substantial cemetery of similar character have been examined just south of the town (Williams (2013); Dawson *et al.* (2017)).

59   For an outline plan, see Frere (1984) 301.
60   See Fitzpatrick-Matthews (2014) 47–49; (2016).
61   A classic 'backland burial' pattern, as defined by Esmonde Cleary (2000) 136–37.
62   Witkin (2009) 275–77.
63   See further below; for grave locations, Leach with Evans (2001) 9, fig. 5.
64   Cooke and Mudd (2014) 126–27.
65   Simmonds *et al.* (2023).
66   Jones (2003) 21–36.

At the other end of the scale, Late Roman burials could occur as single individuals or in groups of varying size, although some of the smaller groups can be less easily assigned to the Late Roman period with confidence in the absence of dating evidence. Another question concerns the extent to which very small burial groups can be considered to constitute formal cemeteries. For the purposes of a review of Later Roman burial in the Upper Thames valley region, analysis[67] was confined to groups of 10 or more burials. This arbitrary number may be misleading, and it is usually inappropriate to consider even individual burials as 'casual' – whatever that might mean but smaller groups in this region generally consisted of isolated ones and twos rather than more coherent clusters. Traditions of rural burial adjacent to field boundary features, for example, were long established in some regions,[68] and where such burials occurred as twos and threes, or even singletons, the interments were not necessarily any less purposive or respectful than burials of otherwise identical character (typically, unaccompanied extended inhumations) widely encountered in more 'formal' cemetery locations. Extended inhumation aligned upon or within boundary ditches was a common enough feature in both urban and rural burial contexts.

The complexity of characteristics of cemetery arrangement is shown particularly clearly by remarkable evidence from Amesbury, Wiltshire. Here, 5 separate cemetery groups have been examined, spread over some 700 m from west to east. All may have related to settlement lying to the north but between the cemeteries and settlement lay a substantial prehistoric linear boundary. This survived as a still significant landscape feature used to separate the realms of the living and the dead, while the ditch itself served as the location for a significant number of burials, associations suggested as connecting the Romano-British burial landscape to a mythic past.[69] The most westerly of the cemeteries was focused on very different features, two small square ditched enclosures, one containing a single grave, the larger enclosing two features, an empty grave (or possible cenotaph) and a larger grave with a stone coffin containing burials of an adult female and a child with unusual preservation of some environmental material (including evidence for cork-soled shoes). This grave appears to be of 3rd c. date. Five inhumation burials were dug into its enclosure ditch, and before this was completely filled, 15 cremation burials were set in the ditch, the upper fills consisting largely of pyre debris. A further 115 inhumation burials, quite closely spaced and including at least three distinct

clusters, lay adjacent to the grave enclosures, mainly on the south and east sides. The broadly NNW-SSE alignment of the principal enclosed burial determined the alignment of some but by no means all, of the surrounding burials, and no other enclosing features are apparent. Just over half of the burials were in nailed coffins. Dating evidence, mainly from coins and pottery, indicates a later 3rd–4th c. range for these burials.[70] The internal burial clusters suggest a diversity of groups contributing to this cemetery, as does the appearance of cremation burials within the sequence, while the overall number of discrete cemeteries indicates a similar situation writ large. While it is possible that chronological variation also contributes to this diversity, all 5 cemeteries are broadly Late Roman in date.

Aspects of Burial Practice

Cemetery Location, Definition, and Grave Orientation

Many aspects of Late Roman burial practice were common to both urban and rural contexts. The varying degrees of definition (or lack thereof) of burial space have already been mentioned. Individual burials and even cemetery groups were not necessarily placed within clearly defined enclosures but even when formal enclosures were lacking, burials were often aligned in close relation to existing boundaries, as seen at Margidunum (above). The enclosure within which the majority of the Lankhills burials were placed may or may not have been set out specifically to contain these burials but it is clear that the principal burial alignment was initially at right angles to the south-east/north-west line of the adjacent main (Winchester to Cirencester) road, and that as burial progressed eastwards, orientation gradually shifted to match the east-west line of the northern cemetery boundary, consolidating for a while at and within the north-south eastern boundary ditch of the site before then extending eastwards beyond that boundary. In general, where present, either in primary or secondary use to contain burials, enclosures were defined by ditches: evidence for associated upstanding elements such as banks, fences, or hedges has generally not survived, and there is little good evidence for the presence of walled cemeteries, particularly in rural contexts in the Late Roman period. Exploitation of pre-existing boundaries to define burial alignments meant that these were not determined by considerations such as belief systems that might (perhaps) have prescribed particular practices. At NIAB, Huntingdon Road, Cambridge, for

67   Booth (2001).
68   E.g. Pearce (1999).
69   Gibson (2013) 108–110.

70   Wessex Archaeology (2008); McKinley (2017) 273–74.

example, inhumation burials occurred in a number of enclosures aligned in relation to major boundaries and a trackway.[71] These include two small but tightly packed groups of burials plausibly identified as 'cemeteries' but a third, larger, group of 45 burials was placed within a similarly-aligned enclosure which was nevertheless clearly intended to contain it[72] and might possibly have been sited to block the trackway.

Factors determining grave alignment in the absence of defined boundaries or other structural features are less easily identified but could include a relationship to specific individual features, as seen at Amesbury, although there the key consideration seems to have been proximity rather than adherence to a common orientation. A general west-east alignment for inhumation burials is quite common in the Late Roman period but may be based on existing features rather than consciously determined (see further below). In rural contexts, north-south alignments are also frequently seen, as for example at Sutton Courtenay, Oxfordshire and numerous earlier cemetery excavations in this region.[73] These also occur in major cemeteries such as Poundbury and Lankhills, where discrete groups of north-south burials contrast markedly with the prevailing, broadly west-east, alignments and may well indicate the presence of distinct burying communities. The stark contrast between north-south and west-east alignments at sites such as Butt Road, Colchester and Poundbury has sometimes been linked to the adoption of a specifically Christian burial rite.[74] Unlike in the case of Butt Road, however, the contrast was not always straightforwardly sequential; for example, relationships between north-south and west-east graves might have varied in different parts of a cemetery. Alternatively, lack of close dating evidence might make it impossible to determine the sequence between spatially distinct groups of graves on contrasting alignments.

Principal Rites: Cremation and Inhumation
Questions of alignment relate principally to inhumation burials. The cremation rite occurred as a minority practice in the Late Roman period, although we should be cautious in assuming that this necessarily represented the survival of widespread Early Roman traditions rather than, perhaps in some cases at least, localised reintroduction associated with particular burying communities. The RRS dataset records 256 cremation burials for the regions covered by the present review (as defined

above) – just over 5% of all Late Roman burials, and also shows that the proportion of Late Roman cremation burials contained within urns is significantly lower than in the Early and Middle Roman periods;[75] un-urned burials have to be dated on other criteria.

At Biddenham Loop, Bedfordshire, scattered cremation and inhumation burials (by no means all of Late Roman date) were characteristic, while more closely grouped graves, totalling 30 inhumations in 3 groups were associated with one farmstead.[76] Amongst the dispersed burials was a single *bustum* (a cremation burial in which the pyre is constructed over a pit in which the cremated remains are often left in their original anatomical position) of 4th c. date.[77] Burials of this distinctive type are rare in Late Roman contexts but occur at a number of rural sites such as Denham, Buckinghamshire, as well as in urban contexts such as Lankhills, where 7 examples were dated to the 4th c., with at least 1 assignable to the very end of the century.[78] As these examples show, cremation and inhumation burials tend to be associated in both urban and rural contexts – cemeteries consisting largely or entirely of cremation burials appear to be unknown in the Late Roman south, although such burials could occur as distinct clusters within larger cemeteries, as for example at Radley Barrow Hills, Oxfordshire.[79]

The Denham site[80] is notable in several respects. Set out on a broadly NNE-SSW alignment related to that of an earlier field system (and possibly referencing a Bronze Age feature) but with its settlement context unknown, the cemetery comprised a core area of 11 inhumation burials (fairly certain, although human bone only survived in 4 cases), all but one quite closely surrounded by at least 7 *bustum* burials and a further 11 features variously interpreted as pyre and cremation-related deposits. A scatter of peripheral features 20–55 m distant consisted of a further three *busta*, a pyre and 4 cremation-related deposits. It is, however, possible that at least 3 of the 'pyre' features in the core area, and the peripheral example, were also *busta* in which the human remains (still in anatomically correct position in the other examples) had been disturbed or partly reworked.[81] All the identified human remains were of adults and if the proposed feature type reinterpretations are accepted the individuals cremated on the *busta* included 6 males and 4 females. Grave goods were largely absent but nailed

71   E.g. Smith (2018) 246, fig. 6.31.
72   E.g. Chapman *et al.* (2014) 356, fig. 20.
73   Booth (2001) 22.
74   See e.g. Petts (2003) 140–49; and further below.

75   Smith (2018) 160–261, fig. 6.42.
76   Luke (2016) 251, fig. 5.28; 315, fig. 5.53.
77   Luke (2016) 310–16.
78   Booth *et al.* (2010) 502–504, with discussion of further examples.
79   Chambers and Boyle (2007).
80   Recently but rather summarily, published in Pine (2018).
81   But see McKinley (2017) 260, 265–67.

footwear was quite common and nails from the *busta* suggest the use of biers or coffins on the pyre, while only one of the inhumation burials contained any evidence for a coffin. Chronology is based mainly on 4 radiocarbon dates (on charcoal), three from *busta*. Those from a pyre and one of the *busta* are effectively the same and indicate use of the cemetery in the 4th c. or perhaps into the early 5th. The other two *busta* are clearly later, however, with one most probably securely within the 5th c. and another perhaps in the 5th c. but more likely in the 6th or even early 7th c. (AD 429–495 (22.6% probability), 527–642 (74.6% probability)). The extremities of these date ranges suggest remarkable continuity and consistency of practice over a very long period which, given the small number of burials involved in total, may seem unlikely. If all the *busta* were dated between (say) the mid-4th c. and the early 7th (i.e. assuming that the undated examples fall within the date range indicated by the radiocarbon sample), this would give little more than one burial of this type for every generation, a scenario which is perhaps not impossible but raises many questions about the size and nature of the community sustaining this practice. A much more condensed time frame in which the two later *busta* fell within the 5th c. is easier to imagine, and is just possible but rather strains the radiocarbon evidence. This seems at present to be the only case where burials of this kind are securely dated later than the 4th c.

Containing the Dead

Containers for cremation burials other than ceramic vessels (the latter already noted as in use in less than half the identified examples) were very rare – boxes (more common in earlier periods) occurred occasionally, as in an isolated burial at Heathrow Terminal 5.[82] Inhumation burials received much more diverse treatment. At its simplest this consisted of placement in earth-cut graves with no lining (presumably clothed, perhaps shrouded but this is often uncertain). Provision of wooden coffins, usually identified from the presence of iron nails (less often from stains in the ground and occasionally, in the absence of both these, from the position of the body suggesting initial decay in a void) was common but far from universal. The RRS data suggest that between 20% and 25% of Late Roman rural burials were contained in coffins,[83] but in some cemeteries the figure could be substantially higher, as at Amesbury (above). As a generalisation, individual burials or those in very small groups were less likely to be placed in coffins. Variation in the frequency of coffin provision in urban contexts

could also be considerable. For example, at Winchester approximately 78% of burials at Lankhills were coffined while coffins were provided in less than 45% of cases at three other contemporary sites at the town.[84] Lead lining was an uncommon but consistently occurring feature of wooden coffins in both urban and rural contexts and was also found in some stone sarcophagi (as at Ilchester, mentioned above) – although these were more usually unlined. The presence of elaborate decoration on some lead coffins suggests that they were intended to be viewed by the living prior to burial[85] and thus provide a further insight into the variety of potential practices around the funeral. The rural distributions of both lead lined and stone coffins are shown by Smith.[86] Both but particularly the latter, show concentrations in western England (where suitable stone was more readily available) and around London. While such obvious higher-status coffins could occur in small groups or in isolation (as for example in the temple-mausoleum at Lullingstone, built *ca*. AD 300, mentioned above), graves containing them were just as likely to be found within cemeteries alongside simpler burials, as in a recently-excavated example at Ebrington, Gloucestershire,[87] sometimes with a focal role as at Amesbury (above). In both urban and rural contexts, there are some hints of correlations between isotopic indications of a richer diet and aspects of burial rite such as provision of coffins.[88]

A more widespread tradition involved the placing of stones, sometimes upright, within graves. These could have served as packing to hold a wooden coffin in place, or could have formed cists of varying degrees of completeness and quality of construction, with stones forming the base and also capping the grave.[89] Large tiles were also sometimes used in this way.[90] Leaving aside northern sites, the cist grave tradition is very much a western one[91] and remained common in this region in the post-Roman period, often being considered particularly characteristic of the 5th–7th c. (see further below).

---

82   Framework Archaeology (2010) 308.
83   Smith (2018) 254.

84   Booth *et al.* (2010) 481–83, with further comparative discussion; 534, table 8.2, now partly enhanced by Holbrook *et al.* (2017) 131 table 7.1.
85   Weekes (2016) 430.
86   Smith (2018) 256.
87   Neil Holbrook pers. comm.
88   E.g. Cummings (2009) 80–81.
89   Cf. Hart *et al.* (2016) 94, fig. 9; Holbrook *et al.* (2017) 56, fig. 3.87, from locally adjacent sites.
90   E.g. at Alchester, Oxfordshire: Booth *et al.* (2001) 161.
91   See Smith (2018) 258, fig. 6.40 for distribution but including Late Iron Age and Early Roman as well as the more common Late Roman sites.

Placing the Dead

Body position in Late Roman inhumation burials could be highly variable. The majority position was extended and supine but even under this heading there was room for variation, for example involving crossing or bending of the legs. More particularly, a wide range of different arm positions is noted in extended inhumations, with hands together or crossed at the waist amongst common arrangements.[92] The significance of the many different arm and hand (and, to a lesser extent, leg) positions is uncertain. Woodward[93] considered these issues in comparative terms at some length in the discussion of Poundbury. From her comparative sample it was concluded that leg positions were predominantly straight but arm positions characteristically involved one or both arms being bent onto the pelvis, the occurrence of straight arms being "surprisingly rare".[94] At Cannington, where straight arm positions were relatively common (32% of an analysed sample of 159 burials) flexed arm positions were still more common. A more striking arrangement, with arms crossed over the chest, was considered to be a specifically Christian characteristic but such burials were in a minority (10% of the sample).[95]

Less common alternatives to the extended supine body position are well known. Crouched burials, a prehistoric tradition in many parts of Britain, continue to be found occasionally in rural contexts but are often not well dated. A partly flexed position, with the body usually laid on the side,[96] was more common, being present in many cemeteries[97] where crouched burials were completely absent. Unfortunately, the RRS analysis takes the view that because of inconsistent use of terminology in original reports, flexed and crouched burials have to be grouped together (under the heading 'flexed') for statistical purposes.[98] These burials occur at 21% of the 420 Late Roman sites with burials (across the country – including the north) but total only 184 burials,[99] therefore accounting for less than 3.5% of the period total, amongst which in turn truly 'crouched' burials probably formed only a very small proportion. It remains unclear if the flexed body position can be considered a distinct tradition with a meaning separate from that of extended inhumation.

Much more attention has been paid to distinctive supposedly 'deviant' rites of prone and decapitated burial. While the former is encountered throughout the Roman period, decapitation was much more common in the Late Roman period than earlier,[100] but in rural contexts neither practice accounted for more than about 4% of all Late Roman burials, although there was potentially considerable variation in their frequency from one site to another, as noted by Smith.[101] As with other practices both these were encountered in urban cemeteries as well as in the countryside. Their significance has been much debated over an extended period.[102] Evidence from sites such as Lankhills and Horcott, however, indicates that in terms of location within the cemetery and the provision of coffins and grave goods, there was little discernible distinction between decapitated and other burials. By contrast, the evidence for prone burials is somewhat more mixed in this regard,[103] but at Horcott, it is clear that the prone burials were marginally located, relatively shallow and poorly furnished, and these characteristics are supported by isotope evidence from both sites that showed significant depletion of δ^{15}N in the sampled prone individuals compared to other members of these cemetery populations regardless of their spatial location.[104] Together, these indications suggest significant status differentiation between (at least) prone and other burials, although at Lankhills isotope evidence showed that both prone and decapitated individuals had depleted carbon levels compared to the majority of the population but that nitrogen levels in the decapitated individuals were more variable.[105] By contrast, at Little Keep, Dorchester, just south of Poundbury, where a remarkable 12 of a total of 29 burials were prone, there was no clear distinction between these and the others in terms of location, depth of grave cut and occurrence of nailed footwear.[106] Overall, therefore, while prone burial was often a rite with associations of marginalisation, complemented by evidence that some prone burials may have had their hands bound,[107] this was not always the case and the full significance of these associations remains unclear.

---

92   E.g. Ottaway *et al.* (2012) 280, fig. 111.

93   Woodward (1993) 222–26.

94   Woodward (1993) 222.

95   Rahtz *et al.* (2000) 81, 84, 417.

96   E.g. Hayden *et al.* (2017) 150, figs. 7.20 and 7.21.

97   E.g. Horcott, Gloucestershire, with 7 examples out of 59 burials; ibid.

98   Smith (2018) 230.

99   Ibid.

100   Smith (2018) 226–29, fig. 6.18.

101   Ibid.

102   Notably by Macdonald (1979), Harman *et al.* (1981); Philpott (1991) 77–90; Boylston *et al.* (2000); for recent views see e.g. Taylor (2008); Tucker (2015); Crerar (2016); Smith (2018) 228 for a concise summary of the debate.

103   For Lankhills, see Booth *et al.* (2010) 476–78.

104   Booth (2017b) 419 with references.

105   Cummings and Hedges (2010) 417–18.

106   Egging Dinwiddy (2009); McKinley and Egging Dinwiddy (2009).

107   E.g. Holbrook *et al.* (2017) 133–34.

The range of variation in body position is found in inhumation burials of all kinds, whether in cists or coffins or uncoffined. In some cases, however, the position of particular bones may result from the various decomposition processes subsequent to burial (particularly where the deceased was placed in a coffin), and the potential complexity of these needs to be clearly understood.[108] In uncoffined burials, features such as the use of a shroud or other tight wrapping can sometimes be inferred from the constricted position of the skeleton, as for example at Sutton Courtenay.

Clothing and Equipping the Dead

The preservation conditions at most cemetery excavations mean that basic questions about the nature of clothing or wrapping of the corpse (prompted by the occasional evidence suggestive of the use of shrouds as mentioned above) can rarely be answered with confidence. In this period, the use of distinctive clothes fastenings such as brooches and belts is relatively uncommon – the Lankhills cemetery, which is particularly well-known in this respect, is quite atypical, and also shows that such items could have been placed in the grave and were not necessarily worn on the body. The question of whether the dead were buried in their typical attire or were specially clothed before interment or cremation merits consideration but can rarely be answered. Very often the best-represented aspect of clothing is footwear, seen in the form of shoe nails but even this category of evidence is not unproblematic (quite apart from the question of the likely use of a range of unnailed shoe types, for which evidence will not normally survive), as shoes very likely had symbolic as well as practical significance[109] and careful observation again allows distinction between cases where the shoes were worn or placed away from (although sometimes very close to) the feet.[110] Consideration of such provision and that of a wide range of other grave goods formed a fundamental part of Philpott's seminal work.[111] Since then, developments in thinking about the way grave assemblages might have been constructed to reflect the persona of the deceased, and the burying community, rather than forming a straightforward 'Spiegel des Lebens'[112] have led to new approaches. These include consideration of the relationship of grave goods to the life course of the deceased[113] and a much clearer realisation that variation in the quantity and type of grave goods could correlate very closely with particular age, gender, and social roles and identities. At the same time, the problems of inferring ethnicity from grave goods have been considered much more critically (see below).

There is a clear chronological trend in the provision of grave goods, with a decrease in their use over time through the Roman period.[114] The RRS dataset shows that for the Late Roman period some 21% of all rural graves contained grave goods, although the pattern was regionally variable, with the RRS 'South' region showing significantly higher levels of provision than the adjacent 'Central Belt' (where the majority of Later Roman rural burials were to be found – see below), with figures of 36% and 17% of graves respectively. These figures, however, include footwear, the one category of material that shows a really significant increase in frequency (or, at least, visibility) through the Roman period. Smith[115] shows the broad chronological trends in the incidence of principal categories of grave goods – from which it is clear that in a significant number of cases, footwear will have been the only grave good type present in the Late Roman period. However, this illustration relates only to the rural picture – in urban and some other contexts (for example the northern fort at Brougham), it is clear that very significant numbers of earlier and mid-Roman cremation burial deposits could contain evidence of nailed footwear.[116] It remains uncertain if nailed footwear was of decreasing importance in the 4th c., as has sometimes been claimed, when at least some of the burial evidence may support a contrary view. As mentioned above, the extent to which footwear may be considered 'normal' grave goods may be debateable, and the greatly variable incidence of footwear in selected major urban cemeteries has been discussed previously.[117] It suggests that factors beyond simple fashion trends may have been at work. The Tetbury Road Cirencester analysis helpfully juxtaposes distributions of graves with nailed footwear[118] and other grave goods[119] – this seems to be a useful and potentially important distinction.

Footwear apart, pottery vessels are the most common grave good type in Late Roman burials, occurring

---

108   E.g. Duday (2009).

109   E.g. van Driel Murray (1999); although see also Crummy (2011) 48.

110   E.g. Booth *et al.* (2010) 498–99.

111   Philpott (1991).

112   E.g. Pearce (2013a) 6–8.

113   E.g. Gowland (2016a); Moore (2016); both with further references.

114   Philpott (1991) 225; Smith (2018) 264–65.

115   Smith (2018) 268, fig. 6.48.

116   Crummy (2011) 48.

117   Booth *et al.* (2010) 534–35; see also Philpott (1991) 171–73; Cool (2011) 309–310.

118   Perhaps as many as 44% of all graves in this cemetery; Holbrook *et al.* (2017) 132.

119   Holbrook *et al.* 2017, 136–37, figs. 7.3 and 7.4.

in some 31% of rural graves of this period which contain grave goods of any kind,[120] roughly 7% of all graves of this period (potentially including, of course, cremation as well as inhumation burials). Animal remains, coins, and bracelets are the other types most commonly present, all found in around 10% of those graves with grave goods (and thus with overall occurrence levels of *ca.* 2–2.5% of all rural graves in this period). As always, there is substantial variation from site to site.[121] As with footwear there are cases where grave goods such as jewellery (for example, bracelets and necklaces) are placed beside the body rather than worn. Detailed work on patterns of this kind by Clarke[122] in his analysis of the earlier Lankhills excavations led to conclusions about the ethnicity of some individuals associated with particular patterns of placement of grave goods, which subsequent isotope-based work (see further below) demonstrated were not sustainable. This does not invalidate consideration of this sort of analysis,[123] but does underline the need for caution in interpretation. The position of some objects types has been argued to reflect belief in their symbolic value or aspects of religious practice. Examples include placement of coins in or near the mouth and therefore linked to traditional provision of the fee for the ferryman Charon. This association is seen at Lankhills in a number of graves but deposition of coins in other locations, including in twos or threes probably wrapped in fabric, was also noted here and elsewhere.[124] Such groups of coins may have served a similar function but this is unknown. A different aspect of practice is seen in the apparently deliberate placement of a nail in or on the mouth, encountered at several Dorchester sites including Poundbury.[125] The possible role of nails in mortuary and ritual contexts to ward off evil spirits or to 'fix' the dead has long been appreciated,[126] but the particular significance of placing a nail in the mouth is unclear. The identical positioning of a flint in the mouth of a burial in the small Late Roman cemetery at Crowmarsh, Oxfordshire, is notable.[127]

That the location of most objects in graves will have been significant, or at least a reflection of customary practice, is indicated by recurring patterns of deposition, most evident in the placement of the commonest grave good types such as pottery vessels. The meaning

of these positions is, of course, debateable. Distinctions between objects placed within the coffin, those placed beside it in the grave, and those placed on the top of the coffin, may indicate differences of meaning but may also simply reflect sequences of action in the funeral process.

People

The greatest advance in the study of Late Roman burial in Britain in the last 20 years or so has come through improvements in the analysis of human remains themselves. This is not the primary focus of the present review but is of fundamental importance and the recent specialist literature is very extensive and complex. Detailed osteological analysis should be routine.[128] This takes us far beyond basic figures for age, sex, and stature, although accurate identification of these characteristics remains fundamental.[129] An obvious example of the importance of this issue relates to the proportions of male and female burials in cemeteries – significant inequalities in these number having implications for interpretation of the workings of Romano-British society at the level of individual burying communities and more widely.[130] Some earlier work is thought likely to have overestimated numbers of males (who can display more readily recognisable skeletal characteristics): again an example is provided by Lankhills, where Gowland's re-examination of the 1960s–early 1970s assemblage[131] suggested a more equal breakdown of males and females than indicated by the initial assessment of Harman.[132] Here, as in most cemetery populations, the presence of a significant number of adult skeletons that could not be securely assigned to sex means that uncertainties remain but the unassigned are perhaps unlikely to have been heavily dominated by one sex or the other. In this case, at least, a reassessed population of very closely similar numbers of males and females potentially leads to interpretations of that population quite different from ones based on a 6:4 male:female ratio.[133] Nevertheless, it is necessary to be alive to the possibility that cemetery

120   Smith (2018) 268, fig. 6.48.

121   For some urban variations, see Booth *et al.* (2010) 534, table 8.2.

122   Clarke (1979) 377–403.

123   See e.g. Cool (2010).

124   Booth *et al.* (2010) 266.

125   Egging Dinwiddy and Bradley (2011) 165; Farwell and Molleson (1993) 148, pl. 50.

126   E.g. Black (1986) 223; Dungworth (1998) 153.

127   Henig and Booth (2000) 133.

128   For a useful overview of the potential of wide-ranging analyses of human remains in a specifically Romano-British context, and the importance of placing these within a framework of well-informed social theory, see Gowland (2017).

129   With nuanced understanding of the limits of the available techniques, which have seen development and reassessment in recent years; e.g. Samworth and Gowland (2007); Moore (2016) 323.

130   E.g. Davison (2000).

131   Gowland (2002).

132   Booth *et al.* (2010) 346–47.

133   For the problematic assumptions underlying some 20th c. sex interpretations, see e.g. Waldron (2014).

groups, or subgroups within them, might not always contain 'typical' populations, and consider the reasons for this such as the consequences of social construction involved in burial practice.

Amongst the many variables observable in Late Romano-British cemeteries are the spatial patterns relating to the buried population in terms of the most basic characteristics of age and sex. To begin with, the general absence of perinates and very small children from some of these cemeteries is a well-known characteristic. Some cemeteries lack burials of perinates altogether (although in some cases this might be a consequence of the destructive effects of agriculture on graves which were often characteristically very shallow) and their occurrence in settlement contexts has been variously interpreted but presumably reflects perceptions of the personhood of very small children[134] and established traditions of burial of such individuals within settlements rather than elsewhere. Notable groups of neonatal burials occur for example at the villa sites of Barton Court Farm, Oxfordshire[135] and particularly at Hambleden, Buckinghamshire, where interpretation of some 93 infant burials originally excavated before the First World War[136] has been much disputed. Some of these have been claimed as providing evidence for infanticide,[137] while the argument that there is no clear case for this practice in Roman Britain has been put by Gowland and others.[138] On balance, continuation of a long tradition of burial of neonates in settlement contexts,[139] sometimes in locations within or closely related to structural features,[140] seems much more likely than that a Mediterranean practice became widespread in rural Roman Britain.

In some contexts, however, the spatial distinction between burials of neonates and older individuals is less clear. This is apart from the occasional occurrence of neonates/perinates in graves with adults, in which case it is likely that the mother died in childbirth or very shortly after, for example (amongst numerous others) at Horcott,[141] while a graphic indication of the potential difficulties of childbirth is presented by grave 1014 at Poundbury containing the dismembered remains of a foetus probably removed from the womb by embryotomy.[142] Poundbury is a case where perinates, and other infants under 12 months of age, did form a significant part of the main cemetery population.[143] Out of a total (incomplete) population of over 1,400 individuals, of which the 'main' west-east group amounts to about 1,100 burials, neonates[144] totalled some 132 skeletons out of a total of more than 400 subadults from the cemetery (there are slight numerical discrepancies between some of the neonate and infant totals presented in different tables in the report), occurring in several distinct clusters within the cemetery but not confined to these areas.

The occurrence of neonates as a significant proportion of the cemetery population has been noticed elsewhere in the south-west, for example at Cannington and Bradley Hill, Somerset.[145] The substantial numbers of neonates in some of these cemeteries does seem to distinguish them from many of the sites mentioned above. The differences may be in part a chronological trend, the cemeteries with greater numbers of neonates (and slightly older infants – see below) being on the whole later in date than the majority, suggesting development of practice from the widespread tradition of burial of neonates in settlement contexts. Alternatively, they may suggest a different attitude to the burial of neonates and very small children from what has been discussed hitherto, a characteristic that has been noted as one of the criteria for identification of potentially Christian cemeteries.[146] The two factors may have been linked but while contrasts are often drawn between cemeteries such as Poundbury on the one hand and Lankhills on the other, the overall percentages of subadults in the two populations are quite similar. Comparison of the numbers for the two main phases of excavation at Lankhills[147] shows significant differences, suggesting that specific spatial factors were at play, as is also seen at Poundbury[148] – in some cases, at least, an apparently 'unbalanced' burial population may simply be a result of the location of the excavated sample.

The trend towards inclusion of small children in certain cemeteries to a much greater extent than in others may extend beyond neonates to encompass burials of infants and young children up to about the age

134   Gowland (2016a) 312; Moore (2016) 325–26.

135   Miles (1986) 15–16 and fiche 4:C8–D1.

136   Cocks (1921).

137   Mays (1993); (2003); Mays and Eyers (2011).

138   Gowland and Chamberlain (2002); Gowland *et al.* (2014); Millett and Gowland (2015); Gowland (2016a) 311–12.

139   Moore (2016) 325–26.

140   The exact significance of which is debated, see e.g. Gowland (2016a) 312; Moore (2009); (2016) 326; Scott (1991).

141   Hayden *et al.* (2017) 166–67, 174–75, 329, graves 463 and 3313.

142   Farwell and Molleson (1993) 15–16, pl. 9, 24 fig. 15.

143   However, a comparative study showed that the percentage of perinates was slightly lower than in other major urban cemeteries in the sample (Rohnbogner and Lewis (2017) 212).

144   These are assigned to several clearly distinguished categories – Farwell and Molleson (1993) 171–76, see 173, table 31.

145   Rahtz *et al.* (2000) 142–43; for Bradley Hill, see Leech (1981) and for recent radiocarbon dates from there, Gerrard (2011).

146   E.g. Woodward (1993) 236–37.

147   Booth *et al.* (2010) 348, tables 5.10 and 5.11.

148   Farwell and Molleson (1993) fig. E.

of 5. Infants, up to the age of 12 months, were a cohort well-represented at Poundbury,[149] and older children were also present in some numbers.[150] Generally, a high proportion of subadults in cemetery populations will be a closer reflection of a representative overall mortality curve.

Once the more problematic early years of childhood were passed, numbers of deaths were reduced for a time – Rohnbogner and Lewis's analysis,[151] for example, showing the lowest percentages of pre-adult mortality in the middle teenage group. Significant stages in the life course may be indicated by some grave good assemblages – particularly associated with probable young females but the relevant evidence shows great variability from one site to another.[152] A very high incidence of grave goods associated with adolescents is seen at Lankhills, for example, and age-related patterning was characteristic of some (but not all) grave good types there,[153] and in some cases may reflect an association with a sense of loss through *mors immatura*,[154] perhaps in relation to loss of child-bearing potential. In this context, it is notable that recent work suggests that Romano-British females would probably not have been able to bear children until their late teens,[155] a picture that is consistent with other evidence from Britain.[156] The unusual character of grave good representation at Lankhills compared to some other urban cemeteries is clear,[157] and in these cases, and in the majority of rural cemeteries, objects rarely seem to have been used to indicate key life course stages.

Assessment of patterns of age at death is complicated by issues concerning aging techniques (see above) and the influence that a few sites that may have been atypical for one reason and another perhaps had on more general trends.[158] The RRS analysis shows that amongst the young adults from rural burial contexts women were more common than men, and despite the possibility that ratios were skewed as a result of migration of young males for work purposes,[159] the more likely explanation surely relates to the problems associated with child-bearing. For the three RRS regions for which meaningful Late Roman data were recovered (albeit in rather broad age ranges), the patterns were roughly similar: for age groups 18–25, 26–45 and >45, the (rounded) percentages of the total recorded Late Roman population were 8%, 22%, and 9% (East), 1%, 5%, and 3% (South, where approximately 65% of the burials recorded for this period were of perinates and infants up to 1 year old), and 11%, 24%, and 16% (Central Belt).[160] In all cases but particularly in the East, a significant proportion of adult burials could not be assigned to an age bracket. Even in the Central Belt, with much the largest body of data, the overall numbers are such that relative percentages of sexed adults in relation to rural settlement category (i.e. potentially indicating different mortality patterns depending on the type of site with which the deceased were associated) are not likely to have been very meaningful. As already noted, females significantly outnumber males in the 18–25 age group in all regions, and in the East in the over 45 age bracket, whereas males are more numerous in other groups.

These broad-brush patterns form a background against which individual cemetery groups can be assessed;[161] the rounded percentages of the three age categories used above were 6%, 35%, and 48% but detailed comparisons are often difficult because of the different age ranges used in osteological recording of site assemblages. This can be seen in discussion of three key urban sites, Lankhills, Poundbury and Colchester Butt Road.[162] At the last of these a very substantial proportion of adults were assigned to a broad 30–50 year old age range, with about 16% of the aged adults belonging to an 'over 50' category. At both Poundbury and Lankhills, a higher proportion of the adults were defined as 'older', and at both sites some were identified as 'much older' – over 60 at Lankhills, where these individuals amounted to almost 20% of all the (143) aged adults from the OA excavations of 2000–2005, and over 65 at Poundbury, where 5.6% of aged adults were assigned to this age bracket. In the western cemetery of Cirencester, almost 14% of all the aged adults were assigned to the 'over 45' category.[163]

Identification of a specific 'much older adult' (i.e. *ca.* 60+) age category is therefore uncommon in Romano-British cemeteries (and has not been used in the RRS analysis). It may be particularly dependent on good skeletal preservation of elements such as the pubic symphysis (assessment of dental attrition, the most widely used aging methodology, does not allow precision above the threshold of about 45 years). The

149 Farwell and Molleson (1993) 174–76.
150 Poundbury appears to be in some respects not an entirely representative cemetery population, see e.g. Rohnbogner and Lewis (2017); Rohnbogner (2017) 224.
151 Rohnbogner and Lewis (2017) 212.
152 Moore (2016) 326–29.
153 Booth *et al.* (2010) 307.
154 See also Moore (2016) 327–28.
155 Arthur *et al.* (2016); Gowland (2017) 183.
156 Allason-Jones (2004) 281.
157 E.g. Moore (2016) 327, fig. 16.1; Keegan (2002).
158 E.g. Rohnbogner (2017) 333.
159 Rohnbogner (2017) 334.

160 Rohnbogner (2017) 292–94, figs. 7.6, 7.8 and 7.10.
161 For example, at Horcott (Hayden *et al.* (2017) 329.
162 Booth *et al.* (2010) 350–53.
163 Holbrook *et al.* (2017) 106.

status of the oldest members of the population may be uncertain.[164] In some cases older adults are apparently distinguished by particular grave goods, one of the more obvious associations being that of combs with older women, although this association was also seen occasionally with males as well.[165] The association is the more notable when seen in cemeteries where grave goods are very scarce.[166] The numbers of Romano-Britons of this 'much older' category are unknown. Tombstones from lowland (i.e. essentially non-military) sites in Britain (all earlier than our period) record occasional individuals of 70 years and more; one lady, from Lincoln,[167] was exceptionally recorded as 90 years of age, although rounding of ages and related issues are well known.[168] However, as Gowland has noted, "The notion that elder members of past societies were uniformly treated with respect is not consistent with the evidence from Roman Britain".[169]

Modern osteological analysis, now routine, allows detailed consideration of a whole range of aspects of health and development and the social implications that can be drawn from such data, some already alluded to. Macroscopic analyses are now complemented by further examination of health and origin, through examination of (inter alia) carbon and nitrogen isotopes and strontium, oxygen and, (less commonly) lead isotopes respectively.

Origins

Origins are considered here in terms of the biological and scientific evidence. They can be directly related to ethnicity but the latter is now widely seen as much as a social construct as a matter of 'race'.[170] In the specific context of Late Antiquity, these issues have generated a huge literature, mostly based around interpretations of the artefactual evidence from burials.[171] Origins are most frequently considered through analysis of strontium and oxygen isotopes, best used in combination but physical characteristics of the skull can be indicative of ancestry, although the problems associated with craniometric studies are well known.[172] Ideally, the osteological data will be combined with isotope analysis.[173] A rare osteological indicator of non-local origins is seen at

Poundbury, where the identification of thalassaemia (a genetic anaemia strongly linked to Mediterranean communities) in two children suggests that these were probably the offspring of immigrant parents.[174]

In a Late Roman context, isotopic analyses have tended to concentrate on high profile sites or specific examples, often initially triggered by the identification of unusual graves on the basis of artefact and other evidence and with a particular focus on elucidation of individual origins.[175] Attention has tended to focus on a small number of individuals who are demonstrably of non-British origin but strontium and oxygen isotopes in combination can be useful for indicating non-local origin. At Lankhills analysis of 40 individuals suggested that 21 of these were probably from Winchester or surrounding areas and a further 8 from (probably various) more distant parts of Britain. Of the remaining 11, characterised as incomers, 10 were from warmer areas and one from a colder area, probably in central Europe, although the data does not allow specific areas of origin to be assigned. The analysis demonstrated conclusively that there was no correlation between broad areas of origin as indicated by the isotopes and the local/Pannonian distinctions identified by Clarke[176] based on characteristics of the grave assemblages.[177]

Application of this approach in a rural context has been less common but appears to have produced interesting results at Wasperton, Warwickshire, where three Late Roman individuals had isotopic signatures thought to suggest origins in the western Mediterranean area.[178] More recently, advances in aDNA technology have allowed this analysis to be deployed, not only in relation to questions of origins but also to consider sex and physical characteristics, and potentially identify a variety of pathogens.[179]

Carbon and nitrogen isotopes primarily provide information about diet (see below) but can be informative about origin if they reveal atypical dietary characteristics. A good example, from near Gravesend, Kent is from an unusual 4th c. sequence amongst a group of north-west/south-east aligned burials. One grave contained a large (1.9 m long) nailed coffin with an adult probable male. The grave was cut by a secondary burial

164   E.g. Moore (2016) 330–31.
165   E.g. Booth *et al.* (2010) 307.
166   For example, at Queenford Farm, Dorchester-on-Thames: Chambers (1987) 45.
167   *RIB* 263.
168   E.g. Revell (2005).
169   Gowland (2017) 184; see further Gowland (2016b).
170   See, concisely, Ivleva (2016) 246–47.
171   E.g. Theuws (2009) amongst many examples.
172   E.g. Gowland (2017) 184–85.
173   Gowland (2017) 184–85.

174   Lewis (2012).
175   Amongst numerous examples, see e.g. Eckardt *et al.* (2009); Chenery and Evans (2012); Shaw *et al.* (2016); more generally Eckardt (2010); Eckardt *et al.* (2014).
176   Clarke (1979) 377–403.
177   Booth *et al.* (2010) 427–28; see above.
178   Montgomery *et al.* (2009).
179   For a limited, localised study integrating these analyses with isotopic and conventional osteological techniques, see Redfern *et al.* (2017).

of another adult male with nailed footwear; remains of the first adult, also including nailed footwear, were then redeposited above those of the second in a condition suggesting that when recut, the first burial had not been in place very long and that it was important for the disturbed remains to be re-associated with those of the second burial. A 1–2-year-old infant in the same grave lay to one side of the coffin position but it is not clear if it was originally associated with the first or the second adult.[180] The second adult had notably high carbon isotope levels, which on further analysis suggested a diet based on C4 cereals (such as millet), which are not native to Britain, and therefore most probably an origin for this individual in an area such as (for example) northern Italy.[181]

Health

One consequence of the greater mobility of individuals in Roman Britain might have been to increase the spread of infectious diseases. Many of these will not have registered as signatures in the skeleton but tuberculosis and leprosy are amongst those that did occur. While the former probably originated in rural communities through contact with cattle, the latter was presumably an introduction into Britain. Recent analysis of individuals from a number of cemeteries with isotope data indicating mobility showed "significant differences between migrant and local populations" in a number of respects, suggesting that "migrants transformed patterns of disease in the Romano-British period and, combined with the changes to settlement patterns and environment, created new disease risks for both groups."[182]

The implications of such analyses and potential for further work examining them are evident. Already, however, the quantity of data now available allows increasingly wide ranging analyses of patterns of health across whole sections of the Romano-British population, marking significant advances on the important overview presented by Roberts and Cox,[183] which, although encompassing a total of 5,716 individuals (of all dates within the Roman period), was only based on 52 sites.[184] The broadest recent review has considered rural populations across the Roman period in Britain.[185] In a similarly diachronic view of urban and rural differences, Redfern *et al.* (2015) focus on Dorset. By contrast, Pitts and Griffin (2012) concentrate specifically on the Late

Roman period and integrate osteological and artefactual data from a range of site types in central and southern England.

Consideration of diet and nutrition is fundamental to issues of health in Later Roman Britain and can be approached through the physical characteristics of the skeleton which may reveal particular deficiencies, and also from the evidence of carbon and nitrogen isotopes.[186] Such data can also be used to examine questions such as the age of weaning and other aspects of breast-feeding.[187] Isotope studies relevant to the region covered by the present review tend to be based on key urban assemblages such as Poundbury,[188] Cirencester,[189] and Lankhills,[190] while rural data comes, for example, from Gloucestershire.[191] The broad picture that emerges from these studies is that, predictably, there were notable dietary differences between urban and rural populations. Carbon isotope levels, which are more consistently enhanced in most urban groups[192] suggest a more varied urban diet (supported, of course, by palaeobotanical evidence), with greater access to marine resources such as fish, although the real extent of consumption of the latter continues to be debated – low levels of fish consumption in the countryside probably owed much to cultural factors. Rural populations show considerable variation in the extent of carbon enhancement, for example at Horcott, while at the same site low levels of $\delta^{15}N$ were correlated with rites such as prone burial.[193] Horcott evidence also showed that it may be possible for changes in diet to be identified in the same individual when different bones are sampled.[194]

An obvious correlate of dietary quality (although also affected by other factors) is stature. A reduction in average adult height compared to preceding and succeeding periods has been demonstrated for Dorset by Redfern and DeWitte (2011), although whether the greater height of early post-Roman populations[195] might also reflect in part the arrival of an immigrant population may also need to be considered.[196]

Beyond the general questions of diet, there is now a very large body of osteological evidence for physical

180   Allen *et al.* (2012) 413–14.
181   Pollard *et al.* (2011).
182   Redfern *et al.* (2018).
183   Roberts and Cox (2003) 107–163.
184   Roberts and Cox (2003) 108.
185   Rohnbogner (2018).

186   Müldner (2013) for a useful summary, with references.
187   E.g. Fuller *et al.* (2006).
188   Richards *et al.* (1998).
189   Cummings (2008); for summary, Cummings (2009).
190   Cummings and Hedges (2010).
191   Cheung *et al.* (2012).
192   Müldner (2013).
193   See above; Hayden *et al.* (2017) 154.
194   Hayden *et al.* (2017) 155.
195   See e.g. Booth *et al.* (2007) 162–63 and 174–75 for the Upper Thames Valley region.
196   See Roberts and Cox (2003) 195.

health in terms of diseases (although many will not have had identifiable impacts on the skeletal remains, while on the other hand the aetiology of some skeletal conditions may be uncertain or multi-factoral), degenerative conditions and trauma which can only be summarised very superficially here. Aspects of the health of children have received particular attention in recent studies,[197] and while these are mostly diachronic across the Roman period, the greater dominance of inhumation burial in the Later Roman period means that much of this evidence is of direct relevance here. Of these studies, the most wide-ranging for Britain is that of Rohnbogner (2017), with a dataset that excludes the distinctive site of Poundbury (see above), already the subject of a specific study by Lewis (2010) and subsequently compared more widely using many of the data from the other paper.[198]

Rohnbogner and Lewis related aspects of children's health to the types of settlement with which they were associated, concluding that poor health was common and that children from all site types were affected by metabolic disease, hematopoietic (blood-system related) disturbances, and infection.[199] Diseases related to living environment, such as tuberculosis and vitamin D deficiency, were found in urban contexts but even the former was not exclusive to urban contexts. Vitamin C deficiency and *cribra orbitalia*, for example, affected rural children at higher rates.

Some of the key aspects of the most recent synthesis of evidence for the physical character of the (adult) rural population as recorded for the RRS project are summarised graphically by Rohnbogner[200] where they are compared with a single urban group, from Lankhills.[201]

As already noted in relation to children, conditions such as *cribra orbitalia*, indicative of iron deficiency and anaemia in childhood, is fairly well-represented in adults. Further indications of early childhood stress, non-specific but perhaps caused by fever or malnutrition, were represented by dental enamel hypoplasia which affected almost 11% of the rural population, although enamel hypoplasia and *cribra orbitalia* were twice as common at Lankhills. Other conditions which are likely to reflect the immediate environment include sinusitis, which was rare in the countryside but affected

almost 12% of individuals at Lankhills. Other differences were less marked but cases of tuberculosis and even of leprosy were occasionally encountered in rural contexts (the former affecting 1% of the population) but absent in the Lankhills adults.

Dental disease was widespread, with calculus and caries recorded in just over a quarter of the rural population and ante-mortem tooth loss in about 20%. The corresponding figures for Lankhills were rather higher but these differences perhaps reflect greater longevity in this population rather than (or as well as) dietary and other factors affecting teeth. Be that as it may, joint degeneration (usually age-related), principally in the spine, was less common at Lankhills than in the rural populations (spinal joint degeneration occurring in just over a quarter of the latter). Conversely, however, Schmorl's nodes, indicative of spinal stress, were almost twice as common at Lankhills as in the rural populations,[202] for reasons which are not clear.

Trauma of various kinds was inevitably evidenced in a significant proportion of the rural adult population (12%), although less common than at Lankhills. Much of this was represented by fractures which, like degenerative joint disease, will have been a direct consequence of individual's lives involving heavy physical labour, principally in agriculture. Unsurprisingly, fractures were more common in males than females, although in the case of joint disease, there was variation in the patterns affecting men and women depending on the joint involved but also from region to region within southern Britain.[203] Trauma – principally in the form of healed fractures – was usually most common in the ribs but lower limbs, shoulders, hands, and spines were all affected. Some fractures, and more specifically sharp force trauma, are indicative of inter-personal violence.

Society

Burial evidence provides insights into Romano-British society in a variety of ways. These include consideration of location of cemeteries and individual burials and their relationships one to another and to associated settlements. Details of burial rites and grave furnishing as discussed above shed light on the burying communities, their social frames of reference and potentially, although much more problematic, on aspects of belief systems and attitudes to the afterlife. The skeletons themselves provide direct evidence of life expectancy, health and other aspects of living conditions.

197   Redfern and Gowland (2012).
198   Rohnbogner and Lewis (2017).
199   Rohnbogner and Lewis (2017) 222.
200   Rohnbogner (2018) 289, fig. 7.2.
201   Clough and Boyle (2010); while gratifying to the present author it must be pointed out that this is a relatively small sample from what is not necessarily the most representative Late Roman urban cemetery in Britain, with a population suggested overall as being "a group in good health" (Clough and Boyle (2010) 403).

202   Rohnbogner (2018) 290 table 7.3.
203   Rohnbogner (2018) 339.

A key element of the RRS analyses of the rural dead, both from the point of view of the cemeteries[204] and that of the people contained within them[205] is the consideration, even if only in broad terms, of the evidence in relation to the character of associated settlements and to wider geographical distributions. The variety in cemetery size, noted above, is a characteristic of some significance for social organisation. In many cases it is clear enough that burials associated with an individual settlement were of inhabitants of that settlement. In other cases, however, the numbers of burials involved, and/or the lack of a clearly associated settlement context, suggest other arrangements. The settlement context of the NIAB Cambridge cemetery (see above), for example, remains uncertain. At Horcott, the settlement adjacent to the Late Roman settlement saw only low level activity at this time and the cemetery itself, with some 61 burials, is very likely to have served a wider rural estate of which the identified settlement was but one small component.[206] Such an arrangement might help to explain the distinct shortage of burials associated with individual farmstead sites,[207] but the more likely conclusion drawn from that lack is that even in the Late Roman period interment was not a universal practice, only now could it "… start to be considered as a 'normative' funerary rite, and even then this was mostly restricted to some of the larger complex farmsteads, villas and nucleated settlements, paralleling the situation at larger Roman towns …"[208] Another important outcome of the RRS study is the demonstration that a disproportionate number of burials in Late Roman Britain come from the 'Central Belt' region defined by that project. This region alone accounts for just over two thirds (some 3,340 burials) of all those from the RRS regions covered by the present review: the South and East regions contribute roughly 23% and 8% respectively, with negligible numbers from the others.[209] The reasons for the concentration of burials in the Central Belt may be complex (perhaps reflecting inter alia the sheer volume of archaeological work in this area) but an important factor may be a relationship with the extensification of agriculture that is such a notable feature of the region at this time. It is possible that rural societies here were particularly heavily exploited and controlled,[210] with the implication that an increased level of provision and

organisation of cemeteries was one aspect of that control. Such 'big picture' interpretation is not inconsistent with evidence for poor health in rural communities and emphasises the importance of the burial evidence for understanding of wide social and economic trends.

That overall the rural population experienced poorer health than their urban counterparts is an important conclusion from several of the wider studies (see above) and contrasts with a more typical view of urban centres as net consumers of population (as a result of poorer living conditions and consequent higher mortality rates); it has far-reaching implications. Equally, the idea that some Late Roman 'urban' cemeteries included burials of individuals drawn from surrounding rural settlements, suggested some time ago in relation to Poundbury,[211] remains uncertain, although it may receive some support from the osteological evidence.[212] There is a distinction to be drawn between urban cemeteries that routinely serviced rural settlements in their hinterland and those that contained burials of individuals of rural origin who subsequently moved to the town. This issue is but one aspect of the social complexity to be expected in urban cemeteries, although not always easily observed there. It is potentially also present in rural contexts, where the presence of scattered small groups of burials can plausibly (but rarely demonstrably) be related to the actions of individual family units. Related aspects could include the decisions made about the location of cemeteries in relation to local landscapes.[213] Consideration of the sorts of individual communities that might have had responsibility for establishing and using particular cemeteries or parts of cemeteries, perhaps obvious enough in some cases but less so in others, can be another useful way of thinking about the diversity of Romano-British society. Religious affiliation might have been one characteristic defining such communities, although direct evidence is lacking except perhaps in relation to Christianity, for which it is much debated, as discussed below. Without very specific evidence "it is impossible to answer questions about belief from archaeological evidence, except in very general terms"[214] and no such attempts will be made here.

The 5th c. and Beyond

The great majority of the burials discussed so far, both demonstrably and by implication, will have been of

---

204   Smith (2018).
205   Rohnbogner (2018).
206   Booth (2017b) 420.
207   Smith (2018) 278.
208   Smith (2018) 278.
209   Smith (2018) 211, table 6.2.
210   Smith (2018) 278.

211   Woodward (1993) 237.
212   E.g. Rohnbogner and Lewis (2017) 221.
213   Booth (2017a) 199–202.
214   Black (1986) 228.

4th c. date. Often the chronology is inferred from association and, given the frequent absence of grave goods,
close dating may not be possible. This is most often the
case in the countryside, and for this reason it is understandable (if disappointing) that the RRS analysis does
not move beyond broad periodisation of rural burial to
consider what evidence there is for its very latest stages.
In many cases this would not necessarily be a problem
were it not for our teleological understanding that perhaps by AD 450 much of 'Roman' Britain would look
greatly different from its appearance in the previous
century. This being the case, it becomes much more
important to be able to date the latest burials and cemeteries as closely as possible in order to understand the
extent to which they continued in a recognisable Late
Roman form after about AD 400 – was the trajectory of
cultural change in burial practice in Britain the same as
that for (apparently) aspects of architecture and material culture, or were there different trends? Amongst
other issues, the evidence for continued use of cemeteries in a traditional manner,[215] particularly in an urban
context, may be potentially important for debates about
questions such as urban survival (town life, as opposed
to life in towns) into the 5th c. More widely, there is the
question of the extent to which the much longer-term
tradition of 'Roman style' inhumation burial in western
Britain represented continuity/evolution of Late Roman
practice or was largely independent of it, and the issue
of whether this development can only be seen within a
framework of Christian practice.

   The forms of Late Roman dating evidence are well
known. They comprise late coins and other closely
datable objects, sequences of burials post-dating earlier well-dated graves, and radiocarbon dates. There
is artefact-based evidence for the survival of at least
some key urban cemeteries at the end of the 4th c. At
Lankhills, Winchester, for example, this is demonstrated
by graves containing coins of the House of Theodosius,
providing a *terminus post quem* of at least AD 388, while
at Kingsholm, Gloucester, the objects associated with
the so-called 'Gloucester Goth' can be dated to the first
half of the 5th c., although a date before *ca.* AD 410 is
suggested for the arrival of their wearer in Britain (but
not necessarily, of course, for his decease and burial).[216]
Comparable evidence can be adduced for individual
burials elsewhere, although the extent to which these
might indicate routine continued use of the cemeteries
in question can always be debated. It is worth pointing

out a potential issue relating to the late Lankhills burials. There is uncertainty over the length of time during
which the Theodosian coins, few of which were probably struck after *ca.* AD 395,[217] remained in circulation
but from the point of view of dating, it makes a considerable difference if coins of this type were placed in
graves in the final decade of the 4th c. or up to (perhaps)
30 years later.[218] For this reason two of the apparently
closely coin-dated graves at Lankhills were included in
the programme of radiocarbon dating for that site but
with the exception of a single cremation burial (not
dated by coins) all the radiocarbon dates from this site
returned calibrated ranges broadly from the mid-3rd to
the end of the 4th c.,[219] a somewhat unexpected and still
unexplained outcome.[220]

Central England

Elsewhere in central England an important sequence of
radiocarbon dates has been obtained from Dorchester-
on-Thames, 11 dates from one of the large cemeteries
(Queenford Farm) associated with the small town and 5
from an Early Anglo-Saxon cemetery (Berinsfield) barely
500 m north of it.[221] The calibrated radiocarbon dates
indicate that while burial at the two sites was essentially
sequential, there was "both artefactual and 14C evidence
for a contiguous succession in the first half of the fifth
century". The Berinsfield cemetery "came into use while
the last burials at Queenford Farm were taking place".[222]
At one level, this result is no more than might have been
expected but it is significant from a 'Roman' point of
view in demonstrating fairly clearly what can only be
suggested at sites such as Lankhills (and elsewhere) – a
level of continued use of a major cemetery into the second quarter of the 5th c.

   Cemeteries with direct physical juxtaposition of
'Romano-British' and 'Anglo-Saxon' burials, rather than
the close proximity seen at Dorchester on Thames,
remain very rare. One of the clearest examples is
Wasperton, Warwickshire, where the case for continuity of use through the 4th–6th c. was made on the
basis of detailed analysis of the cemetery stratigraphy –
horizontal as well as vertical – alongside the associated
material culture. Fourteen radiocarbon dates supported
the argument up to a point, although the two main
groups of dates centred some distance apart with little

215   I.e. not just 'random' burials (or indeed unburied corpses)
          in ditches etc. – see e.g. Wacher (1995) 322 and 417 for this
          scenario.
216   Ager (2012).

217   Moorhead and Walton (2014) 102.
218   Moorhead and Walton (2014) 112–13.
219   Booth *et al.* (2010) 450–52.
220   Booth *et al.* (2010) 455; see also Gerrard (2015a).
221   Hills and O'Connell (2009).
222   Hills and O'Connell (2009) 11.

clear overlap,[223] with the key point of 'culture change' argued on this basis to lie about AD 480.[224] Despite this possible chronological disjuncture, however, it seems perverse to suggest that the spatial association of burials of Romano-British and Anglo-Saxon character represents anything other than probably continuous use of the cemetery, whatever other changes occurred. The burials in question were mostly extended inhumations, initially mainly placed within a rectangular enclosure, although 27 "culturally Anglo-Saxon" cremation burials were also recovered, dated from the later 5th c. onwards.[225]

Wasperton remains one of the most striking (and still very rare) examples of this kind of superimposition of traditions, and interpretation of the significance of this sequence is far from straightforward.[226] At sites such as Mucking on the Thames estuary, 'Romano-British' and 'early Anglo-Saxon' cemeteries are physically close but do not show the same direct overlap. A further particularly interesting contrast is seen in the fact that distinctive graves of Late Roman character are found not in the 'Roman' cemeteries but in both Anglo-Saxon cemeteries I and II[227] where they are dated to the early to mid-5th c.[228] and include (but are not confined to) graves with distinctive military equipment, including the famous quoit-brooch style belt set from grave 117 in cemetery I.[229] These associations are suggested as implying "the existence of a terminal Roman settlement phase ... that essentially involved an 'Anglo-Saxon' community".[230] In a broadly similar vein, it is worth noting that the largest single Early Anglo-Saxon cremation cemetery in Britain, at Spong Hill in Norfolk, seems, on the basis of exhaustive analysis, to have its inception immediately after a phase of Romano-British settlement, and its origins are now dated to the first quarter of the 5th c.[231] There is no question of association of Roman and later burials here but the point is that in eastern England, at least, the dating of the earliest phases of Anglo-Saxon cemeteries to the early 5th c. rather than later means that a direct link between Late Roman and Early Anglo-Saxon (settlement and) cemetery chronologies can be seen as inherently plausible rather than remarkable. Sites where these links are particularly

close are therefore very important for consideration of the interactions of the communities involved.

A notable if enigmatic association of burial traditions is seen at Cherry Hinton, Cambridgeshire where a trapezoidal and two approximately square enclosures were associated with a small group of cremation and inhumation burials of 2nd–3rd c. date. Two further cremation burials were of the 4th c. The north-east to south-west alignment of the Roman features was followed precisely by a substantial Early Anglo-Saxon inhumation cemetery of perhaps 128 graves, most lying just north-east of the Roman burial enclosures but some within them. Two graves surrounded by small circular gullies were late in the sequence, which overall is dated provisionally to the later 5th to mid-6th c. A further particularly notable feature is a substantial posthole structure (or pair of structures) on the same alignment as the other features and forming a tight boundary on the north-east side of the complex. An Early Anglo-Saxon date seems almost certain but such a structure is extremely unusual in a funerary context of this date, adding to the overall remarkable nature of the various associations of this site.

In midland England, even close juxtapositions of this kind are rare but radiocarbon dating is important for clarifying uncertain situations. In the upper Thames valley at Horcott, modelled radiocarbon dates for an inhumation cemetery of some 56 graves indicate a mid-3rd to mid-4th c. range (although use of the cemetery into the later 4th c. may be suspected), while a discrete group of 13 graves (notable for containing exclusively burials of women and children) on a different alignment but of distinctly Roman-British character was of early 5th to mid-6th c. date.[232] A close relationship between these two groups in terms of the parent burying community is almost certain but not directly demonstrable because of their slight spatial separation. At Tubney Wood, Oxfordshire a more direct sequence of radiocarbon dated burial from the later 4th c. into the 5th or early 6th is clear[233] and is notable for the use of three small sub-square enclosures in the post-Roman phase.[234]

South-West England

Further west, Late Roman to 'post-Roman' sequences are more common but because of a widespread scarcity (and often total lack) of datable grave goods are particularly dependent upon radiocarbon dating for definition of their chronology. Key sites occur in Somerset and beyond. The classic, and much the largest, example is

---

223   Carver *et al.* (2009) 45–48; 86–87.
224   Carver *et al.* (2009) 116.
225   Carver *et al.* (2009) 116.
226   E.g. Harland (2017).
227   For these, see Hirst and Clark (2009).
228   Lucy and Evans (2016) 436–39.
229   Hirst and Clark (2009) 366–68; for quoit brooch style metal-work, see now Swift (2019).
230   Lucy and Evans (2016) 438–39.
231   Hills and Lucy (2013) 229.

232   Hayden *et al.* (2017) 22–29 for the radiocarbon chronology.
233   Simmonds *et al.* (2011).
234   See also Booth (2017) 189–91 and further below.

Cannington,[235] with perhaps as many as 542 excavated individuals[236] buried on a broadly west-east alignment on the western side of a small hill with a circular summit structure, of uncertain purpose (possibly a shrine[237]) but probably of Late Roman date, forming a focal feature towards the eastern margin of burial and a small mound over a slab-marked grave a little to the south forming another important focal feature.[238] It is clear that the cemetery was originally much larger than the excavated sample.[239] The overall chronological range is somewhat uncertain but on balance "may be summed up as late Roman to late seventh/eighth centuries AD."[240]

The incompleteness of the Cannington cemetery presents problems for wider interpretation, and the general (and complex) issues relating to a whole class of cemeteries with broadly comparable characteristics are beyond the scope of this paper. The occurrence in this region of other cemeteries in hilltop locations with relationships to shrine sites is notable, however. It is seen for example at Henley Wood, Somerset, where some 75 burials probably represent most of the cemetery, dated broadly to the 5th–7th c.,[241] with burial potentially starting early in the 5th c. (if not earlier) but considered not to have been contemporary with the use of the latest of the sequence of Romano-Celtic temples, itself dated after AD 367–375.[242]

More recent excavations (both Cannington and Henley Wood were dug in the 1960s) of these generally poorly dated west-east aligned inhumation cemeteries include a site near Kenn, Devon,[243] where 111 graves (of which some 45 were excavated) were part of a larger cemetery.[244] A good example is seen at Tolpuddle Ball, Dorset. Here, there were 50 graves, forming a complete or very nearly complete unenclosed cemetery, mostly arranged in north-south rows on a west-east axis, and with only a single case of intercutting of the graves. Two graves had possible evidence for a timber coffin (based on differential fills – nails were absent) and two others contained possible packing stones for coffins. In the complete absence of grave goods, the chronology is entirely dependent upon a series of 5 radiocarbon

dates. Three produced calibrated ranges (95% confidence level) of broadly mid-6th to mid-7th c. date, while a fourth was entirely confined within the 7th c. The fifth date, however, had a significantly earlier range of AD 250–450. This came from a burial in a north-south row on a slightly different alignment from the others and interpreted as probably the earliest component of the cemetery, which it is suggested was probably in continuous use from about AD 400 to 700.[245] A further cemetery of very similar character and size to Tolpuddle Ball, comprising 51 graves, was excavated at Filton, near Bristol in 2005.[246] The graves, many poorly preserved, were mostly arranged in rows with a predominant WNW-ESE alignment but with some variation, assigned to 9 separate groups. The largest of these, group 2, consisted of 24 graves arranged around a central 'special' burial of a young adult female distinguished inter alia by very unusual treatment of the lower leg bones. Possible stone lining was noted in one grave but evidence for coffins and grave goods was otherwise absent.

There is no known settlement context for the Filton cemetery. The Tolpuddle Ball cemetery lay close to a 2nd–4th c. Romano-British farmstead but its Late Roman and post-Roman settlement context is uncertain.[247] The cemetery at Kenn may have originated in the Late Roman period, perhaps associated with a nearby high-status settlement of 4th c. date.[248] Cannington and Henley Wood, however, were both most probably associated with nearby hillforts where 'post-Roman' occupation is attested.[249] The extent to which burial continued after the end of the 4th c. in association with established nucleated Roman settlements may be a different question. Remaining in the south-west, Dorchester (Dorset) is the obvious focus, and particularly the cemeteries of Poundbury which, as has been pointed out[250] have not had the benefit of a radiocarbon dating programme, although radiocarbon dates on material from "corn drying ovens" in the settlement which perhaps overlapped the late use of the burial ground "place their use in the fifth to sixth century".[251] The cemetery chronology is therefore bounded by understanding of the Late Roman grave goods and the overall site sequence – how far this might be extended into the earlier 5th c. is a matter of speculation.[252] At the roadside settlement of Shepton Mallet, 30 inhumation burials were found in three

---

235   Rahtz *et al.* (2000).
236   Rahtz *et al.* (2000) 132.
237   Rahtz *et al.* (2000) 51.
238   Rahtz *et al.* (2000) 51–57; the importance of these and other features in the "accumulation of memories" by local communities is reemphasised by Williams (2006) 211–14.
239   Rahtz *et al.* (2000) 23–26.
240   Rahtz *et al.* (2000) 392.
241   Watts and Leach (1996) 69.
242   Watts and Leach (1996) 69.
243   Weddell (2000).
244   For some analogous sites, see Webster (2004).

245   Hearne and Birbeck (1999) 227.
246   Cullen *et al.* (2006).
247   Hearne and Birbeck (1999) 230–31.
248   Weddell (2000).
249   For caution on this point, Rahtz *et al.* (2000) 31.
250   Hearne and Birbeck (1999) 230.
251   Sparey-Green (2004) 109; see also Eagles (2018) 32.
252   But see Sparey-Green (2004) 106–107.

discrete areas and a further 15 were more scattered. Some 25 graves were assigned to period 5, for which a later 4th to 7th c. date range is given.[253] Only 5 burials have radiocarbon dates, mostly with rather wide calibrated ranges. One of these is firmly within the Roman period but the others include one spanning the late 3rd–late 6th c. and two with early 5th–late 7th/late 8th c. ranges, while the fifth date is later still.[254] Differences of burial style perhaps suggest different dates within the wide radiocarbon range but this is not certain. Further west, at Ipplepen, Devon, a 'post-Roman' cemetery with at least 30 graves is closely associated with a Roman roadside settlement (itself a significant novelty in this part of Britain) or, perhaps more realistically, with a successor of that settlement. As elsewhere, the graves were arranged in rows but with some intercutting.[255]

Overall, the sites discussed in this section have significant features in common. The broad approach to burial is that of mainstream Late Roman practice – extended supine inhumation being the dominant tradition. The alignment is usually (at least approximately) west-east but some of the burial group at Shepton Mallet, for example, retained a north-south alignment that was common in many 4th c. cemeteries in central England. Careful organisation of the cemetery is most obvious at Tolpuddle Ball but elements of rows of comparably aligned burials can be found almost anywhere. Burials can be tightly juxtaposed but frequent intercutting is not often seen, except perhaps in cases of superposition of burials observed at Cannington but the significance of this is uncertain and it may have been a deliberate practice involving members of the same family. If so, this has implications for the nature of memory and perhaps the marking of individual graves. Evidence for use of coffins is much less common than earlier, for example being effectively absent at Cannington, by contrast with Poundbury where approximately 90% of burials in the main Late Roman cemetery were in coffins,[256] although dated 'post-Roman' examples of lead lining are present at Horcott and Shepton Mallet. Partial or complete stone lining of graves, sometimes considered a specifically post-Roman practice in the south-west, is common but by no means universal – relatively common at Henley Wood, for example but rare at Cannington, and effectively absent at Tolpuddle Ball. Grave goods are universally scarce.

A Late/post-Roman feature lacking from the sites just mentioned but encountered elsewhere is the use of small enclosures defining either a single grave or a small subset within a larger cemetery. The linear feature can define a complete rectangle or have an opening in the east side. Enclosures of this type have been usefully reviewed by Webster (2004) but in the specific context of their occurrence in south-western cemeteries for which 5th–7th c. date ranges were suggested,[257] although Lankhills and Poundbury were suggested as providing Late Roman models for the origin of the feature type.[258] While it is clear that distinctive features such as the presence of these enclosures and the use of stone lining in some graves are particularly characteristic of the 5th c. and later cemeteries of the south-west, there is increasing evidence that further east these features were more common than has been appreciated. In any case, the relatively frequent occurrence of graves with various forms of cist-like structure or other stone lining, many of 4th c. date, was discussed by Philpott,[259] who indicated a fairly clear correlation of their distribution with the geology of the limestone belt of central England, a point underlined by more recent work.[260] Notable examples in the English midlands include Bletsoe, Bedfordshire[261] and much more recently a site at Bourton-on-the-Water, Gloucestershire[262] already mentioned. At Lynch Farm, near Peterborough,[263] recent radiocarbon results suggest a 4th c. date for the tradition.[264] Curiously, Smith, in noting the occurrence of cist burials in the RRS central belt, suggests that these may indicate "possible population movement from areas further west or north",[265] and potentially links this with the occurrence of 'flexed' burials in the same part of the central belt in the Later Roman period, with a similar explanation.[266] This seems a rather retrograde step in interpretative terms and fails to convince. However, it is of interest that at Bancroft, the graves of 4 adults and 4 subadults, aligned perpendicular to a north-south enclosure ditch dug between an earlier Roman temple-mausoleum (mentioned above) and a 4th c. circular shrine to the west, were mostly lined with a variety of stone derived from the demolished temple-mausoleum structure. Two of these burials produced early 5th c. radiocarbon dates and the group as a

253   Leach with Evans (2001) 14.
254   Leach with Evans (2001) 288, table 43.
255   Chapman et al. (2016) 346.
256   For selected comparative Late Roman data, see Booth et al. (2010) 534, table 8.2.

257   Webster (2004) 74.
258   Webster (2004) 78.
259   Philpott (1991) 61–66.
260   See e.g. Smith (2018) 258, fig. 6.40.
261   Dawson (1994).
262   Hart et al. (2016).
263   Jones (1975).
264   Gerrard (2015b).
265   Smith (2018) 259.
266   Smith (2018) 230.

whole was discussed in terms of the south-western traditions considered by Rahtz,[267] although this presumably reflects a lack of regional comparanda at the time of publication.

Graves in small rectilinear enclosures are also found at a variety of Late Roman contexts across central England beyond the limited urban examples already referenced. As many as 7 or 8 such enclosures lie within part of a cemetery excavated at Puckeridge, Hertfordshire, in 2011–2014. The dating is broadly 3rd–4th c.[268] with no suggestion of later activity. Also notable is the fact that the enclosures are on varied alignments including north-south as well as east-west. A key site, although a somewhat older excavation, is Kempston, Bedfordshire.[269] Three phases of Late Roman (mid-3rd/4th c.) burial were set within a sub-rectangular ditched enclosure aligned north-east/south-west. The earliest phase involved 44 burials, 21 of which were placed in rows. Alignment on the north-east/south-west axis of the enclosure was fairly common but far from dominant. A second phase of burial, of early-mid 4th c. date, consisted of 22 graves in 4 clusters. In the final phase, some of the 20 graves were in ditched 'enclosures'.[270] Four of these were circular or sub-circular but none was a complete ring. Each contained a single inhumation – three aligned south-west/north-east and one north-east/south-west. Six further enclosures were more nearly square/rectangular but only two were more or less square. All of these may originally have had full circuits but two were incomplete. Each contained a single inhumation, two aligned NNW-SSE, the others *ca.* ENE-WSW. One further length of L-shaped gully might have been a further grave-defining feature, with an ENE-WSW aligned grave in the right place south-west of the surviving corner. This final phase is assigned to the mid-late 4th c. but this is based on conventional dating material and the site sequence, without the benefit of radiocarbon dates. A final example, heading back to the region where this discussion started, is from Bestwall Quarry, Wareham, Dorset. Here, 2 of 5 inhumation burials were placed within small ditched 'enclosures', both set close to the grave cuts and apparently incomplete. All were in wooden coffins and all had nailed footwear but no other grave goods. The dating is "late or final

Roman",[271] and it is notable that two of three associated cremation groups were also dated to the 4th c.

It is argued here that there was a closer connection, as might be expected, between aspects of mainstream Late Roman burial practice in central Britain and what is observed in a number of particularly prominent south-western sites. There has been a tendency for the latter to be seen specifically from a regional viewpoint and at least implicitly (and often explicitly) within a framework of Christian practice. Other dichotomies have also arguably been overstated – particularly the contrast between north-south and west-east burials, as set out for example by Petts,[272] with a broad characterisation of the north-south burial group (Petts' group 2) as artefact-rich and including prone and decapitated burials, while the west-east group differs in all these aspects. These differences do exist but they do so on a continuum, rather than being absolute in every case. Moreover, interpretation of their significance remains questionable.[273] Some of the cases mentioned above make it clear that in the 4th c. the basic features which are thought of as specifically characterising 'post-Roman' Christian burials in the south-west can all be found further east, particularly in central England, and it is notable that the particular prominence of some of these features in the RRS 'Central Belt' is independently identified by Petts in the western part of this area "in some of the areas of the province of Britannia Prima which had been most heavily Romanised in the 3rd and 4th centuries".[274] The primary characteristics are west-east supine body positions and a scarcity (sometimes total absence) of grave goods. More specific elements include the use of slab lined graves and the occurrence of ditched enclosures, usually defining individual graves. These features were not unique to the south-west.

The most important issues here appear to relate to the chronology of the late cemeteries of the south-west, and to the question of Christian associations. With regard to chronology, there seem to be enough points of contact with 4th c. practice in the central belt, in particular, to negate a claim that the south-western west-east inhumation cemeteries were effectively a 'post-Roman' phenomenon. They are surely genuinely late antique. It remains true that the majority of the radiocarbon dates available for these cemeteries place them in the 5th–7th c., and that they were particularly prominent in this period is undeniable. That they apparently only emerge at the point when diocese-wide Roman

---

267 Williams and Zeepvat (1994) 115–41, 592 for the radiocarbon dates.

268 The detailed chronology of the site is not worked out in the assessment report; PCA (2014).

269 Dawson (2004).

270 Dawson (2004) 226.

271 Ladle (2012) 39.

272 E.g. Petts (2004) 77–81.

273 E.g. Quensel-von-Kalben 2000, 228–29.

274 Petts (2004) 81.

administration in Britain had collapsed, however, seems very curious (and indeed fundamentally implausible since most of the area in question was as firmly embedded in the mainstream of Late Roman Britain as areas further east). Much more work is needed on the chronology of these cemeteries but the difficulties of the radiocarbon calibration curve for this period may hinder rapid progress.

The question of the extent of Christianisation, and the fundamental issue of the identification of Christian burials, is the elephant in the room. The most recent short survey of the subject concludes judiciously:

> The intractable nature of the evidence for Roman Christianity in Britain means that there is very little consensus on its extent during the fourth century. The success or otherwise of the Romano-British church has important implications for understanding the growth of Christianity in western and northern Britain in the fifth and sixth centuries.[275]

Foci of scholarly interest on related questions have included the nature of, and mechanisms behind, the development of post-Roman Christian epigraphy.[276] The well-known documentary evidence for the 4th and 5th c. tells us about institutional connections which inevitably have an urban focus, while unequivocal structural evidence is relatively scarce. In this circumstance, the evidence of burial could make a fundamental contribution to understanding but it is in fact as problematic as the other categories of evidence. The difficulties, already mentioned, with simple assumptions about the identification of Christian burials on the basis of orientation and other specific characteristics were summarised by Thomas.[277] Subsequent writers[278] attempted a refined definition of criteria that might be used to distinguish Christian and 'pagan' burials. This was important in encouraging systematic consideration of burial characteristics but involved a crucial (and longstanding) assumption, that in the 4th c. there were specifically Christian locations and modes of burial which would allow them to be identified in contradistinction to other practices. Insofar as 'Christian' burial practice existed, would it necessarily have taken physical, and therefore archaeologically identifiable, forms that distinguished it from the burial practices of non-Christian communities, with the overall potential for diversity that those involved? In this connection it should be noted that some of the particular characteristics of sub-adult health noted at Poundbury, and considered to be atypical, have been categorised as "non-local cultural habits"[279] and potentially linked to aspects of specifically Christian dietary practice.[280] If this association can be securely established, it offers a potentially useful line of investigation of the question contrasting with approaches based on documentary evidence.

On the question of the existence of Christian cemeteries in the 4th c., however, it has been argued that "the texts have, for the most part, been sought out to account for an institution whose existence was presupposed."[281] It can be argued that much of the archaeological evidence has been approached similarly, despite which the view that Christian cemeteries can be identified on archaeological criteria is accepted by many.[282] Continental evidence, however, suggests that a distinctively Christian burial rite is not formalised until as late as the 7th c.[283] On this basis, identification of whole cemeteries as Christian in the 4th and 5th c. must be problematic[284] as has been argued, for example, by the present writer in the context of the Lankhills cemetery.[285] To underline the point one more time, the argument that an absence of grave goods indicates (or at least suggests) Christian burial would require us to believe not only a majority of the Late Romano-British dead in urban contexts were of this persuasion (Lankhills remains exceptional in its proportion of furnished burials) but that this applied in the countryside as well – a situation that is not supported by any other evidence.

This is not, of course, to deny that there were potentially many burials of Christians in Late Roman Britain, although these might have been fewer than imagined if the religion was on the back foot in the later 4th c., as has been suggested by Frend and Watts.[286] Be that as it may, the point is that positive rather than speculative identification of such burials archaeologically will only be possible in rare cases where the evidence of particular structures, tombstones with specific inscriptions or other very special characteristics are present. Beyond this, identifications will have to be tentative and based on understanding of the constraints on interpretation discussed in the works referenced above.

275 Petts (2016) 674.
276 E.g. Handley (2001); Knight (2010); Petts (2014).
277 Thomas (1981) 230–34.
278 E.g. Watts (1991); (1993); Woodward (1993) 236–37.
279 Rohnbogner and Lewis (2017) 222.
280 See also Cool (2006) 238–42.
281 Rebillard (2013) 229.
282 E.g. Petts (2003) 145–49.
283 E.g. Brown (2003) 24–25; Esmonde Cleary (2006); (2013) 164–66.
284 *Inter alia*, Harries (1992) 61; Millett (1995); Rebillard (2009).
285 Booth *et al.* (2010) 464, 470, 521–22.
286 Frend (1992); Watts (1998) 134–36.

Conclusions and Ongoing Themes

The most significant developments in recent work on Romano-British burials stem largely from the great increase in the number of excavated burials resulting from changes in planning legislation implemented in 1990. A majority of these burials are of Late Roman date, although much more routine application of radiocarbon dating is still required in order to clarify and refine the chronology of burial within the conventionally defined Roman period and after AD 400. It is now possible to see more of the complexity of trajectories of development in practice, and significant regional variation in these trajectories. Important is the negative conclusion that while inhumation in various forms was the dominant Late Roman rite, the observed burials probably only represent a part of the total population, and that even in the Late Roman period, formal (archaeologically recoverable) burial might still have been afforded only to certain elements of the overall population. Further development in understanding has come from more nuanced consideration of aspects of burial practice, and particularly the provision of grave goods, in relation to osteological data for sex and age. This shows distinct non-random patterning. Thinking about ethnicity and other aspects of identity, formerly also considered mainly in relation to grave goods, has been transformed by theoretical advances and the application of stable isotope analyses, and the potential of aDNA analyses is just beginning to be realised. Perhaps the most important advances have come from the routine application of detailed osteological analysis of skeletal material, and the combination of these data with the full range of other evidence from individual graves and from cemeteries. Used together these approaches offer huge opportunities for greatly improved understanding of Romano-British society at many levels.

Taking a wider view, both geographically and chronologically, it is important that 'post-Roman' cemetery developments characteristic of south-west England should not be seen as an isolated phenomenon but considered within a framework of developing late antique burial practices having their roots firmly in the 4th c., if not earlier. The role of Christian belief and practice in the evolution of these cemeteries is currently uncertain and under-theorised. If considered carefully within the wider framework, it can be clarified. Both this and a more integrated comparative view of 'Romano-British' and 'Anglo-Saxon' burial practices through the 5th c. and beyond have the potential to make important contributions to understanding of the development of late antique society across the whole of southern Britain.

Acknowledgements

I am grateful to the organisers of the Late Antique Archaeology seminar series for the opportunity to contribute to this volume. Many colleagues, including Martyn Allen, Neil Holbrook, Jacqueline McKinley, Richard Mortimer, Stuart Palmer, Victoria Ridgeway and John Thomas, have provided information that has helped inform this discussion. The anonymous referees' suggestions were helpful. Particular thanks are owed to John Pearce, Jake Weekes, Louise Loe and Thomas Matthews-Boehmer for further suggestions, comments and general inspiration.

Bibliography

Ager B. (2012) "Kingsholm, Gloucester, burial B1 revisited", *Transactions of the Bristol and Gloucestershire Archaeological Society* 130 (2012) 107–113.

Allason-Jones L. (2004) "The family in Roman Britain", in *A Companion to Roman Britain*, ed. M. Todd (Oxford 2004) 273–87.

Allen T., Donnelly M., Hardy A., Hayden C., and Powell K. (2012) *A Road through the Past: Archaeological Discoveries on the A2 Pepperhill to Cobham Road-scheme in Kent* (Oxford Archaeology Monograph 16) (Oxford 2012).

Arthur N., Gowland R. L., and Redfern R. C. (2016) "Coming of age in Roman Britain: skeletal markers of pubertal timing", *American Journal of Physical Anthropology* 159 (2016) 698–713.

Barber B. and Bowsher D. (2000) *The Eastern Cemetery of Roman London, Excavations 1983–1990* (Museum of London Archaeology Service Monograph 4) (London 2000).

Bayliss A., Hines J., Hoilund Nielsen K., McCormac G., and Scull C. (2013) *Anglo-Saxon Graves and Grave Goods of the 6th and 7th centuries AD: a Chronological Framework* (Society for Medieval Archaeology Monograph 33) (London 2013).

Black E. W. (1986) "Romano-British burial customs and religious beliefs in south-east England", *Archaeology* 143 (1986) 201–239.

Booth P. (2001) "Late Roman cemeteries in Oxfordshire: a review", *Oxoniensia* 66 (2001) 13–42.

Booth P. (2014) "A late Roman military burial from the Dyke Hills, Dorchester on Thames, Oxfordshire", *Britannia* 45 (2014) 243–73.

Booth P. (2017a) "Some recent work on Romano-British cemeteries", in *Death as a Process: The Archaeology of the Roman Funeral* (Studies in Funerary Archaeology 12) edd. J. Pearce and J. Weekes (Oxford 2017) 174–207.

Booth P. (2017b) "The Roman and post-Roman cemeteries [Discussion]", in *Horcott Quarry, Fairford and Arkell's Land, Kempsford: Prehistoric, Roman and Anglo-Saxon settlement and burial in the Upper Thames Valley in Gloucestershire* (Oxford Archaeology Thames Valley Landscapes Monograph 40), edd. Hayden C., Early R., Biddulph E., Booth P., Dodd A., Smith A., Laws G., and Welsh K. (Oxford 2017) 411–22.

Booth P., Evans J., and Hiller J. (2001) *Excavations in the Extra-mural Settlement of Roman Alchester, Oxfordshire, 1991* (Oxford Archaeology Monograph 1) (Oxford 2001).

Booth P., Dodd A., Robinson M., and Smith A. (2007) *The Thames through Time; the Archaeology of the Gravel Terraces of the Upper and Middle Thames. The Early Historical Period: AD 1–1000* (Oxford Archaeology Thames Valley Landscapes Monograph 27) (Oxford 2007).

Booth P., Simmonds A., Boyle A., Clough S., Cool H. E. M., and Poore D. (2010) *The Late Roman Cemetery at Lankhills, Winchester, Excavations 2000–2005* (Oxford Archaeology Monograph 10) (Oxford 2010).

Boylston A., Knüsel C. J., Roberts C., and Dawson M. (2000) "Investigation of a Romano-British rural ritual in Bedford", *JAS* 27 (2000) 241–54.

Brandt J. R. (2015) "Introduction: ritual, change, and funerary practices", in *Death and Changing Rituals: Function and Meaning in Ancient Funerary Practices* (Studies in Funerary Archaeology 7), edd. J. R. Brandt, M. Prusac, and H. Roland (Oxford 2015) ix–xix.

Brooks H. (2006) *A Roman Temple-tomb at Colchester Royal Grammar School, 6 Lexden Road, Colchester, Essex, August–September 2005* (CAT Report 345) (Colchester 2006).

Brown P. (2003) *The Rise of Western Christendom: Triumph and Diversity, A.D. 200–1000* (Oxford 2003).

Burnham B. C. and Wacher J. (1990) *The 'Small Towns' of Roman Britain* (London 1990).

Carver M., Hills C., and Scheschkewitz J. (2009) *Wasperton: A Roman, British and Anglo-Saxon Community in Central England* (Woodbridge 2009).

Casa-Hatton R. and Wall W. (2006) "A late Roman cemetery at Durobrivae, Chesterton", *Proceedings of the Cambridge Antiquarian Society* 95 (2006) 5–24.

Chambers R. A. (1987) "The late- and sub-Roman cemetery at Queenford Farm, Dorchester-on-Thames, Oxon.", *Oxoniensia* 52 (1987) 35–69.

Chambers R. and Boyle A. (2007) "The Romano-British cemetery", in *Excavations at Barrow Hills, Radley, Oxfordshire, 1983–5. Vol. 2: The Romano-British Cemetery and Anglo-Saxon Settlement* (Oxford Archaeology Thames Valley Landscapes Monograph 25), edd. R. Chambers and E. McAdam (Oxford 2007) 13–64.

Chapman E. M., Hunter F., Booth P., Wilson P., Pearce J, Worrell S., and Tomlin R. S. O. (2014) "Roman Britain in 2013", *Britannia* 45 (2014) 307–462.

Chapman E. M., Hunter F., Wilson P., Booth P., Pearce J., Worrell S., and Tomlin R. S. O. (2015) "Roman Britain in 2014", *Britannia* 46 (2015) 281–420.

Chapman E. M., Hunter F., Wilson P., Booth P., Pearce J., Worrell S., and Tomlin R. S. O. (2016) "Roman Britain in 2015", *Britannia* 47 (2016) 287–415.

Charles-Edwards T. M. (2013) *Wales and the Britons 350–1064* (Oxford 2013).

Chenery C. and Evans J. (2012) "Results of oxygen, strontium, carbon and nitrogen isotope analysis for the 'Kingsholm Goth'", *Transactions of the Bristol and Gloucestershire Archaeological Society* 130 (2012) 89–98.

Cheung C., Schroeder H., and Hedges R. E. M. (2012) "Diet, social differentiation and cultural change in Roman Britain: new isotopic evidence from Gloucestershire", *Archaeological and Anthropological Science* 4 (2012) 61–73.

Clarke G. (1979) *The Roman Cemetery at Lankhills* (Winchester Stud 3: Pre-Roman and Roman Winchester Part II) (Oxford 1979).

Clough S. and Boyle A. (2010) "Inhumations and disarticulated human bone", in *The Late Roman Cemetery at Lankhills, Winchester, Excavations 2000–2005* (Oxford Archaeology Monograph 10), edd. P. Booth, A. Simmonds, A. Boyle, S. Clough, H. E. M. Cool, and D. Poore (2010) (Oxford 2010) 339–404.

Cocks A. H. (1921) "A Romano-British homestead in the Hambleden Valley, Bucks", *Archaeologia* 71 (1921) 141–98.

Collingwood R. G. and Richmond I. (1969) *The Archaeology of Roman Britain* (London 1969).

Cooke N. and Mudd A. (2014) *A46 Nottinghamshire: The Archaeology of the Newark to Widmerpool Improvement Scheme, 2009* (Cotswold Archaeology Monograph 7 / Wessex Archaeology Monograph 34) (Cirencester 2014).

Cool H. E. M. (2006) *Eating and Drinking in Roman Britain* (Cambridge 2006).

Cool H. E. M. (2010) "Finding the foreigners", in *Roman Diasporas: Archaeological Approaches to Mobilty and Diversity in the Roman Empire* (JRA Suppl. 78) ed. H. Eckardt (Portsmouth 2010) 27–44.

Cool H. E. M. (2011) "Funerary contexts", in *Artefacts in Roman Britain: Their Purpose and Use*, ed. L. Allason-Jones (Cambridge 2011) 293–313.

Cooper L. (1996) "A Roman cemetery in Newarke Street, Leicester", *Transactions of the Leicestershire Archaeological and Historical Society* 70 (1996) 1–90.

Creighton J. and Fry R. (2016) *Silchester: Changing Visions of a Roman Town. Integrating Geophysics and Archaeology: The Results of the Silchester Mapping Project 2005–10* (Society for the Promotion of Roman Studies Britannia Monograph Series 28) (London 2016).

Crerar B. (2016) "Deviancy in later Romano-British burial," in *The Oxford Handbook of Roman Britain*, edd. M. Millett, L. Revell, and A. Moore (Oxford 2016) 381–405.

Crummy N. (2011) "Travel and transport", in *Artefacts in Roman Britain: Their Purpose and Use*, ed. L. Allason-Jones (Cambridge 2011) 46–67.

Crummy N. and Crossan C. (1993) "Excavations at Butt Road 1976–79, 1986, and 1988", in *Excavations of Roman and Later Cemeteries, Churches and Monastic Sites in Colchester, 1971–88* (Colchester Archaeol. Rep 9), edd. N. Crummy, P. Crummy, and C. Crossan (Colchester 1993) 4–163.

Cullen K., Holbrook N., Watts M., Caffell A., and Holst M. (2006) "A post-Roman cemetery at Hewlett Packard, Filton, South Gloucestershire: excavations in 2005", in *Two Cemeteries from Bristol's Northern Suburbs* (Bristol and Gloucestershire Archaeological Report 4), ed. M. Watts (Circencester 2006) 51–96.

Cummings C. (2008) *Food and Society in Late Roman Britain: Determining Dietary Patterns using Stable Isotope Analysis* (Ph.D. diss., Univ. of Oxford 2008).

Cummings C. (2009) "Meat consumption in Roman Britain: The evidence from stable isotopes", in *TRAC 2008 Proceedings of the Eighteenth Annual Theoretical Roman Archaeology Conference, Amsterdam 2008*, edd. M. Driessen, S. Heeren, J. Hendriks, F. Kemmers, and R. Visser (Oxford 2009) 73–83.

Cummings C. and Hedges R. (2010) "Carbon and nitrogen stable isotope analyses", in *The Late Roman Cemetery at Lankhills, Winchester, Excavations 2000–2005* (Oxford Archaeology Monograph 10), edd. P. Booth, A. Simmonds, A. Boyle, S. Clough, H. E. M. Cool, and D. Poore (Oxford 2010) 411–21.

Davies S. M., Bellamy P. S., Heaton M. J., and Woodward, P. J. (2002) *Excavations at Alington Avenue, Fordington, Dorchester, Dorset, 1984–87* (Dorset Natural History and Archaeological Society Monograph 15) (Dorchester 2002).

Davison C. (2000) "Gender imbalances in Romano-British cemetery populations: a re-evaluation of the evidence", in *Burial, Society and Context in the Roman world*, edd. J. Pearce, M. Millett, and M. Struck (Oxford 2000) 231–37.

Dawson M. (1994) *A Late Roman Cemetery at Bletsoe, Bedfordshire* (Bedfordshire Archaeology Monograph 1) (Newcastle 1994).

Dawson M. (2004) *Archaeology in the Bedford Region* (BAR-BS 373) (Oxford 2004).

Dawson T., Falys C., Mundin A., Pine J., and Platt D. (2017) *The Southern Cemetery of Roman Dorchester-on-Thames. With Evidence for Roman and Medieval Settlement: Archaeological Investigations on High Street, Wittenham Lane and Orchard Haven* (Thames Valley Archaeological Services Monograph 29) (Reading 2017).

Derrick M. (2009) "The excavation of a Roman cemetery at 21–23 Newarke Street, Leicester", *Trans Leicestershire Archaeological and Historical Society* 83 (2009) 63–87.

Duday H. (2009) *The Archaeology of the Dead: Lectures in Archaeothanatology* (Oxford 2009).

Dungworth D. (1998) "Mystifying Roman nails: *clavus annalis, defixiones* and *minkisi*", in *TRAC 97 Proceedings of the Seventh Annual Theoretical Roman Archaeology Conference, Nottingham*, edd. C. Forcey, J. Hawthorne, and R. Witcher (Oxford 1998) 148–59.

Eagles B. (2018) *From Roman Civitas to Anglo-Saxon Shire: Topographical Studies on the Formation of Wessex* (Oxford 2018).

Eckardt H. (ed.) (2010) *Roman Diasporas: Archaeological Approaches to Mobility and Diversity in the Roman Empire* (JRA Suppl. 78) (Portsmouth 2010).

Eckardt H., Chenery C., Booth P., Evans J. A., Lamb A., and Müldner G. (2009) "Oxygen and strontium isotope evidence for mobility in Roman Winchester", *JAS* 36 (2009) 2816–25.

Eckardt H., Müldner G., and Lewis M. E. (2014) "People on the move in Roman Britain", *World Archaeology* 46 (2014) 1–17.

Egging Dinwiddy K. (2009) "A late Roman cemetery at Little Keep, Dorchester, Dorset", http://www.wessexarch.co.uk/projects/dorset/dorchester/little-keep.

Egging Dinwiddy K., and Bradley P. (2011) *Prehistoric Activity and a Romano-British Settlement at Poundbury Farm, Dorchester, Dorset* (Salisbury 2011).

Ellis P. and King R. (2014) "Gloucester: the Wotton cemetery excavations, 2002", *Britannia* 45 (2014) 53–120.

Esmonde Cleary S. (2000) "Putting the dead in their place: burial location in Roman Britain", in *Burial, Society and Context in the Roman world*, edd. J. Pearce, M. Millett, and M. Struck (Oxford 2000) 127–42.

Esmonde Cleary S. (2006) "Christianity in Roman Britain by D Petts [Review]", *Britannia* 37 (2006) 514–15.

Esmonde Cleary S. (2013) *The Roman West, AD 200–500: An Archaeological Study* (Cambridge 2013).

Farwell D. E. and Molleson T. I. (1993) *Excavations at Poundbury Volume 2: The Cemeteries* (Dorset Natural History and Archaeological Society Monograph Series 11) (Dorchester 1993).

Fitzpatrick-Matthews K. J. (2014) "The experience of 'small towns': utter devastation, slow fading or business as usual", in *AD 410: The History and Archaeology of Late and Post-Roman Britain* (Society for Promotion of Roman Studies), ed. F. K. Haarer (London 2014) 43–60.

Fitzpatrick-Matthews K. J. (2016) "The cemeteries of Roman Baldock", *Fragments* 5 (2016) 34–60.

Frere S. S. (1984) "Roman Britain in 1983, I. Sites explored", *Britannia* 15 (1984) 266–332.

Frend W. H. C. (1992) "Pagans, Christians, and 'the barbarian conspiracy' of A.D. 367 in Roman Britain", *Britannia* 23 (1992) 121–31.

Fuller B. T., Molleson T. I., Harris D. A., Gilmour L. T., and Hedges R. E. M. (2006) "Isotopic evidence for breastfeeding and possible adult dietary differences from late/sub Roman Britain", *American Journal of Physical Anthropology* 129 (2006) 45–54.

Gerrard J. (2011) "New radiocarbon dates from the cemetery at Bradley Hill, Somerton", *Proceedings of Somersetshire Archaeological and Natural History Society* 154 (2011) 189–93.

Gerrard J. G. (2015a) "Synthesis, chronology, and "Late Roman" cemeteries in Britain", *AJA* 119 (2015a) 565–72.

Gerrard J. G. (2015b) "New radiocarbon dates from the Lynch Farm Romano-British cemetery, near Peterborough", *Northamptonshire Archaeology* 38 (2015b) 241–43.

Gibson C. D. (2013) "Out of time but not out of place. Tempo, rhythm and dynamics of inhabitation in southern England", in *Memory, Myth and Long-term Landscape Inhabitation*, edd. A. M. Chadwick and C. D. Gibson (Oxford 2013) 99–123.

Gowland R. L. (2002) *Examining Age as an Aspect of Social Identity in Fourth to Sixth Century England through the Analysis of Mortuary Evidence* (Ph.D. diss., Univ. of Durham 2002).

Gowland R. L. (2016a) "Ideas of childhood in Roman Britain: the biological and material evidence", in *The Oxford Handbook of Roman Britain*, edd. M. Millett, L. Revell, and A. Moore (Oxford 2016) 303–320.

Gowland R. L. (2016b) "That "tattered coat upon a stick" the ageing body: evidence for elder abuse and marginalisation in Roman Britain", in *Care in the Past: Archaeological and Inter-disciplinary Perspectives*, edd. L. Powell, W. Southwell-Wright, and R. L. Gowland (Oxford 2016b) 71–92.

Gowland R. L. (2017) "Embodied identities in Roman Britain: a bioarchaeological approach", *Britannia* 48 (2017) 177–94.

Gowland R. L. and Chamberlain A. T. (2002) "A Bayesian approach to ageing perinatal skeletal material from archaeological sites: implications for the evidence for infanticide in Roman Britain", *JAS* 29 (2002) 677–85.

Gowland R. L., Chamberlain A. T., and Redfern R. C. (2014) "On the brink of being: re-evaluating infanticide and infant burial in Roman Britain", in *Infant Health and Death in Roman Italy and Beyond* (JRA Suppl. 96), edd. P. M. Carroll and E-J. Graham (Ann Arbor 2014) 69–88.

Graham E-J. (2015) "Corporeal concerns: the role of the body in the transformation of Roman mortuary practices", in *Death Embodied: Archaeological Approaches to the Treatment of the Corpse* (Studies in Funerary Archaeology 9), edd. Z. L. Devlin and E-J. Graham (Oxford 2015) 41–62.

Handley M. (2001) "The origins of Christian commemoration in late antique Britain", *Early Medieval Europe* 10 (2001) 177–99.

Harland J. M. (2017) "Rethinking ethnicity and 'otherness' in early Anglo-Saxon England", *Medieval Worlds* 5 (2017) 113–42.

Harman M., Lambrick G., Miles D., and Rowley T. (1978) "Roman burials around Dorchester-on-Thames", *Oxoniensia* 43 (1978) 1–16.

Harman M., Molleson T., and Price J. L. (1981) "Burials, bodies and beheadings in Romano-British and Anglo-Saxon cemeteries", *Bulletin of the British Museum Natural History Geology* 35 (1981) 145–88.

Harries J. (1992) "Death and the dead in the late Roman west", in *Death in Towns: Urban Responses to the Dying and the Dead, 100–1600*, ed. S. Bassett (London 1992) 56–67.

Hart J., Geber J., and Holbrook N. (2016) "Iron Age settlement and a Romano-British cemetery at the Cotswold School, Bourton-on-the-Water: excavations in 2011", *Transactions of the Bristol and Gloucestershire Archaeological Society* 134 (2016) 77–112.

Hawkes S. C. and Dunning G. C. (1961) "Soldiers and settlers in Britain, fourth to fifth century", *Medieval Archaeology* 5 (1961) 1–70.

Hayden C., Early R., Biddulph E., Booth P., Dodd A., Smith A., Laws G., and Welsh K. (2017) *Horcott Quarry, Fairford and Arkell's Land, Kempsford: Prehistoric, Roman and Anglo-Saxon Settlement and Burial in the Upper Thames Valley in Gloucestershire* (Oxford Archaeology Thames Valley Landscapes Monograph 40) (Oxford 2017).

Hearne C. M. and Birbeck V. (1999) *A35 Tolpuddle to Puddletown Bypass DBFO, Dorset, 1996–8 Incorporating Excavations at Tolpuddle Ball 1993* (Wessex Archaeol Rep 15) (Salisbury 1999).

Heighway C. (2012) "Goths and Saxons? The late Roman cemetery at Kingsholm, Gloucester", *Transactions of the Bristol and Gloucestershire Archaeological Society* 130 (2012) 63–88.

Henig M. and Booth P. (2000) *Roman Oxfordshire* (Stroud 2000).

Hills C. M. and Lucy S. (2013) *Spong Hill Part IX: Chronology and Synthesis* (Cambridge 2013).

Hills C. M. and O'Connell T. C. (2009) "New light on the Anglo-Saxon succession: two cemeteries and their dates", *Antiquity* 83 (2009) 1–13.

Hirst S. and Clarke D. (2009) *Excavations at Mucking: Volume 3, The Anglo-Saxon Cemeteries* (Museum of London Archaeology Monograph) (London 2009).

Holbrook N. and Bateman C. (2008) "The South Gate cemetery of Roman Gloucester: excavations at Parliament Street, 2001", *Transactions of the Bristol and Gloucestershire Archaeological Society* 126 (2008) 91–106.

Holbrook N., Wright J., McSloy E. R., and Geber J. (2017) *The Western Cemetery of Roman Cirencester Excavations at the Former Bridges Garage, Tetbury Road, Cirencester, 2011–2015* (Cirencester Excavations VII) (Cirencester 2017).

Ivleva T. (2016) "Britons on the move Mobility of British-born emigrants in the Roman empire", in *The Oxford Handbook*

Empire", in *Families in the Roman and Late Antique world*, edd. M. Harlow and L. Larsson Loven (London 2012) 111–40.

Redfern, R. C., DeWitte S. N., Pearce J., Hamlin C., and Egging Dinwiddy K. (2015) "Urban-rural differences in Roman Dorset, England: a bioarchaeological perspective on Roman settlements", *American Journal of Physical Anthropology* 157 (2015) 107–120.

Redfern R. C., Marshall M., Eaton K. and Poinar H. N. (2017) "'Written in bone': new discoveries about the lives and burials of four Roman Londoners", *Britannia* 48 (2017) 253–77.

Redfern R. C., DeWitte S., Montgomery S., and Gowland R. L. (2018) "A novel investigation into migrant and local health-statuses in the past: A case study from Roman Britain", *Bioarchaeology* 2 (2018) 20–43.

Reece R. ed. (1977) *Burial in the Roman World* (CBA Report 22) (London 1977).

Revell L. (2005) "The Roman life course: a view from the inscriptions", *EJA* 8 (2005) 43–63.

Richards M. P., Hedges R. E. M., Molleson T., and Vogel J. C. (1998) "Stable isotope analysis reveals variations in human diet at the Poundbury Camp Cemetery Site", *JAS* 25 (1998) 1247–52.

Roberts C. and Cox M. (2003) *Health and Disease in Britain: From Prehistory to the Present Day* (Stroud 2003).

Rohnbogner A. (2017) "Listening to the kids: the value of childhood palaeopathology for the study of rural Roman Britain", *Britannia* 48 (2017) 221–52.

Rohnbogner A. (2018) "The rural population", in *New Visions of the Countryside in Roman Britain, Volume 3: Life and Death in the Countryside of Roman Britain* (Britannia Monograph 31), edd. A. Smith, M. Allen, T. Brindle, M. Fulford, L. Lodwick, and A. Rohnbogner (London 2018) 281–345.

Rohnbogner A. and Lewis M. E. (2017) "Poundbury Camp in context – a new perspective on the lives of children from urban and rural Roman England", *American Journal of Physical Anthropology* 162 (2017) 208–228.

Samworth R. and Gowland R. L. (2007) "Estimation of adult skeletal age-at-death: statistical assumptions and applications", *International Journal of Osteoarchaeology* 17 (2007) 174–88.

Scott E. (1991) "Animal and infant burials in Romano-British villas: a revitalization movement", in *Sacred and Profane, Proceedings of a Conference on Archaeology, Ritual and Religion Oxford, 1989* (Oxford Univ Comm for Archaeol Monograph 32), edd. P. Garwood, D. Jennings, R. Skeates, and J. Toms (Oxford 1991) 115–21.

Shaw H., Montgomery J., Redfern R., Gowland R. L., and Evans J. (2016) "Identifying migrants in Roman London using lead and strontium stable isotopes", *JAS* 66 (2016) 57–68.

Simmonds A., Marquez-Grant N., and Loe L. (2008) *Life and Death in a Roman City; Excavation of a Roman Cemetery at 120–122 London Road, Gloucester* (Oxford Archaeology Monograph 6) (Oxford 2008).

Simmonds A., Anderson-Whymark H., and Norton A. (2011) "Excavations at Tubney Wood Quarry, Oxfordshire, 2001–2009", *Oxoniensia* 76 (2011) 105–172.

Simmonds A., Allen M., McIntyre L., and Champness C. (2023) "Agriculture and population: Occupation and burials in the extramural area of Margidunum on the Fosse Way in Nottinghamshire", *Britannia* 54 (2023) 75–112.

Smith A. (2018) "Death in the countryside: rural burial practices", in *New Visions of the Countryside in Roman Britain, Volume 3: Life and Death in the Countryside of Roman Britain* (Britannia Monograph 31), edd. A. Smith, M. Allen, T. Brindle, M. Fulford, L. Lodwick, and A. Rohnbogner (London 2018) 205–280.

Smith A., Allen M., Brindle T., and Fulford M. (2016) *New Visions of the Countryside in Roman Britain, Volume 1: The Rural Settlement of Roman Britain* (Britannia Monograph 29) (London 2016).

Smith A., Allen M., Brindle T., Fulford M., Lodwick L., and Rohnbogner A. (2018) *New Visions of the Countryside in Roman Britain, Volume 3: Life and Death in the Countryside of Roman Britain* (Britannia Monograph 31) (London 2018).

Sparey-Green C. (2004) "Living amongst the dead: from Roman cemetery to post-Roman monastic settlement at Poundbury", in *Debating Late Antiquity in Britain AD300–700* (BAR-BS 365), edd. R. Collins and J. Gerrard (Oxford 2004) 103–111.

Stoodley N. (1999) *The Spindle and the Spear: A Critical Enquiry into the Construction and Meaning of Gender in the Early Anglo-Saxon Burial Rite* (BAR-BS 288) (Oxford 1999).

Swift E. (2019) "Re-evaluating the Quoit Brooch style: economic and cultural transformations in the 5th Century AD, with an updated catalogue of known Quoit Brooch style artefacts", *Medieval Archaeology* 63 (2019) 1–55.

Taylor A. (2008) "Aspects of deviant burial in Roman Britain", in *Deviant Burial in the Archaeological Record*, ed. E. M. Murphy (Oxford 2008) 91–114.

Theuws F. (2009) "Grave goods, ethnicity, and the rhetoric of burial rites in Late Antique Northern Gaul", in *Ethnic Constructs in Antiquity: The Role of Power and Tradition*, edd. T. Derks and N. Roymans (Amsterdam 2009) 283–319.

Thomas C. (1981) *Christianity in Roman Britain to AD 500* (London 1981).

Thomas J. (2017) "New light on Leicester's southern Roman cemetery: recent excavations at the junction of Oxford Street and Newarke Street", *Transactions of the Leicestershire Archaeological and Historical Society* 91 (2017) 45–96.

Tucker K. (2015) *An Archaeological Study of Human Decapitation Burials* (Barnsley 2015).

Van Driel-Murray C. (1999) "And did those feet in ancient time … Feet and shoes as a material projection of the self", in *TRAC 1998: Proceedings of the Eighth Annual Theoretical Roman Archaeology Conference Leicester 1998*, edd. P. Baker, C. Forcey, S. Jundi, and R. Witcher (Oxford 1999) 131–40.

Wacher J. S. (1995) *The Towns of Roman Britain* (London 1995).

Waldron T. (2014) "Crooked timber: the life of Calvin Wells (1908–1978)", *Journal of Medical Biography* 22 (2014) 82–89.

Watts L. and Leach P. (1996) *Henley Wood, Temples and Cemetery Excavations 1962–69 by the Late Ernest Greenfield and Others* (CBA Report 99) (London 1996).

Watts D. (1991) *Christians and Pagans in Roman Britain* (London 1996).

Watts D. (1993) "An assessment of the evidence for Christianity at the Butt Road site", in *Excavations of Roman and Later Cemeteries, Churches and Monastic Sites in Colchester, 1971–88* (Colchester Archaeol. Rep. 9), edd. N. Crummy, P. Crummy, and C. Crossan (Colchester 1993) 192–202.

Watts D. (1998) *Religion in Late Roman Britain* (London 1998).

Webster C. J. (2004) "Square-ditched burials in post-Roman Britain", in "A seventh-century AD cemetery at Stoneage Barton Farm, Bishop's Lydiard, Somerset and square-ditched burials in post-Roman Britain", C. J. Webster and R. A. Brunning, *ArchJ* 161 (2004), 63–81 [54–81].

Weddell P. (2000) "The excavation of a post-Roman cemetery near Kenn", *Proceedings of the Devon Archaeological Society* 58 (2000) 93–126.

Weekes J. (2016) "Cemeteries and funerary practice", in *The Oxford Handbook of Roman Britain*, edd. M. Millett, L. Revell, and A. Moore (Oxford 2016) 425–47.

Wessex Archaeology (2008) "Boscombe Down Phase VI excavation, Amesbury, Wiltshire, 2006–7, Interim assessment on the results of the Byway 20 Romano-British cemetery excavations", unpublished Wessex Archaeology Report 56246.04.

Williams G. (2013) "11 Wittenham Lane, Dorchester-on-Thames, Oxfordshire, Archaeological excavation report" (John Moore Heritage Services unpublished report 2415).

Williams H. (2006) *Death and Memory in Early Medieval Britain* (Cambridge 2006).

Williams R. J. and Zeepvat R. J. (1994) *Bancroft: A Late Bronze Age/Iron Age Settlement Roman Villa and Temple-Mausoleum, Vol 2 Finds and Environmental Evidence* (Buckinghamshire Archaeological Society Monograph Series 7) (Aylesbury 1994).

Witkin A. (2009) "The human skeletal remains", in *Between Villa and Town Excavations of a Roman Roadside Settlement and Shrine at Higham Ferrers, Northamptonshire* (Oxford Archaeology Monograph 7), edd. S. Lawrence and A. Smith (Oxford 2009) 275–87.

Woodward A. B. (1993) "Discussion", in *Excavations at Poundbury Volume 2: The Cemeteries* (Dorset Natural History and Archaeological Society Monograph Series 11), edd. Farwell, D. E. and Molleson, T. I. (Dorchester 1993) 216–39.

Burial in Late Antiquity: Evidence from Londinium

Victoria Ridgeway and Sadie Watson

Abstract

This paper details advances in the study of late antique burials in London over the past two decades, with an emphasis on unpublished examples. Investment in bioarchaeological techniques and their significance to demographic studies are outlined. Evidence suggests that the population of London was highly diverse and there was mobility across the Empire through the Late Roman period. Specific examples are discussed, as the analysis of two sites excavated in Southwark, on the south bank of the Thames, illustrates the broad extent and wide diversity of practices at play in Late Roman London. This forms a case study, which might act as a model for consideration of the rest of London's cemetery areas.

Introduction

London is the most thoroughly excavated provincial capital in the Roman Empire[1] and there is a vast volume of data relating to burials of all periods with many hundreds of sites excavated, some more than once. The last large-scale synthesis of Roman burials was by Jenny Hall[2] and an update is now overdue.[3] This chapter and the volume within which it sits offer fresh insights into the study of burials in the late antique period across the Roman Empire and will be of particular value for studies of London during the period. It should be noted that 'late antique' is not a term generally used in London's archaeological chronology, nor do we have a chronology for the arrival and spread of Christianity in the London area, although Perring has suggested some possible Christian influence over later burial locations.[4] The Roman period is taken to conclude during the mid-5th c. with Londinium largely abandoned by AD 450,[5] although this enforces strict period definitions that can conceal the nuances that transitional phases contain. In this specific case, the term 'late antique' refers to the Late Roman period; there are early Saxon cemeteries in London but they are not covered here. In this paper we will illustrate topics within the general subject by highlighting selected excavations, focussing on significant (some as

yet unpublished) sites which allow us to reconsider the period. Key to this is an examination of funerary practice and what it indicates in terms of the population of the town, their beliefs, and traditions.

Late Antique Roman London

The tumultuous changes across the Roman Empire during the late 3rd c. were reflected in London with the construction of the riverside wall, which completed the defensive circuit. This blocked access to the waterfront, which saw little subsequent development or reconstruction. Similarly, some minor roads in the town declined or fell into disuse during the later 3rd c. The major routes persisted, however, as did some of the major monuments of the town, including the amphitheatre and baths, although the disuse and demolition of most of the forum-basilica at the end of the 3rd c. is significant.[6] The character of the later town undoubtedly altered from the trading centre it had been since its foundation to a less dynamic but nevertheless important administrative centre. Taxation and local economic successes contributed to the higher status buildings we see in London from the 3rd c. onwards.[7] There were also continued links with the Continent as part of a complex social network with established hierarchies. This would have been reflected in funerary and burial activities, with high status burials at Spitalfields showing that 4th c. London retained a wealthy 'Roman' elite of Continental origins. We can view the Late Roman period as a continuation of long-established societal structures, into which the inhabitants of London had fundamentally invested. The urban lifestyle persisted,[8] reflected in the continued use of existing cemeteries into the late 3rd and 4th c. Burials were located alongside the roads leading out of the town on both sides of the Thames, as well as on derelict land, disused roads,[9] amongst the ruins of substantial buildings[10] or abandoned monuments, even within the walled area.[11]

---

1   Wallace (2014) 1.
2   Hall (1996) 57–84.
3   Pearce (2015) 143.
4   Perring (2015) 37.
5   Hingley (2018) 238.

6   Brigham (1990) 92–94.
7   Hill and Rowsome (2011) 450–51; Gerrard (2016) 856.
8   Pearce (2015) 143.
9   Watson (2006) 64–66.
10   Telfer (forthcoming); Cowan (1992) 56–58; Cowan (2003) 72–73; Mackinder and Whittingham (2013).
11   Bateman *et al.* (2008) 91–92.

© KONINKLIJKE BRILL BV, LEIDEN, 2024 | DOI:10.1163/9789004687974_005
Alexandra Dolea and Luke Lavan (eds) *Burial and Memorial in Late Antiquity*
(Late Antique Archaeology 13) (Leiden 2024), pp. 630–646

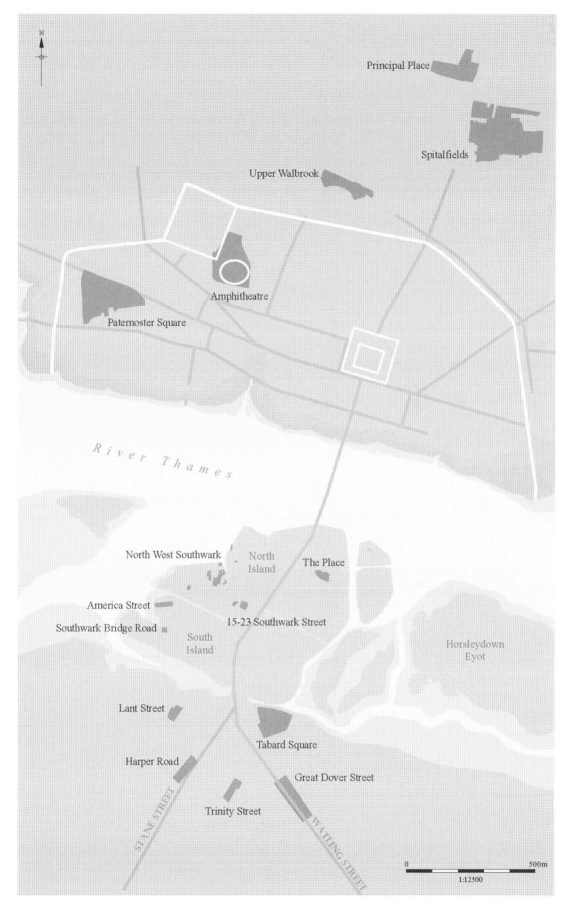

FIGURE 1   Map showing site outlines for the principal sites discussed in the text, in relation to 4th-century *Londinium*.
©PRE-CONSTRUCT ARCHAEOLOGY

There is clear evidence of disturbance of earlier burials, with reused stone from funerary monuments incorporated into the riverside wall and in the bastions added to the landward wall in the 4th c.[12] Several large monuments, including that of the procurator Julius Classicianus, were dismantled (presumably legally) and fragments from them would have been clearly visible within the wall.[13] Hingley suggests the position in which reused funerary sculptures were placed in the landward wall at Camomile Street reflects burial practices and they might have been subject to a second 'burial' in the wall.[14] There is no indication that occupation of London continued beyond *ca.* 450 but excavations at only one site (St. Martin-in-the-Fields church, London WC2, west of the Roman town) seem to provide convincing evidence for continuity of occupation (including burials) from the Roman into the post-Roman period.[15] There is also some evidence from the same general area for a number of small Early Saxon settlements and cemeteries.[16]

The Study of Late Antique Burials in London

Excavation in London has been funded and organised through development control since the 1990s,[17] which has resulted in a focus on site-based narratives. That said, some synthetic reporting, principally by geographic area, has been possible.[18] The significant volume of data available for research should encourage a higher level of synthesis and publication in the future. Constraints on what has been possible have included pressures of client confidentiality, programming issues, project-specific funding, and the manner in which the funding and management of commercial projects is organised.

Projects are not generally research-led or initiated but undertaken before or during development groundworks. There are constraints, as noted above but generally the excavations are carried out to a high standard of national, professional and ethical guidelines[19] and data is readily comparable between different contracting organisations. The locations of Roman cemeteries and burial areas tend to be peripheral to the historic urban core; in London, this has worked in archaeologists'

favour, given that many of the larger cemeteries are in areas subject to redevelopment, particularly from the mid-1980s onwards. This would include the 'eastern cemetery',[20] Spitalfields to the north-east of the Roman town,[21] much of Southwark's cemeteries on the south bank of the Thames,[22] and areas to the north of the modern city of London, around Liverpool Street station and Shoreditch.[23] In addition, the legal framework within which burial archaeology operates[24] offers the opportunity to fully excavate each skeleton, leading to a complete record of skeletal and associated material. The study of London also benefits from an embedded understanding of the chronology of the Roman period, leading to cemeteries often having relatively tightly dated sequences. This enables us to ascertain relatively complex phasing structures in the absence of stratigraphic relationships caused by a lack of intercutting burials.

The topography of London offers many different preservation conditions, from waterlogged river valleys[25] to the higher, level ground of the gravel terraces,[26] with materials of all types surviving in London, contributing to the large dataset. Roman cemeteries of most periods and locations have been published over the last two decades[27] and there have been synthetic or related articles in the academic sphere, particularly that of bioarchaeology.[28] A wide range of burial practice has been identified from London, with cremation burial growing increasingly rare through the period. Inhumation burial rites observed include prone and multiple burials, in coffins of wood and, less often, lead and stone. Grave goods vary: from simple ceramic vessels, to hobnailed boots, food offerings, personal items, and jewellery. Funerary activity and associated ritual were both extremely varied, presumably due to the diverse and multicultural population.

Previously studies have classified sites according to their relative locations to the urban core.[29] In fact,

---

12   Hill *et al.* (1980) 88–93.
13   Barker *et al.* (2018) 321–42.
14   Hingley (2018) 234.
15   Telfer (forthcoming).
16   Blackmore (2012) 147–58; Cowie and Blackmore (2012); Cowie (2008) 49–53.
17   DoE (1990).
18   Barber and Bowsher (2000); Harward *et al.* (2015); Ridgeway *et al.* (2013).
19   E.g. Mitchell and Brickley (2017).

---

20   Barber and Bowsher (2000).
21   McKenzie and Thomas (2020).
22   Ridgeway *et al.* (2013).
23   Harward *et al.* (2015); Ranieri and Telfer (2017).
24   To include licences from the relevant Ministry of Justice/ Church faculty.
25   Watson (2003); Harward *et al.* (2015); Ranieri and Telfer (2017).
26   Barber and Bowsher (2000).
27   Barber and Bowsher (2000); Mackinder (2000); Watson (2003); Butler (2006); Melikian and Sayer (2007); McKinley (2009); Butler and Ridgeway (2009); Ridgeway *et al.* (2013); Harward *et al.* (2015); Ranieri and Telfer (2017).
28   Redfern (2003); Bateman *et al.* (2008); Powell *et al.* (2014); Redfern and Bonney (2014); Redfern *et al.* (2016); Shaw *et al.* (2016); Redfern *et al.* (2017).
29   Hall (1996) 57–84 used the cardinal points to enable comparison of four burial areas and this descriptive terminology has

burial grounds appear irregularly scattered beyond the edges of the settled areas. In terms of definition, most burials took place within ditched, hedged, or occasionally walled enclosures – probably distinct burial grounds – and to a contemporary, an overarching concept such as 'northern cemetery' would have meant little. Esmonde-Cleary's assertion of a town being 'ringed by its ancestors'[30] may be a pattern that only developed in the Later Roman period. Smaller cemeteries will have become subsumed into larger areas, with inevitable deterioration in their individual character.[31] Southwark lacks evidence for formally defined boundaries; nevertheless, the majority of burials lie in a broad arc beyond the Borough Channel, which forms the southern shores of the braided channels of the Thames. To the west of Londinium, Roman finds have been relatively rare and mostly close to the city,[32] but excavations at St. Martin-in-the-Fields Church[33] emphasise the need for more research into burials and settlements in the wider hinterland.

The Nature of the Evidence

Topographic and Spatial Aspects

As outlined above, the cemeteries of London are ranged around the edge of the Roman urban core, located adjacent to (and probably aligned with) topographic and structural features such as roads, ditches, and buildings. The vast majority of Late Roman burials in London are extended supine inhumations, with a general emphasis upon single occupancy graves. Timber coffins are common, although they do not generally survive beyond a stain and the presence of iron nails. The shrouding of bodies does not appear to have been widespread. There are rare examples of double burials from the later period,[34] but no evidence has been found for mass graves. Throughout the later periods, intercutting or reuse of broadly contemporary graves is generally minimal, suggesting there was room to expand the burial areas.[35] This is not to say, however, that there was not reuse of earlier cemeteries, or more complex factors at

play, as with Spitalfields, where certain smaller delineated burial grounds appear to have been more in use than others, without any obvious topographical reason for this.[36]

Southwark, comprising that part of Londinium south of the Thames, presents a discrete area for study, and one where much new data has been gathered in recent years, illustrating a broad range of practices and intimating the extent of the buried population. Sometimes described as an extra-mural suburb, Southwark is perhaps better regarded as an integral part of Londinium. Its development and subsequent success lie in its location at the convenient crossing point it provided for the Thames, from routes to the south-west via Stane Street and south-east via Watling Street. Occupying two islands, or eyots, within the braided river valley, and spilling over onto the south bank of the Thames, or 'mainland' area, Southwark lacks any evidence for formally constructed boundaries. An extramural Romano-Celtic temple complex, established in the 2nd c., lies at the southern extent of settlement, which is otherwise defined by burials.

Within this main cemetery area burial rites vary but include relatively high proportions of grave goods,[37] evidence for coffins, burial on a chalk-like substance, and prone burials. Alignments varied but at both sites, burials appear to follow one of two predominant alignments, defined not according to the compass points but to ditches defining plots or other landscape markers and with no apparent chronological progression to the use of one alignment or the other. Limited intercutting suggests either that graves were not permanently marked but may have remained visible for some time, or that disturbance of earlier burials was not an issue.

Whilst the area of Southwark south of the Borough Channel forms the principal focus of burial south of the river, a second area of more intense burial has recently been identified towards the western tip of the southern island. Much of the evidence for this extensive cemetery area remains largely unpublished,[38] but it includes 166 burials of late 2nd–4th c. date. Chronological resolution of this sequence remains undefined but includes a variety of inhumation practises, including lime-packed wooden coffins, double and triple stacked, prone, crouched and cremation burials, a possible family group (parents and an infant), a horse skull interred with an

stuck e.g. 'eastern cemetery' (Barber and Bowsher (2000)); 'western cemetery' (Watson (2003)).

30   Esmonde-Cleary (2000) 137.

31   Harward *et al.* (2015) 136.

32   Watson (2003); Langton (1991) 278; Bentley and Pritchard (1982) 134–72; MacLaughlin and Scheuer (no date).

33   Telfer (forthcoming).

34   E.g. Harward *et al.* (2015) 143–44.

35   But see evidence from the western tip of Southwark's south island below; Melikian and Sayer (2007); Ridgeway *et al.* (2013).

36   McKenzie and Thomas (2020) 116–17.

37   At Lant Street, 38% of the Late Roman burials were accompanied with grave goods, at Trinity Street around 50% – here interpreting grave goods as objects deliberately placed in the grave, rather than accidentally incorporated, or worn by the deceased.

38   Including the largest cemetery group to date at America Street; Melikian and Sayer (2007) 14–23.

adult male, and an iron-socketed spear head puncturing the feet of an adult inhumation. One of the latest burial features included a pit containing the dumped remains of four individuals.

One of the more remarkable features noted here is the sheer density, with a heavily intercutting cluster of 18 burials and 8 'empty graves' identified at Southwark Bridge Road,[39] all of 4th c. date, representing a northern extension of this cemetery. This evidence is at odds with the other cemetery areas identified in Southwark, and indeed the other major burial areas around London[40] and denotes a practice so far unique to this part of Londinium. The reason for the pronounced density and even direct superimposition of burials here is not immediately obvious. It may reflect the fact that grave markers were not used, although avoidance of earlier interments may not have been considered important or indeed preferable; within this population there may have been deliberate desire to bury in the location of a previous interment. Topographic factors may play their part. Located at the western tip of the southern eyot, space available for burial was no doubt restricted, in contrast to other burial areas.

Elsewhere, the presence of disarticulated human bone from later levels of Roman dumping[41] indicates a general incidence of skeletal material, although not necessarily from contemporary burials. Three adult burials at Guildhall on the banks of the disused amphitheatre are part of the small number of intra-mural burials dating to the 3rd and 4th c.[42] These may reflect awareness of (or adherence to) Christianity but are more likely to reflect the lessening control over central urban areas previously occupied by commercial or residential activity. However, their location might be of specific relevance. Similarly, five inhumations at Paternoster Square were installed into a disused metalled road surface.[43] There were no contemporary burials alongside these; suggesting that the land either side of the road had been used for other purposes, probably agriculture[44] and was therefore avoided for burial.

This phenomenon is paralleled on Southwark's north island where some later burials apparently cluster around former masonry buildings, frequently being inserted through robbed-out wall foundations. This group of burials lies within the core of the settlement, away from the main cemetery areas and has generally been interpreted as representing the contraction of settlement towards the northern bridgehead.[45] Here, numerous isolated observations comprise mainly antiquarian collections and records of vessels that may have accompanied inhumations or cremations are frequently poorly provenanced.[46] This group includes vessels recorded in the vicinity of 15–23 Southwark Bridge Road[47] where later excavation revealed 13 burials clustered around the apparently partly demolished remains of a large masonry building tentatively interpreted as a *mansio*.[48] Nine of the burials encroached on the robbed-out remains of the former building, and all followed its north-south and east-west alignments. Three burials were accompanied by grave goods, 7 buried with a plaster or chalk-like substance. Quarrying of the structure for building materials may have continued into the medieval period suggesting that a core of the building remained around which burials clustered.[49] No 5th c. or later diagnostic Saxon items were recovered, and the burials are considered to be 4th c. in date.[50]

Similarly, to the north-west, 7 burials were focussed on and respected the robbed-out remains of a large masonry building, all but one demonstrably cut into robber trench backfills.[51] Further east, two burials cut into robbed-out foundations, while another two were seemingly contained within the outline of a building provisionally interpreted as a temple of Romano-Celtic form (on the basis of its ground plan).[52] A further 4 burials at Guy's Hospital,[53] though close to large masonry buildings on St. Thomas Street, are less clearly associated with any particular structure. With the exception of the burials clustered around the putative *mansio*, which have been assumed to be Late Roman on the grounds of stratigraphic and other dating evidence, none of these inhumations was accompanied by grave goods. The perceived 4th c. 'contraction' of the settlement to an area around the bridgehead may be more complex, perhaps reflecting a more 'rural' phenomenon, with small settlement foci and the referencing of previously significant features through burial. It is worth noting that no infants have been identified within these groups.

39   Ridgeway *et al.* (2013) 26–27.
40   Bentley and Pritchard (1982); Whytehead (1986); Beard and Cowan (1988); Langton (1990); Hall (1996); Barber and Bowsher (2000); Mackinder (2000); Swift (2003); Watson (2003).
41   Bateman *et al.* (2008) 91.
42   Bateman *et al.* (2008) 93.
43   Watson (2006) 76.
44   Watson (2006) 78.

45   Hall (1996) 57–84; Barber and Hall (2000); Cowan *et al.* (2009).
46   Hall (1996).
47   Dean (1981).
48   Cowan (1992).
49   Cowan (1992) 53–59.
50   Cowan (1992) 58.
51   The robbing has been dated on artefactual evidence to AD 350–400.
52   Mackinder and Whittingham (2013).
53   Sitecode: GHR82.

FIGURE 2   Juvenile burials interred into a disused road surface at Paternoster Square (PNS01).
© MOLA

In the Upper Walbrook cemetery area, a late 3rd c. grave was cut into a disused metalled surface. It contained a young woman accompanied by worn and unworn jewellery.[54] There were other contemporary burials on this unusual cemetery[55] at this date, so the location may have been chosen to avoid disruption to the skeletal remains in an area where fluvial erosion had clearly disturbed other earth-cut graves.

At Spitalfields, some of the earlier graves were organised in rows within ditched enclosures, perhaps in family groups, although this could have been managed by a landowner, a civic or administrative organisation. The later (i.e. AD 250+) burials mostly respected these earlier graves, indicating that they had been delineated, although little evidence of grave markers was found. It is likely that topographic landmarks, particularly rectilinear ditched enclosures aligned on the major north-south road (Ermine Street) to the west, remained an influence on grave alignments; the city wall would also have been a major landmark by AD 200. Whether the lack of intercutting and the presence of organised burial plots provide evidence of managed cemeteries at this period is not easily determined, given the wide variation between sites across either side of the Thames.

North-east of Spitalfields, a large, mixed cemetery area dating predominantly to the 3rd and 4th c. has been identified, with evidence of cremations persisting through the 3rd c. and unusually, one bustum (a

structure for *in situ* cremation).[56] Several of the inhumations were aligned north-south, presumably following the major road to the east. Associated ditches formed discrete burial plots. The vast majority of inhumations were adults in coffins and although analysis is ongoing, there appears to be significant differences between these burials and those seen to both the south-east[57] and south-west.[58]

Mausolea are rare in Roman Britain, although the earlier examples ranged along Watling Street in Southwark[59] indicate a similarity with the tombs seen elsewhere in the Empire. They were perhaps evidence of a localised tradition, as there are large funerary monuments ranged along the road east of London towards Canterbury. Mausolea probably represented a distinct social class or civic position, with the mausoleum of the procurator Julius Classicianus a rare example in London.[60]

The Watling Street evidence comprises a 2nd c. mausoleum, temple mausoleum and walled burial enclosures to the south, interpreted on the basis of finds and structural evidence as being indicative of high status and wealth,[61] which were largely abandoned by the mid-3rd c. However, between AD 250–400, the complex continued to attract isolated inhumations and a

---

54   Harward *et al.* (2015) 59–60, 140–41.
55   Harward *et al.* (2015) 58–62.
56   Daykin (2016); Daykin (2017).
57   McKenzie and Thomas (2020).
58   Harward *et al.* (2015).
59   Mackinder (2000).
60   Hingley (2018) 57–59.
61   Mackinder (2000) 39.

FIGURE 3   Stone sarcophagus (left of image), disturbed following burial, inserted through the chalk
            foundations of a late 3rd c. mausoleum at Harper Road, Southwark.
            PHOTOGRAPH STREPHON DUCKERING ©PRE-CONSTRUCT ARCHAEOLOGY

cremation. Across the road, to the north, three isolated burials lying beyond the eastern extents of the temple complex at Tabard Square might be considered part of this group: broad date ranges provided by two radiocarbon determinations suggest a 3rd to late 4th or 5th c. date, whilst stratigraphic evidence pushes this into the latter years of this range.[62]

Further west, fronting Stane Street, the eastern extent of chalk foundations of a probable mausoleum were identified, constructed around the last quarter of the 3rd c.[63] Much of the structure lay beyond the limits of excavation but the eastern wall foundation was truncated by the interment of a woman buried in a stone sarcophagus. This burial had been heavily disturbed during the post-Medieval period; nevertheless, sufficient evidence remained to suggest that the foundation had been reinstated following the interment of the sarcophagus. The suggested interpretation of this event is that the body was interred beneath the threshold of the building, given that the burial truncated that element facing the road. Grave goods were few; however, a stone intaglio depicting a Bacchic motif, in the form of a satyr, escaped theft.

While mausolea and walled cemetery areas containing masonry structures lay adjacent to the road, other less ostentatious areas of burial were generally set back from the road, as observed elsewhere.[64] By the 4th c., some mausolea along the eastern approach route in Southwark may have been falling into disrepair,[65] but away from the road burial appears, if anything, to have intensified.

Demography

A detailed exploration of demography across London's cemeteries is beyond the scope of this paper and would entail a major review of all the existing evidence. Instead, we focus here on the treatment given to neonates, infants, and juveniles. It has been suggested that by 4th c. Roman Britain, children were afforded extensions of the adult burial rites, with coffins and grave goods. This would include the small group at Paternoster Square, with the graves of one infant, two juveniles and two adults with some redeposited infant bone cut into a disused road.[66] One juvenile was laid on a bed of reused tiles, and both were in graves with rudimentary stone linings. No familial association was established, although developing bioarchaeological techniques could provide further details on this case and others like it. There may have been distinct locations where children were buried, perhaps confirming Gowland's assertion that funerary

62   Killock *et al.* (2015).

63   Grosso (2018); the exact alignment and location of this road
      was unknown prior to 2017.

64   Pearce (2000) 7.

65   Mackinder (2000).

66   Watson (2006) 64–66.

practice and belief were closely associated with the age of the deceased.[67]

In the Upper Walbrook cemetery, the 3rd c. burial of an adult with a neonate on the chest[68] was furnished with Nene Valley Colour Coated beakers, a form more commonly associated with children than adults. One beaker was a miniature, another common theme in child burials, as is a copper alloy bell, which may have been the child's toy. This cemetery shows an increasing percentage of sub-adults over time, with a clear preponderance of males[69] persisting through the later periods, unlike other cemeteries such as Spitalfields where a pronounced male gender bias dissipates after *ca.* 250.[70] Additionally, Spitalfields had an earlier phase containing an area seemingly set aside for the specific burial of sub-adults,[71] whereas in the later period sub-adults seem to be more evenly distributed among the graves of adults. Notably, sub-adults (neonates, infants and juveniles) were poorly represented in the nearby Principal Place cemetery area,[72] although, of course, different burial grounds might be expected to serve different contributing populations. If so, this would suggest that familial groupings were not the only factor influencing burial location.

Within the significant sarcophagus group at Spitalfields was evidence for a timber-lined vault containing the remains of a child of around 8 years old, buried with a group of extremely fine, probably late 4th c. glass vessels, of types rarely found in Britain.[73] The glass was probably imported from north Gaul or the Rhineland,[74] although the child's ancestry is unknown. Analysis of mitochondrial DNA extracted from the rib of the young woman buried in fine clothes with elaborate rites and a diverse range of goods in the stone sarcophagus indicated a genetic sequence (from a maternal ancestor) which was localised to southern Europe. Stable isotope analysis showed that she had grown up in southern Europe, possibly even in Rome before migrating to London.[75] These richly furnished graves illustrate the presence of a cosmopolitan and mobile elite in London's 4th c. population.

Two recently excavated cemetery areas in Southwark, at Trinity Street and Lant Street,[76] provide evidence for low key burial commencing in the 2nd c., along with division of the land by ditches into which disarticulated human bone was deposited, which subsequently intensified particularly during the 4th and into the 5th c.[77] An intensification of burial in the 4th c. has been noted elsewhere, with new cemeteries established in some towns, a phenomenon which might be related to changing attitudes to the dead, including an increase in inhumation over cremation as the dominant burial rite.[78] The Southwark evidence suggests areas of 4th c. and later burial both overlying[79] and set in new enclosures adjacent[80] to earlier burial grounds. There is clearly an increased intensity of burial into and through the 4th c. as demonstrated by the archaeological record. Given the small areas investigated, this would appear to represent a significant population, although whether this urban location attracted burials from the rural hinterland remains unknown.

Adults dominate both assemblages, with slightly higher female to male ratios than elsewhere.[81] Children remain underrepresented; juveniles and adolescents form 24% of the population at Lant Street. This may be a false representation, as interments of small children with attendant small coffins, may have been more shallowly buried than their adult counterparts.[82] Amongst this group was a triple burial comprising a young adult male interred with a baby lying on his stomach and an infant at his feet, suggests near contemporary mortality for the three individuals,[83] perhaps through accident or fatal illness. A *tettina* or 'feeding bottle' buried with this group is a poignant reminder of the baby's age at death. It is tempting to surmise that this forms a family group; DNA analysis of this, and other, similar groupings[84] would be useful in testing this hypothesis.

Bioarchaeology

Recent advances in bioarchaeology are used to address questions concerning the life histories and diets of human populations. In contrast to other urban centres in Roman Britain, such as York, Dorchester or Winchester,[85] our present knowledge of diet and population origin in

---

67   Gowland (2016) 314.
68   Harward *et al.* (2015) 58–59.
69   Harward *et al.* (2015) 107.
70   McKenzie and Thomas (2020) 118–19.
71   McKenzie and Thomas (2020) 20–22, 119–20.
72   Daykin (2016); Daykin (2017).
73   McKenzie and Thomas (2020) 81.
74   McKenzie and Thomas (2020) 81.
75   McKenzie and Thomas (2020) 145–47.
76   Killock *et al.* (forthcoming); Ridgeway *et al.* (2013) 11–15.

77   27 of 44 burials at Trinity Street and 74 of 86 at Lant Street were dated to the 4th c. or later.
78   E.g. Cirencester, Colchester, Dorchester, and Winchester; Esmonde Cleary (2000).
79   Trinity Street.
80   Trinity Street and Lant Street.
81   E.g. the Eastern Cemetery; Barber and Bowsher (2000).
82   A phenomenon observed in more recent burial grounds, e.g. Proctor *et al.* (2016).
83   Ridgeway *et al.* (2013) 13–14.
84   E.g. Melikian (2002) 27.
85   E.g. Leach *et al.* (2009); Leach *et al.* (2010); Redfern *et al.* (2010); Cummings and Hedges (2010); Chenery *et al.* (2010).

Roman London and its hinterland is notably poor. Stable isotope analysis is increasingly being used to elucidate aspects of past diet (C, N), place of origin, and movement of people through their lifetime (O, Sr, Pb); yet, this remains a relatively new (and developing) discipline and is not routinely undertaken as part of developer-funded projects. Within the context of Roman London, studies to date are limited.[86] The resources available for such analyses (the human remains themselves) are finite and the techniques used are destructive. Recent guidelines on the destructive sampling of human remains, issued by the Advisory Panel on the Archaeology of Burials in England,[87] advocate that the significance of any potential findings arising from such research should be weighed against the potential destruction of material which such analyses may incur. Furthermore, advances in technology mean that it is becoming increasingly possible to obtain results from smaller samples and, thus, caution is advised when undertaking destructive analysis (Sylvia Warman, pers. comm.)

Prior to 2015, such data for the London region in the Roman period was limited to only two individuals, the 'Spitalfields Lady' who, it is suggested on the basis of lead isotope data, may have spent her childhood in Rome[88] and the 'Harper Road Woman' (buried in Southwark ca. AD 50–70). The latter, whilst clearly lying outside the period we are dealing with here, nevertheless illustrates some of the potential of such analyses; an initial assessment of mobility isotopes[89] confirmed that she is likely to have grown up in Britain, whilst the assessment of her ancestry suggested she was White European. Bioarchaeological investigations revealed age at death at ca. 21–38 years, whilst cranial and pelvic morphology indicate that she was a woman. Intriguingly, assessment of aDNA identified male chromosomes, probable evidence of a chromosomal intersex condition; the accompanying grave goods indicated that this individual was most probably identified as a woman by her community.[90]

Recent stable isotope analysis of two burial groups from Southwark, at Trinity Street and Lant Street, has shown the potential of such analyses when applied to large-scale commercially-excavated assemblages. The discovery of an ivory-handled folding knife in the form of a leopard, which could only be paralleled in

Carthage, from within a richly furnished grave at Lant Street inspired a programme of collaboratively funded stable oxygen isotope analysis. This indicated that of 22 individuals tested (18 of whom were from 4th c. burials), a relatively high proportion appeared to be immigrants from the southern Mediterranean.[91] The interpretation of the results varies but, based on criteria outlined by Chenery et al.,[92] 13 individuals from Lant Street should be considered migrants from a warmer climate than that of London, whilst on a more conservative basis, only 5 should be.[93] Further macromorphoscopic analyses identified 4 individuals with African, and 2 with Asian ancestry.[94] Clearly, this was a population with diverse origins. Strontium and lead stable isotope analyses were not undertaken but might have helped to refine the likely place of origin for most of these individuals. Subsequent mDNA analysis of the burial with the leopard knife by the Museum of London demonstrated that she had blue eyes, and her maternal ancestry could be traced to south-eastern Europe and west Eurasia, at the eastern fringes of the Roman Empire.[95] The identification of a diverse population in Roman London should not surprise us, particularly given new epigraphic evidence;[96] yet, the application of stable isotope and mDNA analyses add detail.

The cemetery area at Trinity Street appeared superficially similar to Lant Street in terms of layout, comprising inhumation burials, predominantly on two main alignments, set within ditch-defined areas.[97] Trinity Street was perhaps a little less ostentatious in terms of grave goods but comparable grave goods, burial practices and rites were noted. While strontium isotopes fell within the predicted range for London, with one exception, oxygen isotope compositions are perhaps slightly more typical of the western than the eastern side of Britain,[98] but still fall well within the British range. Origin from across large areas of Europe cannot be ruled out but these individuals lack the strong indicators of an immigrant population identified at Lant Street. The results, if not strongly diagnostic, are consistent with a London childhood.

These two populations demonstrate some differences in dietary preferences, particularly with regard to fish consumption. Faunal evidence from London suggests that whilst fish consumption may have

---

86   Millard et al. (2013); Montgomery et al. (2010); Redfern et al. (2017); Shaw et al. (2016).

87   Mays et al. (2013).

88   Montgomery et al. (2010) 217–19.

89   Held in an unpublished Museum of London report, Budd (2003); reinterpreted by Montgomery et al. (2010) 4.

90   Redfern et al. (2017) 5.

91   Redfern et al. (2016).

92   Chenery et al. (2010).

93   Millard et al. (2015) 70.

94   Redfern et al. (2016).

95   BA November December (2016); Redfern et al. (2017) 14–19.

96   Tomlin (2016) 54.

97   As yet unpublished; Killock et al. (forthcoming).

98   Evans et al. (2010).

FIGURE 4   Ivory handled folding knife carved to resemble a leopard, found accompanying the burial of a young
            woman at Lant Street in Southwark.
            ©PRE-CONSTRUCT ARCHAEOLOGY

increased following the conquest through the spread of 'Romanizing' influences[99] (in particular, those products imported from the Spanish and African provinces), following a period of little or no fish consumption in the Iron Age,[100] fish and fish-products remained a minimal contributor to overall diet. Preservation issues may be at play here, although there are a small number of particularly large collections, with plaice, flounder, eel, and a variety of white fish, including cod and gadid dominating.[101] It has been suggested that fish, whether fresh or preserved, did not form a common part of the household diet but may have been available in specialised restaurants.[102] Recent dietary stable isotope work suggests that whilst adults in the region would have consumed terrestrial animal protein and marine fish, juveniles were more likely to be fed locally-derived freshwater fish, particularly in Later Roman Londinium.[103]

At Trinity Street, analyses identified that the diet of certain individuals may have featured a contribution of millet but also fish, in particular from freshwater sources.[104] Diet does not appear to have been influenced by an individual's sex; however, there were distinctive differences between the diets of individuals buried with grave goods and those without, particularly in relation to the suggested consumption of millet, which correlated with the presence of grave goods. Pork consumption was inferred through the presence of articulated pig remains in graves. Within the Lant Street samples, carbon isotope results showed little variation in comparison with other Roman sites in the UK, indicating a purely terrestrial diet, with no evidence for consumption of marine-based foods. The results indicated by nitrogen isotope values, however, are more surprising, indicating that this population consumed at best very small quantities and quite possibly no freshwater fish. This group appears to have a very different isotopic pattern from other populations of Roman Britain investigated to date; whilst low marine food consumption has been linked to lower-status graves elsewhere in the UK, based on grave goods, this does not appear to be the case here.

Sample sizes here are clearly relatively small, and the Trinity Street sample was particularly poorly preserved. Nevertheless, if we take the evidence of these two populations at face value, we might interpret the evidence as indicative of a series of discrete sub-cemeteries, serving different elements of the population. We now need to expand the dataset to include burial samples from the waterlogged burial ground of the Upper Walbrook valley and elsewhere.

99   King (1984).
100   Garnsey (1999).
101   Locker (2007).
102   Locker (2007) 151.
103   Redfern *et al.* (2018) 1038.
104   Craig (2015).

Grave Goods, Grave Furniture and Environmental Evidence

The concept that treatment of the deceased at burial might reflect status in life is obvious, although interpretations of 'rich graves' equating to the wealth or social standing of an individual are over-simplistic. Formal burial itself may have reflected a certain status.[105] The complex relationship between age, sex, and gender and the relationship of these and other aspects of identity as reflected in grave goods forms an important focus of study,[106] as does evidence for physical divisions in age groupings and the treatment of infants and the young.[107] Statistical work that examines the relationship between sex, age, and grave good provisions in large Romano-British cemetery populations is beginning to reveal complex patterning.[108] Despite the ever-expanding literature on the meaning of burial good provision,[109] few studies face up to the problem that on most Late Roman sites, it is a relatively rare rite (e.g. at Spitalfields only 22% of burials dated *ca.* AD 250–400 had goods), only rarely involving costly items, making generalisations to contemporary social structures problematic.

White has highlighted the potential of examining the provisioning of animal food offerings.[110] A preponderance of pig bones has been noted within graves in Southwark, both at Southwark Bridge Road and at Lant Street, which may represent graveside offerings or the residue of feasting. Other less robust organic offerings, such as textiles, plant foodstuffs, or flowers are rarely preserved. The richly furnished female lead coffin and sarcophagus burial at Spitalfields provided an environment that had preserved fragments of textiles.[111] The corpse wore a damask silk tunic, which incorporated wool and gold thread tapestry decoration. This grave also provides the first evidence for the use of aromatic resins in a Roman burial in London, although there are examples from elsewhere in Britain[112] and further afield in Trier.[113] The resins may have been used to preserve the corpse, to mask the smell of decomposition and/or for religious reasons. They are an ostentatious display of wealth as they would have been imported and not widely available.

Meanwhile, establishing patterns that connect grave goods with the age and sex of the deceased remains problematic, with establishing age at death remaining difficult. Cox has demonstrated that it is difficult to age skeletal remains above the age of 45,[114] though some studies push this to 50.[115] This may have the effect of making past populations appear younger than they really were. Establishing biological sex becomes easier with age but it remains difficult to reliably sex skeletal remains below the age of 18. Furthermore, artefacts incorporated in the grave may convey numerous complex messages relating not only to the status of the deceased but also to the mourners themselves. Burial is as much reflective of the concerns of the living, as with those of the dead; funerals and their attendant rituals are bound up in social display, political power, and social identity; they are the focus of conspicuous consumption.[116] A detailed consideration of grave good evidence from late antique burials in London is long overdue but lies beyond the scope of the present paper.

Discussion

Recent Work

The foregoing text has provided an overview of some aspects of burial in late antique Londinium. It illustrates the impact of developer-funded excavation on datasets and highlights the lack of overall syntheses of this data in recent years. Using data from Southwark as an example, Hall's review of the cemeteries of Roman London[117] lists 38 cremation burials and 48 inhumations from the Southwark area as a whole.[118] A more recent assessment[119] put the figure at around 460 (excluding disarticulated bone), illustrating the extent of recent excavation work.

Late antique burial rites across Londinium are, without exception, dominated by inhumations. This should not surprise us; it reflects the prevalent situation in Rome.[120] However, Britain, particularly the London area, appears more complex and less 'formulaic' than has been previously assumed;[121] nevertheless, inhumation appears to have been the dominant rite. Of the 374 or more burials identified since 1996, only half a dozen were cremation burials. This is unlikely to be

105   Milllett and Pearce, pers. comm. in Struck (2000).
106   E.g. Lucy (2000); Stoodley (2000).
107   E.g. Pearce (2001); Gowland (2001); Martin-Kilcher (2000); Scott (2001).
108   Booth *et al.* (2010) 512; Cool (2004).
109   E.g. Pearce (2013).
110   White (2007).
111   McKenzie and Thomas (2020) 145–47.
112   Brettell *et al.* (2018).
113   Reifarth *et al.* (2006).

114   Cox (1996).
115   E.g. Gowland (2001).
116   Williams (2004) 89.
117   Hall (1996).
118   Hall (1996).
119   Ridgeway *et al.* (2013) 106–116.
120   Philpott (1991) 8.
121   Barber and Bowsher (2000) 300.

coincidental and it is important to note the part played by survival and truncation. In this urban context, 18th and 19th c. construction attracted the attentions of antiquarians and collectors, for whom cremation urns made valuable display pieces, with the result that these artefacts survive, whilst other information may have been lost. Additionally, during this period the increasingly deep construction of cellars and basements removed the upper parts of Roman sequences. Cremations, being generally buried more shallowly, are less likely to have survived, potentially skewing the dataset.

Archaeological evidence for burial practices is dominated by the moment of interment in the ground; attendant rituals are much harder to identify archaeologically.[122] Evidence for graveside feasting or other funerary practices can be elusive. Nevertheless, it is clear that there is much diversity in the evidence that survives. This largely inhumation-based late antique tradition can be broadly divided into four groups according to location and type. The evidence for these comprises:

1)   occasional isolated inhumations focussed on temples, mausolea and the walled enclosures surrounding them, set along the approach roads into Londinium

2)   large, predominantly inhumation cemeteries, sometimes set back from but also fronting roads commonly within ditch- and/or hedge-defined plots

3)   a concentration of unusually heavily intercutting burials on the western tip of the southern island in Southwark

4)   small clusters of inhumations focussed on the remains of former monuments, roads and large masonry buildings within formerly occupied areas.

Amongst the evidence for late antique burial in Londinium, the inhumations clustered around former monuments, other buildings, and cut into metalled surfaces, within former occupation areas, present the most distinct departure from earlier Roman traditions. Within Southwark, this focus of late burials on the remains of earlier masonry structures has generally been taken to be indicative of decline, the contraction of the settlement and retreat towards the bridgehead, and with ideas of disposal of the dead becoming less formal.[123] An alternative and more complex scenario might be envisaged here, which would see focus of burial on nodal points within the landscape as a different way of doing things. Heard[124] has suggested that burials may have

been focussed around surviving parts of buildings which served as ritual foci.[125] If the burials identified here are of Late Roman (and not later) date, as assumed, a number of scenarios might be envisaged. These dispersed burials may reflect a series of small settlement foci within the broader landscape, or may represent 'special' burial practices focussed on the ruins of former important or significant buildings, perhaps with ancestral links to the buried population. They perhaps bear comparison with Pearce's 'dispersed dead', albeit that the latter are within a rural context.[126] The placing of burials on the site of earlier occupation has been associated with a connection to long-term or ancestral occupation of a place; a phenomenon which might have particularly characterised the Later Roman period.[127]

Conclusions and Further Work

London is well-studied and complex phasing of excavated material is possible; however, detailed study of cemetery development and change over time would be a very positive addition to the available data. There is clearly a highly nuanced picture with significant variations between areas to be painted. Additionally, the quantitative study of disarticulated bone across the later phases of London would contribute to the overall picture of population size and density and associated changes over time. Prompt publication of excavated sites is always preferable and there are some Roman cemeteries that have languished overlong. It would also be very helpful if contracting organisations provided osteological finds and contextual data digitally in an open access format, to enable synthesis and comparative study.[128] This is true of all archaeological data but the manner in which human remains are excavated and recorded is highly standardised, so this type of site data would be relatively simple to make available.

The evidence suggests dispersed and varied responses to death, with clear indications that different subsets of the population might have utilised different areas for burial and followed different practices. What is sometimes less clear from the physical evidence are differences in the lifestyle and mobility of particular groups as borne out in the stable isotope work undertaken in Southwark. This has demonstrated variability in the mobility and dietary preferences of individuals buried in apparently similar and nearby cemetery areas. We

---

122   E.g. Pearce (2017); Weekes (2017).

123   Drummond-Murray *et al.* (2002) 5–6; Mackinder and Whittingham (2013).

124   Heard *et al.* (1990).

125   Also see Rogers (2011) 172–75.

126   Pearce (1999).

127   Pearce (1999) 158.

128   Pearce (2015) 157.

should all strive to improve and increase our investment in bioarchaeological studies, from these detailed datasets come results, which are hugely relevant to a wider audience. Modern political discourse does not always encourage the expert voice but when scientific methods offer incontrovertible evidence of aspects of the human past such as mobility, ethnicity, and health, we should embrace the opportunity to elucidate on the development of our towns and cities within broader society. The success of exhibitions hosted at the Museum of London Docklands[129] has also vividly illustrated the interest the general public have in Roman funerary archaeology and how the respectful display of burials can stimulate interest in past inhabitants of the city.

We should also expand our Roman temporal zone beyond traditional assumptions of a compact city, which contracted swiftly. The concept of 'urban' burials and cemeteries is unhelpful when extra-mural burials are encountered beyond traditional understandings of the hinterland of London. The Southwark examples provide a challenging counterpoint to discoveries across the Thames but should be considered part of the same Roman London dataset when synthesis is attempted. These sites also highlight the potential of the application of DNA and isotope studies for understanding aspects of the Late Roman population. This should become a standard feature in all future project designs. Systematic use of scientific dating and modelling would also be of benefit to refine our understanding of when the various burial grounds fell into disuse. Further research should attempt to clarify the apparent differences between burial grounds in Southwark and those north of the river. These may result in part from the unusual topographic situation, less intensive use by the population of the smaller southern part of the settlement and better preservation due to less intensive post-Roman development but should be tested as a model for consideration of London's other cemetery areas. The temptation to assume that burial and other aspects of Roman society become more homogenous through time is also to be resisted. The evidence from the examples given in this paper illustrate the variety of funerary tradition across London and its hinterlands, rather than confirm a standard method of burial or belief.

Acknowledgements

The authors would like to thank the Editors of this volume for the invitation to contribute and the anonymous referees who provided very useful comments. We would also like to thank Cate Davies for the illustrations that accompany this publication. In addition, Sadie Watson would like to thank Michael Mulryan for the invitation to speak at the "Fieldwork in Late Antique Archaeology. Burial and Funerary Practice" conference; to Alison Telfer for providing unpublished information, Andy Chopping and Margaret Cox for supplying photographs, and Sue Hirst and the late Bruno Barber for editing. Victoria Ridgeway would like to thank Kevin Rielly (PCA) for discussing fish consumption in Roman London and Dr James Gerrard (Newcastle University) for discussing many aspects of Late Roman Southwark and London, burial included. The stable isotope analyses undertaken on burials from both Lant Street and Trinity Street are very much the product of collaborative analyses, supported by external funding. We are grateful to Dr Rebecca Redfern, Curator of Human Osteology at the Museum of London for her assistance with analysis of the Lant Street individuals, and Dr Andrew Millard, Dr Darren Grocke, and Lucie Johnson of Durham University for carrying out the analyses. Thanks are also extended to Dr Gundula Müldner of Reading University for assistance with the Trinity Street samples and Lauren Craig (Reading University) and Dr Jane Evans (BGS) for carrying out the analyses; this work was made possible through the generous provision of a grant from Southwark and Lambeth Archaeological Excavation Committee.

Bibliography

Barber B. and Bowsher D. (2000) *The Eastern Cemetery of Roman London: Excavations 1983–1990* (MoLAS Monograph 4) (London 2000).

Barber B. and Hall J. (2000) "Digging up the people of Roman London: roads, roadside settlements and the countryside", in *London Underground: The Archaeology of a City*, edd. I. Haynes, S. Sheldon, and L. Hannigan (Oxford 2000) 102–120.

Barker S., Coombe P., and Perna S. (2018) "Re-use of Roman stone in London city-walls," in *Roman Ornamental Stones in North-Western Europe. Natural Resources, Manufacturing, Supply, Life and After-life*, edd. C. Coquelet, G. Creemers, R. Dreesen, and E. Goemaere (Namur 2018) 321–42.

Bateman N., Cowan C., and Wroe-Brown R. (2008) *London's Roman Amphitheatre, Guildhall Yard* (MoLAS Monograph 35) (London 2008).

---

129   The Tunnel exhibition between February and September 2017 had more than 80,000 visitors and over 50,000 online visits (Jackie Keily pers. comm.). The Roman Dead exhibition during 2018 focused on bioarchaeological information and the stone sarcophagus from Southwark.

Beard D. and Cowan C. (1988) "Excavations at 15–23 South-wark Street", *London Archaeologist* 5 (1988) 375–81.

Bentley D. and Pritchard F. (1982) "The Roman cemetery at St Bartholomew's Hospital, London", *Transactions of the Middlesex Archaeological Society* 33 (1982) 134–72.

Blackmore L. (2012) "New light on the origins, development and decline of the Middle Saxon trading settlement of Lundenwic", in *The Very Beginning of Europe? Early-Medieval Migration and Colonisation*, edd. R. Annaert, K. de Groote, Y. Hollevoet, F. Theuws, D. Tys, and L. Verslype (Brussels 2012) 147–58.

Booth P., Simmonds A., Boyle A., Clough S., Cool H. E., and Poore D. (2010) *The Late Roman Cemetery at Lankhills, Winchester; Excavation 2000–2005* (Oxford Archaeology Monograph 10) (Oxford 2010).

Brettell R., Schotsmans E., Martin W., Stern B., and Heron C. (2018) "The final masquerade: resinous substances and Roman mortuary rites", in *The Bioarchaeology of Ritual and Religion*, edd. A. Livarda, R. Madgwick, and R. M. Santiago (Oxford 2018) 44–57.

Brigham T. (1990) "A reassessment of the second basilica in London, AD 100–400: excavations at Leadenhall Court, 1984–6", *Britannia* 21 (1990) 53–97.

Budd P. (2003) "Combined O-, Sr- and Pb-isotope analysis of dental tissues from a Neolithic individual from Shepperton and an Iron Age individual from Southwark, London", Unpublished report, *Archaeotrace Ltd.*

Butler J. (2006) *Reclaiming the Marsh: Archaeological Excavations at Moor House, City of London* (PCA Monograph 6) (London 2006).

Butler J. and Ridgeway V. edd. (2009) *Secrets of the Gardens: Archaeologists Unearth the Lives of Roman Londoners at Drapers' Gardens* (London 2009).

Chenery C., Evans J., Lamb A., Muldner G., and Eckhardt H. (2010) "Oxygen and strontium isotope analysis", in *The Late Roman Cemetery at Lankhills, Winchester. Excavations 2000–2005* (Oxford Archaeology Monograph 10), edd. P. Booth, A. Simmonds, A. Boyle, S. Clough, H. Cool, and D. Poore (Oxford 2010) 421–28.

Cool H. E. (2004) *The Roman Cemetery at Brougham, Cumbria; Excavations 1966–67* (Britannia Monograph Series 21) (London 2004).

Cowan C. (1992) "A possible mansio in Roman Southwark: excavations at 15–23 Southwark Street, 1980–86", *Transactions of the London and Middlesex Archaeological Society* 43 (1992) 3–191.

Cowan C. (2003) *Urban Development in North-West Roman Southwark: Excavations 1974–90* (MoLAS Monograph 16) (London 2000).

Cowan C., Seeley F., Wardle A., Westman A., and Wheeler L. (2009) *Roman Southwark: Settlement and Economy* (MOLA Monograph 42) (London 2009).

Cowie R. (2008) "Descent into darkness: London in the 5th and 6th centuries", in *Londinium and Beyond* (CBA Rep 156), edd. J. Clark, J. Cotton, J. Hall, R. Sherris, and H. Swain (York 2008) 49–53.

Cowie R. and Blackmore L. (2012) *Lundenwic: Excavations in Middle Saxon London, 1987–2000* (MOLA Monograph 63) (London 2012).

Cox M. (1996) *Life and Death at Spitalfields 1700 to 1850* (York 1996).

Craig L. (2015) *An Investigation to Determine the Extent of 'Roman' and Cultural Influences on the Dietary Inhabitants of the Residents of the London Borough of Southwark using Stable Carbon and Nitrogen Isotopic Analysis* (Unpublished diss., Univ. of Reading 2015).

Cummings C. and Hedges R. (2010) "Carbon and nitrogen stable isotopes analysis", in *The Late Roman Cemetery at Lankhills, Winchester. Excavations 2000–2005* (Oxford Archaeology Monograph 10), edd. P. Booth, A. Simmonds, A. Boyle, S. Clough, H. Cool, and D. Poore (Oxford 2010) 411–20.

Davies G., Gardner A., and Lockyear K. edd. (2001) *Tenth Annual Theoretical Roman Archaeology Conference* (Oxford 2001).

Daykin A. (2016) Principal Place (Commercial), Worship Street, London EC2: A Post-excavation Assessment and Updated Project Design (Unpublished MOLA report) (2016).

Daykin A. (2017) *Principal Place (Residential), Worship Street, London EC2: A Post-excavation Assessment and Updated Project Design* (Unpublished MOLA report) (2017).

Dean M. (1981) "Evidence for more Roman burials in Southwark", *London Archaeologist* 4.2 (1981) 52–53.

DoE (1990) *Planning Policy Guidance 16, Archaeology and Planning* (London 1990).

Esmonde Cleary S. (2000) "Putting the dead in their place: burial location in Roman Britain", in *Burial, Society and Context in the Roman World*, edd. J. Pearce, M. Millet, and M. Struck (Oxford 2000) 127–42.

Fulford M. and Holbrook N. edd. (2015) *The Towns of Roman Britain. The Contribution of Commercial Archaeology since 1990* (London 2015).

Hingley R. (2018) *Londinium: A Biography. Roman London from its Origins to the Fifth Century* (London 2018).

Gerrard J. (2016) "Economy and power in Late Roman Britain", in *The Oxford Handbook of Roman Britain*, edd. M. Millett, L. Revell, and A. Moore (Oxford 2016) 850–67.

Gowland R. (2016) "Ideas of childhood in Roman Britain", in *The Oxford Handbook of Roman Britain*, edd. M. Millett, L. Revell, and A. Moore (Oxford 2016) 303–320.

Gowland R. (2001) "Playing dead: implications of mortuary evidence for the social construction of childhood in Roman Britain", in *Tenth Annual Theoretical Roman Archaeology*

Conference, edd. G. Davies, A. Gardner, and K. Lockyear (Oxford 2001) 152–68.

Grosso I. (2018) *25–29 Harper Road, Southwark, London, SE1. An Archaeological Assessment* (Unpublished PCA report) (2018).

Hall J. (1996) "The cemeteries of Roman London: a review", in *Interpreting Roman London: papers in memory of Hugh Chapman*, edd. J. Bird, M. Hassall, and H. Sheldon (Oxford 1996) 57–84.

Harward C., Powers N., and Watson S. (2015) *The Upper Walbrook Roman Cemetery: Excavations at Finsbury Circus* (MOLA Monograph 69) (London 2015).

Hill C., Millett M., and Blagg T. (1980) "The Roman riverside wall and monumental arch in London, excavations at Baynard's Castle, Upper Thames Street, London, 1974–76", *Transactions of the London and Middlesex Archaeological Society Special Paper* 3 (1980) 88–93.

Hill J. and Rowsome P. (2011) *Roman London and the Walbrook Stream Crossing: Excavations at 1, Poultry and vicinity, City of London (Part II)* (MOLA Monograph 37) (London 2011).

Killock D., Shepherd J., Gerrard J., Hayward K., Rielly K., and Ridgeway V. (2015) *Temples and Suburbs: Excavations at Tabard Square, Southwark* (PCA Monograph 18) (London 2015).

Killock D., Gerrard J. and Langthorne J. (forthcoming). *Excavations at 28–30 Trinity Street.* (PCA Monograph).

Langton B. (1990) *Excavations and Watching Brief at 1–4 Giltspur Street, 24–30 West Smithfield and 18–20 Cock Lane, EC4 (WES89)* (Unpublished MoL report) (1990).

Langton B. (1991) "Fieldwork round-up", *London Archaeologist* 6 (1991) 278.

King A. (1984) "Animal bones and the dietary identity of military and civilian groups in Roman Britain Germany and Gaul", in *Military and Civilian in Roman Britain: Cultural Relationships in a Frontier Province* (BAR-BS 136), edd. T. F. C. Blagg and A. King (Oxford 1984) 187–217.

Leach S., Ekhardt H., Chenery C., Muldner G., and Lewis M. (2009) "A lady of York: migration, ethnicity and identity in Roman Britain", *Antiquity* 84 (2009) 131–45.

Leach S., Lewis M., Chenery C., Muldner G., and Eckhardt H. (2010) "Migration and diversity in Roman Britain: a multidisciplinary approach to the identification of immigrants in Roman York, England", *American Journal of Physical Anthropology* 140 (2010) 546–61.

Lucy S. (2000) *The Anglo-Saxon Way of Death* (Gloucester 2000).

Mackinder A. (2000) *A Romano-British cemetery on Watling Street: Excavations at 165 Great Dover Street, Southwark, London* (MoLAS Studies 4) (London 2000).

Mackinder A. and Whittingham L. (2013) *The Place, Formerly New London Bridge House, 25 London Bridge Street, London SE1, London Borough of Southwark, Post-excavation Assessment* (Unpublished MoLA report) (2013).

MacLaughlin S. and Scheuer L. (no date) "Human bone from Giltspur Street, London (WES89)" (Unpublished MoL report).

Martin-Kilcher S. (2000) "Mors immatura in the Roman World – a mirror of society and tradition", in *Burial, Society and Context in the Roman World*, edd. J. Pearce and M. Millett (Oxford 2000) 63–77.

Mays S., Elders J., Humphrey L., White W., and Marshall P. (2013) *Science and the Dead: A Guideline for the Destructive Sampling of Archaeological Human Remains for Scientific Analysis* (Frome 2013).

McKenzie M. and Thomas C. (2020) *In the Northern Cemetery of Roman London: Excavations at Spitalfields Market, London E1, 1991–2007* (MOLA Monograph 58) (London 2020).

McKinley J. I. (2009) "Inhumation burial in a ditch", in *Living and Working in Roman and Later London* (Wessex Archaeology Report 25), edd. Birbeck V. and Schuster J. (Maidstone 2009) 13–14.

Melikian M. and Sayer K. (2007) "Recent excavations in the 'Southern Cemetery' of Roman Southwark", in *Proceedings of the Seventh Annual conference of the British Association for Biological Anthropology and Osteoarchaeology* (BAR-IS 1712), edd. S. R. Zakrzewski and W. White (Oxford 2007) 14–23.

Mitchell P. M. and Brickley M. (2017) *Updated Guidelines to the Standards for Recording Human Remains* (Chartered Institute for Archaeologists and British Association for Biological Anthropology and Osteoarchaeology) (Reading 2017).

Montgomery J., Evans J., Chenery S., Pashley V., and Killgrove K (2010) "'Gleaming, white and deadly': using lead to track human exposure and geographic origins in the Roman period in Britain", *JRA Suppl.* 78 (2010) 199–226.

Parker Pearson M. (1999) *The Archaeology of Death and Burial* (Stroud 2003).

Pearce J. (2016) "Status and burial", in *The Oxford Handbook of Roman Britain*, edd. M. Millett, L. Revell, and A. Moore (Oxford 2016) 341–62.

Pearce J. (1999) "The dispersed dead: preliminary observations on burial and settlement space in rural Roman Britain", in *Proceedings of the Eighth Annual Theoretical Roman Archaeology Conference*, edd. P. Baker, C. Forcey, S. Jundi, and R. Witcher (Oxford 1999) 151–62.

Pearce J. (2001) "Infants, cemeteries and communities in the Roman provinces", in *Tenth Annual Theoretical Roman Archaeology Conference*, edd. G. Davies, A. Gardner, and K. Lockyear (Oxford 2001) 125–42.

Pearce J. (2013) *Contextual Archaeology of Burial Practice: Case Studies from Roman Britain* (London 2013).

Pearce J. (2015) "Urban exits: archaeology and the study of death in the towns of Roman Britain", in *The Towns of Roman Britain. The Contribution of Commercial Archaeology since 1990*, edd. M. Fulford and N. Holbrook (London 2015) 138–66.

Pearce J. (2017) "Introduction: death as a process in Roman funerary archaeology", in *Death as a Process*, edd. J. Pearce and J. Weekes (Oxford 2017) 1–26.

Pearce J., Millett M., and Struck M. (edd.) (2000) *Burial, Society and Context in the Roman World* (Oxford 2000).

Pearce J. and Weekes J. edd. (2017) *Death as a Process* (Oxford 2017).

Perring D. (2015) "Recent advances in the understanding of Roman London", in *The Towns of Roman Britain. The Contribution of Commercial Archaeology since 1990*, edd. M. Fulford and N. Holbrook (London 2015) 20–43.

Philpott R. (1991) *Burial Practices in Roman Britain; A Survey of Grave Treatment and Furnishing A.D. 43–410* (BAR 219) (Oxford 1991).

Powell L. A., Redfern R. C., and Millard A. R. (2014) "Infant feeding practices in Roman London: evidence from isotope analysis", in *Infant Health and Death in Roman Italy and Beyond, JRA Suppl.* 96, edd. M. Carroll and E. J. Graham (Ann Arbor 2014) 89–110.

Proctor J., Gaimster M., and Langthorne J. Y. (2016) *A Quaker Burial Ground at North Shields: Excavations at Coach Lane, Tyne and Wear* (PCA Monograph 20) (London 2016).

Ranieri S. and Telfer A., with Walker D and Yendell V. (2017) *Outside Roman London: Roadside Burials by the Walbrook Stream* (Crossrail Archaeology Series 9) (London 2017).

Redfern R. (2003) "Sex and the city: a biocultural investigation into female health in Roman Britain", in *TRAC 2002, Proceedings of the Twelfth Annual Theoretical Roman Archaeology Conference*, edd. G. Carr, E. Swift, and J. Weekes (Oxford 2003) 147–69.

Redfern R. C., Hamlin C., and Beavan Athfield N. (2010) "Temporal changes in diet: a stable isotope analysis of late Iron Age and Roman Dorset, Britain", *JAS* 37 (2010) 1149–60.

Redfern R. and Bonney H. (2014) "Headhunting and amphitheatre combat in Roman London, England: new evidence from the Walbrook valley", *JAS* 30 (2014) 1–13.

Redfern R. C., Gröcke D. R., Millard A. R., Ridgeway V., Johnson L., and Hefner J. T. (2016) "Going south of the river: A multidisciplinary analysis of ancestry, mobility and diet in a population from Roman Southwark, London", *JAS* 74 (2016) 11–22.

Redfern R. C., Marshall M., Eaton K., and Poinar H. N. (2017) ""Written in bone": new discoveries about the lives and burials of four Roman Londoners", *Britannia* 48 (2017) 253–77.

Redfern R., Gowland R., Millard A., Powell L., and Gröcke D. (2018) "'From the mouths of babes': a subadult dietary

stable isotope perspective on Roman London (Londinium)", *JAS* 19 (2018) 1030–40.

Reifarth N., Boenke N., Teegen W-R., and Wiethold J. (2006) "Das spätantike Grab 279 aus St. Maximin in Trier. Textiltechnologische, anthropologische und archäobotanische Untersuchungen. [The late Roman grave 279 from St Maximin in Trier, Germany. Studies of textiles and anthropological and archaeobotanical analysis]", *Ausgrabungen und Funde im Bezirk Trier* 38 (2006) 58–70.

Ridgeway V., Leary K., and Sudds B. (2013) *Roman Burials in Southwark: Excavations at 52–56 Lant Street and 56 Southwark Bridge Road* (PCA Monograph 17) (London 2013).

Scott E. (2001) "Unpicking a myth: the infanticide of female and disabled infants in antiquity", in *Tenth Annual Theoretical Roman Archaeology Conference*, edd. G. Davies, A. Gardner, and K. Lockyear (Oxford 2001) 143–51.

Shaw H., Montgomery J., Redfern R., Gowland R., and Evans J. (2016) "Identifying migrants in Roman London using lead and strontium stable isotopes", *JAS* 66 (2016) 57–68.

Stoodley N. (1999) *The Spindle and the Spear; A Critical Enquiry into the Construction and Meaning of Gender in the Early Anglo-Saxon Burial Rite* (BAR 288) (Oxford 1999).

Stoodley N. (2000) "From the cradle to the grave; age organisation and the early Anglo-Saxon burial rite", *World Archaeology* 31 (2000) 456–72.

Struck M. (2000) "High status burials in Roman Britain (first-third century AD) potential interpretation" in *Burial, Society and Context in the Roman World*, edd. J. Pearce and M. Millett (Oxford 2000) 85–96.

Swift D. (2003) *Roman Burials, Medieval Tenements and Suburban Growth: 201 Bishopsgate, City of London* (MoLAS Studies 10) (London 2003).

Telfer A. (forthcoming) *Archaeological Discoveries at St Martin-In-The-Fields Church, St Martin's Lane, London, WC2*.

Tomlin R. (2016) *Roman London's First Voices: Writing Tablets from the Bloomberg Excavations, 2010–4* (London 2016).

Wallace L. M. (2014) *The Origins of Roman London* (Cambridge 2014).

Watson S. (2003) *An Excavation in the Western Cemetery of Roman London: Atlantic House, City of London* (MoLAS Studies 7) (London 2003).

Watson S. (2006) *Development on Roman London's western hill: Excavations at Paternoster Square, City of London* (MoLAS Monograph 32) (London 2003).

Weekes J. (2016) "Cemeteries and funerary practice", in *The Oxford Handbook of Roman Britain*, edd. M. Millett, L. Revell, and A. Moore (Oxford 2016) 425–47.

Weekes J. (2017) "Funerary archaeology at St Dunstan's Terrace, Canterbury", in *Death as a Process*, edd. J. Pearce and J. Weekes (Oxford 2017) 83–122.

White C. C. (2007) "Catering for the cultural identities of the deceased in Roman Britain: interpretative potential and problems", in *Proceedings of the Sixteenth Annual Theoretical Roman Archaeology Conference*, edd. B. Croxford, N. Ray, R. Roth, and N. White (Oxford 2007) 115–32.

Whytehead R. (1986) "The excavation of an area within a Roman cemetery at West Tenter Street, London E1", *Transactions of the London and Middlesex Archaeological Society* 37 (1986) 29–31.

Williams H. (1997) "Ancient landscapes and the dead: the reuse of prehistoric and Roman monuments as early Anglo-Saxon burial sites", *Medieval Archaeology* 41 (1997) 1–32.

Williams H. (1998) "Monuments and the past in Early Anglo-Saxon England", *World Archaeology* 30 (1998) 90–108.

Williams H. (2004) "Artefacts in early medieval graves – a new perspective", in *Debating Late Antiquity in Britain AD300–700* (BAR-BS 365), edd. R. Collins and J. Gerrard (Oxford 2004) 89–102.

New Cemetery Evidence from Late Roman Canterbury: the Former Hallet's Garage Site in Context

Elizabeth Duffy, Adrian Gollop and Jake Weekes

Abstract

This article focuses on a Late Roman cemetery excavated at the former Hallet's Garage, Canterbury in 2010 and 2011, on the north-west side of the Late Roman town. In all, 140 burials were investigated, the largest number, at that time, to have been archaeologically excavated in Canterbury. More recently, contemporary and extensive cemetery sites have been investigated in the south-east of the walled town, at Rhodaus Town and the former Peugeot Garage respectively; these are also introduced in summary here. Initial results of a bioarchaeological study of the Hallet's Garage material are then presented, a project that will extend to the many new *comparanda* from the southern Canterbury cemeteries in due course, and with the dead of other urban centres in Late Roman Britain. A methodological statement on archaeologically reconstructing the funerary process follows, along with some initial considerations of the funerary process at Hallet's and how it compares with the other new sites in Canterbury.

Introduction

At the end of March 2011, an intensive three-month excavation came to a close on the site of the former Hallet's Garage on the corner of St. Dunstan's Street and Station Road West in Canterbury, approximately 100 m from the medieval Westgate, which lies on the alignment of the Late Roman wall (Fig. 3.1).[1] Early Roman cemeteries were already known to lie further out from the town centre in St. Dunstan's (as elsewhere in Canterbury), reflecting the more extensive pre-wall topography of Durovernum and the influential Roman rule of siting cemeteries beyond the town limits.[2] Later Roman cemeteries at Canterbury are closer to the walled circuit, which evidently 'cut off' several existing parts of the town in approximately 270–290 AD,[3] and most obviously St. Dunstan's, thereby establishing the area as 'outside the town' and a suitable place for the dead. However, early to mid-Roman St. Dunstan's does not seem to have been heavily urbanized prior to this, seeing rather sporadic occupation and

industrial activities. Indeed, before the use of the land at Hallet's as a cemetery, the plot contained only some ditched land divisions and two or three sunken-featured buildings near the road.

Canterbury's Late Roman inhumation cemeteries had seldom been subjected to modern standards of excavation and are a scarce resource; moreover, until that time, no large Late Roman cemetery areas had been excavated to anything like a modern standard at Canterbury.[4] While isolated finds of inhumation burials in the immediate vicinity of Hallet's Garage suggested a larger cemetery focus there,[5] nothing on the scale of the subsequent findings could be predicted. Sadly, therefore, under funding pressure from a competitive tendering process prior to work commencing and little curatorial flexibility or control during the iterative discovery process, the excavation ran into difficulty and quickly became a salvage project. In the end, Canterbury archaeologists rallied round and excavated at weekends free of charge. Through this 'embedded economy', most of the burials and other features were thereby rescued.[6]

Introducing the Rhodaus Town and the former Peugeot Garage Sites

These more recently discovered extensive Late Roman cemeteries on the southern side of the Late Roman town have apparently been subjected to realistic funding and 'research aware' treatment. Sites at Rhodaus Town and the former Peugeot Garage,[7] while they can only be summarized here, will provide excellent comparative material for the Hallet's Garage assemblage, and include a broadly contemporary shrine and two very different cemetery plots set within a fascinating late antique suburban setting (Fig. 2).

---

1 NGR 61477 15822; note that areas of later truncation are left blank on this and other plans of the Hallet's cemetery.
2 Cf. Weekes (2017a) 84ff.
3 see Weekes (2014) 247–49.

4 Weekes (2011).
5 Pilbrow (1871); Jenkins (1951); Tatton-Brown (1983); Rady (2009); see Weekes (2011) 32ff.
6 12 clearly identified burials had unfortunately to be sacrificed as time ran out, and no further information for these is now available; volunteer work has been necessary in order to bring post-excavation analysis to its current state of publication.
7 Canterbury Archaeological Trust (2015); (2017).

© KONINKLIJKE BRILL BV, LEIDEN, 2024 | DOI:10.1163/9789004687974_006
Alexandra Dolea and Luke Lavan (eds) *Burial and Memorial in Late Antiquity*
(Late Antique Archaeology 13) (Leiden 2024), pp. 647–666

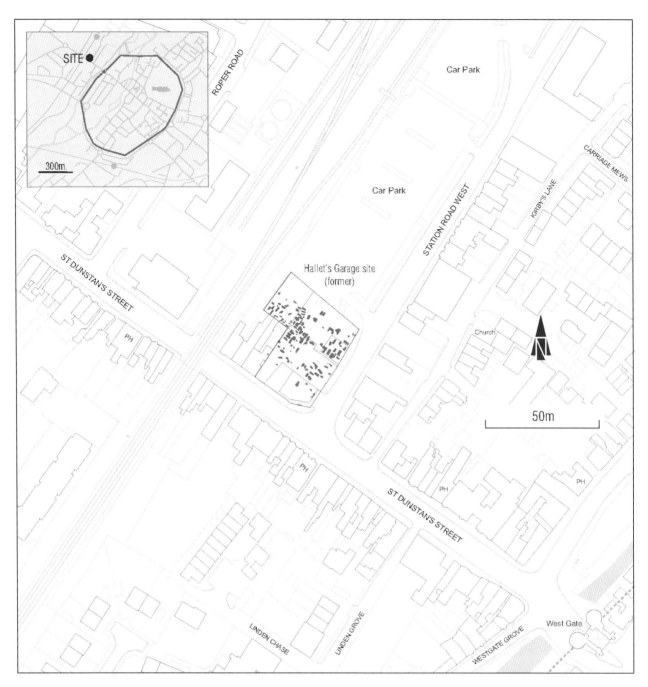

FIGURE 1   The former Hallet's Garage late Roman Cemetery; St Dunstan's Street follows the line of the extra-mural Roman Road (1:1600).

The smaller, Rhodaus Town example,[8] excavated in 2013, contained 20 burials within a clearly delimited cemetery plot. About half of the graves contained coffin outlines and/or coffin nails, and several had earth-cut ledges, while some may have been embellished with timber shoring. The burial population here presented an interesting age and sex profile, with perhaps 5 children, 1 adolescent female, 2 female young adults, 9 adults (including 2 males and 4 possible females) and three older adults (a male and a female present). In respect of this, it might be noted that the dead from a single extended family could have populated the cemetery for over 40 years or so (a group of say 25, at a crude death rate of one deceased every two years, extrapolated from a rough equivalent to a postulated 20 per 1000 annually).[9] Perhaps the most defining characteristic of this cemetery plot, however, was the provision of accessory items,

8   https://issuu.com/alfalfa2/docs/canterburys_archaeology_2013_2014/14.

9   This is about the upper limit of international crude death rates in the 'developing world' today; see https://data.un.org/Data.aspx?d=PopDiv&f=variableID%3A65.

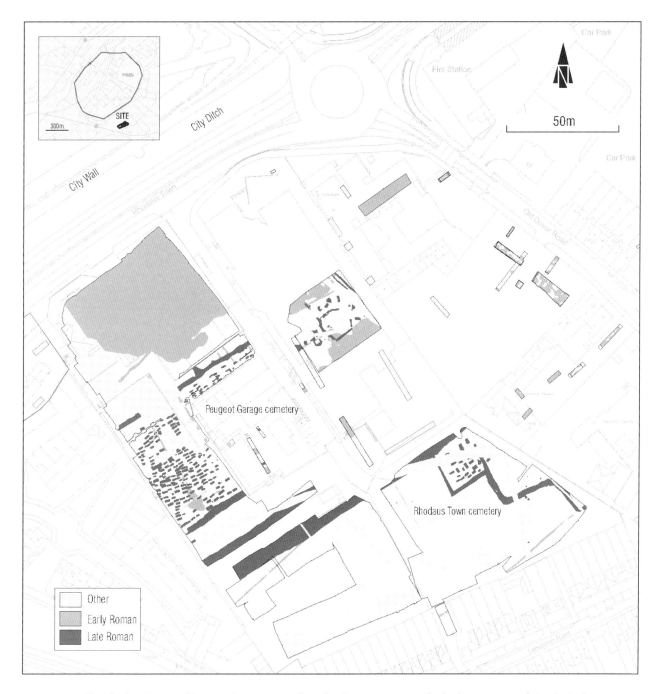

FIGURE 2   The Rhodaus Town and Peugeot Garage sites within a late Roman extra-mural suburb containing a shrine (1:1600).

supplied either during laying out or during depositional phases of the funerals. The possible 'laying out of goods' included items of dress and other accessories, such as the footwear in some cases worn by the corpse (graves 4, 6, 8, and 11), anklets (grave 1), a bracelet (grave 16), hairpins (graves 12 and 16), glass beads and a shale 'ring' (grave 17). Further objects apparently located within the coffin outline are also likely to have belonged to a laying out phase, then carried with the corpse to the burial site. This is quite typical in the case of the glass *unguentarium* from grave 6, for example but perhaps less usual for pots as, apparently, in graves 1, 7, 8, 12, and 16 at least. Other

objects seem more likely to have been 'grave goods' associated with the burial itself. This would perhaps apply to a particularly interesting box/casket, reconstructed as lying above the knees of the adolescent female occupant of grave 6, which contained an odd assortment of apparently old and worn items in a bag: a broken brooch, a coin, a 'boar's tusk' and a pebble (perhaps apotropaic items?). Another particularly interesting find from this small cemetery was a very large and perhaps unique Oxfordshire styled beaker with extraordinary decoration, including the representation of a moustachioed face, from grave 8.

To the west of the Rhodaus Town plot, a much larger cemetery area was also uncovered in near the former Peugeot Garage, where 219 inhumations and one Late Roman cremation burial produced the remains of 195 men, women, and children. 153 of these graves contained some form of evidence for a timber coffin. Stone packing or lining was recorded in 72 graves, with one burial incorporating a re-used column fragment; another burial was in a cist, utilizing roof tiles (*tegulae*). Two decapitation burials were present, the first to be securely identified at Canterbury. Interestingly, both decapitated individuals were young children (1–5 years). Across this cemetery area as a whole, accessory objects seem to have been rare, and tended to be dress accessories and personal ornaments, including copper alloy bracelets, brooches and pins, a few worked bone objects (a needle, a decorated pin, and a hair comb) and footwear represented by iron hobnails. 6 coins were recovered from burials. It will be noted once again that many, if not all, of these items were likely placed with the corpse at the ritual laying out stage, prior to the deceased's transportation to the cemetery.

The Rhodaus Town and Peugeot Garage cemeteries briefly described above both appear to have floruits in the 4th c. and perhaps went out of use early in the 5th c. Further developer funded post-excavation analysis is ongoing on these and other sites around Canterbury. Importantly, results are anticipated for aDNA and isotope analyses on both Rhodaus Town and Peugeot Garage assemblages and there are hopes that new excavations may reveal further burials in the area at the time of writing.[10] It is also hoped that the Hallet's Garage and other material might be sampled for comparison if further funding can be found. In fact, a separate excavation has also taken place recently in the vicinity of Hallet's Garage site, almost certainly within the same cemetery plot, at Station Road West.[11] While the Station Road West burials are so far only known to have been formally assessed for its significance and appropriate mode of publication, any available data will hopefully in time provide vital comparative material.

Hallet's Garage: Location, General Characteristics, Development and Chronology

In situ dating evidence for the Hallet's Garage site was sparse and ambiguous, and we have as yet no radiocarbon dates but circumstantial evidence strongly suggests that the Hallet's Garage cemetery was established in the late 3rd and developed in the 4th c., making it contemporary with the sites summarized above. A good number of the Hallet's burial backfills in the vicinity of these earlier structures contained concentrations of residual 1st to 2nd, and some early 3rd c. potsherds along with other cultural material. The overall date of this material could suggest a hiatus of perhaps 50–75 years between cessation of earlier occupation of land and the first funeral processions being directed there. Of the 140 inhumation burials recognized in the excavation, some interesting general characteristics emerge. A full catalogue is currently being checked and edited for online publication but it is already clear that very few of the burials produced anything other than human remains, remnants or other evidence of coffins, or grave packing. Only 6 burials contained accessory objects, all of which seem to represent laying out, rather than the grave rite (see below). No actual grave goods *per se*, such as accessory vessels, were found in the burials at Hallet's Garage. Further characteristics are most interesting, however, and, in particular, the taphonomic reconstruction of burial in coffins or otherwise. Further detail is considered within its proper context in the funerary sequence later in this paper.

Apart from such clues, it is also just possible to propose scenarios for the development of the cemetery plots with reference to burial orientations (Fig. 3). That the cemetery was managed is surely clear from the overall layout and relative lack of intercutting of graves. There is an emphasis on grave orientation in relation to the nearby road, with many aligned parallel ('Group 1' on the plan), and many others perpendicular ('Group 2') to the road alignment. The reader may agree, from a qualitative assessment, that those burials, which seem to adhere less stringently to this rule ('Group 3'), suggest either a 'slackening' of strict spatial management in the north-west and south-east of the excavated area, or perhaps even an overall subtle shift of alignment. These could, therefore, represent later burials and, in the few instances of intercutting, the stratigraphy appears supportive. Radiocarbon dating is required in order to test this hypothesis but it will also be noted below that possible commensurate variations of funerary practice can be discerned.

---

10   R. Helm pers. comm.

11   See http://www.swatarchaeology.co.uk/pdf/assesments/SR West%20Draft%20complete%20Report.pdf.

FIGURE 3   Initial grouping of grave orientations (1:250).

Initial Bioarchaeological Analysis of the Adults Buried at Hallet's Garage

Elizabeth Duffy

A full osteological analysis and report having been conducted and prepared as part of the developer-funded project,[12] E. Duffy conducted a bioarchaeological pilot study on the remains for her Master's research at the University of Las Vegas, Nevada, re-examining the human skeletal remains at the Canterbury Archaeological Trust's stores. The aim of this project was to investigate what adult life in Late Roman Canterbury was like by focusing on the health status of adult individuals from Hallet's Garage cemetery and to develop an approach and methodological framework that highlights areas of further research that could be applied to other Late Roman cemetery sites in the area. Based on previous work which has highlighted significant and

12   Bailey (2015).

variable health effects following the Roman occupation of Britain,[13] the following questions were developed to guide research on Hallet's:

1. Are there health disparities across adult age and sex groups?
2. Are certain age and/or sex groups more at risk for particular types of health-related stress?
3. How does health status of this adult cemetery population compare to published data from cemetery populations in other regions of Late Roman Britain?

The findings are discussed in terms of potentially interesting trends in the health data collected, which should be the subject of further research. These health patterns are also considered against that of some published Romano-British sites to further understand how Hallet's fits into the wider context. Finally, selected individuals are considered in order to reveal some possible differential experiences as evidenced by osteobiographies.

The Adult Cemetery Population

From the 140 inhumation graves identified in the field, 82 individual adult skeletons were available for analysis. An estimate of 35 non-adult individuals were present,[14] but were not included here as they were beyond the scope of the project. However, any further research should include the non-adult individuals, as they would contribute valuable information, particularly in regards to health status. Bone preservation in the brickearth context was not ideal; many individuals that were lacking diagnostic criteria for estimating age and biological sex, or were very fragmentary, could not be included in the data collection.

Data was collected on biological sex, age-at-death, stature, pathology and trauma, and this information was then used to help construct a narrative of each individual in the form of an osteobiography. Guidelines in Buikstra and Ubelaker (1994) were used for the collection and coding of data. Further literature was consulted for any skeletal anomalies observed.[15] For individuals with ambiguous or incomplete features, the methods developed by Calce (2012) and Bruzek (2002) using morphology of the hip were included when applicable to aid in age and sex group categorization. Estimations were made using a combination of these methods to

increase accuracy wherever possible. The biological sex and age-at-death categories used were male, female, and indeterminate, and young adult (18–35), middle adult (36–50), and old adult (50+), respectively. It is important to note that these categories only represent biological realities that may not correspond to culturally informed ideas of gender and ageing.

Of the 82 adults, 40% were sexed biologically as males and 29% as females (Table 1). Age-at-death estimation revealed 37% of the population died between the ages of 18–35 followed by around 22% of the population in the 36–50 age range (Fig. 4). Only 4 individuals were identified as old (>50 years), however, for over 35% of skeletons, age-at-death could not be estimated beyond adulthood due to poor preservation and completeness.

Characteristic aspects of the demographic structure of this sample of the adult cemetery population are as follows:

> Males are more highly represented than females.
> There is a general under-representation of older adults.

The over-representation of males at urban centres has been observed at other Romano-British sites, with possible interpretations proffered including seasonal influxes of men for military and economic reasons (trade, craftsmen, legionaries), selective infanticide, and selective migration between males and females.[16] The lack of old adults in Romano-British cemeteries has also been discussed in light of biases both in the funerary record and with the consistency and accuracy of skeletal ageing methods, particularly for elderly individuals.[17] It should be remembered on both counts that about 35% of the population could not be assessed for age or sex due to poor preservation; thus, the current demographic patterns may not reflect the true structure for this population. Furthermore, the excavation included only a part of the cemetery, with many burials within the examined area either disturbed or destroyed by later activity, and a further number extending beyond the excavation area. The extent of the cemetery remains unknown.

While the difference between males (n=33; 40%) and females (n=24; 29%) is only slight and qualified in any case as a finding by circumstances of recovery, it is interesting that there appear to be more males dying at a younger age than females in the sample (Fig. 5). Males generally had higher rates of pathology across all categories of health, and this could reflect the suggested

---

13   E.g. Roberts and Cox (2003); Peck (2009); Redfern *et al.* (2012); Gowland (2015).

14   Bailey (2015).

15   Ortner (2003); Roberts and Manchester (2005); Waldron (2009); Wedel and Galloway (2013).

16   McWhirr *et al.* (1982); Farwell and Molleson (1993); Watts (2001); Peck (2009); Bonsall (2013).

17   Gowland (2007).

TABLE 1   Biological sex and adult age-at-death estimation from Hallet's Garage (N=82).

MALE				FEMALE				INDETERMINATE			
40% [33/82]				29% [24/82]				31% [25/82]			
Young	Middle	Old	N/A	Young	Middle	Old	N/A	Young	Middle	Old	N/A
45% [15/33]	27% [9/33]	3% [1/33]	24% [8/33]	50% [12/24]	33% [8/24]	8% [2/24]	8% [2/24]	16% [4/25]	4% [1/25]	4% [1/25]	76% [19/25]

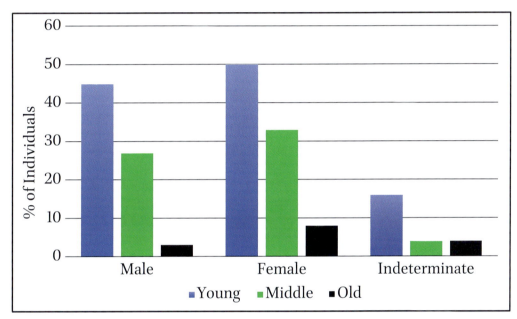

FIGURE 4   Biological sex and adult age-at-death from Hallet's Garage.

differences in biological adaptations between males and females.[18] Previous research has provided evidence for this in Roman Dorset, demonstrating that female biological advantages (i.e. enhanced immune system) provided a buffer that outweighed the apparent cultural buffering in males from their generally elevated status in society.[19]

Moreover, despite biases of sampling, it is notable that the average stature for males and females in the Hallet's assemblage is consistent with averages both from Britain and in other areas of the Empire. For example, an average of 153 cm for females and 169 cm for males had been recorded for Roman Dorset[20] and at Herculaneum, 155 cm for females and 169 cm for males

have been estimated.[21] There are, however, 4 notably tall (180 cm) and short (158 cm) outliers for male stature in the collection; these are robust young males, one exhibiting numerous pathologies.

General Health Patterns

The current bioarchaeological findings from Hallet's suggest there were some health disparities between males and females potentially related to divisions in activity but that, overall, most of the population did not exhibit evidence of health stress as a result of inequality or violence. Several studies have shown that Iron Age child-rearing practices were less detrimental

18   Redfern and DeWitte (2011).
19   Hamlin (2007); Redfern (2006); Allason-Jones (2012).
20   Redfern (2008).
21   Laurence (2004).

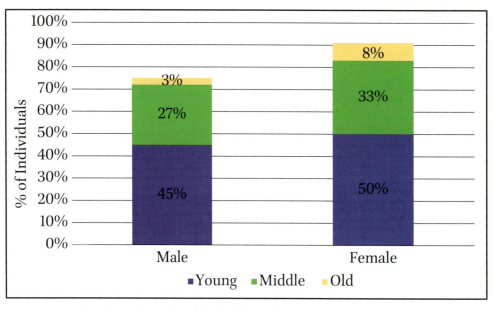

FIGURE 5   Age distribution for males and females from Hallet's Garage showing percentage of young, middle and old aged adults.

to the health of infants and children, whereas skeletal indicators of nutritional or environmental stress (e.g. *cribra orbitalia*, periosteal lesions) increases for these age groups in the Roman period.[22] Moreover, previous bioarchaeological studies have illustrated that the shift from the Iron Age to the Roman period had a negative effect on health in many communities, with an overall increase in skeletal indicators of stress and trauma.[23] The frequency of *cribra orbitalia*, only present in 7 individuals (8.5% crude prevalence rate (CPR)), and one potential case of systemic infection in a young adult male indicates that a small portion of the population was exposed to childhood stress and/or unhygienic living conditions. Additionally, trauma that is accidental or caused by interpersonal violence is patterned and often distinguishable.[24] The large majority of individuals with trauma at Hallet's is more indicative of accidental causes or habitual overuse, with only two cases of peri-mortem trauma, likely a result of some form of conflict. An overall low incidence of skeletal stress indicators and peri-mortem trauma, and comparatively normal stature estimations, could indicate that this adult population experienced low levels of health-related stress but this warrants further investigation. Comparative analysis with Late Iron Age individuals and other Late Roman cemeteries from Canterbury would allow us to contextualize and explore these findings further.

The cemeteries at Dorchester, Ancaster, London and Winchester represent a mix of small and large towns from different regions for comparison, and present easily available and appropriately collected data, which was similar to that of this study (Fig. 6). Dorchester and Ancaster represent smaller towns and London and Winchester larger, public towns. However, while some of the comparative data derived from older studies is reported similarly, recent studies have generally used more nuanced methods. The study of Hallet's used crude prevalence rates for comparability with other sites considered herein; further work will consider true prevalence rates. Compared to Romano-British sites at Dorchester, Ancaster, London, and Winchester, the Hallet's sample had a higher CPR among adults of *cribra orbitalia*, periosteal lesions, trauma and joint disease compared to the examples from smaller towns, with some equal or higher frequencies for some categories compared to the larger town samples (Table 2).

Further examination of sex differences was considered alongside data from Ancaster and Winchester. Bonsall's study had clearly reported data from both males and females and used comparable methods of data collection to those used in this study.[25] Interestingly, the results from Hallet's suggest males had higher frequencies of skeletal indicators of stress than females but both male and female frequencies were lower across all categories, except joint disease, when compared to Ancaster and Winchester (Table. 3). Incidences of joint disease at Hallet's was higher, especially for males compared to both sites. These patterns could indicate social, environmental or possibly regional differences.

22   Gowland and Redfern (2010); Redfern *et al.* (2012); Redfern *et al.* (2015).

23   Roberts and Cox (2003); Redfern and Roberts (2005); Peck (2009); Redfern and DeWitte (2011); Gowland (2015).

24   Judd (2004); Knüsel and Smith (2013); Gilmour *et al.* (2015).

25   Bonsall (2013).

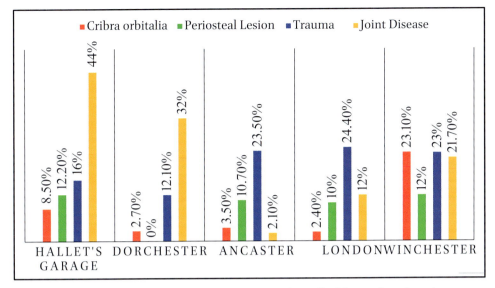

FIGURE 6   Crude percentages for adult individuals with markers of health stress from Canterbury
(Hallet's Garage), Dorchester, Ancaster, London and Winchester.

TABLE 2   Crude prevalence in adult individuals with skeletal indicators of stress from Hallet's Garage, Dorchester, Ancaster, London and
Winchester. References note where totals and percentages were found.

Site	N	*Cribra orbitalia* (%)	Periosteal lesions (%)	Trauma (%)	Joint Disease (%)	Reference
Canterbury *Hallet's Garage*	82	7/82 (8.5)	10/82 (12.2)	13/82 (16)	36/82 (44)	
Dorchester (*Alington Avenue*)	109	3/109 (2.7)	0/109 (0)	13/107 (12.1)	35/109 (32)	Waldron (1989)
Ancaster	271	5/145 (3.5)	21/196 (10.7)	46/196 (23.5)	7/327 (2.1)	Cox (1989); Bonsall (2013)
London (*Eastern Cemetery*)	550	13/550 (2.4)	55/550 (10)	134/550 (24.4)	67/550 (12)	Conheeney (2000)
Winchester	330	25/108 (23.1)	24/200 (12)	46/200 (23)	43/198 (21.7)	Roberts and Cox (2003); Bonsall (2013)

TABLE 3   Male and female comparative frequencies and percentages of skeletal indicators of stress from Hallet's Garage, Ancaster
and Winchester.

Site	N	*Cribra Orbitalia* (%)		Periosteal lesions (%)		Trauma (%)		Joint Disease (%)		Reference
		Males	Females	Males	Females	Males	Females	Males	Females	
Hallet's Garage	82	4/33 (12)	2/24 (8)	4/33 (12)	1/24 (4)	7/33 (21)	2/24 (8)	20/33 (61)	11/24 (46)	
Ancaster	271	13/68 (19.1)	5/49 (10.2)	15/105 (14.3)	6/78 (7.7)	30/105 (28.6)	14/78 (17.9)	38/105 (36.2)	19/78 (24.4)	Bonsall (2013)
Winchester	330	15/56 (26.8)	10/48 (20.8)	9/93 (9.7)	9/67 (13.4)	31/93 (33.3)	12/67 (17.9)	27/93 (29)	14/67 (20.9)	

Activity Related Patterns of Stress

While it is nearly impossible without a large preponderance of convincing evidence (usually not afforded in Romano-British contexts) to connect ancient individuals with specific occupation, trauma and joint disease can help elucidate patterns of every day wear and tear.[26] In the Hallet's sample, patterns of trauma and joint disease yielded some interesting results. Again, while it cannot be said definitively whether the cause of these injuries was accidental or violent/intentional, several individuals exhibited injuries and degenerative changes that appeared to be caused by activity-related mechanisms (i.e. falls, overuse, excessive strain). When ligaments or tendons undergo repetitive stress, this can lead to the new bone formation at the attachment sites called enthesophytes.[27] 7 cases of characteristic enthesophyte development, some accompanied by healed fractures, were observed in ligamentous attachment sites of the tibia and fibula. Of those 7 cases, all of the individuals whose biological sex could be estimated were young to middle-aged males. Other observed injuries included healed fractures to the upper arm and collarbone. High rates of lower leg injuries disproportionately affecting males has been found in provincial contexts in Britain[28] and other areas of the Roman Empire such as Croatia[29] and Hungary,[30] suggesting gendered differences in activity was widespread. It is possible that these injuries reflect engagement in activity, particularly by males, that predisposes certain areas of the body to stress and strain.

Another observation of possible significance is the patterning of joint disease between males and females. The crude prevalence of spinal and extra-spinal osteoarthritis and Schmorl's nodes was higher in young adult males compared to age-matched females but this trend reversed in the middle-aged adult group with females exhibiting a higher crude prevalence of degenerative changes. These results were not significant but sample sizes were not large enough in any case to make any statistically sound observations. This could be explained by biologically based differences between males and females, where females are often considered at a higher risk of developing osteoarthritis and osteoporosis in later years of life as the protective qualities of oestrogen on cartilage and joint inflammation steadily decline with menopause.[31] However, the presence of osteoarthritis

and Schmorl's nodes among young males, considered together with the presentations of lower limb injuries, suggests there may have been increased mechanical stress affecting this age group. Further exploration of this might provide interesting results.

The information presented thus far represents preliminary but exciting findings. As more skeletal data becomes available from other sites in Canterbury, important considerations such as differential frailty among age and sex groups and changes in population growth[32] should be explored to examine these results further. Even so, the findings that are consistent with those of other Romano-British sites could represent repeated patterns occurring across time and space and could thus contribute to the interpretation of Romano-British bioarchaeological datasets.

Osteobiographies

Osteobiographies are detailed accounts of an individual's skeleton, which aim to highlight multiple dimensions of life experience of that specific person.[33] The value of osteobiographies in bioarchaeology has been increasingly recognized, as it helps humanize the past by offering individualized perspectives of daily life and is well suited to research with smaller, fragmentary assemblages (as is the case with Hallet's). Moreover, osteobiographies are complementary to population level analysis because the detailed information gleaned from an individual's remains can both explain variations in statistical data and reveal hidden heterogeneity in the circumstances structuring life. Thus, considered together with a population method, and the funerary context itself, such an approach enhances our understanding of the past by offering an opportunity to explore and link different life stories between individuals across time and space in Late Roman Canterbury. Two individuals from Hallet's with interesting pathologies are presented here to illustrate the approach and highlight some potential aspects of life not represented by the population-based data.

Skeleton 303 is the remains of a middle-aged adult male with possible Perthe's disease or slipped femoral capital epiphysis, who likely lived with a significant disability. As these two potential diagnoses are both childhood afflictions, in addition to the progressive deformation and osteoarthritis, this individual would have lived with this condition for some considerable time. In addition to the affected hip joint, degenerative changes were found in his left elbow, wrist and shoulder.

26   Roberts and Cox (2003).
27   Waldron (2009) 71.
28   Redfern (2003); Gowland (2004).
29   Novak and Šlaus (2010); Šlaus et al. (2012).
30   Gilmour et al. (2015).
31   Weiss and Jurmain (2007); Li and Jiang (2010).

32   See DeWitte and Stojanowski (2015).
33   Buikstra (2019) 29–30.

Previous analysis has suggested this represents evidence for the use of a crutch,[34] as the condition would have disrupted walking. Considering the evidence for males being engaged in quite laboured tasks in this population, this condition is likely to have made many forms of work very challenging, if not impossible. The acknowledgement of care in the past has received increasing interest in bioarchaeological literature and it is very possible that this individual depended on others to some degree to survive to this age.[35]

Skeleton 430, a male of unknown age-at-death, represents the only case of cranial peri-mortem trauma for this population, and the most convincing case of violence. The characteristics of the cranial defects (clearly visible both *in situ* and upon observation post-excavation) include two apertures that align diagonally just above the brow line on the front of the cranium and near the base of the cranium on the back. The characteristics of the defect (anterior diamond-shaped aperture, external beveling, radiating fracture lines, collapsed bone) suggest injury, perhaps by a sharp, pointed object, inflicted with considerable applied force at or around time of death.[36] Evidence of peri-mortem and ante-mortem cranial injuries linked to projectile weapons has been cited frequently in Iron Age sites,[37] but amongst Romano-British sites the typical finding is of intentional decapitation.[38] A sharp force cranial injury, attributed to a sword, has been cited in a male adult at Cirencester,[39] which also showed evidence of medical treatment in the form of trepanation. In an ancient Roman gladiator cemetery, numerous peri-mortem cranial injuries have been identified, one of which is in fact described as diamond-shaped and inflicted by a Roman gladius or sica (swords).[40] In the Hallet's case, the relationship between the two apertures is not clear, and it cannot be concluded if they were the result of a single blow to the head or two separate events without further investigation. It is notable that this individual was not the only one exhibiting an unhealed and possible weapon-related injury. Two further cases of unhealed sharp force injuries were present but these affected the shoulder joint and the lower leg just below the knee.

These osteobiographies illustrate that while some members of this population were probably engaged in laborious activity, care for potentially less physically able members of society existed. Also, for at least three individuals living in Roman Canterbury, their experience included some level of violence in death. This initial analysis offers an approach that highlights some multidimensional aspects of life, which can be considered in the context of the funerary evidence for a more detailed and integrated study into the events and social actions surrounding the life and death of the inhabitants of Late Roman Canterbury. Furthermore, there are significant opportunities for future research with the new skeletal data emerging from other sites in Canterbury such as Rhodaus Town and Peugeot's Garage. The findings from this preliminary study, enhanced through advanced imaging and chemical analytical approaches such as radiographic work, Stable Isotope Analysis and aDNA (which are already in progress), and applied to a much larger, integrated bioarchaeological dataset, would be a substantial contribution to the field of Roman and late antique studies.

Analytical Frameworks, and Interim Notes on the Funerary Process

Jake Weekes

Analysis of the funerary process from archaeological remains is established in Romano-British studies as an approach that takes us beyond mere comparisons of grave contents.[41] A specific methodology for Canterbury sites including a St. Dunstan's cemetery plot has been used[42] and is set out in table form here for reference (Table 4), although this is not presented as exhaustive since the method and understanding continue to evolve. The focus is on systematically reconstructing the funeral through specified classes of evidence: human remains, associated material, and archaeological features and layers, for each of several stages/aspects[43] of the funerary ritual. These have been deemed 'Selection', 'Preparation', 'Modification', 'Location', 'Deposition', and 'Commemoration'.

---

34   Bailey (2015).
35   Tilley (2015).
36   Symes *et al.* (2012).
37   E.g. Hooper (1984) and (1991); King (2009); Redfern (2009).
38   E.g. Harman *et al.* (1981); McKinley (1993); Boylston *et al.* (2000); Anderson (2001); Müldner *et al.* (2011); Redfern and Bonney (2014).
39   Redfern and Roberts (2005) 124.
40   Kanz and Grossschmidt (2006).

41   Weekes (2016).
42   Weekes (2017a) 91ff.
43   It will be noted for example that 'Modification' and 'Location' aspects can be relevant to more than one stage.

TABLE 4   Evidence types for reconstructing the funerary process.

Human remains[a]	Materials in direct association with human remains, including all placed deposits	Archaeological features / layers
Selection		
Presence/absence Demography: minimum number of individuals (MNI), age, sex Geographical origin Familial groups, Diet/deficiencies etc. Congenital factors Occupation/class/lifestyle Cultural markers (e.g. hair, tattoos) Disease/injury Cause of death (N.B. good/bad deaths/cenotaphs)	Cause of death (N.B. 'good' and 'bad' death Placed deposits that are cultural markers for gender, age, occupation etc. Personal objects? Mass produced, curated, broken or defective objects Re-use of existing materials, monuments, sarcophagi etc. Objects specifically produced for mortuary practices? Environmental evidence Biological factors (e.g. parasites?) Selection of objects for placed deposits	Use of existing feature (e.g. a well or a ditch), interface, layer or burial place? Size, depth and form of burial cut
Preparation		
Posture for laying out Taphonomic considerations, such as rigor mortis, secondary flaccidity, autolysis and decomposition Bone disposition and other osteological evidence for decomposition in a void or not, coffins, shrouds or other bindings, biers etc. Hair styling, cosmetics etc. Evidence for preliminary burial or storage?	Dress accessories and clothing Cosmetics/insect repellents (containers) Shrouds, coffins, biers, vehicles and their production Objects within the shroud, coffin or on bier etc., mixed with cremated bone deposits Environmental evidence Biological factors relating to post-mortem interval (e.g. carrion or scavenging, *Diptera*/*Coleoptera*) associated with laying out? Assemblage of objects for placed deposit Evidence of cooking and other preparations	New feature? Grave cut (size, shape, design for body or other shape, made to measure or template, spacious or constraining, deep or shallow, etc.) Grave structure, vaulting, lining etc. Monumentalisation: including sarcophagi and production of commemoration materials (e.g. grave stones or tombs produced prior to death)
Modification		
Evidence for: Mutilation Binding/constraints 'Preservation' and other treatments including removal of organs or other body parts such as decapitation Installation arrangement of body(ies) in feature Exposure Excarnation Preliminary burial Embalming Mummification Burning	Pyre material Pyre goods Material at charnel sites or sites for continued manipulation of remains 'Killing' of objects at human remains modification stage based on context Environmental evidence Biological factors associated with modification sites (e.g. carrion or scavenging, or *Diptera*/*Coleoptera*)	Excarnation sites Pyre sites Crematoria Destruction, re-use from earlier phases or previous use, funerary or otherwise

a   Taphonomic considerations are derived from Duday (2009) and Blaizot (2014).

TABLE 4   Evidence types for reconstructing the funerary process (*cont.*)

Human remains	Materials in direct association with human remains, including all placed deposits	Archaeological features / layers
Modification		
Cremation (fragmentation, colour variation etc.) Cannibalism Curation Etc.		
Location		
Conceptual arrangement or location in relation to settlement/cemetery (places for the living and the dead, inter-visibility; continued access?) Conceptual arrangement or location in relation existing monuments, to cosmology etc. Orientation and directional posture Binding or other constraints for control (physical and potentially otherwise) during transport and following deposition? Flaccid movement during transport?	Equipment and modes of transport: shrouds, coffins, biers, vehicles Environmental evidence for locale (e.g. charred plants at modification site) Containers of placed deposits, suggesting transport	Conceptual location in relation to cemeteries: plots, morphology, organization development, foci monuments and other structures Pre-existing liminal places and their qualities, structures etc.
Deposition		
MNI (collection for secondary deposit) Posture/arrangement/'lack of arrangement' (taphonomic caveats; also, relativity to preparation stage) Separation from modification site Inclusion of pyre material Derivation of pyre material (e.g. multiple token deposits from single pyre) Relative location of skeletal elements in feature or container Taphonomy	Pyre material Pyre goods Material at charnel sites or sites for continued manipulation of remains Environmental evidence; Biological factors (e.g. carrion or scavenging, *Diptera*/*Coleoptera*) associated with deposition sites? Combinations of objects for placed deposition; Spatial arrangement in vertical and horizontal, conceptual and symbolic (e.g. cosmological or in relation to human remains) Objects used to restrain the corpse Closure ritual evidence such as discard of objects during backfilling Material representing earlier events in the funerary process (e.g. including incense and containers?)	Closure/backfill deposits

TABLE 4   Evidence types for reconstructing the funerary process (*cont.*)

Human remains	Materials in direct association with human remains, including all placed deposits	Archaeological features / layers
Commemoration		
MNI (addition of further individuals to existing funerary deposit; degree of mixing)	Material in accessible burials or other funerary contexts	Methods of continued access for manipulation, offerings etc, such as cists, superstructures, surfaces,
Continued access and manipulation	Site closure placed deposits	platforms, troughs etc.
Posture in relation to access (e.g. hand positioned in tube to surface, removable lid of cist/container etc.)	Lids and other objects in graves suggesting continued access and object placement	Markers, structures and build-
	cemetery surface deposits	ings, cemetery plots, enclosures,
Evidence of addition, mixing, further treatment or removal of human remains	Other offerings or 'feasting' deposits, animal burials etc.	mounds and monuments
	Environmental evidence	
Taphonomy	Biological factors associated with commemoration sites (e.g. carrion or scavenging, *Diptera/Coleoptera*)	

Selection

'Selection' refers to those individuals evidently chosen for a given type of (archaeologically visible) funerary treatment, with the obvious caveats on findings that a) only part of a cemetery has been excavated, and b) information has been lost through post-depositional processes. The overall distribution of age and sex of the cemetery population in the Hallet's assemblage is not that unusual, although it has been noted that infants are over-represented and older adults under-represented compared with contemporary Romano-British sites.[44] There are hints of an early preponderance for infants and children zonally (graves 14, 20, 26, 27, 31, 38, 68, 74, 77, 80, 97, 101, and 106; see Fig. 7) especially in the apparently most strictly organized area of the site, might be of note, if this is also an early phase, suggesting specialization. Two other factors of this potential group, namely that grave cuts are generally adult sized even for infants and children, and that only females, some with peri-mortem injuries (graves 20, 68, and 97) are positively identified in the row, might be significant. The grave of one of the infants (grave 101) seemed to excavators to have been focused on a (presumably unused and derelict) sunken featured building. These locational clues (returned to below), along with potential evidence of good/bad death considerations relating to peri-mortem trauma, could suggest a possible selectivity in this area, which may have been a factor of early funerary practice on the site. It is also very notable that only infants and children were certainly afforded coffins in this group. Another

possible early zone of children, infant and 'bad death' has been noted to the south-east, where infant and child bones are residual in a group of later burials (graves 57, 60 [probably a pit], 62, 115, and 125), and in a loose cluster of infant and child burials (graves 79, 118, 123, and 127). Another burial in this area contained the remains of a woman and a breech-birth baby *in situ* (grave 102). In another possible case where the type of death perhaps has had a bearing on the funerary process, Hallet's Garage may indeed have evidence of a decapitation burial in grave 116 (unplanned); this grave was only partially visible but skull fragments were located next to the *in situ* foot bones in an apparently undisturbed remnant of the grave cut.

A small number of accessory funerary objects were recovered, which could imply the selection of certain of the dead for funerary specialism: some beads in child grave 10, a pin (grave 106, a middle-aged female), a bone comb (grave 66, an elderly female), probably shoes (grave 89, a middle-aged female), and coins (graves 84 and 129, the sex of these adults is unknown). There is a possibility then that children and mature females were given particular funerary treatment, at least by some, as part of the laying out procedure during preparation.

Preparation

Having already noted that adult-sized graves were provided for infants and children in a given area of the cemetery plot, it should also be said that this goes for very many of the adults in the rest of the excavated areas, with numerous examples of grave design bearing no relation to coffin size or the size of un-coffined

44   Bailey (2015) 66.

FIGURE 7   Sex and age distributions across the cemetery (1:250).

individuals earmarked for burial in them. This suggests that different agencies were involved in laying out and cemetery preparations respectively, that an adult or regular grave size was symbolic in itself and overrode particular size considerations, or both (see also *Deposition*, below).

In preparations of the body, shrouding or binding has been tentatively diagnosed in nearly 30 cases of adult burials, considering anatomical disposition of the bones, lack of coffin evidence, and maintenance

of 'tight' postures within the grave.[45] There was a focus of adult shrouding/binding in the central area of the excavation, whereas over 40 adults elsewhere bear many of the hallmarks of having been laid out in coffins, the evidence including actual coffin stains or stratigraphy, convincing coffin nails and fittings surviving *in situ*, packing around the positions of coffins, and again bone

---

45   Cf. Duday (2009) and Blaizot (2014).

dispositions, the reconstructed taphonomy of decom-position within a coffin-shaped void.[46]

As noted above, some at least had been presented in death with dress accessories. The shortlist included the child burial in grave 10, from whose coffin derived red amber beads (8 complete and 5 frags), green glass beads (14 complete) and 2 jet beads, along with an uni-dentified copper alloy object associated with the skull. A middle-aged female in grave 106 appears to have worn a copper alloy brooch, while the elderly female in grave 66, supine within the coffin, had a bone hair comb located at the back of the skull, perhaps where it had been worn as part of a funerary hair styling. Coins from graves 84 and 129 also suggest preparatory procedures (although locations of these objects were not precisely recorded), and a middle-aged female in grave 89 prob-ably wore hobnailed shoes. All of the above, however, seem notable for being exceptions to a more general rule of denying the dead such objects in this cemetery.

Modification

The possible decapitation burial (grave 116) would be a clear example of either peri-mortem or funerary modifi-cation but there are many examples at Hallet's Garage of more subtle modifications, again at the laying out stage: the possible binding of remains (again based on tapho-nomic considerations) and the manipulation of corpses into clear postures. Many of the potentially shrouded individuals presented with the hands crossing in the pelvic area, while arms by the sides or across the lower abdomen may have been more typical of bodies placed in coffins, taking into account the effects of secondary flaccidity whilst transported in a (probably closed) box, and decomposition effects.[47] Post-depositional pro-cesses may account in many cases for burial postures deviating from these general patterns but a small num-ber of graves suggest an alternative rite. The middle-aged man in grave 4 was buried with both forearms raised so that his hands would have lain on his chest. His was the only grave with this posture certainly represented but graves 3, 26, 86, 89, and 113 all had one hand in a similar location, with the other either in a different posture, or missing; flaccid movement during closed coffin transfer, could account for some of these presenting with only one hand elevated in the grave.

Location

A processional funerary route out of the town would seem an obvious part of this reconstruction, at least for the majority in the Hallet's cemetery but what were the

intra-cemetery locational factors? Some possibilities have already been referred to in relation to clues to the selection of groups for certain funerary treatment, with zonality suggested for the young in particular, and pos-sibly 'bad death' considerations in tandem. It was also noted that coffins were apparently reserved for infants and children in at least one of these *foci*, with adults pos-sibly shrouded, while coffins predominated for adults elsewhere in the cemetery. Another interesting possibil-ity is that infant burial 101 was indeed focused within the remains of a then derelict earlier structure, represented archaeologically by a sunken feature. The alignment of this structure perpendicular to the road perhaps fore-shadows the strict locational axis for burial, at least in the beginning.

Apart from this, there are sufficient indicators for the area of the Hallet's site becoming part of a well-managed cemetery, with regular grave layout and lack of inter-cutting. Further evidence of organization is provided by the physical orientation of human remains within the graves. In nearly all of the 'group 1' north-west to south-east aligned graves (Fig. 3), parallel to the road, the head lay at the north-west end (the only proven exception to this rule was grave 103). In nearly all of the 'group 2' south-west to north-east aligned graves, per-pendicular to the road, the head lay at the south-west end (only graves 17 and 119 flouted this apparent 'rule'). The conceptual connection with the road for these burials is somehow strengthened by such associations. Alternative head orientation was a further variant of several of the less stringently aligned graves of 'group 3', and actually burials relatively close or adjacent to each other (graves 82 [north-east], 84 [north-east], and 89 [south-east]). This becomes more interesting if we note that discrepant north-west/south-east aligned graves 79 and 103 are nearby: another potential spatial cluster? South-west/north-east aligned graves 17 and 119 were also relatively near each other at the north-east limit of excavation.

Deposition

The discrepancy between grave cut and the size of cof-fin or occupant requires further consideration at the depositional stage. In some cases (for example graves 15 and 35), there may even have been modifications to the grave cuts when the deceased and mourners arrived, allowing for coffins to be placed in new pits cut into the base of the pre-prepared pit, or into pits deliberately deepened. Certainly 'packing' of stone or other mate-rial was provided in a number of cases (graves 31, 52, 66, 67, 68, 77, 87, 100, 112, and 114) outlining a coffin into the corner or along one edge of the larger pit. The possibly shrouded elderly male in grave 91 lay diagonally across

46   Cf. Duday (2009) and Blaizot (2014).
47   Cf. Duday (2009) and Blaizot (2014).

a wide grave. In fact, narrow graves were the exception at Hallet's, like the child burial in grave 79, for whom a child-sized grave was provided. The pit for grave 34 was notably narrow and shallow, the disposition of the bones suggesting that the decomposing body was to an extent shaped by the pit, rather than shroud or any other container. On the same taphonomic premises, grave 132 looks to have been placed more directly in a rather irregular grave cut: an anomaly in depositional terms for this cemetery, although still supine. Nearly all of the burials lay supine within the grave, the majority having been brought thence within a shroud or a coffin but others (graves 6, 36, and 80) could be proven to have been buried lying on their sides, while further graves also suggest such a practice (graves 61, 95, and 117).

Commemoration

The severely truncated site offered no clues to what may have occurred at the cemetery surface by way of commemoration. No grave markers survive, even in secondary contexts. However, it is clear that ample opportunity for ongoing focus on particular dead would have been afforded by the roadside location, the managed rows, including potential cemetery zonation, a general lack of intercutting, etc. Moreover, while many grave backfills contained clearly residual older material, particularly near the road and in the vicinity of known earlier buildings, some contained scraps of broadly contemporary pottery at least. The latter suggests some use of pottery in the cemetery, and most likely some commemorative use, such as food offerings.

Late Roman Funerary Ritual Action at Hallet's Garage

I hope that the foregoing consideration of comparative funerary profiles and application of draft methodology for studying them demonstrate that styles of ritual action are worth studying in themselves, and can be approached in a systematic and meaningful way. Acknowledgement of the funerary sequence builds an arrow of time into our understanding of the evidence, so that each funeral can be seen as a fragmented artefact we must reconstruct and compare, before any attempt at discerning 'meaning'.[48] My long-held view,[49] in any case, is that funerary ritual, and ritual generally, is essentially about specialized action, even more than any particular meanings intended by it, or read into or from it. If there is any one general meaning to be discerned from funerals, perhaps it is that specialized actions allow

for polysemy and fluidity of meanings for participants, a liminal phase of catharsis and societal mediation in response to the natural fact of death. It can be suggested that it is indeed the primacy of ritual action that makes such transformation possible, marking out funerals as an important context for structuring social change.

That said, what does the overall funerary profile at Hallet's Garage suggest? The founding of a new cemetery near the new wall, with possible initial zoning of infants and children, several of whom were placed in adult-sized graves, is an interesting development in itself, in keeping with a generic 'Roman' model in terms of location but perhaps affording the young a place in this too. There is also suggestion of central organization of the cemetery, perhaps more stringent at first. In fact, while some slight degrees of variation in terms of age, gender, and perhaps types of death have been noted, in areas of preparation, modification, and location, the general sense seems one of a fairly uniform practice applied to all: a kind of 'levelling' of status in death. This compares well with initial understanding of the large Peugeot Garage cemetery but again highlights the contemporaneous diversity of practice of, and between, those segregated in the small Rhodaus Town plot. As ever it seems, the popular culture of Romanitas has been interpreted by local folk culture in divergent ways. With further in-depth comparison, in tandem with the additional detailed osteobiographies planned, and more understandings opened up through archaeological science, we may well be able to develop and challenge such generalizations in fascinating ways.

Future Research into Death and Life in Late Antique Canterbury

Aware as we are that the investigation of the Late Roman cemetery at the former Hallet's Garage is a 21st c. rescue excavation, there is much hope that more can be derived from this material in terms of the bioarchaeology and funerary custom, and that important and meticulous comparisons with the other new sites in Canterbury await. The nearby finds from Station Road West must be integrated into a more detailed analysis, and clearly the cemetery represented by this and Hallet's has more in common with the Peugeot Garage cemetery than that at Rhodaus Town in terms of its morphology, development, laying out and grave goods but there are many further areas of study that should be applied to the group as a whole.

Contemporaneity is a key issue, and a broader sample of radiocarbon dates must be sought. Then there is the hope that aDNA and stable isotope studies, already

---

48   Weekes (2017b).
49   See Weekes (2002).

underway at the southern Canterbury sites,[50] might be funded for the St. Dunstan's Late Roman cemetery also. Moreover, we look forward to combining funerary and bioarchaeological studies in a unified approach to taphonomic evidence of social responses to the post-mortem interval. More than this, the osteological data needs to be brought into a contextual relationship with further evidence of life and the living in Late Roman Canterbury and beyond,[51] including the funerary.

Bibliography

Allason-Jones L. (2012) "Women in Roman Britain", in *A Companion to Women in the Ancient World*, edd. S. L. James and S. Dillon (Oxford 2012) 467–77.

Anderson T. (2001) "Two decapitations from Roman Towcester", *International Journal of Osteoarchaeology* 11 (2001) 400–405.

Bailey A. (2015) "Osteological report on the human bones from the former Hallet's Garage, 21–24 St. Dunstan's Street, Canterbury", Unpublished Archive Report (2015).

Blaizot F. (2014) "From the skeleton to the funerary architecture: a logic of the plausible", *Anthropologie* 52 (2014) 263–84.

Bonsall L. (2013) *Variations in the Health Status of Urban Populations in Roman Britain: A Comparison of Skeletal Samples from Major and Minor Towns*. (Ph.D. diss., Univ. of Edinburgh 2013).

Boylston A., Knüsel C. J., Roberts C. A., and Dawson M. (2000) "Investigation of a Romano-British rural ritual in Bedford, England", *JAS* 27 (2000) 241–54.

Bruzek J. (2002) "A method for visual determination of sex, using the human hip bone", *American Journal of Physical Anthropology* 117 (2002) 157–68.

Buikstra J. and Ubelaker D. (1994) *Standards for Data Collection from Human Skeletal Remains* (Arkansas Archaeological Survey Research Series 44) (Fayetteville 1994).

Buikstra J. E. ed. (2019) *Ortner's Identification of Pathological Conditions in Human Skeletal Remains* (London 2019).

Calce S. E. (2012) "A new method to estimate adult age-at-death using the acetabulum", *American Journal of Physical Anthropology* 148 (2012) 11–23.

Canterbury Archaeological Trust (2015) "Rhodaus Town", in *Canterbury's Archaeology 2013–2014. Annual Review of the Canterbury Archaeological Trust*. https://issuu.com/alfalfa2/docs/canterburys_archaeology_2013_2014/14.

Canterbury Archaeological Trust (2017) "Rhodaus Town revisited", in *Canterbury's Archaeology 2015–2016. Annual Review of the Canterbury Archaeological Trust*. https://issuu.com/alfalfa2/docs/canterburys_archaeology_2015_2016/20.

Conheeney J. (2000) "The inhumation burials", in *The Eastern Cemetery of Roman London* (MoLAS Monograph 4), edd. B. Barber and D. Bowsher (London 2000) 277–97.

Cox M. (1989) *The Human Bones from Ancaster* (English Heritage Ancient Monuments Laboratory Report 93/89) (London 1989).

Deetz J. (1996) *In Small Things Forgotten: The Archaeology of Early American Life* (New York 1996).

DeWitte S. N. and Stojanowski C. M. (2015) "The osteological paradox 20 years later: past perspectives, future directions", *Journal of Archaeological Research* 23 (2015) 397–450.

Duday H. (2009) *The Archaeology of the Dead: Lectures in Archaeothanatology*. Translated by A. M. Cipriani and J. Pearce (Oxford 2009).

Farwell D. E. and Molleson T. I. (1993) *Poundbury Volume 11. The Cemeteries* (Dorset Natural History and Archaeological Society) (Dorchester 1993).

Gowland R. L. (2004) "The social identity of health in Late Roman Britain", *Theoretical Roman Archaeology Journal* (2004) 135–46.

Gowland R. L. (2007) "Age, ageism and osteological bias: the evidence from late Roman Britain", *JRA-SS* 65 (2007) 153–69.

Gowland R. L. (2015) "Entangled lives: Implications of the developmental origins of health and disease hypothesis for bioarchaeology and the life course", *American Journal of Physical Anthropology* 158 (2015) 530–40.

Gowland R. L. and Redfern R. (2010) "Childhood health in the Roman World: perspectives from the centre and margin of the Empire", *Childhood in the Past* 3 (2010) 15–42.

Gilmour R. J., Gowland R., Roberts C., Bernert Z., Kiss K. K., and Lassányi G. (2015) "Gendered differences in accidental trauma to upper and lower limb bones at Aquincum, Roman Hungary", *International Journal of Paleopathology* 11 (2015) 75–91.

Hamlin C. (2007) *The Material Expression of Social Change: The Mortuary Correlates of Gender and Age in Late Pre-Roman Iron Age and Roman Dorset* (Wisconsin 2007).

Harman M., Molleson T. I., and Price J. L. (1981) "Burials, bodies and beheadings in Romano-British and Anglo-Saxon cemeteries", *Bulletin of the British Museum of Natural History Geology* 35 (1981) 145–88.

Helm R. and Weekes J. "The early development of a Canterbury suburb? Romano-British and medieval archaeology at nos 19 and 45–7 Wincheap", *Archaeologia Cantiana* 135 (2014) 235–49.

Hooper B. (1984) "Anatomical considerations", in *Danebury: an Iron Age Hillfort in Hampshire, Volume 2: The Excavations, 1969–1978: The Finds* (CBA Report 52), B. Cunliffe *et al.* (London 1984) 463–74.

---

50 R. Helm, *pers. comm.*

51 Cf. Pearce (2013).

Hooper B. (1991) "Anatomical considerations", in *Danebury: an Iron Age Hillfort in Hampshire, Volume 5: The Excavations, 1979–1998: The Finds* (CBA Report 73b), B. Cunliffe and C. Poole (London 1991) 425–31.

Jenkins F. (1951) "Archaeological notebook, Canterbury, 1949–51", *Archaeologia Cantiana* 64 (1951) 66–67.

Judd M. (2004) "Trauma in the city of Kerma: ancient versus modern injury patterns", *International Journal of Osteoarchaeology* 14 (2004) 34–51.

Kanz F. and Grossschmidt K. (2006) "Head injuries of Roman gladiators", *Forensic Science International* 160 (2006) 207–16.

King S. S. (2009) "Warfare and violence in the Iron Age of East Yorkshire", *American Journal of Physical Anthropology* 138 (2009) 91.

Knüsel C. and Smith M. edd. (2013) *The Routledge Handbook of the Bioarchaeology of Human Conflict.* (London 2013).

Laurence R. (2004) "Health and the life course at Herculaneum and Pompeii", in *Health in Antiquity*, ed. H. King (London 2004) 105–118.

Li H. and Jiang L. (2010) "Role of estrogen in the development of osteoarthritis and osteoporosis", *Orthopaedic Journal of China* 18 (2010) 474–78.

McKinley J. I. (1993) "A decapitation from the Romano-British cemetery at Baldock, Hertfordshire", *International Journal of Osteoarchaeology* 3 (1993) 41–44.

McWhirr A. D., Viner L., and Wells C. (1982) *Romano-British Cemeteries at Cirencester, vol. 2* (Cirencester 1982).

Müldner G., Chenery C., and Eckardt H. (2011) "The 'headless Romans': multi-isotope investigations of an unusual burial ground from Roman Britain", *JAS* 38 (2011) 280–90.

Novak M. and Šlaus M. (2010) "Bone traumas in late antique populations from Croatia", *Collegium anthropologicum* 34 (2010) 1239–48.

Ortner D. J. (2003) *Identification of Pathological Conditions in Human Skeletal Remains* (London 2003).

Pearce J. (2013) *Contextual Archaeology of Burial Practice: Case Studies from Roman Britain* (BAR-BS 588) (Oxford 2013).

Peck J. J. (2009) *The Biological Impact of Culture Contact: A Bioarchaeological Study of Roman Colonialism in Britain* (Ph.D. diss., Ohio State Univ. 2009).

Pilbrow J. (1871) "Discoveries made during excavations at Canterbury in 1868", *Archaeologia* 43 (1871) 151–64.

Rady J. (2009) *Excavations at North Lane, Canterbury, 1993 and 1996* (Canterbury Archaeological Trust Occasional Paper No. 6) (Canterbury 2009).

Redfern R. (2003) "Sex and the city: a biocultural investigation into female health in Roman Britain", in *TRAC 2002: Proceedings of the Twelfth Annual Theoretical Roman Archaeology Conference*, edd. G. Carr, E. Swift, and J. Weekes (Kent 2002) 147–70.

Redfern R. and Roberts C. A. (2005) "Health in Romano-British urban communities: reflections from the cemeteries", in *Fertile Ground: Papers in Honour of Susan Limbrey. Symposia of the Association for Environmental Archaeology*, edd. D. N. Smith, M. B. Brickley, and W. Smith (Oxford 2005) 115–29.

Redfern R. C. (2006) *A Gendered Analysis of Health from the Iron Age to the End of the Romano-British Period in Dorset, England (Mid to Late 8th century BC to the End of the 4th century AD)* (Ph.D. diss., Univ. of Birmingham 2006).

Redfern R. (2008) "A bioarchaeological investigation of cultural change in Dorset, England (mid-to-late fourth century BC to the end of the fourth century AD)", *Britannia* 39 (2008) 161–91.

Redfern R. C. (2009) "Does cranial trauma provide evidence for projectile weaponry in late Iron Age Dorset?", *OJA* 28 (2009) 399–424.

Redfern R. C. and DeWitte S. N. (2011) "A new approach to the study of Romanization in Britain: a regional perspective of cultural change in late Iron Age and Roman Dorset using the Siler and Gompertz – Makeham models of mortality", *American Journal of Physical Anthropology* 144 (2011) 269–85.

Redfern R. C., Millard A. R., and Hamlin C. (2012) "A regional investigation of subadult dietary patterns and health in late Iron Age and Roman Dorset, England", *JAS* 39 (2012) 1249–59.

Redfern R. and Bonney H. (2014) "Headhunting and amphitheatre combat in Roman London, England: new evidence from the Walbrook Valley", *JAS* 43 (2014) 214–26.

Redfern R. C., DeWitte S. N., Pearce J., Hamlin C., and Dinwiddy K. E. (2015) "Urban-rural differences in Roman Dorset, England: A bioarchaeological perspective on Roman settlements," *American Journal of Physical Anthropology* 157 (2015) 107–20.

Roberts C. A. and Cox M. (2003) *Health and Disease in Britain: From Prehistory to the Present Day* (Gloucester 2003).

Roberts C. A. and Manchester K. (2005) *The Archaeology of Disease*, 3rd edition (Ithaca 2005).

Šlaus M., Novak M., Bedić Ž., and Strinović D. (2012) "Bone fractures as indicators of intentional violence in the eastern Adriatic from the antique to the late medieval period (2nd–16th century AD)", *American Journal of Physical Anthropology* 149 (2012) 26–38.

Symes S. A., L'Abbe E. N., Chapman E. N., Wolff I., and Dirkmaat D. C. (2012) "Interpreting traumatic injury to bone in medicolegal investigations", in *A Companion to Forensic Anthropology,* ed. D. C. Dirkmaat (London 2012) 340–89.

Tatton-Brown T. W. (1983) "An Anglo-Saxon pendant from Canterbury", *Kent Archaeological Review* 71 (1983) 9.

Tilley L. (2015) *Theory and Practice in the Bioarchaeology of Care* (New York 2015).

Waldron T. (1989) "The effects of urbanism on human health: the evidence from skeletal remains", in *Diet and Crafts in Towns. The Evidence of Animal Remains from the Roman to the Post-Medieval periods* (BAR-BS 199), edd. D. Serjeanston and T. Waldron (Oxford 1989) 55–73.

Waldron T. (2009) *Palaeopathology* (Cambridge 2009).

Watts D. J. (2001) "The silent minority: women in Romano-British cemeteries", *ArchJ* 158 (2001) 332–47.

Wedel V. L. and Galloway A. (2013) *Broken Bones: Anthropological Analysis of Blunt Force Trauma*, 2nd edition (Springfield 2013).

Weekes J. (2002) "Acculturation and the temporal features of ritual action", in *TRAC 2001: Proceedings of the Eleventh Annual Theoretical Roman Archaeology Conference, Glasgow 2001*, edd. M. Carruthers, C. van Driel-Murray, A. Gardner, J. Lucas, L. Revel, and E. Swift (Oxford 2002) 73–82.

Weekes J. (2011) "A review of Canterbury's Romano-British cemeteries", *Archaeologia Cantiana* 131 (2011) 23–42.

Weekes J. (2014) "The development of Roman and Medieval Wincheap", in "The early development of a Canterbury suburb? Romano-British and medieval archaeology at nos 19 and 45–7 Wincheap," R. Helm and J. Weekes, *Archaeologia Cantiana* 135 (2014) 246–49.

Weekes J. (2016) "Cemeteries and funerary practice", in *The Oxford Handbook to Roman Britain*, edd. L. Revell, M. Millett, and A. Moore (Oxford 2016) 425–47.

Weekes J. (2017a) "Funerary archaeology at St Dunstan's Terrace, Canterbury", in *Death as a Process. The Archaeology of the Roman Funeral*, edd. J. Pearce and J. Weekes (Oxford 2017) 83–122.

Weekes J. (2017b) "Afterword – process and polysemy: an appreciation of a cremation burial", in *Death as a Process. The Archaeology of the Roman Funeral*, edd. J. Pearce and J. Weekes (Oxford 2017) 287–300.

Wedel V. L. and Galloway A. (2013) *Broken Bones: Anthropological Analysis of Blunt Force Trauma*, 2nd edition (Springfield 2013).

Weiss E. and Jurmain R. (2007) "Osteoarthritis revisited: a contemporary review of aetiology", *International Journal of Osteoarchaeology* 17 (2007) 437–50.

Levis aesto terra – Early Christian Elite Burials from St. Maximin, Trier (Germany)

N. Reifarth, H. Merten, W.-R. Teegen, J. Amendt, I. Vanden Berghe, C. Heron, J. Wiethold, U. Drewello, R. Drewello and L. Clemens

Abstract

The Early Christian community at Trier left behind a wide range of fascinating evidence which enables us to shed light on their origins, social backgrounds, burial rites, and individual fates in times of radical political and cultural change between the 4th and 8th c. AD. The findings discussed here refer to burials from a 4th c. cemetery basilica discovered beneath the church of the former Benedictine abbey of St. Maximin. The exceptionally large late antique burial hall, and the special quality of its inscriptions, textiles and other finds can be explained by the patronage of the imperial court at Trier and highlight its position in comparison to other Early Christian centres in the surrounding area.

Periodisation and History of Scholarship

The city of Trier's outstanding importance in Late Antiquity can be attributed to its dual function as an imperial residence and episcopal see. However, Trier and the Trier region had already experienced an economic and political heyday in the period from the early 1st to the end of the 3rd c. AD. Trier competed with Reims as the provincial capital of Gallia Belgica and perhaps even replaced it as the seat of the provincial governor. It is certain that Trier was the seat of the financial procurator of Gallia Belgica and the two Germanias. For almost 200 years, the city experienced a time of peace and prosperity as is vividly illustrated by numerous representative large buildings.

This period of peace and prosperity came to an end in the mid-3rd c. with the turmoil associated with the so-called Gallic Empire. Consolidation of the situation brought about a profound reorganisation of the Roman Empire under Emperor Diocletian and the first Tetrarchy in AD 284–305. In 286, Trier became an imperial residence. The transformation of the city into a metropolis reflects its newly won prestige as a 'cosmopolitan city'. From a political perspective, Trier was the most important city in the west of the Roman Empire outside of Italy. The headquarters established here governed and administered an area that stretched from Scotland to North Africa.

In addition to the city's outstanding importance in political and administrative terms, Trier also played a significant role as a centre of Early Christian worship in the Gallic-Germanic region. Christianity had reached Trier perhaps by the end of the 2nd but no later than the 3rd c. Probably established in the final third of the 3rd c., the bishop's see at Trier was the oldest north of the Alps; the first incumbent was Bishop Eucharius, followed by Valerius and Maternus. As successors to the three founding bishops, an uninterrupted list of bishops' names important figures such as Agricius, Maximinus, and Paulinus for the early period; these churchmen not only promoted the Christian faith and its dissemination but also influenced the course of political events. Against this background, the study of the Early Christian era in Trier is of crucial importance from an historical and archaeological point of view.[1] The most recent large-scale archaeological excavation at St. Maximin between 1978 and 1990 focused mainly on the complex history of construction at the site.[2] The excavations carried out within the church identified and partially uncovered approximately 1,000 sarcophagi, 30 of which were retrieved with their preserved contents for further study.[3]

State of Research

Mortuary Space

Rescue excavations are a common occurrence in Trier due to the fact that Roman remains are located beneath large sections of today's city. The Roman necropolises of Trier have largely been covered over by modern development and were never systematically excavated. They lined the arterial roads to the north and south beyond the urban residential areas (Fig. 1). The two Christian cemeteries evolved from these large pagan burial

---

1 Wightman (1970); Wightman (1985); Heinen (1985); Heinen (1996) 53–168; Heinen (2017).
2 Clemens and Seferi (2022); Neyses (2001).
3 Merten (2011) 6–8, 15–16; Merten (2018b) 101–103; Schwinden (2018) 59–66. Scientific examinations have been carried out for 21 sarcophagi so far (Reifarth (2013a)). The main results are presented in 'State of Research' and 'Biological Data' sections of this contribution.

Alexandra Dolea and Luke Lavan (eds) *Burial and Memorial in Late Antiquity*
(Late Antique Archaeology 13) (Leiden 2024), pp. 667–691

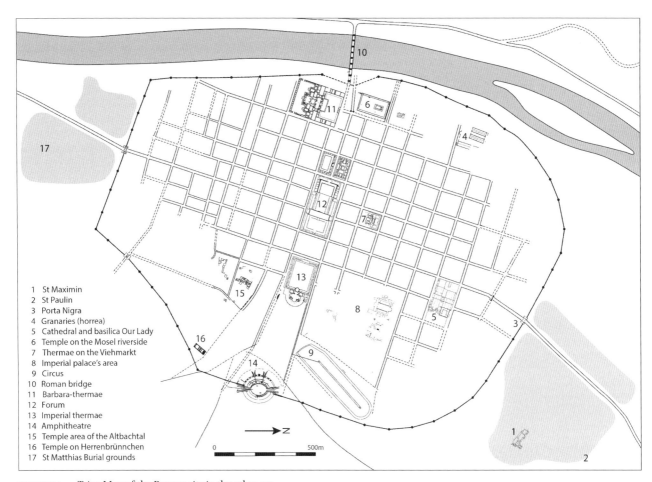

FIGURE 1   Trier. Map of the Roman city in the 4th c. AD.
CHART: © F.-J. DEWALD, RHEINISCHES LANDESMUSEUM TRIER

1   St Maximin
2   St Paulin
3   Porta Nigra
4   Granaries (horrea)
5   Cathedral and basilica Our Lady
6   Temple on the Mosel riverside
7   Thermae on the Viehmarkt
8   Imperial palace's area
9   Circus
10 Roman bridge
11 Barbara-thermae
12 Forum
13 Imperial thermae
14 Amphitheatre
15 Temple area of the Altbachtal
16 Temple on Herrenbrünnchen
17 St Matthias Burial grounds

FIGURE 2   Trier, St. Maximin. Map of the graves inside the Early Christian cemetery basilica.
CHART: © MUSEUM AM DOM TRIER

FIGURE 3   Trier, St. Maximin. Epitaph for Urania.
MUSEUM AM DOM TRIER; INV. MAD TRIER MAX. NO. 598.1; PHOTO: © TH. ZÜHMER,
RHEINISCHES LANDESMUSEUM TRIER

grounds, which had emerged around the early 1st c. AD and had remained in use into Late Antiquity. Both cremations and inhumations in sarcophagi have been uncovered dating from this period. Both cemeteries contained the remains of some of the first bishops of Trier and the veneration of these saints' graves prompted the establishment of Benedictine monasteries near them from approximately the 7th c. AD onwards. Whilst the monastery of St. Maximin in the north was dissolved in the period of secularisation, St. Matthias' Abbey in the south is still in existence today.

On the eastern edge of the northern cemetery, an edifice, consisting initially of a building with a central hall, was erected in the early 4th c. AD. Over the course of the century, it was altered and extended in several phases into a hall-type building with luxurious fixtures and fittings. The construction was a so-called cemetery basilica, which was apparently used exclusively by influential and wealthy members of the Trier Christian community as their main burial ground (Figs. 2A–B).[4]

The popularity of the burial ground is clearly reflected in numerous late antique Christian inscriptions, the main attraction undoubtedly being the burials of Bishop Agricius (313–329?) and his successor, Bishop Maximinus (329/30–346?).[5] A burial *ad sanctos*, i.e. near the tombs of saints, was desirable for Early Christians as proximity

to the saints, it was hoped, would ensure intercession with God on their behalf. The particularly fervent veneration of Maximinus is mirrored by, amongst other things, the fact that the cemetery basilica, which by then had been transformed into a church, was rededicated to him as early as the mid-6th c.[6] His veneration is directly manifest in an inscription, which explicitly states that a deceased lady called Urania is being entrusted to the intercession of Maximinus (Fig. 3).[7]

In contrast to the area north of ancient Trier, where the Christian burial ground was dominated by an imposing cemetery basilica, the southern cemetery around today's Benedictine abbey of St. Matthias has yielded numerous burial chambers and burial vaults dating from the 3rd and 4th c.[8] A relief sarcophagus, a very rare example of Early Christian art from Trier, was found in the southern cemetery. Its central image shows Noah, his family, and numerous animals in a box-shaped ark. The burials around St. Matthias deserve particular attention because they are quite early in date.[9] The popularity of the area as a burial ground was attributable to the graves of the first bishops of Trier, who were all buried there.

---

4   Neyses (2001) 20–61.

5   Neyses (2001) 24–28.

6   Resmini (2016) 66–77, 592–97, and 606–611.

7   Merten (2018a) Cat. 29: '*Urania hic conmendata / spirito Maximini in nomine / Dei*' – 'Urania is here commended / by the spirit of Maximinus in the name / of God'.

8   Siedow (2016); Clemens and Wilhelm (2001) 181–85.

9   Heinen (1985) 282–85.

This was attested to by an inscription, unfortunately now lost, which mentioned the construction of an altar near the tombs of Bishops Eucharius and Valerius by their successor Cyrillus around the mid-5th c.[10] Given the number of burials and inscriptions,[11] the area around St. Maximin appears to have replaced the southern cemetery as the preferred burial ground at Trier.

Funerary Inscriptions

Both cemeteries at Trier yielded remains of mortuary enclosures and foundations of large burial monuments. A family cemetery in the form of a small temple came to light in the northern cemetery, whilst the southern cemetery yielded the remains of numerous funerary monuments. The most important category of finds is that of the Early Christian funerary inscriptions which have now been comprehensively examined and have given detailed insight into the history of social, demographic, and ecclesiastical development in Late Antiquity and the Early Middle Ages. Some 1,300 inscriptions from Trier date from the period between the 4th and early 8th c., with a distinct emphasis on the 4th and the first half of the 5th c. There are hardly any examples of inscriptions that are clearly rooted in the pagan belief system dating from Late Antiquity at Trier to counter this vast amount of evidence for Christian worship. The most obvious marker for a Christian inscription is the use of a Christogram as a decorative motif. The presence of Christograms in the Trier inscriptions from the 4th c. onwards clearly points to an overwhelming acceptance of the Christian faith amongst the wealthier strata of society. The use of a Christogram in a funerary inscription turns it into a profession of faith.[12]

Trier stands out even more clearly in view of its number of Early Christian inscriptions in comparison to other large cities in the western part of the Roman Empire. The city of Rome has yielded a most impressive assemblage of Early Christian inscriptions numbering more than 42,000. The next biggest group of Christian inscriptions is known from Carthage, which yielded a mere 3,000 specimens. At 100 to 400 examples, other seats of imperial power such as Aquileia, Milan, Sirmium and Ravenna have yielded much smaller groups of Early Christian inscriptions than Trier. Similar observations can be made for the cities in the Germanic provinces and Gaul, where Early Christian funerary inscriptions make up much smaller assemblages, numbering between 30

and just under 200.[13] The inscriptions, mainly found on marble slabs, were used to mark the graves. The thin slabs were often fitted into large frames (Fig. 12). Probably in the context of *refrigeria*[14] – some inscriptions have been found embedded in low table-like pedestals (Fig. 4). We may also assume that inscriptions were hung on the walls of funerary monuments.

Burial Forms

Cremation was the almost exclusive funerary rite practiced at the Trier cemeteries in the period from the 1st to 4th c. AD. At about the same time as the spread of Christianity as far as Trier, we can observe a gradual shift towards inhumation with the deceased being buried in stone sarcophagi. The transition from funerary columns with relief decoration and a chamber for the urn to undecorated sarcophagi was marked by a small number of relief sarcophagi. These showed scenes from everyday life and often included large inscription plaques. They might have been used by wealthy families that had not yet converted to the Christian faith. Given their rich decoration, they must have been on display in burial vaults and funerary monuments.[15] The sarcophagi from the Christian period were undecorated and no longer on display but buried in the ground. However, traces of heavy wear identified on the lids of sarcophagi from the cemetery basilica of St. Maximin indicate that the sarcophagi were dug into the ground only as far as the upper rim of the chest, while the lid was visible above ground and, in some cases, contained the marble inscriptions.

The graves in the basilica were predominantly east-west aligned in very closely packed rows with as many as three stacked on top of each other, showing how popular this Early Christian burial ground was (Figs. 2B and 4). Most of the sarcophagi were monolithic and made of sandstone extracted from local quarries. They exhibited a nidged surface finishing with a characteristic wavy, 'drapery'-like pattern ('*Gardinenschlag*'). The dimensions of the sarcophagi were directly linked to the size of the deceased and varied accordingly.

As a rule, only one individual was buried in each sarcophagus. Among the rare exceptions were a few monolithic double sarcophagi, so-called *bisoma*,[16] with two separate chambers (Fig. 12). One of these contained a man and a woman, presumably a couple, whose sequence of interment was determined based on entomological and micro-stratigraphical analyses.[17] Another

---

10   Gauthier (1975) Cat. 19; Newel (1995).
11   Gose (1958); Clemens and Wilhelm (2001) 181; Schwinden (2001) 189–94.
12   Merten (2018a) 20.

13   Merten (2018a) 18–19.
14   See below 'Refrigeria'.
15   Schwinden (1999).
16   EDCS [14.3.2018]: 157 epigraphical mentions of *bisomum*.
17   See section 'A couple in a double sarcophagus'.

FIGURE 4   Trier, St. Maximin. Epitaph for Exsuperius. The inscription was found lying on the sarcophagus. In contrast to most other
cases, this allowed a direct linking between an inscription and a burial. Both the sarcophagus and the inscription were severely
disturbed by medieval and 19th c. construction work, resulting in a loss of the burial.

MUSEUM AM DOM TRIER; INV. MAD TRIER MAX. NO. 174; PHOTO: © TH. ZÜHMER, RHEINISCHES LANDESMUSEUM TRIER

multiple burial was found in a simple stone sarcophagus, which contained a young woman together with two *ca.* 3-year-olds, possibly twins (Fig. 5). This find might correspond to the tragic inscription for a young mother of noble ranking (*femina clarissima*) and her (new-born) daughter who died within a short period of each other.[18]

Inscriptions which mention several persons dying and being buried simultaneously[19] were also found. In these cases the deceased may well have shared a grave (and sarcophagus).

---

18   Gauthier (1975) Cat. 192: '[... *h*]*ic posita est clarissima femina /* [*mater*] / *q*]*uae meruit miserante deo, ut funus ⤐[acerbum]* / *nesciret natae, quae mox in pace se/[cuta est]. / Concessum est solamen ei n[atam superesse ? / [q]u(a)e potuit cr[edi multos victura per annos ?]*' – 'Here is placed the most illustrious woman [mother] who deserved the mercy of God so that she

should not know of the [bitter] funeral of her daughter, who soon followed her in peace. It was a comfort granted to her to predecease her daughter, who could have been expected to live for many years'; for a matching fragment see Merten (2018a) Cat. 77; see also section 'Social status and Professions'.

19   Gauthier (1975) Cat. 6: a brother and sister, Cat. 27: 3 brothers, Cat. 57: 2 women, Cat. 70: 6 people; Merten (1990) Cat. 10: 2 children; Merten (2018a) Cat. 57: 3 people.

FIGURE 5
Trier, St. Maximin, grave 174. Sarcophagus with a young
woman (A) with two infants (B + C) at her feet. The woman
was first wrapped in broad strips of silk damask with a
separate silk cloth on her face. Her body was then covered
with additional, resin-soaked burial shrouds. In contrast,
the (bodies of the) children were first treated with umbra
pigments and then dressed or wrapped in precious silk
fabrics. Individual iron nails were placed next to the heads
of all three deceased.

Besides stone coffins, only a few other burial types were discovered at St. Maximin. They included graves lined with stone slabs, a few brick-lined graves, simple inhumations and numerous wooden coffins, the latter being identified predominantly by virtue of the presence of coffin nails. In a single case, a neonate was interred in a clay pot. Other, as yet unique cases included a lead-lined stone coffin with the remains of a *ca.* 7-year-old child and a neonate interred in a gypsum-filled lead casket placed in a stone coffin. Analysis of the lead isotopes in the first case points to deposits in the Eifel region, whereas the lead casket for the neonate can be linked to British deposits, thus perhaps indicating a secondary use.[20]

Funerary Rituals

Preparation of the Grave

As part of an interdisciplinary research project, the contents of 21 sarcophagi were examined *in situ* largely using non-destructive methods, which meant that the contents of the graves remained in their original positions within the sarcophagi. Only micro-samples for special scientific analyses were taken. The combination of archaeological, textile-analytical, anthropological, archaeobotanical, and forensic methods provided basic insight into the contents, periodisation, and sequencing of individual phases of funerary rites practiced at Late Roman and Early Christian Trier. This included the use of special substances in the preparation of the dead for burial, as well as the significance of certain types of fabric in the funerary context and the sophisticated techniques used in their manufacture.

General Features

The 21 sarcophagus burials examined so far show clear similarities in all significant aspects including burial goods and the positions of the dead, which can be seen as characteristic of late antique Trier's Roman or Romanised upper echelons of society. Overall, there were no age- or sex-related differences regarding the burial goods of female, male, or children's graves. As a rule, the deceased were buried in an extended supine position. One of only a few exceptions were the two children from the multiple burial mentioned above found lying on their sides at the feet of a young woman, perhaps their mother (Fig. 5). The deceased were not usually placed directly on the base of the coffin but on various kinds of padding. Three types of padding can be distinguished, all of which were probably regularly used in the same period: the burials were filled with either

gypsum (calcium sulphate dihydrate), wood shavings, or myrtle twigs.

Gypsum 'Package'

Burials of bodies encased in gypsum- or calcite-based plaster were diagnostic of the Late Roman period. The use of plaster is known from almost all types of inhumation graves, regardless of the individuals' age and sex.[21] Remarkably, one of the regular features among the plaster burials found at St. Maximin was that the head area always remained uncovered and was often found in a slightly raised position on top of a concentration of gypsum acting much like a 'pillow', thus creating the illusion of a bed for the deceased.[22] As far as the motives behind this type of interment are concerned, practical reasons can be assumed for the graves from St. Maximin, as encasing the body in gypsum gives an almost airtight seal, which would also have functioned as a liquid absorber during decomposition of the body. It would, therefore, have helped prevent the occurrence of odours inside the large funerary building, which was constantly being used for ritual purposes.

Wood Shavings

The second type of interment involved a layer of wood shavings beneath the body and another layer covering it (Figs. 5 and 13). Remarkably, fir (*Abies* sp.) or white fir (*Abies alba*) was exclusively used in all examined graves from St. Maximin.[23] Because this species was not indigenous to the region around Trier in Late Antiquity, it had to be imported. In contrast to the very popular plaster burials, there are hardly any records of wood shavings being used in other late antique burial contexts. However, there might be a taphonomic bias due to the perishable nature of organic materials in archaeological contexts.

Myrtle Twigs

So far, two sarcophagi – one containing the remains of a woman aged 25–35 years and the other those of a girl aged 3–6 years – have been recorded where the bodies

21   The custom of plaster burials has been well studied in particular for Roman Britain (e.g. Green (1977); Philpott (1991); Sparey-Green (1993); on scientific analyses see e.g. Green *et al.* (1981) and Schotsmans *et al.* (2014)). A compilation of Roman plaster burials from Germany, England, Italy (only Rome), Hungary, Spain, and Tunisia shows the variety of different types of graves (Reifarth (2013a) 433–75). Remarkably, recent analyses of a mass grave from the catacomb of St. Peter and Marcellinus in Rome indicate that the buried bodies were plastered with a mixture of gypsum, powdered amber and sandarac (Devièse *et al.* 2017).

22   Reifarth (2013a) 31–40.

23   Reifarth *et al.* (2006); Reifarth (2013a) 27–30.

20   Durali-Mueller (2006); Durali-Mueller *et al.* (2007).

lay on a bed of myrtle twigs (*Myrtus communis* L.).[24] The girl also wore a wreath wrought from myrtle twigs. This evergreen plant, indigenous to the Mediterranean and Middle East, could have been either imported from the Southern Alpine region, or may have been cultivated as a garden or potted plant at the imperial court at Trier. Based on the high number of berries found in the graves, the burials of both deceased can be estimated to have taken place in the autumn/winter months, which would correspond with the absence of necrophagous flies from both graves.[25]

Dressing the Dead

All individuals examined were dressed or wrapped in the most precious luxury goods available in Late Antiquity, including extremely finely spun gold threads, silk cloth, and murex purple wool, which were turned into precious fabrics and garments using highly advanced skills and served as status symbols for the elite that frequented the imperial court at Trier. This combination of silk, purple, and gold textiles is a distinctive feature, which enables us to 'fingerprint' the Roman elite in Late Antiquity and to trace the long-distance trade in luxury goods even in peripheral (and less important) provinces within the Roman Empire.[26]

During the late antique period, it was not the style or level of decoration alone that was used to signify rank or status. What was more likely to have made it clear would have been the quality of the clothes; that is to say the type of weaving technique, the fineness of the weave, and the use of special fibres and expensive dyes. Thanks to the wealth of material, the textile finds from Trier allow us to show the difference between the ordinary and the sublime. When comparing the extremely fine silk and half-silk fabrics and their exotic and very expensive dyestuffs with items of everyday clothing,[27] it quickly becomes apparent what it was that signified luxury at the time and how it was demonstrated and flaunted even beyond death.

Silk Fabrics

The deceased at St. Maximin were often dressed in two garments: a silk tunic with tapestry bands (*clavi*) made of purple wool and a monochrome, purple, woollen under-tunic underneath it. Importing precious raw materials, chiefly among them *Bombyx mori* silk from China, must have played a significant role in long-distance trade with the East.[28] High demand for silk products inevitably led to western attempts at establishing local silk manufacturing. As a consequence, western traders not only imported the finished silk textiles but also silk yarns. This is attested to by written sources[29] and probably also by archaeological finds.[30] The silk fabric from the graves at St. Maximin can, thus, be divided into two basic categories:

One category includes silk cloth in plain tabby weave, which was probably traded as a finished product. i.e. as already-woven fabric and, based on its unspun yarns, standardised weaving density and the typical bale width of 45–53 cm, probably corresponds to the Chinese *juan* silk (Fig. 6A).[31] The second category consisted of silk fabrics woven in special twill varieties with check patterns, the so-called *vestis scutulata* (block damask silk).[32] The weave and the twisted warp threads are special features of this type of fabric, suggesting that they were manufactured outside of China (Fig. 6B). These fabrics were probably woven from imported silk yarns in the Western Roman Empire, possibly using a special horizontal loom.[33] Of particular significance in this context is a Latin inscription, i.e. a maker's mark, embroidered onto a *scutulatus* silk found together with numerous other silk fabrics in the grave of St. Paulinus at Trier,[34] for which J. P. Wild[35] cautiously suggests that they might have been finished at the emperor's private textile workshop, the court *gynaeceum*,[36] at Trier. Additional decorative strips of purple wool were often incorporated, as

---

24   Reifarth (2013a) 255 (grave 169), 408 (grave 571); see also Reifarth (2013a) 40–42, with further references for the identification of special plants and flowers in late antique inhumation burials.

25   See 'Entomological analysis'.

26   Wild (2013); Reifarth (2013a) 80–90.

27   A recent overview of Roman textile finds from military and civilian contexts in Germany is given by Möller-Wiering and Subbert (2012) 163–76.

28   See in particular Hildebrandt with Gillis (2017).

29   Hildebrandt (2017).

30   Discussed in Reifarth (2013a) 83–87, with further references.

31   See e.g. Kuhn and Zhao Feng (2012) 521–29.

32   Wild (1964). Interestingly, besides check-patterned silk cloth, the making of high-quality *vestis scutulata* woven out of wool is attested to by recent finds from Roman Egypt (Wild and Wild 2014, with further references).

33   Wild (1987) argues that, given the mention of a special loom for weaving silk *vestis scutulata* in Diocletian's 'Edict of Maximum Prices' (AD 301), anyone across the Empire could, in theory, have bought such a loom and woven silk damasks for themselves. Although the tower tombs of Palmyra yielded various silk textiles, including two silk damasks (Schmidt-Colinet *et al.* (2000) Cat. 319 and 453) which are considered to have been made in Syria or even in Palmyra (De Jonghe and Tavernier (1977–1978); Stauffer (1996)), there is no evidence, archaeological or otherwise, which would point to the existence of an industrial weaving centre there.

34   Dreyspring and Schrenk (2007).

35   Wild (2012); see also Dreyspring and Schrenk (2007).

36   Written sources attest two *gynaecea* in Trier in Late Antiquity, one for weaving clothing for the army and one for clothing for the court (Wild 1976); see also Luik (2003).

 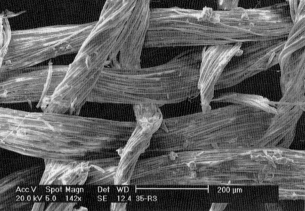

FIGURE 6   Trier, St. Maximin, Scanning electron micrographs of silk fabrics: a) a silk tabby made of unspun yarns from Grave 4, corresponding to Chinese silk fabrics. b) a damask silk (scutulatus) with z-spun warp threads from Grave 219.

can be seen in three silk tunics from St. Maximin.[37] It is also possible that imported, already-woven silk fabrics were unravelled and rewoven locally, though this is still under discussion and not clearly attested to by any written sources.[38] Damask silks with motifs that resemble the western *scutulatus* silk are also occasionally found in tombs in the Tarim Basin in Central Asia, e.g. at Yinpan. These finds appear to indicate that, from the 3rd and 4th c. onwards, silk was not just traded from east to west but also perhaps in the opposite direction.[39]

Half-silk Fabrics

These two groups of fabrics, consisting entirely of silk, can be classified as *holoserica* and terminologically distinguished from *subserica,* 'half-silken' fabrics, i.e. combinations with other materials.[40] Whilst the undergarments found at St. Maximin initially only seemed to contain purple wool, microscopic examination revealed a crucial detail in terms of the warp thread system which had almost completely decayed. Minute remnants, however, were identified as silk fibres and the undergarments can, therefore, be classified as mixed half-silk fabrics or perhaps *subserica.*[41]

Enigmatic Gold Ribbons

Gold threads were used to create decorative patterns consisting of extremely delicate floral motifs.[42] Some of them share amazing stylistic and technological

similarities to Late Roman finds from France, Greece, and Hungary.[43] The gold threads consisted of gold strips measuring 0.1–0.2 mm in width and 2–3 micron in thickness, twisted around a silk fibre core.[44] The result was a thread with a diameter of no more than 0.1 mm, barely visible to the naked eye (Figs. 7A–B). Remarkably, there are single narrow ribbons of gold threads, which occur frequently among the burials examined.[45] They are all of a uniform size and exhibit the same technological features. They were placed on different parts of the body – running across the face but also the pelvic region and legs – and were not linked in any obvious way with the other funerary textiles. They quite closely correspond to a rather inconspicuous detail on an Egyptian linen *dalmatica*, which has been interpreted as a weaver's mark.[46] The obvious conclusion is that these ribbons were decorative elements from a tunic, possibly made of linen, which has not survived due to the usually acidic conditions inside the sarcophagus. On the other hand, they perhaps represent previously unknown parapher-nalia in the context of late antique burial practices. The use of signs and symbols as 'apotropaic tools' was clearly an important part of life in Late Antiquity and even bits of twisted cord or cloth could be imbued with amuletic properties.[47]

37   Reifarth (2013a) graves 35, 219, 279.
38   On the Roman sources, see Hildebrandt (2012); on the Chinese sources, see Liu Xinru (2017); on archaeological evidence for unravelled and rewoven silk from the Tarim Basin, see Zhao Feng (2017) 101–102.
39   Zhao Feng (2017); Liu Xinru (2017).
40   Hildebrandt (2017) 39.
41   Reifarth (2013a) 58–59, table 4.
42   Reifarth (2013a) 60–72, and in particular table 5 (62–63).

43   Desrosies (2000); Moulherat C. and Spantidaki S. (2011); Sipos, E. (1990).
44   Technological details discussed in Reifarth (2013a) 73–78.
45   Reifarth (2013a) 61–67; see also Reifarth (2013 b).
46   Granger-Taylor (2006) Cat 116; Wild (2012 a) Cat 2.6; discussed in Reifarth (2013a) 64–67.
47   On clothing in Late Antiquity see in particular Pennick Morgan (2018). Also Han Dynasty silk fabrics with interwoven characters, recovered from the tower tombs of Palmyra, were associated with amuletic properties (von Falkenhausen (2000) 62–63). In some burials at St. Maximin the remains of individual ribbons made of murex purple wool (*clavi*) were found running down from the shoulders (Reifarth (2013a)

FIGURE 7A–B   Trier, St. Maximin, Grave 302. The facial area of a *ca.* 1-year-old child shows a fragmented tooth crown within whitish, crystallised bone structures and remains of delicate gold threads.

Red and Purple Dyes

Besides the use of different weaving techniques and the combination with other types of fibres in *subserica*, another significant clue pointing to a local processing of Chinese silk is the presence of dyestuffs. All silk textiles from St. Maximin exhibit a distinctive reddish colour.[48] Dyestuff analysis revealed evidence for madder root (*Rubiaceae* sp.), which was widely used, and for the presence of the anthraquinone dye compounds rhein, aloee-modin and chrysophanol,[49] all evidence of dyeing with rhizomes and roots of rhubarb (*Rheum* sp.), dock and sorrel (*Rumex* sp.) and with the bark or fruit of buckthorn species (*Rhamnus* sp.).[50] Of particular importance, however, is the remarkable abundance of textiles that were dyed with murex purple. It was detected in 14 textiles, most of which belonged to the wool-silk under-tunics as well as decorative woollen elements on the silk tunics.[51]

However, a silk tabby, which had been used to wrap an infant, also contained murex purple,[52] and even insect faeces taken from another, highly decomposed infant burial revealed the distinctive indigoid components of this precious dye.[53] Whilst the silk was imported from the East, dyeing must have taken place in one of the facilities in the eastern Mediterranean.

A remarkable feature is the consistent red and purple colouring of all burial clothes at St. Maximin, be it from female, male, or children's burials. The frequency of red and purple dyed textiles in late antique funeral contexts may not have been simply for demonstrating high status but contemporary written sources allude to the apotropaic nature of the colour red, which was seen as a protective force against evil.[54] A recent study by F. Pennick Morgan impressively indicates that specific details were added on garments probably for reasons of protection, in particular on children's tunics.[55] The use of red tapestry and various embellishments around the neckline or front of tunics, and also red trim on the cuffs and hems, appears to have been intended to protect the 'entrances' of a garment (and its wearer) from the incursion of evil spirits.[56]

---

graves 124, 174, 201, 287). The obvious conclusion was that these were decorative elements on tunics which had not survived. It is also possible, however, that the *clavi* were placed as separate elements on the body, perhaps in a *pars pro toto* sense. Remarkable in this context is evidence of reuse of such decorative items, as shown, for instance, by radiocarbon dating of a tunic fragment now in Brussels, which revealed that the applied, tapestry-woven embellishments were considerably older than the tunic itself (De Moor *et al.* (2010) 36–37).

48   Reifarth (2013a) 55, table 3.

49   The component chrysophanol was earlier identified on cashmere wool fibres which were found in conjunction with gold threads and wild silk fibres in a 3rd c. sarcophagus burial from Weilerswist-Klein-Vernich, close to Cologne (Stauffer (2011)).

50   Cardon (2007) 86–96, 674; Bechtold and Mussak (2009) 157–58.

51   Reifarth (2013a) 56–57 and 58–59, table 4.

52   Reifarth (2013a) 267, grave 174.

53   Reifarth (2013a) 387, grave 303.

54   See e.g. Hermann (1969); Elliott (2016) 257–58; on the apotropaic properties of red on Roman floor mosaics, see e.g. Reich (2013).

55   Pennick Morgan (2018) 32–64.

56   The extraordinary well-preserved mummies from the Tarim Basin (Xinjiang Uyghur Autonomous Region, China) seem to underline this not only by red stitching on their clothes but

FIGURE 8A–B   Trier, St. Maximin, Grave 304. Fragment of a multi-layered, finely pleated linen shroud (left) with loose, sharp-edged resin particles between the textile layers, shown by cross-sectional view (right).

Treatment with Resins and Earth Pigments

Having been fully dressed, most of the deceased were wrapped or covered in different types of shrouds, including silk damask, linen tabby weaves and even finely pleated linen fabrics (Figs. 8A–B). As an exception to the usual practice of first dressing a body and then wrapping it in burial shrouds, the body of one young woman, including her hands and feet, was first meticulously wrapped in broad strips of silk damask. Her face, however, was covered with a separate small silk cloth (Fig. 5).[57] Almost all burial shrouds in the sarcophagi were soaked or otherwise treated with oily or resinous substances. For this purpose, pistacia resin (*Pistacia* sp.) was mainly used. In some cases it was mixed with resins from conifer trees (*Cupressaceae* sp., *Pinaceae* sp.), or with balsamic resins, probably gum resins, and other aromatic substances.[58] The popularity of this practice is well-attested to by recent molecular analyses carried out at other sites in the Western Roman Empire and it can be considered an integral component of Late Roman funerary rites.[59]

Microscopic analysis of the finds from St. Maximin revealed that the resinous substances were applied to the burial shrouds in different ways. In some of the plaster burials, several layers of fabric were generously coated with a thick resin paste or even sprinkled with loose resin particles before wrapping the body in the fabric (Figs. 8A–B). In other cases, the liquefied substances were directly poured over the deceased's head and chest after the body had been covered in burial shrouds. The purpose of these measures was probably not to conserve the body in the proper sense of 'mummifying' or 'embalming' it but more likely to eliminate the odours of decay. Of course, it cannot be excluded that these measures were integrated in the existing ritual practices. The number of written reports attesting to the participation of priests (*presbyteri*) and bishops (*episcopi*) in the funeral ceremony as religious representatives does, however, increase after the reign of Constantine I (306–337 AD).[60] Early Christian literary sources might point to a similar practice under the term 'anointment of the dead', which involved the cleric pouring oil over the corpse.[61] Of special interest in this respect are a few small glass vials found in some of the sarcophagus burials from St. Maximin which still contained remains of organic substances.[62] They are currently being analysed and the results will show if they were aromatic resin mixtures that might have been poured over the body. So far unique is the special preparation of two infants

---

red woollen yarn was even inserted into the nostrils of the deceased (see e.g. Barber (1999)).

57   Reifarth (2013a) 262 and 264.

58   Reifarth (2013a) 91–114.

59   On indications and evidence for the use of resinous substances in Roman burial contexts, see Reifarth (2013a) 492–511. Systematic molecular analyses on burials from Late Roman Britain revealed a comprehensive database regarding the application of *Pinaceae* sp., *Pistacia* sp., *Boswellia* sp. (frankincense), and probably *Liquidambar orientalis* (Brettell *et al.* (2015); see also Brettell *et al.* (2014)). Recent analysis on textile remains of two sarcophagus burials from Jaunay-Clan (France), dating from 3rd – 4th c. AD, proved a treatment with

Boswellia sp. (frankincense) and *Cupressaceae* sp. (Rast-Eicher *et al.* (2017) 78).

60   Volp (2002) 195–96.

61   Dion. Ar. *EH* 7,2, cited in Volp (2002) 205.

62   Reifarth (2013a) 101–102 and figs. 29–30.

from the multiple burial mentioned above (Fig. 5). Their whole bodies, including the head, were covered with a considerable layer of earth pigments (umbra). Microscopic examinations revealed that pieces of cloth were coated with umbra pigment and then wrapped around the bodies.[63] Following this procedure, the bodies were wrapped in precious silk fabrics.[64]

Refrigeria

Overall, the inscriptions bear no evidence of graveside rituals. Low pedestals measuring approximately 30 cm in height placed on top of a grave may point to the consumption of simple meals at the graveside, for example on anniversaries or similar occasions. The funerary inscriptions were embedded in the surfaces of these pedestals. They may have served as tables for *refrigeria* and also to clearly mark the graves (Fig. 4).[65]

Assemblages

Glass Bottles

Christian graves in Trier are generally devoid of any grave goods. However, small glass unguent bottles are occasionally found which probably contained fragrant essences.[66]

Shoes

A pair of small leather shoes was found in the burial of a *ca.* 1-year-old child.[67] They had been placed on the gypsum cover when it was still soft. No other shoes were found in the St. Maximin graves, although the deposition of shoes (as a grave offering, not as an item of clothing) was commonplace in late antique burials.[68]

'Magic' Nails?

Interestingly, several graves at St. Maximin contained individual iron nails near the head of the deceased.[69] There was no apparent functional reason such as wooden constructions. Various written sources suggest that nails were seen as magical means of averting evil.[70] Parallel finds of individual nails placed in graves are known from numerous Hellenistic Greek, Roman, and Early Christian cemeteries. As well as nails, a great variety of artefacts of apotropaic significance are regularly found in late antique mortuary contexts, particularly

in the eastern part of the Mediterranean region.[71] The phenomenon has been studied in detail with regard to the city of Rome.[72] A particularly interesting source is a *tabella picta* from an Early Imperial columbarium on *Via Latina* in Rome which bore the inscription '*Quicumque hinc clavos exemerit in oculos sibi figat*'.[73] In this case the nail was intended to protect the deceased and to punish anyone who tried to defile the grave. In the 4th c. AD people in the Roman Empire still had a deep faith in magic as can be seen from several examples of Early Church Fathers launching attacks against magic and witchcraft, as well as imperial edicts against soothsayers and sorcerers.[74] In spite of its vehement rejection in late antique literary sources, apotropaic magic was still practiced amongst Christians, and even with the collaboration of the clerics and must be seen as a permanent feature of Early Christian life.[75]

Biological Data

Preliminary Results of Osteoarchaeological and Demographic Analysis

Material and Methods

The 21 graves examined contained a total of 24 individuals including a double burial (*bisoma*) probably of a married couple (Fig. 13) and a single grave of a young woman with two infants (Fig. 5). All other sarcophagi contained one body each. As part of a separate project, some 50 further burials are currently being analysed.[76] Most of the skeletal remains were highly fragmented and displayed a very advanced stage of bone decomposition. This is mainly caused by the conversion of hydroxyapatite of bone into another mineral, brushite, which tends to crack the bone apart due to its expanding crystalline structure. Thus, only the enamel caps of the teeth were slightly better preserved (Fig. 7A). However, if the burials had been filled with gypsum, the skeletons would usually be in a better condition, due to the different pH values in the sarcophagi. The skeletal material was examined using the established anthropological and palaeopathological standard procedures to determine sex and age, metric data, and evidence of pathological changes.[77] However, the accuracy in determining

---

63   Reifarth (2013a) 277.
64   Reifarth (2013a) 267–68.
65   Neyses (1999); Merten (2018a) Cat. 10, 28, and 29.
66   See above, 'Treatment with resins and pigments'.
67   Reifarth (2013a) 331–43, grave 249.
68   Reifarth (2013a) 118–19, with further references.
69   Reifarth (2013a) 115–16.
70   A compilation of written sources and archaeological evidence in Reifarth (2013a) 116–18, with further references.

71   See e.g. Bollok (2013).
72   Ceci (2001).
73   CIL 6.7191 (cited in Ceci (2001) 90).
74   See Engemann (2007) 295–301; Leglay (1987) 247.
75   On the role of ecclesiastics in the persistence of the ancient magical tradition among Christians see also Frankfurter (1997).
76   See 'Future Perspectives'.
77   On the methods applied, see Pirson *et al.* (2011) 146.

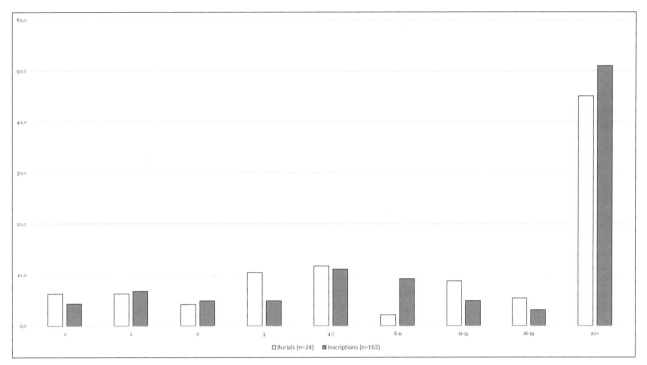

FIGURE 9   Subadult mortality according to skeletal material in comparison with inscriptions from Late Roman and Early Medieval Trier.

age and sex was significantly limited by the poor state of preservation of the skeletons.

Age Distribution

Age determination of the subadults according to long-bone length and dental development was generally quite successful. As mentioned above, the state of preservation of the skeletal remains meant that the age of the adults had to be determined mainly by examining the degree of tooth abrasion. This method, however, only identified the minimum age because tooth abrasion in high-status individuals can result in ages that are 10–30 years too low. Often, the age could only be determined as 21+ years. The individuals represent all age groups from neonates up to 60+. 11 of the 24 individuals in total were identified as adults (20–40 years), though 2 may have belonged to the mature age group (40–59 years). 7 burials contained children in the age group infans I (0–6 years), 3 other children belonged to the age group infans II (7–12 years) and 3 individuals were determined as juveniles (13–18/20 years). The age distribution of about 50% of the subadults corresponds to the information found in the late antique funerary inscriptions from Trier (Fig. 9).[78]

Sex Distribution

Sex determination on the basis of osteological features was only possible for a small number of graves, largely due to the very poor state of preservation of the skeletal remains. However, the sex of some individuals was quite firmly identified based on hair analysis. Since Roman women never wore their hair short, remnants of hair provided additional information for the anthropological analysis. Whilst the men displayed plain short haircuts, often paired with a trimmed beard, several female burials show that their long hair was arranged in crown braids. Most of the children had short hair; only the girl with the myrtle wreath[79] wore her hair long and plaited in two braids arranged around her head. 11 individuals in total, including 9 children or adolescents, bore no identifiable sex-specific features. The individuals in 7 of the graves were quite probably female, including 1 child and 1 adolescent, whilst the other 6 were probably male.

Pathological Changes

In view of the severity of the bone decay, we did not expect to find much evidence of disease or even causes of death. However, since the teeth in the majority of graves were relatively well preserved, they may add to our knowledge of social differentiation based on the diseases identified. The palaeopathological analysis, therefore, focused especially on so-called non-specific stress markers that become manifest as evidence of impaired growth on long bones (Harris' lines), in dental enamel (enamel hypoplasia) and in the roots of the teeth (root hypoplasia or periradicular bands).[80] For a long time,

78   See below, 'General mortality according to the inscriptions'.

79   See 'Preparation of the grave'.

80   Teegen (2004).

enamel hypoplasia was seen as an indicator of poverty and malnourishment. Recent research, however, has shown that it is also found in members of the upper classes.[81] The condition can be caused by a variety of diseases and deficiencies.[82] The high frequency of this kind of non-specific stress marker among the examined individuals from St. Maximin is remarkable: 14 out of 23 individuals showed linear enamel hypoplasia, 3 out of 23 individuals exhibited point-like enamel hypoplasia and 7 out of 9 individuals had root hypoplasia. In most cases, dental development had been affected between the ages of 2 and 7. Sometimes it began just after birth or at below 2 years of age. In some individuals enamel hypoplasia is present on the third molar, pointing to stress around the age of 11 or 12. High frequencies of linear enamel hypoplasia and other developmental defects on teeth have also been found in other elite burials from the Roman period. However, in this sample, the severity of the defects is quite significant and the social status was much higher. Since the 1980s, similar signs of impaired growth have quite regularly been found in Roman and Early Medieval populations in central Europe so that diachronic studies are available for comparison.

Two individuals had so-called mulberry molars.[83] This deformity on the permanent first molars is relatively rare in the osteoarchaeological record and is usually associated with syphilis, although it is not pathognomonic. In this case, venereal syphilis can be excluded. Congenital syphilis can also be excluded due to the fact that the dental lesions on our skeletons developed at approximately 2 years of age. The most likely cause could, therefore, be a severe inflammatory process or some other disease such as rickets (vitamin D deficiency). Due to the poor condition of the skeletons, no further information is available concerning the general health of these two individuals. One of the adult individuals had severe bowing of the left femur. Rickets can be excluded because neither the tibias nor the fibulas were affected. A possible cause could have been fibrous dysplasia of the left femur, a tumorous condition mainly found in younger people. Another possible diagnosis could have been a poorly healed fracture of the upper femur. In summary, we can conclude that infant mortality was high even amongst the leading families of the Western Roman Empire. Stresses in infancy were also common. These were probably not related to malnutrition but to weaning stress or diseases in infancy. Children of wealthy families probably fell ill quite often

too. However, their families could obviously afford a good-quality diet, care, and medical treatment.

Mortality Rate based on the Inscriptions in Trier

The Early Christian funerary inscriptions often give remarkably precise ages in years, months, days and sometimes even hours, and can, therefore, be statistically analysed.[84] This analysis shows that most funerary inscriptions refer to young women and to children aged from infancy to approximately 9 years of age. A total of 163 inscriptions from Late Roman and Early Medieval Trier provided information about the ages of the deceased. At 48 or 52% respectively, subadult and adult mortality rates were almost the same, which correlates with the data from the skeletal material recovered from the sarcophagi at St. Maximin (Fig. 9).

According to the epigraphic sources, there were two clusters of high mortality rates, the first amongst infants aged less than 4 and the second amongst the 20–35-year-old adults. Smaller peaks can be seen in the 40–44 and 50–54 and in the 60–69 age groups (Fig. 10). Female mortality was highest between 20 and 30 years of age, where it surpassed male mortality rates. Childbirth in antiquity was associated not just with high risk to the infant, as evidenced by the high rate of infant mortality but also to the mother – as perhaps attested to by the multiple burial of a young woman and two children (Fig. 5) and by the inscription for a young mother and her new-born child.[85] Male mortality rates, on the other hand, were higher between 35 and 60 years (Fig. 10). A closer look at the infant mortality rates, however, revealed that neonates and infants under 12 months (4%) were underrepresented, both in the burials and in the inscriptions. In general, neonate mortality was approximately the same as that of the other subadults.

The inscriptions show a mortality peak between November and February (Fig. 11), pointing to so-called excess winter mortality also seen in present-day Europe.[86] In contrast, the highest mortality rates in Rome were in September (approx. 47%)[87] and in Egypt in June,[88] which indicates that both high and low temperatures are correlated with higher death rates.[89] In this, outdoor temperatures are relevant. Recent investigations have revealed that average indoor temperatures

81   Pirson *et al.* (2011) 146–65 (with further references).
82   See Jälevik and Norén (2000).
83   Hillson (2014).

84   Schwinden (1986); Teegen (2006).
85   Gauthier (1975) Cat. 192, see above note 18; for Roman Pergamum, see Teegen (2016).
86   Liddell *et al.* (2016).
87   Scheidel (1996); Scheidel (2001) 17.
88   Shaw (2006) 104 fig. 4–5; see also Scheidel (1996); Scheidel (2001); Shaw (1996).
89   This can be observed throughout the world, e.g. for China see Han *et al.* (2017).

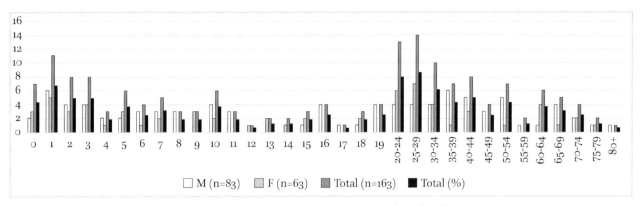

FIGURE 10   General mortality according to the inscriptions from Late Roman and Early Medieval Trier.

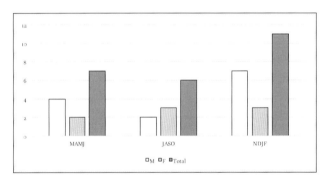

FIGURE 11   Seasonal mortality according to the Late Roman
and Early Medieval inscriptions from Trier. Day of
death or burial divided into 4 month periods in %.
MAMJ = March, April, May, June; JASO = July, August,
September, October; NDJF = November, December,
January, February.

below 18°C are not suitable for sedentary persons.[90]
Women and the elderly are particularly affected by
this. Insufficient heating in winter impacts not only
people's general physical wellbeing but also their state
of mental health. An on-going research project has
detected a great variety of pathological conditions in the
better-preserved human remains from St. Maximin,[91]
both on the cranial and postcranial skeletons. Diseases
of the upper respiratory tract were found in many of the
deceased, which at least in part explains the causes of
the excess winter mortality.[92]

Entomological Analysis
The microscopic examination of 21 Late Roman sar-
cophagi revealed the remains of insects in 9 of them. All
these burials were padded with wood shavings. Insect
finds from two further sarcophagus burials from St.
Maximin dating from the post-Roman period (6th–8th c.
AD), were also included in the entomological analysis.
Further analyses are currently being carried out on other

post-Roman burials.[93] The insect species from the 11 sarcophagi examined so far are highly diverse and include
representatives of at least 12 families of articulate animals. They can be divided into two large groups.

Detritivores, Material Pests and Predators/Parasites
One group is made up of fungivores and detritivores
(*Coleoptera* (beetles): *Cryptophagidae* and the millipedes:
Diplopoda), various wood and material pests (*Coleoptera*
(beetles): *Dermestidae*, *Curculionidae* and *Lepidoptera*
(butterflies, moths): *Tineidae*) and predators/parasites
(*Coleoptera* (beetles): *Carabidae*, *Hymenoptera* (wasps):
Chalcidoidea, the pseudoscorpiones to be assigned to
the arachnids, and centipedes: *Chilopoda*). These were
found in almost all of the graves. The insects may have
found their way into the sarcophagi at various stages
after burial, even several hundred years later, and may
have lived in them. In view of their feeding preferences,
we cannot exclude the possibility that both the fungivores and detritivores chose the sarcophagi as their hab-
itats due to the presence of human remains. However,
the wood shavings and various textiles in an advanced
state of decay may also have served as a source of food.
Larder beetles (*Dermestidae*) are known mainly as material pests (e.g. museum beetles) but can also feed on
dried or mummified carrion. Ground beetles (*Carabidae*
cf. *Platynus assimilis*), pseudo-scorpiones, and centipedes (*Chilopoda*) can be termed predators since they
hunt other insects and would not be interested in cadav-
ers or sarcophagus materials. They may have fed on
necrophagous insects or material pests present within
the graves. The latter can be also stated for the parasitic
wasps of the *Chalcidoidea*, who often develop in the
pupae of necrophagous flies.

90   Jevons *et al.* (2016).
91   See 'Future Perspectives'.
92   Liddell *et al.* (2016) 806–807 and 810.

93   See 'Future Perspectives'.

FIGURE 12   Trier, St. Maximin. Epitaph for Rusticula.
RHEINISCHES LANDESMUSEUM TRIER; INV. PM 20544; PHOTO: © TH. ZÜHMER,
RHEINISCHES LANDESMUSEUM TRIER

Necrophagous Flies

7 of the sarcophagi contained remains of necrophagous flies which are highly likely to have developed on the bodies of the deceased. Such flies depend on the presence of dead human or animal tissue and because the different stages of decomposition are of interest to various species of flies, each of the stages is characterised by the presence of a typical fauna. The necrophagous flies identified in the sarcophagi had gone through at least one complete lifecycle from eggs to various larval stages to pupation and, finally, to the hatching of adult flies. Under favourable conditions, archaeological contexts usually contain mainly the puparia, which are created during the pupal stage. Interestingly, blow flies (*Calliphoridae*), which are usually predominant in the presence of freely accessible dead bodies, were completely absent from the graves at St. Maximin. Although they are usually the first insects to be found on a dead body, they appear to have been kept at bay quite efficiently.[94] The only flies found were from the *Phoridae* and *Muscidae* families, known for their ability to sense and colonise bodies that are difficult to access, even those that are buried up to several metres deep. They also prefer to feed on bodies

at an advanced stage of decomposition. The absence of *Calliphoridae* could have been caused by several factors. Firstly, the deceased were probably laid out for relatively short periods only. This is confirmed by the only inscription from St. Maximin which includes both the date of death and the date of interment. A 22-year-old woman named Rusticula (Fig. 12) died on 10th January and was buried two days later, on 12th January some time after AD 450.[95]

Moreover, the bodies were carefully prepared for burial. Evidence of a variety of such measures was found in almost all examined Late Roman graves, including
- careful wrapping of the deceased in cloth – both beneath and over the clothing
- separate covering of the facial areas
- preparation with aromatic resins and oils
- embedding the body in and covering it with a layer of gypsum.

And finally, the time of year at which a person died must also be taken into account, as with most insects in our latitudes, the lifecycles of necrophagous flies are mainly limited to the warmer summer months and they are most active from June to September. Our own analyses have shown that these flies (*Calliphoridae*) exhibit

94   Accordingly, entomological analysis of a Late Roman plaster burial in a lead coffin from Évreux (France) revealed only two Calliphoridae puparia (Pluton-Kliesch *et al.* (2013)). However, taphonomic loss must also be taken into account.

95   Gauthier (1975) Cat. 153; for another inscription possibly giving both date of death and date of interment see Gauthier (1975) Cat. 227.

FIGURE 13A–C Trier, St. Maximin, Grave 189. a) Monolithic double sarcophagus (bisoma) with a man (left) and a woman (right). b–c) The clothed bodies are covered with wood shavings, whereas only the man's body is covered with an additional shroud above the wood shavings.

almost zero activity in the months from November to February, which means that colonisation of a dead body cannot be excluded but is highly unlikely.[96] According to the inscriptions, the mortality rates in Late Roman Trier were lowest in summer and highest in winter (Fig. 11).

However, the conclusion which might, at first glance, seem to be the obvious one to draw, that the graves without flies were dug during the winter months, is unfortunately not without its problems. Other scenarios are also possible, such as the preparation of the body as mentioned above, which prevents the insects from colonising it. Similarly, the reverse conclusion that the graves that did contain flies were dug in the summer months, does not automatically apply either. It has been shown that both *Phoridae* and *Muscidae* can colonise bodies that have been dead for several months and it is, therefore, possible that bodies that were buried in winter were colonised by these flies the following spring or even summer. Apart from one exception it was, therefore, not possible, based on the insects present, to identify the precise time of year at which the Late Roman graves were dug.

The exception was a double sarcophagus with two burials that exhibited colonisations of varying intensity, thus providing invaluable clues with regard to the time of interment. The two Early Medieval burials contained particularly large numbers of empty *Muscidae* puparia, pointing to a high degree of colonisation in spite of the deposition in sarcophagi. On one hand, we can assume that the bodies were interred in the summer at a time of high insect activity; on the other hand, the ongoing examinations appear to show that almost all Early Medieval graves at St. Maximin contained noticeably large numbers of puparia, which may suggest a change in the funerary rites. These preliminary observations align with other features concerning the preparation of the bodies, which exhibited marked differences compared to the Late Roman burials.[97]

A Couple in a Double Sarcophagus and the Order in which they were Interred

Only one of the sarcophagus burials dating from the Late Roman period contained a substantial number of *Muscidae* puparia. It was a male burial in a monolithic

96   Fremdt and Amendt (2014).

97   See 'Future Perspectives'.

double sarcophagus (*bisoma*) with two separate chambers (Fig. 13a). Interestingly, there were no *Muscidae* puparia on the female individual in the second chamber, confirming the theory that the two bodies were buried at different times, the male individual in the summer, the female in the colder winter months. Moreover, analysis of the microstratigraphic sequence and textile-technological features allowed us to conclude that the male had predeceased the female.[98] The left arm of the man was covered with a hardened layer of rubble. A similar accumulation of rubble was found in the chamber of the woman but *beneath* her right shoulder. It is possible that rubble had ended up in both chambers when the lid of the sarcophagus was opened during the course of the second burial and that it partially covered the man, who had already been buried there, whilst the woman was then placed on top of it. The position of the female body also suggests that it was buried second, because it was located on the side and very close to the interior wall of the sarcophagus, whilst the male individual was found in a supine position in the centre. Another, striking indication of the burial sequence was a unique textile-technological feature in the male burial. Wood shavings generally formed the topmost layer in the stratigraphic sequence, on top of the body, which was fully clothed and covered with cloth. In contrast, the wood shavings in this particular burial were found beneath another layer of fabric (Figs. 13B–C), which was severely decayed but had probably been treated with resins or oils and had perhaps been placed on top of the male body, which was already in a state of decomposition when the woman's body was placed in the sarcophagus.

Social Data

Social Status and Professions

The funerary inscriptions are the most fertile category of sources for gathering 'social data'. Despite their brevity and formulaic nature, inscriptions allow us, for instance, to trace familial structures. The kinship relations between the deceased and the sponsors of the graves are usually precisely outlined in the inscriptions. When examining familial structures, the members of aristocratic families are particularly interesting, as attested to by two examples that stand out amongst the St. Maximin inscriptions. Along with a funerary inscription for a mother and her daughter, who died in quick succession,[99] two other examples are the only

ones amongst the entire body of inscriptions at Trier that mention families from the senatorial rank. Whilst Flavius A ..., as a *vir perfectissimus*[100] may have been part of the urban Roman nobility and probably came to the imperial residence at Trier because of the post he held in the imperial administration around the turn of the 4th c. AD,[101] the two *feminae clarissimae*[102] are more likely to have belonged to local Gallic aristocratic families. These families may have been awarded the rank purely as honorific titles, without actually having a seat or vote in the Roman Senate.

In some rare cases, professions are mentioned. People who worked at or on the periphery of the imperial court, enjoyed a high social status. Members of the imperial staff included two imperial clothes administrators (*a veste sacra*),[103] a palace official (*palatinus*)[104] and a member of the imperial guard (*protector domesticus*).[105] They were all Christians, in contrast to the inscription for Hariulfus, a young officer of the imperial guard (*protector domesticus*),[106] who was the son of a Burgundian nobleman, includes no symbols that would point to his family being of the Christian faith. Both Hariulfus and his uncle Reutilo, who is named as the sponsor of the tombstone, were apparently members of the imperial staff. The presence of Burgundian noblemen at the imperial court would not have been unusual in the second half of the 4th c., since the Burgundians had provided military aid to the Roman Empire on several occasions.

---

98   Reifarth (2013a) 283–300.
99   Gauthier (1975) Cat. 192, see above note 18.

100   Merten (2018a) Cat. A 287: '*Callosiae Clamosae co(n)i/ugi carissimae quae vexit / annis XXVIIII et m(enses) V d(ies) n(umero) XVIIII / cui Fl(avius) A.[...] v(ir) p(erfectissimus) p(rae)p(ositus) v/inorum coniux eius faci/undum curavit*' – 'To Callosia Clamosa, dearest wife, who lived for 29 years, 5 months and 19 days. For her, her husband [coniunx] Flavius A ... a most perfect man, [a steward] in charge of the wine, built this'.
101   Schwinden (1996).
102   Merten (2018a) Cat. 5: '*Quae iacet hoc saxo maternis moribus / aequa cunctorumque dolor casta Boethio / la nobiliter nata claríssima femina Amand / i coniunx consimilis, qui posuit titulum / O quam saeva dies bissenos ímptulit ann / os quí(bu)s vixít sancte coniuge cum proprio. Boethiola c(larissima) f(emina) vixit anni / s XXV et menses VIIII dies III quae fuit / [uxor] Amandi v(iri) c(larissimi) annos XII et dies XVIIII*' – 'The woman who lies under this stone, fair/just in her maternal ways, a cause [in her death] of sorrow to all, chaste Boethiola, a nobly born and most illustrious woman, wife of Amandus, a husband of similar character, who erected the slab. O how cruel the day that ended the twelve years that she lived in holiness with her husband, Boethiola, a most illustrious woman, lived 25 years and 19 months and 3 days, who was the wife of Amandus, a most illustrious man, for 12 years and 19 days'; Gauthier (1975); Gauthier (1975) Cat. 192, see above n. 18.
103   Gauthier (1975) Cat. 37 and 126.
104   Gauthier (1975) Cat. 148.
105   Gauthier (1975) Cat. 130.
106   Gauthier (1975) Cat. 5; Schwinden (1984) Cat. 186.

FIGURE 14   Trier, St. Maximin. Epitaph for Valerius Leo.
RHEINISCHES LANDESMUSEUM TRIER; INV. RLM TRIER 2000, 2 NO. 643; PHOTO: © TH. ZÜHMER, RHEINISCHES
LANDESMUSEUM TRIER

With the collapse of the Western Roman Empire, the administrative structures also dissolved with the gap filled by Church administration and hierarchy. These structures had survived the fall of the Empire, which is attested to by an important source: the uninterrupted list of Trier bishops. The Church hierarchy offered opportunities for advancement under the episcopal leadership that evolved in the 6th c. both to members of the local nobility and to groups of lower social status.[107] From the 5th c. onwards, official titles of clerics (such as *subdiaconus* or *presbyter*) began to replace secular occupational titles in the funerary inscriptions.

Children

The formula used in the inscriptions was the same for both children and adults. This was probably due to the fact that from the 4th c. onwards, children were christened. The children of Christian parents could be christened as infants or toddlers, making them full members of the community regardless of their age. The tender treatment of deceased children is clearly reflected in the types of burial. Like adults, children were buried wearing expensive dress in stone sarcophagi and their graves were marked with inscriptions which were often inserted into large frames. Two inscriptions for children[108] found

lying *in situ* in the northern side aisle of St. Maximin suggest that there may have been a specific funerary site for children within the cemetery basilica, as known from many of the catacombs in the city of Rome.

Ethnicities and Names

Some of the inscriptions provide information on a person's origins. The use of the Greek language in the Latin-speaking West always points to someone of foreign ethnicity. From a chronological point of view, most of the Greek inscriptions can be linked to a great wave of migration from the East, mainly from Syria, which reached the Latin West around the turn of the 5th c. AD. By the use of their mother tongue on grave inscriptions, immigrants expressed close ties to their homelands.[109]

The use of certain formulaic elements which do not occur in the majority of Trier inscriptions may also be seen as indicating migration. The set phrase *levis aesto terra*,[110] used in the funerary inscription for a 6-year-old boy called Leo (Fig. 14), was widely used on the Iberian Peninsula and in Africa. The phrase *contra votum*

---

107   Gauthier (1975) 39–40; Binsfeld (2015); Merten (2018a) Cat. 7, 33, and 56.
108   Merten (2018a) Cat. 16 and 22.

109   Schwinden (2012).
110   Merten (2018a) Cat. 31: '*V(alerio) Leoni<i> insonti levis / aesto terra precamur / qui vixit annis (V)I*' – 'We pray that the earth should lie lightly upon the innocent Valerius Leo'.

posuerunt,[111] which was used for the 8-month-old baby, Paula, is found on inscriptions in Rome, Milan, Aquileia, and in Gallia Cisalpina. We can assume that the parents of both children brought the custom of making a vow to ensure its welfare and the phrases themselves from their homelands.

The names themselves also give an indication of where the deceased originated from. All names are given in Latin or Latinised Greek and generally point to people's origins in the Latin West. Names like Maurus or Numidius were based on geographical terms and probably point to their African origins.[112] Explicitly Christian nomenclature did not begin to evolve in the Roman West until the late 4th c. at the earliest. Names like Maria and Paula[113] were already known and widely used in a pagan context; their Christian connotation, however, might have advanced their use in Late Antiquity.[114] Germanic names are surprisingly scarce in the inscriptions from the 4th to 8th c. at Trier and it is not until the turn of the 8th c. that they become more commonplace. Contrary to the rest of Gaul, where Germanic names quickly became popular after the fall of the Roman Empire, Trier maintained its Roman character and the traditional Latin names continued to be used almost up to the end of the Merovingian period. Whilst the Germani adopted the Christian faith, they did not take on the Latin script or the Roman custom of placing inscriptions on their graves; this would explain the lack of Germanic names in Christian inscriptions.[115] There is one example, however, which impressively shows that two generations of the same Germanic family converted to Christianity without, however, renouncing their Germanic origins: a sorrowful mother, Ebrechildis, placed a tombstone on her son Ebraharius' grave, adding a Latin inscription which follows the usual Trier formula.[116] Ebraharius' family is an example of a successful process of acculturation.

Change and Continuity

The Early Christian inscriptions from Trier can only be tentatively dated. Apart from two exceptions, none of the inscriptions can be precisely dated because the consuls in office are not named.[117] Relative dating is largely based on the evaluation of the formula used. The latter grew increasingly longer up to the mid-5th c. and then remained largely unchanged up to the 8th c. A small number of inscriptions can be dated by coins found in their immediate surroundings.[118] However, most inscriptions were no longer *in situ* but were reused elsewhere. Dating their time of creation by means of the archaeological context, therefore, is largely futile. The Early Christian inscriptions themselves, however, contain some indications to suggest that the earliest examples were probably created in the first few decades of the 4th c.[119] Whilst new elements were added to the formula and new ornaments were developed all over Gaul from the second half of the 5th c. and earlier elements ceased to be used, the people of Trier held on to the 5th c. formula. This led to a situation, where Trier and the region around the River Moselle became quite insular in terms of its epigraphic output, with the outmoded formula surviving continuously for almost another 300 years. It was not until the 8th c. that Trier gradually began to absorb outside influences, which marked the beginning of a new era in the wake of the rise of the Carolingian dynasty.[120]

The Early Christian funerary inscriptions from the 4th to 8th c. at Trier overall give a reflection of an educated and wealthy section of society. A striking element is the retention of outmoded traditions of classical antiquity, probably by a Roman population, which had remained at Trier throughout the period of upheaval. Following a phase which appears to be visible at St. Maximin, during which Roman and Germanic funerary rites co-existed, a period of acculturation set in during the 7th c. One of the more obvious traits of this period was that people with Germanic names adopted the Roman custom of placing inscriptions on graves using the traditional formula. The boundary between Late Antiquity and the Middle Ages only became recognisable with the onset of the Carolingian period, when the formal design of the inscriptions changed and they began to feature people with mainly Germanic names. The Early Christian inscriptions from Trier clearly show this transition from

---

111   Merten (2018a) Cat. 22: *'Severus et Kalen / dia dulcissimae fi / liae Paulae contra / votum posueru<n>t / qui vixit in (Christo) mens(es) / VIII dies III'* – 'Severus and Kalendia erected this, against a vow, to their sweetest daughter Paula, who lived in Christ 8 months and 3 days'.

112   Gauthier (1975) 83–84; Merten (1990) Cat. 12; Merten (2018a) Cat. 20.

113   Merten (2018a) Cat. 12, 22, and 48.

114   Gauthier (1975) 84–85.

115   Gauthier (1975) 80–81.

116   Merten (2018a) Cat. 8: *'Hic requiescit Ebra / harius qui vixit an / nus plus minus / XXXV Ebrechildis / mater sua cum doloris / et lacrimis plina VI K(a)l(endas) / Iunias titulum posuit in pa / ce'* – 'Here rests Ebraharius who lived or more or less 35 years. Ebrehildis his mother, with pain and full of tears, erected this slab in peace on the 6th day of the Kalends of June'.

117   Gauthier (1975) Cat. 93 (dated to AD 409) and Cat. 211 (dated to AD 383).

118   Merten (2016).

119   Gauthier (1975) 27–31; Merten (2015); Merten (in print).

120   Boppert (2003) 135; Krämer (1974) 44–47 and 54–55; Fuchs (2015) 72–74; Matijević (2015) 134–35.

Antiquity to the Middle Ages, which occurred at a rather slow pace at the turn of the 8th c.[121] On the other hand, the grave furnishings changed fundamentally, as several sarcophagi from the post-Roman era, which were also recovered during the archaeological excavations at St. Maximin, attest to.

Future Perspectives

Various other finds and features from St. Maximin are currently being examined as part of a separate research project with its own set of research questions.[122] The project deals with the period from the 4th to the 7th c. AD. This period was characterised by profound change in many areas. The spread of Christianity and the associated demise of the old religions were particularly important. A crucial event for the late antique imperial residence of Trier was an influx of Frankish people after the fall of the Roman Empire. In the years that followed, Germani began to ascend the political, military, and church hierarchy. This raises the question as to the indicators of change on one hand and of continuity on the other. Answers to this question can be found in changes to the funerary rites amongst other things. These changes can be seen in the burials themselves and also in the grave goods and other finds.

Frankish burials generally yield rich grave goods, precious items of attire and valuable jewellery in particular, which also provide important insight into the social status of the deceased. A group of 11 graves at St. Maximin mirrors the wealth of grave goods that one would expect from the Frankish period (late 5th to 8th c.). Jewellery was found in both adult and children's graves. A large disc brooch from St. Maximin[123] deserves special attention. A variety of strap fittings attest to the elevated level of metalworking artisanship at the time.[124] Likewise, preliminary results from textile analyses carried out on the post-Roman graves show marked technological differences compared to the earlier burials, including the absence of aromatic resins or oils, so far. The deceased were no longer laid on gypsum or wood shavings but on straw. Even the fauna in the graves, i.e. the colonisation

patterns of the necrophagous insects, also points to very different burial customs.[125] Thanks to the sometimes excellent preservation of the human remains, it will also be possible to carry out further palaeopathological investigations, and in particular stable isotope analysis in order to answer questions concerning diet and mobility. In combination with the funerary inscriptions from the same period, this group of post-Roman graves forms the basis upon which to examine the question of continuity and new beginnings at the transition from Late Antiquity to the Early Middle Ages.[126]

Acknowledgements

We wish to thank the editors Alexandra Dolea and Luke Lavan for their kind invitation to contribute to this volume. This project has been supported by funding from the Deutsche Forschungsgemeinschaft, DFG (L. C., H. M., N. R., W.-R. T.), the Fördererkreis des Rheinischen Landesmuseums, the Fritz Thyssen Foundation, the Studienstiftung des Deutschen Volkes (N. R.), the Ludwig-Maximilian University Munich (W.-R. T.), and the EU-funded project *Clothing and Identities. New Perspectives on Textiles in the Roman Empire* (*DressID*), initiated by the Reiss-Engelhorn Museum Mannheim (N. R.). Furthermore, we are grateful to the Museum am Dom Trier and the Rheinisches Landesmuseum Trier for providing access to the archaeological finds and records. Our sincere thanks go to Sandy Hämmerle (Prehistrans, Galway) for her linguistic revision and partial translation of the manuscript. We are also grateful to John Peter Wild and the two anonymous reviewers for their invaluable advice and constructive comments. Robert Maltby translated the funerary inscriptions.

Bibliography

Primary Sources

Dion. Ar. *EH* = G. Heil and A. M. Ritter ed. *Pseudo-Dionysius Areopagita. De Coelesti Hierarchia, De Ecclesiastica Hierarchia, De Mystica Theologia, Epistulae* (Patristische Texte und Studien 67) (Berlin 2012).

Secondary Sources

Barber E. (1999) *The Mummies of Ürümchi. Did Europeans Migrate to China 4000 Years Ago?* (London 1999).

Bechtold T. and Mussak R. edd. (2009) *Handbook of Natural Colorants* (Chichester 2009).

---

121 Merten (2018a) Cat. 1, 7, 8, 17, 25, 26, 33, 36, 38, 46, 56, 89, 108, 141, 153, and 223.

122 The interdisciplinary research project *Early Christian burial traditions in Late Antiquity and the Early Middle Ages. Findings from burial contexts in the cemetery basilica beneath St Maximin, Trier* is held at the department of Ancient History, University of Trier, and supported by the Deutsche Forschungsgemeinschaft, DFG (project number 291089196).

123 St. Maximin Grave 278, FN 200.1: Merten (2010) 72–73.

124 Neyses (2001) 59 fig. 27; 77–87 figs. 36–46.

125 See 'Necrophagous flies'.

126 Fuchs (2015) 63; Merten (2018a) 27–30.

Binsfeld A. (2015) "Kirchliche Würdenträger in Trierer Inschriften", in *Frühchristliche Grabinschriften im Westen des Römischen Reiches. Beiträge zur Internationalen Konferenz "Frühchristliche Grabinschriften im Westen des Römischen Reiches", Trier, 13.–15. Juni 2013* (Interdisziplinärer Dialog zwischen Archäologie und Geschichte 3), edd. L. Clemens, H. Merten, and C. Schäfer (Trier 2015) 37–60.

Bollok A. (2013) "Apotropaion and burial in Early Byzantium: some preliminary considerations", in *Byzanz und das Abendland: Begegnungen zwischen Ost und West*, ed. E. Juhász (Budapest 2013) 227–41.

Boppert W. (2003) "Frühchristliche Grabsteine in den gallisch-germanischen Grenzprovinzen", in *Reallexikon der germanischen Altertumskunde* 25 (Berlin 2003) 132–38.

Brettell R. C., Schotsmans E. M. J., Walton Rogers P., Reifarth N., Redfern R. C., Stern B., and Heron C. P. (2015) "Choicest unguents: molecular evidence for the use of resinous plant exudates in Late Roman mortuary rites in Britain", *JAS* 53 (2015) 639–48.

Brettell R. C., Stern B., Reifarth N., and Heron C. P. (2014) "The "semblance of immortality"? Resinous materials and mortuary rites in Roman Britain", *Archaeometry* 56/3 (2014) 444–59.

Cardon D. (2007) *Natural Dyes. Sources, Tradition, Technology and Science* (London 2007).

Ceci F. (2001) "L'interpretazione di monete e chiodi in contesti funerari: esempi dal suburbio romano", in *Römischer Bestattungsbrauch und Beigabensitten in Rom, Norditalien und den Nordwestprovinzen von der späten Republik bis in die Kaiserzeit* (Palila 8), edd. M. Heinzelmann, J. Ortalli, P. Fasold, and M. Witteyer (Wiesbaden 2001) 87–97.

Clemens L. and Wilhelm J. C. (2001) "Sankt Matthias und das südliche Gräberfeld", in *Das römische Trier* (Führer zu archäologischen Denkmälern in Deutschland 40), ed. H.-P. Kuhnen (Stuttgart 2001) 175–87.

Clemens L. and Seferi M. (2022) "Der christliche Großbau aus Spätantike und Frühmittelalter unter St. Maximin vor Trier", in *Der Untergang des Römischen Reiches. Begleitband zur Ausstellung im Rheinischen Landesmuseum, im Museum am Dom Trier und im Simeonstift Trier. 25. Juni 27. November 2022* (Schriftenreihe des Rheinischen Landesmuseums Trier 44), ed. H. P. Henrich (Darmstadt 2022) 336–41.

De Jonghe D. and Tavernier M. (1977–1978) "Die spätantiken Köper-4-Damaste aus dem Sarg des Bischofs Paulinus in der Krypa der Paulinus-Kirche zu Trier", *TrZ* 40/41 (1977–1978) 145–74.

Desrosiers S. (2000) "Textiles découverts dans les deux tombes du Bas Empire à Naintré (Vienne)", in *Archéologie des textiles des origins au Vᵉ siècle: actes du colloque de Lattes* (Monographies Instrumentum 14), edd. D. Cardon and M. Feugère (Montagnac 2000) 195–207.

Devièse Th., Ribechini E., Castex D., Stuart B., Regert M., and Colombini M. P. (2017) "A multi-analytical approach using FTIR, GC/MS and Py-GC/MS revealed early evidence of embalming practices in Roman catacombs", *Microchemical Journal* 133 (2017) 49–59.

Dreyspring B. and Schrenk S. (2007) "Seidenfragmente mit Spuren einer Stickerei aus dem Paulinusgrab", in *Konstantin der Große: Imperator Caesar Flavius Constantinus*, edd. A. Demandt and J. Engemann (Mainz 2007) Kat. 11.4.34 (on CD-ROM or www.dreyspring-textilrestaurierung.de/paulinusgrab.htm, accessed 07.07.2018).

Durali-Mueller S. (2006) *Roman Lead and Copper Mining in Germany: Their Origin and Development through Time, Deduced from Lead and Copper Isotope Provenance Studies* (Ph.D. diss., Johann Wolfgang Goethe-University, Institute of Geoscience, Frankfurt 2006) http://publikationen.ub.uni-frankfurt.de/frontdoor/index/index/docId/2824 [30.07.2018].

Durali-Mueller S., Wigg-Wolf D., Brey G. P., and Lahaye Y. (2007) "Roman lead mining in Germany: its origin and development through time deduced from lead isotope provenance studies", *JAS* 34/10 (2007) 1555–67.

Engemann J. (2007) "Magie", in *Konstantin der Große: Imperator Caesar Flavius Constantinus*, edd. A. Demandt and J. Engemann (Mainz 2007) 295–301.

EDCS Epigraphik-Datenbank Clauss-Slaby (EDCS) http://www.manfredclauss.de [14.07.2018].

Elliott J. H. (2016) *Beware the Evil Eye. The Evil Eye in the Bible and the Ancient World, 2: Greece and Rome* (Eugene 2016).

von Falkenhausen L. (2000) "Die Seiden mit chinesischen Inschriften", in *Die Textilien aus Palmyra: Neue und alte Funde* (Damaszener Forschungen 8), edd. A. Schmidt-Colinet, A. Stauffer, and K. Al-Ascad (Mainz 2000) 58–81.

Frankfurter D. (1997) "Ritual expertise in Roman Egypt and the problem of the category 'magician'", in *Envisioning Magic. A Princeton Seminar and Symposium* (Numen Book Series 75), edd. P. Schäfer and H. G. Kippenberg (Leiden, New York, and Cologne 1997) 115–35.

Fremdt H. and Amendt J. (2014) "Species composition of forensically important blow flies (Diptera: Calliphoridae) and flesh flies (Diptera: Sarcophagidae) through space and time", *Forensic Science International* 236 (2014) 1–9.

Fuchs R. (2015) "Epigraphische Zeugnisse des frühen Mittelalters in Trier. Einige methodische Überlegungen" in *Frühchristliche Grabinschriften im Westen des Römischen Reiches. Beiträge zur Internationalen Konferenz "Frühchristliche Grabinschriften im Westen des Römischen Reiches* (Interdisziplinärer Dialog zwischen Archäologie und Geschichte 3), edd. L. Clemens, H. Merten, and C. Schäfer (Trier 2015) 61–74.

Gauthier N. (1975) *Première Belgique* (Recueil des inscriptions chrétiennes de la Gaule antérieures à la Renaissance carolingienne 1) (Paris 1975).

Gose E. (1958) *Katalog der frühchristlichen Inschriften in Trier* (Trierer Grabungen und Forschungen 3) (Berlin 1958).

Granger-Taylor H. (2006) "Kat. 116 Dalmatic", in *Constantine the Great: York's Roman Emperor*, edd. E. Hartley, J. Hawkes, and M. Henig (York 2006) 162–65.

Green C. (1977) "The significance of plaster burials for the recognition of Christian cemeteries", in *Burial in the Roman World* (CBA Report 22), ed. R. Reece (London 1977) 46–53.

Green C., Paterson M., and Biek L. (1981) "A Roman coffin-burial from the Crown Building site, Dorchester: with particular reference to the head of well-preserved hair", *Proceedings of the Dorset Natural History and Archaeology Society* 103 (1981) 67–100.

Han J., Liu S., Zhang J., Zhou L., Fang Q., Zhang J., and Zhang Y. (2017) "The impact of temperature extremes on mortality: a time-series study in Jinan, China", *British Medical Journal Open* 7 (2017) e014741. doi:10.1136/bmjopen-2016-014741 [07.07.2018].

Heinen H. (1985) *Trier und das Trevererland in römischer Zeit (2000 Jahre Römisches Trier)* (Trier 1985).

Heinen H. (1996) *Frühchristliches Trier. Von den Anfängen bis zur Völkerwanderung* (Trier 1996).

Heinen H. (2017) "Trier", in *The Eerdmans Encyclopedia of Early Christian Art and Archaeology*, ed. P. Corby Finney (Grand Rapids 2017) II.651–52.

Hermann A. (1969) "Farbe", in *Reallexikon für Antike und Christentum 7*, edd. T. Klauser *et al.* (Stuttgart 1969) 358–447.

Hildebrandt B. with Gillis C. edd. (2017) *Silk. Trade and Exchange along the Silk Roads between Rome and China in Antiquity* (Ancient Textiles Series 29) (Oxford 2017).

Hildebrandt B. (2017) "Silk production and trade in the Roman Empire", in *Silk. Trade and Exchange along the Silk Roads between Rome and China in Antiquity* (Ancient Textiles Series 29), edd. B. Hildebrandt with C. Gillis (Oxford 2017) 34–50.

Hildebrandt B. (2012) "Some thoughts on the unravelling of Chinese silks in the Roman Empire. A reassessment of Lucan, *Bellum Civile* 10.141–143", in *Textiles and Dress in Greece and the Roman East: A Technological and Social Approach. Proceedings of a Conference held at the Department of History and Archaeology and Cultural Resource Management of the University of Peloponnese in Kalamata in collaboration with the Department of History and Archaeology of the University of Crete on March 18–19, 2011*, edd. I. Tzachili and E. Zimi (Athens 2012) 107–115.

Hillson S. (2014) *Tooth Development in Human Evolution and Bioarchaeology* (Cambridge 2014).

Jälevik B. and Norén J. G. (2000) "Enamel hypomineralization of permanent first molars: a morphological study and survey of possible aetiological factors", *International Journal of Paediatric Dentistry* 10 (2000) 278–89.

Jevons R., Carmichael C., Crossley A., and Bone A. (2016) "Minimum indoor temperature threshold recommendations for English homes in winter – a systematic review", *Public Health* 136 (2016) 4–12.

Krämer K. (1974) *Die frühchristlichen Grabinschriften Triers* (Trierer Grabungen und Forschungen 8) (Mainz 1974).

Kuhn D. and Zhao Feng edd. (2012) *Chinese Silks. The Culture and Civilization of China* (New Haven, London and Beijing 2012).

Leglay M. (1987) "La magie et la mort", in *La mort les morts et l'au-delà dans le monde romain*, ed. F. Hinard (Caen 1987) 245–48.

Liddell C., Morris C., Thomson H., and Guiney C. (2016) "Excess winter deaths in 30 European countries 1980–2013: a critical review of methods", *Journal of Public Health* 38 (2016) 806–14.

Liu Xinru (2017) "Looking towards the West – how the Chinese viewed the Romans", in *Silk. Trade and Exchange along the Silk Roads between Rome and China in Antiquity* (Ancient Textiles Series 29), edd. B. Hildebrandt with C. Gillis (Oxford 2017) 1–6.

Luik M. (2003) "Römische Wirtschaftsmetropole Trier", *TrZ* 64 (2003) 245–82.

Matijević K. (2015) "Frühchristliche Grabinschriften von der Untermosel: Kobern-Gondorf und Umgebung", in *Frühchristliche Grabinschriften im Westen des Römischen Reiches. Beiträge zur Internationalen Konferenz "Frühchristliche Grabinschriften im Westen des Römischen Reiches"* (Interdisziplinärer Dialog zwischen Archäologie und Geschichte 3), edd. L. Clemens, H. Merten, and C. Schäfer (Trier 2015) 125–35.

Merten H. (1990) *Katalog der frühchristlichen Inschriften des Bischöflichen Dom- und Diözesanmuseums Trier* (Kataloge und Schriften des Bischöflichen Dom- und Diözesanmuseums Trier 1) (Trier 1990).

Merten H. (2010) "Reiche Bestattungen des frühen Mittelalters", in *Einblicke wahrnehmen*, ed. M. Groß-Morgen (Trier 2010) 72–73.

Merten H. (2011) "Christliche Epigraphik und Archäologie in Trier seit ihren Anfängen", *RömQSchr* 106 (2011) 5–26.

Merten H. (2015) "Frühchristliche Grabinschriften in Trier. Stand der Bearbeitung", in *Frühchristliche Grabinschriften im Westen des Römischen Reiches. Beiträge zur Internationalen Konferenz "Frühchristliche Grabinschriften im Westen des Römischen Reiches"* (Interdisziplinärer Dialog zwischen Archäologie und Geschichte 3), edd. L. Clemens, H. Merten, and C. Schäfer (Trier 2015) 29–36.

Merten H. (2016) "Pausat in pace – Inschriften als früheste Zeugnisse des Christentums in Trier", in *Costantino e i Costantinidi: L' innovazione Costantiniana. Le sue radici e i suoi sviluppi. Acta XVI Congressus Internationalis Archaelogiae Christianae Romae 22.–28.9.2013* (Studi di antichità cristiana 66), edd. O. Brandt and G. Castiglia (Rome 2016) 1197–1205.

Merten H. (2018a) *Die frühchristlichen Inschriften aus St. Maximin bei Trier* (Kataloge und Schriften des Museums am Dom Trier 8) (Trier 2018).

Merten H. (2018b) "Die frühchristlichen Grabinschriften aus St. Maximin in Trier", in *Die Abtei Trier-St. Maximin von der späten Antike bis zur frühen Neuzeit* (*Quellen und Abhandlungen zur mittelrheinischen Kirchengeschichte* 142), edd. M. Embach and B. Simon (Mainz 2018) 101–108.

Merten H. (2019) "Wo sind sie geblieben? Zeugnisse paganen Lebens im frühchristlichen Trier", in *Himmelwärts und erdverbunden? Religiöse und wirtschaftliche Aspekte spätantiker Lebensrealität* (Menschen – Kulturen – Traditionen 15. Studien aus dem Forschungscluster 7 des Deutschen Archäologischen Instituts), edd. R. Haensch and P. von Rummel (Rahden 2019).

Mitschke S. and Paetz gen. Schieck A. (2012) "Dressing the dead in the city of Rome: burial custom according to textiles", in *Dressing the Dead in Classical Antiquity*, edd. M. Caroll and J. P. Wild (Stroud 2012) 115–33.

Möller-Wiering S. and Subbert J. (2012) "Germany: Roman Iron Age", in *Textiles and Textile Production in Europe from Prehistory to AD 400* (Ancient Textiles Series 11), edd. M. Gleba and U. Mannering (Oxford and Oakville 2012) 153–81.

Moulherat C. and Spantidaki S. (2011) "Les tissus à bandes d'or du bas-empire: l'exemple de Thessaloniki", in *Textiles and Dress in Greece and the Roman East: A Technological and Social Approach. Proceedings of a Conference held at the Department of History and Archaeology and Cultural Resource Management of the University of Peloponnese in Kalamata in collaboration with the Department of History and Archaeology of the University of Crete on March 18–19, 2011*, edd. I. Tzachili and E. Zimi (Athens 2012) 35–46.

Newel N. (1995) "Die Cyrillus-Inschrift von St. Matthias in Trier (Gauthier, RICG 1 19). Neue Quellen zu ihrer Überlieferungsgeschichte, Auswertung ihres Formulars", *TrZ* 58 (1996) 211–65.

Neyses A. (2001) *Die Baugeschichte der ehemaligen Reichsabtei St. Maximin bei Trier* (Kataloge und Schriften des Bischöflichen Dom- und Diözesanmuseums Trier 6.1–2) (Trier 2001).

Ortner D. J. (2003) *Identification of Pathological Conditions in Human Skeletal Remains*, 2nd ed. (San Diego 2003).

Pennick Morgan F. (2018) *Dress and Personal Appearance in Late Antiquity. The Clothing of the Middle and Lower Classes* (Leiden 2018).

Philpott R. (1991) *Burial Practices in Roman Britain. A Survey of Grave Treatment and Furnishing A.D. 43–410* (BAR-BS 219) (Oxford 1991).

Pirson F., Japp S., Kelp U., Nováek J., Schultz M., Stappmanns V., Teegen W.-R., and Wirsching A. (2011) "Der Tumulus auf dem Ilyastepe und die pergamenischen Grabhügel", *IstMitt* 61 (2011) 146–65.

Pluton-Kliesch S., Devièse T., Kliesch F., Leconte L., Moulherat C., Pilon F., and Yvinec J.-H. (2013) "Un cercueil antique en plomb découvert à Évreux: étude pluridisciplinaire", *Gallia* 70.2 (2013) 1–18.

Rast-Eicher A., Nowik W., and Garnier N. (2017) "Textiles from two Late Roman graves found in a mausoleum in Jaunay-Clan near Poitiers, France", in *Archaeological Textiles – Links Between Past and Present. NESAT XIII – North European Symposium for Archaeological Textiles*, edd. M. Bravermanová, H. Březinová, and J. Malcolm-Davies (Liberec and Prague 2017) 73–80.

Reich D. (2013) "Rot gegen das 'Böse Auge' – die apotropäische Rolle der roten Farbe auf römischen Fußbodenmosaiken", in *Rot – Die Archäologie bekennt Farbe. 5. Mitteldeutscher Archäologentag vom 04. bis 06. Oktober 2012 in Halle (Saale)* (Tagung des Landesmuseums für Vorgeschichte Halle 10), edd. H. Meller, C.-H. Wunderlich, and F. Knoll (Halle 2013) 353–58.

Reifarth N., Teegen W. R., Boenke N., and Wiethold J. (2006) "Das spätantike Grab 279 aus St. Maximin in Trier. Technologische, anthropologische und archäobotanische Untersuchunge", *Funde und Ausgrabungen im Bezirk Trier* 38 (2006) 58–70.

Reifarth N. (2013a) *Zur Ausstattung spätantiker Elitegräber aus St. Maximin in Trier. Purpur, Seide, Gold und Harze* (Internationale Archäologie 124) (Rahden 2013).

Reifarth N. (2013b) "Rätselhafte Goldgewebestreifen in spätantiken Sarkophagen aus St. Maximin in Trier", in *Die Macht der Toga. Dresscode im Römischen Weltreich* (Publikation der Reiss-Engelhorn-Museen in Kooperation mit dem Roemer- und Pelizaeus-Museum 56), edd. M. Tellenbach, R. Schulz and A. Wieczoreck (Regensburg 2013) 242–47.

Resmini G. (2016) *Die Benediktinerabtei St. Maximin vor Trier* (Germania sacra 3. F., 11) (Berlin 2016).

Scheidel W. (1996) "Seasonal mortality in the Roman Empire", in *Measuring Sex, Age and Death in the Roman Empire. Explorations in Ancient Demography* (JRA Supplementary Series 21), ed. W. Scheidel (Ann Arbor 1996) 139–63.

Scheidel W. (2001) "Roman age structure: evidence and models", *JRS* 91 (2001) 1–26.

Schmidt-Colinet A., Stauffer A., and Al-Ascad, K. (2000) *Die Textilien aus Palmyra: Neue und alte Funde* (Damaszener Forschungen 8) (Mainz 2000).

Schotsmans E. M. J., Wilson A. S., Brettell R., Munshi T., and Edwards H. G. M. (2014) "Raman spectroscopy as a non-destructive screening technique for studying white substances from archaeological and forensic burial contexts", *Journal of Roman Spectroscopy* 45 (2014) 1301–1308.

Schwinden L. (1984) "Grabinschrift für Hariulf", in *Trier – Kaiserresidenz und Bischofssitz. Ausstellungskatalog, Rheinisches Landesmuseum Trier* (Mainz 1984) 349–50 cat. 186.

Schwinden L. (1986) "Kinderleben und Kindersterblichkeit nach antiken Denkmälern aus Trier", *Funde und Ausgrabungen im Bezirk Trier* 18 = *Kurtrierisches Jahrbuch* 26 (1986) 30–37.

Schwinden L. (1996) "Praepositus vinorum. Ein kaiserlicher Weinverwalter im spätrömischen Trier", *Funde und Ausgrabungen im Bezirk Trier* 28 (1996) 49–60.

Schwinden L. (1999) "Zur Herkunft des Formulars der frühchristlichen Inschriften von Trier. Neue Sarkophage als missing links", in *Atti, Congresso Internazionale di Epigrafia Greca e Latina 11, Roma, 18–24 settembre 1997* (Rome 1999) II. 729–38.

Schwinden L. (2001) "Sankt Maximin: Antiker Bestattungsplatz und frühchristliche Verehrungsstätte im Norden Triers", in *Das römische Trier* (Führer zu archäologischen Denkmälern in Deutschland 40), ed. H.-P. Kuhnen (Stuttgart 2001) 188–201.

Schwinden L. (2012) "Einführung: Griechen und Orientalen im römischen Trier. Griechische Sprache und Schriftzeugnisse", in *Inscriptiones Graecae Treverenses. Edition der spätantiken und frühchristlichen griechischen Inschriften in Trier mit Übersetzung und Kommentar*, edd. M. Siede and L. Schwinden (Trier 2012) 1–17.

Schwinden L. (2018) "Sankt Maximin – die archäologischen Beobachtungen und Untersuchungen", *in Die Abtei Trier-St. Maximin von der späten Antike bis zur frühen Neuzeit*, edd. M. Embach and B. Simon (Mainz 2018) 57–84.

Siedow, M. (2016) *Der Baukomplex auf dem Friedhof zu St. Matthias in Trier: Überlegungen zur Genese spätantiker Coemeterialbauten* (Ph.D. diss., Univ. of Trier 2016).

Shaw B. D. (1996) "Seasons of death: aspects of mortality in imperial Rome", *JRS* 86 (1996) 100–138.

Shaw B. D. (2006) "Seasonal mortality in imperial Rome and the Mediterranean: three problem cases", in *Urbanism in the Preindustrial World. Cross-Cultural Approaches*, ed. G. R. Storey (Tuscaloosa 2006) 86–109.

Sipos E. (1990) "Heténypusztai Római kori Textilek Vizsgálata, A Textil – És Ruhaipari Múzeum Évkönyve", *Journal of the Museum for Textiles and Dress* 7 (1990) 7–13, figs. 1–8.

Sparey-Green C. (1993) "The rite of plaster burial in the context of the Romano-British cemetery at Poundbury, Dorset (England)", in *Römerzeitliche Gräber als Quellen zu Religion, Bevölkerungsstruktur und Sozialgeschichte* (Archäologische Schriften des Instituts für Vor- und Frühgeschichte der Johannes-Gutenberg-Universität Mainz 3), ed. M. Struck (Mainz 1993) 421–32.

Stauffer A. (2011) "Antiker Luxus aus römischen Särgen. Die mittelkaiserzeitlichen Goldgewebe aus Weilerswist-Klein-Vernich und Rommerskirchen", in *Textilien in der Archäologie* (Materialien zur Bodendenkmalpflege im Rheinland 22), ed. J. Kunow (Bonn 2011) 61–68.

Stauffer A. (1996) "Textiles from Palmyra. Local production and the import and imitation of Chines silk weaving", in *Les Annales Archéologiques arabes syriennes* (Revue d'Archéologie et d'Histoire 42) 425–30.

Teegen W.-R. (2004) "Hypoplasia of the tooth root. A new unspecific stress marker in human and animal paleopathology", *American Journal of Physical Anthropology Suppl.* 38 (2004) 193.

Teegen W.-R. (2006) "Zur saisonalen Sterblichkeit im spätantiken und frühmittelalterlichen Trier", *Funde und Ausgrabungen im Bezirk Trier* 38 (2006) 52–57.

Teegen W.-R. (2016) "Case study: the burial of a pregnant woman from the Roman South-East necropolis at Pergamon (Bergama, Prov. Izmir, Turkey)", in *Rencontre autour de la mort des tout-petits. Mortalité fœtale et infantile: Actes de la 11e Rencontre du Gaaf à Saint-Germain-en-Laye les 3 et 4 décembre 2009* (Publication du Gaaf 5), edd. É. Portat, M. Detante, and M. Guillon (Saint-Germain-en-Laye 2016) 91–101.

Volp U. (2002) *Tod und Ritual in den christlichen Gemeinden der Antike* (Supplements to VigChr 65) (Leiden 2002).

Wightman E. M. (1970) *Roman Trier and the Treveri* (London 1970).

Wightman E. M. (1985) *Gallia Belgica* (Oxford 1985).

Wild J. P. (1964) "The textile term scutulatus", *CQ* 14/2 (1964) 263–66.

Wild J. P. (1976) "The *gynaecea*", in *Aspects of the Notitia Dignitatum*, edd. R. Goodburn and P. Bartholomew (BAR S15) (Oxford 1976) 51–58.

Wild J. P. (1987) "The Roman horizontal loom", *AJA* 91 (1987) 459–71.

Wild J. P. (2012) "Makers' marks – on textiles?", in *Dating and Interpreting the Past in the Western Roman Empire. Essays in Honour of Brenda Dickinson*, ed. D. Bird (Oxford 2012) 245–54.

Wild J. P. (2013) "Luxury? The north-west end of the silk-purple-and-gold-horizon", in *Luxury and Dress. Political Power and Appearance in the Roman Empire and its Provinces*, edd. C. Alfaro Giner, J. Ortiz García, and M. Martínez García (Valencia 2013) 169–80.

Wild J. P. and Wild F. C. (2014) "Berenike and the textile trade on the Indian Ocean", in *Textile Trade and Distribution in Antiquity. Textilhandel und -distribution in der Antike*, ed. K. Droß-Küpe (Wiesbaden 2014) 91–109.

Zhao Feng (2017) "Domestic, wild or unravelled? A study on tabby taqueté and jin with spun silk from Yingpan, Xinjiag, third-fourth centuries", in *Silk. Trade and Exchange along the Silk Roads between Rome and China in Antiquity* (Ancient Textiles Series 29), ed. B. Hildebrandt with C. Gillis (Oxford 2017) 95–103.

Funerary Patterns in Late Roman Cities (3rd to 7th c.): Reviewing Archaeological Data in Northern Italy

Alexandra Chavarría Arnau

Abstract

One of the principal transformations underlined by researchers analysing urban landscape during Late Antiquity concerns changes in funerary patterns and the progressive development of intramural burials. It is a phenomenon that has traditionally been linked to processes of Christianisation, the construction of churches inside cities and particularly a change in the relationship between people and the bodies of the dead, especially those of martyrs and saints. In this paper, I shall try to demonstrate that between the 4th and 6th c., burials inside city walls are rare and almost never related to Christian buildings. At least in northern Italy, Roman and Ostrogothic populations continued respecting Roman traditions, burying their dead in existing cemeteries located in suburban areas outside the city walls. Some of these burial areas had existed since Republican and Imperial times and contained pagan and Christian burials alike. Others seem to have been created, again in the suburbs, during the 3rd c. and developed a century later into large Christian areas. Real changes in burial practices inside the city would only begin from the end of the 6th c. with the multiplication of scattered burials and still later the development of intramural cemeteries linked to private chapels and, more rarely, episcopal churches.

Introduction

Archaeological evidence reveals two major changes relating to burial practices in Late Antiquity and the Early Middle Ages in Italy.[1] The first took place from the 3rd c., which saw a series of transformations in burial ritual, with the abandonment of cremation, the decline of grave-goods depositions and the reorganisation of earlier Roman burial areas. The second, possibly more dramatic break, took place from the end of the 6th c. onwards with the entry of burials into cities and, in the countryside, the appearance of row cemeteries with furnished (sometimes armed) graves.[2] This second period coincides with the arrival and settlement of the Lombards in 568/569. In contrast, 3rd c. changes in funerary practices can probably be linked to different phenomena taking place in this period of still poor archaeological study, transformations which are of major significance for the understanding of Late Antiquity. Until now, urban Roman funerary archaeology in northern Italy has mainly concentrated on some major sites such as Milan,[3] Verona,[4] Concordia,[5] Bologna,[6] or more recently Padova,[7] among others.

In this paper, I will analyse characteristics and evolution of burial practices in urban contexts between the 3rd and 6th c., attempting to understand how Christianity affected the way in which families buried their dead and how these changes modified the uses of urban space. I shall focus on three main questions:

1. How did Christianisation modify the way in which Romans buried their dead in urban contexts and when do these changes start to be documented in the archaeological record?
2. Was there a real change of burial customs in urban contexts with the officialising of Christianity and the construction of monumental churches?
3. When did intramural burial first appear and what caused this break with past traditions?

It is important to underline that the characteristics of mortuary practices are linked to the central role cities held in their territories during the late antique period, at least until the arrival of the Lombards, and the figures of bishops as continuators of Roman laws and traditions. While in many cities there was continuity of this function, in other centres, due to particular political and strategic circumstances, their role changed, or they experienced radical alterations in the function of their intra- and extramural spaces. The chronology of cemeteries is significantly complicated by the general lack of grave goods and the few systematic radiocarbon dates available for cemeteries of the 3rd and 4th c. For these reasons, I will use a limited number of examples, which have been the subjects of recent archaeological research.

---

1 Research on this paper was funded by the University of Padua (Progetto di Ateneo 2012 – Bird: 2019–2021 PI: Alexandra Chavarría Arnau).
2 On which, see Possenti (2014) and Giostra (2017).

3 Bolla (1988) and Bolla (1992).
4 Cavalieri Manasse and Bolla (1998); Bolla (2005).
5 Anibaletto (2010); Rinaldi and Vigoni (2015).
6 Brizzolara (1983).
7 Rossi (2016); Pettenò and Rossi (2015).

Alexandra Dolea and Luke Lavan (eds) *Burial and Memorial in Late Antiquity* (Late Antique Archaeology 13) (Leiden 2024), pp. 692–704

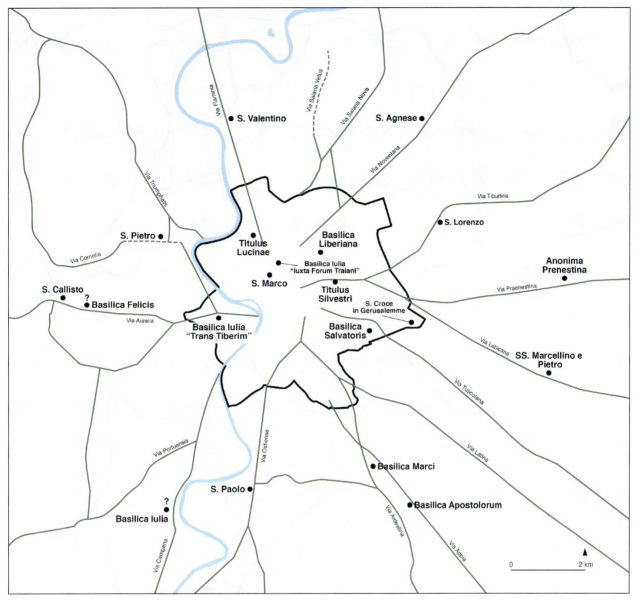

FIGURE 1 Rome, main roads leading from and to the city and cemeteries quoted in the text. Fiocchi Nicolai in Chavarría Arnau (2023) 90 figs. 10–11.

Christianisation and Burials

The death of a person, the fate of the soul, hopes for salvation and the Final Judgement on the day of *parousia* were dramatic aspects of Early Christianity and are essential to understanding the earliest Christian archaeological evidence. Reason for this lies in the fact that Early Christians believed that Jesus accomplished his mission of redemption and salvation not only with prophecies, miracles, and signs but first and foremost, with his death, burial, and resurrection.[8] The oldest archaeological evidence for Christianisation in the West relates consequently to funerary cults and, in particular,

sarcophagi, mosaics, paintings, and objects used in cemeteries (such as lamps) depicting Christian subjects, symbols, and formularies relating to death and the life beyond.[9]

Archaeologically, the first clear evidence of Christian burials appear at the very end of the 2nd and from the 3rd c.; for example, at the Vatican cemetery in relation to the grave of St. Peter and in cemeterial areas by the *Via Appia*[10] (Fig. 1). And we know from some written sources that bishops started to manage Christian cemeteries from the 3rd c., where the faithful could bury their loved ones and fulfil funerary rites. The first notice about Rome refers to Callixtus, tasked by Pope Zephyrinus (199–217)

8   Stancati (2006).

9   Bisconti (2007).

10   Spera (2009) 774–76.

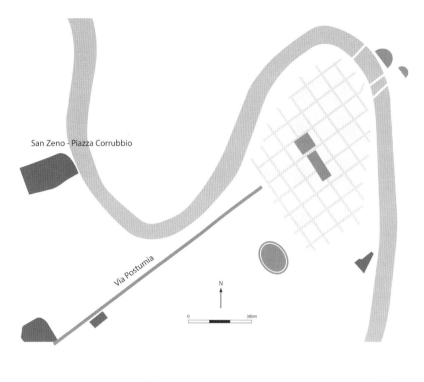

FIGURE 2
Verona, Via Postumia and funerary area of
Piazza Corrubbio-San Zeno.
PLAN BY PAOLO VEDOVETTO

FIGURE 3
Verona, funerary area excavated in Piazza
Corrubio, close to the suburbian basilica of
San Zeno (from Lusuardi Siena and Baratto in
Bass and Cavalieri Manasse (2013) 180 fig. 19).

with organising a cemetery on the *Via Appia*. This activity continued with Pope Fabian (226–250), who '*multas fabricas per cimiteria fieri iussit*', and Pope Dionysius (259–268) was remembered because '*cymiteria et parrocias diocesis constituit*'.[11] Cemeteries owned and used by the Roman Christian comunity developed not only in the southern suburbs of the city (e.g. cemetery of Callixtus) but also in the northern area (e.g. Priscilla's, Bassilla's and Agense catacombs), in the west by the *Via*

Aurelia (e.g. Calepodio's catacomb) and east (e.g. cemeteries of Ippolito and Novaziano) among others.[12]

Recent investigations by Vincenzo Fiocchi Nicolai highlight the extraordinary importance of a systematic study of the number of burials in the most ancient Christian cemeteries in Rome. The results, although still provisional and calculated by default, are extremely interesting. Callixtus Area I, that is the cemetery founded at the time of Zephyrinus and managed by his collaborator Callixtus, counted at least 1,500 burials in the *ca.* 280 m of underground tunnels between

---

11   For a recent review of the evidence, see Spera (2009) 778–80.

12   Fiocchi Nicolai (2006).

AD 230–240. By the middle of the 3rd c., the Arenario region of the catacomb of Priscilla and the adjacent areas of Eliodoro and Tyche housed 1,200 burials. The so-called Good Shepherd and Flavi Aureli 'A' regions of the catacomb of Domitilla housed at least 250 burials, while those of the Scala Maggiore and Scala Minore of the cemetery of Pretestato, about 600. The cemetery on the Aurelia of Calepodio, where Callixtus was deposed in 222, accounted for about 350 burials by the middle of the 3rd c. In a few decades, therefore, many thousands of believers had already been housed in these cemetery areas.[13] In light of the archaeological, epigraphic, and literary documentation, the doubts raised by Éric Rebillard on the communitary Christian character of some Roman cemeteries[14] are not convincing. The collective character of the first cemetery areas of Rome constitutes a seemingly undeniable fact.[15]

Other suburban cemeteries created *ex novo* in the 3rd c. and which became the focus of later monumental Christian cemeteries *ad sanctos* could be taken as evidence of this process of Christianisation. In many cases, these cemeteries developed in areas previously occupied but then abandoned by residential or industrial quarters. Traditionally, these abandonments have been linked to the insecurity caused by Alamanni and other barbarian raids, an hypothesis that finds support in the contemporary or later building of defensive walls. In any case, profound transformations were affecting the function of the suburbia of Roman cities and the organisation of funerary areas in some cases dismantled for the construction of the new walls.[16] Recent excavations at Verona confirm that suburbia suffered radical transformations during the second half of the 3rd c. (Fig. 2). Entire residential quarters which had existed since the Early Imperial period and developed in the proximity of the city walls were abandoned and destroyed during the reign of Gallienus (253–268) in order to rebuild the fortifications and to leave a security space around them.[17] The new construction, ordered by the emperor, as is recorded in an inscription,[18] was finished in 8 months

under the direction of Julius Marcellinus, possibly the urban curator, and the *curator dux ducenarius* Aurelius Marcellinus.[19] The city's funerary areas also seem to have been reorganised at this point. In the eastern suburb, along the *Via Gallica* connecting Verona to Brescia, excavations at Piazza Corrubio (2011–2013) have brought to light a large, monumental area originating in the 3rd c. and which saw development until the beginning of the 8th (Fig. 3).[20]

Excavations have uncovered some 450 burials comprising simple earth graves, stone or brick structures, amphorae burials (mostly for infants), as well as some mausolea. A church dedicated to San Procolo was built at the end of the 5th c., perhaps as an evolution of an earlier cult space, which could have developed around an important Christian tomb. It is difficult to say whether this area was conceived of as a Christian cemetery from the outset or whether some walled areas inside the cemetery could indicate any kind of religious differentiation among the graves. The burial in this area of St. Zeno, bishop of Verona, and the nearby presence of a church devoted to one of Verona's first martyrs, St. Proculus, 4th bishop of Verona, could point in this direction. Further systematic research is, however, needed in order to fully understand the significant changes which took place in the suburbs during the second half of the 3rd c., to clarify the significance of the abandonment of residential and industrial quarters, and investigate who led the reorganisation of funerary space.

A cemetery created also in the 3rd c. has been widely excavated and studied in the southern court of the Catholic University in the Western suburb of Milan.[21] In this case, burials have been identified as those of the soldiers linked to the imperial palace and their families, with some allochthonous presences detected by anthropology and some of the grave-goods. The cemetery seems to be organised in familiar groups and there are few indicators of a Christian presence (Fig. 4). The cemetery was abandoned during the 5th c. around the time Milan lost its status as imperial capital with the flight of the imperial court to Ravenna, while Christian cemeteries linked to the churches *ad sanctos* were growing close by, such as the churches of Sant'Ambrogio and San Vittore in Ciel d'Oro.

Evidence is too scarce to provide any understanding of the development of other 3rd c. cemeteries in suburban areas of cities such as Aquileia, Padova, Vicenza, Treviso, among others. During the period of the Christian

---

13   Fiocchi Nicolai (2006).

14   Rebillard (1997) and later Rebillard (2009) based on a lexicological discussion about the word *caementerium* in early sources and in the chronology of the main source, the *Liber Pontificalis*, which is not contemporary to the facts it describes.

15   Guyon (2005); Duval (2000) 448–57; see also Fiocchi Nicolai (2016) for a more recent critique of the negationist hypothesis made by Rébillard (1997).

16   Cantino and Lambert (1998) 103. Similar evolutions in Spain include the suburban funerary areas of the Parc Central in Tarragona and Santa Eulalia in Mérida (see for a synthesis Chavarría (2019) 631–34 with a wider bibliography).

17   Cavalieri Manasse and Bruno (2003) 51.

18   CIL 5.3329 = ILS 544.

19   Brogiolo (2011) 90–92

20   Cavalieri Manasse and Meloni (2012); Cavalieri Manasse (2017).

21   Sannazaro (2009).

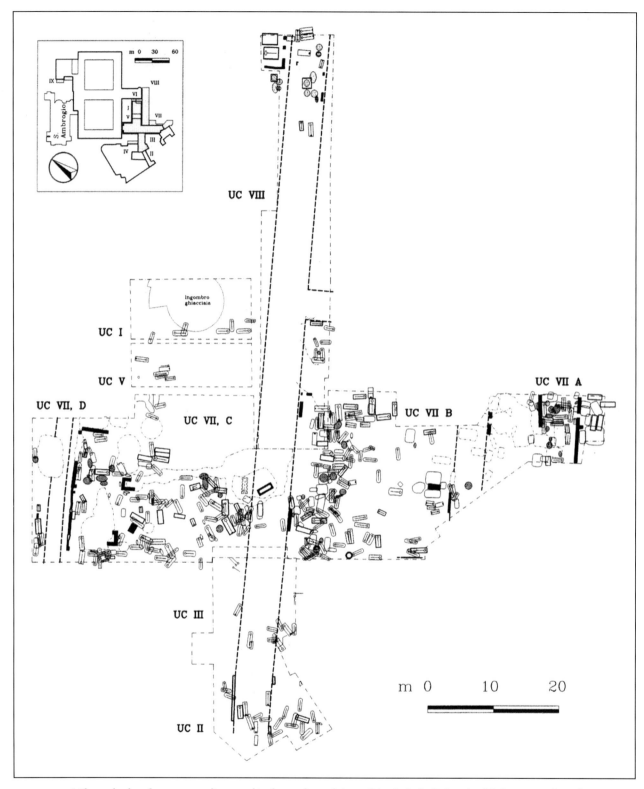

FIGURE 4   Milan, suburban funerary area discovered in the southern cloister of the Catholic University. (M. Sannazaro, Cronologia
e topografia dell'area funeraria nei cortili dell'Università Cattolica, in M. Sannazaro (ed.), *Ricerche archeologiche nei cortili
dell'Università Cattolica. La necropoli tardoantica* (*Atti delle giornate di studio, Milano 25–26 gennaio 1998*) (Contributi di
Archeologia 1) (Milan 2001) (39–58) p. 51, fig. 1).

persecutions and particularly during the 3rd and the beginning of the 4th c., martyrs were buried in some of these suburban cemeteries, either new establishments or in continuity with Early Imperial burial areas. Their tombs became places of devotion for the Christian population of the cities, saw the building of elaborate monuments as cultic focal points and in turn attracted the graves of the faithful.[22]

Was There a Real Change in Burial Customs in Urban Contexts with the Officialising of Christianity after the 4th c. and the Construction of Monumental Churches?

40 years of studies in Late Roman Christian urban topography have clearly established how, during the early 4th to the 6th c., urban churches carried out two completely different functions: the cathedral (*ecclesia mater*), located inside the city, was used as a meeting place and for the regular liturgy, while suburban churches (generally called *basilicae*) served to honour martyrs and as a place of burial and commemoration of the Christian dead.[23] In fact, one of Constantine's first actions after he arrived in Rome after his victory at Milvian Bridge was the renewal and monumentalizing of martyrs' graves in suburban cemeteries. In collaboration with the bishop of Rome, Constantine constructed large churches over the graves of the main Roman martyrs and invited other members of the administration to restore 'those places that had become sacred thanks to the corpses of the martyrs and to build churches above them'.[24] The function of these churches was not only to honour the memory of the martyrs but also to be used as covered cemeteries (*coemeteria subteglata*), where ceremonies linked to funerary cults took place, although very soon other liturgical ceremonies were performed within them.[25] The presence of martyrs and their relics and the conduction of liturgical ceremonies, in addition to continued use of these areas from earlier centuries, attracted the favour of the highest urban elites, from bishops – who throughout the Early Middle Ages were mainly buried in such suburban 'basilicas' near the earlier graves of martyrs – to the secular elite. External monumental mausolea built by the churches or in their vicinity testify to this attraction.

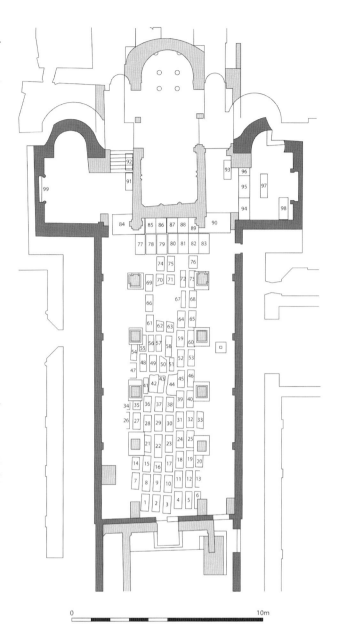

FIGURE 5   Trento, funerary suburban basilica of San Vigilio, plan of the funerary area inside the church: Rogger and Cavada (2011).

The space inside churches seem to have been used in a highly hierarchical fashion. In the martyrial basilica of St. Vigilius at Trento, erected close to the porta Veronensis at the southern suburbium, the original floor of the basilica was dismantled in the 5th c. and a grid of 200 *loculi* was built to be used as graves (Fig. 5).[26] Grave-goods are practically absent and limited to a fibula and some fragments of glass in grave 18. Only 7 of about 30 inscriptions belonged to members of the clergy[27] and the sex ratio does not seem to indicate a massive number of clergy (73 males, 64 females, 14 adolescents and

22   A recent useful synthesis in Lusuardi Siena and Baratto (2014).
23   Gaillard, Prévot, and Gauthier (2014). See also Lorans (2014) for a comparison between funerary patterns linked to Christian topography in Gaul and England.
24   Euseb. *Vit. Const.* 2, 23, 40.
25   Fiocchi Nicolai (2016) 630.

26   Rogger and Cavada (2001) fig. 5.
27   Mazzoleni (2001).

0   10 m

a

b

FIGURE 6
Aosta, church of San Lorenzo, plan and funerary area
inside the church (R. Perinetti "La chiesa di San Lorenzo.
Appunti per una tipologia delle tombe", in *La chiesa di
S. Lorenzo in Aosta. Scavi archeologici* (Rome 1981) 47–92.

24 infants younger than 10–14 years). These results suggest a far more diversified use of the basilica than simply a limited use for clerics. At the basilica of St. Vigilius,
some graves were occupied by a single burial, while others contained a large number of corpses (up to 10). The
reuse of graves for multiple burials was widely adopted
during this period, especially in church contexts. At the
suburban church of San Lorenzo in Aosta (Fig. 6), multiple burials mainly appear inside the church, with the
exception of the sarcophagus that preserved the corpse
of Bishop Agnellus, while burials outside the church
were used only once.[28] Wider research about this sub-

ject is needed on the location and chronology of multiple burials.[29] Genetic research may be able to detect
whether these graves were conceived as family mausolea (the most plausible hypothesis) or whether there
were other dynamics that justified the presence of multiple burials.[30]

---

28   On this church and the identification of the privileged buri-
      als as bishops and other churchmen, see Perinetti (1981) and

Bonnet (1981), including the possibility of burials belonging to
non-ecclesiastics.

29   See Gleize (2007).

30   See Bolla (2015) for wider discussion and Italian examples.

When Did Intramural Burials Start?

Archaeology reveals that by the 7th c. and in some areas like Emilia Romagna as early as the 3rd to 4th c., scattered burials were placed inside the original limits of the majority of ancient cities.[31] In Italy, these burial 'plots' were generally very small – between 1 and 10 burials – and can often be related to abandoned private and public buildings. Scattered burials have been found in almost all Italian cities. While their dating is not always easy to establish, they seem to start from the end of the 5th c. or later.[32] In some cases, such as various cities in Abruzzo, grave-goods date the burials accurately to the end of the 6th/beginning of the 7th c.[33] These burials tend to be quite simple, in earth or stone and brick structures, sometimes with floors and covers built with tiles 'alla cappuccina,' and with very few or no grave goods. 20 years ago, G. P. Brogiolo suggested that examples discovered in Brescia belonged to a low status, possibly servile, population working for Lombard elites,[34] as they were located near sunken huts in an area belonging to the Lombard royal court. A total of 65 scattered tombs are now known in late antique/Early Medieval Brescia and anthropological analysis seems to confirm this interpretation.[35] Comparable data has been recently synthesised and reviewed at other north Italian cities such as Verona, Pavia, Cividale, Piacenza and Alba, and follow Brogiolo's interpretation.[36] Recent bioarcheological research on the osteological materials confirms for these individuals precarious life conditions with clear signs of malnutrition and young deaths.[37]

Nevertheless, burial inside the city is not to be only viewed as a sign of marginalisation or low social status, and can sometimes denote privilege: at Verona, the burial place of the first Lombard king, Alboin, was under the staircase of his palace,[38] while in the same city, a very high status female tomb dated to the beginning of the 7th c. was discovered in the area of Palazzo Miniscalchi/Cortalta (*Curtis alta*).[39] At Cividale, a sarcophagus containing rich mid-7th c. grave goods was recovered in 1874, possibly associated with some form of public or elite building.[40] The characteristics and grave goods of some of the burials recovered in Bergamo, via Osmano-vicolo Sant'Andrea, reveal élite Lombard populations and again the graves seem to be linked to some kind of public building.[41]

One must underline the extreme variability of the data and the related interpretations which indicate multiple ideological, social, and economic traditions. The occurrence of formal burial activity inside the city at the end of the 6th and the first decades of the 7th c. is, therefore, not necessarily an indicator of Christianisation or evidence for the establishment of a church but more probably relates to a change in the conception and use of urban space in the post-Roman period. In fact, it is noticeable that intramural churches, and in particular cathedrals, in Italy did not attract formal burial grounds until a later date and never before the 7th c.[42] Some of the earliest burials that have been found close to cathedrals seem to be linked to other contexts. Some may well pre-date the construction of the church or are connected to a period when this building could have been abandoned, such as in the examples of Alba,[43] Trento,[44] Brescia,[45] Cividale,[46] and Padua, where recent detailed stratigraphic excavation and a range of radiocarbon dates have clearly attested the complete destruction of at least part of the episcopal complex – specifically the baptistery – at the beginning of the 7th c., followed by a residual settlement of two huts with a cemetery (tombs 7, 8, 13, 14 with 2 adults and 2 infants) (Figs. 7 and 8).[47] The area would not have a religious function again until the 10th or 11th c., when a large building (maybe the baptistery) was built, with a large, privileged funerary area for infants attached to its walls and northern area.[48]

It is interesting to underline that the earliest 7th c. graves which can reliably be linked to cathedrals probably belonged to lay elites and not to members of the church hierarchy.[49] At San Salvatore in Turin, inhumations, radiocarbon-dated to between AD 660 and 770, were identified by anthropological analyses to be

31 Lambert (1997) and (2003).
32 Lambert (2003). For Ravenna and Classe: Ferreri (2011) and (2014). For Rome: Meneghini and Santangeli Valenzani (1995) and Fiochi Niccolai (2003); Verona: Bedini and Bartoldi (2008).
33 For Amiternum, Castrum Truentinum, Interamnia-Castrum Aprutensium, Corfinium, among others, see Staffa (1998).
34 Brogiolo (1994) 560.
35 Brogiolo (2011) 49–50, with wider discussion on the uses of urban spaces for burial, 139–46.
36 Giostra (2014).
37 Chavarría Arnau (2020); Chavarría, Marinato, Lamanna in this volume.
38 Paulus, *HL* 2, 28.
39 Cipolla (1907).
40 Brogiolo (2001); Lusuardi, Giostra, and Spalla (2012) 277–78.
41 Fortunati *et al.* (2014) 141–44.
42 Chavarría and Giacomello (2014).
43 Micheletto (1999) 34; Lambert (2003) 230.
44 Guaitioli (2013) 116–21.
45 Breda (2007) 240–42.
46 Borzacconi (2003).
47 Brogiolo, Chavarría, and Nuvolari (2017).
48 Specifically on the burials, see Canci, Marinato, and Zago (2017).
49 The earliest textual references to ecclesiastical burials in cathedrals (presbyters and bishops) seem to come slightly later, from the 8th to 9th c. (Picard (1988)).

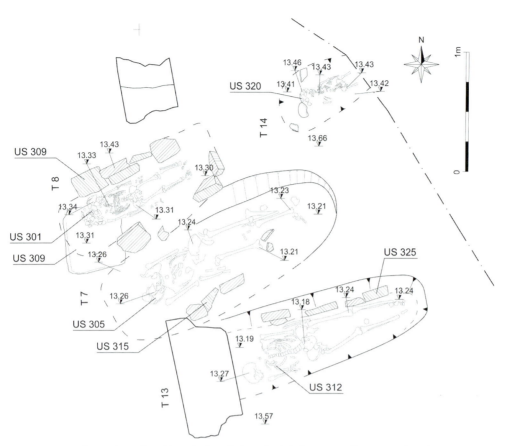

FIGURE 7   Padua, early medieval burials identified north of the baptistery (from *Ricerche sul centro
episcopale di Padova. Scavi 2011–2012*, ed. A. Chavarría Arnau (Mantua 2017) fig. 17, p. 25).

FIGURE 8   Padua, tombs 7, 8 (in *Ricerche sul centro episcopale di Padova. Scavi 2011–2012*, ed.
A. Chavarría Arnau (Mantua 2017) fig. 19, p. 26).

members of the military aristocracies of the city.[50] At Mantua, recent excavations on the via Rubens have unearthed a monumental baptistery in which a typically Lombard grave with the characteristic "wooden house" structure and gold grave goods had been located in the internal deambulatory. This building was in use during the 7th c., as well as another baptistery known in the area of the Cortile del Seminario where 7th c. burials with weapons or clothing with gold brocade were also discovered. In this case. the existence of two contemporary baptisteries is interesting and seems to point to two cathedrals, probably reflecting the co-existence of Arian/Catholic communities.[51] Between the end of the 7th and the 8th c., a large number of churches and monasteries were constructed with the support of urban aristocracies, generally of Lombard origin, inside and outside cities. Amongst their various functions was frequently that of family mausolea. It is perhaps at this moment and by this means that the distinction between urban and suburban and that between the living and the dead finally disappeared.

Conclusion

Archaeological documentation for Italy shows that many changes in the organisation of urban cemeteries took place during the 3rd c. Not only did inhumation cement its place as the preferred burial practice during this century but radical transformations were taking place in the suburbs, where new cemeteries were sometimes created at the expense of previous residential and industrial areas. The reason for the abandonment of these earlier spaces was probably related to the insecurity of the period and the reorganisation of urban fortifications. Further research is needed but the wider evolution of these cemeteries, with the burial of martyrs and their monumental development into funerary churches during the 4th and 5th c., could also point to a Christian origin for some cemeteries as early as the 3rd c. A hypothesis, which still requires future confirmation, would see bishops acquiring abandoned areas of the suburbs to allow the creation of cemeteries for their Christian flocks, as written sources suggest.

During the 4th to 6th c., no major changes seem to affect the burial customs of Late Roman populations, which continued to use suburban cemeteries, mostly developing around martyrial churches, and employing burial forms already existing in Imperial times and,

therefore, respecting Roman laws. Dramatic changes would only begin from the end of the 6th c., when graves start being more frequently documented inside cities and occupying earlier residential or public structures. These burials are rarely connected to churches and, therefore, they cannot be interpreted as a consequence of Christianisation. They can generally be related to the deposition of low status urban inhabitants, who were buried close to their houses (generally sunken huts) or next to the craft workshops they were probably employed as servants. Rarely elite burials were located by their own urban palaces. On the other hand, 7th c. burials in intramural churches seem to correspond to lay elites and, on rare occasions, bishops. Other members of the ecclesiastical hierarchy and the majority of the urban population continued to prefer suburban locations linked to martyrial basilicas for their graves. Discontinuity, therefore, does not seem to be related to Christianisation but to the arrival of new populations in Italy, in particular the Lombards.

Bibliography

Primary Sources

Euseb. *Vit. Const.* = A. Cameron and S. Hall ed. and transl., *Life of Constantine* (Clarendon Ancient History Series) (Oxford 1999).

Paulus, HL = W. D. Foulke transl., *Paul the Deacon, Historia Langobardorum* (Philadelphia 1906).

Secondary Sources

Anibaletto M. (2010) *Il paesaggio funerario di Iulia Concordia* (Rome 2010).

Ariès P. (1974) *Western Attitudes Toward Death from the Middle Ages to the Present* (Baltimore 1974).

Bedini E. and Bartoli F. (2008) "Gli inumati medievali: studio antropologico, paleopatologico e paleonutrizionale", *L'area del Capitolium di Verona. Ricerche storiche e archeologiche*, ed. Cavalieri Manasse G. (Verona 2008) 591–94.

Bisconti F. (2007) "La « cristianizzazione » delle immagini in Italia tra Tarda Antichità e Alto Medioevo", in *La cristianizzazione in Italia fra tardoantico e altomedioevo. IX Congresso Nazionale di Archeologia Cristiana (Agrigento, 20–25 novembre 2004)*, edd. R. M. Carra Bonacasa and E. Vitale (Palerm 2007) 151–67.

Bolla M. (1988) *Le necropoli romane di Milano, Rassegna di Studi del Civico Museo Archeologico e del Civico Museo Numismatico di Milano* (Milano 1988).

Bolla M. (2015) "Sepoltura non perpetua: la riapertura delle tombe e il caso concordiense", in *Le necropoli della media e tarda età imperiale (III–IV sec. d.C.) a Iulia Concordia e*

---

50   Pejrani Baricco (2003) 316.
51   Menotti and Manicardi (2004); Manicardi (2015) 56–61 for via Rubens.

nell'arco altoadriatico. Atti del Convegno di Concordia Sag-ittaria (*giugno 2014*), edd. F. Rinaldi and A. Vigoni (Rubano and Padua 2015) 357–77.

Bonnet Ch. (1981) "L'église cruciforme de Saint-Laurent d'Aoste. Etude archéologique (les fouilles de 1972 à 1979)", in *La chiesa di S.Lorenzo in Aosta. Scavi archeologici* (Rome 1981) 11–46.

Borzacconi A. (2003) "Gli scavi nelle sacrestie del Duomo di Cividale: dati acquisiti e problemi aperti nella conoscenza delle aree adiacenti al complesso episcopale", *Forum Iulii* 17 (2003) 155–72.

Breda A. (2007) "Archeologia degli edifici di culto di età medievale nella diocesi di Brescia", in *Società bresciana e sviluppi del romanico* (*XI–XIII secolo*). *Atti del convegno di studi* (*Brescia 9–10 maggio 2002*), edd. G. Andenna and M. Rossi (Milan 2007) 235–79.

Brissolara A. M. (1983) "Analisi distributiva della documentazione funeraria di Bononia. Contributo alla definizione funzionale del suburbio", in *Studi sulla città antica: l'Emilia Romagna* (Studia Archaeologica 27), ed. G. A. Mansuelli (Rome 1983) 211–43.

Brogiolo G. P. (1994) "La città longobarda nel periodo della conquista (569-in VII sec.)", in *La storia dell'alto medioevo italiano alla luce dell'archeologia*, edd. R. Francovich and G. Noyé (Forence) 555–66.

Brogiolo G. P. (2001) "Urbanistica di Cividale nell'alto medio-evo", in *Paolo Diacono e il Friuli altomedievale* (*secc. VI–X*). *Atti del XIV Congresso Internazionale di Studi sull'Alto Medi-oevo* (*Cividale del Friuli-Bottenicco di Moimacco, 24–29 set-tembre 1999*) (Atti dei Congressi 14) (Spoleto 2001) 357–85.

Brogiolo G. P. (2011) *Le origini della città medievale* (PCA Studies 1) (Mantua 2011).

Brogiolo G. P., Chavarría Arnau, A., and Nuvolari S. (2017) "Frammenti di storia del complesso episcopale di Padova. Lo scavo archeologico a nord del battistero (2011–2012)", in *Ricerche sul centro episcopale di Padova. Scavi 2011–2012*, ed. A. Chavarría Arnau (Mantua 2017) 13–48.

Brown P. (1982) *The Cult of the Saints: Its Rise and Function in Latin Christianity* (Chicago 1982).

Canci A., Marinato M., and Zago M. (2017) "Le aree cimite-riali: studio bioarcheologico", in *Ricerche sul centro epis-copale di Padova. Scavi 2011–2012*, ed. A. Chavarría Arnau (Mantua 2017) 131–50.

Cantino Wataghin G. (1999) "The ideology of urban buri-als", in *The Idea and Ideal of the Town between Late Antiq-uity and the Early Middle Ages*, edd. G. P. Brogiolo and B. Ward-Perkins (Boston 1999) 147–80.

Cantino Wataghin G. and Lambert C. (1998) "Sepolture e città. L'Italia settentrionale tra IV e VIII secolo", in *Sepolture tra IV e VIII secolo* (Documenti di Archeologia 13), edd. G. P. Bro-giolo and G. Cantino Wataghin (Mantua 1998) 89–114.

Cavada E. (1998) "Cimiteri e sepolture isolate nella città di Trento (secoli V–VIII)", in *Sepolture tra VI e VIII secolo* (Documenti di Archeologia 13), edd. G. P. Brogiolo and G. Cantino Wataghin (Mantua 1998) 127–37.

Cavalieri Manasse G. (2017) "L'area di San Zeno in oratorio in età romana e tardoantica", *Annuario Storico Zenoniano* 24 (2017) 1–18.

Cavalieri Manasse G. and Bolla M. (1998) "Osservazioni sulle necropoli veronesi", in *Bestattungssitte und kulturelle Iden-tität. Grabanlagen und Grabbeigaben der frühen römischen Kaiserzeit in Italien und den Nordwest-Provinzen, Kollo-quium* (*Xanten, 1995*), edd. P. Fasold, T. Fischer, H. von Hes-berg, and M. Witteyer (Cologne 1998) 103–141.

Cavalieri Manasse G. and Bruno B. (2003) "Edilizia abitativa a Verona", in *Abitare in città. La Cisalpina tra impero e medio-evo. Atti del Convegno* (*Roma 1999*) (Palilia 12), edd. J. Ortalli and M. Heinzelmann (Wiesbaden 2003) 47–64.

Cavalieri Manasse G. and Meloni F. (2012) "Piazza Corru-bio. Lo scavo dell'area cimiteriale 2009–2011", *Quaderni di Archeologia del Veneto* 27 (2012) 79–81.

Chavarría Arnau A. (2018) "People and landscapes in North-ern Italy: interrogating the burial archaeology of the Early Middle Ages", in *Interpreting Transformations of Land-scapes and People in Late Antiquity*, edd. P. Diarte-Blasco and N. Christie (Oxford 2018) 163–78.

Chavarría Arnau A. (2019) "Christian landscapes in the Iberian Peninsula: the archaeological evidence (fourth–sixth cen-turies)", in *The Oxford Handbook of Early Christian Archae-ology*, edd. W. R. Caraher, T. W. Davis, and D K. Pettegrew (Oxford 2019) 623–44.

Chavarría Arnau (2020) "Il contributo delle analisi bioarche-ologiche allo studio della stratificazione sociale in Italia tra Tardoantico e alto Medioevo", *Archeologia Medievale* 47 (2020) 321–332.

Chavarría Arnau A. ed. (2023) *Cambio de Era. Chavarría Arnau y el Mediterràneo Cristiano* (Córdoba 2023).

Chavarría Arnau A. and Giacomello, F. (2014) "Riflessioni sul rapporto tra sepolture e cattedrali nell'altomedioevo", *Hor-tus Artium Medievalium* 20 (2014) 209–220.

Cipolla C. (1907) *Una tomba barbarica scoperta nel palazzo Miniscalchi a Verona* (Verona 1907).

Ferreri D. (2011) "Spazi cimiteriali, pratiche funerarie e identità nella città di Classe", *Archeologia Medievale* 38 (2011) 59–74.

Ferreri D. (2014) "La città dei vivi e la città dei morti. La ridefinizione degli spazi urbani e le pratiche funerarie a Ravenna e nel territorio circostante tra la tarda antichità e l'alto medioevo", *Hortus Artium Medievalium* 20 (2014) 112–22.

Fiocchi Nicolai V. (2003) "Elementi di trasformazione dello spazio funerario tra tarda antichità e altomedioevo", in *Uomo e spazio nell'alto medioevo. Settimane di Studio del*

Centro Italiano di Studi sull'Alto Medioevo (Spoleto, 4–8 aprile 2002) (Spoleto 2003) 921–69.

Fiocchi Nicolai V. (2006) "Gli spazi delle sepolture cristiane tra il III e il v secolo: genesi e dinamica di una scelta insediativa", in *La comunità cristiana de Roma. La sua vita e la sua cultura dalle origini all'Alto Medioevo*, edd. L. Pani Ermini and P. Siniscalco (Vatican City 2006) 341–69.

Fiocchi Nicolai V. (2016) "Le aree funerarie cristiane di età costantiniana e la nascita delle chiese con funzione sepolcrale", in *Costantino e i costantinidi. L'innovazione costantiniana, le sue radici e i suoi sviluppi. Acta XVI Congressus Internationalis Archaeologiae Christianae (Romae, 22–28.9.2013)*, edd. O. Brandt, V. Fiocchi Nicolai, and G. Castiglia (Vatican City 2016) 619–70.

Fiocchi Nicolai V. (2023) "Los primeros espacios de culto y la primera topografia cristiana", in *Cambio de Era. Còrdoba y el Mediterràneo Cristiano*, ed. A. Chavarría Arnau (Córdoba 2023) 83–90.

Fortunati M., Caproni R., Garatti E., Ghiroldi A., Resmini M., Rizzotto A., and Vitali M. (2014) "Recenti ritrovamenti longobardi in territorio bergamasco", in *Necropoli Longobarde in Italia. Indirizzi della ricerca e nuovi dati*, ed. E. Possenti (Trento 2014) 137–62.

Gaillard M., Prévot F., and Gauthier N. (2014) *Topographie Chrétienne des Cités de la Gaule, des origines au milieu du VIIIᵉ siècle, Quarante ans d'enquête (1972–2012)* (Paris 2014).

Giostra C. (2014b) "I longobardi e le città: forme materiali e scelte culturali", *Hortus Artium Medievalium* 20 (2014) 48–62.

Giostra C. ed. (2017) *Archeologia dei Longobardi: dati e metodi per nuovi percorsi di analisi* (Mantua 2017).

Gleize Y (2007) "Réutilisations de tombes et manipulations d'ossements : éléments sur les modifications de pratiques funéraires au sein de nécropolesdu haut Moyen Âge", *Aquitania* 23 (2007) 185–205.

Guaitioli M. T. (2013) "Trento, Santa Maria Maggiore", in *Chiese trentine dalle origini al 1250 (APSAT 10)*, edd. G. P. Brogiolo, E. Cavada, M. Ibsen, N. Pisu, and M. Rapanà (Mantua 2013) 116–21.

Guyon J. (2005) "A propos d'un ouvrage récente: retour sur "les dossiers" des origines des catacombes chrétiennes de Rome", *Rivista di Archeologia Cristiana* 81 (2005) 235–53.

Lambert C. (1997) "Le sepolture *in urbe* nella norma e nella prassi (tarda antichità-alto medioevo)", in *L'Italia centro-settentrionale in età longobarda*, ed. L. Paroli (Florence 1997) 285–93.

Lambert C. (2003) "Spazi abitativi e sepolture nei contesti urbani", in *Abitare in città. La Cisalpina tra impero e Medioevo (Palilia 12)*, edd. J. Ortalli and M. Heinzelmann (Wiesbaden 2003) 229–39.

La Rocca M. C. (1989) "Trasformazioni della città altomedievale in 'Langobardia'", *Studi Storici* 4 (1989) 993–1011.

Lorans E. (2016) "Funerary patterns in towns in France and England between the fourth and tenth centuries: a comparative approach", in *Making Christian Landscapes in Atlantic Europe: Conversion and Consolidation in the Early Middle Ages*, ed. T. Ò Carragain (Newcastle 2016) 303–323.

Lusuardi Siena L. and Baratto C. (2013) "Sguardo sull'edilizia religiosa e civile nella Venetia et Histria in età tardoantica", in Storia dell'Architettura nel Veneto. L'età romana e tardoantica, edd. P. Basso and G. Cavalieri Manasse (Venice 2013) 166–217.

Lusuardi Siena S., Giostra C., and Spalla E. (2000) "Sepolture e luoghi di culto in età longobarda: il modello regio", in *II Congresso Nazionale di Archeologia Medievale (Brescia, 28 settembre–1 ottobre 2000)*, ed. G. P. Brogiolo (Florence 2000) 273–83.

Lusuardi Siena S., Rossignani M. P., and Sannazaro M. edd. (2011) *L'abitato, la necropoli, il monatero. Evoluzione di un comparto del suburbio milanese alla luce degli scavi nei cortili dell'Università Cattolica* (Milano 2011).

Lusuardi Siena S. and Sannazaro M. (2001) "I battisteri del complesso episcopale milanese alla luce delle recenti indagini archeologiche", in *L'edificio battesimale in Italia. Aspetti e problemi. (atti dell'VIII congresso nazionale di archeologia cristiana: Genova, Sarzana, Albenga, Finale Ligure, Ventimiglia, 21–26 settembre 1998)* (Istituto Internazionale di Studi Liguri 5), ed. D. Gandolfi (Bordighera 2001) 650–57.

Manicardi A. (2015) *Mantova: topografia e potenziale archeologico della civitas vetus dalla tarda antichità all'alto medioevo* (Mantua 2015).

Mazzoleni D. (2001) "Reperti epigrafici dalla basilica vigiliana di Trento", in *L'antica basilica di San Vigilio a Trento. Storia Archeologia Reperti, II*, edd. I. Rogger and E. Cavada (Trento 2001) 379–412.

Meneghini R. and Santangeli Valenzani R. (1995) "Sepolture intramuranee a Roma tra v e VII secolo d.C. Aggiornamenti e considerazioni", *Archeologia Medievale* 22 (1995) 283–90.

Micheletto E. (1999) "Archeologia Medievale ad Alba: note per la definizione del paesaggio urbano (v–XIV secolo)", in *Una città nel medioevo. Archeologia e architettura ad Alba dal VI al XV secolo*, ed. E. Micheletto (Turin 1999) 31–60.

Pejrani Baricco L. (2003) "L'isolato del complesso episcopale fino all'età longobarda", in *Archeologia a Torino. Dall'età preromana all'Alto Medioevo*, ed. L. Mercando (Turin 2003) 301–317.

Perinetti R. (1981) "La chiesa di San Lorenzo. Appunti per una tipologia delle tombe", in *La chiesa di S. Lorenzo in Aosta. Scavi archeologici* (Rome 1981) 47–92.

Picard J. C. (1988) *Le souvenir des évêques. Sépultures, listes épiscopales et culte des évêques en Italie du Nord, des origines au Xᵉ siècle* (Rome 1988).

Possenti E. ed. (2014) *Necropoli longobarde in Italia. Indirizzi della ricerca e nuovi dati* (Trento 2014).

Rebillard E. (1997) "L'Église de Rome et le développement des catacombes. À propos de l'origine des cimetières chrétiens", in *Mélanges de l'École Française de Rome. Antiquité tardive* 109 (1997) 741–63.

Rebillard E. (2009) *The Care of the Dead in Late Antiquity* (Ithaca 2009).

Rinaldi F. and Vigoni A. (2015) "… redditur enim terrae corpus. Le necropoli di Opitergium tra media e tarda età imperiale", in *Le necropoli della media e tarda età imperiale (III–IV sec. d.C.) a Iulia Concordia e nell'arco altoadriatico. Atti del Convegno di Concordia Sagittaria (giugno 2014)*, edd. F. Rinaldi and A. Vigoni (Rubano and Padua 2015) 225–44.

Rogger I. and Cavada E. edd. (2001) *L'antica basilica di San Vigilio a Trento. Storia Archeologia Reperti, II* (Trento 2011).

Rossi C. (2015) *Le necropoli urbane di Padova Romana* (Rome 2015).

Spera L. (2009) "Forme di autodefinizione identitaria nel mondo funerario: cristiani e non cristiani a Roma nella tarda antichità", in *Miscellanea in onore di Roberto Pretagostini* (Rome 2009) 769–803.

Staffa A. R. (1998) "Sepolture urbane in Abbruzzo (secc. VI–VII)", in *Sepolture tra IV e VIII secolo, Settimo Seminario sul TardoAntico e l'Alto Medioevo in Italia Centro-Settentrionale (Gardone Riviera 24–26 Ottobre 1996)*, edd. G. P. Brogiolo and G. Cantino Wataghin (Mantua 1998) 161–78.

Stancati S. T. (2006) *Escatologia, morte e risurrezione* (Naples 2006).

Funerary Practices in Late Antique Sardinia: Overview and Potential

Mauro Puddu

Abstract

This paper offers an overview of state-of-the-art funerary archaeology of late antique Sardinia. It will expose the most recurrent issues faced by archaeologists working in the discipline. To do so, this paper will highlight some renowned studies and recent results coming from major excavations in south and central Sardinia, such as Cornus and Pill'e Matta. While providing a synthesis of the work done so far, this paper will eventually single out one often overlooked piece of evidence that has recently gained more attention internationally: burial manipulation. This involves the structured, often respectful, reuse of tombs. While aiming at increasing the relational understanding of the archaeological evidence by observing the interaction between late antique communities and their more or less recent past, this paper highlights the potential held by burial manipulation studies to answer some key questions about late antique Sardinia.

An Archaeological Overview of Late Antique Sardinia

Late Antiquity in Sardinia was a period rich in events which had an impact on the reorganization of communities at a local level. However, late antique archaeology in Sardinia cannot yet rely on a consistent corpus of evidence, such as that available for the classical or medieval periods. This is all the more true when it comes to burials, their human remains, and grave goods. Fig. 1 displays this situation, showing the flimsy archaeological evidence available for late antique Sulci (in purple), one of the most renowned Mediterranean archaeological sites, if compared to the Punic and Roman periods (in green). Despite this relative lack of evidence, the last 20 years have marked a solid increase of available data due to both well-run new excavation projects and systematic reordering of paperwork relating to excavations conducted in the 19th and 20th c. – today stored in the archives of the Soprintendenza Archaeologica della Sardegna. For these reasons, the quantity of the forthcoming archaeological evidence for late antique Sardinia is due to increase further in the next 5 to 10 years, allowing us to forecast a growth of our knowledge of late antique burial practices in the near future.

Looking at the late antique burial evidence available, two main research lines have been traditionally applied: one has consistently related funerary practices to Christianization; the other has focused on archaeological signs as indicators of ethnic identity. Both lines of study fit the research framework of an archaeology of identity in a rather two-dimensional way. Even if caution is explicitly applied by scholars, the tendency is "to see artefacts as 'signatures' or 'representations' of specific cultures"[1] determined by a religious or ethnic nature. In both cases, archaeological studies of late antique burials of Sardinia have relied heavily on the identification of burials and grave good typologies. Less consistent attention has been given so far to human remains in a broad sense, and to burials as the product of dynamic practices in the making, composed by a set of multiple gestures. However, this trend has been changing rapidly and the remarkable potential of the results is already visible in some recent studies.

This paper will give space to all the aforementioned aspects. Section 2 will look at the main challenges of the discipline, highlighting the differences and similarities with Roman archaeology, which has a consistent chronological and thematic overlap. Section 3 will focus on the important scholarly tradition of grave goods studies. Section 4 will display two of the few relevant and recent studies on completely excavated necropolises of Sardinia: Cornus and Pill'e Matta. Section 5 will introduce the rich evidence of the moving of burial remains in late antique Sardinia, singling out two types: Byzantine period collective burials of the centre and south, and the 4th and 5th c. manipulated burials in the centre. In order to fit these topics in the paper, I had to give it a geographical limitation. For this reason, the paper's general review of the discipline refers to the whole island, but when it comes to specific case studies, it focuses on some that, despite their importance for the whole island, come from southern and west-central Sardinia.

Late Antique and Roman Archaeology of Sardinia: Similarities and Differences

When I started preparing this paper, I had to question how much an account of funerary archaeology of late antique Sardinia would differ from one on Roman Sardinia. This question concerns not only a

---

1   Casella and Fowler (2004) 1.

Alexandra Dolea and Luke Lavan (eds) *Burial and Memorial in Late Antiquity*
(Late Antique Archaeology 13) (Leiden 2024), pp. 705–726

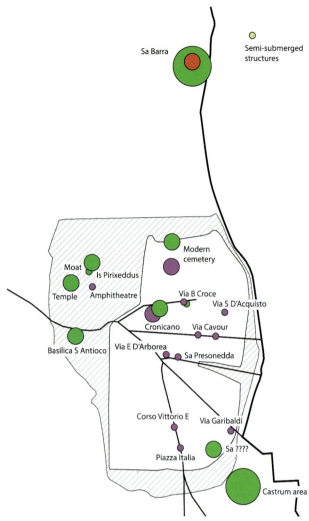

FIGURE 1   Late antique evidence at Sulci (pink shades indicate
             late antique sites; green shades indicate Roman period
             sites); Cisci and Martorelli (2016).

tries to neatly frame a period of history, Late Antiquity cannot be defined with precision without making generalizations that do not satisfy the same criteria in every region analysed. Whether one has it start in the 3rd or in the 5th c., it is evident that Late Antiquity overlaps with Roman times. Late Antiquity also shares similar archaeological evidence, methodology, case studies, and interpretive frameworks with the latter. This paper will specifically deal with Sardinian case studies dating between the 4th and 6th c. AD. The overlap with Roman archaeology is evident.

In 2013, Tronchetti provided an overview of Roman period funerary studies and it is the aim of this section to verify whether or not this overview fits for late antique funerary studies as well. For Tronchetti, burial studies of Roman Sardinia are based on data coming from excavations carried out until the 1960/1970s, often obtained without applying a proper stratigraphic method, and whose information – when published – centred on three elements: number of graves, grave goods typology, and their disposition inside the burial. For him, when it comes to Roman Sardinia, it is more accurate to talk about a tradition of studies of single graves rather than of entire necropolises.[3] Accordingly, Sirigu's account on the subject added a discrepancy between the prominent scholarly attention given to a small number of elite burials, often studied as self-contained contexts that did not interact with the rest of the site, and the lack of focus on the large majority of non-elite burials.[4]

In her account of late antique burials of Sardinia,[5] Martorelli underlined similar limitations to those highlighted by Sirigu and Tronchetti for Roman studies. She highlights the lack of comprehensive studies of funerary spaces as a whole and flags three more aspects that affect the interpretation of late antique sites specifically. Firstly, numerous 19th c. excavations were almost solely interested in classical – i.e. Roman – burials, and, therefore, frequently compromised post-classical layers. Secondly, the clarity of late antique archaeological layers is often heavily affected in 17th c. Counter-Reformation, when Catholic bishops sent diggers all over Europe to search graveyards for 'corpi santi' – the bodies of the saints. The Catholic Church did so to prove, with physical evidence, the existence of martyrs that at the time was being challenged due to the long-lasting effects of the Protestant Reformation. This situation is seen in Sardinia, where Bishop Gavino Manca de Cedrelles in Sassari and Bishop Francesco De Esquivel in Cagliari

chronological perspective, but also one related to the nature of scholarship. The first periodization of Late Antiquity, such as that proposed by Brown or even earlier by Marrou,[2] framed a time between the 3rd and the 8th c. AD. These terms shifted back and forth with the advancement of the studies in the last decades – some scholars have Late Antiquity start with the triumph of Christianity in the 4th c., others with the fall of the Western Empire in the 5th, but they are all still broadly valid and taken into account. A chronological discordance emerged also amongst the papers presented at the LAA conference held at Birkbeck, University of London, on 25 November 2017, on which this volume is based. Different speakers referred to Late Antiquity in different regions – from Egypt to Britain, from Spain and Sardinia to Slovenia and Turkey – using very different chronological spans. Like every other abstraction that

2   Brown (1971).

3   Tronchetti (2013).
4   Sirigu (2003) 111–13.
5   Martorelli (2003).

ordered the opening of the graves to look for Sardinia's local saints.[6]

Third, uniquely to late antique archaeology, the interpretation of graves has often been biased towards the application of a syllogism based on Early Christian ideology to the archaeological evidence. It has long been an accepted truism that the Church Fathers asked Christian communities to bury their dead in modesty, with no personal possessions, in order to reach the afterlife in simplicity and purity. Most 19th and 20th c. European scholarly interpretations tended to equate Christian burials with the lack of grave goods alongside the dead.[7] Accordingly, until the late 1990s, burials with no grave goods in Sardinia were constantly, often erroneously, interpreted as Christian.[8] These postulations were fed, amongst others, by the idea of the self-imposed modesty of the first Christian communities buried in Rome's catacombs.[9] However, a few scholars, amongst whom Bollok's work stands out, have started to explicitly question whether the Church Fathers' teachings around the destiny of the body after death and mortuary behaviours find material correspondence in the archaeological record.[10] A thorough engagement with those written sources shows that the Church Fathers did not really encourage the excessive care of the dead body; nor did they express any opinion towards the local uses of graves and offerings in burials. The Church Fathers' criticism was more towards the luxuries of the wealthy, both in life and in burial excess,[11] than towards local burial customs followed by the large majority. Henceforth, the fixed application of a forced, uniform Christian thought regarding the origins of burial evidence needs to be kept in mind when reassessing the numbers and typologies of late antique graves provided by previous scholarship.

A fourth characteristic that can be added to Martorelli's list is, as Gastaldo noticed 20 years ago,[12] a lack of theoretical investigation in the interpretive process of late antique burials. Gastaldo invited archaeologists to go beyond the attribution of the dead to ethnic/religious categories and to investigate what social processes led to their formations.

These aspects have been faced consistently by archaeologists in the last 25–30 years. One of the limitations of late antique archaeology in Sardinia that has been challenged with more intensity is the attempt to extract useful information from 17th and 18th c. excavations undertaken by the Church in search of the 'corpi santi'. In this regard, the study carried out by Mureddu, Salvi, and Stefani, at the end of the 1980s, is still significant today. In the conclusions of the book *Sancti Innumerabiles*, Salvi pointed out that the interpretations of the burials given by the people in charge of the 17th c. excavations were aimed at creating a narrative that helped to reconstruct the life of the saints.[13] In order to do that, 17th c. researchers had to look for details from which information could be extracted about the lives of the saints and their names: their focus was on graves with inscriptions and on their messages. By doing so, only the burials of those individuals whose status allowed them to display writing on their graves were counted, neglecting all those – the majority – who did not have access to it. This attitude recalls Sirigu's statement about Roman funerary studies being too focused on the elite minority (see n. 4). Nevertheless, even in these documents Salvi, Stefani and Mureddu came across numerous useful details for current archaeological research. For instance, the chroniclers and notaries that followed the 17th c. excavations registered in detail all data that could have been useful to reconstruct the research being carried out.[14] From this data, it was possible to reconstruct the forms of the graves of Cagliari – mainly simple rectangular pits – and the presence of funerary mosaics related to inscriptions. Conversely, the information on grave goods that could be extracted is very limited, as the majority of graves opened in the 17th c. contained few or no ritual objects, and only rare personal possessions.[15]

This overview shows that late antique and Roman archaeologies of funerary practices share several aspects and methodological issues, particularly when it comes to the nature of interpretive frameworks used to make sense of material evidence. Indeed, both leading paradigms for the respective periods, Romanization – for example Millett's model[16] – and Christianization, are often applied uncritically to the study of burials as homogenising ways of identification between the archaeological record and the identities of the communities whose burials are under study. Establishing a more solid contact between the two disciplines will certainly benefit both. However, this section has also shown that late antique archaeology has to deal with issues that affect its materiality and stratigraphy in a unique way. The rest of the paper will focus on these aspects.

6   Lai (2010).

7   Bollok (2018) 246.

8   Martorelli (2003) 301.

9   On the currently debated ideas around the origins of Christian catacombs, see Lewis (2016) and Rebilliard (2009).

10   Bollok (2018).

11   Bollok (2018).

12   Gastaldo (1998).

13   Salvi (1988) 89.

14   Salvi (1988) 89.

15   Salvi (1988) 91.

Historical and Archaeological Sources

Sardinia faced some important changes during Late Antiquity, which influenced its local communities too. Some of them have had a crucial political impact, like the passage of the island to the administration of the Vandals during the mid-5th c., and back to the Romans in 534. Other events have had a significant social impact, as the first attested arrival in Sardinia of members of Rome's Christian community in AD 190, sent to the island as *damnati ad metalla* – forced labourers in the mines. Written sources refer indirectly to Sardinia's society and to its people's practices, such as the edicts from the various synods. Two of them, the synods of Auxerre, held in 568,[17] and that of Macon, held in 585,[18] made clear that it was illicit to reopen burials already hosting a body. In inviting local Christians[19] – if not involving other areas beyond – to reject such a practice, these synods show indirectly that it was a common practice.

Moving from the historical to the archaeological sources, the evidence gets more abundant. The quantity of burial sites in Sardinia attributed to the early historical period is decent. However, many of them, especially those excavated in the 19th and early 20th c., have been generically defined by the excavators as Roman grave grounds. This is why a revision of the unpublished materials stored in museums, and of the information reported day-by-day in archaeological journals written during excavation operations is essential.

A general, although indirect picture of late antique burial sites is provided by website www.anthroponet.it, where the Department of Anthropology of the University of Cagliari has published a list of all human remains found in Sardinia. In fact, despite the website not yet being set up for late antique searches, 'Roman Imperial period' searches (Fig. 2) provide 84 site results, many of which include late antique burials, as the periodization of Anthroponet includes graves dated between the 1st and the 5th c. AD. Likely, many of the 84 Imperial period sites recorded by Anthroponet were in use during the late antique period, either in continuation with an earlier usage, or started anew – as is the case for all cemeteries founded around a Christian basilica and specifically for Cornus, which will be treated later in this paper. Despite the uncertainty around the archaeological sources for late antique Sardinia, there is also some good news. Archaeology of late antique Sardinia has

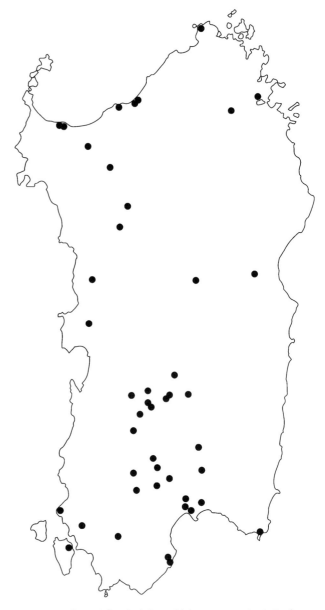

FIGURE 2   Imperial period sites with human remains in Sardinia (www.anthroponet.it).

received a big boost in the last two decades, particularly thanks to the studies of Anna Maria Giuntella, Rossana Martorelli, Sabrina Cisci, and Donatella Salvi, who have carried out both new excavations and dedicated time to put together the data from unpublished 19th and 20th c. excavations. The most frequently studied type of evidence to come from such old excavations is grave goods. The next section will provide an overview of the patterns derived from their study.

Grave Goods Analysis, Patterns, and General Trends in Sardinian Cemeteries

If one looks at the relationship between personal and utilitarian items found in late antique graves, a few neat

---

17   De Clercq (1963) canon 17: 246.
18   De Clercq (1963) canon 15: 267.
19   Bollok (2018) 261 warns that "even greater caution needs to be exercised when studying the material record of regions in whose case we have to turn by necessity to the works of authors living in more distant lands."

patterns emerge. The diagrams in Fig. 3 synthesise the results of Martorelli's study on two grave good trends in late antique Sardinia. Firstly, buckles, brooches, and other metallic items used as part of the dressing of the dead increased consistently over time, starting from small numbers in the 3rd–5th c. AD to total more than one third of objects introduced in 6th c. graves. Similarly, the number of other personal items such as bracelets and necklaces increased. Secondly and conversely to the previous trend, pottery, which had a prominent role at the beginning of Late Antiquity, became less common in the following centuries. Pottery constituted more than two thirds of objects in Sardinian graves between the 3rd and the 5th c. AD, only to drop to a quarter of the material culture found in 6th c. burials. Glass and coins followed the same trend as pottery, being quite widely used in the late 3rd c., and much less so from the 5th c. onwards.

Martorelli, who called for a long-needed 'redefinition' of the grave goods distinguishing them between objects that belonged to the deceased and objects that did not,[20] underlined how these trends reached a peak from AD 534 to the 11th c., when the island was a Byzantine *thema*.[21] The distinction between 'personal' and 'ritual' objects has been used since the late 1990s, with the former used for objects linked to the personal ornament of the deceased – often significant of their role in life – and the latter for objects used to perform burial related rituals.[22] Despite pottery still being introduced into graves by the Byzantine period, remaining an important chronological indicator, personal objects like earrings, buckles, and necklaces with pendants began to outnumber it. This pattern emerges even more clearly in the graves of soldiers sent to the island by Justinian I, and who were likely buried in their military clothes, such as the set of belt buckles and weapons found in Siurgus Donigala.[23]

As stated at the beginning of this paper, due to the numerous excavations carried out in the 18th and 19th c. without detailed attention to the stratigraphic relationships, grave goods have been for a long time the main, often only, source of archaeological interpretation. The study of grave goods composition, production, provenance, and choice has allowed archaeologists to draw major interpretations on social status, ethnic and religious affiliation, tradition and change of the buried people and their communities.[24] It is

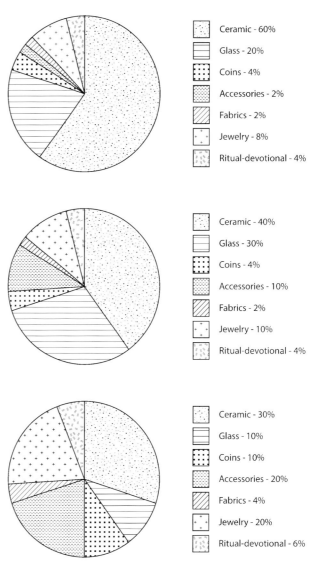

FIGURE 3   Grave goods patterns in late antique Sardinia; Martorelli (2003).

fundamental to continue studying grave goods today, possibly from secure contexts, to understand what kind of assumptions lie behind decades of ethnic, religious, or identity-driven interpretations. Such structures need to be deconstructed or reviewed to some extent, and the consistent study of grave goods will help to breed a balanced critique of the culture-historical connections between objects and people that we still often use.[25]

This section has dealt with grave goods at a broad level, highlighting that the patterns of increase in personal ornaments and decrease in utilitarian vessels are shared everywhere in Sardinia. The next sections will use two recently excavated funerary sites as optimal case studies: Cornus in west-central Sardinia, and Pill'e Matta in the south. They show neatly the two research lines mentioned earlier – Christianization and ethnic

20   Martorelli (2003) 303.
21   Martorelli (2003) 308.
22   Giuntella (1998) 65.
23   Serra (1990) 112–13.
24   Martorelli (2003) 303.

25   Pitts (2007).

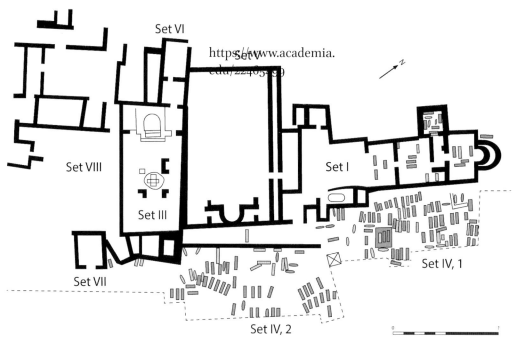

FIGURE 5   Columbaris-Cornus: plan of site; from Giuntella (2002): drawing by L. Saladino and M.C. Somma.

FIGURE 6   Grave types at Columbaris-Cornus (from the left: *alla capuccina* graves, *enchytrismoi*, sarcophagi); Giuntella (2002).

have been applied too rigidly by many archaeologists in the past, who identified all graves without grave goods as members of the Early Christian communities.[47]

An interesting aspect of the funerary apparatus from the graves of Cornus is the presence of luxury objects. Some items, such as earrings and rings were carved in gold and in silver[48] with crosses and other Christian motives; some others were made of luxurious materials not commonly found in other funerary contexts of the island, such as bracelets and necklaces in amber (Fig. 6). Moreover, a few graves located either inside or by the early basilica to the north-west (Fig. 4) were sealed by

an inscribed marble slab. One of them is the burial of a 25-year-old woman, Patriga Honesta Femina, whose name was written on the surface of her burial. Inside, she was wrapped in a mantle fixed by a silver brooch with a bronze barb – i.e. brooch pin.[49] The presence of inscribed marble slabs, rare elsewhere in the island, together with the presence of personal items made of precious material, constitute a good indication of the presence of a privileged elite – maybe even Christian elites – at Cornus. A few small hoards, rather than a single coin, were left in burials.[50] This evidence adds

47   Martorelli (2003) 301; Giuntella (1998) 65 n.14.
48   Giuntella (1998) 66.
49   Giuntella (1998) 66.
50   Amante Simoni (1990) 232; Giuntella (1998) 70.

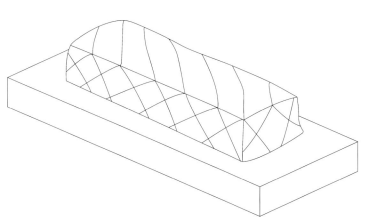

FIGURE 7   *Mensa* surrounding a singular grave in Cornus: photo and graphic reconstruction; Giuntella (1985).

another element of economic wealth to the picture of Cornus' necropolis.

Utilitarian grave goods such as ceramic and glass vessels were both inside and outside the graves. Some of them were found *in situ*, often containing the remains of a meal,[51] which are to be interpreted as a continuation of the traditional practices of collective eating and drinking held by non-Christian communities in Roman cemeteries. Compared to the other sites of Sardinia, Cornus offers unique evidence of banqueting practices: the *mensae*. These were a series of slabs, either surrounding single graves or connecting multiple burials to one another, on which abundant remains of banqueting were found. *Mensae* are related to a practice seen mainly in North Africa and not anywhere else outside western-central Sardinia, the *refrigerium* – whose etymology Testini linked to archaeological sources.[52] In these cases, the collective activities of eating and drinking at the funeral were held on a permanent flat surface, archaeologically documented, made of limestone and pot fragments bound together by mortar, and covered in white or pink plaster installed by the burials.[53] These permanent structures are some of the main material

elements distinguishing Cornus from other Sardinian necropolises. Site excavation exposed several 4th c. archaeological deposits with abundant remains of broken vessels and animal bones scattered around the single graves, covered by prismatic structures with vaulted sections – *tombe a cupa* – were surrounded by the high pavement constituting the *mensa* (Fig. 7).

The first strata involving documented *mensae* has them set up around one grave only, but from the 5th c., similar features were created tying multiple graves together (Fig. 8). This can be interpreted as a sign that, over time, the *refrigerium* became a collective practice, which involved the families of more than one individual, and denotes a wider openness towards the community than in the past.

Beyond the remains of elite burials and *refrigeria*, Cornus offers some evidence for funerary practices that need more attention than they have been given so far. Both Giuntella[54] and Pani Ermini[55] mention an abundant evidence of burial manipulations.[56] These are indicated by signs of reuse of old burials – even at a short distance from the original – and by the scattered presence of human bones outside the graves. We know

51   Giuntella (1998) 67, 72.

52   Testini (1980) 141.

53   Giuntella (1999) 132; Giuntella (1998) 69.

54   Giuntella (1998) 72.

55   Pani Ermini (1990) 26.

56   Pani Ermini (1990) 26.

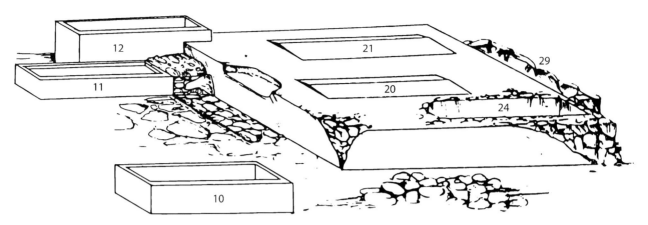

FIGURE 8   Columbaris-cornus: eastern funerary area: reconstruction of quadrangular complex of graves provided with mensa; Giuntella
(1995): drawing by C. Sassetti.

indirectly about the practice of reusing burials from 6th c., when the Council of Macon in 585 and the synod of Auxerre in 588 acknowledged that '*Comperimus multos necdum marcidata mortuorum membra sepulchra reserare et mortuos suos superimponere vel aliorum*'[57] ('We learn that many reopen burials and [remove] the remains of the dead and overlap their dead over others' dead'), and stated that '*non licet mortuum super mortuum mitti*'[58] ('it is not allowed to place the body of the dead on top of another').[59] Despite both councils being of local or regional importance and hence very likely referred to customs witnessed in the southern regions of the Gallo-Frankish realm, it is likely that the same habit was deeply-rooted in other provinces as well. This hypothesis is supported, for instance, by the epigraphic evidence found in Sardinia, with inscriptions cursing those who would have dared reopening sealed graves (i.e. see below, and n. 85 of this paper). The evidence of burial reopening and reuse is also witnessed abundantly in archaeological data. Such material evidence is commonly reported in the same way in relation to other funerary sites in Sardinia: it is often briefly and generically mentioned in publications and in excavation journals, but it has been rarely explored in a systematic way so far. The topic will be broadened in Section 5 of this paper.

Pill'e Matta and the South of Sardinia

Numerous sites have been excavated in the south of Sardinia, and a few patterns emerge from their study. The area is dominated by the cities of Karales and Sulci. In a recently published census of the late antique archaeological material of Sulci, Cisci and Martorelli[60]

retrieved a remarkable amount of data from a review of the 1950s excavation journals. These journals familiarize us with the techniques used in the recent past to excavate the hypogeal graves. In 1954, Giuseppe Lai, assistant of the *Soprintendenza Archeologica*, revealed in his journal that vertical shafts were dug to reach one chamber grave, from which the archaeologists preceded horizontally, breaking through the separation wall of one chamber to proceed into the next.[61] This anecdote provides further evidence of the difficulty of retrieving any stratigraphic information from old excavation campaigns, while reinforcing the importance of reviewing past excavation journals to extract useful information.

One of the most interesting phases of Sulci's burial grounds is late antique reuse – with the adoption of Christian rites – of graves dug in the Punic period, and obliterated in the 1st c. AD. These are now located below the church of Sant'Antioco.[62] Late antique communities dug through the originally divided chamber graves, creating a catacomb-like path that united the single chambers into something of an interconnected hypogeal system, used until the 7th c.[63] Below the basilica, burials with material culture bearing Jewish symbols, like the menorah and Hebrew names, were found too. Initially interpreted as Punic graves reused in Late Antiquity, they have been recently reinterpreted as graves dug *ex novo* in the 5th–6th c.[64] The presence of a Jewish community in Sulci fits the wide diversity of practices – that may and may not correspond to a multiethnic diversity – that the city shows in its funerary record from Punic and Roman times. A plethora of different but co-existing funerary rites – some of which create hybrid burial types, such

57   De Clerq (1963) 267.
58   De Clerq (1963) 246.
59   Author's translations.
60   Cisci and Martorelli (2016).

61   Cisci and Martorelli (2016) 285.
62   Tronchetti (1989) 32–38.
63   Tronchetti (1989) 60–65; Martorelli (2011b) 68–76; Cisci and Martorelli (2016) 280.
64   Serra (2002) 77.

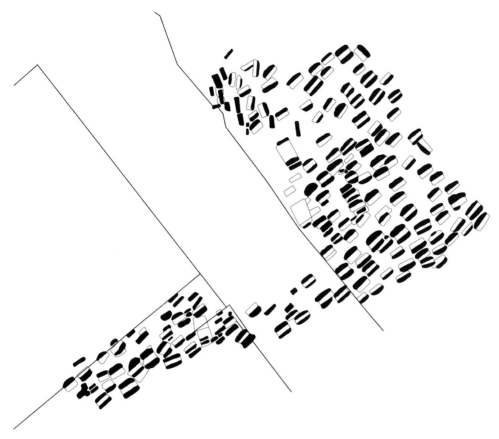

FIGURE 9   Quartucciu. Necropolis of Pill'e Matta; elaborated on from Salvi (2015).

as fusions of *enchytrismoi* and *alla capuccina* graves –
occurred from the Late Republican period onwards.[65]
Certainly, the role played by Sulci in the trade of lead
and copper made the Roman *municipium* a pole of
attraction for numerous peoples with varying doctrines
and practices.[66]

A similar funerary site to Sulci, for archaeological
and historical importance, is the necropolis below the
Church of San Saturnino in Cagliari. The area has been
subject to numerous investigations.[67] Occupied since
the Republican period, this area of Karales included both
funerary buildings, which influenced the conformation
of the area, and pit graves outside such buildings.[68] Both
Christian and non-Christian burials co-existed in the
area, as attested elsewhere, but several of these graves
were subjected to non-stratigraphic excavations in the
17th c., from which not much information is left.[69] One
specific set of data that the necropolis of San Saturnino
has in common with both Cornus and Sulci is the abundance of epigraphic material, amongst which was found

one poem.[70] Such inscriptions, and the setting of these
graves around the tomb of the martyr give very strong
indications that the people buried there belonged to the
elites of Karales. Further funerary evidence is scattered
around the city of Cagliari. One comprehensive publication is that on the excavation of Vico III Lanusei,[71] in
the area of Castello where a few late antique pit graves
were found and could be connected to the nearby
Republican/Early Imperial cemetery underneath the Ex
Albergo La Scala di Ferro.[72]

South-east of Karales is another site of south
Sardinia – the *municipium* of Nora. Here, Punic and
Roman necropolises have been extensively documented, and a few graves were installed in the 4th and
5th c. What is relevant here is that numerous graves at
Nora housed grave goods of a wide chronological range,
generally from the 2nd to the 5th c. AD. An example of
such grave apparatus is Grave 1, a pit grave with slab
cladding, from the necropolis of Su Guventeddu. This is
explained by La Fragola[73] as the presence of infiltrated
later materials in an older grave. Despite more detailed
information is not available, the case of Su Guventeddu

65   Tronchetti (1990) 174.
66   Bartoloni (2008) 25.
67   Pani Ermini (1992); Mureddu, Salvi, and Stefani (1988).
68   Salvi (2002b) 215.
69   Mureddu, Salvi, and Stefani (1988) 73–74.

70   Salvi (2002b) 220.
71   Martorelli and Mureddu (2006).
72   Locci (2012).
73   La Fragola (2003).

FIGURE 10   Buckles from Grave 100, Pill'e Matta.
SALVI (2015)

matches numerous other similar contexts of the necropolises looked at in this article, where the reuse of old graves is often attested, such as at Pill'e Matta.

The necropolis of Pill'e Matta, only 10 km inland, north of Cagliari, was the subject of several archaeological seasons, yielding more than 200 graves. The plan of the cemetery in Fig. 8 shows that almost all graves were aligned north-east/south-west. The ones coloured in red (Fig. 9) date to the late antique period, mainly between the 5th and 6th c., whereas the few graves to the north (in green) are as early as the 3rd c. BC.

Compared to Cornus, the solutions adopted at Pill'e Matta could not be more different. Sarcophagi – the most frequent burial type at Cornus – are not common at Pill'e Matta. After the use of *enchytrismoi* and *alla capuccina* graves in the 2nd and 3rd c. AD, hypogeal chamber graves were used from the 4th c. onwards. Their structure comprises a vertical shaft of a maximum 2 m deep, rectangular in plan, at the base of which two or three chamber graves were dug sidewise, and then sealed with rectangular slabs. This type of grave, new to Sardinia, has a few parallels in Sétif,[74] Algeria, during the Early Imperial period, and outside the Mediterranean in central Europe. It is noteworthy that these late antique chamber graves followed the south-west/north-east orientation of the Early Roman period. This evidence suggests that some late antique practices were set-up in continuity with those of the Early Imperial period.

To the south, Grave 100 is one of the most superficial burials in the cemetery.[75] It is very representative of all other burials at Pill'e Matta, but does have some unique features. Closed with 5 slabs placed vertically against the entrance of the chamber, 3 of which were broken by the collapse of the vault, Grave 100 housed one dead body only. This was laid on its back, with its arms down by its sides. The grave goods distribution around the body is in line with the pattern repeated across

the whole necropolis. In this case, one cup containing two lamps and one beaker were by the feet – another repeated pattern across the site of Pill'e Matta. The grave goods introduced in Grave 100, particularly one glass beaker of Isings 196c form and dated consistently to the second half of the 4th c. Moreover, by the waist and underneath the backbone of the deceased was a set of metallic plaques and buckles not usual for Sardinia. The whole system of the belt, the so-called *cingulum militiae*[76] is not frequently found in its entirety even outside the island. The two horseshoe-shaped buckles – to the centre of Fig. 10 – are common among Roman soldiers in Sardinia and are often found in the necropolis of Quartucciu. However, the vaguely triangular one – to the right in Fig. 10 – decorated with the *kerbschnitt* technique, chip carving, is much less common. Some close parallels come from the Croatian island of Brioni. This type of buckles was generally worn by Late Imperial soldiers from other provinces of the Empire, as Scorton in Britain,[77] and is sometimes found in Byzantine period contexts in the Mediterranean.

In general terms, the excavation of the necropolis of Pill'e Matta has provided plenty of information on the disposition of the dead body and of the grave goods around it. Despite the way that grave goods were placed not being entirely standardized,[78] it is still possible to single out some repetitive patterns: for instance, the presence of an African Sigillata dish or cup with one lamp or glass inside seen in Grave 100 is almost a constant at Pill'e Matta,[79] as is the presence of one or two coarse ware Campidanese jugs near the hips of the deceased.[80]

Bringing all these elements together, particularly the use of chamber graves and the presence of objects

74   Guery (1985).
75   Salvi (2015).
76   Salvi (2015) 196.
77   Eckardt (2015) 191–223.
78   Salvi (2002a) 473.
79   Salvi (2005).
80   Salvi (2010) 241, 242.

rarely attested in this area of the Mediterranean, Salvi advanced the interpretation – amongst others – that the necropolis of Pill'e Matta can also be analysed as a potential ethnic indicator. In line with the interpretive trends amongst Sardinian scholars underlined at the beginning of this paper, Salvi cautiously ascribes the funerary rituals held at Pill'e Matta to Sarmatians.[81] Salvi backs up her interpretation by highlighting that, not just one aspect of it, but the whole funerary ritual registered at Pill'e Matta is different from all other contemporary communities of Sardinia. The presence in the graves of numerous used lamps; the burial type with vertical shaft and lateral niche chamber replacing the popular *alla cappuccina* graves in the 3rd c.; and the consistently high number – higher than that registered in other burial grounds of Sardinia – of grave goods are elements that do not find any other comparison in the island.[82] Particularly the burial typology is considered typical of Sarmatians and finds comparison only in Eastern Europe, such as the Eurasian steppe,[83] Crimea, Chersonese, and Poland. The only other example of this niche grave is from Spain, where it represents only around 2.4% of the small sample of 247 graves dug in the cemetery.[84] The quantity of niche graves present in Spain is outnumbered by the 208 found at Pill'e Matta.[85] Salvi relates the people buried at Pill'e Matta with the historical sources referring of the arrival of the peasants/warriors *Sarmati Gentiles* to Italy on several occasions, one of which was ordered by Constantine I who sent 300,000 of them to repopulate the agricultural sites of Italy.[86] Some of these could have been sent to Sardinia.

While proposing and testing the ethnocentric interpretation that links the late antique cemetery of Pill'e Matta to the Sarmatians, Salvi explicitly states that certain objects are not sufficient to define the ethnic or social group of the deceased.[87] For instance, Possenti underlines the archaeological ephemerality of the Sarmatians, even when they are attested by written sources.[88] Nevertheless, the numerous novelties yielded by the study of the graves at Pill'e Matta caused scholars

to attempt a working hypothesis that will need to be tested under different approaches in the future.

Late Antique Practices of Burial Reuse

One of the most recurrent types of archaeological evidence encountered in preparing this paper is the reuse of burials. The evidence of burial reopening and of the manipulation of their content was touched upon several times by different speakers during the conference held in November at Birkbeck College, London, from which this paper derives. However, the so-called reuse is only one type of many possible interactions that can occur between the members of a community and the old burials in the cemetery they inherited and used. This has already emerged in this paper – i.e. in Cornus[89] and in Nora.[90] This section looks at the diversity of such interactions, stressing the importance of the insights that a systematic study on burial manipulations can generate in terms of funerary archaeology, identity studies, and understanding of the late antique communities of Sardinia both as a whole and at a local level.

The archaeological evidence of burial reopening is abundantly supported by epigraphic sources. One inscription from San Giorgio del Sinis, Cabras, west coast of Sardinia, is interesting in its peculiarity. It is a curse against those who would have dared opened the grave for their own use. The composer of the inscription's verses wishes them to contract leprosy and end up with Judas in Hell.[91] More confirmation of the practice of reopening old graves comes from several Christian councils, like those of Macon and Auxerre, held in the 6th c., and mentioned in Section 2. There, the Christian authorities of the area and from other regions agreed that it was illicit to open old burials and disturb the dead. As specified above,[92] the two councils bear witness largely to customs present in the southern regions of the Gallo-Frankish realm. It is well known that participants to the councils came from all regions of the Roman Empire. Nevertheless, these specific ones were called by secular Frankish authorities, and the participants were all from what is now France. It does not mean that similar practices may not have been rooted in other provinces too. Beyond the information that can be gathered from written sources, the archaeological evidence of

81   Salvi (2015) 201.
82   Salvi (2015) 201.
83   Kazanski (1991) 57; Kazanski (2002) 405–406 attribute the niche-graves to generally Iranian-linked people and specifically to Alan-Sarmatian people are discussed by Salvi (2015) note 39.
84   *contra* Martinez (2006) 276, and see also its brief discussion in Salvi (2015) n. 42.
85   Salvi (2015) 201–202.
86   Salvi (2015) 202.
87   Salvi (2015) 202.
88   Possenti (2012) 154–55. See also the discussion of Possenti (2012) in Salvi (2015) n. 44.

89   Pani Ermini (1990) 26.
90   La Fragola (2002) 101.
91   Corda (1999) 181: *ABEAT PARTEM CUM JUDA ET LEBRAM GIEZI*
92   Bollok (2018) 261; see n. 19 above.

burial reopening, reuse, and manipulation is abundant, although not yet central to funerary discourses.

In archaeological terms, burial reopening is the result of at least three divergent practices that can be synthesised in the following material evidence:

1. the reuse of graves where the bones of the original burial were moved to one side to make space for the new one: reduced bones are found tidily put aside, together with remains of original grave goods[93]

2. the presence of scattered human remains inside and outside collective graves

3. the manipulation of old graves

The first type of evidence is the result of one of the most known phenomena of antiquity: the reuse, often for practical and economic reasons, of already dug and occupied graves. In this case, the mourners and community members of the deceased have moved away from the proximity of the burial; they may not have kept their dead in a burial for longer than a certain period, or a long time had passed and the memory of specific deceased had faded away, leading to burials being emptied of the original human remains. Some bones though, were kept and put aside to make more room for the next deceased. Precisely because this phenomenon is well-known, the tendency has been, so far, to treat all human remains not belonging to the main individual buried in a specific grave as reduced bones from an older burial. However, this economic aspect tends to flatten discrepant types of evidence and does not really contribute to the explanation of certain types of human remains present in some burials, as shown by the trailblazing work by Aspöck, Klevnäs and Müller-Scheeßel (2020). For this reason, the first group of archaeological evidence is not treated here. This section will instead focus on the evidence of n. 2 and n. 3 listed above.

A new study published by Salvi and Fonzo,[94] focuses on a specific type of burial interaction: a set of collective burials of rectangular shape, made of a semi-hypogeal part dug into the ground, and a *sub divo* half, clad with rectangular slabs. Generally dated from the 6th c. onwards, these so-called Byzantine tombs[95] appeared only in south and central Sardinia, and as far south-west as Sulci, Sant'Antioco. Among the most thoroughly excavated of them is the one at Monastir, south Sardinia, 20 km north of Cagliari. The burial lays on top of the hill dominated today by the church of San Sebastiano, near Neolithic burials. This is why, at the moment of its first discovery in 1978, the grave was believed to be

prehistoric as well. However, the stratigraphic excavation of the grave of San Sebastiano, held in 2006–2007,[96] yielded unexpected results. The grave, built of limestone blocks held together by small stones and mortar made from a base of mud, was cut into the schist rock of the hill in a rectangular shape – 2.3 m long × 1 m wide and around 0.9 m deep – with the walls narrowing slightly towards its ceiling.[97] The analysis of the material culture proved that the semi-hypogeal chamber was used in the Byzantine period, as a collective burial for 4 deceased.[98]

For the issues faced in this section, the most relevant characteristics of the grave of San Sebastiano are the well-preserved anatomical lay-out of the majority of bones of the 4 individuals, and the absence of some bones from their bodies. Similar collective graves have been excavated at Nuraminis,[99] where 3 dead were buried; at Dolianova, Riu Sicci, which housed 11 skeletons tidily aligned to the entrance wall and parallel to one another;[100] at Sant'Antioco, Samassi,[101] Quartucciu,[102] Decimoputzu,[103] and Tratalias.[104]

The recent excavation of the latter, followed by thorough anthropological analyses, has generated important evidence. The section of the burial of Tratalias in Fig. 12 – half of the grave was cut accidentally by the installation of a modern pipe – is indicative of the general characteristics of the Byzantine collective burials: their narrowness did not allow much room for spacing out the dead or even for much movement around the burial. The result is what Salvi and Fonzo describe as "an unusual burial deposit due to the quantity of overlapping and manipulated skeletons".[105] The analyses and statistical count of the bone remains showed that the grave hosted a minimum number of 32 individuals, deposited here during the late 6th c. AD or slightly after. This was determined by a chrono-typological study of the round earrings with loop-hooking and three little bells found *in situ* near their crania, which provide a *terminus post quem*.[106]

The discovery of skeletons in anatomic lay-out but missing some parts, and of a high number of skeletal remains no longer in anatomical form testifies, for Salvi and Fonzo, that the manipulation and movement of

93   See Duday (2009) for other examples and definition.
94   Salvi and Fonzo (2016).
95   Salvi and Fonzo (2016) 447.

96   Casagrande (2015).
97   Salvi (2016) 448.
98   Salvi (2016) 448.
99   Serra (1990); Serra (2007).
100   Salvi and Fonzo (2016) 449.
101   Serra (1990) 136, 137.
102   Serra (1990) 144.
103   Casagrande (2015) 808.
104   Salvi and Fonzo (2016) 452.
105   Salvi and Fonzo (2016) 451.
106   Salvi and Fonzo (2016) 451 and fig. 21, 2.

FIGURE 11   Tratalias, South Sardinia, Monti Pranu.
             PHOTO BY A. ZARA

bodies from the single inhumations to the collective grave happened after different periods of time. Salvi and Fonzo describe a broad variety of bones conservation in Tratalias, starting from the state of anatomic form. At the time of the excavation, 6 individuals were anatomically complete and distinct from many other human bones that, despite some partial anatomic connection, were not attributable to a specific body.[107] This means that the inhumed bodies were exhumed from their original graves at different times. Those found in almost complete anatomical connection had clearly been exhumed not long after their first inhumation, when the majority of their ligaments were still intact. Conversely, the numerous bones found anatomically disconnected are a sign that they belonged to individuals exhumed much later than the former, when even their strong ligaments had decayed. There is no standard decay time for ligaments, and is dependent on numerous cultural and especially geological factors (see below). The nature of ligaments also explains why most of the big bones were found in anatomical connection, especially femurs, whereas the small bones (knuckles) were found scattered all over the grave,[108] or even outside it, as they got lost during transport. The recent excavation of the communal grave of Tratalias presents important archaeological evidence, raises numerous questions about the funerary practices of the Late Antiquity, and has the potential to answer those questions through specific studies.

There are not many comparative case studies for the collective burials of Sardinia. One of them comes from the necropolis of Alqueria de Rubio, Valencia, dated roughly to the 6th and 7th c. AD.[109] The anthropological picture of the Spanish case studies is characterised by the connection of numerous bones, and by the absence of others, few of which – i.e. crania and long bones – were moved to the side of the graves. Generally, such graves in Spain are connected to the disposal of the dead during the spread of epidemics. This interpretation is not applicable to Sardinian collective burials, where the bones do not show signs of such pathologies. They rather show the more usual enamel erosion, abscesses, tooth decay, and arthrosis,[110] study of which can advance the interpretation of the late antique community of Tratalias in terms of diet and attached social dynamics.

The practices centred around these collective graves in Sardinia involved the moving of buried individuals whose ligaments had not decayed entirely. Hence, it concerned deceased that had been buried not long before their displacement from their original grave, and whose memory was probably still vivid in the community. Understanding why this reopening and moving happened, whether for practical reasons of space redistribution, for a change of land control, or as a creative solution for the community to drive specific messages of cohesion, control of the past, or identity statements is a research path to explore. The rich evidence provided by

107   Salvi and Fonzo (2016) 459.
108   Salvi and Fonzo (2016) 454.
109   Alapont and Ribera (2006) 182; Alapont (2009) 154.
110   Salvi and Fonzo (2016) 465.

the well-conducted stratigraphic excavations may facilitate such understanding.

Evidence of burial manipulation of the third type of the list provided above comes from an earlier phase of Sardinia's Late Antiquity, between the late 3rd and 5th c. There is information about numerous remains of burial manipulations, especially in western-central Sardinia, the most detailed of which comes from Sa Mitza Salida, Masullas. Used between 1st and late 6th c., the necropolis was located on top of a small hill along the main road *a Tibula Karales* that still unites south and north Sardinia – Strada Statale Carlo Felice. Its excavation yielded 54 pit graves, with mostly single depositions,[111] and almost all aligned south-west/north-east (Fig. 12). Until the late 3rd c., the community settled in the area followed a consistent funerary practice, repeating with precision the same gestures that composed the burial set-up characterised by a high degree of uniformity across the whole site. Inside the majority of them, the body of one deceased was laid on its back with legs straight, arms either down by its sides or folded on the chest, and surrounded by ceramic and glass vessels. Their mutual positions and the resultant pattern were repeated for centuries until the late 3rd/early 4th c. AD, when a change in the funerary ritual occurred. Human remains from old burials were no longer moved around the same grave to make space for a more recent deceased, but likely they were moved to another grave entirely. The space of one single grave, respected in terms of individual boundaries until then, was now extended to the whole cemetery within a ritual that involved the space around the original burial.

The data, treated before in terms of identity interpretation,[112] provides evidence of burial manipulation consisting of the introduction of crania inside two graves: MAS-43B and MAS-9bis. This was only mentioned in excavation journals written in 1997[113] and was classified as another case of bone reduction of earlier depositions through burial reuse, commonly attested in Masullas. However, the taphonomic evidence challenges this explanation. The recognised signs of reduction – bones left aside, bone variety, remains from previous grave goods – are not present in these two cases. Looking at the remains of the crania is crucial to understand when and how they were removed from their original resting place to be laid inside two late antique graves. From these perspectives, the study of the mandibular bone is an important source. In anatomical terms, the mandibular ligament is amongst the most persistent in the human body: it decays around 12 months after death, although this varies depending on a whole range of environmental[114] and cultural features such as coffin type used and the depth at which the burial is placed.[115] Hence, the presence or absence of the mandibular ligaments in the crania placed inside graves MAS-9bis and MAS-43B is a crucial sign to interpret what happened.

Grave MAS-9bis was arranged by placing a cranium without mandible in upright position, at the feet of the primary deceased occupying the grave, together with only one grave good: a Isings 34 form glass beaker decorated with water leaves,[116] dated to the 4th c. AD (Fig. 13). The dead in MAS-43B was deposited with several objects, among them a Hayes 50 form Sigillata African Dish dating to the 4th c., and a contemporary *campidanese* jug, with three crania laid over the body of the main deceased. Only one had its mandible bone still in place: hence, the skull was removed from a relatively recent burial (less than one-year-old), before the mandibular ligament had decayed but after weaker bone ligaments had. Skeletal analysis carried out by Unida for her MA thesis[117] proves that this skull belongs to a woman in her mid-20s, likely a deposition previously occupying the grave. Its arrangement is not to be classified as as reduction: instead, it has been given the same treatment as the other two crania without mandible, and placed over the latest primary inhumation.

If these crania were separated from their original skeletons after the mandibular ligaments decayed, it is a good idea to look for potential sources of crania inside other burials in the necropolis of Masullas. In 4 cases, from 1st, 2nd and 3rd c. AD, the mandible was still in place despite the absence of the skull and there were no further signs of disturbance.[118] For this reason, it would be important to carry out cross skeletal analysis of the crania deposited in the two graves, and of the bones of the deceased where the head is missing, in order to understand the kind of practice performed at Masullas during Late Antiquity. This analysis might

---

111   Manos and Floris (2005); Puddu (2019) 68.

112   Puddu (2018) 239–60 analyses the manipulated graves of Masullas as a foundational moment of the late antique identity of the local community as it creates a meaningful discontinuity with the social dimension of the past of the site while establishing a strong, physically visible, link with the material dimension of its past.

113   21 March 1997, notes taken by Sannia and Mureddu, both from *Soprintendenza Archeologica della Sardegna*

---

114   Di Maio and Di Maio (2001) 21–41.

115   Pinheiro (2006) 87.

116   Isings (1957) 48.

117   Unida (2005).

118   Puddu (2019a).

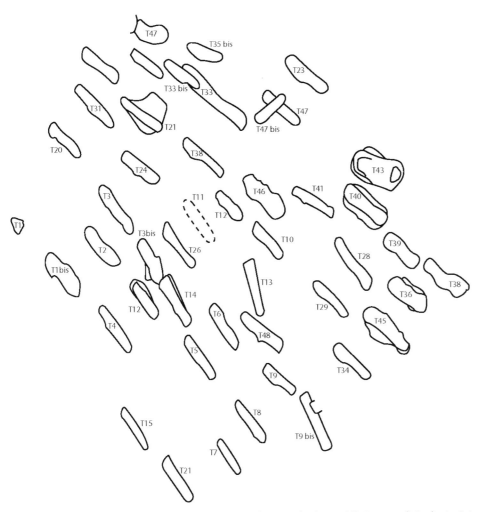

FIGURE 12   Plan of Sa Mitza Salida, Masullas; *Soprintendenza Archeologica delle Province di Cagliari e Oristano.*

help us understand if there was a kinship link between the individual buried in their primary inhumations and the crania belonging to the manipulated one. If that hypothesis was excluded, further investigation would be required into the structures of broader social bonds and power relationships linking the community of Masullas and the forces organising the area. While waiting for such specific aDNA analyses, these interpretive threads are already being unravelled and developed through the thorough exploration and experimental application of theoretical frameworks,[119] which are proving fundamental to the understanding of the complex materiality of Masullas as a result of dynamic and fluid identities.

The case studies of burial and human remains manipulations presented in this section show that both anthropological and historical enquiries are necessary in the future. The archaeological evidence usually attributed to a generic 'burial reuse' needs to be discerned from different evidence looking at the archaeological details that can provide interpretive links to the different practices that created them, following the research agenda that looks at graves reopening as a European phenomenon (Klevnäs, Aspöck, Noterman, van Haperen, and Zintl (2021)). Exploration of the practices that generated this archaeological evidence – collective burials, manipulation of crania treated as grave goods – is fundamental because they show a conscious interaction of regional and local communities with a more or less antique past in the form of old graves. As such, they are capable of providing further insights into community identity, adding depth to the often flat identifications that occur when interpretations rely only on static objects, burial, and generic ritual types like inhumation/cremation.

119   See Puddu (2019b) on the application of Gramsci's theory of subalterns to the crossing of the archaeological evidence of Masullas and the historical evidence of a social tension registered in 4th c. amongst peasants and slaves of Sardinia due to the stressful conditions of work and social divisions created by the introduction of *emphiteusis* as a system of agricultural land organization.

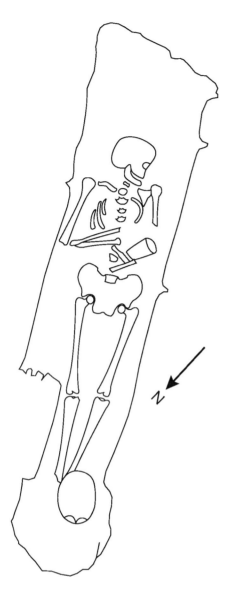

FIGURE 13   Grave 9bis, Masullas, Sa Mitza
             Salida; *Soprintendenza Archeologica*
             delle Province di Cagliari e Oristano.

Where Next? Future of Late Antique Funerary Archaeology of Sardinia

This paper reviewed the literature on the most pursued interpretive trends of burial-related practices in late antique Sardinia. It highlighted the abundance of data available from old excavations and the increasing quality of more refined data that new excavations are yielding. It highlighted the cutting edge techniques and methodologies that allowed the collection of an outstanding set of data, but also the limitations and interpretive hardships, as well as the the strong potential for future research that characterise the discipline of funerary archaeology. This paper demonstrated that some difficulties in late antique research are inherent to its nature: they derive

from the great interest in Late Antiquity that developed during the 17th and 18th c. and saw the Church's search for the bodies of saints compromise stratigraphic relationships in a way that is unique and incomparable to Punic, Roman, and Medieval archaeologies. For this reason, the late antique archaeology of Sardinia has already benefitted remarkably from the development of works aiming at reconstructing the excavations carried out in those centuries – i.e. *Sancti Innumerabiles*[120] – to recover a picture of material evidence that was considered lost. More historiographical studies of the kind are needed to refine the discipline's methodology and expand the amount of secure data further. This paper postulated that new stratigraphic excavations, combined with the recovery and interpretation of excavation journals written during the 20th c. stratigraphic digs, will provide the discipline with an increasingly more reliable material base for chronological and cultural understanding of this period. If this trend keeps the same pace it has over the last decade, much more secure data and solid interpretations are expected to be published in the next few years.

This paper also shows that some pre-dominating models of archaeological interpretation, such as the paradigms of Christianization and ethnic identification that create a flatter and static version of much more complex interpretive identities, have some basic problems that have been exposed by international scholarship and of which Sardinian scholarship is also aware. The next step to take is to use this awareness as a stimulus to actively investigate the theoretical roots of identity studies in relation to late antique burials. Critical work of those models and of the way archaeological evidence has been used to fit them has already started and can be expected to become wider and more consciously adopted even at excavation stage. Studying the centuries of conjunction between Late Antiquity and the Late Roman period, recognising in a firm sense the chronological overlap would also contribute to redefine such paradigms. For instance, the 3rd and 4th c. – i.e. Masullas in section 5 – provide a lot of material evidence from past excavations which needs to be critically assessed and whose study will provide outstanding results that will help to refine our interpretive paradigms. One way to go beyond those paradigms is focusing on the concept of practice – literally what people do[121] – involving the whole community or part of it, when the evidence of collective activities allows. From this perspective, despite it representing a unique set of data, Giuntella's work on *refrigeria*

---

120   Mureddu, Salvi, and Stefani (1988).
121   Gardner (2007) 19.

practices held in Columbaris-Cornus is a model to refer to when dealing with material evidence of possible collective practices in funerary contexts.

The aid of anthropological analysis on the necropolises dug in the past will be determinant in providing a solid data support to the critical approach that late antique archaeology can and will embark on. The amount of data on human remains that has already been collected is rich and anthropological analyses on them are easily practicable. In particular, this paper has shown that significant anthropological data comes from the contexts of burial manipulations, which are probably the richest prospect for late antique burial studies of Sardinia. This paper suggests that the area of human and material culture remains of burial manipulations is the fastest growing and more promising archaeological areas on which to concentrate future analytical and interpretive efforts. This data can help reconstruct funerary rites and provide understanding of the relationships between local communities of the Mediterranean and their dead and their past. This will grant further insights into local communities in a broad temporal sense, which would allow the picturing of them in strict relation with the material remains left by previous funerary practices and hence with the material dimension they have inherited from the world they lived in. An important development for the future of late antique burial studies, in Sardinia and beyond, will be the questioning of certain types of burial manipulations as archaeological problems bearing an unexplored socially-bound interpretive potential. The manipulations analysed here, as those seen at Tratalias and Masullas, have specific contextual meaning and are not just generic re-depositions of human skeletal material in a long-lived cemetery. This is why great attention must be paid to their depositional details, while contextualising them with historical and other archaeological sources.[122]

New methodologies and interpretive frameworks for late antique burial manipulations will help to undermine the tendency to culture-historical equivalence. This paper has highlighted that this attitude has permeated most interpretations of late antique Sardinia sites. Nevertheless, such identification-bound frameworks are being used more cautiously than in the past and with a fast-growing awareness by scholars – i.e. Salvi's critical approach of her own interpretation of Pill'e Matta.[123] Cautious identifications between categories of objects found in the burials and ethnic/religious group are a recurrent pattern of many interpretations of Sardinian archaeology, but they are also a problem in archaeology worldwide. It is not an easy task to deconstruct multiple essentialisms, as they are closely linked to the material nature of archaeology's object of investigation. Materials are, by themselves, one-dimensional and static. It takes an important theoretical awareness to make them appear dynamic. From this point of view, the archaeology of late antique burials of Sardinia has a lot of room for improvement. Bringing an explicit theoretical engagement with identity debates to the interpretive agenda of late antique (and Roman) Sardinia – so far mostly neglected – will certainly be a way forward in the understanding of the material relations between objects and groups of people.[124] The abundant evidence of burial manipulations and vast cemeteries so far unaccounted for constitute an ideal stage on which to perform and test such theoretical ideas in an active and challenging way that cannot but benefit the discipline.

Acknowledgements

I am grateful to Luke Lavan and Michael Mulryan for inviting me to the stimulating conference on *Fieldwork in Late Antique Archaeology: Burial and Funerary Practices* in November 2017, at Birkbeck, University of London: this paper is a result of that conference and of the discussions following the presentation of each paper. I hence thank all the speakers present at the conference, because through their ideas and research results I could contextualise the position of Sardinia's late antique archaeology in the Mediterranean much more clearly. I am very thankful to the University of Cambridge and to my Ph.D. supervisor Martin Millett for allowing me to stay connected with interesting webs of researchers, and to my examiners, John Peirce and John Robb who helped me refine my research questions. This project has received funding from the European Union's Horizon 2020 research and innovation programme under the Marie Sklodowska-Curie grant agreement No. 893017.

Bibliography

Alapont L. (2009) "El mundo funerario en el limes visigodobizantino:el territorio valenciano", in *Contextos funeraris a la Mediterrània nordoccidental (segles VVIII)*, edd. J. Pinar Gil and T. Juarez Villena (Gausac 2009) 145–58.

Alapont L. and Ribera A. (2006) "Los cementerios tardoantiguos de Valentia: arqueologia y antropologia. Espacios y

---

122 See Puddu (2018).
123 Salvi (2016).

124 See, for instance, Remotti (1996) 60, for an invitation to anthropologists to engage theoretically with identity debates.

usos funerarios en la ciudad histórica", *Anales de Arqueología Cordobesa* 17 (2006) 161–94.

Amante Simoni C. (1990) "Sepoltura e moneta: obolo viatico-obolo offerta", in *Cuglieri IV. Le Sepolture in Sardegna dal IV al VII secolo* (1990) 231–42.

Amante Simoni C. and Martorelli R. (1986) "Cultura, materiali e fasi storiche del complesso archeologico di Cornus: primi risultati di una ricerca. I corredi funerari e la suppellettile metallica", in *Cuglieri I. L'archeologia romana e altomedievale nell'Oristanese. Atti del I Convegno. Mediteranno tardoantico e medievale. Scavi e ricerche* 3, ed. A. M. Giuntella (Taranto 1986) 161–89.

Aspöck E., Müller-Scheeßel N., and Klevnäs A. (2020) *Grave Disturbances: The Archaeology of Post-depositional Interactions with the Dead* (Oxford 2020).

Auffarth C. (2009) "Religio migrans: Les « religions orientales » dans le contexte religieux antique. Un modèle théorique", in *Trivium. Revue franco-allemande de sciences humaines et sociales-Deutsch-französische Zeitschrift für Geistes-und Sozialwissenschaften* 4 (2009).

Bartoloni P. (2008) "Da sulky a Sulci", with the contribution of A. Gavini, in *Epigrafia romana in Sardegna: atti del I. convegno di studio*, Sant'Antioco, edd. F. Cenerini and P. Ruggeri (Rome 2008) 15–32.

Bollok A. (2018) "Mortuary display, associated artefacts, and the resurrection of the body in Early Christian thought: some considerations for archaeologists", *Antaeus* 35–36 (2018) 245–70.

Brown P. (1971). *The World of Late Antiquity* (New York 1971).

Casagrande M. (2015) "Tomba ipogeica di Decimoputzu, loc. San Giorgio", in *Isole e terraferma nel primo cristianesimo. Identità locale ed interscambi culturali, religiosi e produttivi*, Atti XI Congresso Nazionale di Archeologia Cristiana, edd. R. Martorelli, A. Piras, and P. G. Spanu (Cagliari 2015) 807 814.

Cisci S. and Martorelli R. (2016) "Sulci in età tardoantica e bizantina", in Storia e Archeologia di Sant'Antioco: dai Nuraghi all'Alto Medioevo *Atti della Pontificia Accademia Romana di Archeologia (serie III)* (Rendiconti 88), edd. P. Bartoloni *et al.* (2016) 277–331.

Cisci S. and Tatti M. (2013) "Cagliari: indagini archeologiche entro il bastione di santa Caterina", in *Quaderni della Soprintendenza per i Beni Archeologici delle province di Cagliari e Oristano* 24 (2013) 1–24.

Corda A. M. (1999) *Le iscrizioni Cristiane della Sardegna Anteriori al VII Secolo* (Vatican City 1999).

Corda A. M. (2007) *Breve introduzione allo studio delle antichità cristiane in Sardegna* (Ortacesus 2007).

De Clerq C. ed. (1963) "*Concilia Galliae*" = Corpus Christianorum CXLVIII A (Turnholt 1963).

Di Maio D. and Di Maio V. J. (2001) *Forensic Pathology* (Boca Raton 2011).

Eckardt H., Muldner G., and Speed G. (2015) "The late Roman field army in northern Britain? Mobility, material culture, and multi-isotope analysis at Scorton (N Yorks)", *Britannia* 46 (2015) 191–223.

Fiocchi Nicolai V. and Spera R. (2015) "Sviluppi monumentali e insediativi dei santuari dei martiri in Sardegna", in *Isole e terraferma nel primo cristianesimo. Identità locale ed interscambi culturali, religiosi e produttivi, Atti dell'XI Congresso Nazionale di Archeologia Cristiana*, edd. R. Martorelli, A. Piras, and P. G. Spanu (Cagliari 2015) https://www.academia.edu/22465499.

Floris P. (2005) *Le Iscrizioni Funerarie Pagane di Karales* (Bari 2005).

Giuntella A. M. (1985) "Materiali ceramici", in *Mensea e riti funerari in Sardegna. La testimonianza di Cornus. Mediterraneo tardoantico e medievale. Scavi e ricerche*, edd. A. M. Giuntella, G. Borghetti, and D. Stiaffini (Taranto 1985) 69–116.

Giuntella A. M. (1990) "Sepoltura e rito: consuetudini e innovazioni", in *Cuglieri IV. Le Sepolture in Sardegna dal IV al VII secolo* (Taranto 1990) 215–29.

Giuntella A. M. (1998) "Note su alcuni aspetti della ritualità funeraria nell'alto medioevo. Consuetudini e innovazioni", in *Sepolture tra IV e VIII secolo. 7° Seminario sul Tardo Antico e l'Alto Medioevo*, edd. G. P. Brogiolo and G. Cantino Wataghin (1998) 61–75.

Giuntella A. M. (1999) "Cornus 3.2. L'area cimiteriale orientale", in *Mediterraneo tardoantico e medievale. Scavi e ricerche* 13 (Oristano 1999) 41–46.

Giuntella A. M. (2002) "Brevi note sull'area cimiteriale orientale di Cornus (Cuglieri provincia di Oristano)", in *Insuale Christi. Il Cristianesimi Primitivo in Sardegna, Corsica e Baleari* (Scavi e Ricerche 16), ed. P. G. Spanu (Oristano 2002) 245–52.

Giuntella A. M. and Amante Simoni C. (1992) "L'uso degli Spazi, Sepolture, e Riti Funerari", in *La Civitas Cristiana. Urbanistica delle Citta' Italiane tra trarda antichita' e altomedioevo, Atti del I seminario di studio. Mediterraneo Tardoantico e medievale*, edd. P. Demeglio and C. Lambert (Turin 1992) 127–43.

Gregorius Magnus S. (1982) *Registrum epistularum* (Turnhout 1982).

Grossi W., Knobloch R., and Lumacone A. (2008) "I rituali funerari", in *Bollettino di Archeologia On-Line. International Congress of Classical Archaeology* (Rome 1982) 29–37.

Guery R. (1985) "La nécropole orientale de Sitifis (Sétif, Algérie), fouilles de 1966–1967", in *Etudes d'Antiquités Africaines. Revue des Mondes Musulmans et de la Méditerrané* (1985) 176–77.

Kazanski M. (1991) *Les Goths (Ier–VIIe s. ap. J.C.)* (Paris 1991).

Kazanski M. (2002) "Les antiquités germaniques de l'époque romaine tardive en Crimée et dans la région de la mer d'Azov", *Ancient West and East* 1/2 (2002) 393–441.

Klevnäs A., Aspöck E., Noterman A. A., van Haperen M. C., and Zintl S. (2021) "Reopening graves in the early Middle Ages: from local practice to European phenomenon", *Antiquity* 95 (2021) 1005–1026.

La Fragola A. (2003) "La necropoli romana", in *Ricerche Su Nora II (1990–1998)*, ed. C. Tronchetti (Elmas 2003) 99–115.

Lai R. (2010) [De Esquivel F. 1617]. *Relazione sulla "Inventio" dell'illustre martire e apostolo della Sardegna, San Antioco nella sua propria chiesa di Sulci*. Extracted from: *Relacion de la invencion de los cuerpos santos que en los años 1614, 1615 y 1616 fueron hallados en varias yglesias de la ciudad de Caller y su arçobispado. A la santidad de n.s. Paulo papa 5. Por don Francisco de Esquiuel*, transl. by C. Bombasaro, with explicative notes by M. Massa. (Sant'Antioco 2010).

Lewis N. D. (2016) "Reinterpreting 'Pagans' and 'Christians' from Rome's late antique mortuary evidence", in *Pagans and Christians in Late Antique Rome. Conflict, Competition, and Coexistence in the Fourth Century*, edd. M. R. Salzman, M. Sághy, and R. L. Testa (Cambridge 2016) 273–90.

Locci C. (2012) "Tipologie funerarie nella necropoli romana dell'ex albergo 'La Scala di Ferro' – Cagliari", in *Quaderni della Sorpintendenza Archeologica di Cagliari e Oristano* 23 (Cagliari 2012) 108–133.

Manos A. and Floris R. (2005) "La necropoli di *Mitza Salida* – Masullas – Oristano (OR)", in *Rendiconti Seminarion Facolta di Scienze Universita di Cagliari* 75 (Cagliari 2005) 65–73.

Martorelli R. (2003) "Proposte Metodologiche per un uso dei corredi funerari come fonte per la conoscenza dell'età tardoantica e medievale in Sardegna", in *Fonti Archeologiche e Iconografiche per la Storia e la Cultura degli Insediamenti nell'Alto Medioevo*, ed. S. Lusuardi Siena (Milan 2003) 301–321.

Martorelli R. (2007) "La diffusione del Cristianesimo in Sardegna in epoca Vandala", in *La Cristianizzazione in Italia fra Tardoantico e Alto Medioevo. Atti del Cognresso Nazionale Archeologia Cristiana, Agrigento, 2002*, edd. G. Bertelli, M. Corrente, M. Minchilli, and L. F. Tedeschi (Palermo 2007) 281–323.

Martorelli R. (2011a) "Usi e consuetudini funerarie nella Sardegna centro-occidentale fra tarda antichità e altro medioevo", in *Oristano e il suo Territorio*, edd. P. G. Spanu and R. Zucca (Rome 2011) 700–759.

Martorelli R. (2011b) "Le catacombe di Sant'Antioco", in *S. Antioco da primo evangelizzatore di Sulci a glorioso Protomartire "Patrono della Sardegna*, edd. R. Lai and M. Massa (Sant'Antioco 2011) 59–76.

Martorelli R. (2015) "Cagliari bizantina: alcune riflessioni dai nuovi dati dell'archeologia," *European Journal of Post-classical Archaeology* (2015) 175–99.

Martorelli R. and Mureddu D. (2006) *Archeologia Urbana a Cagliari. Scavi in Vico III Lanusei* (Cagliari 2006).

Mastino A. (2005) *Storia della Sardegna antica* (Nuoro 2005).

Millett M. (1990) *The Romanization of Britain: An Essay in Archaeological Interpretation* (Cambridge 1990).

Mureddu D. (1990) "Alcuni contesti funerari cagliaritani attraverso le cronache del seicento", in *Le Sepolture in Sardegna dal 4° al 7° secolo. Convegno sull'Archeologia Tardoromana e Medievale* (Cuglieri 1987) 179–206.

Mureddu D., Salvi D., and Stefani, G. (1988) *Sancti Innumerabiles: Scavi nella Cagliari del Seicento: Testimonianze e Verifiche* (Oristano 1988).

Piepenbrink K. (2009) *Christliche Identität und Assimilation in der Spätantike: Probleme des Christseins in der Reflexion der Zeitgenossen* (Heidelberg 2009).

Pinheiro J. (2006) "Decay process of a cadaver", in *Forensic anthropology and medicine*, edd. A. Schmitt, E. Cunha, and J. Pinheiro (New York 2006) 85–116.

Pitts M. (2007) "The emperor's new clothes? The utility of identity in Roman archaeology", *AJA* 111 (2007) 693–713.

Possenti E. (2012) "Movimenti migratori in eta' tardoantica: riscontri archeologici negli insediamenti rurali della Venetia", in *La Trasformazione del Mondo Romano e le Grandi Migrazioni. Nuovi Popoli dall'Europa Settentrionale e Centro-Orientale Alle Coste del Mediterraneo. Atti del Convegno Internazionale di Studi*, edd. C. Ebanista and M. Rotili (Cimitile 2012) 143–62.

Puddu M. (2018) "Testo, rizoma e cultura materiale. Riflessioni semiotiche sull'identità sociale in archeologia", in *Semiotica generale – semiotica specifica. Sémiotique générale – sémiotique spécifique*, edd. A. Gałkowski and T. Roszak (Lodz 2017) 239–260.

Puddu M. (2019a) *Funerary Archaeology and Changing Identities: Community Practices in Roman-Period Sardinia* (London 2019).

Puddu M. (2019b) "An archaeology of the subalterns' disaggregated history: interpreting burial manipulations of Roman-period Sardinia through Gramsci's Theory", *Theoretical Roman Archaeology Journal* 2 (2019).

Rebillard E. (2009) *The Care of the Dead in Late Antiquity*, transl. by E. Trapnell Rawlings and J. Routier-Pucci. (*Cornell Studies in Classical Philology* 59) (London 2009).

Salvi D. (1988) "Conclusioni. Considerazioni generali – Le tipologie tombali", in *Sancti Innumerabiles: Scavi nella Cagliari del Seicento: Testimonianze e Verifiche*, edd. D. Mureddu, D. Salvi, and G. Stefani (Oristano 1988) 89–101.

Salvi D. (2002a) "Quartucciu, Località Pill'e Matta: la Necropoli Tardo-Romana", in *Insulae Christi: il Cristianesimo Primitivo in Sardegna, Corsica, e Baleari*, ed. P. G. Spanu (Oristano 2002) 473–74.

Salvi D. (2002b) "Cagliari: l'area cimiteriale di San Saturnino", in *Insulae Christi. Il Cristianesimo Primitivo in Sardegna, Corsica e Baleari*. ed. P. G. Spanu (Oristano 2002) 215–24.

Salvi D. (2005) *Luce sul Tempo: la Necropoli di Pill'e Matta, Quartucciu* (Cagliari 2005).

Salvi D. (2007) "San Saturnino, progetti di variante", in *Ricerca e Confronti 2006: giornate di studio di archeologia e Storia dell'arte* (Cagliari 2007) 349–58.

Salvi D. (2010) "La Campidanese. Ceramica comune da mensa della Sardegna meridionale nei contesti chiusi di eta' tardoantica della necropoli di Pill'e Matta, Quartucciu (Cagliari – Sardegna – Italia)", in *LRCW3 Late Roman Coarse Wares and Amphorae in the Mediterranean* (BAR-IS 2185), edd. S. Menchelli, S. Santoro, M. Pasquinucci, and G. Guiducci (Oxford 2010) 235–43.

Salvi D. (2015) "La tomba 100 di Pill'e Matta e altri Militaria nella necropoli tardoantica di Quartucciu (CA)", in *Quaderni Friulani di Archeologia* XXV (Udinese 2015) 195–206.

Salvi D. and Fonzo O. (2016) "La tomba bizantina di San Sebastiano a Monastir, con novità e considerazioni sulle tombe impogee altomedievali e note di antropologia sulle sepolture collettive di bivio Monte Pranu, Tratalias, e T4, Sett. I di San Saturnino, Cagliari", in *Quaderni della Soprintendenza Archeologica di Cagliari e Oristano* (2016) 447–80.

Serra P. B. (1990) "Complesso Sepolcrale Bizantino nel Mastio del Nuraghe Su Nuraxi di Siurgus Donigala – Cagliari", in *Le Sepolture in Sardegna dal IV al VII Secolo* (Cagliari 1990) 107–131.

Serra P. B. (1990) "Tombe a camera in muratura con volta a botte nei cimiteri altomedievali della Sardegna", in *Le sepolture in Sardegna dal IV al VII secolo, IV Convegno sull'archeologia tardoromana e medievale* (Oristano 1990) 133–60.

Serra P. B. (2002) "Elementi di cultura materiale di ambito ebraico: dall'alto impero all'alto medioevo", in *Insulae Christi. Il Cristianesimo Primitivo in Sardegna, Corsica, e Baleari*, ed. P. G. Spanu (Cagliari 2002) 67–110.

Serra P. B. (2007) "Documenti di età altomedievale: la tomba a camera in muratura voltata a botte in località San Costantino", in *Villa dei Greci. Una Villagreca inedita fra storia, archeologia e arte*, ed. N. Rossi and S. Meloni (Dolianova 2007) 65–73.

Sirigu R. (2003) "Un percorso di lettura nell'ipertesto museale. La 'morte povera' in età romana", in *Quaderni del Museo: Soprintendenza archeologica delle Province di Cagliari e Oristano* (Cagliari 2003) 107–150.

Tronchetti C. (1989) *S. Antioco (Sardegna Archeologica. Guide e Itinerari 12)* (Sassari 1989).

Tronchetti C. (1990) "La necropoli romana di Sulci. Scavi 1978: relazione preliminare", in *Quaderni della Soprintendenza Archeologica di Cagliari e Oristano* 7 (Cagliari 1990) 173–92.

Spanu P. G. and Zucca R. (2004) *I Sigilli Bizantini della Sardegna* (Milan 2004).

Tronchetti C. (1996) *La ceramica della Sardegna romana* (Milan 1996).

Tronchetti C. (2013) "Necropoli, tombe e società nella Sardegna Romana. Note a margine", in *Societa' dei vivi, comunita' dei morti: un rapporto (ancora?) difficile. Atti del Convegno di Studi 2013.* (forthcoming).

Unida S. (2005) *Analisi osteometrica sui reperti di età romana della necropoli di Mitza Salida (OR). Tesi di Laurea* (Cagliari 2005).

Volp U. (2002) *Tod und Ritual in den christlichen Gemeinden der Antike* (Supplements to *Vigiliae Christianae* 45) (Leiden and Boston 2002).

Zucca R. (1987) *Neapolis e il suo Territorio* (Oristano 1987).

Zucca R. (1988) "Osservazioni sulla storia e topografia di Cornus", in *Ampsicora e il territorio di Cornus. Atti del II Convegno sull'archeologia romana e altomedievale nell'Oristanese Mediterraneo tardo antico e medievale. Scavi e ricerche* 6 (Taranto 1988) 31–57.

Burial Rites in Byzantine Sicily – New Approaches and Discoveries

Valentina Caminneci, Maria-Serena Rizzo and Martin Carver

Abstract

Early Byzantine Sicily shows the full repertoire of Mediterranean mortuary practice for the period: rock-cut and earth-cut graves (*formae*), stone-built and lidded tombs, arched niches (*arcosoli*), subterranean catacombs and chambers (*ipogei*), burial in sarcophagi and in amphorae (*enchytrismòs*), graves cut from ground level (*sub divo*), and tombs standing above ground (*subdiali*). Sicilian archaeologists since Paolo Orsi in the 19th c. have explored and cherished this inheritance, asking questions about the meaning of its diversity, and whether it be regional, temporal, social or religious. This chapter focuses on two recent campaigns of especial interest: first that at Agrigento, of all Byzantine burial-places in Sicily the most comprehensively and scientifically explored; and second the contribution of a European Research Council project *Sicily in Transition* (SICTRANSIT) which is examining the mortuary practice and biomolecular properties of 253 individuals in 22 cemeteries, 13 of which are mainly Byzantine in date. Burials of both the Early (5th to 8th c.) and Middle (9th to 13th c.) Byzantine periods are discussed.

Introduction

The authors of a recent review of burial practice in Byzantine Sicily, as important as it was useful, divided the island into three parts: the south, taking in the area from Mazara to Agrigento and Gela; the north-west, including Lilybaeum (Marsala), Palermo and Cefalù, and the east, around the coast from Messina, to Taormina, Catania, Syracuse and inland to Ragusa.[1] They mapped the seats of its 13 dioceses, which are all on the coast, two in the south (at Agrigento and Triocala), 5 in the north-west (Marsala, Carini, Palermo, Termini, Cefalù) and 6 in the east (Patti, Messina, Taormina, Catania, Syracuse, Lentini), each commanding territories of different sizes and with different levels of surviving monumentality. Only two basilicas are known in the south (Sofiana and Eraclea Minoa), 5 in the north-west (Salemi, Palermo, Ciminna, Castelbuono, Castellana Sicula) and 22 in the east (Fig. 1).[2]

The map gives a primary indication of Early Christian investment. The funerary evidence is widely spread, but its role in reporting social and religious change is more elusive. The tombs themselves are vulnerable – many have been ransacked, while a majority of the larger tombs have been re-opened a number of times to admit new burials. A basic hierarchy of investment may be observed: at the higher end, cellular underground chambers (*ipogei*), *arcosoli* (above and below ground) and tombs standing above ground; at the lower end, graves *sub divo* cut into rock or lined with uncut stones (Fig. 2). Catacombs are communal underground cemeteries consisting of chambers and corridors and may feature a wide variety of depositions.[3] In general, the diversity of tomb types is at its highest in the 3rd to 7th c.; thereafter the stone-built family tombs *subdiali* and the simpler forms of unfurnished graves *sub divo* prevail. The cemeteries are distributed between towns, former towns, the countryside and along the roads, especially those connecting the coast with the hinterland.[4]

Some explanation of the distribution of types appears to have been geological: the limestone regions in the west and south favour subterranean *ipogei, arcosoli* and rock-cut graves. In the area of Enna and Gela, only 20% of the burials are subterranean and the larger tombs are built of quarried blocks, while in Catania the subsoil of volcanic lava discourages the digging of underground chambers.[5] Tombs may be dated by grave goods, by association with a datable church or by virtue of their implantation in abandoned Roman suburbs. There are many examples of the reuse of the underground burial chambers of previous periods (for example at Lilibeo), as well as of their cisterns or in one case an olive press.[6] Syracuse is famous for its *latomie,* artificial square chambers cut into the faces of the deep quarry left by the builders of the monumental Greek city. Association with Rome and Byzantium is evident in the use of Latin and Greek inscriptions, but also noted were a number of cultural links with North Africa: the *arcosoli* at Palermo, the tomb superstructures at Contrada Sant'Agata, the architecture and mosaics of the church at San Miceli,

---

1   Carra Bonacasa *et al.* (2015). The authors were Giuseppina Schirò (south), Emma Vitale (north-west) and Giuseppe Falzone (east), the whole overseen by Maria Rosa Carra Bonacasa.

2   Fig. 1 draws on Carra Bonacasa *et al.* (2015) 176–78, figs. 1–4.

3   For example at Villagrazia di Carini: Carra Bonacasa *et al.* (2015) 147.

4   Carra Bonacasa *et al.* (2015) 137, 162.

5   Carra Bonacasa *et al.* (2015) 138, 153.

6   Contrada Muratore: Carra Bonacasa *et al.* (2015) 144; Alfano (2006–2007) 166, fig. 11.

© KONINKLIJKE BRILL BV, LEIDEN, 2024 | DOI:10.1163/9789004687974_010
Alexandra Dolea and Luke Lavan (eds) *Burial and Memorial in Late Antiquity*
(Late Antique Archaeology 13) (Leiden 2024), pp. 727–751

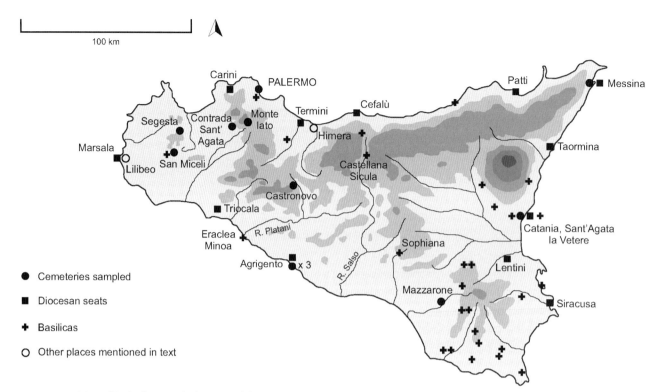

FIGURE 1   Map of Sicily showing the location of the seats of dioceses, basilicas and cemeteries researched by SICTRANSIT (Cecily Spall
             FAS Heritage, after SICTRANSIT and Carra Bonacasa *et al.* (2015) figs. 1–4).

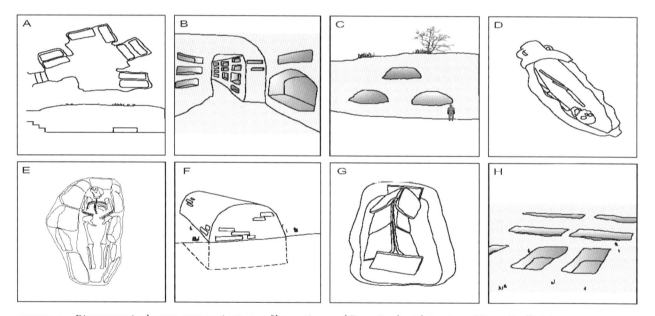

FIGURE 2   Diagrammatic glossary, representing types of late antique and Byzantine burial structures (Carver/Spall) A: ipogeo
             B: catacomba C: arcosoli D: enchytrismòs E: tomba a cassa litica F: tomba a cupa G: tomba a cappuccina H: tombe a formae.

and the enclosed *cocciopesto* platform beside the *ipogei*
at Agrigento, which has parallels at Tipasa in Algeria.[7]

The 2015 review was concerned to use the geogra-
phy of burial to document the arrival and spread of
Christianity. No evidence for Christian symbolism or
ritual was noted earlier than the 3rd c., and the Christian

burial corpus was taken as those tombs that could be
dated between the 3rd c. and the 7th–8th. These burials are proposed as 'useful guiding fossils' for tracking
the new religion.[8] The authors urge that, by virtue of its
variety of burial rites and its 'funeral avenue' which

7   Carra Bonacasa *et al.* (2015) 137, 148, 150, 161.

8   Carra Bonacasa *et al.* (2015) 160 – ""*utili fossili guida*" *per deter-
     minare l'incidenza della nuova religione*" – ""useful guide fossils" to
     determine the impact of the new religion".

connects the *sub divo* graves and the community catacomb to the groups of private *ipogei*, Agrigento should be considered a model for urban funerary organisation in Sicily more generally.[9]

Another chapter in the same volume broadened and enhanced the study and interpretation of the Sicilian corpus, by putting to one side the assumption that all the unmarked burials were Christian or necessarily assigned to a documented religion.[10] Paola De Santis recommended a study of the burials at three levels – the indications of individuality through personal effects, the message conveyed by the building and furnishing of the tomb by others, and the re-integration of the dead through post-burial performance – these representing layered aspects of the interpretation of mortuary practice as discerned by archaeology. Examples of personal attributes are rare encounters, in which fragments of clothing, and gold thread stand out.[11] Tombs are prepared and furnished by burial parties to a varying degree, and do not have to correlate with documented religious thinking or ethnic alignment. At Quartucciu in Sardinia, lamps carrying both Jewish and Christian symbols were included, suggesting "substantial indifference to their ideological content".[12] Affectionate attention continues after the tomb is built: feasting rituals were noted, with the provision of stone 'tables' and traces of cooking, frequent visits and methods of feeding the deceased through an orifice. De Santis cites a poignant inscription by a daughter in memory of her mother, describing just such a prescription of feasting as a way of healing grief.[13] These observations encourage the view that a specific allegiance to one of the well-documented faiths is rarely identifiable or sufficient: "rather we see a micro-reality where groups express a particular ritual and behavioural code that is not reducible to a religious identity."[14]

In urging this change of focus, De Santis is citing earlier thinking by Février and Ariès and building on a body of theory that has developed in Europe and the Mediterranean aimed at addressing the interpretation of its material record.[15] Reviewing the theoretical scene in 1985, Bruno D'Agostino emphasised that, while we want to use burials to recognise inherited tradition, external influence, allegiance to social group, ethnicity, wealth,

religious affiliation and mobility, the meaning expressed by such diverse desiderata depends largely on context. As he demonstrated at Pithecusae in the Bay of Naples, rich grave goods can mean a rich person, a sacred person or a hero. The dead do not bury themselves and hence are not responsible for the message of the identity signalled by the grave. Collectively, 'signalled identity' (burial location, burial rite) needs to be reconciled with physical identity (genetic descent, diet, health). But burials never mean nothing. Understanding the dead is our problem, not their problem; it requires the reconciliation of interpretations of every kind, best aided by a knowledge of the context.[16] It is probably no accident that, in Europe at least, the favoured analogy in burial studies has moved from an anthropological to a literary platform. While prehistorians may find this unhelpful, in Classical and medieval studies we have embraced the concept of expressive and even declamatory memorials, contextualised by inscriptions, art and historical contexts. In the case of low investment burials, the silence is also significant.[17]

The research project *Sicily in Transition*, which began in 2016, is dedicated to amplifying this agenda by studying the location, layout, burial rites and physical anthropology of 253 individuals in 22 excavated Sicilian cemeteries, ranging in date from the Byzantine through the Islamic into the Norman and Swabian periods (5th to 13th c.).[18] The choice of cemeteries was guided by Sicilian archaeologists, and dependent on the availability of viable bone for analysis. The aim is to characterise the mortuary repertoire and its messages and how they changed through successive regimes over these

---

9   Carra Bonacasa *et al.* (2015) 135, 161.

10   De Santis (2015).

11   Earrings and brooches at Contrada Sant'Agata and San Miceli (Sicily); textile fragments in the *ipogei* of Tanca di Borgona and the silver pin with the young woman in Tomb 80 at Cornus (Sardinia).

12   De Santis (2015) 206.

13   De Santis (2015) 207, 209.

14   De Santis (2015) 210.

15   Février (1977); Ariès (1980).

16   D'Agostino (1985) 52–54. "*Le campionature si potrebbe moltiplicare: dal loro confronto, soprattutto quando sono parti di un contesto unitario, è possibile verificare la validità delle interpretazioni, la compatibilità delle diverse letture. Nel campo dell'ideologia funeraria. … questo sembra l'unico metodo possibile* (p. 57) – "The samples could be multiplied: by comparing them, especially when they are part of a unitary context, it is possible to verify the validity of the interpretations and the compatibility of the different readings. In the field of funeral ideology. … this seems to be the only possible method". See also Cerchiai (2018), a discussion of D'Agostino's construct in the light of later transatlantic theory.

17   E.g. for the Early Medieval period, Carver (2000), (2001) and (2002), which extends the relationships between archaeological evidence, monumentality and the various functions of texts.

18   Sicily in Transition, acronym SICTRANSIT is funded by a 5-year advanced grant from the European Research Council (AdvG 693600). The three partners are the University of Rome Tor Vergata (Prof. Alessandra Molinari) the University of Salento at Lecce (Prof. Girolamo Fiorentino) and the BioArch laboratory at the University of York (Prof. Oliver Craig) with Martin Carver (York) as PI.

900 years, deploying archaeological, bioarchaeological and biomolecular methods. The priority was to date as many individuals as possible by radiocarbon, in order to anchor them securely in time, whether or not they were accompanied by grave goods. Depending on the type and conservation of bone, each individual was further characterised by staple isotopes of carbon, nitrogen, oxygen and strontium, and by aDNA, in order to provide a measure of their diet, mobility and ancestry. This procedure meant that an individual could play a part in the study of transition, even when their grave had been disturbed by pillage or later burials or other kinds of rummaging. These data were then integrated with the location and layout of each cemetery and the burial rites deployed in order to gain a holistic impression of the community and its context, as a product of its sampled members.

Thirteen of these cemeteries are largely Byzantine in date and will be considered in what follows. It was evident that their archaeological character represents moments in a long continuum, and their rites were to a great extent anticipated in the preceding Punic, Archaic, Classical, Hellenistic and Roman periods. The radiocarbon dating also showed that many of the culturally Byzantine burials belonged to the period of Islamic governance and continued with some slight modifications into the Sicily of the Norman and Swabian regimes. The establishment of context, therefore, requires us to look back and forward several hundred years from the Early Byzantine period. As anticipated, no place in Sicily better encapsulates what might be termed the Byzantine mortuary experience than Agrigento, which is where we will begin our presentation.

Late Antique and Early Byzantine Burial in Agrigento

The archaeological evidence for late antique and Early Byzantine burial in Agrigento features three fundamental nuclei: one in the Valley of the Temples, another in the so-called Hellenistic-Roman Quarter (Quartiere Ellenistico Romano, or QER), and the third at the ancient port at the mouth of the Akragas river (Fig. 3). The first systematic study of *sub divo* and hypogean funerary architecture in the Valley of the Temples was published by Catullo Mercurelli in 1948.[19] In the 1950s, the excavations into the inhabited sector known as the Hellenistic Roman Quarter unearthed several tombs from the Byzantine period placed among the derelict houses.[20] In the 1980s, the research of Rosa Maria Carra from the University of Palermo in an unexplored sector of the

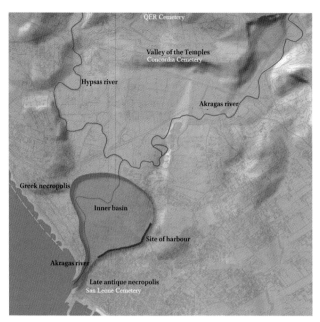

FIGURE 3   Agrigento. Locations of the harbour and the three cemeteries discussed (Temple ridge, San Leone and QER). (Caminneci).

sub divo cemetery was also important for expanding our knowledge of the necropolis in the Valley of the Temples.[21] For the first time in Agrigento the investigations made use of osteological analyses of the buried remains as well as archaeometric analyses on the pottery fabrics. The research itself, which lasted over 30 years, also clarified our understanding of the chronology of the burials dated from the 3rd c. to the 6th c. AD, along with their topographic organisation, the most important discovery of which was a road, the *Via dei Sepolcri*, reusing an ancient water conduit to serve the necropolis by linking the groups of tombs.

Burials amongst the Temples

The most conspicuous cemetery is that which developed between the Temples of Juno and Hercules during Late Antiquity, probably, from the 3rd to the 6th c. AD.[22] Unfortunately, most of the tombs were opened in ancient times, and in the case of tombs investigated between the end of the 19th c. and the beginning of the 20th, the documentation is often seriously flawed, especially with regard to the anthropological data. Groups of *formae* dug into the limestone bedrock, are located on the terraces among the temples, as well as on the north side of the hill, but it has been difficult to establish their exact chronology. From the 6th c., the former Greek Temple of Concordia provided an important focus for the cemetery, since at that point it was converted into

19   Mercurelli (1948).
20   De Miro (2009).

21   Bonacasa Carra (1995); Carra and Ardizzone (2007).
22   An accurate description of the necropolis in Schirò (2014).

FIGURE 4   Agrigento. The Temple of Concordia, with *formae sub divo* graves in the foreground
(Caminneci).

TABLE 1   Agrigento: Radiocarbon dates from the Temple group and San Leone (harbour group) of tombs (Scottish Universities
Environmental Research Centre, June 2021).

Site name, code	Sample no.	Tomb/Area/US/Ind.	Lab no. (SUERC)	Date at 95.4% probability (SUERC)
AGC	BN1	Concordia/T6-I/1C	93052	cal AD 1055–1275
AGC	BN2	Concordia/T-I/2C	93053	cal AD 1060–1285
AGC	BN3	Concordia/T67-I/1C	93057	cal AD 980–1150
AGC	BN4	Concordia/T3-I/1C	93058	cal AD 140–395
AGC	BN5	Versante NE/US3/T2-I/1D	93059	cal AD 1470–1790
AGC	BN7	Concordia/T40/Ind.1: adult	96733	cal AD 345–575
AGC	BN8	Concordia/T21/Ind.1: adult	96734	cal AD 755–1005
AGC	BN9	Giunone/T100/Ind.1: adult	96735	cal AD 255–515
SL	BN1	T5/Ind.4: infant	97697	cal AD 265–540
SL	BN2	T4/8/Ind.3: M, adult	97698	cal AD 360–555
SL	BN3	T2/Ind.4	97699	cal AD 260–525
SL	BN4	T3	97700	cal AD 260–535

a church (Fig. 4). Radiocarbon dating of 8 individuals by the SICTRANSIT project has shown that the cemetery was in use from at least the 3rd c. up to the 13th (Table 1).[23] The chronology of three inhumed individual in *formae* near the Temple of Juno and the Temple of Concordia between the late 2nd and the 4th c. AD is very

significant for understanding the changes to the city at the end of antiquity.

There are also significant examples of subterranean funerary architecture in Agrigento. The largest Agrigentine communal catacomb, known as the Grotta Fragapane, traverses the southern line of the city walls underground, and reuses the Greek bell-shaped cisterns as funerary rooms, or rotundas, where *formae* and *arcosoli* were dug (Fig. 5). This reuse during Late Antiquity attests not only to a change in the use of the Greek

23   Not counting a burial of Early Modern times (15th–18th c.) from the area near the Church of St. Blaise on the eastern slopes of acropolis, not far from the Valley of the Temples.

FIGURE 5   Agrigento. *Ipogeo* reusing a Greek cistern (Caminneci).

FIGURE 6   Agrigento. Former *arcosoli* cut into the Greek town wall (Caminneci).

cisterns, but also to the shrinking of the city, which no longer relied upon the walls to stop potential invaders. Indeed, some tombs were also dug into the southern walls near the main temples of the Greek city, most likely between the 4th and the 5th c. AD. On the inner face of the surviving walls, groups of damaged *arcosoli* are visible today (Fig. 6). It is assumed that the *ipogei* east of Fragapane and those now incorporated in the garden of Villa Aurea, a few metres from the Temple of Concordia, may have been owned by individual families (Fig. 7). The stone sarcophagi and the *a cupa* tombs (with barrel-shaped cover) may have been the prerogative of the richer classes.

This necropolis is likely to be an indication of a large Christian community. No funerary inscriptions have been found across the entire necropolis of Agrigento, so we know very little about the people who were buried there. However, such a large and articulated cemetery may very well have been a project of the local bishopric. While it is not easy to make sense of the evidence of ritual gestures in this cemetery, the few oil lamps found do display the symbolic iconography of Christianity (such lamps are common in all contexts) whereas the ceramic and glass tableware recovered near the *sub divo* tombs might also indicate, according to the discoverers, the rite of *refrigerium*, or a meal consumed by the family on the

FIGURE 7   Agrigento. A family *ipogeo* (Caminneci).

tomb of the deceased, who was imagined to be present during the banquet.[24] The remains of *mensae* for the memory of the dead were also found, which also served the purpose of preserving one's social status. Tombs with multiple occupation were also present, accommodating two or three infants, sometimes together with adults.[25] Some *sub divo* burials have also provided data about the age and health of the deceased.[26]

Death and Memory in the Port of Agrigento in Late Antiquity

An important part of the funerary archaeology in late antique Agrigento is the necropolis found in the port district. Thanks to a recent research project, the ancient port, once mentioned in written sources as an Emporion

or Emporeion, has been located at the mouth of the river Akragas, only a few kilometres from the southern walls of the ancient city (see Fig. 3).[27] In this area, today called San Leone, where modern holiday homes are located, the research, although episodic and conditioned by the dense urbanisation, has unearthed some sectors of the necropolis on the river's left bank, dating back to between the 4th and 7th c. AD.[28] While documentation from the first excavations conducted in the last century is missing, and current archaeological access is limited in the busy town, it has proved possible to gain an indication of the location of buildings and cemeteries by mapping the chance discoveries of tombs, walls and artefacts. The most recognisable discovery has been burials in the *enchytrismòs* rite, in which the skeleton is contained in amphorae.[29] The containers used could be more than one, sometimes without the neck or stub, wedged one inside the other or bonded together with a little plaster so as to carefully cover and protect the mortal remains. Other examples used only a "blanket" of fragments in layers, sawing off excess parts, patching cracks with sherds, and closing the mouth of the amphorae, to create an overall casing. These are single burials, except in the case of an ossuary tomb made of several assembled amphorae, which testifies to the existence of exhumation practices and the selection of

24   Aug., *conf.* VI, 2: "… et si multae essent quae illo modo videbantur honorandae memoriae defunctorum, idem ipsum unum, quod ubique poneret, circumferebat … cum suis praesentibus per sorbitiones exiguas partitetur" – "And if there were many oratories of departed saints that ought to be honoured in the same way, she still carried round with her the selfsame cup, to be used everywhere; and this … she would distribute by small sips to those around."

25   As in the case of Tomb 19, where two women in their thirties were buried together with two infants (6 months and 1 year old), and three children who died at the age of 2–3, which coincides with the age of weaning. The remains displayed vitamin-nutritional stress on the teeth (cavities and hypoplasia of the enamel) as well as sideropenic syndromes on the skeletal system (*cribra orbitalia*): Ronco (1995).

26   From a sample of 46 individuals, 13 were under 6 years of age and, of these, 6 were under 1 year old, suggesting that by the age of 5, 30% of the population had died: Ronco (1995).

27   As part of a recent geo-archaeological study, the existence of an internal port basin in antiquity has been proposed as a working hypothesis: Caminneci, Cucchiara and Presti (2016).

28   Caminneci (2014); (2020).

29   Caminneci (2012b).

FIGURE 8   Agrigento-San Leone. *Enchytrismos* burials (Caminneci).

bones (Fig. 8).[30] The chronology of four *enchytrismoi,* found in the Emporion dated to the 5th c. on the basis of the African amphorae reused in the burials, has been confirmed, even if within a wide range, by radiocarbon analysis commissioned by SICTRANSIT project.[31]

Although some have argued that a metaphorical or social interpretation of this burial rite should be excluded,[32] these terracotta containers reveal, in their concern for protecting the dead, a deliberate and attentive level of care. Large fragments of amphora lying under the chin and over the heart, the base of an amphora with its tip positioned between the femurs under the coccyx, or the sherds at the height of the pelvis found in two Agrigentine *enchytrismoi,* could be

manifestations of care for the body of the deceased.[33] The neck of an amphora fixed next to the burial or grafted vertically onto the containers that made up the tomb also suggests a libation rite. Similar devices for the introduction of offerings have been reported in the necropolis of the Catholic University in Milan, in the cemeteries of Isola Sacra at Ostia, in Aquileia, and at *Turris Libisonis* (Porto Torres, Sardinia), where necks of amphorae have been affixed to the tombs capped *alla cappuccina.*[34] Offering libations to the deceased in Early Christian times, documented by various literary sources, is an expression of a cult of the dead that also implies

30   Like the *enchytrismos* of an adult in a secondary burial in the late antique necropolis of Milan: Sannazaro (2001) 71.

31   See Table 1.

32   Costantini (2013) 675.

33   Caminneci (2015a). Augustine, *De cura pro mortuis gerenda,* considered the treatment of the body and the funerary rites superfluous for the dead, but important for the living to prepare mourning, strengthening faith in the afterlife.

34   Boninu, Pandolfi *et al.* (2008) 1792–94; Spalla (2005).

the practice of frequenting the grave after burial.[35] The bottom of the amphora placed on the burial of an infant in a Keay 27 amphora, perhaps served as a *signaculum*, to ensure the visibility of the tomb prescribed by the sacred texts.[36] Other burials of children placed in a lateral position in Keay 27 amphorae have also been found in Tuscany, in the necropolis of St. Victor, and in Sicily, in Messina and Milazzo.[37] At San Leone, a small coarse-ware jug was positioned close to the mouth of the amphora in one burial, while in another *enchytrismòs* an illegible bronze coin (AE5), and a bronze *tintinnabulum* were found amongst the grave goods.[38] Also at San Leone, some small jugs, together with two fibulae of Syracuse and Balgota types, were recovered in the assemblages of 4 tombs made of stone slabs, dating them to the middle of the 7th c. AD.[39]

The practice of burial in amphora is often found in Late Roman contexts and in the vicinity of port facilities, where it was easy to find such containers.[40] The evidence of the *enchytrismòs* necropolis testifies to the availability of African amphorae in the area of the ancient Emporion of Agrigento, which documents the prevalence of African imports over other productions.[41] The Agrigentine *enchytrismoi* reused forms Keay 35 B which came from the workshop of Sidi Zahruni,[42] Keay 27 B, from the Carthage area, together with Keay 36 and its variants (El Mahrine).[43] The Keay 62 R and 62 variant and the Keay 61 form, datable to between the end of the 5th and the 7th c. AD, are attributable to the workshops of Sidi Zahruni and Henchir ek Chekaf. The close link with the workshops active in the area of the Gulf of Hammamet is a constant theme in the late antique and Byzantine sites of western Sicily, which had an almost

exclusive relationship with North Africa.[44] The funerary context of Rue de Malaval in Marseille demonstrates a significant affinity with the evidence from Agrigento, due to the type of reused amphorae, mostly from the area of Nabeul (Tunisia).

Who were the people who lived in the Emporion? In addition to the archaeological evidence from the late antique port, we have a hagiographic text, the *bios* of the Agrigentine Bishop Gregory, written by the monk Leontius around the 8th c. Some elements narrated in the text permit us to recognise the period as consistent with the context of events dating to the 7th c.[45] Gregory's voyages, detailed in their travel times, cross a peaceful Mediterranean Sea from Carthage to Constantinople. Leontius mentions the Emporeion of Agrigento several times as the suburban quarter on the river where ships landed or departed.[46] From the *bios*, the central role of the port of Agrigento in navigation across the sea and along the coast emerges, as well as the direct relationship with North Africa which has already been archaeologically documented.[47] The story tells us of the existence near the emporion of a monastery dedicated to *Theotokos Panymnetos*, equipped with cells, a meeting room and a church, led by a *hegoumenos*.[48] The community that inhabited the port suburb accompanied its Bishop into the city, going up the road along the river in a processional ascent, conducted by Gregory in prayer with his people. The topographical references of the *bios*, as subliminal inputs, stimulate the collective memory, linking venerated figures to places, which are also objects of devotion and pilgrimage destinations.

Burials amongst the Houses

Beginning around the first decades of the 6th c., burials were placed inside the former city of Agrigento, in a way that was similar to those of many other Mediterranean cities of the period. According to research so far, however, burials were not attracted to the public spaces of the ancient city. Only two tombs have ever been found within the area of the ancient agora, which later became the forum of the Roman city, and no burials have been

---

35 See Prud. *Cath.* X, 169–172: "… *et frigida saxa liquido spargemus odore*" – "… and we will sprinkle the cold rocks with liquid perfume." Paolino pours *liquores* in the *foramina* on the tomb of St. Felice (*Patrologia Latina* 61, 594–595). Spera (2005) 25–32.

36 Caminneci and Di Giuseppe (2018). On visible death, Stasolla (2013) 378. An example is Tomb S1 identified near the external wall of the *Porticus Aemilia* near Rome: Contino and D'Alessandro (2014) 328.

37 Costantini (2013) fig. 6 (Tuscany); Bonifay, Roth Congès (2009) 23 (St. Victor in Marseille); Tigano (1997–1998) (Sicily).

38 Tomb III; Caminneci (2012a) 116; On the symbolic value of objects in funerary assemblages and on the persistence of the use of Charon's obole, Papparella (2009) 25–41.

39 The tombs were found a short distance from the mouth of the river in the 1950s.

40 Numerous late antique *enchytrismoi* found near the ports, in Caminneci (2012b).

41 Caminneci (2020).

42 Ghalia, Bonifay and Capelli (2005).

43 Bonifay (2004) 132.

44 These are the results of a recent project about African pottery in Sicily by Malfitana, Bonifay (2016).

45 Motta (2004) 268, 273, n. 352.

46 "ἐν τοῖς μέρεσιν Ἀκραγάντου ἐν τῷ ποταμῷ εἰς τό περίπολιν τό λεγόμενον Ἐμπορεῖον" (A. Berger 1994 *Leontios, Presbyteros von Rom. Das Leben des Heiligen Gregorios von Agrigent*, Berlin, 1989).

47 Caminneci (2015b).

48 There are no archaeological traces of the monastery, but the dedication to the Mother of God is an unequivocal sign of the Byzantine dominion which intended to restore orthodoxy against the Arian religion of the defeated Goths.

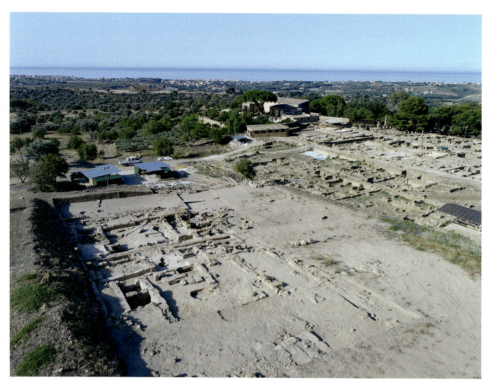

FIGURE 9   Agrigento QER. Insula IV (foreground), with Insula III, II and I beyond (Rizzo).

discovered in the area of the Hellenistic-Roman gymnasium or in that of the ancient theatre, although the latter is still only partially excavated. However, since the 1950s, several groups of tombs have been found in the ancient residential district known as the Quartiere Ellenistico Romano (QER) (Fig. 9). The burials are found in tombs generally located in small groups installed in the rooms of certain of the ancient houses, and often reusing their walls. The tombs are almost all made with slabs of limestone fixed vertically inside the grave dug into the ground and covered with slabs of the same type of stone. In some cases, the cover slab overlaps the crest of the contiguous wall, suggesting that the height of the wall surviving today was the same at the time of the tomb's construction. The graves were dug into the fill of the abandoned rooms of the ancient *domus* in Insula I (Tomb 1, Tomb 8), in Insula II (Tombs 1–6, Fig. 10), in Insula III (Tomb 3), and in the *ambitus* that divided Insula III in an east-west direction (Tomb 8, Fig. 11). Three graves were also found in the pool of the *frigidarium* of a small thermal complex recently investigated in sector B of Insula IV.

The tombs generally have an east-west orientation, with the skull of the deceased to the west, with the exception of cases where the orientation is adapted to the pre-existing walls. In some instances, the position of the legs of those buried, or the discovery of bronze pins, suggest that the deceased was wrapped in a shroud. The arms are usually stretched out along the sides, or in some cases one arm is bent over the pelvis. The tombs

in the QER are all multiple burials, containing a variable number of deceased, the bones of the earliest burials often being displaced in favour of the later, either pushed to one side or put back on top. Thus, it is not easy to establish the order of burial. In some cases, however, the contextual deposition of two or more bodies can be documented (Table 2). Tomb 1/2014 in Insula I contained the remains of 7 individuals, the earliest being a woman accompanied by a 6th c. bottle and a pin (*spillone*) used to fix the hair. She was followed by two male children, a man aged 45–55, a woman aged 45–55, with a small jug (*brocchetta*) of 6th/7th c. date. Also in the tomb were the bones of a neonate and a toy rattle or windchime (*tintinnabulum*) perhaps associated with the two children (Fig. 12).[49] In Insula II, Tomb 2/2013, the earliest deposition consisted of two individuals, an adult male over 40 years of age and a child of about 30 months (Fig. 13). The adult was in a supine position with the skull to the west, his arms at his sides and the left hand on the shoulder of the child, who was also in a supine position between the legs of the adult. The man probably died from a blow to the skull, the only case in which a violent death has been documented. A necklace, made of glass beads and perforated bronze coins, was in all likelihood placed around the neck of the buried child. Another female child followed, and the most recent burial was that of a young woman with a hairpin,

49   Fanelli (2016) 2–3.

FIGURE 10   Agrigento QER. Insula II, House II, Room a1 and h. From left to right: Tomb 5, Tomb 4 and
            Tomb 2/2013 (Rizzo).

TABLE 2   Tombs in each insula at Agrigento-QER with stratified sequences of deposition (latest by stratification uppermost).

Insula I Tomb 1	Individual	Date at 95.4% probability	Insula II Tomb 2	Individual	Date at 95.4% probability	Insula III Tomb 3	Individual	Date at 95.4% probability
102a	Adult		10L	Female, 15–19 years old, articulated, with hairpin, gilt bronze earring, brooch		7a	Adult, 30–40 years old	
106a	Female, 45–55 years old, with small 6th–7th-century jug	560–680 (BN 2)	9L	Female child Also Male 35–40 years old	475–660 (BN24)	8a	Male (or female by DNA), 21–24 years old	775–1005 (BN 6)
110a	Male, 45–55 years old	565–750 (BN1)	11L	Female child [contemporary with 13L]. c. 2.5 years old Necklace of glass beads and perforated coins		9a	Male (or female by DNA), 22–28 years old.	775–1010 (BN28)
104a, 111a	2 male children; also a neonate	595–810 (BN 30) 590–770 (BN 31)	13L	Male, >40 years old	430–635 (BN10)	18a:	Male, 45–55 years old	775–1005 (BN3)
109a	Female adult, with mid-6th-century bottle, bone hairpin	495–660 (BN26)				16a: [unstratified] 17a: 2a:	Female, adult Female, 17–25 years old. unsexed, unstratified	715–990 (BN5) 700–975 (BN4) 670–925 (BN29)

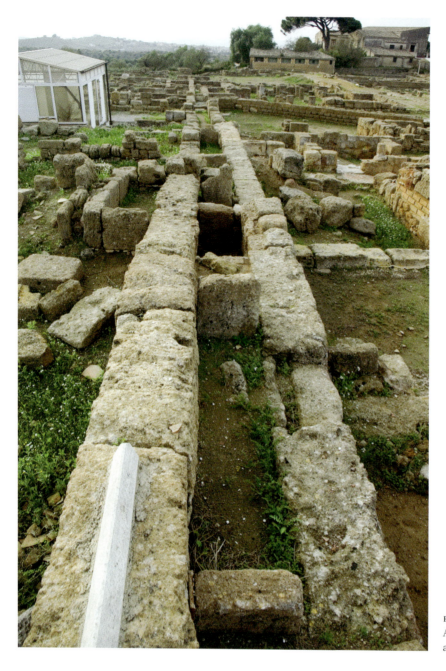

FIGURE 11
Agrigento QER. *Ambitus* between Insula II
and III (Rizzo).

earrings, and brooch.[50] In Insula III, Tomb 3 contained at least 7 individuals in 4 phases of deposition: (1) a male 45–55 years old; (2) a female 17–25 years old; (3) two bodies interred together, both in their late twenties;[51] (4) an adult 30–40 years old. There were unstratified remains from three other unstratified individuals.[52]

Tomb 3B, in the pool of the *frigidarium* in sector B of Insula IV, contained the remains of 4 very young children, the two most recent of whom were placed together. The fill of the tomb contained much lime, perhaps to separate the different burials. Four jugs of similar shape, found inside the tomb, were probably each

related to one of the small burials (Fig. 14). The jugs, thanks to a comparison with similar vessels found in the Byzantine necropolis of San Leone, can be dated to the 7th c.[53] Other burials of children are documented in other sectors of the area; of note is the young age of the deceased and the significant frequency of infants and children generally.

Unlike the circumstances uncovered in the *sub divo* necropolis excavated in the 1980s and 1990s, where almost no objects were found inside the tombs (though external depositions following the celebration of *refrigerium* rites occurred), some burials in QER contained items in the funerary assemblage that were both personal and ritual.

50 Di Giuseppe (2015) 96–98.
51 Both were determined as female by aDNA.
52 Fanelli (2016) 4.

53 Bonacasa Carra (1987) pl. VI, 4.

FIGURE 12
Agrigento QER. Insula I, House IC, Room r,
Tomb 1/2014. (Rizzo).

Personal objects were found in tomb 2/2013 for example, in connection with two different burials: an earring and a ring fibula in gilded bronze, which seem to belong to the same set and must have been worn at the time of burial by the most recently deceased, a young woman. A necklace, made of glass beads and perforated bronze coins, was in all likelihood placed around the neck of the buried child placed on the pelvis of the adult male inside the same tomb. Particularly widespread in the barbarian world, the practice of perforating coins to use them as pendants, with an ornamental and talismanic function, was already known in Roman times[54] and has also been found in Sicily; at least one pierced coin has been found in the so-called Early Christian necropolis of Agrigento. The coins placed in the funerary assemblage, found in some burials, served a ritual function[55] as well as a protecting the deceased. The operculum of

an *Astraea rugosa* seashell, found in the same Insula II, Tomb 2, perhaps originally inserted in a jewel, probably also had a talismanic function.[56] Some of the deceased, especially children, were buried with jugs,[57] vessels that were frequently included in late antique and Early Medieval tombs, which in this context assumed a ritual and symbolic meaning probably connected with water and its purifying value.[58] It was precisely these vessels that offered a first indication of a chronological nature, allowing us to date some of the tombs investigated to a period from the beginning of the 6th to the beginning of the 7th c.

These dates have been endorsed by the radiocarbon analyses commissioned by the York laboratory as part of the SICTRANSIT project, which identified the time of deposition of most of the artefacts accompanying

54   Perassi (2011/2012)
55   Perassi (2001); Duchemin (2012).

56   Fanelli (2016) 355, fig. 3.
57   Di Giuseppe (2015) figs. 30–31; Fanelli (2016) figs. 1–2.
58   Stasolla and Marchetti (2010).

FIGURE 13   Agrigento QER. Insula II, House IIC, Room h, Tomb 2/2013. (Rizzo).

the burials to be in the 6th/7th c. The radiocarbon programme was also able to date directly the original deposition of displaced bone. Among the most important results was that the practice of burying inside the QER, using traditional methods, continued into the 8th and 9th c., that is until the end of the Byzantine period and perhaps even after the Islamic conquest. As can be seen from Table 2, the 5 dates obtained from Tomb 1 in Insula 1 centre in the 6th to 8th c., and in Insula II, Tomb 2, the two dated individuals belong to the 5th to 7th c. In Tomb 3 in Insula 3, the three unstratified individuals were buried after 670, 700, and 715 respectively, and the three later individuals after 775, with a probability of 95.4%. As a group, they can be placed no earlier than the 7th and no later than the 11th c. Near this part of the QER (Insula III), settlement traces of the Early Middle Ages have been contacted in the form of lamps and grooved amphora handles, dateable between the 7th and the 9th c.,[59] and a nearby rectangular building was built on a thick layer of fill covering the most ancient structures and ignoring the alignments of the original urban

plan.[60] Given its proximity to Tomb 3, it is not excluded that the building had a ritual function (Fig. 15).

From the early 6th c., the QER was, thus, radically transformed. The previously inhabited area was reorganised into scattered nuclei in which groups of the rooms of former houses were adapted, some for burial, some for craft and production and some for residence.[61] It was a new way of living, but also a new way of mourning and remembering deceased loved ones, buried near their home, with tombs that were periodically reopened for new depositions. The relationship between the small cemetery areas of the QER and the great Early Christian necropolis on the hill of the temples still remains to be clarified. Although mainly used between the 4th and the 5th c., the necropolis on the hill continued to receive interments until at least the 11th c. (Table 1). It is not entirely clear whether the arrival of burial in the inhabited area near the houses was a result of the large cemetery in the valley being abandoned, or whether the two funerary areas and the two different burial methods coexisted and were used, perhaps, by different social groups.

VC, M-SR.

59   The grooved handles are dated to the 9th c. by Ardizzone (2010) 61.

60   Cirelli (2019) 150.
61   Rizzo (2018).

FIGURE 14
Agrigento QER. Insula IV,
Tomb 3B/2018 (Rizzo).

The SICTRANSIT Project – Agenda and Prospects

The ERC project *Sicily in Transition* is a joint project of the Universities of York, Rome Tor Vergata and Salento at Lecce, aimed at throwing light on the social and economic experience of farmers, merchants, and their families, between the 5th and the 13th c. The study of cemeteries forms one part of this bigger objective and has its own programme intended to appear in a monograph on open access in 2022.[62] The present article is concerned only with burial in the Byzantine/Christian style, and this section intends to provide a backdrop for the outstanding work at Agrigento summarised above and offer some general trends indicated by the other

10 cemeteries that form part of the SICTRANSIT programme. In what follows "Byzantine" is used archaeologically to refer to a range of burial types which have in common the enclosure of the body or bodies in a tomb or grave, cut into rock, made of stone, or lined with stone in the form of slabs or token stone pieces and belonging to periods from the 5th to 8th c. ('early Byzantine') and 9th to 13th c. ('middle Byzantine').[63] The cemeteries concerned are located in the west, centre and east of Sicily in both urban and rural contexts (Fig. 1 and Table 3).

---

62   Carver *et al.* (forthcoming).

63   Correlating with the Early Byzantine (4th–7th c.), 'Dark Age' or Transitional (7th–9th c.) and Middle Byzantine (10th–13th c.) periods used in the larger cultural zone, e.g. Poulou-Papadimitriou *et al.* (2012) 377.

FIGURE 15   Agrigento QER. Insula III, Tomb 3/2014 and adjacent building (Rizzo).

TABLE 3   SICTRANSIT sites with burials of Byzantine type, summarising periods of use as determined by radiocarbon analysis
(The collaboration of the research directors in each case is gratefully acknowledged).

Location	Site	Burials	Date range
Palermo			
Palermo, VG	Via Guardione	At least 60 burials in cemetery	Used between the 6th and 12th century
West			
Contrada Sant'Agata (SA)		Rural cemetery of at least 100 burials	5th–7th century with one outlier of 11th–12th century
San Miceli (SM)	Church	Over 60 burials with church	5th–7th century
Segesta (SGo)	Cemetery o (SG o)	Five tombs	7th–8th century
Centre			
Agrigento (AGC)	Temple ridge	nine tombs sampled (out of many)	4th to 13th century
Agrigento town (QER)	Quartiere Ellenistico-Romano	Insula I/Tomb 1: sixth/seventh century; Insula II/Tomb 3: fifth–sixth century; Insula III/Tomb 3: eighth–ninth century	5th–9th century
Agrigento San Leone (SL)	San Leone	Amphora burials	5th–7th century
Castronovo (CV)	Capelvenere	90 Rock-cut tombs; 15 re-excavated	5th–7th century
Castronovo (CLESP)	On plain next to Casale San Pietro (Int. 4)	Two children's graves	6th–7th century
East			
Catania (SAV1)	Sant'Agata la Vetere, Cemetery 1	Eleven tombs	7th–8th century [not radiocarbon dated]
Catania (SAV2)	Sant'Agata la Vetere, Cemetery 2	Eight tombs	11th–12th century
Mazzarrone (MZZ)		A single rock-cut tomb	7th–9th century
Messina (VM)	Via dei Mille	A single tomb in Isolata 145	7th–8th century

Some of the principles adopted were aired in the introduction. Each cemetery examined has been deemed to be a window on a particular community, and to that purpose the intention is to synthesise the location of the burial ground, its organisation, its burial rites, the physical and molecular properties of those buried, and most essentially the radiocarbon date-span in which each burial took place. The diversity of mortuary practice, overall, is seen as socially and ideologically meaningful, but only when the context is well defined, and the definition requires comparisons not only with contemporary practice in other regions, but in pre-Christian practice in Sicily itself – which is a suitable place to begin.

Before the late antique and Byzantine periods, Sicily had already experienced a millennium of monumental mortuary practice inherited from Punic, Archaic, Classical, Hellenistic and Roman times. Cemeteries excavated on a large scale, for example the Punic cemetery at Caserma Tuköry outside the west gate of Palermo, the battle cemetery (480 BC) of Himera at Termine Imerese, and the long-lived Greek and Roman burial ground of Lilibeo in Marsala show us the prodigious range of subterranean burial chambers and graves at ground level that were built: underground chambers approached by a ramp, *enchytrismoi*, sarcophagi, tile graves *alla cappuccina*.[64] Although these particular examples were of course revealed in the 20th and 21st centuries, it is clear that the burial parties of the Byzantine period would be aware of the types, and more aware than we are of their meaning. At Agrigento, there are cemeteries of the 6th c. BC at Maddalusa and Contrada Pezzino south of the Valley of the Temples, and the late antique *enchytrismoi* and *ipogei* emerged from a background of many centuries of subterranean burial. At Lilibeo, the tombs retained the forms typical of the Punic world for a long period after the Roman conquest.[65] There a Punic *ipogeo* was reworked as a 4th c. catacomb later modified by the insertion of four *arcosoli*. A 6th c. Christian cemetery developed over the former *decumanus maximus* which contained an *enchytrismòs* burial, as well as a matching pair of sarcophagi laid side by side, each carrying Greek Christian inscriptions along the interior long sides, and crosses set in circles on the inside short

walls. These were all painted in red, giving unequivocal declarations of Christian belief.[66]

While Agrigento provides the most exemplary account of this referencing of the past and its development into the first millennium (see above), other Sicilian urban cemeteries also exhibit continuity. At Palermo, an area at the west end of the Cassero, between via del Bosco and vicolo Ballarò, south of the river Kemonia, has been shown to be the site of a series of rock-cut subterranean chambers (*ipogei*) along the rocky right (south) face of the riverbank. The cemetery at San Michele Arcangelo featured two connected chambers, one containing numerous rock-cut and *arcosoli* tombs of the late antique period, and the other, with many rock-cut east-west tombs, took the form of a basilica with an altar at the east end. Medieval re-use of the tombs was dated by pottery from the mid-10th to the 11th c.[67] At SS Crispino e Crispiniano, a little further south, was an extensive open (*sub divo*) cemetery, part of which was excavated in 2009. Three phases were defined: a residential street running north to south dating to the 10th c., followed by a cemetery of stone-lined, slab-lidded single occupation east-west tombs dated by pottery from the end of the 10th to the first half of the 11th c. The occupants were laid supine with hands crossed, and some were accompanied by finger-rings and earrings. A third phase, dating from the end of the 12th to the start of the 13th c. featured numerous burials in broad communal graves buried side by side with heads to the west; one contained 19 individuals.[68]

The tally of these late graves has been augmented by recent rescue work. Discovered in 2018 in via Guardione, Palermo, during the construction of the tramway at Piazza Tredici Vittime, was a cemetery of Byzantine type about 400m² in extent containing some100 skeletons in around 60 tombs.[69] It is likely that these formed part of an Early Christian burial ground covering an extensive area outside the northern wall of the fortified city. In 1863, a Byzantine cemetery had been encountered under the Palazzo Saponara in neighbouring via Cavour, and an inscribed stone was found (now in the Salinas Museum) which featured the epitaph of Pietro Alessandrino (i.e. Peter of Alexandria), a linen merchant who died on 22 January 602. Other undated burials have been discovered at various times between via Cavour and the Piazza Tredici Vittime, some of which may have

64 Di Stefano (2002) 553–65; (2009); Spatafora (2010c–d); Spatafora (2014); Vassallo and Valentino (2012); Lonoce *et al.* (2018); Giglio (2016).
65 Giglio (2016) 111–12: '*Le tombe lilibetane, infatti, continuano a conservare le forme tipiche del mondo punico per un lungo periodo successivo alla conquista romana*' – 'The Lilibetan tombs, in fact, continued to preserve the typical forms of the Punic world for a long period after the Roman conquest.'
66 Giglio (2007) figs. 6–14; Giglio (2016) 108–109, fig. 9.
67 Ardizzone and Pezzini (2014) 287–89; Spatafora *et al.* (2020) 345–49, fig. 2.
68 Spatafora *et al.* (2020) 350–58.
69 *La Repubblica* (Archivio La Repubblica.it 22 March 2018).

been Muslim.[70] Six samples from the newly discovered tombs have been dated by radiocarbon, placing these individuals in the Early Byzantine to Norman periods (7th to 13th c.), suggesting that the Christian cemetery was used through the period of Islamic governance.

Still in Palermo, a later phase of burial was encountered south of the town along the Corso dei Mille during rescue excavations in advance of the installation of a tramway in 2013–2015.[71] Thirty burials were recorded within 4 out of 16 or more archaeological test areas, stratified above an Islamic period workshop producing knives with horn handles and dated to the 9th to 11th c.[72] In area 134/144, there were 17 supine burials all in wooden coffins (deduced from the presence of nails) in an area of c. 50m.2[73] In Area 126 (12m²), there were three supine burials, two in wooden coffins placed in graves lined with stone slabs, some with traces of plaster, and covered by pitched roofs alla cappucina. In Area 120, contained within an area of c. 15m², there was a row of 4 burials with the body laid on the right side and the head facing south-east, following the Muslim rite, and (further east) a group of 6 supine burials. There was no indication of a stratigraphic order between the rites. Twenty out of the 30 burials have been examined anthropologically and determined as 6 children, two adult females and 9 adult males.[74] Radiocarbon dating has determined that the individuals in Area 134/144 were buried between the 12th and the 14th c. and those in Area 120 between the early 13th and the 15th c. The supine burials are ostensibly Christian but not necessarily so: the excavator has proposed that they may have been Jewish.[75]

In the countryside, the principal Early Byzantine cemeteries sampled by the SICTRANSIT project are at Contrada Sant'Agata (5th/6th c.) and at the church of San Miceli (5th–7th c.), both excavated on a large scale. Contrada Sant'Agata lies in the area of the Piana degli Albanesi, 30 km south-west of Palermo.[76] Field survey revealed the presence of adjacent settlements dating from the Hellenistic to the Late Medieval periods, covering about 4 hectares south-east of the cemetery. The pottery included African imports of the 6th c. and Roman Forum Ware of the 9th c. The cemetery explored

(Sector A) consisted of 250+ stone-lined tombs disposed on the steep southern and eastern slope of the Mandra Sant'Agata. The more northerly are oriented north-south, while those in the south-east quarter are oriented west-east. The north- south tombs are arranged in at least 7 east-west rows of c. 15 tombs, which include both adults and children. For this reason, they are probably to be interpreted as family rows. The tombs are rectangular or trapezoidal and dug into the chalky rock. They were generally covered with a monolithic slab of this stone, on top of which was a heap of mortared stones, which may have originally been a plastered tomba a cupa, a barrel-shaped roof – a type of monument also known in the Mediterranean especially in North Africa.[77] The plan shows that the north/south tombs were in the majority. The east-west tombs appear to have been added on the east side. If there are few obvious examples of burials cutting each other, this could be because the north/south tombs were clearly visible by virtue of their mortared stone grave-markers. Eight out of the 10 radiocarbon-dated individuals are placed in the 5th to early 7th c., one in the 7th–8th was in the east-west group, while the tenth was dated 1050–1255 at 95.4% confidence, more than three centuries later. Although identified by chance, it does indicate a later medieval use of the cemetery.

The large cemetery at San Miceli was associated with an extant church, which is situated on a south-facing hillside in the district of Salemi (TP). It is located on the southern stretch of the Via Valeria from Palermo, at a point where it turned westward to Marsala. San Miceli was probably the site of an Archaic temple, followed by a Roman villa which was in decline and abandoned in the early 3rd c. AD. The villa was followed by a large agricultural town ('agritown'), probably the ad Olivam of the Antonine Itinerary, where amphorae remained in use until the 7th c. Originally a building of the 4th c., the church was demolished and rebuilt in the 6th c. and abandoned in the mid-7th c. The church, together with 58 associated tombs, was originally excavated in 1893 by A. Salinas. The Late Roman tombs took the form of rectangular graves cut into bedrock, with stone linings and covered with large limestone slabs. The majority were oriented east-west with the skull to the west, like the apse. They typically contained one skeleton, more rarely two, and grave goods included hoop earrings, rings, necklaces, buckles, glass and ceramic containers.

Recent excavations from 2013 onwards conducted by Andrews University (USA), have revealed more tombs.[78] Three stone-lined tombs were excavated, each covered

70   Di Stefano (1989) 601, 603; Arcifa et al. (1989) 336.
71   Directed by Giuseppina Battaglia to whom I am indebted. Battaglia et al. (2018a).
72   Battaglia et al. (2018b).
73   Indicated by iron nails: Battaglia et al. (2018a) fig. 7.
74   Battaglia et al. (2018a).
75   Battaglia et al. (2018a). In 1170, the Jewish traveller Benjamin of Tudela reported at least 1,500 Jewish families living in Palermo.
76   Greco et al. (1991) fig. 1.

77   Greco et al. (1991) 163, fig. 7
78   Lesnes and Younker (2016); (2018).

with limestone slabs, two situated at the entry to the nave on the east side (Tomb 1 and 2), while a third (Tomb 4) was found at the north-west corner of the north nave. Tomb 1 contained a woman and a man, and Tomb 2 two male adults.[79] The woman in Tomb 1 had silver loop earrings with pendants. A ceramic jug, a finger-ring and a coin were also found in this tomb. Tomb 2 had no grave goods, but there was a fragment of a necklace in the backfill. In the tomb of the female burial in the north nave near the front of the church (Tomb 4) were two silver loop earrings with more elaborate dangles. Two shallow graves were also found in the north aisle. One (F17) contained the remains of two very young children (2–3 years old) and the other (F28) the disturbed remains of an adult woman. The fills of both included tesserae, sometimes with mortar still attached, originating from mosaic A, showing that they were dug through the final floor of the church. These are interpreted as hasty burials made by survivors not long after a final episode of destruction.[80]

Burial at the major Greek and Roman monumental centre of Segesta took place from the 6th to the 13th c. at three separate sites: Byzantine, Islamic and Swabian. Five Byzantine tombs were found in the late antique agora/forum, three of the inhumations were located in the walkway in the south sector of the cryptoporticus (site code SAS4) and another two about 30 m to the south-west (SAS3) on the disused paved access road to the cryptoporticus which rose in a series of large steps.[81] SAS3 Tomb 1, that of a man, was oriented north-west/south-east with its north-west end against the wall bordering the paved road. The other three sides were formed of slabs of stone laid against the cut, and 4 horizontal slabs, probably reused, covered the grave. The occupant was laid supine with hands across the pelvis and the head turned towards the west. There were no grave goods. SAS3 Tomb 2 was located about 2 m to the south of Tomb 1 on the third step of the paved road. It was 0.43 m wide, but its full length was not determined. Here too the dug grave was lined with stone slabs placed vertically against the cut, and 4 horizontal slabs were employed as a cover. These had probably served previously as door jambs or thresholds. The occupant was a woman who had been laid on her back directly on the surface of the road, with the head turned towards the west. Here too there were no grave goods.[82] Both

SAS3 Tombs 1 and 2 returned remarkably late radiocarbon dates, after 690 and after 715.

The Islamic occupation at Segesta was noted for its hilltop village and adjacent mosque, with a cemetery in the Muslim rite situated nearby along the upper rim of the Greek theatre. It counted 75 graves, a group of 13 stratified beneath a larger group of 62. The graves were often coffined and stone-lined and lidded with stone slabs, some with grave goods in the Byzantine manner, although the bodies lay on their right side with the faces turned to the south or south-east in accordance with Islamic practice.[83] The children's tombs were covered by semi-circular roof tiles (*kalipter*). Of the 8 radiocarbon-dated individuals, the earliest must date before 970 and the latest after 1170. The Muslim presence ended before 1275 in all cases but one.

A Norman (Latin Christian) presence was imposed at Segesta's Monte Barbaro from the end of the 12th c., with a castle, an expanded settlement area, a church and a cemetery.[84] The church was built on a terrace below the castle and its cemetery developed on its west side cutting through the remains of Muslim period buildings. The church was oriented with the apse to the south-east. The tombs, oriented east-west, were stone-lined and stone-lidded, and hosted multiple occupancy in the Byzantine style. Of the 16 dated individuals, the earliest date to before 1200 and the latest after 1250, most burials belonging to the 13th c. A similar situation occurred at the former Greek city of Monte Iato where excavators encountered a cemetery of Christian graves of single occupation. There was also a neighbouring and contemporary Muslim cemetery on the rim of the Greek theatre in the 12th to 13th c.

At Castronovo di Sicilia in the centre of the island were the undated remains of *arcosoli* cut into a south-facing rock-face at Capelvenere on top of which was a cemetery of c. 90 rock-cut graves arranged in 5 groups with a variety of orientations. A single bone surviving *in situ* from previous clearance of the tombs returned a radiocarbon date of 415–540. On the plain below, an isolated pair of small stone-lined graves was discovered within an extensive area of late antique occupation. They contained two children less than two years old and some neonates. One of the children, suffering from scurvy, gave a radiocarbon date of 570–750, and was accompanied by a *brochetta* (small jug) marked on each side with a scratched cross.[85]

SICTRANSIT is studying 5 cemeteries in the east of Sicily, of which three date to the broader Byzantine

79   Lesnes and Younker (2016) 97; Di Salvo (2016).
80   Lesnes and Younker (2016) 98–99; (2018).
81   Serra (2010) 23; Facella (2013) 297–99; Fabbri and Farina (2010).
82   Serra (2010) 23–24.

83   Di Salvo (2004) 403. This can also be inferred from the plans.
84   Firmata *et al.* (1995) 626–31.
85   Carver *et al.* (Forthcoming).

period. At Sant'Agata La Vetere in Catania there were two cemeteries, one following the other, both classifiable as Byzantine. The earliest (Cemetery 1) is a group of 11 stone-lined and lidded tombs, stratified above Late Roman strata and beneath a layer of dumping that contained material no later than the 9th c.; the cemetery can, therefore, be securely dated between the 6th and the 9th c. Each of the tombs was occupied by a single person, except Tomb I which had two persons. Here Individual A was laid on the side with the face turned to the north while Individual B was on the back with the arms crossed over the chest (*incrociati*). The occupants of Tombs II, IV,V and VI also had the arms crossed over the chest (with the arms forming a V); while those of Tombs III, VI, VIII, IX, X, and XI had the arms folded (*conserte*; i.e. with the arms parallel).[86] This cemetery has been seen as a burial area *ad sanctos* in recognition of Sant'Agata's incarceration on the spot, although the so-called prison itself has produced no evidence for the Early Christian or Early Medieval periods.[87] The later of the two cemeteries (Cemetery 2) consisted of 8 tombs with stone linings bonded with a coarse mortar containing fragments of bone and ceramics. These tombs, dated to the 10th–12th c. by associated pottery and radiocarbon determinations, had already been disturbed on rediscovery and had lost most of their covering of slabs or tiles. Together the two cemeteries represent an urban narrative of continuous Christian burial from the 6th to the 12th c., save for a hiatus during the 9th.[88]

A single tomb was sampled in Messina. Discovered during excavations in the via dei Mille (isolato 145, Tomb A) on the remains of an obliterated Roman house, it was oriented north-west/south-east and strongly, if irregularly, built of stones, brick and tile bonded with mortar and finished internally with a thin layer of plaster. It contained a mass of scrambled bone deriving from 9 adults and a small 7th c. amphora found at one corner. Two individuals were radiocarbon-dated to 689–940 and 670–885, thus deposited after the late 7th c.[89]

Another single rock cut tomb showed that there were high investment family tombs in the countryside at an even later date. It was discovered by a hunting party near Botteghelle in Contrada da Grassura in Mazzarone (CT) and studied by archaeologists from the Soprintendenza and University of Catania in 2012.[90] The tomb had been

cut into tufa with a level base and ledges to support the slab covers. Inside were the remains of 11 individuals, and the order of deposition was deduced to have begun with disarticulated burials accompanied by three pitchers of the 5th/6th c., followed by an adult radiocarbon-dated to775–990 with two finger-rings, a second adult dated 725–990 with a mid-7th c. belt buckle, and 5 disarticulated subadults. These were covered by a layer of soil 10 cm thick on top of which was deposited an adult dated 720–990, the tibia in contact with a grooved handle dated to the 8th/9th c., a child 6–7 years old dated 725–1020, and finally an adult with a blade wound dated 740–995.[91] All the adults were under 35 and their dates suggest that they died within a short space of time and perhaps even as a result of a single traumatic event.

A final vivid example is provided by the free-standing tomb excavated by Roger Wilson beneath wind-blown sand in a room (Room 5) within House 6 at Punta Secca, Kaukana. Dating to the first half of the 7th c., the tomb and its immediate surroundings provided strong evidence of periodic feasting, including a hole in the plaster lid, probably for pouring libations.[92] The occupant was a woman aged 20–25, placed in the tomb with a child some 3–5 years old, shown by aDNA to be consanguineous. The woman had suffered a depression in the skull in life, interpreted as likely to have resulted in seizures and it was suggested that she manifested special powers. There was an incised cross on one of the grave slabs and the room featured artefacts with Christian insignia as well as objects connected to eating and drinking. The inscribed symbol on the lid mixed prehistoric with Christian references.[93] This example invites us to return to the matters raised in the introduction (above). While the expectation is that the tomb was allied to the Christian church, the archaeological evidence suggests that there is a corpus of significant anterior beliefs that vary with locality, deserving of further investigation.

MOHC

Discussion

The sampled cemeteries we have are diverse in their location, tomb type, levels of investment and date range, something probably best explained as due to the

---

86   Arcifa (2010) 357; Patané, Calì and Tanasi (2010) 340.

87   Arcifa *et al.* (2016) 38–39.

88   Biomolecular analysis is in progress.

89   Bacci (2001) 9–18.

90   Turco *et al.* (2013).

91   Arezzo *et al.* (2016) 50–51.

92   Wilson (2011); (2017).

93   Wilson (2017) 25–30. The symbol comprised a Greek inscription with 'holy, holy, holy' written backwards within a 'magical design' deriving from the Bronze Age (p. 26).

diversity of communities practising ostensibly Christian burial rites over the 7 centuries examined, the 6th to 13th centuries. The classical high-investment forms of burial – the *ipogei, arcosoli, enchytrismoi* – inherited from the deep Punic, Archaic, Classical and Hellenistic past, survive into the first millennium AD, as exemplified at Agrigento and Lilibeo. The creation of the *Basilica of the Apostles* inside the Greek Temple of Concordia in the 6th c. at Agrigento was probably a turning point, after which middle-investment stone-built stand-alone multiple burial family tombs colonised the QER, continuing until at least the 9th c., while the low-investment rock-cut graves on the Temple ridge continued until at least the 11th c. This sequence is reflected outside Agrigento. High-end *ipogei* and *arcosoli* were in use in Lilibeo, and have been located in Palermo by the river Kemonia, as well as in large numbers in the east. These monuments seem to represent a traditional ideology, succeeded in Lilibeo for example by 6th c. tombs in which the Christian affiliations were clear. At Contrada Sant'Agata, the single and multiple occupation north/south stone-lined tombs belonged to the 5th to early 7th c., with a later group of east-west tombs (one dated 7th–8th c.) perhaps marking a conversion or alignment to Christianity. After this, the stone built multi-occupant family tombs continued in use in the east at Messina and Mazzarone, spanning dates from the late 7th and late 8th centuries respectively. Although these multiple tombs are generally assumed to be those of an extended family, there are examples, such as Mazzarrone, where the occupants may have been thrown together by other events. Graves cut into earth and lined with loose stones with a greater or lesser formality appear to be the later medieval inheritors of the local tradition, both in Islamic cemeteries (at Segesta) and among those Christians assigned by radiocarbon to the Norman and Swabian periods (at Segesta, Monte Iato, and other hill-top sites). The Byzantine 'thread' thus continued to run in Sicily over the period of the 6th to the 13th c., and notably throughout the period of Islamic governance.

If a strong inheritance bearing on medieval Sicilian mortuary practice was provided by the Greek past, potent influence came also from contemporary neighbours: broadly Rome, Byzantium and North Africa. The North African link is visible in burials at San Leone, Contrada Sant'Agata, the *arcosoli* at Palermo, and the mosaics and church at San Miceli. As for the example of Punta Secca, it reminds us of the value of high precision examination of each burial to discover its affiliations and anomalies. Given a continuing brisk rate of investigation and publication, it should soon be possible to begin mapping social, biological and even ideological trends by locality and century in medieval Sicily. Early signs are that this will be a patchwork of differing expressions, each allowing us a privileged insight into the aspirations and anxieties of ordinary people released at a moment of high emotion.

Acknowledgements

As PI of the SICTRANSIT project I would like to offer my warm thanks to my co-authors and to the archaeologists, excavators and scholars who have provided documentation and samples for the cemeteries discussed in this paper.

Bibliography

Alfano A. (2006–2007) *Necropoli tardoantiche e Bizantine nel territorio della Provincia di Palermo* (Tesi di Laura, Università degli studi di Palermo) (Palermo 2006–2007).

Arcifa L., Di Stefano C. A., de Floris M. H., and Pesez J.-M. (1989) "Lo scavo archeologico di Castello S. Pietro a Palermo", *BCA Sicilia* 6–8 (1989) 30–41.

Arcifa L. (2010) "Da Agata al Liotru. La costruzione dell'identità urbana nell'altomedievo", in *Tra Lava e Mare. Contributo all' all'archaiologhia di Catania*, edd. M. G. Branciforti and V. La Rosa (Catania 2010) 355–86.

Arcifa L., Lanza G., Mussumeci G. and Trapani F. (2016) "Il Sacro Carcere di S. Agata a Catania. Analisi architettonica e trasformazioni urbanistiche", in *Architetture del Mediterraneo. Scritti in onore di Francesco Tomasello* (Thiasos Monografie 6), edd. N. Bonacasa, F. Buscemi, V. La Rosa, and F. Tomasello (Rome 2016) 35–64.

Ardizzone F. (2010) "Nuove ipotesi a partire dalla rilettura dei dati archeologici: la Sicilia occidentale", in *La Sicile de Byzance à l'Islam*, edd. A. Nef and V. Prigent (Paris 2010) 51–76.

Ariès Ph. (1980) *L'uomo e la morte dal medioevo a oggi.* (Rome/Bari 1980).

Arezzo C., Calabrese A., Ferlito F., Lisi S., Turco M., and Turco Me. (2016) "Nuove riflessioni sulla tomba altomedievale di Mazzarrone", in *Dopo l'Antico Ricerche di archeologia medievale*, edd. L. Arcifa and L. Maniscalco (Palermo 2016) 47–52.

Bacci G. M. (2001) "Isolato 145 via dei Mille", in *Da Zancle a Messina II. Un percorso archeologico attraverso gli scavi*, edd. G. M. Bacci and G. Tigano (Messina 2001) 9–22.

Battaglia G., La Mantia M., Miccichè R. and Riolo L. (2018a) *A Norman Age Necropolis with a Mixed Ritual in Palermo* (Palermo 2018a).

Battaglia G., Riolo L. and Aniceti V. (2018b) "Produzioni artigianali nella Palermo Islamica", in *La Città che produce. Archeologia della produzione negli spazi urbani*, edd. V. Caminneci, M. C. Parello, and M. S. Rizzo (Bari 2018b) 91–97.

Bonifay M. (2004) *Etudes sur la céramique romaine tardive d'Afrique* (BAR-IS 1301) (Oxford 2004).

Bonifay M. and Roth Congès A. (2009) "Les sépultures en amphores du cimetière de Saint-Victor", in *Saint-Victor de Marseille. Études archéologiques et historiques, Actes du colloque de Saint-Victor, Marseille, 18–20 novembre 2004*, edd. M. Fixot and J. P. Pelletier (Turnhout 2009) 17–24.

Bonifay M., Capelli C., and Moliner M. (2011) "Amphores africaines de la Rue Malaval à Marseille", in *SFECAG, Actes du Congrès d'Arles, 2–5 juin 2011* (Marseille 2011) 235–54.

Boninu A. and Pandolfi A. (2008) "Colonia Iulia Turris Libisonis. Dagli scavi archeologici alla composizione urbanistica", in *L'Africa romana: Le ricchezze dell'Africa: risorse, produzioni, scambi, Atti del XVII Convegno di studio, Sevilla 14–17 dicembre 2006* (Rome 2008) 1777–1818.

Caminneci V. (2012a) "Enchytrismos. Seppellire in vaso nell'antica Agrigento", in *Parce sepulto. Il rito e la morte tra passato e presente*, ed. V. Caminneci (Palermo 2012) 111–32.

Caminneci V. (2012b) ""Animam sepulcro condimus"; sepolcreto tardoantico in anfore presso l'Emporion di Agrigento (Sicilia, Italia)", in *Rei Cretariae Romanae Fautorum Acta, 27th Congress of the Rei Cretariae Romanae Fautores, Belgrade 19–26 September 2010* (Bonn 2012) 259–66.

Caminneci V. (2014) "Alla foce dell'Akragas. Storia e archeologia dell'Emporion di Agrigento", in *Le opere e i giorni. Lavoro, produzione e commercio tra passato e presente*, ed. V. Caminneci (Palermo 2014) 151–80.

Caminneci V. (2015a) "'Carnem suam quisque naturaliter diligit' (August. de cura pro mortuis, 7,9). La cura dei corpi in una necropoli tardo antica dell'Emporion di Agrigento", in *VII Congresso Nazionale di Archeologia Medievale, Lecce 2015*, edd. P. Arthur and M. Leo Imperiale (Florence 2015) 50–54.

Caminneci V. (2015b) "Sulle sponde del Mediterraneo. Il porto di Agrigentum in età tardo antica e bizantina", in *Isole e terraferma nel primo Cristianesimo. Identità locale ed interscambi culturali, religiosi e produttivi, Atti XI Congresso Nazionale Archeologia Cristiana, Cagliari 23–27 settembre 2014*, edd. R. Martorelli, A. Piras, and P. G. Spanu (Cagliari 2015) 481–90.

Caminneci V., Cucchiara V., and Presti G. (2016) ""Εἰς τό περί πόλιν τό λεγόμενον Ἐμπόριον" (*PG* 98, col. 581). Nuove ipotesi sulla topografia dell'Emporion di Agrigentum", in *Paesaggi urbani tardo antichi, Atti delle VIII Giornate Gregoriane, Agrigento, 29–30 novembre 2014*, edd. M. C. Parello and M. S. Rizzo (Bari 2016) 63–75.

Caminneci V. (2020) "Sepolture tardoantiche e bizantine nell'Emporion di Agrigento", in *From Polis to Madina, La trasformazione delle città siciliane tra Tardoantico e Alto Medioevo*, edd. L. Arcifa and M. R. Sgarlata (Bari 2020) 285–95.

Caminneci V. and Di Giuseppe Z. (2019) "Sepoltura in anfora di infans dall'Emporion di Agrigento", in *Una favola breve. Archeologia e antropologia per la storia dell'infanzia*, ed. C. Lambrugo (Florence 2019) 109–115.

Caminneci V., Parello M. C., and Rizzo M. S. (2020) ""*Hic corpus reparans mentemque relaxans*" (Anth. 119R): Le terme dell'Insula IV del Quartiere Ellenistico-Romano di Agrigento", in *Le forme dell'acqua. Approvvigionamento, raccolta e smaltimento nella città antica. Atti delle XII Giornate Gregoriane*, edd. V. Caminneci, M. C. Parello, and M. S. Rizzo (Rome 2020) 185–97.

Carra R. M. and Ardizzone F. edd. (2007) *Agrigento dal tardoantico al medioevo. Campagne di scavo nell'area della necropoli paleocristiana. Anni 1986–1999* (Todi 2007).

Carra Bonacasa R. M. (1987) *Agrigento paleocristiana. Zona archeologica e Antiquarium* (Palermo 1987).

Carra Bonacasa R. M. (1995) *La necropoli paleocristiana* sub divo *di Agrigento* (Roma 1995).

Carra Bonacasa R. M., Falzone, G., Schirò, G., Vitale, E., and Sanna, E. (2015) "Le aree funerarie fra isole e terraferma: esempii dalla Sicilia e dalla Sardegna", in *Isole e terraferma nel primo cristianesimo. Identità locale ed interscambi culturali, religiosi e produttivi (Atti XI Congressi Nazionale di Archeologia Cristiana)*, edd. R. Martorelli, A. Piras, and P. G. Spanu (Cagliari 2015) 135–80.

Carver M. O. H (2000) "Burial as poetry: the context of treasure in Anglo-Saxon graves", in *Treasure in the Medieval West*, ed. E. Tyler (York 2000) 25–48.

Carver M. O. H (2001) "Why that, why there, why then? The politics of early medieval monumentality", in *Image and Power in Early Medieval British Archaeology. Essays in Honour of Rosemary Cramp*, edd. A. Macgregor and H. Hamerow (Oxford 2001) 1–22.

Carver M. O. H. (2002) "Marriages of true minds: archaeology with texts", in *Archaeology: The Widening Debate*, edd. B. Cunliffe, W. Davies, and C. Renfrew (Oxford 2002) 465–96.

Carver M. O. H. (2019) *Formative Britain. An Archaeology of Britain, Fifth to Eleventh century AD* (London and New York 2019).

Carver M. O. H. et al. (forthcoming). *Remembering the Dead in Medieval Sicily: A Multi-disciplinary Study* (SICTRANSIT Monograph 3) (Florence forthcoming).

Cerchiai L. (2018) "Società dei vivi, comunità dei morti: qualche anno dopo," *Annali di Archeologia e Storia antica* 25 (2018) 151–58.

Cirelli E. (2018) "I materiali di età tardo-antica e alto-medievale", in *Agrigento I: nuove ricerche nell'insula III del quartiere ellenistico-romano (2016–2017)*, edd. G. Lepore *et al.* (2018) www.fastionline.org/docs/FOLDER-it-2018-405.

Cirelli E. (2019) "La fase tardoantica e medievale. I materiali e le strutture", in *Agrigento I. Quartiere Ellenistico-Romano: Insula III. Relazione degli scavi e delle ricerche 2016–2018* edd. G. Lepore *et al.* (Rome 2019) 153–59.

Contino A. and D'Alessandro L. (2014) "Materiali ceramici dagli scavi della Porticus Aemilia (Testaccio, Roma). Campagne di scavo 2011–2012", *Rei Cretariae Romanae Fautorum Acta* 43 (2014) 323–34.

Costantini A. (2013) "Il reimpiego delle anfore tardoantiche considerazioni sulle sepolture ad enchytrismòs" in Toscana, *Archeologia Classica*, 64 (2013) 657–75.

D'Agostino B. (1985) "Società dei vivi, comunità dei morti: un rapporto difficile", *Dialoghi di Archeologia* 3.3.1 (1985) 47–58.

De Miro E. (2009) *Agrigento. L'abitato antico. Il Quartiere ellenistico-romano* (Rome 2009).

De Santis P. (2015) "Riti practiche funerarie nel processo di costruzione di una memoria identitaria: esempi da Sardegna e Sicilia", in *Isole e terraferma nel primo Cristianesimo. Identità locale ed interscambi culturali, religiosi e produttivi (Atti XI Congressi Nazionale di Archeologia Cristiana)*, edd. R. Martorelli, A. Piras, and P. G. Spanu (Cagliari 2015) 203–20.

Di Giuseppe Z. (2015) "Le tombe del Quartiere Ellenistico Romano, campagna di scavo 2013", in *Agrigento Romana. Scavi e Ricerche nel Quartiere Ellenistico Romano. Campagna 2013*, edd. M. C. Parello and M. S. Rizzo (Caltanissetta 2015) 89–110.

Di Salvo R. (2004) "I Musulmani della Sicilia Occidentale. Aspetti antropologici e paleopatologici", *MÉFRM* 116-1 (2004) 389–408.

Di Salvo R. (2016) "La necropoli paleocristiana di San Miceli: aspetti antropologici e paleopatologici", *SicArch* 108 (2016) 235–40.

Di Stefano C. A. (1989) "Castello San Pietro", *Kokalos* 34.2 (1989) 595–606.

Duchemin J.-P. (2012) "Numismatique et archéologie du rituel: réflexion sur le rite dit de l'« obole à Charon » à partir de l'exemple de la nécropole tardo-antique de Nempont-Saint-Firmin (Pas-de-Calais, France)", *Journal of Archaeological Numismatics* 2 (2012) 127–98.

Fabbri P. F. (1995) "Scavo e studio antropologico delle sepolture medievali del SAS2", in *Segesta. Parco archeologico e relazioni preliminari delle campagne di scavo 199–1993, Annali della Scuola Normale Superiore di Pisa* 25 (1995) 632–56.

Fabbri P. F. and Farina L. (2010) "Note antropologiche su alcune sepolture tardoantiche (SAS 3&4) 2007–08", *Annali della Scuola Normale Superiore di Pisa* 5.2/2 (2010) 21–25.

Facella A. (2013) "Nuove acquisizioni su Segesta tardoantica", *Annali della Scuola Normale Superiore di Pisa* 5.1/1 (2013) 285–318.

Fanelli R. (2016) "Il Quartiere Ellenistico-Romano tra Tardoantico e Altomedioevo: le indagini archeoantropologiche del 2014", in *Paesaggi urbani tardo antichi. Casi a confronto, VIII Giornate Gregoriane, Agrigento, 29–30 novembre 2014*, edd. M. C. Parello and M. S. Rizzo (Bari 2016) 353–58.

Février P. A. (1977) "A propos du repas funéraire : culte et sociabilité," *Cahiers Archéologiques* 26 (1977) 29–45.

Ghalia T., Bonifay M., and Capelli C. (2005) "L'atelier de Sidi-Zahruni: mise en évidence d'une production d'amphores de l'Antiquité tardive sur le territoire de la cité de Neapolis (Nabeul, Tunisie)", in *LRCW 1, Late Roman Coarse Wares, Cooking Wares and Amphorae in the Mediterranean: Archaeology and Archaeometry* (BAR-IS 1340), edd. J. Ma. Gurt i Esparraguera, J. Buxeda i Garrigós, and M. A. Cau Ontiveros (Oxford 2005) 495–508.

Giglio R. (2007) "La cristianizzazione di Lilibeo attraverso le recenti scoperte archeologiche", in *La Cristianizzazione in Italia tra tardoantico e altomedioevo*, edd. R. M. Bonacasa Carra and E. Vitale (Palermo 2007) 1779–1813.

Giglio R. (2016) "La Necropoli di Lilibeo alla luce delle ultime scoperte", in *Se cerchi la tua strada verso Itaca … Omaggio a Lina Di Stefano*, edd. E. Lattanzi and R. Spadea (Rome 2016) 101–114.

Giglio R. and Canzonieri E. (2009) "Nuovi dati dalle necropoli ellenistiche e tardo antiche di Lilibeo", in *Immagine e immagini della Sicilia e di altre isole del Mediterraneo antico, Vol II*, ed. C. Ampolo (Pisa 2009) 573–80.

Giglio R., Palazzo P., Vecchio P., and Canzonieri E. (2012) "Lilibeo (Marsala). Risultati della campagna 2008", in *Sicilia occidentale. Studi, rassegne, ricerche*, ed. C. Ampolo (Pisa 2012) 225–37.

Greco C., Mammina G., and Di Salvo R. (1991) "Necropoli tardoromana in Contrada S. Agata (Piana degli Albanesi)", in *Di terra in terra: nuove scoperte archeologiche nella provincia di Palermo*, ed. C. A. Di Stefano (Palermo 1991) 161–88.

Lesnes E. and Younker R. W. (2016) "Verso una nuova storia di San Miceli (Salemi TP) Risultati preliminari delle campagne di scavo 2014–2015", *SicArch* 108 (2016) 1–257.

Lesnes E. and Younker R. W. (2018) *'Quod vult deus': L'inizio della Cristianità a San Miceli (Catalogo della Mostra, Museo di Salemi* (Berrien Springs 2018).

Lonoce N., Palma M., Viva S., Valentino M., Vassallo S., and Fabbri P. F. (2018) "The western (Buonfornello) necropolis (7th to 5th BC) of the Greek colony of Himera (Sicily, Italy): Site-specific discriminant functions for sex determination in the common burials resulting from the battle of Himera (ca. 480 BC)", *International Journal of Osteoarchaeology* 28 (2018) 766–74.

Malfitana D. and Bonifay M. (2016) *La ceramica africana nella Sicilia Romana / La céramique africaine dans la Sicile romaine* (Catania 2016).

Marchetta I. (2016) "Gli oggetti in tomba e il loro significato simbolico alcuni esempi da necropoli lucane di V–VII secolo", in *Territorio, insediamenti e necropoli fra tarda antichità e alto medioevo. Atti del Convegno internazionale di studi. Cimitile-Santa Maria Capua Vetere, 19–20 giugno 2014*, edd. C. Ebanista and M. Rotili (Naples 2016) 387–411.

Mercurelli C. (1948) "Agrigento paleocristiana", in *Memorie. AttiPontAcc* III.8 (1948) 1–105.

Motta D. (2004) *Percorsi dell'agiografia. Società e cultura nella Sicilia tardoantica e bizantina* (Catania 2004).

Papparella F. C. (2009) *Calabria e Basilicata: l'archeologia funeraria dal IV al VII secolo* (Reggio 2009).

Parello M. C. and Rizzo M. S. (2016) "Agrigento tardoantica e bizantina: nuovi dati dal quartiere residenziale e dalle aree pubbliche", in *Paesaggi urbani tardo antichi. Casi a confronto, VIII Giornate Gregoriane, Agrigento, 29–30 novembre 2014*, edd. M. C. Parello and M. S. Rizzo (Bari 2016) 51–62.

Patané A., Calì D., and Tanasi D. (2010) "Indagini archeologiche a Sant'Agata la Vetere e Sant'Agata al Carcere", in *Tra lava e mare: contributi all'Archaiologhia di Catania: atti del convegno*, edd. M. Branciforti and V. La Rosa (Catania 2010) 337–54.

Perassi C. (2001) "Le monete della necropoli: osservazioni sul rituale funerario", in *Ricerche archeologiche nei cortili dell'Università Cattolica. La necropoli tardoantica* (Milano) 101–114.

Perassi C. (2011/2012) "Monete romane forate. Qualche riflessione su «un grand thème européen» (J.-P. Callu)", *Aevum* 85 (2011/2012) 257–315.

Piepoli L. (2008) "Sepolture urbane nell'Apulia tardo antica e altomedievale. Il caso di Herdonia", in *Ordona XI. Ricerche archeologiche a Herdonia*, edd. G. Volpe and D. Leone (Bari 2008) 579–94.

Pinna A., Sfligiotti P., and Firmati M. (1995) "Segesta. Lo Scavo del Area 2000 (SAS2", *Annali della Scuola Normale Superiore di Pisa* 25 (1995) 614–31.

Poulou-Papadimitriou, N., Tzavella E., and Ott J. (2012) "Burial practices in Byzantine Greece: archaeological evidence and methodological problems for its interpretation", in *Rome, Constantinople and Newly-Converted Europe. Archaeological and Historical Evidence* Vol. 1, edd. M. Salamon, M. Wołoszyn, A. Musin, P. Špehar, M. Hardt, M. P. Kruk, and A. Sulikowska-Gąska (Leipzig and Warsaw 2012) 377–428.

Rizzo M. S. (2018) "Dopo le terme: spazi abitativi e impianti produttivi nell'Insula IV del quartiere residenziale di Agrigento alla fine dell'antichità," in *La città che produce. Archeologia della produzione negli spazi urbani* (Atti delle X Giornate Gregoriane), edd. V. Caminneci, M. C. Parello, and M. S. Rizzo (Bari 2018) 99–105.

Ronco D. (1995) "Studio antropologico del materiale scheletrico", in *La necropoli paleocristiana sub divo di Agrigento*, ed. R. M. Bonacasa Carra (Rome 1995) 328–56.

Sannazaro M. (2001) *La necropoli tardoantica. Ricerche archeologiche nei cortili dell'Università Cattolica* (Milan 2001).

Serra A. (2010) "Area del criptoportico e sepolture tardoantiche (SAS3 & 4; 2007–08)", *Annali della Scuola Normale Superiore di Pisa* 5.2/2 (2010) 20–24.

Spalla E. (2005) "Strutture per libagioni nella ritualità funeraria romana: i dati archeologici", in *La Signora del sarcofago. Una sepoltura di rango nella necropoli dell'Università Cattolica*, edd M. P. Rossignani, M. Sannazaro, and G. Le Grottaglie (Milan 2005) 47–54.

Spatafora F. (2010a) "La Necropoli di *Panormos*", in *L'ultima città: rituali e spazi funebri nella Sicilia nord-occidentale di età arcaica e classica*, edd. F. Spatafora and S. Vassallo (Palermo 2010) 31–40.

Spatafora F (2010b) "Ritualità e simbolismo nella necropoli punica di Palermo", in *Atti della Giornata di Studi in onore di Antonella Spanò*, ed. R. Dolce (Palermo 2010) 23–39.

Spatafora F. and Vassallo S. (2010) *L'ultima città: rituali e spazi funebri nella Sicilia nord-occidentale di età arcaica e classica* (Palermo 2010).

Spatafora F., Canzionieri E. and Cavallaro N. (2020) "Palermo tra tarda antichità e età normanna: nuovi dati di topografia urbana", in *From Polis to Madina. La trasformazione delle città siciliane tra Tardoantico e Alto Medioevo*, edd. L. Arcifa and M. Sgarlata (Bari 2020) 343–61.

Spera L. (2005) "Riti funerari e "culto dei morti" nella tarda antichità: un quadro archeologico dai cimiteri paleocristiani di Roma", *Augustinianum* 45 (2005) 5–34.

Stasolla F. M. and Marchetti M. I. (2010) "Ceramiche dai contesti funerari tardoantichi ed altomedievali: aspetti simbolici e formali", in *LRCW3 Late Roman Coarse Wares, Cooking Wares and Amphorae in the Mediterranean. Archaeology and Archaeometry. Comparison between Western and Eastern Mediterranean* (BAR-IS 2185) (Oxford 2010) 131–38.

Stasolla F. R. (2013) "Vescovi e rituali funerari: quadro normativo e realtà archeologica", in *Atti del XV Congresso internazionale di archeologia cristiana, Toledo, 8–12 settembre 2008* (Vatican City 2013) 373–79.

Tigano G. (1997–1998) "Messina. Interventi di scavo lungo la via C. Battisti; Milazzo. Scavi e ricerche tra il 1994 e il 1997", *Kokalos* 43–44 (1997–1998) 487–506; 513–45.

Turco M., Arezzo C., Calabrese A., Ferlito F., Lisi S. and Turco Me. (2013) "Dal recupero di emergenza al dato scientifico: lo scavo della tomba alto-medievale di Mazzarrone (CT)", in *Ollus leto datus est. Architettura, topografia e rituali funerari nelle necropoli dell'Italia meridionale e della Sicilia fra antichità e medioevo*, edd. S. Bonomi and C. Malacrino (Reggio 2013).

Vassallo S. and Valentino M. (2012) "Scavi nella necropoli occidentale di Himera, il paesaggio e le tipologie funerarie", in *Sicilia occidentale. Studi, rassegne, ricerche,* ed. C. Ampolo (Pisa 2012) 49–58.

Vitale L. (2015) "Lo spazio degli infanti nei cimiteri tardoantichi: organizzazione e distribuzione spaziale fra ritualità e consuetudini sociali", in *Isole e terraferma nel primo cristianesimo. Identità locale ed interscambi culturali, religiosi e produttivi, Atti XI Congresso Nazionale di Archeologia* *Cristiana, Cagliari, 23–27 settembre 2014,* edd R. Martorelli, A. Piras, and P. G. Spanu (Cagliari 2015) 197–202.

Wilson R. J. A. (2011) "Funerary feasting in Early Byzantine Sicily: new evidence from Kaukana", *AJA* 115 (2011) 263–302.

Wilson R. J. A (2017) "Dining with the dead in Early Byzantine Sicily" (*Eleventh Babesch Byvanck Lecture*; http://www.babesch.org/downloads/BABESCH_Byvanck_Lecture_2017_Wilson.pdf).

Late Roman Burials in Slovenia

Kaja Stemberger

Abstract

The chapter examines the state of research on Late Roman cemeteries in Slovenia. Dated between the late 3rd and the 6th c., Slovenian Late Antiquity coincides with the Langobardic movement from Pannonia into Italy and with the Slavic settlement in modern Slovenian territory. Accordingly, the Late Antique period is typically studied with the Early Middle Ages in Slovenian scholarship, that is to say, separate from both Roman and Classical archaeology. The chapter summarises the research on Late Roman burials in Slovenia published until 2018, and discusses some of the persisting theoretical issues.

Introduction

My specialisation is in Roman mortuary archaeology, and Late Antiquity is just outside my expertise. This paper, written in 2018, is therefore based on existing overviews, predominantly on the work of Slavko Ciglenečki.[1] For context and clarity, a brief discussion of certain aspects of the Slovenian archaeological tradition is provided below. In Slovenia, the study of Late Antiquity is usually associated with the Early Middle Ages. It is, however, generally separated from both Roman and Classical archaeology; the latter is concerned mostly with the art and architecture of the Greek and Roman period, while the former focuses on all other aspects of the Roman period. Somewhat confusingly, Late Antiquity is sometimes referred to in Slovenian archaeology as 'the Early Middle Ages' (*zgodnji srednji vek*), 'the Late Roman period' (*pozna rimska doba*), 'the Great Migration period' (*čas preseljevanja ljudstev*), or 'the Early Byzantine period' (*zgodnje bizantinsko obdobje*). According to Ciglenečki's chronology,[2] Slovenian Late Antiquity starts between the reigns of Diocletian and Constantine and finishes at the end of the 6th c. This partially overlaps with the abandonment of hill fort settlements, the movement of Langobardic tribes from Pannonia to Italy, and the period of Slavic settlement, which begins in the late 6th c. and continues into the 7th c. Despite this general chronological delimitation, the term 'Late Antiquity' can be justifiably used for the urban settlements along the Adriatic coast which persisted into the 7th c., accompanied by African and Eastern imports, at locations including present-day Koper, Piran, Sveti Jurij, and others.[3]

It is worth noting that such terminology regarding the period of Late Antiquity was discussed by Irena Mirnik Prezelj,[4] who criticised among other things the atomistic treatment of the material along ethnic or cultural lines common in Slovenian archaeology – e.g. focusing only on the Langobardic material as though it existed in isolation from Roman traditions. She also criticised the associated practice of applying broad and generalised 'interpretations' to the material using temporal and ethnic descriptors such as 'late antique', 'native', 'Slavic', and 'Early Medieval'.[5] Her work was in turn criticised for being too "western-oriented" and "ignoring the important contributions and established practices of continental scholarship",[6] such as Alexander Demandt's *Die Spätantike. Römische geschichte von Diocletian bis Justinian.* However, I find her argument that the natural development of the Late Roman period cannot be understood and studied without taking into consideration the various ethnic groups cohabiting with the Roman population in the area at the time reasonable. The conception of identity in the Roman period in Slovenian archaeology is still strongly tied to and sometimes simply conflated with ethnicity (and not only for the Late Roman period). The problem with this concept is that it not only excludes other important factors such as profession, social class, age, gender, and language from the discussions of identity,[7] but that it is based on an overly deterministic and indeed binary understanding of ethnicity,[8] which is itself often conflated with other discrete aspects of identity. In the case of Late Antiquity, the binary 'Roman' vs. 'non-Roman' is frequently assumed to correspond with 'Christian' vs. 'non-Christian'. The issues raised by Mirnik Prezelj regarding the study of the Late Roman period in Slovenia[9] echo the theoretical considerations that pertain to the study of the entirety of Roman Slovenia. For example, crude pottery is automatically attributed exclusively to the pre-Roman

---

1 Ciglenečki (1997); (1999a).
2 Ciglenečki (1999a) 289.
3 Vidrih Perko (2005); Vidrih Perko and Župančič (2005).
4 Mirnik Prezelj (1998).
5 Mirnik Prezelj (1998) 370.
6 Ciglenečki (2007).
7 Mattingly (2010) 285.
8 Stemberger (2018) 40.
9 Mirnik Prezelj (1998).

© KONINKLIJKE BRILL BV, LEIDEN, 2024 | DOI:10.1163/9789004687974_011
Alexandra Dolea and Luke Lavan (eds) *Burial and Memorial in Late Antiquity* (Late Antique Archaeology 13) (Leiden 2024), pp. 752–763

occupants of the territory of modern Slovenia, and in much the same way only high-quality pottery is ascribed to the so-called 'Romans'. The rather straightforward proposition that, since it remained in use throughout the entire Roman period, crude pottery likely served as a locally-specific form of cooking vessels, has not been explored.

The Late Roman period was defined by Ciglenečki in his overview of Late Roman settlements in Slovenia as falling roughly between AD 300 and 476.[10] In my discussion of Slovenian Late Antiquity, I will focus on Late Roman culture and will not address Langobardic and Hunnic material. I will, however, address slightly earlier Roman material where this is relevant to the discussion of the Late Roman period in Slovenia. In addition to the problems that stem from equating material culture with ethnicity, I would like to emphasise that the burial sphere is a specific context in which the identity of the deceased is negotiated, proverbially not by the dead themselves, but by the people who outlived them.[11] According to post-processual theories, the assortment of grave goods is not a random collection of items. It is a carefully chosen arrangement that expresses something about the deceased, but does not necessarily correspond exactly to who and what the individual was while alive, nor does it necessarily reflect how the deceased perceived themselves.

History of Research

The concept of Late Antiquity in Slovenia was first mentioned and briefly discussed by Balduin Saria, Jože Kastelic, Jaroslav Šašel, and Peter Petru,[12] but only in the 1970s was the term introduced properly into Slovenian archaeology to denote a separate historical period. The rise in late antique interest was closely linked to the exploration of the *Claustra Alpium Iuliarum*,[13] which to this day is among the most thoroughly researched remains from the period. Two forts, Hrušica and Ajdovski gradec[14] were studied in the context of an international collaboration, which lent importance to the concept of Slovenian Late Antiquity. A subsequent series of colloquia on the Early Middle Ages served to cement the theoretical importance of the period.[15]

The development of the notion of Late Antiquity coincides with one of the most productive phases of Slovene archaeology, the Yugoslav period. Just after the Second World War, Slovenia became one of the 6 federal republics of Socialist Yugoslavia. Although culture was to a significant degree instrumentalised by politics, heritage studies were one of the exceptions since they were linked to pre-Yugoslav institutions[16] and were concerned with eras which were not a priority for the new system; a fortunate circumstance for the study of Late Antiquity.[17] Since, however, it was politically more favourable to study Late Antiquity in conjunction with the Early Medieval period and Slavic studies rather than with the Roman period, no clear continuity in the interpretations between the Roman period and Late Antiquity was achieved. This distinction has been maintained ever since almost solely due to inertia, especially in recent decades.

Although the Second World War had left many top institutions facing a shortage of experts, the post-war period was characterised by a massively positive development, namely pan-Yugoslav archaeological congresses, which resulted in a well-organised, regular, and systematic output of publications, and a plan for engaging with the general public.[18] From this period originates the majority of plans, finished and unfinished, for the publication of cemeteries and other Roman sites. A major drawback of the archaeological agenda of the time is that it heavily prioritised research related to Slavic settlement of the Western Balkans. After Slovenia gained its independence in 1991, the Yugoslav research and publication plan continued to be followed for a few years, and the last attempt to unify research output was made in 1999 by Ciglenečki in the form of systematic overviews for each research period.[19] Even at the time, the problems with late antique and more specifically Late Roman cemeteries were highlighted. Especially for the Late Roman period, the need to have a systematic overview of the cemeteries, which were poorly researched in comparison with the much larger scope of data on the settlements, was obvious.[20]

In the last three decades since Slovenia has become independent, a few publications did attempt to provide broader, if not comprehensive overviews. First and foremost, there is Ciglenečki's massive compilation

10   Ciglenečki (1997) 191.
11   Parker Pearson (2003).
12   Saria (1939) 142–48; Kastelic (1964–1965); Šašel (1975a) and Petru (1964–1965) 90–92.
13   Šašel and Petru (1971)
14   Petru and Ulbert (1975); Ulbert (1981).
15   Ciglenečki (1999a).
16   In spite of the fact that the majority of museums as well as the Institute of Archaeology were formally established only after the war; for further details: see Plestenjak (2013).
17   Plestenjak (2013); Stemberger (2018) 30–32.
18   E.g. Plestenjak (2013).
19   Ciglenečki (1999a).
20   Ciglenečki (1997).

of Slovenian late antique archaeology.[21] Rok Ratej compiled a well-written overview of burial manner in Slovenia between the 5th and 11th c. in the form of an MA thesis, covering the shape of grave pits, orientation of the skeletons with additional emphasis on arm placement, and planning of the cemeteries, with brief comments on grave goods as well.[22] Another MA thesis discussing social structures on the basis of late antique cemeteries was written by Kaja Pavletič.[23] Noteworthy is also the history of Slovenian and neighbouring lands covering the period from the military emperors to the end of the 7th c. by Rajko Bratož.[24]

Burials and the State of Research

There exists a solid body of bibliography on the subject of Late Antiquity in Slovenian archaeology, the most prominent work being the aforementioned 1999 overview by Ciglenečki. Besides settlements and material culture, this overview also contains a section on burials. Ciglenečki separated the cemeteries of the period into two categories according to his chronology based on the patterns of settlement.[25] During the discussed period, the Roman Empire and consequently the territory of modern Slovenia underwent several changes. The outset of Late Antiquity sees the dynamics of the period marked by the Tetrarchy and Diocletian's reforms. As a consequence of the renewed stability, major Roman settlements in modern Slovenia flourished for the last time in the 4th c. (e.g. *Colonia Traiana Ulpia Poetovio, Colonia Iulia Emona, Municipium Claudia Celeia, Municipium Flavium Latobicorum Neviodunum*). After that, there was a short period when the settlements were still being used, but by the first half of the 5th c., they were fading fast, seeing only perhaps short-term occupation. During this decline in the population, the residential areas of the settlements were shrinking, and in some cases (e.g. *Colonia Traiana Ulpia Poetovio*) burials can be found in abandoned parts of the towns.[26] The 'Roman' inhabitants of the cities either relocated to hill forts or further away. Bratož's historical research also shows that indigenous Christian communities persisted into 8th c.[27]

The cemeteries from the early phase, which includes the 4th and the first half of the 5th c., are relatively well

documented. Usually, they belonged to settlements that had been continuously inhabited, but because the population had declined significantly, residential parts were being used as burial grounds in Late Antiquity. The most prominent examples of this practice are the cemeteries of Poetovio (modern Ptuj),[28] Carnium (modern Kranj),[29] the numerous sites associated with Emona (modern Ljubljana),[30] and to a lesser degree Celeia (modern Celje).[31] Several smaller settlements also had adjunct cemeteries, such as Colatio (modern Slovenj Gradec).[32] Finally, the Late Roman cemetery at Kapucinski vrt near Koper is frequently referenced by Slovenian scholars,[33] but it is unfortunately not yet published.

Based on a handful of well-furnished graves, it seems that the cemeteries were internally divided along cultural or ethnic lines: Germanic burials for example were separated from 'Roman' ones.[34] This early phase is also characterised by the appearance of hill forts such as Brinjeva Gora,[35] Javorniki,[36] and Ajdovski gradec[37] and their respective cemeteries. The second phase, from the 5th until the end of the 6th c., is also relatively well known since there are at least two systematic overviews of the period. Davorin Vuga's work focuses on cemeteries in the Sava valley related to the migration period.[38] Bierbrauer on the other hand concentrates on the north-western part of the country.[39] The most notable cemeteries of the second phase are Rifnik,[40] at which different cultural groups were recorded; Bled, a large Late Roman cemetery[41] for which osteological analyses were done;[42] Tinje nad Loko pri Žusmu, notable for its child burials;[43] Tonovcov grad, a settlement near Kobarid with several sacral objects and a cemetery which continued in use

---

21 Ciglenečki (1999a).
22 Ratej (2015).
23 Pavletič (2018).
24 Bratož (2014).
25 Ciglenečki (1999a) 295–98.
26 Klemenc (1950); Curk (1978); Ciglenečki (1993); (1997).
27 Bratož (1996).

28 Ciglenečki (1999a); Jevremov, Tomanič Jevremov and Ciglenečki (1993); Curk (1966); Tušek (1997); Korošec (1999); Vomer-Gojkovič and Tušek (1997).
29 Stare (1980); Sagadin (1987).
30 Plesničar Gec (1972); Petru (1972); Vuga (1985); Korošec (1951); Miškec *et al.* (2020).
31 Ratej (2018).
32 Pleterski and Beljak (2002).
33 E.g. Žerjal and Vidrih Perko (2017).
34 Ciglenečki (1999a) 295.
35 Pahič (1969).
36 ANSL (1975) 152.
37 Bachran (1975).
38 Vuga (1980).
39 Bierbrauer (1984) 52–58.
40 Bolta (1971); Vičič (1990).
41 Kastelic (1960); Pleterski (2008); (2014); the settlement layers of Bled are not preserved as they were presumably built over during the construction of Bled castle, but next to the Late Roman cemetery, a later Slavic cemetery was found.
42 Leben-Seljak (1996).
43 Ciglenečki (1992).

into the Middle Ages;[44] and the recently excavated Vrajk near Gorenji Mokronog,[45] for which osteological analyses were also done.[46] Other cemeteries from the period are relatively small, such as Ajdna nad Potoki[47] and Črnomelj.[48] Finally, there is Podloka, which, similar to Kapucinski vrt, is often referred to but not yet published.

Most Late Roman sites in Slovenia belong broadly to one of two types. The first are the already mentioned burials associated with large settlements like Carnium, Emona, and Poetovio. Emona in particular, with its large numbers (over 450) of recently excavated, but unpublished graves, shows that inhumations are usually further away from the roads and aligned in rows,[49] a practice observed also at other cemeteries such as Rifnik.[50] At smaller cemeteries, inhumations sometimes appear in clusters. The second type comprises several hill-fort cemeteries with an overall smaller number of burials. According to Ciglenečki,[51] the second group is composed of smaller cemeteries[52] and mound burials.[53]

Burial Manner and Grave Goods

The predominant burial form in Slovenian Late Antiquity appears to have been single inhumation, typically oriented in the direction from west to east.[54] As noted by Ratej,[55] the majority of single inhumations were stretched out and lying on their backs. The arms were positioned either next to the body or on the chest.[56] Crouched burials are rarer and are sometimes referred to as Hocker burials. Ratej argues, based on several parallels from Pannonia, that such burials were reserved for the lower classes.[57] Based on the drawings included in the major catalogues,[58] it is sometimes impossible to predict whether the person was buried with or without a shroud and whether or not wooden coffins were present. The former was indisputably present only at the site

of Kranj-Lajh,[59] where threads of fabrics were found covering entire skeletons.[60] The latter are mainly documented with illustrations of nails, which in some cases visibly form the outline of a wooden box, but in other cases their pattern is less telling. In recent excavations, more attention was paid to documenting the remains of potential wooden objects. Exceptional are stone chests as inhumation containers, which are, regardless of their decoration, called sarcophagi (*sarkofag*) in Slovenian. They are, however, distinguished from stone chests (*kamnita skrinja*) used as containers for urns or pyre remains and usually pre-date inhumations. Other forms of burials are extremely rare. At Emona, which I am the most familiar with, only a handful of double burials and three *a cappuccina* burials were found among the several thousand graves in total from the cemetery that spanned almost 5 centuries. Inhumations in wooden boxes or coffins were present at Poetovio as well; their number is not clear from the publications.[61] Multiple inhumations also exist but are much rarer. At Emona, there are 9 cases of double and 2 cases of triple inhumations.[62] Multiple bodies were deposited in the same grave at the same time at Celeia as well.[63]

Osteological analyses were not consistently carried out and/or published for most excavations (with early exceptions such as analyses of the bone remains from the cemetery of Vranje pri Sevnici by Orožen-Adamič *et al.*).[64] Therefore, potential patterns of bone manipulation and pathology cannot be observed systematically. The large volume of publications produced mostly in the 1970s and 1980s included a great deal of material that was excavated much earlier,[65] precluding in many cases an osteological assessment. In certain examples, outstanding finds were recorded as curiosities (e.g. skull burials at Emona) during these older excavations, but details (e.g. cut marks, presence of mandibula etc.) were omitted. Specific observations, however, can be made. Body manipulation, more precisely disembodiment, was observed at at least two sites, Gorenje Vrhpolje and Roje pri Moravčah, according to Ciglenečki.[66] From *Colonia Iulia Emona*, there are also three graves,

---

44   Modrijan and Milavec (2011) 18.
45   Bavec (2003).
46   Leben-Seljak (2003).
47   Bitenc and Knific (2001).
48   Manson (1998).
49   E.g. Mulh (2008).
50   Bolta (1981).
51   Ciglenečki (1997) 167.
52   E.g. Pahič (1969); Petru and Šribar (1956); Stare (1952); Zavrtalnik (1984).
53   Pahič (1972).
54   Ratej (2015) 88.
55   Ratej (2015).
56   Stemberger (2018) ch. 3; Ratej (2015); (2018) 20.
57   Ratej (2018) 22.
58   E.g. Plesničar Gec (1972); Petru (1972).

59   For this multi-period site, results from different excavations were collated and synthesised into several partial interpretations of ethnicity, status, sex/gender, and age of the deceased from Late Antiquity: Knific (1995); (2005); Knific and Lux (2010), summarised by Pavletič (2018) 14.
60   Stare (1980) 15; Ratej (2015) 33.
61   Istenič (1999) 50; Ferk (1890) 25.
62   Stemberger (2018) ch. 3.
63   Ratej (2018) 23–25.
64   Orožen-Adamič *et al.* (1975).
65   E.g. Petru (1972); Istenič (1999).
66   Ciglenečki (1999a) 297.

published only in a preliminary report, where stones were inserted into the head cavities.[67] A trend of secondary burials also existed in this time period, illustrated by the 21 human skulls buried in what seemed to be a coffin in Celeia.[68] To a lesser degree, similar practices were noted at Ajdovski gradec[69] and Ptuj-Zgornji Breg.[70] In terms of pathology, various sites yielded several deformed skulls, which have been argued by Marijan Slabe to be related to the Germanic population.[71] In general, more osteological reports have been published in the last 30 years.[72]

Tombstones from Late Antiquity are also rare. It is typical for the Slovenian territory that tombstones were displaced or reused in later centuries. This applies to tombstones from the entire Roman period, not only from Late Antiquity. The most prominent example is that of Gaudentius from Celeia, supposedly from the 6th c., but as with other late tombstones, the dating is uncertain and potentially too narrow. The research on funerary rituals is mostly limited to comparisons between the 1st and 2nd c. AD and the rest of antiquity. The general observations are that after the shift to Christianity in the 3rd c., the number of grave goods declined, a phenomenon that is usually attributed to Christianity. Other elements that are studied are comparisons with the newcomers, usually associated with a noticeably Germanic material culture.

Material culture is one of the foremost interests of Slovenian archaeology, regardless of period. The most prominent feature of Late Antiquity are elements of costume and jewellery, although they are sometimes perceived as an 'impoverished version' of 1st and 2nd c. AD material in terms of artistic expression and forms, possibly also due to the comparatively elaborate contemporary Germanic artefacts. The main item of personal adornment found in Late Roman burials are brooches, which come in several forms. The most recognisable are crossbow brooches and animal shapes, frequently interpreted as having a Christian connotation. Other typical items are bracelets, simple earrings (multi-faced, ornamented with crosses, dots, lines), and hairpins with multi-faced heads. An important element of clothing are simple belt buckles, which developed into complex and large forms in the second half of the 6th c., presumably under Byzantine influence.[73]

The rest of late antique material culture mainly consists of crude cookware, coins, and occasionally combs in the graves. The interpretational level of material studies focusses either on using certain types of items to determine aspects of identity or on using a dataset to indicate which item types could be associated with certain aspects of identity.[74] In contrast, interpretations of cemeteries as a whole are mainly limited to determining the gender of the deceased (usually based on dress) and occasionally their age. A recent study of osteological remains in connection with grave goods[75] has confirmed previous observations that infant and child burials are underrepresented across Slovenian sites. Furthermore, it has shown that female graves tend to be better furnished than male graves, a phenomenon that has been noted already on the basis of grave goods.[76]

There are several studies of material culture, of which some include the funerary material as well, but publications covering the material remains from the graves in their own right, such as that by Maja Pogačnik on military belts from the graves of Noricum and Pannonia,[77] are rare. More commonly, Late Roman material culture is discussed in the context of broader studies such as the comprehensive glass artefact overview by Irena Lazar,[78] or various pottery[79] and metal studies.[80] A separate study by Saša Čaval focusses on late antique stylus-type pins.[81] There are too many general studies of small finds in Slovenia to provide a full account here, but Ciglenečki's work can serve for further investigation on the topic.[82]

The strong emphasis on material culture observable in Slovenian archaeology is firmly rooted in the predominance of cultural-historical paradigms that pervade the Slovenian archaeological research of all time periods, although they are most pronounced in prehistoric research. Nonetheless, a gradual shift away from prioritising artefacts to the exclusion of most other data and information has been observable since around the year 2000. A slowly growing number of scholars are pointing out that the 'traditional' interpretations derived exclusively from material culture are becoming increasingly

---

67   Tomažinčič (2011).
68   Ratej (2018) 26.
69   Bachran (1975).
70   Curk (1966) 56.
71   Slabe (1980).
72   E.g. Leben Seljak (1996); (2003); (2018); Miškec *et al.* (2020).
73   Ciglenečki (2007).

74   E.g. Pogačnik (2007).
75   Pavletič (2018).
76   E.g. Stemberger (2020).
77   Pogačnik (2007).
78   Lazar (2003).
79   Petru (1969); Mikl Curk (1972); (1973); Vidrih Perko and Župančič (2005); Vidrih Perko and Žbona Trkman (2005); Vidrih Perko (2005); Gaspari *et al.* (2007); Žerjal and Vidrih Perko (2017).
80   Ibler (1991).
81   Čaval (2013).
82   Ciglenečki (1999a); (2007).

irreconcilable with modern theoretical approaches in archaeology.

There are also several studies that aim to overcome this entrenched methodology in practice, such as Mikl Curk's 1997 paper that discusses the drawbacks of the 'traditional' approach. It aimed to interpret the religious affiliation and, partly, social standing of the deceased by including typically overlooked data such as traces of perishable items and body position. More recent examples are the studies of late antique grave goods in combination with anthropological remains[83] and burial manner.[84] Such works connect different categories of data in order to extract a more comprehensive account of the material. The case study of a military belt burial from Emona[85] shows how different aspects of the identity of the deceased can be more fruitfully addressed through a combination of osteology and material culture.

Problems of the Research

In addition to the general lack of up-to-date publications, there are at least two major issues with Late Roman burials that need to be addressed and further discussed. The first one is the common generalisation by which inhumation graves without artefacts are attributed to the spread of Christianity. The discussed period was influenced by an important new social dynamic – a shift in the perception of the religion. It went from imperial persecution under Diocletian, to legalisation by the Edict of Milan, and then to faith of the imperial family within the first decades of the 4th c.[86] The presence of Christianity in Slovenia is highlighted by the finds of churches in the cities like Poetovio,[87] Emona,[88] Celeia,[89] Neviodunum, Carnium,[90] and Aegida,[91] as well as in hill fort settlements.[92] However, apart from the overall shift to inhumation, there is precious little direct and unambiguous evidence to support the interpretation

of graves without artefacts as 'Christian'.[93] For example, at Colonia Iulia Emona, an early *intra muros* Christian centre is documented,[94] but of the up-to-date published graves, only one contains any item clearly related to Christianity: a round silver-alloy mirror depicting 4 crosses.[95]

That is not to say that no grave lacking religious grave goods should be considered an early Christian burial, but rather that, conversely, the lack of grave goods by itself cannot suffice for such an interpretation. Automatically assuming that all the deceased from inhumation graves were Christians is a methodological fallacy. Cremation graves without artefacts from the 1st and 2nd c. AD, for example, are usually explained as having been damaged during excavation, poorly documented,[96] or indeed unfurnished, likely due to the social standing of the deceased. Inhumations, however, are attributed to the 3rd c. or later since they are believed to have been a Christian funerary practice.[97] Thus, similar phenomena are interpreted from two different aspects, one religious and the other social, but the two are applied separately depending on the assumed context.[98]

Modern publications continue to attribute inhumations to the Christian tradition,[99] even though a small proportion of inhumation graves demonstrably predate the spread of Christianity.[100] For many, if not most inhumations, it is in fact impossible to even determine a date, much less associate them with a particular religion, in part precisely because their grave goods are few and not particularly revealing. This is based mostly on the fact that the number of overall grave goods in Emona's graves declines in the 3rd c.,[101] the explanation for which is sought by circular argument in Christianity, where food, drink, and furnishing are not necessary provisions for the afterlife. Now, similarly 'unfurnished' inhumations would be interpreted as a result of religious expression.[102] A practice that could signal connection of the deceased to Christianity is the placement of one glass beaker per grave, interpreted by Slovenian researchers along the lines of the Eucharist.[103]

83   Pavletič (2018).
84   Ratej (2018).
85   Tomažinčič (2018).
86   Ciglenečki (1999b).
87   E.g. Tušek (1982); Horvat (2003) 159; Bratož (2013).
88   Plesničar Gec (1973); Plesničar Gec *et al.* (1983) and Plesničar Gec (1999).
89   Bratož (2013); Lazar (2003).
90   Sagadin (1991).
91   Knific (1991) 12.
92   For about 20 different locations: see Ciglenečki (1987) and Knific (1991); for more information: see Knific (1991) 11–32; Bratož (1996).

93   First noted by Iva Mikl Curk as early as 1997, and later again by Stemberger (2018) and Županek (2018).
94   Plesničar Gec (1999).
95   Petru (1972) 65, T.46.6.
96   Early excavations sometimes did not offer more data than a grave number, e.g. Petru (1972).
97   E.g. Plesničar Gec (1967) 145.
98   Stemberger Flegar (2020a).
99   E.g. Gaspari (2014); (2010); Plesničar Gec (1977) 66–68.
100 Stemberger (2018) ch. 3.
101 Stemberger (2018) app. D.
102 E.g. Plesničar Gec (1972).
103 E.g. Gaspari (2014).

However, there are also certain examples of graves that do not fit into the narrative of the deceased being buried without grave goods as a form of religious expression. Some of the very richly furnished female graves[104] and at least one military-related grave,[105] all late inhumations, seem to continue Roman funerary traditions where the grave goods were chosen for their significance to either the deceased or, more likely, the mourners. Moreover, seemingly empty graves cannot simply be interpreted as 'humble'. Many objects such as expensive fabrics and any other items made of organic materials would simply not be preserved. Burials now seen as 'without artefacts' could therefore have conveyed much more information at the time of burial than they do now, as dress alone could communicate social standing beside the visible gender and age of the deceased.

Directly related to the 'lack of artefacts' phenomenon is the underrepresentation of graves from the 3rd c.[106] This was noted during some older excavations at Emona.[107] One of the reasons for this might also be that the local crude pottery is sorely understudied and as such cannot be used for dating graves. Chronologies for graves from the 1st and 2nd c. AD are normally based on imports, especially on thin-walled cups and beakers, and of course on terra sigillata. Even though both the new (not yet fully published) and recently published excavations[108] include significant numbers of late burials, they will likely not change the overall picture.[109] One of the explanations for this underrepresentation is that many graves preliminarily dated to the 4th c. could in fact belong to the 3rd c., but they are largely indistinguishable[110] due to mostly unchanging burial practices and poor furnishings. This effectively blurs the lines for a whole century as to when inhumation burials became common, and also renders Ciglenečki's year AD 300 as the start of the Late Roman period tentative by the same margin.

While the shift towards inhumation could have been reinforced by the spread of Christianity, there are no solid grounds to assume that it was completely dependent on it. It could well be that Slovenian sites simply mirror the wider shift in burial manner observed elsewhere in the Empire in the same period.[111] A modern analogy for a shift in burial style not motivated by religious considerations comes from the end of the 19th and beginning of the 20th c., when cremations started becoming as popular as inhumations in Europe.[112] A similar 'spontaneous' change could have happened in the Roman period as well.

The second problem I argue originates from Roman archaeology in Slovenia in general, where equating sex with gender, and culture with ethnicity, is a longstanding problem and has been discussed elsewhere.[113] Since studies focussing on social and cultural aspects of burials are relatively few in Slovenian archaeology of any period, the wider timeframe of Late Antiquity is taken into consideration here.

For Late Antiquity, one of the innovative studies that sought to overcome the problems of missing anthropological analyses was an attempt at interpreting the burials from Rifnik by Boris Vičič:[114] after tentatively determining sex/gender on the basis of grave goods, the author analysed the horizontal stratigraphy of the graves. Four different clusters of graves emerged that he interpreted as 4 distinct family units, and the patterns further indicated that two different cultural traditions must have been present at the cemetery. No distinction, however, was made between sex and gender, or between ethnicity and culture.

A brilliant example of complex interpretation comes from the already mentioned burial from Emona, where a military belt was placed in the grave of a young male who was too young to have served in the army based on his (osteologically determined) age.[115] Recent studies such as that of social structure in Late Antiquity[116] are attempting to dispel the notion that the world of the dead, i.e. the funerary setting, is a straightforward extension of the world of the living. The theoretical part, based predominantly on Heinrich Härke,[117] is clearly articulated, but pointing out other problematic aspects and missing data would have been welcome, for example perishable grave goods. This topic was covered more in depth (for the Early Slavic period) by Andrej Pleterski, who pioneered different theoretical approaches to the interpretation of cemeteries. Most of his work consciously deviates from numerous predominant practices, among them the interpretation of status and other aspects of identity solely on the basis of grave goods, and incorporates findings of other scientific disciplines, notably ethnology.[118] The work of Pleterski

104   Stemberger (2014).
105   Tomažinčič (2018).
106   Pearce (2001) 136; (2013).
107   Stemberger (2018).
108   E.g. Miškec et al. (2020).
109   Županek (2018).
110   Pearce (2001) 136.
111   Morris (1992).

112   E.g. Rebay-Salisbury (2012) case study 1.
113   Stemberger (2008); Stemberger Flegar (2020a); (2020b).
114   Vičič (1990).
115   Tomažinčič (2018).
116   Pavletič (2018).
117   Härke (1993); further bibliography cited by Pavletič (2018).
118   E.g. Pleterski (2001); (2002).

and a few other researchers such as Štular, particularly his 2007 study of the Early Medieval cemetery of Mali grad,[119] even though not strictly 'Late Roman', are helping pave the way towards more scrupulous interpretations for sites classified as Late Roman and Roman in general.

Conclusions and Suggestions for Future Research

Slovenian Late Antiquity, spanning roughly from AD 300 to 476, is a distinct period closely associated with both the preceding Roman and the following Early Medieval period. To the extent that Roman settlement and material culture persisted into Late Antiquity, it is studied as the Late Roman period in the context of Roman archaeology, whereas the rest is typically included in the study of the Great Migration period. Historical sources suggest it must have been a diverse and dynamic, even turbulent time, but in spite of this, or perhaps in part exactly because of this, it is not as well studied as either the preceding or the following period.

For the 'Roman' part of Late Antiquity – that is to say, for the Late Roman period – in particular, a major obstacle is that compared to the earlier Roman period, significantly less material culture is available for study. Judging by the data from all published excavations, the Slovenian Late Roman period was characterised by scarce grave goods; while numerous Roman graves can be securely dated to the 1st or 2nd c. AD based on the associated material (typically, on imported artefacts), providing also a relatively solid basis for dating similar burials, few graves can confidently be attributed to the 3rd, 4th or 5th c. This in turn means that few reliable patterns can be established with which to chronologically classify other, even less revealing burials. Since the 1st and 2nd c. AD are characterised by cremation and the subsequent 300 years by inhumation, it has become common in Slovenian Roman archaeology to interpret all inhumations from Roman cemeteries with little to no chronologically or otherwise distinctive grave goods as 'Christian' burials from the Late Roman period. Although in specific cases this can be justified, I argue that in the absence of reliable indicators it is too broad a generalisation and methodologically unsound.

Another factor, external and more general, impeding the study of Late Antiquity in Slovenia is the clear division of Slovenian archaeology into discretely defined time periods that originated in the Yugoslav era. For the Late Roman period, this is especially problematic since the whole of Late Antiquity is studied separately from the Roman period, obscuring aspects such as the largely uninterrupted development of the coastal settlements from the turn of the millennium up to the end of the 7th c.

Future research should first and foremost concentrate on catching up with excavations and delivering basic publications. Several big excavations that were carried out before the turn of the century have still not been published. An overall analysis of Late Roman burials is also still lacking as a consequence of missing primary excavation publications, with the exception of burial manner which has been systematically addressed by Ratej.[120] In other words, the problems outlined by Ciglenečki[121] remain essentially unresolved. This does not pertain exclusively to the Late Roman material, but while a period as opulent in material as the 1st and 2nd c. AD can more easily tolerate omissions, they are much more significant for the study of the comparatively less rich Slovenian Late Roman period.

Publications of the recent excavations will hopefully include more osteological and other scientific analyses, which are known to have been carried out in several cases. A significant proportion of the large number of burials unearthed in recent times at Emona, for example, are as yet published only in the form of preliminary reports,[122] but have been osteologically analysed,[123] and more analyses are planned. There is, thus, a large pool of data in processing which will shine a light on the sex, age, and potential diseases and trauma of the deceased. Beyond this, commonly overlooked areas in Slovenian archaeology such as burial processes and body manipulations will hopefully receive more attention. Detailed systematic analyses of the known cemeteries would be more than welcome, even more so if they included artefactual comparisons with the settlements. The works of younger generations of Slovenian researchers[124] are promising signs that more such comprehensive and interdisciplinary studies of the period will be soon undertaken.

Besides preliminary reports, one can for now get a glimpse of what is being researched in the daily press, social media, and various blogs. Quite a few archaeological firms have also started to organise 'open days' at excavation sites in order to engage the broader public.

119   The study includes a discussion about sex vs. gender and is cautious about translating social status in life directly into social status in death.

120   Ratej (2015).
121   Ciglenečki (1997) 196.
122   E.g. Mulh (2008); Tomažinčič (2011).
123   This is frequently referenced by Slovenian scholars as 'unpublished reports'.
124   E.g. Pavletič (2018); Ratej (2018).

The need to involve the public in the work of archaeologists is increasingly being recognised in the entire field, and the Slovenian late antique burial material is also used to demonstrate and illustrate the history of the period. One of the most relatable stories based on Slovenian Late Antiquity, more specifically on 6th c. burials from modern day Kranj, comes from the children's book *Pripovedka iz Karnija ali ni ga čez dober nasvet* ('A tale from Carnium, or you cannot beat good advice') by Verena Vidrih Perko (2009) which focusses on the fictional relationship between two girls, one a 'native Roman' and the other belonging to the new Germanic ruling elite. Even though it is entirely fictional, it references actual artefacts (a specific brooch as well as other pieces of jewellery) from real graves that are on display as part of the permanent exhibition in the Gorenjska Museum in Kranj. Overall, the outlook for the study of Slovenian Late Antiquity is positive, and in a few years' time a large amount of new data should become available that will enable both general and specialised studies to further our understanding and knowledge of this interesting period.

Acknowledgements

I would like to thank the organisers of the *Fieldwork in Late Antique Archaeology: Burial and Funerary Practice* conference, especially Dr Luke Lavan. I would also like to extend my gratitude to Dr John Pearce for his inexhaustible and invaluable support, as well as ddr. Verena Vidrih Perko and Ana Kovačič, not least for their comments and insights that helped improve my paper. Any remaining errors are of course my own.

Bibliography

ANSL (1975) *Arheološka najdišča Slovenije* (Ljubljana 1975).

Bachran W. (1975) "Das Gräberfeld (Grobišče)", in *Vranje pri Sevnici. Starokrščanske cerkve na Ajdovskem gradcu / Frühchristliche Kirchenanlagen auf dem Ajdovski Grdec* (Katalogi in monografije / Catalogi et monographiae 12), edd. P. Petru and Th. Ulbert (Ljubljana 1975) 99–115.

Bavec U. (2003) "Predhodno poročilo o poznoantičnem grobišču na Vrajku v Gorenjem Mokronogu / Preliminary report on the Late Roman cemetery at Vrajk in Gorenji Mokronog", *Arheološki vestnik* 54 (2003) 325–30.

Bešter H. (2012) *Poznorimsko in zgodnjesrednjeveško grobišče Na steni v Solkanu pri Novi Gorici* (*izkopavanja leta 2008*) (BA thesis, Univ. of Ljubljana, 2012).

Bierbrauer V. (1984) "Jugoslawien seit dem Beginn der Völkerwanderung bis zur slawischen Landnahme: die Synthese auf dem Hintergrund von Migrations- und Landnahmevorgängen", in *Jugoslawien. Integrationsprobleme in Geschichte und Gegenwart. Beiträge des Südosteuropa-Arbeitskreises der Deutschen Forschungsgemeinschaft zum V. Internationalen Südosteuropa-Kongreß der Association Internationale d'Études du Sud-Est Européen* (Göttingen 1984) 49–97.

Bitenc P. and Knific T. (2001) *Od Rimljanov do Slovanov. Predmeti* (Ljubljana 2001).

Bolta L. (1981) *Rifnik pri Šentjurju. Poznoantična naselbina in grobišče / Spätantike Siedlung und Gräberfeld* (Katalogi in monografije / Catalogi et monographiae 19) (Ljubljana 1981).

Bolta L. (1970–1971) "Poznoantično grobišče pri Rifniku pri Šentjurju / Spätantikes Gräberfeld auf Rifnik bei Šentjur", *Arheološki vestnik* 21–22 (1970–1971) 127–40.

Bratož R. (2014) *Med Italijo in Ilirikom. Slovenski prostor in njegovo sosedstvo v pozni antiki* (Ljubljana 2014).

Bratož R. (2013) "Raziskovanje zgodnjekrščanske dobe v Sloveniji v zadnjih dveh desetljih: arheologija in zgodovina", in *Oltre i confini: scritti in onore di don Luigi Tavano per i suoi 90 anni*, edd. L. Ferrari and P. Iancis (Gorizia 2013) 17–48.

Bratož R. (1996) "Ecclesia in gentibus: vprašanje preživetja krščanstva iz antične dobe v času slovansko-avarske naselitve na prostoru med Jadranom in Donavo", in *Grafenauerjev zbornik*, ed. V. Rajšp (Ljubljana 1996) 205–225.

Čaval S. (2013) "Poznoantične okrasne igle vrste stilus v Sloveniji / Late Antique decorative pins of the stylus type in Slovenia", *Arheološki vestnik* 64 (2013) 197–248.

Ciglenečki S. (2007) "Poznoantična arheologija v današnjem Slovenskem prostoru", http://iza.zrc-sazu.si/FF/Slavko/PA_splosno.html.

Ciglenečki S. (1999a) "Results and problems in the archaeology of Late Antiquity in Slovenia", *Arheološki vestnik* 50 (2007) 287–304.

Ciglenečki S. (1999b) "Zaton antičnega sveta", in *Zakladi tisočletij. Zgodovina Slovenije od neandertalcev do Slovanov*, edd. B. Aubelj, D. Božič, and J. Dular (Ljubljana 1999) 334–36.

Ciglenečki S. (1997) "Strukturiranost poznorimske poselitve Slovenije / Strukturierung spätantiker Besiedlung Sloweniens", *Arheološki vestnik* 48 (1997) 191–202.

Ciglenečki S. (1993) "Arheološki sledovi zatona antične Petovione", *Ptujski arheološki zbornik ob 100-letnici muzeja in muzejskega društva* (1993) 505–520.

Ciglenečki S. (1987) *Höhenbefestigungen aus der Zeit vom 3. bis 6. Jh. im Ostalpenraum / Višinske utrdbe iz časa 3. do 6. st. v vzhodnoalpskem prostoru* (Dela 1. Razprave. SAZU / Opera Instituti Archaeologici Sloveniae 31) (Ljubljana 1987).

Curk I. (1978) "Poetovio v pozni antiki / Poetovio in der Spätantike", *Arheološki vestnik* 29 (1978) 405–411.

Curk I. (1966) "Poznoantično grobišče na Zgornjem Bregu v Ptuju", *Časopis za zgodovino in narodopisje* 2 (1966) 46–62.

Demandt A. (1989) *Die Spätantike. Römische geschichte von Diocletian bis Justinian (Handbuch der Altertumswissenschaft* III.6) (Munich 1989).

Ferk F. (1890) *Dnevnik Franceta Ferka*. Unpublished notes (1890).

Gaspari A. (2014) *Prazgodovinska in rimska Emona: vodnik skozi arheološko preteklost predhodnice Ljubljane / Prehistoric and Roman Emona. A Guide through the Archaeological Past of Ljubljana's Predecessor* (Ljubljana 2014).

Gaspari A. (2010) *Apud horridas gentis: začetki rimskega mesta Colonia Iulia Emona / Beginnings of the Roman Town of Colonia Iulia Emona* (Ljubljana 2010).

Gaspari A., Vidrih Perko V., Štrajhar M., and Lazar I. (2007) "Antični pristaniški kompleks v Fizinah pri Portorožu – zaščitne raziskave leta 1998 / The Roman port complex at Fizine near Portorož – rescue excavations 1998", *Arheološki vestnik* 58 (2007) 167–218.

Härke H. (1993) "Intentionale und funktionale Daten. Ein Beitrag zur Theorie und Methodik der Gräberarchäologie", *Archäologisches Korrespondenzblatt* 23 (1993) 141–46.

Ibler U. G. (1991) *Studien zum Kontinuitätsproblem am Übergang von der Antike zum Mittelalter in Nord- und Westjugoslawien* (Bonn 1991).

Istenič J. (1999) *Poetovio, zahodna grobišča 1. Grobne celote iz Deželnega muzeja Joanneuma v Gradcu / Poetovio, the Western Cemeteries 1: Grave-groups in the Landesmuseum Joanneum, Graz* (Katalogi in monografije / Catalogi et monographiae 32) (Ljubljana 1999).

Jevremov B., Tomanič Jevremov M., and Ciglenečki S. (1993) "Poznorimsko grobišče na Ptujskem gradu / Spätrömisches Gräberfeld auf dem Ptujski grad", *Arheološki vestnik* 44 (1993) 223–34.

Kastelic J. (1964–1965) "Nekaj problemov zgodnjesrednjeveške arheologije v Sloveniji / Quelques problèmes concernant l'archéologie du haut moyen âge en Slovénie", *Arheološki vestnik* 15–16 (1964–1965) 109–124.

Kastelic J. (1960) *Slovanska nekropola na Bledu*. (Dela 1. reda SAZU / Opera Instituti Archaeologici Sloveniae 13) (Ljubljana 1960).

Klemenc J. (1950) *Ptujski grad v kasni antiki / Le château de Ptuj à l'époque de la décadence romaine* (Dela 1. reda SAZU / Opera Instituti Archaeologici Sloveniae 4) (Ljubljana 1950).

Knific T. (2005) "Gospe iz mesta Karnija", *Kranjski zbornik* (2005) 331–43.

Knific T. (1995) "Vojščaki iz mesta Karnija", *Kranjski zbornik* (1995) 23–40.

Knific T. (1991) "Arheologija o prvih stoletjih krščanstva na slovenskem", in *Pismo brez pisave. Arheologija o prvih stoletjih krščanstva na slovenskem*, edd. T. Knific and M. Sagadin (Ljubljana 1991) 11–33.

Knific T. and Lux J. (2010) "Otroci iz mesta Karnija", *Kranjski zbornik* (2010) 26–36.

Korošec P. (1999) *Nekropola na Ptujskem gradu, Turnirski prostor / Das Gräberfeld an dem Schlossberg von Ptuj: Turnierplatz* (Ptuj 2010).

Korošec P. (1951) "Slovanske ostaline na dvorišču SAZU v Ljubljani", *Arheološki vestnik* 2 (1951) 156–183.

Lazar I. (2003) *Rimsko steklo Slovenije / The Roman Glass of Slovenia* (Opera Instituti Archaeologici Sloveniae 7) (Ljubljana 2003).

Lazar I. (2002) "Celeia", *in The Autonomous Towns of Noricum and Pannonia / Die autonomen Städte in Noricum und Pannonien*, edd. M. Šašel Kos and P. Scherrer (Ljubljana 2002) 71–101.

Leben-Seljak, P. (2018) "Antropološka analiza skeletov", in *Miren. Grobišče iz časa preseljevanja ljudstev*, edd. V. Tratnik and Š. Karo (Ljubljana 2018) 58–70.

Leben-Seljak P. (2003) "Antropološka analiza poznoatičnega grobišča na Vrajku v Gornjem Mokronogu", *Arheološki vestnik* 54 (2003) 397–420.

Leben-Seljak P. (1996) *Antropološka analiza poznoantičnih in srednjeveških grobišč Bleda in okolice / Anthropological Analysis of Late Antiquity and Medieval Necropolises at Bled and Surroundings*. (Ph.D. diss., Univ. of Ljubljana 1996).

Manson P. (1998) "Poznoantični Črnomelj in Bela krajina / Late Roman Črnomelj and Bela Krajina", *Arheološki vestnik* 49 (1998) 285–313.

Mattingly D. (2010) "Cultural Crossovers: Global and Local Identities in the Classical World", in *Material Culture and Social Identities in the Ancient World*, edd. S. Hales and T. Hodos (Cambridge 2010) 283–97.

Mikl Curk I. (1997) "Iz materialne kulture k vprašanjem verstva in premožnosti na slovenskem ozemlju ob koncu 4. st. / Von der materiellen Kultur zur Frage von Religion und Vermögenverhältnissen im heutigen Slowenien am Ende des 4. Jhs.", *Arheološki vestnik* 48 (1997) 179–89.

Mikl Curk I. (1973) "Zapažanja o temni rimski kuhinjski lončeni posodi v Sloveniji / Observations of Roman dark clay cooking pottery in Slovenia", *Arheološki vestnik* 24 (1973) 883–900.

Mikl Curk I. (1972) "Nekaj misli o poznoantični materialni kulturi v Sloveniji / Zum Studium der spätrömischen materiellen Kultur in Slowenien", *Arheološki vestnik* 23 (1972) 376–82.

Mirnik Prezelj I. (1998) "Slovenska zgodnjesrednjeveška arheologija med preteklostjo in sedanjostjo – pogled z "Zahoda" / Slovene Early Medieval archaeology between the past and present – view from the West", *Arheološki vestnik* 49 (1998) 361–81.

Miškec A., Županek B., Karo Š., and Tica G. (2020) *Severno emonsko grobišče – raziskave na najdišču Kozolec* (Situla 45) (Ljubljana 2020).

Modrijan Z. and Milavec T. (2011) *Poznoantična naselbina Tonovcov grad pri Kobaridu. Najdbe / Late Antique Settlement Tonovcov grad near Kobarid. Finds* (Opera Instituti archaeologici Sloveniae 24) (Ljubljana 2011).

Morris I. (1992) *Death-Ritual and Social Structure in Classical Antiquity* (Cambridge 1992).

Mulh T. (2008) *Poročilo o zaščitnih arheoloških izkopavanjih na lokaciji Potniški center Ljubljana 2007/2008 (poročilo št. 1/2003 – BV TM)*. (Ljubljana 2008).

Orožen-Adamič A., Zorc M., and Zupanc D. (1975) "Antropološka obdelava izkopanega gradiva", in *Vranje pri Sevnici. Starokrščanske cerkve na Ajdovskem gradcu / Frühchristliche Kirchenanlagen auf dem Ajdovski Gradec* (Katalogi in monografije / Catalogi et monographiae 12), edd. P. Petru and Th. Ulbert (Ljubljana 1975) 117–22.

Pahič S. (1972) *Nov seznam noriško-panonskih gomil* (Razprave 1. razreda SAZU 7/2) (Ljubljana 1972) 113–212.

Pahič S. (1969) *Antični in staroslovanski grobovi v Brezju nad Zrečami* (Razprave 1. razreda SAZU 6) (Ljubljana 1969) 217–308.

Parker Pearson M. (2003) *The Archaeology of Death and Burial* (Stroud 2003).

Pavletič K. (2018) *Preučevanje družbene sktruture na podlagi poznoantičnih grobišč*. (Unpublished MA diss., Univ. of Ljubljana 2018).

Pearce J. (2013) *Contextual Archaeology of Burial Practice: Case Studies from Roman Britain* (BAR 588) (Oxford 2013).

Pearce J. (2001) "Infants, cemeteries and communities in the Roman provinces", in *TRAC 2000: Proceedings of the Tenth Annual Theoretical Roman Archaeology Conference, London 2000*, edd. G. Davies, A. Gardner, and K. Lockyear (Oxford 2001) 125–42.

Petru P. (1969) *Poskus časovne razporeditve lončenine iz rimskih grobov na Dolenjskem in Posavju / Cronologia della ceramica delle tombe romane nella Carniola inferiore (Dolensko) e della valle della Sava* (Razprave / Dissertationes VI) (Ljubljana 1969).

Petru P. (1964–1965) "Nekateri problemi provincialno rimske arheologije v Sloveniji", *Arheološki vestnik* 15–16 (1964–1965) 65–107.

Petru P. and Šribar V. (1956) "Nove najdbe", *Arheološki vestnik* 7 (1956) 297–304.

Petru P. and Th. Ulbert. (edd.) (1975) *Vranje pri Sevnici. Starokrščanske cerkve na Ajdovskem gradcu / frühchristliche Kirchenanlagen auf dem Ajdovski Gradec* (Katalogi in monografije / Catalogi et monographiae 12) (Ljubljana 1975).

Petru S. (1972) *Emonske nekropole. Odkrite med leti 1635–1960.* (Katalogi in monografije / Catalogi et monographiae 7) (Ljubljana 1972).

Plesničar Gec L. (1999) *Zgodnje krščanski center v Emoni. Zbirka vodnikov.* (Kulturni in naravni spomeniki Slovenije 198) (Ljubljana 1999).

Plesničar Gec L. (1977) *Keramika emonskih nekropol* (Ljubljana 1977).

Plesničar Gec L. (1973) *Starokrščanski center v Emoni / Old Christian Centre in Emona* (Katalogi in monografije / Catalogi et monographiae 21) (Ljubljana 1973).

Plesničar Gec L. (1972) *Severno emonsko grobišče / The Northern Necropolis of Emona* (Katalogi in monografije / Catalogi et monographiae 8) (Ljubljana 1972).

Plesničar Gec L. (1967) "Obeležje in kronologija antičnih grobov na Prešernovi in Celovški cesti v Ljubljani / Caractère et chronologie des tombes antiques sur la Prešernova et la Celovška cesta à Ljubljana", *Arheološki vestnik* 18 (1967) 137–51.

Plestenjak A. (2013) *Vpliv politike na oblikovanje arheološke dediščine: primer prezentacij arheološke dediščine v Ljubljani*. (Unpublished Ph.D. thesis, Univ. of Ljubljana 2013).

Pleterski A. (2014) "Kulturni genom", *Studia mythologica Slavica. Suppl.* 10 (Ljubljana 2014).

Pleterski A. (2008) *Zgodnjesrednjeveška naselbina na Blejski Pristavi. Najdbe / Frühmittelalterliche Siedlung Pristava in Bled. Funde* (Dela 1. reda SAZU / Opera Instituti Archaeologici Sloveniae 14) (Ljubljana 2008).

Pleterski A. (2002) "Od deklice do starke. Od doma do moža", *Arheo* 22 (2002) 53–58.

Pleterski A. (2001) "O nekaterih možnostih interpretiranja zgodnjesrednjeveških grobišč", *Arheo* 21 (2001) 69–71.

Peterski A. and Beljak M. (2002) "Grobovi s Puščave nad Starim trgom pri Slovenj Gradcu / Die Gräber von Puščava oberhalb von Stari trg bei Slovenj Gradec", *Arheološki vestnik* 53 (2002) 233–300.

Pogačnik M. (2007) *Poznorimske pasne spone v grobnih kontekstih na področju Norika in Panonije*. (Unpublished Ph.D. thesis, Univ. of Ljubljana 2007).

Ratej R. (2018) *Poznoantično grobišče "Celeiapark"* (Unpublished MA diss., Univ. of Ljubljana 2018).

Ratej R. (2015) *Način pokopavanja na grobiščih med 5. in 11. stoletjem v Sloveniji*. (Unpublished BA diss., Univ. of Ljubljana 2015).

Rebay-Salisbury K. (2012) "Inhumation and cremation: how burial practices are linked to beliefs", in *Embodied Knowledge: Historical Perspectives on Technology and Belief*, edd. M. L. Stig Sørensen and K. Rebay-Salisbury (Oxford 2012) 15–26.

Sagadin M. (1991) "Najstarejša cerkvena stavba v Kranju", in *Pod zvonom sv. Kancijana*, ed. S. Zidar (Kranj 1991) 31–44.

Sagadin M. (1987) *Kranj – križišče Iskra. Nekropola iz časa preseljevanja ljudstev in staroslovanskega obdobja / Kranj – Iskra Crossroads. A Cemetery from the Migration Period and the Early Slavic Period*. (Katalogi in Monografije / Catalogi et monographiae 24) (Ljubljana 1987).

Slabe M. (1980) *Polhograjska gora* (Maribor 1980).

Slabe M. (1974) "Poznoantični staroselski grob iz Dan pri Starem trgu", *Arheološki vestnik* 25 (1974) 417–23.

Stare V. (1980) *Kranj. Nekropola iz časa preseljevanja ljudstev / Kranj. Necropolis from the Time of the Migration of Peoples* (Katalogi in monografije / Catalogi et monographiae 18) (Ljubljana 1980).

Stare V. (1952) "Pozno antično grobišče na Ravnem brdu", *Arheološki vestnik* 3 (1952) 137–44.

Stemberger, K. (2020) "A study of female-associated burials from Roman-period Slovenia", in *Un-Roman Sex: Gender, Sexuality, and Lovemaking in the Roman Provinces and Frontiers*, edd. T. Ivleva and R. Collins (London 2020) 210–37.

Stemberger K. (2014) "Identity of females buried at Colonia Iulia Emona / Rekonstruiranje identitet žensk z emonskih nekropol", *Arheo* 31 (2014) 69–81.

Stemberger Flegar K. (2020a). "Identity through the looking glass: how the perception of identity in Roman funerary archaeology developed in Slovenia", *Theoretical Roman Archaeology Journal* 3 (2020) 1–15.

Stemberger Flegar K. (2020b) "The importance of being earnest: language and its perception in discussing sex, gender, identity, and Romanisation in Slovenia. Why precise language matters", in *Community and Identity at the Edges of the Classical World*, ed. A. W. Irvin (New Jersey 2020) 243–54.

Šašel, J. (1975) "Kasnoantično in zgodnjesrednjeveško obdobje v Vzhodnih Alpah in arheološke najdbe na Slovenskem", in ANSL (1975) *Arheološka najdišča Slovenije* (Ljubljana 1975) 68–73.

Šašel J. and Petru P. (1971) *Claustra Alpium Iuliarum 1. Fontes*. (Katalogi in Monografije / Catalogi et monographiae 5) (Ljubljana 1971).

Štular B. (2007) "Posamezniki, skupnost in obred v zgodnjem srednjem veku. Primer grobiščnih podatkov z Malega gradu v Sloveniji / The individuals, the community, and the ritual in the Early Middle Ages", *Studia Mythologica Slavica* 10 (2007) 23–50.

Tomažinčič Š. (2018) "Belt types, identity and social status in late antiquity: the belt set in Emona's grave 18", *JRA* 31 (2018) 426–44.

Tomažinčič Š. (2011) *Poročilo o zaščitnih arheoloških izkopavanjih na območju izgradnje podzemnih zbiralnic na Štefanovi 4 v Ljubljani.* Unpublished excavation report (2011).

Tušek I. (1997) "Skupina poznorimskih grobov iz območja izkopa za stanovanjski blok B-2 v Rabelčji vasi -- zahod na Ptuju", *Arheološki vestnik* 48 (1997) 289–300.

Ulbert Th. (ed.) (1981) *Ad Pirum (Hrušica). Spätrömische Paßbefestigung in den Julischen Alpen*. (Munich 1981).

Urek M. (2008) *Analiza poznorimskih grobišč v južnem delu Sredozemskega Norika*. (Unpublished BA diss., Univ. of Ljubljana 2008).

Vičič B. (1990) "Horizontalna stratigrafija poznoantičnega grobišča na Rifniku", *Arheološki vestnik* 41 (1990) 439–54.

Vidrih Perko V. (2009) *Pripovedka iz Karnija ali ni ga čez dober nasvet* (Buča 2009).

Vidrih Perko V. (2005) "Seaborne trade routes in the north-east Adriatic and their connections to the hinterland in the late antiquity", in *L'Adriatico dalla tarda antichità all'età carolingia: atti del convegno di studio Brescia 11–13 ottobre 2001*, ed. G. P. Brogiolo (Florence 2005) 49–77.

Vidrih Perko V. and Žbona-Trkman B. (2005) "Ceramic finds from Ajdovščina – Fluvio Frigido, an early Roman road station and late Roman fortress castra", *Rei Cretariae Romanae Fautorum acta* 39 (2005) 277–86.

Vidrih Perko V. and Županič M. (2009) "Amphorae in western Slovenia and in northern Istra", in LRCW 1: *Late Roman Coarse Wares, Cooking Wares and Amphorae in the Mediterranean: Archaeology and Archaeometry* (BAR-IS 1340), ed. J. M. Gurt Esparraguera (Oxford 2009) 521–36.

Vuga D. (1985) "Moški grob z vrta Narodnega muzeja v Ljubljani. Poznorimske in barbarske ledvičaste pasne spone z ovalnim okovom", *Arheološki vestnik* 36 (1985) 237–54.

Vuga D. (1980) "A study of burying methods in the period of the Great Migration (5th to 6th centuries) in the south-eastern Alpine and Cisalpine world", *Balcanoslavica* 9 (1980) 17–25.

Zavrtanik J. (1984) "Poznoantično grobišče pri Kosovelih", *Goriški letnik* 11 (1984) 85–94.

Žerjal T. and Vidrih Perko V. (2017) "La ceramica orientale da contesti sloveni", *Antichita Altoadriatiche* 86 (2017) 245–68.

Županek B. (2018) "Pokrajine umrlih: struktura in dinamika severnega grobišča Emone", in *Nova odkritja med Alpami in Črnim morjem. Rezultati raziskav rimskodobnih najdišč v obdobju med leti 2005 in 2015. Zbornik 1. mednarodnega arheološkega simpozija, Ptuj, 8. in 9. oktober 2015: Zavod za varstvo kulturne dediščine Slovenije*, edd. M. Janežič, B. Nadbath, T. Mulh, and I. Žižek (Ljubljana 2018) 253–80.

Death at the Edge of Empire: Burial Practices in the Province of Scythia (4th–7th c. AD)

Ciprian Crețu and Andrei D. Soficaru

Abstract

Despite the substantial number of burials dated between the 4th and 7th c. discovered in Scythia Minor, a systematic approach of the mortuary data is still missing. This paper aims to address this knowledge gap. After providing a brief historical narrative, the available archaeological record and the current state of research are discussed, together with major topics such as the mortuary landscape and the diverse burial practices documented in the Lower Danube province during the Late Roman and Early Byzantine periods.

A Short History of the Region

The creation of the province of Scythia[1] – an administrative unit within the Later Roman Empire's diocese of Thrace – stems from the complex and all-embracing program of restructuring initiated during the reign of Emperor Diocletian (284–305).[2] The province covered roughly the territory between the river Danube, enclosing it to the west and north, and the Black Sea to the east. Given its position at the northern periphery of the empire, the strategic importance of this region was acknowledged as such by the church historian Sozomen (active in the first half of the 5th c.), who noted that it 'possessed many natural advantages which rendered it necessary to the Roman Empire, for it served as a barrier to ward off the barbarians.'[3] This commentary was accurate throughout the 3rd to 7th c. period as Scythia faced constant pressure from various peoples from beyond the imperial frontier, most often in the form of plundering raids, but also seeking refuge in the face of greater perils.[4]

From the beginning of the 3rd c., a large number of people of Germanic origin from the north began to constantly migrate towards the Black Sea causing major disturbances in the peripheral areas of the empire. Successive barbarian invasions, especially those of the Goths, in the middle of the century caused serious deterioration of Roman rule in the provinces of Dacia and Moesia, as well as throughout the Balkan Peninsula, in a long-lasting conflict known as the *Bellum Scythicum*.[5] Despite some extended periods of peace, the Goths remained a major threat to the Lower Danube well into the following century, with the imperial armies of Emperor Valens required in the late 360s in order to deal with the danger, ensure peace and rebuild the damaged infrastructure.[6] Events surrounding the disastrous Roman defeat at Adrianople in 378, up to the peace 'treaty' of 382, saw the Goths plunder large areas of the Thracian diocese. The defeat of the Romans meant a serious blow to their military capability, considering that the nucleus of the eastern army was decimated. The disappearance of some important Roman leaders, the Emperor Valens himself above all, together with the destruction of settlements that provided necessary supplies to the army in the Lower Danube region should be added as consequences of this conflict as well. At the same time, the growing necessity for troops compelled the Romans to recruit more units from outside the borders of the empire.

Between 379 and 382, emperors Gratian and Theodosius I undertook military action in an attempt to deal with the Goths victorious at Adrianople. During this period the failure of the Romans led to the emergence of a new and particular configuration of power in terms of Gothic settlement within Roman territory, as *regnum in regno* – a protectorate within the borders of the empire, led by their own leaders. Some kind of agreement may have been reached between the Goths and Romans in October 382. According to this settlement, the Goths were deemed to be *foederati socii*, meaning they received land in the provinces, bearing the juridical status of *hospites* and were obliged to serve

---

1 For the official denomination of the province and its many variants, see Zahariade (2006) 1.

2 Jones (1964) 42–68; Barnes (1982) 209–225; Rees (2004) 24–71.

3 Sozom. *Hist. eccl.* 6.21.3.

4 Such an episode happened in 376, during the reign of Valens, when the Goths sent embassies to the emperor's court seeking asylum within the borders of the empire under the imminent threat of Hunnic invasions from the east. The emperor allows them to cross the Danube and settle in Thrace. Wanke (1990) 111–28; Wolfram (1990) 117–20.

5 This conflict seems to have begun in 238 when the first raid on Roman territory is attested and concluded with a series of important victories on the Roman side culminating with that of Claudius II at Naissus, in 268/269. Wolfram (1990) 42–49; Watson (1999) 215–25; Kulikowski (2007) 18–20.

6 Wanke (1990) 84–110; Lenski (2002) 116–52.

Alexandra Dolea and Luke Lavan (eds) *Burial and Memorial in Late Antiquity* (Late Antique Archaeology 13) (Leiden 2024), pp. 764–778

in the Roman army when required. Even though the assigned land remained Roman sovereign territory, the Goths were considered autonomous.[7] Themistius (*ca.* 317–389), an important senator and imperial spokesman at Constantinople, envisaged Goths as Roman soldiers and tax-paying farmers sharing offerings, tables, military ventures, and public duties with his fellow citizens.[8] During the reign of Theodosius, the Roman perception and dissatisfaction with the Gothic presence remained confined to a rhetoric entailing certain assumptions of nomadism, cruelty, and lack of civilization. According to Zosimus (*ca.*435–501), the garrison commander from the capital city of Tomis, a soldier named Gerontius, engaged in an attack against some barbarians stationed outside the city in order to punish them for 'their attitude and their intention to attack and disrupt the city' and managed to kill all of them, apart from a few who 'took refuge in a building revered by Christians, called an asylum.'[9] Zosimus' account is important for two reasons. This episode not only testifies to the presence of the Goths as settled near a major city within the Roman Empire, but it also speaks about certain animosities between Romans and non-Romans and the resentment of the former, even in times when, at least officially, peace had been restored.

In the last decades of the 4th c., yet another greater threat would rise north of the Danubian border of the empire – the Huns. Real Hunnic domination was established in the region only after the beginning of the 5th c. when the first leader named by Roman sources appears – a certain Uldin/Uldis based along the Danube.[10] In 400, Uldin became an ally of Arcadius after killing the usurper Gainas, who was seeking shelter and support from the Goths, sending his head to the imperial court in a diplomatic gesture. Meanwhile, as Zosimus writes, 'a band of fugitive slaves, and others who had deserted from the armies, pretending to be Huns, pillaged all the country [Thrace], and took whatever they found out of the walls.'[11] For almost a century, until the reign of Anastasius I (491–518) when a period of recovery and restoration of the Danubian border began,[12] the province of Scythia (together with the Balkans) had been subjected to numerous attacks caused by barbarian invasions from the north with short hiatuses following peace agreements. In 422 and 441–447 the Huns

launched an invasion deep into the Thracian diocese – *Thraciam vastaverunt*, as Marcellinus puts it[13] – causing havoc to such an extent that Constantinople itself was at risk.[14] The *Gallic Chronicle of 452* recalls that no less than 70 cities were devastated by the Huns.[15] The attack from 447 was the last to be carried out by the Huns in the eastern provinces of the empire, aimed at forcing the latter to pay higher tribute.

For the 6th c. and the first decades of the 7th c., many peoples invaded across the Danube into Scythia. Ancient written sources recorded them under various names: Huns, Kutrigurs, Bulgars, Slavs and Avars among them.[16] These successive attacks concluded with the collapse of the Danubian *limes* at the beginning of the 7th c. as a natural outcome following the plunder and destruction of settlements and the gradual weakening of Roman military control over the province. Shortly before the accession of Emperor Mauricius (582–602), the destruction caused in the province is noticeable in the archaeological record for several settlements such as Axiopolis (probably destroyed during the Slavic attack of 576–584), Capidava (destroyed after 572/573), Beroe (where all coins discovered in the debris layer are dated before 575/576) and Hamlyris (where two hoards ending with coins from 574–577 were discovered).[17] According to A. Madgearu, these events mark the beginnings of a decline and disintegration process culminating with further massive ravaging in 614–626. The fortifications from Ibida, Ulmetum and Histria perished and lost their military function, together with Tomis – the capital city of the province. Deurbanization began in the last two decades of the 6th c. and continued through the first two decades of the next. One of its final results, as A. Madgearu puts it, was to wipe out the differences between the territory of the South-Danubian provinces and the barbarian North-Danubian area.[18]

This sketch of the main historical events that took place in the Lower Danube region over a period of three centuries underlines the main traits of both the region and the chronological framework. Given its geographical position at the edge of the Roman Empire, the province of Scythia in the 4th–7th c. was a multi-ethnic area, where experiences of war alternated with times of peace, co-operation, and commercial contacts. It has been well-established that the borderline area, the

---

7   Sivan (1987) 762–65; Wolfram (1990) 132–34; Heather (1991) 158–65; Cedilnik (2009).

8   Them. *Or.* 16. 211d.

9   Zos. 4. 40.

10   Kim (2016) 77–79.

11   Zos. 5. 23.

12   For Anastasius' policy concerning the Lower Danube border, see Haarer (2006) 109–114.

13   *Chron. Marcell.* 422. 3.

14   Maenchen-Helfen (1973) 115–25; Croke (1977).

15   *Chron. Gall. 452.* 24.

16   For a detailed account of these various conflicts as mentioned in written sources, see Teodor (2002); (2003); (2004).

17   Madgearu (1996) 38–39.

18   For the disintegration of the Danubian border in the 7th c., see Madgearu (1997); (2001); (2006).

Roman *limes*, had multiple functions: to promote and control economic activity along and across the outer line of political control[19] while manifesting as a barrier in the Roman mental topography between 'us' and 'them' – the psychological frontier of civilization.

There are numerous ancient sources offering details about people from across the Danube receiving permission to settle within the territories of the empire, thus contributing to the multi-ethnic configuration of the province. The account of Zosimus mentioning the Goths camped near the capital city of Tomis, on the Black Sea coast, has already been mentioned. In his *Histories*, Eunapius of Sardis (345/346 to *ca.* 414) describes the events in the aftermath of a victory over the Goths, when 'after many arguments had been aired on both sides in the imperial consistory, the emperor decided to admit the Scythians.'[20] The description of the Black Sea and the people living on its shores by Ammianus Marcellinus should be added to the list. The author mentions the island of Peuce where the Troglodytae, the Peuci, and other lesser tribes dwell, next to the main cities on the coast such as Histria, Tomis and Apollonia.[21] A later source, Procopius of Caesarea (*ca.*500–565) writes about the fort of Ulmetum (located almost halfway between Histria and Capidava) that became wholly deserted, for the barbarian Sclaveni had been tarrying there for a long time. Moreover, during the building restoration program of Emperor Justinian, a new fort named Adina was built as the same people 'were constantly laying concealed ambuscades there against travellers, thus making the whole district impassable.'[22] Lastly, Jordanes' work *De origine actibusque Getarum* (written in or shortly after 551) recounts the events following the death of Attila, king of the Huns, in 453. After the battle of Nedao, the Goths were allowed to settle in Pannonia, following an agreement with the Romans, while further to the east, the Scyri, Sadagarii and 'certain of the Alani' with their leader named Candac received the same treatment and entered Scythia Minor and Lower Moesia.[23]

Despite the narrative shaped by written sources, what is known, from an archaeological point of view and according to the current state of research, is that settlements or cemeteries belonging to these people from beyond the Danube that were settled within the territories of the empire are yet to be found. Nevertheless, isolated discoveries such as skeletons with artificially

deformed skulls[24] or burials with particular grave goods (or associations of specific items)[25] point towards an interesting phenomenon of cultural exchange and amalgamation. Even though the history of most settlements from the province of Scythia ended in the first half of the 7th c., as a consequence of the Roman *limes* collapse and the consequent generalized decline, their (hi)stories are continuously being brought to light and shape by the work of archaeologists and historians alike.

The Archaeological Record and Current State of Research

The earliest funerary discoveries are most likely those from Tomis, from the period when the modern harbour was constructed during which a "large number of graves" was discovered.[26] Vasile Pârvan (1882–1927), known as the founder of Romanian archaeology, began the excavations in the ancient city of Histria in 1914, leading to the discovery of several tombstones, funerary reliefs and stelae.[27] The interest towards archaeological research grew exponentially from the 1950s. Between 1957 and 1976, over 460 graves were unearthed during excavations in the cemeteries of Callatis. The results were published in the monograph of Preda some years later.[28] In addition to the 367 graves published in the monograph, the research carried out between 1975 and 1992, and then after the year 2000, led to the discovery of more than 470 burials, thus making Callatis the archaeological site with the largest number of such findings.[29] Even though burials dated in the interval between the 4th and the 7th c. were discovered within many sites, only 4 sites produced more than a few discoveries: Tomis, Callatis, Ibida and Histria.[30] The most extensive research at

---

24   Sonu (2018).

25   See, for example, the case of an early 7th c. female grave from Enisala where two copper-alloy fibulae (belonging to Werner's class I G) and two bracelets made of copper-alloy circular bars were found, pointing towards a Middle Dnieper origin. However, the authors' conclusion deserves attention: "Even if the [stable isotope] analysis were to prove that she hailed from the Middle Dnieper region, the personal accessories with which she was buried are not primarily badges of her ethnic identity, since that identity most likely did not depend on the place in which she had been born, but on the position she had in the community within which she spent the last years of her life." Ailincăi *et al.* (2014) 75.

26   Barbu (1961) 203; Oța (2015).

27   Pârvan (1916); (1923).

28   Preda (1980).

29   Georgescu and Ionescu (1995–1996) 197; Ionescu *et al.* (2002–2003); Ungureanu and Radu (2006).

30   An unfortunate situation should be acknowledged in the case of Beroe-Piatra Frecăței (located in the north-eastern part of

---

19   Whittaker (1994) 72–84.

20   Eunap. *Hist.* 47.

21   Amm. Marc. 22. 8.

22   Procop. *Aed.* 4. 7.

23   Jord. *Get.* 265. 23–25.

Tomis (1959–1964) led to the discovery of more than 685 burials dated after the 2nd c.[31] In 1988, two domed vaults containing co-mingled human remains were discovered.[32] With excavations taking place for more than a century now, establishing the exact number of funerary discoveries from the cemeteries of the capital city of Scythia is no simple task due to the nature of the published material.

The year 1961 marked the beginning of one of the most important archaeological excavations at Histria, in terms of discoveries concerning burial practices in the Late Roman period. 74 graves spanning from the end of the 3rd c. to the beginning of the 7th c. were discovered on the so-called 'Basilica extra muros' sector. 42 graves belong in the 4th c., while another 19 burials were broadly dated between the 4th and 5th c. This group, accounting for 61 graves, belongs to the "first horizon of burials", or the "first cemetery". A second smaller group of only 10 graves located in the funerary near the church is dated to the 6th c. (or 7th c.).[33] Research was resumed in the area after 2001 with more than 50 burials being excavated since.[34] Excavations of a more recent date were carried out at Ibida between 2001 and 2013, leading to the discovery of almost 200 graves.[35] One of the most important findings is that of an underground vaulted tomb with *dromos* and funerary chamber. This monument was the final resting place for at least 39 individuals of all ages and sexes. Unfortunately, the graves were looted (probably several times) resulting in a thick layer of co-mingled human remains with no skeleton found in complete anatomical form.[36]

A smaller number of burials have been discovered in several sites across the province, such as Carsium (95),[37] Tropaeum Traiani (43),[38] Noviodunum (38),[39] and Dinogetia (29).[40] Even though the total number of findings accounts for thousands of graves, not all of them could be incorporated in an analysis due to the lack of sufficient relevant data. In the case of Carsium, for instance, we know from a paper published 27 years

ago that 45 graves were excavated in Cemetery I, while "more than 50 graves were found" in Cemetery II.[41] The authors are aware that the publication and analysis of the materials are of great importance and could improve our knowledge about Carsium, a little-known archaeological site. However, this statement did not have the expected outcome, as the results remain unpublished thus far.

Most of the early research was primarily focused on describing the graves together with the objects found accompanying the dead. When confronted with a substantial number of funerary discoveries, archaeologists sought to organize and make sense of the archaeological record by developing typologies. As a consequence, each major study about a cemetery came was published with its own typology.[42] Given the constantly growing corpus of discoveries and certain evolutions within the field of archaeology, different approaches and narratives emerged. Archaeologists began to be interested in new topics such as the funerary topography of the sites[43] and the burial treatment for a particular category of individuals (such as children)[44] while anthropologists, together with other specialists from various disciplines, engaged in research projects on complex issues, steering away from the analysis of burial customs *per se*, but integrating it in the same time, in order to tackle topics such as gender, diet, mobility and migratory phenomena.[45]

Scythia) where 1139 burials were excavated. The monograph dedicated to the cemetery is incomplete, discussing only 228 graves largely dated by the author between the 2nd and the 7th c.; Petre (1987) 7–8.

31   Barbu (1961) 204; Barbu (1971) 47.
32   Bucovală (1993).
33   Hampartumian (1971a); Crețu *et al.* (2020).
34   Rusu-Bolindeț *et al.* (2014); Dabîca (2014); (2019).
35   Soficaru (2014).
36   Mirițoiu and Soficaru (2003a).
37   Nicolae (1993) 222–24.
38   Barnea (2004) 19.
39   Baumann (2006).
40   Data from the unpublished fieldnotes of A. Barnea, the excavation director. Soficaru (2011) 88–90.

---

41   Nicolae (1993) 222–24.
42   Barbu (1971) for Tomi; Preda (1980) for Callatis; Petre (1987) for Beroe.
43   Achim (2015).
44   Achim (2012); Rubel and Soficaru (2012); Crețu (2018).
45   Two examples could be cited here: the recent project of Andrei Soficaru, "Women at the Edge of Empire: Female Social Identity in the Lower Danube in 4th–6th Centuries AD" aimed at addressing the role of women as active participants in a plural society by investigating the (trans)formation, (re)articulation and (re)construction of female identity in response to intercultural contact by focusing on the people themselves. The project draws together human osteology, stable isotopes, mortuary behavior, material culture and epigraphy (more details at https://womenattheedgeofempire.wordpress.com/); the Romanian-American joint project Histria Multiscalar Archaeological Project-HMAP designed to address issues related to human mobility, diet and health by an integrated program of archaeological, bioarchaeological and ecological analysis of human osteological material discovered in the cemeteries from Histria (https://microarchlab.github.io /research_romania.html?fbclid=IwAR2cRAyb6A132uEsL _QmIWi_1ZJAf9RNxNRFWTQNooLSVOJgWNgBQ4ZPC4A).

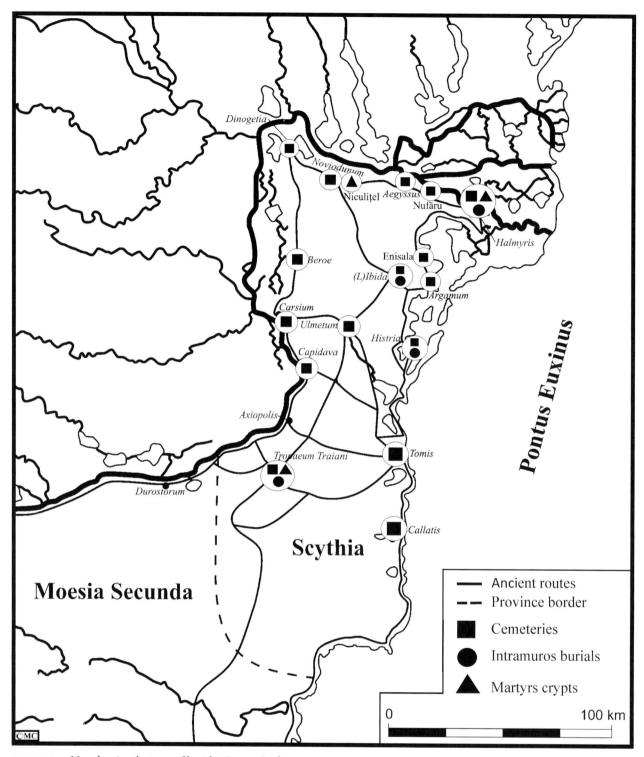

FIGURE 1   Map showing the types of burial in Roman Scythia.

Deathscapes in Late Roman and Early Byzantine Scythia

It has long been established by archaeologists that while cemeteries were created by the living to house and mourn the dead, burial grounds are also significant cultural spaces utilized by and integral to the cultural traditions of the former. Separating the realm of the living from that of the dead was fundamental for many past civilizations, and the Romans were no exception. Establishing a separate space for the deposition of the deceased impacted on the topography of the ancient city through the creation of deathscapes.[46] Most

46   Deathscapes are the places associated with death and for the dead, and how these are imbued with meanings and

people were buried in cemeteries located outside city walls.[47] Changes in mortuary landscape should also be understood in connection to the historical events that occurred in the region. For Histria, the emergence of a new space designed for the deposition of the dead was determined by the significant contraction of the settlement that followed the construction of a new defensive wall. The Early Roman defensive system was destroyed and consequently abandoned after the Gothic attacks of the mid-3rd c. Constructed most probably during the reigns of Aurelian (270–275) and Probus (275–282), the new fortification reduced the city area to less than half its previous size. The former residential districts, now situated *extra-urbem*, eventually lost their original function and became a cemetery at the beginning of the 4th c.[48]

Regardless of its reasons, causes and effects, this separation is rooted in the existence of a dichotomy in the Roman frame of mind between the funerary and the non-funerary realms. Death was a disruptive event that polluted the bereaved family[49] turning them into a *familia funesta*, as opposed to *familia pura*. Civil laws regarding burials differentiated a *locus religiosus*, meaning land on which a body had been interred, from a *locus purus*, land without buried human remains.[50] It took the emergence and spread of Christianity in the region for this attitude toward death to sharply change, with far-reaching consequences for the topography of the ancient city.

In close relation with the Christian faith, a particular form of mortuary practice is worthy of attention – burials inside churches. The term *martyrium* (pl. *martyria*) is used to describe a shrine or structure built or adapted to honour a martyr whose remains are interred inside.[51] In Scythia, burial chambers (*hypogaea*) located under the altars of churches were found at Halmyris, Noviodunum, and Tropaeum Traiani. The Halmyris

crypt is situated under the altar and beneath the pavement of the church and has two rectangular rooms. The first room (2.5 m long) was identified as the *dromos*, an access room reached after walking down 8 descending stairs. The mortuary chamber is a 2 m long, 1.85 m wide and 1.88 m high vaulted room. The scattered remains from two individuals were found inside, suggesting that the grave was looted. Only a few objects were found inside the room: a fragment of an amphora bearing the pentagram sign, a hook from a votive candle, and a fragment of a vase bearing the stylized fish, one of the most distinctive Christian figures.[52] Anthropological analysis revealed that the remains belong to two adult males. Traces of perimortem violence were also documented, such as fractures of the scapulae and destruction of its mandible for one skeleton, while for the other the inferior articular facets were severed from posterior to anterior by a blow produced by a very sharp object, indicating most probably a beheading.[53] The individuals interred under the church altar from Halmyris were the two martyrs Epictet and Astion[54] who died most probably at the beginning of the 4th c., in the same period when other martyrs were killed in the Danubian provinces ruled by Galerius, and were laid to rest inside the church at a later date.[55]

The basilica from Niculițel, located in the vicinity of Noviodunum, was constructed at the end of the 4th c. to shelter the remains of Christian martyrs in a monumental crypt. That particular location was deemed suitable for such a project by virtue of the existence of an older *martyrium* built on the same spot at the beginning of the century on a *villa rustica* property that contained the remains of two locals martyred during the 3rd c. The entrance to the crypt was sealed by a limestone block. A wooden structure served as protection for the remains of 4 individuals laid directly on the stone pavement of the chamber. The anatomical position of the skeletons suggests a primary deposition at a short time after death occurred. On the walls from both sides of the coffin, two Greek engraved and red painted inscriptions read μαρτύρες Χριστοῦ (Christ's martyrs) and the names of the martyrs: Zotikos, Attalos, Kamasis, Philippos.[56] The access to the underground crypt from Tropaeum Traiani, situated under the pavement in the middle nave area, was through a sloping 4.2 m long corridor. The remains

associations: the site of a funeral, and the places of final disposition and of remembrance, and representations of all these. Maddrell and Sidaway (2010) 4–5. The creation of such spaces was sanctioned by official prohibitive official regulations imposing a distinction between the place occupied by the living and that designed for the dead by exclusion of the latter from the residential space reserved for the former, as well as through common, recurrent practice.

47   See Figure 1 for the main settlements discussed in the text.

48   Hamparțumian (1971a); Domăneanțu (1990).

49   For a definition and an anthropological discussion related to pollution by contact with a dead person, see Douglas (1966). The literature discussing the attitude of the Romans towards *pollution* caused by death is substantial: André (1980); Lindsay (2000); Retief and Cilliers (2006).

50   De Visscher (1963) 43–63; Robinson (1975).

51   Eastman (2018) 89.

52   Zahariade (2001–2003); Zahariade (2009).

53   Mirițoiu and Soficaru (2003b); (2007)

54   An inscription discovered on the eastern wall of the mortuary chamber served as the basis for the identification of the two names, see Zahariade (2001–2003) 152, Fig. 19.

55   Madgearu (2012); (2014).

56   Baumann (2015) 123–68.

of 5 individuals were found inside. Unfortunately, the crypt was looted and the domed roof collapsed making more precise observations impossible. The identity of the martyrs remains unknown. The construction of the basilica, provided since its inception with the crypt, was dated around 500.[57]

Of the three basilicas with *martyria*, two were located *intra urbem* – within city walls (those of Hamyris and Tropaeum Traiani) and one on the outskirts of the city cemetery (at Noviodunum). As a consequence of Christians burying the remains of the martyrs in churches within the city, the old taboo that forbade interments in such places disappeared. The exceptional remains of these holy men made a first breach in the city walls as well as in an old way of thinking.[58] Soon after relics were placed inside churches, other burials appeared in their proximity. Speaking about graves in connection with churches, Achim defines two categories: one that contains churches which "attracted" contemporary cemeteries around them and the other made up of isolated graves or small groups of burials in the proximity of churches.[59] Cemeteries developed near basilicas at Tropaeum Traiani in the 4th c. and at Histria two centuries later. A group of 10 graves has been dated in the period between the 6th and 7th c. being contemporary with the so-called 'extra-mural basilica' from Histria. The position of Grave 58 stands out within the funerary landscape by being located in a courtyard that extends eastwards from the apse of the church. The burial was placed 1.2 m east of the apse, following the direction of its longitudinal axis. The grave distinguishes itself also through the unique artefacts found inside: a set of gold footwear items, with two strap ends, two buckles, and two rectangular fittings decorated with incised crosses, together with remains of golden threads from a costume's embroidery.[60] The location of this grave best illustrates the desire of those of the upper social stratum to be buried in a special, highly-visible place. As the grave was probably marked above the ground by a tombstone, it was integrated into the structure of the building and the surrounding landscape through its constant presence within the visual field of the community members who frequented the place. For the survivors who attended services or ceremonies at the church, as well as for those who buried their dead at a later date, such a grave could have functioned as a mnemonic device that

would remind the viewer about the high status of the departed (or their family).

Unlike at Tropaeum Traiani, no crypt was found underneath the basilica from Histria. Even though Born noted that the existence of a northern annex of the basilica together with "privileged" burials in the immediate vicinity are clues for relics sheltering inside the religious edifice,[61] this is not necessarily the case. We are more inclined to believe that the church itself, even without a *martyrium*, was the point of attraction. The church is the place that facilitates the connection of this world with the heavenly paradise, as Brown puts it,[62] so this could be the reason why people considered appropriate to bury their dead near churches. But a church and the graveyard nearby are also places where people meet and came together in acts of worship and remembrance. Consequently, it is equally valid that people would bury their dead in such special places in order to convey a message in the mortuary arena as a space of social negotiations, representations and creating narratives. It is important to acknowledge the material agency[63] exerted by churches *per se* or by the holy remains sheltered inside.

Burials within the city walls have been discovered also at Histria near the Episcopal Basilica. The cult building, situated this time inside the city, was constructed in the period between the last years of the 5th c. and the first half of the 6th c. and functioned as such until the reign of Mauricius (582–602).[64] A group of at least 5 burials were found east of the apse.[65] Considering their placement, the graves were interpreted as belonging to members of the clergy who have performed their duties in the city. Even if a basilica with a crypt existed inside the city at Histria, no burials were discovered nearby.[66]

It is worth noting that for the territories close to the province of Scythia, such as Illyricum, the choice of *intra urbem* interments was linked, at least in part, to a far-reaching phenomenon of urban cores shrinkage – *id est* a 'citadelisation' that replaced the classic urban idea with a new concept whose main purpose was a defensive one that established the city wall(s) as a central

---

57   Barnea (1978); Mirițoiu and Nicolăescu-Plopșor (1978) for the anthropological analysis.
58   Dagron (1977) 11–19.
59   Achim (2015).
60   Hamparțumian (1971b); Crețu *et al.* (2020) 148–50.

61   Born (2012) 83.
62   Brown (1981) 3.
63   The capability of building or objects to affect people's behavior and attitudes.
64   Suceveanu (2007) 38, 98.
65   The precise number remains unclear given that a total of 7 graves are mentioned in the annual reports including one cenotaph and one belonging to an infant, while in the monograph dedicated to the building only 5 burials are discussed; Suceveanu (2007) 37–38.
66   Achim (2005).

point of reference.[67] Consequently, a contraction of the urban peripheries occurred thus demanding the abandonment of extramural quarters. In conjunction with the climate of perpetual insecurity due to foreign people repeatedly plundering the region and considering the stabilization of the Christian faith, it seems somehow natural that the inhabitants sought to bury their dead in cemeteries established around churches located *extra urbem*, near the city's walls, as well as in specially designated places inside the city.

Scythia does not lack examples of cemeteries that developed around extramural churches, such as those from Histria,[68] Tropaeum Traiani,[69] or Beroe.[70] Burials within the city walls are extremely rare. Two newborns and an adult were buried at Ibida,[71] one grave and several dispersed human bones were discovered at Halmyris,[72] two craniums from Tropaeum Traiani,[73] and at least 5 burials at Histria.[74] It is evident that the small isolated group of graves from Histria offers the only case from the province where a space inside the city was allocated and deemed suitable for burying the dead. Northern Illyricum displays a different picture. Numerous *intra urbem* cemeteries were established here either in the proximity of cult buildings such as the Basilica of St. Demetrius from Sirmium, or in an assigned area as it is the case of Singidunum II cemetery located around the city's south-western rampart. As mentioned above, the graves near the Episcopal Basilica in Histria probably belonged to members from the ecclesiastical hierarchy, unlike the individuals from Singidunum II, or those from Sirmium, who were ordinary, non-elite citizens.[75] Therefore, at least in the case of Histria, it seems that burial inside the city was restricted only to a particular category. However, this hypothesis remains dependent on the current state of archaeological research in the province of Scythia.

The consideration of mortuary spaces in the province of Scythia would be incomplete without taking into account the exceptional discovery of a family burial vault at Ibida. The vault was in use for a long period of time between the 4th and the beginning of the 7th c. The interval was established based on the objects found inside the funerary chamber: several glass beads,

fragments from two bone combs, a silver double-loop belt buckle with mobile plate, oval in shape, with three rivets arranged in a triangle (dated second half of the 4th c. to first part of 5th c.), and another iron belt buckle without plate, rectangular with rounded corners (dated largely from the 4th to the 6th c.).[76] It probably belonged to the family of a dignitary and housed the remains of over 40 individuals of all ages (including newborns). The walls of the crypt were rendered and painted in the *a seco* technique, divided in panels delimited by red and dark blue stripes and decorated with vegetal motifs and honeycombs. A raised platform located between the funerary beds was probably used for the placement of offerings, as well as support for *lucernae* and other paraphernalia. The dead were laid to rest in wooden coffins, as proven by the large number of iron nails found inside. Unfortunately, the vault was looted multiple times and no skeleton was found in complete anatomical form. Scattered human bones were also discovered in the *dromos* area outside of the mortuary chamber.[77] This vault with its 1.7 m long *dromos* and a spacious mortuary chamber (4.5 m long × 4.5 m wide) definitely stood out within the cemetery of Ibida both as a topographical point, by virtue of its location near the road leading to a monastic complex that functioned until the beginning of the 7th c.,[78] and as a place of memory and commemoration for the family of the departed. The existence of such a complex structure is indicative of the financial resources that the beneficiaries have at their disposal and their willingness to invest in constructing a place for burying their dead like no other in the cemeteries of the city.

As a type of monument, the vaulted tomb from Ibida is not the only one of its kind in the province of Scythia. Several constructions with similar features were discovered at Callatis. Items found inside these *hypogaea*, such as a golden cross (*engolpion*) with a red gem mounted in the centre,[79] together with the craftsmanship and labour force required to design and build the structures (involving an appropriate remuneration) point yet again towards members of the upper echelons of society who possess the necessary means for such an enterprise. The painted vault from Tomis is probably the best example of an exquisite design for a funerary construction. The walls of the mortuary chamber are completely covered

67   Müller-Wiener (1986); Milojević (1996); Kirilov (2007).

68   Hamparțumian (1971a)

69   Achim (2015) 291–94.

70   Petre (1962) 579.

71   Soficaru (2011) 107–108; Rubel and Soficaru (2012).

72   Discovered near the martyrs' crypt, see Zahariade (2001–2003) 149–50.

73   Found in the vicinity of Basilica D, see Soficaru (2006–2007).

74   See above, n.63.

75   Ivanišević and Bugarski (2018) 98.

76   Aparaschivei *et al.* (2012) 178.

77   Iacob (2002); Mirițoiu and Soficaru (2003a) for the anthropological analysis.

78   A hoard was found inside the monastic complex. It contains one solidus minted during the reign of Justin II (565–578) and 5 solidi from the time of Mauricius (582–602), see Iacob (2005).

79   Barnea (1995–1996).

by a fresco depicting anthropomorphous, zoomorphous and fitomorphous scenes. 4 individuals were deposited in wooden coffins. Among the personal items found with the deceased are a silver *philakterium*, several beads, a fusiform glass *unguentarium*, two bronze earrings and an amphora.[80] Finally, another beautifully painted *hypogeum* was discovered at Durostorum in a funerary area destined for the members of the elite,[81] and 5 simple vaulted tombs featuring rich grave assemblages made of gold and silver were documented at Carsium.[82]

An exceptional discovery, also from Ibida, does not fall in any of the working categories discussed in the paper (cemeteries located *extra urbem*, graves positioned in the proximity of basilicas with *martyria*, and burials within city walls). A mass grave dated in the 4th c.[83] was identified in 2008 when scattered human remains were discovered during the archaeological investigation of the foundation of the 10th tower of the walled enclosure. Analysis revealed that the remains of at least 28 individuals were placed inside the pit. The high frequency of cut marks and other indicators of perimortem trauma suggest violent deaths. Moreover, considering the high degree of fragmentation and disarticulation of the osteological material, it seems that the bodies of the dead already decomposed elsewhere before they were gathered and buried in the same place. By looking at how the funerary space was organized and structured and by considering its relationship with the residential area we sought to gain a better understanding of the intangible driving forces upon which people's actions and intentions are based when they deliberately selected and chose certain places to bury their dead.

Burial Practices – Similarity and Diversity

In the previous section we focused on cemeteries and other groups of burials as constituent parts of the funerary landscape. Three different categories were discussed: cemeteries located *extra urbem*, graves positioned in the proximity of basilicas with *martyria*, and burials within city walls. From this point onwards the focus shifts towards the graves themselves, in an attempt to

discuss the diverse repertoire of funerary solutions documented on the territory of Scythia. In the 3rd c., cremation became obsolete and was eventually replaced by the exclusive practice of inhumation. The only cremation dated to the middle of the 4th c. was discovered at Krapets, 30 km south of Callatis, on the Black Sea coast.[84] Even though inhumation was the only way of disposing of the dead, grave construction presents great variety. For most burials, a simple rectangular pit was dug and the corpse was deposited inside in a container and then the pit was sealed by covering it with soil.[85] A disposal container refers to any element used in transporting or holding the body. The body could be wrapped in a textile shroud and/or deposited in a wooden coffin, usually fastened with nails. If iron nails discovered on the margins of the pit are indicative for a burial in a coffin, the existence of a shroud is more complicated to prove because it involves a careful observation of the position of various anatomical elements of the skeleton. Tightly wrapping the body using a fabric limits the upcoming movement of different parts of the body as the corpse decomposes.[86]

In Grave 23/1961 from the 4th c. cemetery at Histria two young women were buried in supine position.[87] A few clues point toward the use of a shroud to wrap the bodies: displacement of the clavicles to an almost vertical position, the position of the lower limbs closer to each other in the knee area, the preservation of the anatomical connection and position of the patellae and of the bones of the feet. The pit itself could be delimited with rows of stone blocks or bricks, creating a cist-like structure. In the late cemetery (6th–7th c.) located near the extra-mural basilica at Histria, 6 out of a total of 10 graves belong to this category. In addition to the simple pit in which the deceased were deposited, a structure made of tiles was sometimes designed atop. Two main variants of such external structures were documented. Graves were covered either by flat lids made of bricks and tiles or by double-sloped roofs (the so-called *alla cappuccina* graves). A ridge of *imbrices* could be added. In grave 10/1961 from Histria (dated in the 4th c.), the remains of an 11 year-old female was covered with a slanted roof made of tiles. 4 *imbrices* were arranged in perpendicular pairs forming a cross above the roof.[88]

---

80   Barbet and Bucovală (1996).
81   Considering that a high-ranking local magistrate's funeral with a chariot and other gifts and weapons was uncovered nearby, see Atanasov (2007).
82   Nicolae (1993).
83   Based on the stratigraphy of the complex and on the relative dating of the pottery fragments, together with two absolute dates obtained by means radiocarbon dating which provided two absolute dates: 304–406 (1700±30 BP) and 244–398 (1715±35 BP). Soficaru *et al.* (2019).

---

84   Two other instances of cremation were recorded in the 4th c., but at a greater distance from Scythia: at Abritus and further to the west, near the village of Kovachevets. Rusev (2012) 393.
85   A disposal container refers to any container used in transporting or holding the body, such as a shroud or a coffin.
86   Duday (2009) 45–46.
87   Crețu *et al.* (2020) 153, 173.
88   Crețu *et al.* (2020) 151, 168.

Combinations of these internal and external features are attested as well. Many graves from Callatis have stone cists covered with horizontal lids made of limestone slabs. In a similar manner, the individual from grave 33/1963 in the same cemetery was placed in a coffin, and then deposited in a cist grave sealed with a horizontal lid.[89] Niche graves were discovered only in cemeteries from Tomis, Histria, and Callatis.[90] The operational sequences for this type unfolded as follows: at the bottom of a vertical shaft a lateral niche was dug; after the body of the deceased was placed inside, the niche was usually sealed by covering the entrance with stones or tiles. At least 80 niche graves were identified at Tomis. In some of them individuals were deposited inside coffins, as traces and imprints of wood as well as a large quantity of iron nails testify. Niche graves were the prevalent form of burial within the cemetery located outside the city walls at Histria, with 43% of the graves belonging to this category. Unfortunately, for this group there is no data available about the use of coffins. At both sites, where items found inside allowed for the dating of the burials, it is noticeable that they all belong in the 4th c. The chronology was established by dating various items found inside graves, such as a particular type of brooch – the so-called *zwiebelknopffibel* – all belonging in the 4th c.[91]

An interesting correlation between this type of graves and the custom of placing animal bones inside the burial pit was observed at Histria. More than half of the graves with niches also have animal offerings deposited either near the head of the deceased or at the lower extremity of the pit. The deposition of animal body parts in graves was a widespread practice in several cemeteries belonging to the Sântana de Mureş – Chernyakhov groups north of the Danube.[92] On the same note, in the cemeteries of the late Sarmatians (from the 3rd c. onwards)

there is an increase in the number of niche graves in the entire region between the mouth of the Don and the Danube.[93] Under the circumstances, a scenario suggesting influences coming from outside the empire should not be discarded.

Within the same framework of discussing a certain influence exerted by foreigners, if not their presence *per se* in cemeteries from the province of Scythia, a particular category of items found in some graves is worthy of attention. Bilateral bone combs were deposited inside at least 8 graves from Scythia – 4 from Histria,[94] three from Beroe,[95] and one from Tomis[96] – most of them dated in the 6th c. Depositing bone combs, usually in the area near the skull of the deceased (but not restricted to it), was a widespread practice in the Germanic/Gepid environments.[97] This type of bilateral comb is the most widespread form in the during the 5th c. Carpathian Basin. It seems that it appeared in Pannonia during the last decades of the 4th c. and it is later attested in Sarmatian milieus from the first decades of the 5th c.[98]

Whereas numerous historical sources mention successive waves of foreigners crossing the river Danube from the north, starting with the Goths in the 4th c. and continuing later with frequent attacks and invasions of Huns, Avars and Slavs, no barbarian cemeteries are known within the territory of Scythia. The *foreign* character of such rather isolated discoveries was usually assigned based on the grave goods. For example, 8 graves discovered at Ulmetum contained typical Sântana de Mureş-Chernyakhov pottery, together with other Roman items. Two of the skeletons were orientated north-south and were therefore assigned to the Goths. In a similar manner, the presence of two bronze brooches placed on each shoulder of an individual from Argamum determined the archaeologist to consider it a Germanic grave.[99] The preference for a particular type of burial, such as niche graves, together with the choice of specific items and objects (e.g. animal bones deposited in burial pits, bone combs placed inside graves) emphasizing yet

89　Preda (1980) 87–88, 109.

90　Hamparţumian (1971a); Preda (1980) 15–22; Lungu and Chera-Mărgineanu (1982) 176–82; Bucovală and Paşca (1988–1989) 126–42; Creţu *et al.* (2020).

91　In the Tomis cemetery three such brooches were found in niche graves: one brooch of Pröttel 2b type (dated 300–350) in grave 8/1982, another one of Pröttel 1b type (dated 290–320) in grave 37/1982 (a triple burial), and the third and last one belonging to the Pröttel 3/4a type (dated 330–360) discovered in grave 100/1987–1988. At Histria, two brooches were found inside graves from the cemetery outside city walls: one of the Pröttel 1b type in grave 26/1961, and the second one in grave 6/1961 belonging to the Pröttel 3/4d dated 350–400. In the order they were mentioned, for Tomis, see Lungu and Chera-Mărgineanu (1982) 176, 180; Bucovală and Paşca (1988–1989) 139. For Histria, see Creţu *et al.* (2020) 151, 153. For the typology used, see Pröttel (1999).

92　Stanc and Bejenaru (2004); Haimovici (2005).

93　Mordvintseva (2017).

94　Condurachi (1957) 49; Condurachi (1960) 260; Condurachi (1962) 417; Hamparţumian (1971a) 207–208.

95　Petre (1987) 1987, Pl. 182/d, Pl. 210/b, Pl. 214/b.

96　Cheluţă-Georgescu (1974) 363–365, 373, Pl. v/6.

97　The discoveries are very numerous and distributed in a fairly large area. For Moreşti and Bratei (Romania), see Horedt (1979) Fig. 72/2–4, Fig. 72/7, Fig. 74/14, Fig. 89/1; Blăjan and Togan (1981) Fig. 1/2, Fig. 2/4. For Jaksor and Kiszombor (Hungary), see Csallány (1961) Pl. III/12, Pl. IV/9, Pl. v/6, Pl. v/12; Pl. CXIX/2, Pl. CXX/8, Pl. CXXIX/9.

98　Masek (2016) 106.

99　The complex relationship between Roman and foreign mortuary practices in the province of Scythia was recently discussed in Soficaru and Sofaer (2021).

again the complex dynamics at work within the funerary realm, along with the idea that mortuary practices had a flexible and variable nature, echoing the complexity of the social, cultural, and political milieu in which people experienced life and death.

Apart from the ethnic component when discussing preferences and choices in terms of funerary treatment, it seems that age played an important role for the inhabitants of the province, considering that newborns and very small children were dealt with in a special manner – they were buried in amphorae or under fragments of larger pots. Such burials were found at Histria, Ibida and Callatis.[100] Unlike at Histria and Callatis where the graves were found in the cemeteries located outside city walls, at Ibida the infants were interred inside the settlement. Here, the remains of newborns (38 foetal weeks), buried in amphorae, were discovered inside a tower located in the northern part of the city under the foundation of a dismantled wall to the west. In contrast to the situation mentioned above, older children did not receive any special burial treatment. 4 skeletons belonging to infants older than three months were discovered at Ibida, only this time they were buried together with other members of the society in the *extra urbem* cemetery. Moreover, in the case of Histria it was established that there are absolutely no differences between how older children (that is to say except the newborns interred in amphorae) and adults were treated in a mortuary setting. The choices and preferences in terms of grave architecture were similar. The same categories of graves (e. g. niche graves, *alla cappuccina* graves, grave with simple pits) show a symmetrical decrease, from the most to the least common type, regardless of the age of the deceased. On the same note, no discrepancy was noted between children and adult burials and the occurrence of grave goods. For both categories, the items deposited most often were adornments of different types, such as bracelets or beads.[101]

Most individuals were buried in extended supine position and aligned on a west-east axis[102] (with north-west/south-east and south-west/north-east variants) as it was typical of Roman practice at that time. Corpses were usually arranged with their arms stretched alongside the body, or with the forearms bent with the hands placed on the pelvis or sometimes resting on the chest. Items buried together with the deceased, if any, include adornments such as bracelets made from bronze, silver, animal bone and iron, beads made from glass, amber and coral, rings made of bronze, silver and gold, bronze hairpins and earrings, etc. Even though the majority of objects from this category were found in female graves it seems that the use of adornments was not restricted on a gender basis of the deceased individuals. Beads and rings have been found in male graves as well. It seems that the only items found exclusively in graves belonging to women were earrings. In addition to garments, other categories of objects placed inside the burial pit include: pottery, glass vessels, coins, lamps, combs made from animal bone with iron rivets. No weapons were buried together with the deceased.

On the occasion of concluding this brief analysis based on data from a province located at the edge of the Roman world, one main idea should be pointed out. While mortuary practices could be understood as a set of standardized choices, they are also diverse and subject to change. Through the mixture of different lines of evidence, maybe general patterns can be discerned, but it is important to emphasize their variability as well at both intra- and inter-site level, and ultimately to understand that practices, attitudes, and behaviours related to the funerary realm varied geographically as well as temporally.

Conclusion

While engaging with the topic of ancient deathscapes, scholars must be aware that the production of knowledge is conditioned by and dependent upon the frail archaeological record. Its fragmentary nature in conjunction with the disproportionate character of the available data[103] often complicates and limits the analysis. The process of observing and contextualizing[104] the interrelation between the dynamic changes occurring in the mortuary realm and the consequential spatial adjustments enabled us to examine how deathscapes were created and maintained, as well as how they mutated in time. As the basis for this study, we identified three distinct categories of mortuary spaces:

100　Preda (1980) 15–22; Suceveanu (1983) 36–37; Rubel and Soficaru (2012); Crețu *et al.* (2020) 146.

101　Crețu (2021) 228–47.

102　84% of the graves from Histria and 73% from those at Callatis had a west-east orientation (noting that the total number of excavated burials is significantly higher at Callatis).

103　From a quantitative as well as a qualitative point of view. To name only a few shortcomings, in many situations the descriptions of the graves are very brief, lacking important details such as the orientation and position of the skeleton, the presence (or absence) of any objects on the basis of which archaeological features could be dated, detailed plans of the excavations.

104　Contextualization plays an important role, since deathscapes dynamics are inherently dependent and influenced by the social, historical, and political settings.

cemeteries located *extra urbem*, graves positioned in the proximity of basilicas with *martyria*, and burials within city walls. Cemeteries located on the outskirts of settlements represent beyond any doubt the most common articulation of a mortuary landscape not only in the scrutinized region, but throughout the empire. By deliberately selecting a place destined for burying the dead, and through its continuous use, the configuration of the surroundings of the cities was transformed, both *per se* and within the mental topography of the inhabitants.

The emergence and popularity of the Christian faith and of the cult of saints explain the desire to be buried in the proximity of cult buildings. Attitudes regarding the separation of the space for the living from the space for the dead fundamentally changed, in the sense of accepting burials inside settlements, along with the establishment of a set of ideas assumed and promoted by the Christian doctrine. The beginnings of this phenomenon could be linked to the bringing and deposition of the relics of the martyrs in churches inside the cities, followed by the inhabitants' eagerness to bury their dead nearby. However, other explanations should be sought for the burials that are not connected with buildings sheltering martyrs' remains. The general climate of insecurity due to constant barbarian invasions and the inability to defend a place located outside the defensive system of a city is a plausible scenario. The desire of the survivors to bury the dead in a privileged and highly visible position in order to assert their status should be also considered in some cases, such as grave 58 from Histria, located in a courtyard near the apse of the basilica.

The analysis of burial practices gave way to the assessment of the degree of variability and similarity of the mortuary record from the province. Setting aside the Tudorka family vault and the mass grave from Ibida along with the *martyria*, it is worth noting that most of the other grave types and mortuary practices documented in Scythia were also common for the whole Lower Danube region. Be that as it may, it is important to acknowledge the existence of inter-site differences in terms of preferences for particular types of graves or the wide repertoire of burial technologies.[105] Cemeteries and individual burials alike are not the result of societal-level decisions, but where rather organized at a local level, and consequently bear the marks of different agents that acted under specific social, historical, economic and political circumstances.

Our intention with this study is not to provide an in-depth and complete analysis of the burial customs from the 4th to the 7th c. in the province of Scythia, otherwise a lesser-known subject apart from a regional level. Such endeavour is perhaps worthy of a full-length book. The main goal we set out was rather to put forward an overview of the data available in the region by assessing and propounding the multidimensional and multi-layered nature of the research potential that mortuary archaeology allows, and to offer instances or exemplifications in support of such claims. By observing the relation between people from the past and the spaces destined for burying their dead and how this changed in time, we should seek to better understand the reasons on which such attitudes and behaviours are based. The same applies to each topic discussed in this study whether related to the different types of graves or to the custom of placing certain items together with the corpse inside the pit, to give just a few examples. Much work and things to be discovered lie ahead for both the present and the future generations of scholars interested in the mortuary archaeology of late antique and Early Byzantine Scythia. Seeing that knowledge and technology evolve, as it is obvious from the increased interest in interdisciplinary projects involving advanced statistical methods or various chemical analyses (such as radiogenic strontium or oxygen isotope analysis in archaeological and bioarchaeological research), will see new horizons of potential in-depth analysis open up.

Bibliography

Primary Sources

Amm. Marc. = J. C. Rolfe ed. and transl. *Ammianus Marcellinus. History, Volume II: Books 20–26* (Loeb Classical Library 315) (Cambridge 1940).

Chron. Gall. 452 = Burgess R. (2001) "The Gallic Chronicle of 452: a new critical edition with a brief introduction", in *Society and Culture in Late Antique Gaul*, edd. R. W. Mathisen and D. Shanzer (Aldershot 2001) 52–84.

Chron. Marcell. = B. Croke transl. *The Chronicle of Marcellinus* (Sydney 1995).

Eunap. Hist. = R. C. Blockley transl. *The Fragmentary Classicising Historians of the Later Roman Empire: Eunapius, Olympiodorus, Priscus and Malchus. Vol. 2. Text, Translation and Historiographical Notes* (Liverpool 2007).

Jord. Get. = C. C. Mierow transl. *The Gothic History of Jordanes* (Cambridge 1966).

Procop. Aed. = H. B. Dewing and G. Downey transl. *On Buildings. General Index* (Loeb Classical Library 343) (Cambridge 1940).

---

105 By burial technologies we understand the whole set of operations performed at a funeral, such as the position of the body (e.g. the positioning of the hands and legs), its orientation, the deposition of items inside the grave, etc.

Sozom., *Hist. eccl.* = E. Walford transl. *The Ecclesiastical History of Sozomen: A History of the Church from AD 324 to AD 440* (Mercantville 2018).

Them. *Or.* = P. Heather and D. Moncur transl. *Politics, Philosophy, and Empire in the Fourth Century. Select Orations of Themistius* (Liverpool 2001).

Zos. = R. T. Ridley transl. *Zosimus, New History* (Sydney 2006).

Secondary Sources

Achim I. (2005) "Étude d'archéologie chrétienne en Scythie Mineure: la basilique à crypte d'Histria", in *Mélanges Jean-Pierre Sodini*, edd. F. Baratte, V. Déroche, C. Jolivet-Lévy, and B. Pitarakis (Paris 2005) 85–97.

Achim I. (2012) "Early Roman and Late Roman child graves in Dobrudja (Romania). Preliminary considerations", in *Homines, Funera, Astra: Proceedings of the International Symposium on Funerary Anthropology: 5–8 June 2011 "1 Decembrie 1918" University, Alba Iulia, Romania*, edd. R. Kogălniceanu, R.-G. Curcă, M. Gligor, and S. Straton (Oxford 2012) 183–96.

Achim I. (2015) "Churches and graves of the Early Byzantine period in Scythia Minor and Moesia Secunda: the development of a Christian topography at the periphery of the Roman Empire", in *Death and Changing Rituals: Function and Meaning in Ancient Funerary Practices*, edd. J. Rasmus Brandt, H. Ingvaldsen, and M. Prusac (Oxford 2015) 287–342.

Ailincăi S., Constantinescu M., Curta F., and Soficaru A. (2014) "An early seventh-century female grave from Dobruja", *Archaeologia Bulgarica* 18(1) (2014) 65–84.

André J.-M. (1980) "La notion de Pestilentia à Rome: du tabu religieux à l'interprétation préscientifique", *Latomus* 39(1) (1980) 3–16.

Aparaschivei D., Iacob M., Soficaru A. D., and Paraschiv D. (2012) "Aspects of everyday life in Scythia Minor reflected in some funerary discoveries from Ibida (Slava Rusă, Tulcea County)", in *Homines, Funera, Astra: Proceedings of the International Symposium on Funerary Anthropology: 5–8 June 2011, "1 Decembrie 1918" University, Alba Iulia, Romania*, edd. R. Kogălniceanu, R.-G. Curcă, M. Gligor, and S. Straton (Oxford 2012) 169–82.

Atanasov G. (2007) "Late antique tomb in Durostorum-Silistra and its master", *Pontica* 40 (2007) 447–68.

Barbet A. and Bucovală M. (1996) "L'hypogée paléochrétien des Orants à Costanța (Roumanie), l'ancienne Tomis", *Mélanges de l'École française de Rome. Antiquité* 108/1 (1996) 105–158.

Barbu V. (1961) "Considérations chronologiques basées sur les données fournies par les inventaires funéraires des nécropoles tomitaines", *Studii Clasice* 3 (1961) 203–225.

Barbu V. (1971) "Din necropolele Tomisului I. Tipuri de morminte din epoca romană", *Studii și Cercetări de Istorie Veche* 22(1) (1971) 47–68.

Barnea A. (2004) "Adamclisi – Tropaeum Traiani, Sector Necropolă Valea Mare", *Cronica Cercetărilor Arheologice din România. Campania 2003* (2004) 14–21.

Barnea I. (1978) "Bazilica "simplă" (A) de la Tropaeum Traiani", *Pontica* 11 (1978) 181–87.

Barnea I. (1995–1996) "Despre două inscripții paleocreștine de la Callatis (Mangalia)", *Pontica* 28–29 (1995–1996) 183–86.

Barnes T. D. (1982) *The New Empire of Diocletian and Constantine* (Cambridge 1982).

Baumann V. H. (2006) "Isaccea – Noviodunum, Sector Cariera de lut – necropola", *Cronica Cercetărilor Arheologice din România. Campania 2005* (2006) 185–86.

Baumann V. H. (2015) *Sângele Martirilor* (Tulcea 2015).

Blăjan M. and Togan G. (1981) "Descoperiri arheologice fortuite la Bratei (jud. Sibiu)", *Studii și Comunicări* 21 (1981) 87–92.

Born R. (2012) *Die Christianisierung der Städte der Provinz Scythia Minor: ein Beitrag zum spätantiken Urbanismus auf dem Balkan* (Wiesbaden 2012).

Brown P. (1981) *The Cult of the Saints. Its Rise and Function in Latin Christianity* (Chicago 1981).

Bucovală M. (1993) "Cavou din secolul IV d. Chr. Descoperit în necropola de vest a Tomisului", *Pontica* 26 (1993) 207–214.

Bucovală M. and Pașca C. (1988–1989) "Descoperiri recente în necropolele de epocă romană și romano-bizantină la Tomis", *Pontica* 21–22 (1988–1989) 123–61.

Cedilnik A. (2009) "Sklenitev rimsko-gotske mirovne pogodbe leta 382", *Keria Studia Latina et Graeca* 11(1) (2009) 33–74.

Cheluță-Georgescu N. (1974) "Complexe funerare din secolul VI e.n. la Tomis", *Pontica* 7 (1974) 363–76.

Condurach E. (1962) "Șantierul Histria", *Material și Cercetări Arheologice* 8 (1962) 382–437.

Condurachi E. (1957) "Șantierul arheologic Histria", *Material și Cercetări Arheologice* 4 (1957) 9–102.

Condurachi E. (1960) "Șantierul arheologic Histria", *Material și Cercetări Arheologice* 7 (1960) 227–72.

Crețu C. (2018) "Despre moartea infantilă și practicile funerare din lumea romană. Studiu de caz: mormintele de copii de la Histria", *Buletinul Cercurilor Științifice Studențești* 24(1) (2018) 55–66.

Crețu C. (2021) *Practici funerare în mormintele de epocă romană de la Histria (secolele II–VII p. Chr.)* (Ph.D. diss., Univ. of Bucharest 2021).

Crețu C., Dabîca M., and Soficaru A. (2020) "Digging up the archives: a reassessment of burial practices in the cemeteries from the Extra muros basilica Sector at Histria", *Material și Cercetări Arheologice* 16 (2020) 139–80.

Croke B. (1977) "Evidence for the Hun invasion of Thrace in A.D. 422", *GRBS* 18 (1977) 347–67.

Csallány D (1961) *Archäologische Denkmäler der Gepiden im Mitteldonaubecken (454–568 u.Z.)* (Budapest 1961).

Dabîca M. (2014) "The Histria Sud sector. Recent archaeological research on an 'imposing' Early Roman public building", *Materiale și Cercetări Arheologice* 10 (2014) 133–56.

Dabîca M. (2019) "Sector Histria Sud", *Cronica Cercetărilor Arheologice din România. Campania 2018* (2019) 87–90.

De Visscher F. (1963) *Le droit des tombeaux romains* (Milan 1963).

Domăneanțu, C. (1990) "Die spätrömische Festungsmauer von Histria", in *Histria: eine Griechenstadt an der rumänischen Schwarzmeerküste*, edd. P. Alexandrescu and W. Schuller (Konstanz 1990) 265–83.

Eastman D. L. (2018) "Martyria", in *The Oxford Handbook of Early Christian Archaeology*, edd. D. K. Pettegrew, W. R. Caraher, and T. W. Davis (New York 2018) 89–104.

Georgescu V. and Ionescu M. (1995–1996) "Mărturii creștine la Callatis", *Pontica* 28–29 (1995–1996) 187–200.

Haarer F. K. (2006) *Anastasius I. Politics and Empire in the Late Roman World* (Cambridge 2006).

Haimovici S. (2005) "O problemă incomplet rezolvată – studiul resturilor animaliere depuse ca ofrandă în necropole aparținând culturii Sântana de Mureș-Cerneahov", *Arheologia Moldovei* 28 (2005) 327–34.

Hamparțumian N. (1971a) "Contribuții la topografia cetății Histria în epoca romano-bizantină. Considerații generale asupra necropolei din sectorul Bazilicii extra muros", *Studii și Cercetări de Istorie Veche* 22(2) (1971) 199–215.

Hamparțumian, N. (1971b) "Ein gotish-alanisches Grab in Histria", *Dacia* 15 (1971) 335–47.

Heather P. J. (1991) *Goths and Romans 332–489* (Oxford 1991).

Horedt K. (1979) *Morești. Grabungen in einer vor- und frühgeschichtlichen Siedlung in Siebenbürgen* (Bucharest 1979).

Iacob M. (2002) "Ibida – Cavoul Tudorka", *Cronica Cercetărilor Arheologice din România. Campania 2001* (2002) 293.

Ionescu M., Alexandru N., and Constantin R. (2002–2003) "Noi cercetări în necropola paleocreștină callatiană", *Pontica* 35–36 (2002–2003) 225–77.

Ivanišević V. and Bugarski I. (2018) "Transformation of burial space in the cities of Northern Illyricum during Late Antiquity", *Antaeus* 35–36 (2018) 91–118.

Jones A. H. M. (1964) *The Later Roman Empire 284–602: A Social, Economic and Administrative Survey* (Oxford 1964).

Kim H. J. (2016) *The Huns* (London-New York 2016).

Kirilov C. (2007) "The reduction of the fortified city area in Late Antiquity: some reflections on the end of the "antique city" in the lands of the Eastern Roman Empire", in *Post-Roman Towns, Trade and Settlement in Europe and Byzantium. Vol. 2: Byzantium, Pliska and the Balkans*, ed. J. Henning (Berlin-New York 2007) 3–24.

Kulikowski M. (2007) *Rome's Century Gothic Wars: From the Third to Alaric* (Cambridge 2007).

Lenski N. (2002) *Failure of Empire: Valens and the Roman State in the Fourth Century A.D.* (Berkley 2002).

Lindsay H. (2000) "Death, pollution and funerals in the city of Rome", in *Death and Disease in the Ancient City*, edd. V. Hope and E. Marshall (London and New York 2010) 152–73.

Lungu V. and Chera-Mărgineanu C. (1982) "Contribuții la cunoașterea unei necropole creștine a Tomisului (I)", *Pontica* 15 (1982) 175–199.

Maddrell A. and Sidaway J. D. (2010) "Introduction: bringing a spatial lens to death, dying, mourning and remembrance", in *Deathscapes. Spaces for Death, Dying, Mourning and Remembrance*, edd. J. D. Sidaway and A. Maddrell (Farnham 2010) 1–16.

Madgearu A. (1997) "The downfall of the Lower Danubian Late Roman frontier", *Revue Roumaine d'Histoire* 36 (1997) 315–36.

Madgearu A. (2001) "The end of town-life in Scythia Minor", *OJA* 20 (2001) 207–217.

Madgearu A. (2006) "The end of the Lower Danube Limes: a violent or a peaceful process?", *Studia Antiqua et Archaeologica* 12 (2006) 151–68.

Madgearu A. (2012) "Data patimirii sfintilor Epictet si Astion de la Halmyris", *Pontica* 45 (2012) 539–48.

Madgearu A. (2014) "The persecution of Galerius in Scythia, with a special regard to Halmyris", in *Serdica Edict (311 AD). Concepts and Realizations of the Idea of Religious Toleration*, edd. V. Vachkova and D. Dimitrov (Sofia 2014) 121–32.

Maenchen-Helfen O. J. (1973) *The World of the Huns: Studies in Their History and Culture* (Berkley-Los Angeles 1973).

Masek Z. (2016) "The transformation of late antique comb types on the frontier of the Roman and Germanic world – early medieval antler combs from Rákóczifalva (County Jász-Nagykun-Szolnok, Hungary)", *Antaeus* 34 (2016) 105–172.

Milojević M. (1996) "Forming and transforming protobyzantine urban public space", in *The Sixth Century: End or Beginning?* (Byzantina Australiensia 10), edd. P. Allen and E. M. Jeffreys (Oxford 1996) 247–62.

Mirițoiu N. and Nicolăescu-Plopșor D. (1978) "Analiza antropologică a osemintelor descoperite în cripta basilicii „simple" (A) de la Tropaeum Traiani", *Pontica* 11 (1978) 189–207.

Mirițoiu N. and Soficaru A. D. (2003a) "Studiul antropologic al osemintelor din cavoul romano-bizantin „Tudorka" de la Slava Rusă (antica Ibida)", *Peuce* 14 (2003) 511–30.

Mirițoiu N. and Soficaru A. D. (2003b) "Studiu antropologic al osemintelor descoperite în cripta basilicii de la Murighiol (anticul Halmyris)", *Peuce* 14 (2003) 531–80.

Mirițoiu N. and Soficaru A. D. (2007) "Osteobiographical study of the human remains discovered in the crypt of Murighiol (antique Halmyris) basilica", *Il Mar Nero* 5 (2007) 169–90.

Mordvintseva V. I. (2017) "The Sarmatians in the northern Black Sea region (on the basis of archaeological material)", in *The Northern Black Sea in Antiquity. Networks, Connectivity, and Cultural Interactions*, ed. V. Kozlovskaya (Cambridge 2017) 233–83.

Müller-Wiener W. (1986) "Von der Polis zum Kastron. Wandlungen der Stadt im Ägäischen Raum von der Antike zum

Mittelalter", *Gymnasium. Zeitschrift für Kultur der Antike und humanistische Bildung* 93 (1986) 435–75.

Nicolae C. (1993) "Despre topografia anticului Carsium", *Pontica* 26 (1993) 215–29.

Oţa L. (2015) "Cercetările lui Grigore Tocilescu în necropola de la Tomis", *Studii şi Cercetări de Istorie Veche şi Arheologie* 66(1–2) (2015) 123–28.

Pârvan V. (1916) *Histria IV. Inscripţii găsite în 1914 şi 1915* (Bucharest 1916).

Pârvan V. (1923) *Histria VII. Inscripţii găsite în 1916, 1921 şi 1922* (Bucharest 1923).

Petre A. (1962) "Săpăturile de la Piatra Frecăţei", *Materiale şi Cercetări Arheologice* 8 (1962) 565–89.

Petre A. (1987) *La romanité en Scythie Mineure: IIe–VIIe siècles de notre ère: recherches archéologiques* (Bucharest 1987).

Preda C. (1980) *Callatis. Necropola romana-bizantină* (Bucharest 1980).

Pröttel P.-M. (1999) "Zur Chronologie der Zwiebelknopffibeln", *JRGZM* 35 (1999) 347–72.

Rees R. (2004) *Diocletian and the Tetrarchy* (Edinburgh 2004).

Retief F. P. and Cilliers L. (2006) "Burial customs and the pollution of death in ancient Rome: procedures and paradoxes", *Acta Theologica* 26(7) (2006) 128–46.

Robinson O. (1973) "The Roman law on burials and burial ground", *Irish Jurist* 10(1) (1973) 175–86.

Rubel A. and Soficaru A. D. (2012) "Infant burials in Roman Dobrudja. A report of work in progress: the case of Ibida (Slava Rusă)", in *Homines, Funera, Astra: Proceedings of the International Symposium on Funerary Anthropology: 5–8 June 2011 „1 Decembrie 1918" University, Alba Iulia, Romania*, edd. R. Kogălniceanu, R.-G. Curcă, M. Gligor, and S. Straton (Oxford 2012) 163–68.

Rusu-Bolindeţ V., Bădescu A., Lăzărescu V. A., Dima M., Radu C., and Szeredai N. (2014) "Recent research at the Basilica extra muros in Histria at 100 years since the initiation of archaeological research on the site", *Materiale şi Cercetări Arheologice* 10 (2014) 199–219.

Sivan H. (1987) "On *Foederati, Hospitalitas*, and the Settlement of the Goths in A.D. 418", *AJP* 108(4) (1987) 759–72.

Soficaru (2014) "Anthropological data about the funeral discoveries from Slava Rusă, Tulcea County, Romania", *Peuce* 12 (2014) 307–340.

Soficaru A. D. (2006–2007) "Human remains discovered in the Basilica D from Tropaeum Traiani", *Annuaire Roumain d'Anthropologie* 43–44 (2006–2007) 3–8.

Soficaru A. D. (2011) *Populaţia provinciei Scythia în perioada romano-bizantină* (Iaşi 2011).

Soficaru A. D., Radu C., and Tica C. I. (2019) "A mass grave outside the walls. The Commingled Assemblage from Ibida", in *Bioarchaeology of Frontiers and Borderlands*, edd. C. I. Tica and D. L. Martin (Gainesville 2019) 187–211.

Soficaru A. D. and Sofaer J. (2021) "Regional patterns in mortuary practice in the Lower Danube region in the 4th–6th Centuries", *Archäologisches Korrespondenzblatt* 51/2 (2021) 263–85.

Sonu D. (2018) "Practica deformării artificiale a craniului în provincia Scythia", *Buletinul Cercurilor Ştiinţifice Studenţeşti* 24 (2018) 67–90.

Stanc S. and Bejenaru L. (2004) "Animal offerings found in necropoleis belonging to Sântana of Mureş Cerniahov culture from the east and the south extra-Carpathian zones of Romania", in *Behaviour Behind Bones: The Zooarchaeology of Ritual, Religion, Status and Identity*, edd. S. J. O'Day, W. Van Neer, and A. Ervynck (Oxford 2004) 14–19.

Suceveanu A. (1982) *Histria VI: Les Thermes romains* (Bucharest 1982).

Suceveanu A. (2007) *Histria XIII. La Basilique Épiscopale* (Bucharest 2007).

Teodor E. S. (2002) "Epoca romană târzie şi cronologia atacurilor transdanubiene. Analiza componentelor etnice şi geografice (partea întâi, de la 469 la 565)", *Muzeul Naţional* 14 (2002) 3–35.

Teodor E. S. (2003) "Epoca romană târzie şi cronologia atacurilor transdanibiene. Analiza componentelor etnice şi geografice (partea a doua, de 565 la 626)", *Muzeul Naţional* 15(1) (2003) 3–36.

Teodor E. S. (2004) "Epoca romană târzie şi cronologia atacurilor transdanubiene. Analiza componentelor etnice şi geografice (partea a treia, concluzii)", *Muzeul Naţional* 15 (2004) 3–38.

Ungureanu M. and Radu L. (2006) "Cercetări arheologice în necropola romano-bizantină de la Callatis", *Pontica* 39 (2006) 259–78.

Wanke U. (1990) *Die Gotenkriege des Valens. Studien zu Topographie und Chronologie im unteren Donauraum von 366–378 n. Chr.* (Frankfurt 1990).

Watson A. (1999) *Aurelian and the Third Century* (London and New York 1999).

Wolfram H. (1990) *History of the Goths* (Berkley 1990).

Zahariade M. (2001–2003) "The Halmyris episcopal basilica and the Martyrs' Crypt", *Il Mar Nero* 5 (2001–2003) 143–68.

Zahariade M. (2006) *Scythia Minor: A History of a Later Roman Province (284–681)* (Amsterdam 2006).

Zahariade M. (2009) "The episcopal basilica from Halmyris and the crypt of Epictetus and Astion", *Thraco-Dacica* 24 (2009) 131–50.

Burial and Society in the Greek World during Late Antiquity

Joseph L. Rife

Abstract

A large body of evidence and important historical questions exist for the study of burial in the late antique Greek world. This slowly evolving field has long been influenced by trends in classical archaeology, the archaeology of Early Christianity, and folklore studies. The physical remains of funerary ritual, which have been unevenly studied and published, attest to the forms of interment, tombstones, the treatment of bodies and objects, and the topographic settings of burial. Variation in these remains reflects the expression of different identities, including status, family, profession, ethnicity, and the new Christian perspective on death. Mortuary variability can also be traced across space, both between and especially within regions, and over time from the Roman to Byzantine eras, which reveals a paradigm shift in the concepts and uses of burial in Late Antiquity.

Introduction

Greece furnishes copious evidence for the study of burial and society in Late Antiquity. Archaeologists since the birth of the modern discipline in the 19th c. have uncovered thousands of burials of late antique date at sites of all kinds across the Greek world, from churches and fortifications to large cities, small towns, and villages or farms. We also possess a rich corpus of literary and documentary texts pertaining to death and burial, from histories to theology and hagiography. Such varied and abundant sources provide a unique opportunity for the comparative analysis of the physical remains of burial with written testimony that is often sharply focused in place and time. Besides evidence of such quality and quantity, the region's particular history raises interesting questions for researchers. Greece was in many ways geographically, culturally, and politically central. During Late Antiquity, it remained a hotbed of intellectualism with a celebrated classical past; it was a fulcrum in crisscrossing networks of exchange; it emerged as an evangelical centre for the Early Church and became the homeland of powerful bishops; and it straddled the border between the old Roman West and the new Byzantine East. The study of burial in late antique Greece thus has great potential to elucidate global developments in Mediterranean history, including the evolving character of urban and rural communities, the advent and establishment of Christianity, and the creation of new identities.

And yet this potential is largely unrealized. In the area of funerary archaeology, late antique Greece has received less scholarly attention than many other regions of Europe and the Mediterranean basin. My aim is to introduce the subject and to suggest paths forward. Thus I will survey the available evidence and the complexities scholars face in collecting and interpreting it, trace basic patterns of variation, and highlight current advances and future directions in this exciting but nascent field. To the present study I bring the perspective of a historian and archaeologist who has explored burials of Roman to Byzantine date over the past three decades in Greece, with special attention to the north-eastern Peloponnese.[1] Before turning to the physical remains of burial, I will give the geographic and chronological parameters and ideological background of my discussion.

The Greek World in Late Antiquity

I imagine the 'Greek world' to be a geographic zone that was sufficiently coherent in its social, economic, political, religious, and cultural character to justify its consideration as a unit. It encompassed mainland and insular Greece, from Macedonia and Thrace south to the Peloponnese with the Aegean and Ionian islands, though even the outer fringes of Thrace and Crete were significantly linked to the worlds of eastern Europe and north-eastern Africa. Through geopolitical processes such as imperialism, migration, trade, and colonization, the people of this world were historically connected to southern Italy, the northern Balkans, the Black Sea, and Cyprus, and yet in many respects those regions participated in other cultural traditions and exchange networks – southern Italy with Sicily, Tunisia, and central Italy, and Cyprus with Cilicia and Syria. The connection between Aegean Greece and western Asia Minor from the Propontis to Lycia was unusually close during the Roman to Early Byzantine era. Apart from ancestral bonds and deep memories of a Bronze Age to Classical past, the entire Aegean seaboard shared an essential environmental substrate and a provincial

---

1   E.g. Rife (1999), (2022a).

© KONINKLIJKE BRILL BV, LEIDEN, 2024 | DOI:10.1163/9789004687974_013
Alexandra Dolea and Luke Lavan (eds) *Burial and Memorial in Late Antiquity*
(Late Antique Archaeology 13) (Leiden 2024), pp. 779–810

model of urban and rural life, dominated by a civic elite with common cultural interests and political privileges. Moreover, maritime traffic was booming. There are good reasons to separate the study of burial in late antique Asia Minor from its study in late antique Greece, including the particular political, economic, religious, and cultural history of Anatolia over the long term,[2] and the distinct tradition of Turkish archaeology. However, as scholars increasingly explore the trans-Aegean axis, we may well find that the rituals and spaces of burial at late antique Ephesus approximate more closely those at contemporary Corinth than those at contemporary Constantinople or Thessalonica, let alone Ierapetra, Maroneia, or Paphos.

The notoriously mutable concept of 'Late Antiquity' has many definitions in different regions of the Mediterranean world today. The commonest formula in Greek scholarship has been 'Early Christian' (παλαιοχρι- στιανική, πρωτοχριστιανική), a clumsy historical designation that pertains perhaps more effectively to literature and art, while many studies of material culture have adopted as discrete categories 'Late Roman' and 'Early Byzantine'. I view Late Antiquity in the Greek world as a dynamic era of large-scale developments between Classical Antiquity and the Byzantine Middle Ages. These include environmental changes and natural disasters, new political and military alignments with the rise of the eastern empire, socioeconomic and demographic shifts giving rise to different patterns of settlement and population movements, and the full integration of the Church into Greek society. These developments chiefly belong to the 4th to 7th c.; we might extend the range into the 8th c., but evidence for that time in Greece is so thin that it would amount to speculation. We can reasonably identify 3rd c. Greece as a late phase of provincial prosperity in the Roman East and 9th c. Greece as a preliminary phase of the Constantinopolitan efflorescence. Likewise, we can distinguish late antique Greek burial from Middle Roman and Middle Byzantine Greek burial.

One obstacle to surveying burial in the late antique Greek world is the chronological imprecision of published research. Once it was a widespread practice among excavators to identify any remains that post-dated the High Empire, and specifically the founding of Constantinople, as 'Byzantine', mixing late antique with Middle to Late Byzantine graves and tombstones. Even when studying remains they can securely place in the 4th to 7th c., researchers often cannot give a more precise chronology than a 100- to 150-year span, either

because they lack datable finds or because they overlook depositional and structural associations. It can be more reliable to classify late antique burials by period simply as Late Roman (*ca.* 4th–mid-6th c.) or Early Byzantine (*ca.* late 6th–7th c.). In most cases this basic division can be readily applied, and it roughly accords with distinctions in artefactual assemblages and sweeping changes to Greek communities after Justinian.

Ways of Thinking about Late Antique Greek Burial

Research on burial in late antique Greece from the 19th through the 20th c. has been guided by certain perspectives on the past. These dominant epistemological frameworks, which still echo today, have influenced how archaeologists select their evidence, plan their fieldwork, and understand their discoveries. The first is the traditional field of classical archaeology, which from its inception carried certain inherent biases: a privileging of narratives and topographies recorded in textual sources; an overarching interest in cities, particularly the monumental settings of public life and elite experience; the organization of knowledge about the past in terms of classes of objects; a close attention to material and visual culture of perceived aesthetic value or sophistication; and a disproportionate focus on Bronze Age and Classical society, especially the spheres of the Mycenaeans and the Athenians.[3] Part and parcel of this old paradigm was the concept of Late Antiquity as a fateful twilight, a time of tragic catastrophe and abject decline into a dark age. A second approach to the past germane to my discussion is the traditional archaeology of Early Christianity. Prior generations of scholars preferred to examine especially churches to trace the spread of the new religion as a theological and institutional victory over ancient cult that was chronicled in New Testament scripture, the writings of the Fathers, and the lives of the saints.[4] A third intellectual model that has influenced the study of late antique burial is λαο- γραφία, or the Greek discipline of folklore with elements of ethnography.[5] Researchers have assiduously recorded the customs of the countryside, including the activities of burial, in part to chart embedded continuities across time between ancient and modern Greek culture.[6] These three investigative and interpretive strategies

---

2   Mitchell (1993) remains an excellent starting point.

3   E.g. Snodgrass (1987), (2006); Alcock and Osbourne (2012).
4   E.g. Soteriou ([1942] 1962); Orlandos (1952–1954); see in general Frend (1996).
5   E.g. Polites ([1931] 1975); Loukatos (1940), (1978); Megas (1940); Koukoules (1940), (1951); see also Danforth (1982).
6   Herzfeld (1982); Schell (1989).

are well known to scholars of ancient Greece. They are deeply rooted in a complicated history of conservative intellectualism, political thought and rhetoric, and ideological neoclassicism stretching back to the foundation of the modern Greek state and its early formation in the mid- to late 19th c. Moreover, their inherent tendencies have been reinforced by enduring educational curricula, strong popular appeal, and a tourist industry that celebrates a particular view of the past.

Alongside these trends, and in part because of them, research on ancient Greek burial has been slow to embrace major recent advancements in the theory and practice of funerary archaeology. In this regard, south-eastern Europe has lagged behind other continental regions and to a degree behind parts of North Africa and the Middle East, if one considers recent research for example in Tunisia, Egypt, Israel, and Jordan. From the 1990s onward, a key approach emerged for research concerning 'death-ritual and social structure' in prehistoric, Greek and Roman, and Medieval Europe. This approach views burials as the creations of a series of events, or a process, with material, spatial, temporal, and experiential (emotional, cognitive, behavioural) dimensions when people and communities express a sense of self and generate (or obliterate) a memory.[7] Another innovation encapsulated in the rise of survey archaeology over the past half-century is the regional perspective, or the concept of individual sites – in our case burials – as points in a larger continuum of variability that can be traced across a landscape meaningfully delimited by its ancient residents and visitors.[8] Finally, I highlight two scientific fields that remain new to the study of late antique Greek burial. The first is bioarchaeology, or the study of human behaviour and life-experience through the analysis of bones and teeth from archaeological contexts.[9] The second is taphonomy and the study of formation processes, which examine the gradual transformation of a burial's depositional setting and its biological, artefactual, and structural contents due to both environmental and anthropogenic factors.[10]

Seeing this background can help us to understand why burials in late antique Greece have been studied in the way they have been. Frequently archaeologists have treated them piecemeal and briefly, as incidental to earlier or grander remains, so that by far most published graves from Late Antiquity appear as passing mentions

or photographs in the government bulletin Αρχαιολογικόν Δελτίον. With notable exceptions, as we will see below, few syntheses of cities and regions and almost no concerted coverage of small or peripheral communities exist. On the other hand, archaeologists have been especially interested in burials at churches.[11] This has yielded relatively good evidence for elite burials in and around settlements and their relationship to monumental design, but it has also promoted a skewed view of late antique burial as devotedly Christian and palpably aristocratic. Furthermore, we find an abiding fascination with the commemoration of clerics and saints, particularly when they are named in the historical record and, with the spread of Christianity, particularly when burials and churches appear to have supplanted pagan shrines.[12] A steady cross-current in folklore studies has been the search for 'pagan survivals,' or the persistence of fossilized burial practices via simple linear descent from Antiquity to the Medieval or Modern eras, such as leaving money or invoking Charon.[13] Insightful scholarship has examined the funeral liturgy, ecclesiastical depictions of funerals, and sepulchral law mainly during the Byzantine era.[14] Few publications of individual burials or cemeteries from Late Antiquity, however, have explored their full ritual context, or attempted to relate such a process enacted by living members of a community to the particular structures, ideologies, and memories of that community. Until recent years, the scientific analysis of human skeletal remains and their depositional history has been largely absent from the study of late Greek burials. Besides the loss of essential information concerning the dead – biological sex and age at death, health, diet, occupation, genetic affiliation – this state of affairs has obfuscated the complex processes by which burials evolve over time after their creation through reopening, disturbance, and displacement or obliteration – the afterlife of the afterlife, as it were.[15]

In contrast, Late Roman to Early Byzantine epitaphs have always belonged to a lively subfield. Greek epigraphy, as a disciplinary branch of both classical archaeology and classical philology, adopts a comprehensive approach to the documentation of texts in part to trace

7   E.g. Morris (1992); Parker Pearson (1999); Scheid (2008); Scheid and Rüpke (2010); Pearce (2013); Pearce and Weekes (2017).

8   E.g. Morris (1987); Beck (1995); Stone and Stirling (2007).

9   Larsen (1997); Buikstra and Beck (2006).

10   E.g. Schiffer (1987); Mays (1998) 13–32; Duday (2009); Rife (2012); Duday, Le Mort, and Tillier (2014).

11   E.g. Soteriou (1919), (1929); Shelley (1943); Ivison (1996); Oikonomou-Laniado (1998), (2003); Makri (2006).

12   E.g. Stikas (1964); Pelekanides (1978); Pallas (1989); Pelekanides and Mentzos (1990).

13   E.g. Schmidt (1926); Alexiou (1978), (2002). See the critical discussions at Haldon (1997) 327–37; Trombley (2001) 148–51; and Saïd (2005).

14   Kyriakakis (1974); Fedwick (1976); Walter (1976); Emmanouelides (1989); Velkovska (2001). Nalpandis (2002) is a useful summary to accompany a lavish exhibition catalog.

15   E.g. Rakita et al. (2005).

linguistic and onomastic development over the long term. The late epitaphic record with its unusual divergences from the Classical Greek and Imperial Roman corpora has been an enticing sidelight for historians, archaeologists, and epigraphists since the 19th c., who have produced useful collections and commentaries. Furthermore, late antique tombstones often contain Christian invocations, terminology, and iconography that have understandably drawn the attention of scholars of Early Christianity.[16]

This short history of a wide field of inquiry has offered a long view that risks sounding dismissive. An honest assessment does reveal a clear discrepancy in the status of late antique mortuary studies between Greece and other regions and periods, for instance, Roman to Medieval England, France, and Italy. Nevertheless, several contributions over the past century and more have been substantial and enlightening, particularly in the archaeology of churches and the epigraphy of tombstones. I highlight two recent works that unfortunately can be hard to acquire: the magnificent synthesis of mortuary remains that Nikolaos Laskaris prepared as his doctoral thesis at the Sorbonne (1996), (2000), and the painstaking study of the west cemetery at Thessalonica that Despoina Makropoulou prepared for hers at the National and Kapodistrian University of Athens (2007). Moreover, although bioarchaeology falls outside the scope of this discussion, it is worth noting that several studies of human skeletal remains of Late Roman to Early Byzantine date have appeared over the past two decades, including my first attempt to synthesize data from across the Greek world.[17] Indeed, scholars in the new millennium have shown burgeoning interest in all aspects of Late Antiquity in Greece, including burial and society. The field today is not moribund or stagnant; it is a field of growth and opportunity.

The Archaeological Record: A Brief Survey

Bearing in mind these developments and tendencies in the study of late antique Greek burial, I turn to the physical evidence on which it is based. While the importance of literature and documents should be obvious from the foregoing discussion,[18] I will concentrate on archaeological remains as they are recorded on the ground: the interments, their contents, and their location. My survey is organized according to these categories of structural, corporeal, artefactual, and spatial evidence in order to facilitate comparison to existing data and to remains yet to be found. What follows is not a systematic catalogue or gazetteer but a collection of examples selected for their importance and illustrative value. From this survey I will then explore the themes of social structure and regional and diachronic variation.

At the outset we should recognize that vast evidence for funerary practices still lies buried both in the ground and in the depot. Perhaps it is unsurprising, in light of the longstanding tendencies I have observed, that past researchers have not infrequently been loath to excavate late burials, such that there was once a time when they would openly discuss where to dig in order to avoid them. However, since graves are unavoidable in many contexts, particularly dense settlements with long histories, some excavators have uncovered or cleared out late antique burials without care or off the record. Furthermore, countless finds from burials and documents on their recovery have ended up in the storerooms of museums and dig-houses without further analysis or publication and still remain unknown to scholars, teachers and students, and an interested public. So when I survey the available evidence, I am not just discussing uncovered remains but rather uncovered remains that have been analysed and published, which is a drastically smaller subset of the whole. Ultimately, we face the basic challenge of evidentiary significance: are the data we possess sufficiently varied and robust for us to assume that they represent a large and complex geographic region and historical period in a meaningful way? Lest we fall prey to Snodgrass's positivist fallacy, namely, that what we can observe is by definition what is significant,[19] we should be cautious over the limitations of our data, cognizant of the possible importance of what is unknown, or even just hard to see, and committed as much to the broad search for new knowledge as we are to the open dissemination of new discoveries.

Forms of Interment

Any regional survey of ancient burial confronts the intrinsic difficulties of devising a typology. On the one hand, burial typologies, which constitute an especially well-worn subclass of all archaeological typologies, have great practical and heuristic value as formats for organizing large quantities of objective data. On the other, they embody an essentialist understanding of the creation and meaning of material culture in human society; they

---

16   E.g. Bayet (1878a); Aigrain (1913); Jalabert and Mouterde (1926); Guarducci (1976); *ICG*, see further n. 37.

17   E.g. Bourbou (2004), (2016); Tritsaroli (2006), (2017); Bourbou, Fuller, Garvie-Lok, and Richards (2011); Rife (2012); Tritsaroli and Karadima (2017).

18   E.g. Rush (1941); Samellas (2002); see also nn. 4 and 14.

19   Snodgrass (2006) 10.

enforce a positivistic approach to interpreting data; and in their tidy precision they can mask authorial biases.

These advantages and pitfalls are evident in past taxonomies of late antique Greek burial. Pallas collected various terms for graves from Late Roman and Byzantine texts and attempted to match them one-to-one with forms of Middle to Late Byzantine burial found at Ayios Demetrios on Salamis. Such an approach succeeds when words of technical usage can be directly associated with actual burials, such as in the language of *in situ* epitaphs, but it fails for words of generalizing semanticity like those we find in most cultures, such as 'burial', 'grave', 'memorial', 'container' (τάφος, θήκη, μνῆμα, κιβώριον).[20] In his compendium, Laskaris adopted a traditional strategy of classifying burial sites according to elaborate formal criteria, especially the composition and shape of the compartment.[21] Many old reports on Late Roman to Early Byzantine remains, such as those in the Forum and Asklepieion at Corinth, describe the forms of burial in sketchy terms but scrutinize their local associations, specifying in which trenches they were uncovered or which earlier remains they disturbed.[22] If, however, we think of burials in the archaeological record as resulting from a process of past behaviours, we may classify them in terms of the experiences of creating a site for burial and activating it through meaningful behaviour. The physical traits of burials – composition, shape, size, decoration – are all essential to such a classification because they were determined by mourners who decided to invest a certain amount of time, energy, and resources in designing a particular place for funerary ritual.

The simplest burial forms in late antique Greece required the least investment to produce and would not have supported lavish graveside rites, though we cannot in every case rule out ceremonial performance at another locale, such as a church or home. Basic cists, or narrow holes in the ground without flooring, lining, or covering, seem ubiquitous across the Greek world, like those at Corinth, Zygouries, Nemea, Argos, and Perissa on Thera.[23] While this kind of grave is the most poorly documented, presumably due to its simplicity and thus perceived insignificance, myriad published comments point to its frequency during Late Antiquity. Mourners

could enhance this design by adding a covering, sometimes merely a pile of rubble and sometimes an orderly layer of slabs with mortar or even a tent of pitched tiles, like those at Corinth, Argos, Athens, Pylos in Elis, Patras, Nea Anchialos, and Larissa (Figs. 1–2).[24] Inside the cist mourners could variously add rubble or bricks, sometimes freshly manufactured but often collected or recycled, pave the floor, and line the walls. Varying degrees of elaboration are reflected in the regularity of structural elements, which range from incomplete or disorganized to even and tight. Such built cists were prevalent in the burial grounds of late antique Greece, for example, in well documented cases from the Corinthia and Argolid, Olympia, and Gortyn.[25] A popular form that also employed recycled ceramics to contain a body inside a simple cist was the burial of infants or young children inside amphoras or pithoi, which could be easily split for the insertion of the corpse into an effective coffin. Typical examples are reported from the north-eastern Peloponnese, Chalkis, Torone, and Thessalonica.[26]

Mourners who wanted more substantial spaces that could accommodate elaborate rituals of commemoration and visitation built full, formal enclosures for the deceased. In the north-eastern Peloponnese, mourners dug into slopes or rock exposures to make oblique shafts or wide cavities with enclosed compartments inside (Fig. 3).[27] Sculpted sarcophagi are very rare in late antique Greece (e.g. on Ithaca, at Thebes and Tegea, and on Lesbos, Thera, and Rhodes),[28] while simple sarcophagi in marble and very unusually in lead (e.g. at Larissa, Thessalonica, and Philippi) occur most often inside burial chambers.[29] Likewise, iron nails or bits of planking from wooden coffins or biers are rarely discovered (e.g. at

20   Pallas (1951) 167–75.
21   Laskaris (2000) 291–310.
22   E.g. Roebuck (1951) 162–64; Scranton (1956) 29–31.
23   Blegen (1928) 62, 70–72, 73, figs. 62–64; Roebuck (1951) 163; Scranton (1956) 127; Rudolph (1979) 298, 300; Miller (1979) 85, fig. 28e, (1988) 3, fig. 4d; Bookidis and Stroud (1997) 382, 386–88, fig. 53, pls. 58e, 59a–d; Laskaris (2000) 252; Oikonomou-Laniado (1998) 406–408, figs. 5, 8, (2003) 16–17, 29, 31–32, fig. 13.
24   Roebuck (1951) 162–63, fig. 32, pl. 67.4; Travlos and Frantz (1965) 166–67, pl. 42c; Wiseman (1967a) 32–33, pls. 13a, 14a, d; Miller (1981) 48, fig. 12b, (1988) 3, fig. 4c; Coleman (1986) 139, 150, pls. 16b, c, g, 17d; Bookidis and Stroud (1997) 381–87, pls. 57c, 58a, c; Oikonomou-Laniado (1998) 406–407, 408, figs. 5, 8, 9, (2003) 13–14, 28–30, 31–32, figs. 44, 45, 58; Laskaris (2000) 183, 208–209, 215, nos. 328af, 378g, 388f.
25   Wiseman (1967b) 418, 420, pl. 84b, e, (1969) 79, fig. 7; Di Vita (1988) 91–139, figs. 66, 86–158; Oikonomou-Laniado (1998) 406, 407, 408, figs. 3, 5, 7, (2003) 13–14, 15, 16–17, 28–31, 33, figs. 11–13, 40–43, 53–57; Rife (2012) 25–44, 56–71, figs. 2.1–2.21, 2.36–3.56, (2022a); Völling (2018) 68–107, pls. 1–13.
26   Roebuck (1951) 163–64, pl. 67.4; Wiseman (1967a) 32, 34–35, pl. 14c, (1967b) 418; Rudolph (1979) 300; Papadopoulos (1989) 70–71, 76–78, 80, figs. 8b, c, 9a, b, 10; Oikonomou-Laniado (1998) 407–408, (2003) 31, 47, figs. 62, 68, 69; Laskaris (2000) 118, 223–24, 228–29, 234, nos. 336d, 411, 416(a)s, (b)o; Sanders (2005b) 427–28, fig. 16.5; Makropoulou (2007) 423–24.
27   Rife (2012) 177–79.
28   Koch (2000) 353, 354–56.
29   Laskaris (2000) 44, 215, 307, nos. 9, 388b; Marki (2006) 100–103.

FIGURE 1
Isthmia, Grave NEG 69–001, Built cist grave
containing four bodies, mid-late 5th century.
IMAGE COPYRIGHT: RIFE (2012) 43, FIG.
2.20, COURTESY OF THE TRUSTEES OF THE
AMERICAN SCHOOL OF CLASSICAL STUDIES
AT ATHENS

Isthmia, Corinth, Thessalonica, Philippi, and Perissa),[30] though we must accept their under-representation in the archaeological record due to poor preservation. The most impressive forms were chambers constructed either above or below ground that were sometimes free-standing or solitary, sometimes appended to church buildings, and sometimes incorporated into larger complexes (see below). Among these, some rooms were brightly decorated. In contrast to North Africa and Spain during Late Antiquity, burials in the Greek world seldom displayed mosaics. The best examples, found at Philippi and Heraklion, name the deceased in commemorative texts with geometric ornament.[31] Wall-painting flourished in Macedonia. Sepulchral paintings in the cemeteries of Thessalonica depicted both religious symbols, such as the cross and Christogram and perhaps sheep and fish, more traditional sepulchral motifs, such as blooming gardens, chalices, and peacocks, and rarely human or divine figures, including both scenes from real life (portraits of families or households?) and scenes

30   Carpenter (1929) 346; Laskaris (2000) 44, 45, 252, 271–72, nos. 9, 10, 453c; Oikonomou-Laniado (2003) 27, 28, 32; Makropoulou (2007) 51, 61, 89, 147, 186, 187, 190, 196, 213, 246, 350, 381, 383, 424, 449; Rife (2012) 90–96, 165–66, figs. 2.80, 2.81.

31   Laskaris (2000) 44, 70–71, 305, nos. 9, 83, 84, figs. A 22, A 46, A 49.

from the Bible (e.g. Adam and Eve, the sacrifice of Isaac, Daniel and the lions, and the resurrection of Lazarus).[32]

Noteworthy is the absence from many burial sites of installations to serve graveside rituals. We can reasonably assume that certain activities of lamentation and remembrance before, during, and after interment either did not occur at the site of burial or did not require permanent fixtures, such as leaving things on the ground or atop a wooden stand that no longer survives. Among the uncommon instances of graveside facilities, one recurrent feature is a flat surface for placing offerings. Several Corinthian graves were covered with solid, raised platforms.[33] While such structures invoked the form of a *klinê*, whether a figurative bed or a model of the bier, some also had a panel like a table-top. In other examples, such as at Kenchreai, a small, low surface like an implanted tray or a small, raised surface like an altar was built next to the grave (Fig. 3).[34] More elaborate features resembling formal altars or tables are reported, for example, at Eretria, Nea Anchialos, and Thessalonica.[35] Mourners used these fixtures for placing either offerings, such as vessels with consumables, unguents, or incense, or implements, such as lamps. An unusual feature of special stone-lined cists was a hole through the cover fitted with a channel or pipe. This kind of aperture, which is well known in North Africa, is found at the burials of officials or grandees in churches at Knossos, Heraklion, Eleftherna, Corinth, and Athens.[36] It allowed pious visitors to pour libations or oil down to the holy dead.

32   Pallas (1961) 173–74, pls. 72c, 73a, (1975) 9, fig. 14; Laskaris (2000) 485–571, figs. D 1–65; Marki (2006) 120–204, pls. 1–26, 59–68a; Poulou-Papadimitriou, Tzavella and Ott (2012) 381–82.

33   Roebuck (1951) 163; Wiseman (1967a) 32–33, 35, fig. 17, pls. 13c, 14f, (1969) 81–83, 85, figs. 9, 11, pls. 25f, 26a, 27b, e, (1972) 8–9; Rife (2012) 44–54, 178–79, figs. 2.22–2.35.

34   Rife (2022a).

35   Marki (1987) 99–101, 114, 209; Laskaris (2000) 60, 191 n. 425, 234, nos. 39, 338, fig. A 32.

36   Konstantinidis (1881); Frend and Johnston (1962) 194–95, pl. 49a; Stikas (1964) 134, fig. 4, pl. 90; Sodini (1975); Snively (1984); Pallas (1989) 20, 21, fig. 2; Laskaris (2000) 33 n. 29, 70 71, 268–69, no. 83, figs. A 2, A 46; Yangaki (2004) 159, fig. 35.

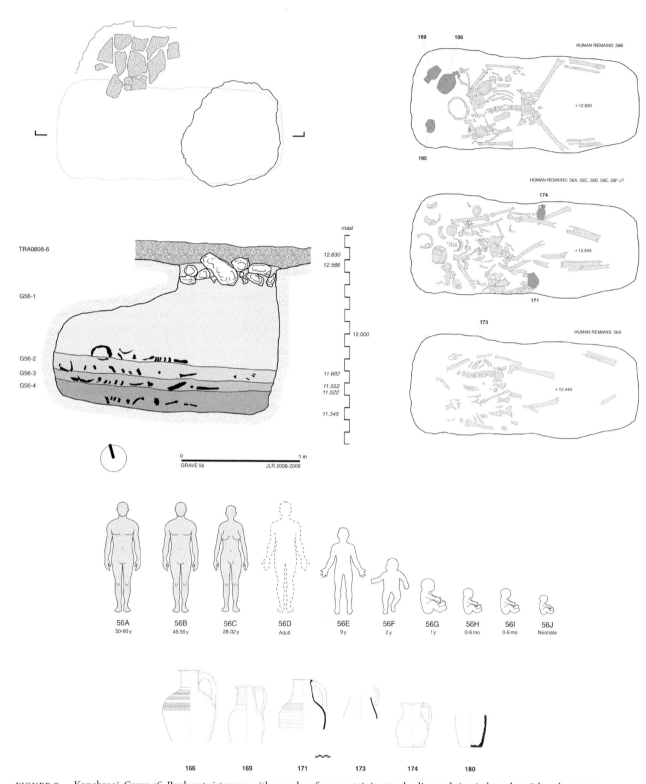

FIGURE 3   Kenchreai, Grave 56, Rock-cut cist grave with paved surface containing ten bodies and six pitchers, late 6th–7th century.

Tombstones

An important part of designing many Greek graves during Late Antiquity was preparing and erecting a tombstone. We are unusually well informed about the epigraphy of death, as I have already noted, possessing several compilations and studies that elucidate especially the habits of Attica, the Corinthia and Argolid, and northern Greece.[37] Besides the unusual cases of painted texts inside burial compartments or chambers, most epitaphs were carved on rectilinear stone slabs, some cut for the purpose but many reused. The few that have been found *in situ*, for example, at Corinth, Kenchreai, Brauron, and Kisamos on Crete, were posted flat or upright above the burial (Fig. 2).[38] Our interpretation of tombstones, however, is substantially hindered both by their ancient or medieval removal to secondary contexts and by the modern custom of publishing them with only bare contextual information or none at all. In either case they are deracinated from the rich sepulchral associations their creators intended. Consequently our study of this important element in funerary ritual often depends on intrinsic features – the stone used, the quality of the writing, and the words above all.

Most late antique epitaphs display brief texts with simple meanings, a few prosaic lines in which the reader learned to whom the grave belongs. And yet the spare details furnish precious evidence for religion, society, and economy. The range of personal names across large and small communities, including both Greek and Roman, polytheistic, Jewish and Christian, make up a diverse onomasticon incorporating both old and new. A fascinating feature of these tombstones is the identification of the dead not just by personal name, sometimes patronym, and very occasionally ethnonym, but also often by profession. The inscriptions supply abundant terminology for vegetable sellers and butchers to barbers, cobblers, muleteers, deacons, and constables.[39] Christian identity was not infrequently marked by crosses at start and finish and by formulae such as 'of blessed memory' (τὴν μακαρίαν μνήμην) or honorific qualifications such as 'most blessed', 'eternal', and 'faithful' (μακαριώτατος, αἰώνιος, πιστός), which at least carry a Christian ethical flavour. A more sweeping innovation

was the currency of the term 'resting place' (κοιμητήριον and its many variants), which evokes the metaphor of death as serene slumber before heavenly salvation.[40] Another distinctive feature of late antique epitaphs is precise reference to the chronometry of death, whether by days in a month, by years in a life, or by periods in an indiction cycle. While verse-epitaphs were very uncommon, some texts betray poetic pretensions in the careful choice of words and sounds, echoing a venerable epigrammatic tradition in what we may call Christian classicism.[41] More mundane but no less interesting are those texts that addressed the acquisition and security of private locales. Some tombstones verified ownership by recording the exact price of the plot, like an inscribed receipt. Others aimed to indemnify exclusive access to a grave for its owner and heirs by prohibiting violation and cursing violators. The penalty of a fine payable to the municipal fisc that was conventional in the eastern provinces was by Late Antiquity giving way to threats of divine punishment and condemnation to the fate of Judas.[42]

Burial Contents: Bodies

Mourners constructed graves in order to contain the remains of a particular person, whom they had prepared at home and carried to the site for deposition. The discovery of dress accessories suggests that the dead were sometimes clothed and even beautified with jewellery. On the other hand, the absence of such objects from many graves and the testimony of written accounts point to the routine use of a shroud or 'winding sheet' (ὀθόνη), which could have covered clothing. Depositing the body in the cist or compartment must have been an emotionally wrenching and physically cumbersome task, but it was not accomplished carelessly. Although excavators of graves have not always recorded the details of burial orientation and corporeal position, we can collect this information from drawings and photographs, when they are available.

We find a marked uniformity in the treatment of the corpse across late antique Greece.[43] The standard practice was to orient a burial with the head in the west. The evidence does not support the hypothesis that the eastward placement was calculated off a precise point on the horizon or in the heavens that migrated seasonally. Instead, unless the general direction of east was common knowledge, mourners probably estimated burial orientation from the sun's broad path at any time of day,

37 Bees ([1941] 1978); Creaghan and Raubitschek (1947); Robert (1960); Kent (1966); Bandy (1970); Pallas and Dandis (1979); Feissel (1983); Feissel and Philippides-Braat (1985); Sironen (1997); Rife (2022c); Walbank and Walbank (2006); *IG* II/III², IV³, X.1.2; *IGC*.

38 Stikas (1955) 78–81, figs. 7, 8; Wiseman (1969) 81, 93, pl. 25f; Diamandis (2004) 387–88, 390, figs. 2, 6, 8, 10; Walbank and Walbank (2006) 269; Rife (2022c); see also Makropoulou (2007) 271, 288, 421, fig. 11 for a possible example at Thessalonica.

39 E.g. Sironen (1997) 401–408; Walbank (2010).

40 Bees ([1941] 1978) 38–39; Rebillard (1993).

41 E.g. Sironen (1997) 168–69, 209, 219–20, 247; Rife (2004–2009).

42 Dandis (1983).

43 Laskaris (2000) 270–76; Rife (2012) 181–87.

and they often adjusted it to account for existing architecture or irregular terrain. In a vast majority of cases the dead body was laid to rest in a supine, extended position with the head facing forward, the arms over the abdomen or chest, and the legs straight. Mourners were especially concerned about the head and arms. Sometimes they propped up the head from the back and sides with stones or tiles like a cushion, and the fact that many skeletons have been found with closed mouths may well demonstrate that mourners also bound up the jaws. They pulled the arms up over the upper body, stomach, or waist, perhaps also tying them in place to facilitate transport and to connote order. Since these parts of the human anatomy are most overtly associated with a living personality, an individual who communicates, creates, and emotes, their delicate handling was a final act of personal care by the bereaved for the departed. The traditional interpretation of this position and orientation remains the most plausible: late antique Greeks placed the dead in the posture of peaceful repose as though sleeping until they would rise to face their saviour arriving in the East. Regardless of whether this specific doctrinal interpretation consciously informed every interment, which seems doubtful, the behaviour arising from this widespread belief clearly became customary.

Late antique Greek graves frequently contained multiple burials in single compartments. Many sites have produced built cists enclosing a few bodies up to over a dozen, aligned in such a way as to indicate their calculated deposition over time, not in rushed or haphazard dumpings of numerous corpses from a single event (Figs. 1, 3).[44] We know from epigraphic and literary sources that such multiple interments represent family tombs. This conclusion is supported by anthropological analyses revealing a typical demographic distribution across an extended family spanning two or three generations, or shared morphological traits that point to genetic affiliation.[45] In such cases we can imagine a graveside scene in which an earlier burial was located, perhaps after some probing if there was no marker or it had fallen; the covering was laboriously removed, and long buried remains in varying states of decay were moved aside as the intact body was placed on top of or beside dead relatives. During this process, mourners sometimes collected bones already in the same cist into piles with a vaguely anatomical arrangement, shifting them to the side or corner to make way for the new corpse, as we see in graves at Isthmia, Knossos, Thessalonica, and Aliki on Thasos.[46]

A parallel practice that also required the meticulous handling and arrangement of dead bodies was secondary burial. Redeposited contents of graves have been reported, for example, at Isthmia, Nemea, Halieis, Thessalonica, and Gortyn.[47] In these cases the disarticulated remains include a small sample of all bones from the body, usually the skull, long bones, and large elements from the shoulder and pelvic girdles, which are concentrated into an orderly pile with the cranium on top, usually in the west, and the appendicular bones on a longitudinal axis. The purpose of this ritual of secondary burial (ἀνακομιδή), which is well known from the Byzantine era down to modern times, was to consolidate the remains of family members into a single locale that could be maintained for visitation, particularly when earlier interments had fallen to disrepair. But without fuller documentation of the osteological evidence in most published burials, when confronting displaced bones inside a single cist, we often cannot ascertain whether they represent earlier burial inside that same cist or earlier burial inside a different cist. This is one reason why we should hesitate to join past researchers in generically calling late antique burial compartments with large deposits of commingled bones 'ossuaries' (ὀστεοθῆκαι, ὀστεοφυλάκια). That term applies to the distinct practice of storing exhumed bones in a communal depository typically attached to a church, which certainly was observed during the Middle Byzantine period but has shadowy origins. Nonetheless, the intimate engagement of mourners with skeletonized remains during Late Antiquity, as in later centuries, is striking. Their conscientious, even respectful handling of defleshed bones indicates a basic recognition of the sanctity of the body and a deliberate act of remembrance.

The grave continued to be a locus of interaction between the living and the dead long after the deposition of the body. The routine activities of cultivation and construction must have on occasion uncovered forgotten burials, especially in areas with deep histories of settlement. A common response to such accidental disturbance was to handle the remains with care, moving aside or resetting the bones to trace a living body, as was typically done in multiple and secondary burials. In other cases, those opening the grave took one bone or a

---

44   E.g. Wesolowsky (1973) 341–42; Makropoulou (2007) 91–93, fig. 6; Rife (2012) 169–71, (2022a); Völling (2018) 93, 104–105.

45   E.g. Gejvall and Henschen (1968); Catling *et al.* (1976) 36–37, 41–42; Rife (2012) 169–70, 291–92.

46   Catling *et al.* (1976) 29–37, fig. 6; Buchet and Sodini (1984) 235–36; Sweetman and Becker (2005) 365–66; Makropoulou (2007) 91–96, fig. 6; Rife (2012) 41–43, 78–81, figs. 2.20, 2.66.

47   Rudolph (1979) 300; Miller (1983) 87, pl. 26e; Di Vita (1988) 107–109, figs. 106–109; Mallegni (1988) 341–42; Makropoulou (2007) 443–45; Rife (2012) 82–85, 199–202, figs. 2.69, 4.2.

few from the fully articulated skeleton, usually a tractable element such as a jaw or a heel. Although this practice has been recognized at only a few sites with burials of late antique or later date, it was undoubtedly more widespread than the sparse published reports might suggest. Extracting remains in this manner implies a desire to locate and to possess a representative piece of the whole form. In some cases, such as the headless body in the so-called 'Bishop's Tomb' with a disturbed cover in the basilica near Knossos,[48] the removal of bones can be persuasively associated with the collection of relics, or intrinsically powerful fragments from the holy dead. In other cases, such as skeletons missing arm, leg, foot bones in the modest cists at Isthmia, Corinth, and Tiryns,[49] it seems unlikely that bones were removed as holy relics. Perhaps they were considered valuable because of their antiquity or apotropaic utility, or as conduits for communing with an ancestral past.[50]

The reopening of graves was not always so reverential; sometimes it was destructive on purpose. This intentional disturbance of burials (τυμβωρυχία), which was prohibited by Civil and Canon Law and condemned by the Church,[51] took the form of graverobbing, vandalism, and desecration. Historical sources tell us about damage to graves and their contents that was ideologically motivated, such as the Emperor Julian's assault on the remains of Babylas, John the Baptist, and Elisha in Syria and Palestine. Such notorious episodes, however, have not been positively identified in the archaeological record. Across the Greek world, we do find copious evidence for the targeted disturbance of late antique graves in the form of compartments with the covers crushed or torn out and the contents mixed up and scattered.[52] Often it is impossible to ascertain the chronology of disturbance, let alone its impetus. The severity and focus of the damage in many cases calls to mind robbers churning through the grave, presumably seeking jewellery or other treasures. Intrusive artifacts found in some disturbed graves reveal that this process of looting, which continues unabated today at many sites, had begun already in the Late Roman to Early Byzantine periods.[53]

Burial Contents: Objects

Of all the material, spatial, and biological dimensions of mortuary behaviour, archaeologists have usually paid closest attention to the artefactual contents of burial, or 'grave goods'. This focus has generated a relatively full published record of the kinds of objects mourners chose to leave with the dead, even if many researchers have missed the ritual significance of those objects. Furthermore, it has been commonplace in Greek archaeology to remark on the paucity of funerary artifacts in late antique burials. While it is true that late graves typically do not contain the quality or number of decorative objects that are typically found, for example, in Archaic to Classical Athenian graves, their contents often compare with those in Greek graves of Hellenistic, Roman, and Byzantine date. The most prevalent classes of finds are vessels, personal adornments, lamps, and coins. It should also be stressed that, while the basic funerary assemblage of Late Antiquity shows striking typological homogeneity across the Greek world, individual interments vary greatly in the number and character of their artefactual contents.

Ceramic and less commonly glass vessels from funerary contexts include chiefly pitchers, cups, and unguentaria in many shapes and sizes, often of regional manufacture (Fig. 3).[54] With the possible exception of unguentaria and certain jugs such as late lekythoi, these vessels do not seem to have been manufactured expressly for funerals but rather were borrowed from the domestic stock. They are found in various positions alongside or above the body. This suggests a particularly close association between corporeal deposition and ritual application, as though mourners brought the vessels in procession and then used them for libation or chrismation, whether pouring, sprinkling, or dabbing wine, honey, or aromatic substances over or around the corpse. An interesting question is whether funerary banqueting at graveside, which is attested in the textual and archaeological records of Roman Greece, persisted in Late Antiquity. That mourners offered food and drink at the burial site during the funeral or later visitation is plausible if we consider the existence of small altars or other flat surfaces. But the small number and limited function of the vessels found in many graves – usually only one or two jugs, very rarely more than half a dozen – point to a symbolic gift, even if it did accompany a shared salute. Of course, we cannot rule out the possibility of commensal rituals in another locale, such

48   Frend and Johnston (1962) 196–97, pl. 49b.

49   Gejvall and Henschen (1968) figs. 2, 3; Kilian (1980) 286, pl. 49.3; Rife (2012) 65, 66–68, 202–204, figs. 2.49, 2.54.

50   Cf. Rife (2012) 225–26.

51   Petrakakos ([1905] 1971) 127–29; Emmanouelides (1989) 454–508; Rebillard (2009) 70–79.

52   E.g. Makropoulou (2007) 470–71; Rife (2022a).

53   E.g. Rife (2022c).

54   E.g. Roebuck (1951) 164, pl. 67.5, 6; Pallas (1961) 173, pl. 72b; Frend and Johnston (1962) 195–96, 231–32, fig. 9; Sodini (1977); Oikonomou-Laniado (2003) 35–50, figs. 75–102; Makropoulou (2007) 458–59; Tzavella (2008) 356–57, 359–62, figs. 4, 7, 8, (2010); Antonaras (2010) 314–16, fig. 10; Papanikola-Bakirtzi and Kousoulakou (2010); Völling (2018) 60–61, 108–116, figs. 14, 15, 17–20, 22; Rife (2022a).

as a meal hosted at the bereaved home. Early excavators of late antique and Byzantine graves sometimes interpreted the mixed sherds they found in fills at graves as the remnants of collective dining.[55] Without complete stratigraphic and artefactual analysis, however, we must admit that such remains could have been ceramic residue unrelated to ritual activity. The rare discovery of numerous joining sherds from single or small groups of cooking or serving vessels strewn at graveside, such as is reported at Isthmia, Corinth, and Thessalonica, seems to indicate a different practice.[56] Mourners apparently brought these pots, perhaps from a meal at home, and smashed them. They may have intended this gesture to punctuate their grief and signify their loss, to 'kill' a ritual tool, or to repel malevolence.

The exploration of large urban cemeteries has revealed intriguing evidence for more elaborate uses for food on site. Assorted pottery including amphoras and serving wares is reported in and around cists and tombs at Argos and Thessalonica, and animal bones and shells, seeds, and burned matter have been found in the west cemetery at Thessalonica.[57] These remains prove that mourners cooked, consumed, and disposed of meat and fruit or vegetables within the cemetery. But we cannot recover the scale of single events, and thus whether mourners always participated in blood sacrifices or in large group meals near the grave, but only offered portions of food and drink to the dead. Three remarkable paintings in chamber tombs at Thessalonica portray dining.[58] One shows 7 persons seated around a semi-circular table; one shows 3 servants bringing platters of fish and bread to a couple reclining at a small table; and one shows a woman lifting a glass opposite a reclining man(?) around a small table with fish and bread. While these scenes reflect common motifs in sepulchral painting at Rome, we cannot be sure whether they depict domestic or funerary dining either real or fictive, a eucharistic meal either liturgical or funerary, or even a symposium of saints, or an abbreviated Last Supper. Moreover, the poor preservation and nebulous dating of the chambers (late 3rd or early to mid-4th c.?) leave open the possibility that this vibrant art belongs rather to the Middle Roman phase of the Thessalonican

burial grounds, that it is pre-Christian, and that it is irrelevant to interpreting the putative ceramic, biological, and botanical evidence for funerary dining at the late antique city. In any case, the most likely setting for banquets in a large cemetery was indeed a chamber tomb. Small buildings with open ground outside or forecourts afforded not only an adequate place for preparing and serving meals but also separation from the dank stench of the burial compartment. Such spaces at certain tombs, for example, in Corinth, Argos, Thessalonica, and Vrondi on Karpathos have been identified as kitchens or dining rooms.[59]

As I have noted, mourners often prepared the dead for burial by dressing them as in life. Seldom do textiles or animal hide survive in the depositional environment, but buckles, buttons, and hobnails from clothes, belts, and footwear sometimes do. Embroidery or appliqué has been reported in unusual instances, such as gold thread certainly or possibly from clerical vestments in burials at Corinth, Patras, Thessalonica, and Philippi.[60] Simple articles variously made from bronze, iron, glass, stone, and shell occur in small but consistent numbers in late antique Greek graves: hairpins, earrings, necklaces, bracelets, finger rings, fibulae.[61] A favourite adornment was the miniature pendant cross either found alone, perhaps having been laid on the corpse or sewn onto the clothing, or strung on a beaded necklace. A notable discovery in graves at Olympia, Kenchreai, Delion, Thessalonica, and Edessa are small metal bells (κωδωνίσκοι),[62] which are also known in funerary contexts across Asia Minor and the Near East. Both kinds of objects seem to be disproportionately represented in the burials of infants and children (Fig. 4). Apart from the decorative function of the cross and its potency as a badge of personal devotion, the cross and the bell have served as prophylactic measures for centuries down to the present. The persistence of both symbols in Greek daily life and burial over the long term, one Christian and one pagan, speaks to their perceived efficacy in

---

55   E.g. Soteriou (1917) 136–38; Keramopoullos (1929) 131–33; Pallas (1951) 164–66.

56   Williams and Zervos (1992) 162–63; Williams *et al.* (1998) 241–42; Makropoulou (2007) 460; Rife (2012) 196–97, 229; see also Grinsell (1961) for ethnographic survey and interpretation of this practice.

57   Oikonomou-Laniado (2003) 34; Makropoulou (2006) 464–69.

58   Perdrizet (1905) 93–94, pl. 11; Pelekanides (1963) 23–25, fig. 9, (1969) 218–20, figs. 7, 8; Laskaris (2000) 501–506, figs. D 7, D 56; Marki (2006) 140–41, figs. 74, 75, pl. 5b–c.

59   Oikonomou (1988) 500; Oikonomou-Laniado (2003) 34; Geraskli (2004) 392, fig. 11; Makropoulou (2007) 325–26, 467–68, fig. 14, pls. 41.6, 62.6, 7.

60   Stikas (1964) 134; Laskaris (2000) 42–45, 182, 213, 232, 242, nos. 8, 9, 328g, 381a, 416b.d1, 425h; Makropoulou (2007) 445.

61   E.g. Davidson (1952); Vikatou (1992) 253–54, figs. 18–22; Antonaras (2010) 319–24, figs. 12, 13; Makropoulou (2007) 445–49, 508–26; Rife (2012) 108–12, figs. 2.96–2.114, (2022a); Meleti (2013) 164; Völling (2018) 54–60, figs. 14–21, 23, 24.

62   Karamanoli-Siganidou (1973–1974) 710, fig. 509d; Makropoulou (2007) 455–56, pl. 72; Hamilaki (2009) 1170, 1176, fig. 12; Pazaras (2009) 102, 150, fig. 196; Völling (2018) 77, 111, fig. 17; Panelas (2022).

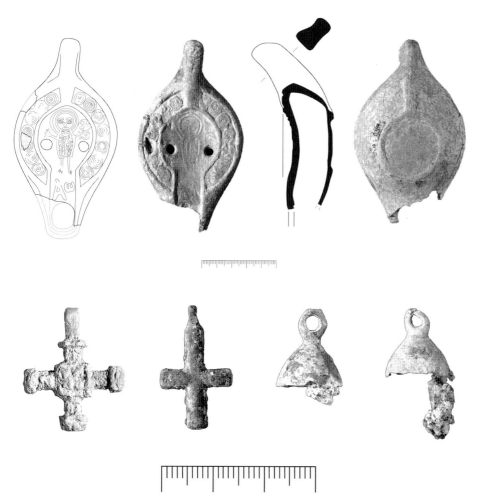

FIGURE 4   Above: Kenchreai, Grave 39, Unglazed moldmade lamp, Athenian imitation of North African type, with image of Jesus Christ the Savior on discus, mid-late 6th century. Below, left to right: Isthmia, Grave T14–991, Bone pendant cross, 7th century or later; Kenchreai, Grave 33, Bronze pendant cross, late 5th-early 7th century; Kenchreai, Grave 46, Bronze pendant bell with iron clapper, late 6th-early 7th century; Kenchreai, Grave 41, Bronze pendant bell with iron clapper, 6th–7th century.

IMAGE COPYRIGHTS: RIFE (2012) 110, FIG. 2.103 AND KORKA AND RIFE (2022) 888, FIG. 19.44, COURTESY OF THE TRUSTEES OF THE AMERICAN SCHOOL OF CLASSICAL STUDIES AT ATHENS

warding off malice and their real power in comforting the wary user.[63]

Mourners typically carried lamps during the funeral or later visitations and left them outside the grave or inside with the body. The commonest form across the Greek world, such as in the well documented cemeteries of Corinth, Kenchreai, Argos, Thebes, Nea Anchialos, Thessalonica, and Thera,[64] was the hand-held terracotta lamp with a decorated discus, though remains at Thessalonica show that glass goblet- and bowl-lamps were also left at graves.[65] The terracotta lamps, many manufactured regionally but also many imported from Asia Minor and North Africa, represent the same types used widely in private and public contexts during Late Antiquity. While we cannot know the thought behind the selection of any one lamp, we can reasonably assume that mourners who used lamps displaying crosses during funeral processions or graveside visits, as many did from the 5th c. onward, recognized the power of the image for spiritual inspiration, emotional succour, and divine protection. Besides their iconography, burning lamps may well have affected the experience of grieving and remembrance in many ways as tools of prayer, as visual focal points and sources of peculiar smells that triggered feelings, and as symbols of salvation, eternity,

63   Psarologaki (2010) 88; Leontsini and Panapoulou (2013) 858–60.

64   Keramopoullos (1917) 103–106, figs. 74–77; Roebuck (1951) 164, pl. 67.1; Soteriou (1956) 113–15, pl. 40a, b; Wiseman (1969) 82–83, pl. 26c, (1972) 8; Oikonomou (1988), Oikonomou-Laniado (1998) 405–407, (2003) 34, 44, 49–50, figs. 106–113; Sanders (2005b) 436–37; Gerousi (2014); Rife (2022b).

65   Marki (2006) 115–16, 208; Antonaras (2010) 314, (2017) 186–87.

or passage. It would be wrong to conclude, as some have, that the chief or exclusive purpose of lamps in such ritual settings was artificial illumination, and therefore that their presence demonstrates burial at night or in bad weather. Likewise, candles in churches are not just lit when the sky or the interior is dark.

Another class of objects that mourners sometimes left with the dead is coins, though the practice seems to have waned into the Byzantine era. These are found alone or in small clusters, rarely in caches that were once gathered in pouches, situated over the mouth, face, neck, or upper body. Late funerary coins invariably belonged to small denominations of little monetary value, and sometimes they were already antique issues at the time of deposition.[66] Most scholars interpret them as a vestige of the ancient practice of paying a toll to Charon, the Stygian ferryman.[67] In Late Antiquity, such coins may have simply betokened a sacrifice or loss on the part of the bereaved without always conjuring vivid notions of a perilous descent to Hades.

The Microtopography of Burial

A crucial decision by mourners when making a burial was where to inter the dead. In some cases, as I have discussed above, the recently deceased was added to a compartment already owned by the family; and yet the question remains why mourners chose that particular site in the first place and then conscidentiously maintained and used it over time. Many factors must have influenced the selection of a burial locale. Open space was of course a requirement, and one that would have been at a premium in dense cemeteries. Placement within a larger burial complex could have created, expressed, or cemented a relationship between the deceased person and a larger community. While the visibility and accessibility of the burial were considerations, we can assume that signs at ground level, together with a lasting memory of local landmarks, helped participants in the funeral and later visitors to locate and to relocate the site. Moreover, since the wider surroundings formed a permanent setting for the dead, mourners must have also considered how to contextualize a special place for active performance, contemplation, and preservation within an existing landscape. For all these reasons, it is worth exploring the spatial distribution of graves on the local and regional scales – the microtopography and macrotopography of burial – in the Greek world during Late Antiquity.

One prevalent pattern is the clustering of burials. We find in many cemeteries, such as those at Corinth, Argos, Patras, Athens, and Thessalonica, even rows of cists built from mortar, rubble, or brick masonry, often sharing walls or coverings.[68] In some cases these tight rows are divided into subgroups, but many show no obvious demarcation. The visual impression of expansive uniformity is striking, like the walls of niches in a Roman *columbarium* rising up toward the sky but instead a floor of graves spreading out across the land. Such a regular formation implies planning and unified execution, which in turn implies corporate control, whether by a neighbourhood, a civic body, or the Church. The socioeconomic underpinnings of organized cemeteries thus fit the operation of a populous town or city. Moreover, we cannot help but see in their bland repetition an anonymous necropolis, a faceless population whose inherent diversity is elided into overarching commonality.

Narrower clusters of burials were gathered inside walled enclosures, both chambers and precincts at or below ground level. The greater size, prominence, and complexity of these constructions presumably reflects a greater household wealth than do seriated graves. Confined concentrations of cists, sarcophagi, or compartments within a hedging wall (περίβολοι) are known in zones of intensive burial, like those at Argos and Thessalonica.[69] Here, groups may well have been concerned to segregate their own from the encroachment of outsiders. Isolated chamber tombs, like those that dotted the suburbs and countryside of cities in the eastern provinces during the early to middle Roman centuries, are rare (e.g. Samos).[70] A common late form of chamber tomb across south-eastern Europe was a vaulted crypt with a short ingress on one end. Mourners placed bodies either directly on the floor or into compartments alongside or within the walls, which were usually cleanly plastered but sometimes lavishly painted. Such chambers are well known in the sprawling cemeteries of Corinth, Veroia, Thessalonica, and Philippi, where in some places they were unevenly arranged and in other places aligned in rows.[71] These precincts and chambers

---

66   Sodini (1977) 13–14; Laskaris (2000) 321–24; Markopoulou (2007) 454–56; Rife (2012) 192–93.

67   Cf. Schell (1989) 104–12; Poulou-Papadimitriou, Tzavella, and Ott (2012) 380.

68   Wiseman (1969) 81, pl. 26a; Laskaris (2000) 149, 150, 184, nos. 280am, 280as, 328aO, figs. A 91, A 92; Oikonomou-Laniado (2003) 30, fig. 55; Makropoulou (2007) 25–44, 55–67, 99–110, 125–88, figs. 1–3, pl. 41; Meleti (2013).

69   Oikonomou-Laniado (2003) 28–29, 30–31, figs. 40–52, 56, 57; Marki (2006) 54, 55, 103–105, figs. 41, 42; Makropoulou (2007) 68–97, 301, 305–307, 309–27, figs. 4–6, 13, 15–17, pls. 41a, b.

70   Laskaris (2000) 68, 601, fig. A 43.

71   Pelekanides (1955) 151–53, 155, figs. 36–39; Williams, MacIntosh and Fisher (1974) 8–10, fig. 2, pl. 2; Ivison (1996) 108–10, figs. 5.3, 5.4; Laskaris (2000) 217, no. 398a, fig. A 127; Marki (2006) 110–19, figs. 48–56, pls. 55, 56; Makropoulou (2007) 414–23.

surely contained families, and their size and the number of skeletons (when recorded) indicate an extended family buried over many years. We may view such elaborate spaces as a monumentalized version of single cists reused multiple times to inter several members of a lineage.

Better known to scholars of Late Antiquity are burials clustered at churches, which have been explored since the beginning of Christian archaeology as a discipline in modern Greece. The textual and archaeological evidence for churches reveals that the sacred building and its vicinity constituted a unique experiential context that served not only the religious but also the social, economic, and cultural interests of the community. The prospect of membership in the group of those interred around a church must have attracted residents who sought divine favour and intercession, though the drive to claim standing within a congregation would have also been compelling. It is not therefore surprising that a late antique church formed its own mortuary micro-environment that was by turns planned and organized, irregular and cumulative, expansive and centralized, mirroring as it were the same spatial distributions that we observe in wider burial grounds around settlements. In churches with long lives, the interior pavements filled with graves, sometimes nearly wall to wall, and the periphery grew crowded with burials competing for proximity to the sanctuary. This late antique phenomenon is well documented at Tigani in the Mani and Philippi, and a striking parallel may be found at the church occupying the ancient Hephaisteion in the Athenian Agora throughout the Byzantine era.[72]

In churches of great importance to their communities, whether due to their historical associations, their elite sponsorship, or their ecclesiastical authority, we often find either formal burial annexes around the sanctuary or burial compartments situated prominently inside it. Chambers above or below ground opened off the aisles, chapels were appended to the building, or richly appointed cists were sunk into the floor in the middle of the *naos* or at the heads of the aisles. Salient examples can be found at the great basilica of Lechaion, the basilica in the Kraneion district of Corinth (Fig. 5), the basilica on that city's north-east outskirts identified with Ayios Kodratos (St. Quadratus), the basilica on the Ilissos at Athens, and the opulent basilicas of Thessalian Thebes (modern Nea Anchialos).[73] These conspicuous

burials belonged to eminent members of the congregation, dedicated in some cases to clergy, bishops, and presbyters and in others to local aristocrats, perhaps donors to the construction or interior décor of the church itself.

Monuments for the veneration of saints and martyrs comprise an important category of sites for Christian worship. Few certain cases are known in Greece. Likely or possible instances at Corinth, Kenchreai, Athens, Knossos, and Philippi are characterized by a symmetrically octagonal, polylobate, or tricameral floor plan with a crypt (Figs. 5, 6).[74] Such *martyria* are often connected to or embedded in a larger complex that could accommodate pious visitors on a regular basis and a commemorative service on festal days. Like prominent churches, these structures are often surrounded by elaborate burials that belonged to elite local families seeking prestige in their community and assistance for the resurrection by interring loved ones in perpetual approach to the holy dead.

An unusual form of communal burial that appeared for the first time in Late Antiquity are the Greek 'catacombs', so-called after the tunnelled necropoleis around the city of Rome. The two most famous sites are located on Melos and near Methone in Messenia.[75] On Melos, residents excavated overlapping corridors with rows of loculi and arcosolia in the walls, sometimes stretching upward in registers, which were cleanly finished and painted with epitaphs and dedications. Residents near Methone cut a cavern out of a hillside and divided it into several irregular chambers with dense burial compartments in the walls and floor. Neither site exhibits ritual furniture apart from stone benches along the walls. While both complexes were used by Christians, we cannot associate them with holy veneration, because neither was centred around a primary burial or attached to a church. Nor does their creation underground prove their use by believers hiding from persecution. Furthermore, the crowded and schematic form of the compartments, which at Melos are estimated to have held thousands of bodies, does not suggest elite interment. Instead both 'catacombs' seem to be rock-cut cemeteries that served nearby communities over an extended period, both apparently organic outgrowths from earlier chambers. They represent local accommodations of the late

72   Dinsmoor ([1941] 1975) 6–15, figs. 1–3; Pelakanides (1955) 150–72; Drandakis and Gioles (1980) 248–50, plan 8; Tzavella (2008) 355–56.

73   Soteriou (1919) 27–30, figs. 28–31, (1935) 59–62, figs. 10, 11, (1955) 135–36, fig. 3; Carpenter (1929) 347, 348–55, figs. 1–3,

pl. VI; Shelley (1943) 176–79, 183 fig. 9–11, pl. XII; Pallas (1961) 173–74, pl. 72c, (1972) 98–99, fig. 1, (1974) 213–19, fig. 6, plan 4, pls. 201–206.

74   Soteriou (1919) 8–14, figs. 7–9, (1927) 52, fig. 39; Shelley (1943) 179–83, figs. 12, 13, pls. XII, XIII; Pallas (1972) 99–102, fig. 1; Sweetman and Becker (2005); Brélaz (2018) 253–55, fig. 10.3; Rife and Andrikou (2022); see also Laskaris (2000) 329–426.

75   Bayet (1878b); Lampakis (1907); Soteriou (1928); Pallas (1968); Laskaris (2000) 429–71.

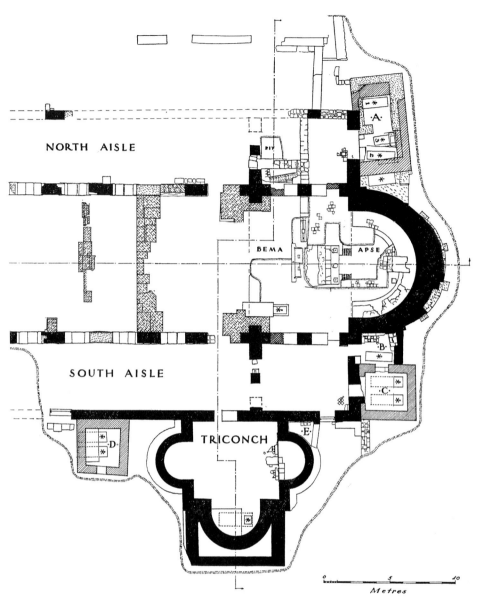

FIGURE 5 Corinth, Christian basilica in Kraneion district surrounded by burial annexes (after Shelley
(1942) pl. XII, courtesy of the Trustees of the American School of Classical Studies at Athens).

antique impulse for dense, collective burial to a karstic landscape of soft sedimentary bedrock, just as occurred in the communities of central Italy, Sicily, and Malta.

The Macrotopography of Burial

In choosing where to bury their dead – at a church, in a cemetery, or elsewhere – members of late antique communities responded to broader trends in the evolution of the Greek mortuary landscape. Residents of the countryside buried their dead on farmsteads, sometimes in isolation, or in small village burial grounds. Large settlements witnessed the continuing growth of cemeteries on the suburban periphery, concentrated around routes of passage or landmarks such as roads and gates, which furnished an accessible and visible setting. Mourners who prepared for burial in renowned burial grounds

would have been aware of their antiquity, as must have occurred in the Kraneion at Corinth, which by Late Antiquity had been in use for over a millennium,[76] but we cannot know if that knowledge spurred mere curiosity or decisive planning. At the same time, acute limitations on space in long-lived settlements forced mourners into unaccustomed spaces. They began to bury their dead in dilapidated houses, inside defunct waterworks, and around standing fortifications.[77] Other manifestations of this same adaptive behaviour are well-documented

---

76 Carpenter (1929) 345–47; Stillwell and Fowler (1932) 77–84; Elderkin (1945).

77 E.g. Carpenter and Bon (1936) 68, fig. 49; Davidson (1937); Stillwell, Scranton, and Freeman (1941) 55–57, pl. II; Broneer (1954) 145–41, plan V; Scranton (1957) 23–24, 30–33; Tsigaridas (1977) 478–79, fig. 1, pls. 439a–440a; Ivison (1996) 114, 118–19;

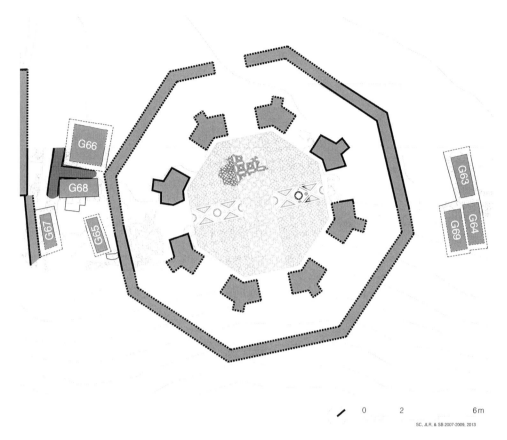

FIGURE 6   Kenchreai, Octagon on north-east headland of harbor surrounded by built cist graves.

in the Corinthia. There mourners repeatedly entered centuries-old tombs for the addition of the Christian dead, sometimes after consecration with the sign of the cross, which may have served to evict demons, or to signpost devotional moments inside the reimagined chamber.[78] Burials in common cists spread across once bustling cult-sites and formerly sacred buildings, as at the sanctuaries of Asklepios and of Demeter and Kore on the north and south edges of the city.[79] We also find exceptional cases of elaborate cists conspicuously cut into the façades of collapsed temples, such as the Antonine Palaimonion at the Isthmian Sanctuary.[80] What is most arresting about these developments, especially from the traditional viewpoint of classical archaeology, is their seemingly flagrant disregard of ancient prohibitions against intramural burial. Longstanding principles of urban planning and religious practice dictated that dead flesh inside city circuits and temple precincts would introduce pollution and thus violate the purity of shrines and homes.

Such repurposing of ruins is among the most distinctive features of late antique Greek burial. The mortuary exploitation of derelict areas has elicited some of the more tendentious interpretations in scholarship on late antique Greece. Some have misunderstood the depositional sequences of burial in houses, drains, and fortifications, or overplayed their architectural associations, viewing them as evidence for distressed people who crammed their dead under the floor or in the sewer, or as the remains of soldiers (or invaders) left at the walls they guarded (or assailed).[81] Others have envisioned a sharp caesura between the old concepts of inviolability and the new realities of burial, either proposing long gaps between the end of Greek temples and the advent of Christian rituals to the same sites, or assuming the erection of whole new civic boundaries to which

Laskaris (2000) 264; Rife (2012) 25–72, 76–82, 124–25, 129, 130, 134, 177, figs. 2.1–2.57, 2.65–2.67.

78   E.g. Walbank (2005) 279; Rife *et al.* (2007) 152–53, 163, 172–73, 174–75; Rife (2012) 113, 171, nn. 50, 118; Walbank and Walbank (2015) 183, 200–201; see also perhaps Deligiannakis (2016) 79–82, 178–79.

79   Roebuck (1951) 161–67; Bookidis and Stroud (1997) 381–91.

80   Scranton (1951) pls. 5, 16, plan v; Williams, MacIntosh, and Fisher (1974) 10, n. 13; Rife (2012) 91–96, 130–34, figs. 2.77–2.81.

81   See n. 77.

extramural burial was now aligned.[82] In many respects these theories are critically cogent; and we must admit that any universal explanation could not account for all local variations in burial and settlement across the Greek world.

We should, nevertheless, consider the possible influence of new worldviews in Late Antiquity. I have already discussed the rise of burial in and around churches, a trend that intensified into the Byzantine Middle Ages. Some churches were erected in the midst of suburban cemeteries, particularly mortuary chapels. But church builders were drawn to other locales regardless of city walls or other formal limits of settlement, whether by a place's legendary associations with an execution or a miracle, or by a place's topographic benefits on a headland, along a shore, or next to a highway. As new churches appeared and burials followed them in towns without walls and in cities where decrepit circuits were being replaced by smaller enceintes that bounded the heart of a settlement but not necessarily all of its residents, such as Athens, Corinth, and Amphipolis, the ancient dichotomy of intramural/extramural must have been fading.[83] Do fundamental shifts in the topography of burial thus reflect the dissolution of the classical Greco-Roman city and the beginning of its medieval Mediterranean successor, a fortified core with orbiting neighbourhoods centred around churches? In this light, we should hesitate to interpret burial strictly in relation to city-walls especially over the transitional era of the late 6th to 8th c.

Alongside changing models of urban topography were evolving attitudes about the past, including the ancient landscape. We need not read into late antique burials among Classical or Roman ruins an experience of desperation or marginalization but rather a strategy of practicality, even a measure of innovation and resilience. Mourners adapted to their ancient environment for advantage in the present. I have suggested elsewhere that the transformation of broken structures for funerary ritual was a conceptual and behavioural analogue to the creative act of spoliation in Late Roman to Early Byzantine masonry and monumental art.[84] Likewise, we should not dismiss burial in abandoned sanctuaries as coincidental or unintended. We cannot know exactly the many ways that late antique Greeks viewed their

mythic and historic past, but we can safely assume that they did remember it in some form, perhaps even with surprising specificity. Did this cultural memory inform the placement of Christian burials over pagan shrines in Greece? It seems unlikely that the gradual and disorganized spread of numerous simple graves over ancient foundations expressed a concerted message of Christian triumph over Hellenic polytheism, as is described in contemporary narratives of Syrian holy men who were interred in pagan temples. But we may reasonably wonder whether Corinthians who buried their dead in the former precincts of Demeter and Kore and of Asklepios desired an appropriate place for gathering and devotion, or just sought relief in the numinous surroundings.

The prominent graves cut into Corinthian temples are more intriguing but no less enigmatic.[85] Although stripped of their superstructure, the tall podia furnished an impressive architectural setting for burial and thus proclaimed the importance of the deceased. The juxtaposition is blatant at the Isthmus, where a late antique grave was conspicuously placed above the mythical crypt of the boy Palaimon. Did mourners intend to translate the heroön of the Middle Roman sanctuary into the funerary monument of an eminent local family of the 5th or 6th c.? And in doing so, did they aim to depose the ancient hero or to glorify their own dead – or to achieve both ends at once?

Not all burials in late antique settlements were controlled and conventional. Unusual circumstances that threatened the prevailing social order from outside or inside the community sometimes generated burials out of place. Mass graves in subterranean cavities have been variously interpreted. Roebuck hypothesized that a large 6th c. deposit of disarticulated human bones inside a reservoir in Lerna Hollow at Corinth contained victims of the pandemic under Justinian.[86] Plague-pits probably were created in large maritime centres like Corinth in AD 542, but we have meagre chronological and stratigraphic evidence for this particular discovery in print. The apparent presence of not only intact amphora burials and funerary lekythoi but also commingled bones raises the possibility of peaceful burial over several generations combined with secondary burial. Another disaster of the 6th c. that had a drastic impact on settlements from northern Greece far south into the Peloponnese was the incursion of bands of Avars or 'Slavs'. Clearing the deep fill inside the Hellenistic tunnel into the Stadium at Nemea uncovered a late grave. Although the excavator speculated that barbarians had

---

82   E.g. Frantz (1965), (1988) 70–71, 92; Spieser (1976) 314–17; Vaes (1984–1986) 326–28; Pallas (1989) 887–88; Avramea (1997) 114–15; Ivison (1996) 110–12; Sanders (2002) 648–49, (2004) 179–80, figs. 6.1, 6.3, (2005a) 14; Poulou-Papadimitriou, Tzavella, and Ott (2012) 383.

83   Cf. Morris (1992) 171–73; Snively (1998); Sodini (2007) 326–28; Tzavella (2008); Baldini (2014).

84   Rife (2012) 134.

85   Rife (2012) 130–34.

86   Roebuck (1951) 164, pl. 28.1, plan A; Sanders (2005b) 434; McCormick (2016) 1027.

brutally dismembered a hapless resident squatting in the hollow, the published osteological, artefactual, and mortuary remains can be more simply interpreted as a typical secondary burial made by local farmers.[87] In contrast, the astonishing discovery of a remote cave near Andritsa in the south-western Argolid does seem to have revealed a secret refuge.[88] Multiple burials associated with clustered amphoras and other habitational debris, perhaps separate domiciles within the cavern, constituted a makeshift village surviving underground around the end of the 6th to early 7th c. This site seems to corroborate colourful historical accounts of city-dwellers fleeing invaders to hide in the mountains and on islands.

Members of communities or interlopers who disrupted the social order sometimes received unorthodox burial. The remains of criminals, the unbaptized, or heretics – all categories for exclusion from formal burial according to the Church[89] – have seldom been positively identified and recorded in the archaeological record. So far as we can tell, outcasts received burials that were antithetical to standard practice in their design, orientation and corporeal position, contents, and location. Rare examples of Late Roman to Byzantine date on Crete and at Corinth, Isthmia, and Athens include bodies thrown into wells or bogs, bodies with mutilated limbs, and bodies stuffed into pits next to animal carcasses.[90] In some cases, the deceased were unwanted newborns who were disposed of before recognition as full members of their families and communities. In other cases, the deceased were apparently branded as social deviants, rejected from society and forcibly erased from collective memory, human garbage cast to oblivion.

People, Communities, and the Dead: Burial and Identity

Mortuary spaces, burial forms, and funerary rituals in late antique Greece bear an important relationship to local social structures, or the systems of association and interaction between persons and groups that were recognized within communities. A person's identity is a complicated amalgam of individual and collective perceptions that shifts according to context. If we can presume that the creation of mortuary space, the design of graves, and the performance of funerary rituals in

Ancient and Medieval Greece, as in other places and times, were deliberate acts by participants, then we may view the archaeological remains of burial as the intended outcome of conscientious decision-making. On some level, beyond a need to assuage emotional anguish and to satisfy personal concern, everyone is motivated to communicate who they are in the face of death, and mindful of the image that creates for posterity. Furthermore, considering not only the textual evidence for death in Roman to Byzantine Greece but also ethnographic analogy, we can be sure that burial furnished a time and a place for expressing selfhood and committing it to collective memory before a local audience. The challenge for us lies in reading the archaeological record of a burial site to interpret a community's social structure and its many identities.

The relationship between burial and status, or a person's relative influence in society deriving chiefly from wealth and authority, was a recurrent subject in Greek thought. Injunctions against sepulchral splendour, which recur in Early Christian writings and persist in the Byzantine tradition, echo a classical literary and philosophical *topos* concerning the transitory nature of earthly achievements that was, among others, famously associated with the Cynic School. The proclaimed aversion to material ostentation was consonant with the wider Christian ethos of vigilant modesty, and it aligned with the theological encouragement to engage in funerary acts that were effective at bringing salvation.[91] To be sure, certain widespread forms of extravagance during the Roman Empire had diminished greatly by Late Antiquity, such as enormous private tombs and costly grave goods, which had been pervasive signs of power and affluence since the Hellenistic era (see below). But they did not utterly vanish: painted chamber tombs continued to flourish in northern Greece, and the special attention to grandiose commemoration once afforded urban elites shifted to the holy dead in the form of ecclesiastical shrines or *martyria*. There is scant indication that the wealthy buried their dead like paupers to express Christian piety, and indeed the repetition of this ethical theme over the centuries rather proves the contrary. Furthermore, while we can imagine the poor saving up fortunes or pooling family funds to pay for unusually expensive burials, we should doubt that they could have acquired for themselves the most costly materials or claimed the most visible locales known from the archaeological record.

In the late antique Greek world, the investment of time, effort, and resources in the funeral, burial, and

---

87 Miller (2001) 134, fig. 247, (2004) 75, 109–10, 195; cf. Rife (2012) 202 n. 192, 217.

88 Kormazopoulou and Chatzilazarou (2010).

89 Petrakakos ([1905] 1971) 41–48, 112–15; Emmanouelides (1989) 90–105.

90 Rife (2012) 72–74, 231–32, figs. 2.58–2.60.

91 See e.g. Engels (1998); Rebillard (2009) 123–39.

commemoration of the dead shows a positive correlation with social status, even if the particular range of preferred objects and spaces had evolved from earlier times. While any precise discrimination between degrees of wealth and authority within a large and complex burial assemblage can be hazardous to undertake, certain gross patterns are observable. By and large, elites were identified in death by prominent burial sites, permanent and orderly chamber tombs or graves, prescribed epitaphs, and valuable adornments on display when the body was carried in procession to interment. Burial near or inside a church expressed both an individual's importance in their community and congregation and their desired place in the heavenly kingdom. The most impressive burials belonged to clerics or grandees around churches or other sites of worship. Sometimes these contained few artifacts or were austere in display, but their distinctions included rich clothing, mural painting, symmetrical and careful design, and a conspicuous and permanent situation within an opulent structure. Chamber tombs not immediately associated with churches in urban cemeteries like those around Corinth, Athens, and Thessalonica exhibit similar features but with considerable variability in the kind and scale of their composition, contents, and prominence.

In those same sprawling burial grounds but also in many narrower ones belonging to smaller communities, from towns and villages to estates and farms, we find numerous cists with few artifacts and inconsistent designs in humble locations. Presumably this differential investment by families reflects in basic outline the socioeconomic diversity within and between different classes of settlement. As we have already noted, the late antique re-use of Roman-era chamber tombs or grand structures like podium-temples for burial could have resonated with cultural memory and Christian ideology, and structural recycling had undeniable pragmatic advantages. It may also reflect a localized scenario wherein non-elites aspired to prestige in death, effectively climbing the social ladder by appropriating ruined buildings as funerary monuments. The isomorphism of status and burial is most stark in the treatment of social deviants, which harshly inverted all phases of mortuary behaviour.[92] The criminal, excommunicated, or otherwise marginalized body, which was mishandled or mutilated and deprived of accompaniment, virtually disappeared into an informal and inaccessible space. The naked truth of these unusual graves was that the deceased had fallen out of the social order and therefore had been erased from memory.

In the rituals of death, mourners expressed other essential elements of identity within their community. As in many pre-modern societies, late antique Greece witnessed higher mortality among infants and young children than in developed countries today due to the prevalence of infectious disease and malnutrition. While we do not find cemeteries exclusively for children, noteworthy concentrations of child burials have been documented, for example, on the north slope of Acrocorinth, on the north-east edge of ancient Athens, north-east of the village at Vergina, and around the basilicas at Aliki on Thasos.[93] These burial grounds might have contained the victims of epidemic, drought, or famine, which disproportionately afflict the most vulnerable members of a biological population. We should also consider the possibility that these areas were intentionally segregated by age, not necessarily to set apart the unbaptized but perhaps to identify persons who had not fully joined the community as productive, legal members. Any discrepancies in ritual treatment between the young and the old are hard to see. The published evidence does suggest that dead infants and children were interred with apotropaic devices more frequently than were adults.[94] Such attention presumably reflects the care of young persons with whom families felt an intense emotional connection, desiring to protect and to nurture them while bemoaning a life cut short. In contrast, among the mortuary remains of both children and adults we find no fundamental variation that can be correlated with the biological sex of skeletal remains. Individual gender was undoubtedly expressed through the position of the bodies, the preparation of the skin and hair, and the choice of clothing and adornment for dead men and women. Likewise, certain intersecting identities, such as marital status and parenthood, were not only marked by the physical appearance of the deceased but also by the words of both the tombstone and the lamentation.

Apart from the bonds of family and home, we find little definite evidence for burial according to group membership in late antique Greece. The commercial sphere of burial and the inner mechanics of the funerary industry (if we may call it that) are fascinating topics about which we know very little. The archaeological and epigraphic records give no certain instances of professional associations or 'burial clubs' like those found in

---

92   Cf. Shay (1985); Papadopoulos (2000); Lindenlauf (2001).

93   Chatzioti (1988) 12–13, pl. 13β; Loverdou-Tsigarida (1985) 45; Bookidis and Stroud (1997) 391; Sodini and Buchet (1984) 212, 215, 234–35, 236, figs. 174, 177; and see in general Laskaris (2000) 288–90.

94   See nn. 62 and 63.

certain eastern cities from Hellenistic to Roman times.[95] Instead, bereaved families typically worked on their own behalf, with or without planning at the occasion of death and surely in some cases with great hardship. Tombstones record the purchase of plots, and churches would have overseen interment at places of worship, if not also on land-holdings remote from basilicas.[96] But to what extent did mourners purchase anew funerary instruments such as flowers, lamps, and pots? And to what extent did they carry objects from home, whether generic or utilitarian objects in store, personal effects of the dead or survivors, or valuables passed down across generations? The Church Fathers spoke against hiring mourners to sing dirges (θρηνῳδοί), but their frequency and role in late antique Greek communities are hard to know.

To be sure, our sources for funerary practice are not devoid of expressions of professional identity. The career of the deceased was frequently marked in the epitaph. While the full range of connotations such references carried for past readers remains unclear, we can trace no clear formal differentiation between the graves of, for example, stoneworkers and butchers, individuals who probably represented the same broad socioeconomic stratum. Professional epithets on tombstones, in other words, identified the dead by a profile familiar to the local community, and did not assert affiliation with a professional group. Likewise, while we can imagine colleagues of the deceased participating in the ceremonies of interment and commemoration, for instance as pall-bearers, presumably they did so as associates or friends and not primarily as corporate agents. Late antique Greek communities did, however, recognize certain roles in society as sufficiently impactful to merit special commemoration. One key case is the exceptional burial of church leaders or holy persons, which, as we have seen, were variously distinguished by ritual, form, location, and content. The ranked organization of the cortège was a significant feature of the funeral, as officials and congregants lined up for adoration by level of influence. Objects buried with the dead can symbolize social roles. As I have noted, burial in gilded vestments commemorated the clergy as important leaders of an earthly community and exemplary followers of the heavenly deity. Rarely do we find tools of duty or craft in late antique Greek burials, like the elaborate medical kit

interred with a doctor during the 3rd c. at Kallion, which in all respects seems to have been extraordinary.[97]

One professional identity that emerges clearly from funerary artifacts is military service. The graves of soldiers have long been a focus of scholarly debate over the Roman-Byzantine transition in the Greek world. Exploration of central and peripheral areas of Corinth during the early 20th c. uncovered 4 cists containing at least 12 persons with iron weaponry, iron and bronze buckles, a handmade beaker, and a silver and bronze ornament, possibly amuletic.[98] Some of these objects were Byzantine products, while others were either brought from the northern Balkans or the broader Central to Eastern European zone, or they were manufactured under the influence of that region's material culture. On one hand, the design of these cists and the handling of the bodies resembled in basic form other standard late antique Greek graves, and they were located in regular areas for burial at Corinth during the late 6th to 7th c. On the other hand, the rare sword and spears clearly marked the deceased as soldiers. Scholars subsequently identified these persons variously as Early Medieval Slavs, Avars, Kutrigur or Onogur Bulgars, or even Middle Byzantine Greeks, noting similarities between the grave goods and contemporary assemblages from much further north, and recounting a massive and violent barbarian invasion during the 580s that advanced southward in waves.[99] In retrospect, we recognize in these discussions the twin distortions of culture-historical theory, whereby a foreign object must belong to an outsider self-identifying with a foreign ethnicity or nationality, and the historiographical narrative of a precipitous 'dark age'. Perhaps the greatest contribution of this debate has been the consensus that certain objects were exotic (whether in origin or inspiration) and would have been viewed as such at Early Byzantine Corinth.

The long shadow of old paradigms has obscured the professional demarcation of these graves. The deceased were soldiers, and it is tempting to read these Corinthian graves as distant echoes of the emerging warrior-culture of Medieval Europe. The recurrence and order of the graves, integrated into the mortuary landscape and in many regards conventional, speak against the identification of the dead as barbarian invaders or 'wanderers'

---

95 van Nijf (1997) 31–69; see in general Rebillard (1999) 280–82 and (2009) 37–56.

96 On epitaphs, see nn. 39 and 40. On burial on church lands, see e.g. Walbank and Walbank (2006) 284 and (2015) 201.

97 Petrakos (1977) 375–78, fig. 319α.

98 Davidson (1937) 228–33, figs. 1–3, (1952) 5–6; Scranton (1957) 27–33; Davidson Weinberg (1974); Ivison (1996) 114–16, figs. 5.6, 5.7.

99 Davidson (1937) 227–28, 235–40, (1952) 5–6 n. 8, 266; Zeiss (1940); Setton (1950), (1952); Charanis (1952); Pallas (1954); Werner (1955), (1956); Davidson Weinberg (1974) 512–13, nn. 3, 4.

with no place in the civic community. One sensible proposal is that they were mercenaries or auxiliaries in the garrison securing the Corinthian fortress (κάστρον) after the incursions of the late 6th to 7th c., when administrative and military control of the Byzantine Peloponnese was considerably weakened. Similar conditions may well have prevailed during this time in the fortified settlement at Tigani in the Mani.[100] Even if they had not travelled from abroad with ordinary troops, the soldiers wore buckles and bore weapons that emblematized an international style of Early Medieval dress.[101]

These controversial burials at Corinth raise the challenging question of the relationship between ethnicity and burial. The communities of late antique Greece were filled with people from other places who must have balanced their ancestral, local, and regional identities. Bereaved families may have identified themselves, for example, as Syrians or Egyptians by bringing personal items to the funeral or leaving them at the grave. A degree of homogenization in practices across the eastern Mediterranean, however, tends to disguise ethnic differentiation, which was more overtly communicated through sepulchral design and decoration in the eastern provinces during the Early Empire. Epitaphs in late antique Greece, for example, did not name the deceased as immigrants. Probably the most striking case of ethnic identification in funerary practice are the 'Slavic' graves found in the 1960s at Olympia and in 2014 at Makri near Tripoli.[102] These burials, which resemble those in the cemeteries of Central and Eastern Europe, contrast starkly with the interments of Christian Greeks of the 7th c. and later. The foreign settlers cremated their dead and collected the ashes in small, plain beakers that they placed in sparsely arrayed, unmarked pits.

Two pervasive dimensions of self-presentation that influenced the funerary practices of late antique Greece were family and Christianity. The importance of the family as the essential unit in society is reflected in the common practice of multiple interment. So far as we can reconstruct from the demographic profiles and datable contents of burial groups, single graves could contain parents and children and siblings, whole nuclear or extended families together for eternity. Mourners created and sustained an ideal picture of familial unity as they added the remains of their beloved dead to a grave already occupied by decaying relatives. This memorialization of the domestic unit, the sepulchral recreation of the household, is expressed in the occasional epitaphic

identification of the grave as a 'house' or 'dwelling' (οἶκος, οἴκημα, οἰκητήριον), a term still used on tombstones today. Furthermore, the metaphor of the Christian congregation as a family, supporting and watching over one another even beyond biological or spousal relationships, coloured participation in funerals, so that fellow believers joined in lamentation, burial, and visitation as devoted brothers and sisters.[103]

Many features of late antique Greek funerary ritual can be understood as expressions of Christian belief. Although we have no evidence for a standard funeral liturgy in the Greek world already in Late Antiquity, various writings show that certain essential rituals had widely circulated among families from the early centuries of Christianity. These include prayer, recitation and singing, and convening with the display of lights and crosses; administration of the Eucharist and engagement with the clergy sometimes occurred but not as a rule.[104] The greatest impact of Christianity on the rituals of death was ideological, not institutional. A whole new eschatological framework guided mourners to lay their dead down for quiet slumber until a heavenly dawn. Reports of the extraordinary deaths of saints and martyrs, wherein scorn gave way to triumph, material poverty to spiritual wealth, stench to perfume, and dolour to joy, painted a glorious picture that could have uplifted ordinary Greeks in their profound sorrow, but it hardly altered the harsh realities of bereavement. The best that Boeotian farmers and Laconian craftsmen could do amid suffering was to prepare the dead for a Christian afterlife. So, as I have discussed above, we observe in graves across the Greek world bodies laid out in a supine, extended position, with the head approximately facing eastward and the arms flexed inward; the conscientious handling of skeletal remains even when disturbed; the formalization or expansion of spaces immediately associated with graves to facilitate gathering and commemoration; and the proliferation of Christian words and symbols on tombstones and objects.

While these widespread practices can be linked to a fundamental belief system, it is unlikely that mourners intended thus to signify a singular identity or exclusive group-membership. Such burials represent communities of Christians, to be sure, and not Christian communities *per se*. We know that Christianity as an institution, a doctrine, a praxis, and even a style was firmly and widely established in Greek society by the 5th c., when many communities boasted church buildings, and we have little or no evidence for the sort of

100   Ivison (1996) 118–20; Vida and Völling (2000) 37–39.

101   Cf. Curta (2005) 130–31.

102   Vida and Völling (2000); Völling (2001) 310–15, figs. 5–8; Athanasoulis (2014).

103   See in general Hoxnes (1997).

104   Rowell (1977); Février (1987); Velkovska (2001); Rebillard (2009) 123–39.

violent destruction or forceful supplanting of ancient shrines that is colourfully recorded in Syria and Egypt. As for the graves of Christian Greeks, we should read in them not an oppositional stance to a static paganism but an adaptive response to a world of many rituals and beliefs, without tempering our estimation of the mourners' sincerity or piety. From this perspective, searching for 'pagan survivals' is far less interesting than tracing the creative combinations of the Christian and the non-Christian in the burials of late antique Greeks. They embraced a novel worldview of ultimate exaltation even while they deployed ancient measures for safety and relief in painful, precarious times: coins, curses, libations, bells, lamps, laments.

Burial and Society across Space: The Regional View

Any researcher on late antique Greek burial is struck by the similarity in sepulchral designs and funerary assemblages across the lower Balkan peninsula and the Aegean basin. Residents of the mainland and the islands built cists in which they interred one or more bodies in a similar position and orientation and they left a few vessels, lamps, coins, and/or adornments. They situated their dead in similar ways to negotiate the spaces of cemeteries, churches, and ruins. Such thorough regularity in the materials and places of burial across such a large area arose in part from fundamental conditions that were shared by myriad interconnected communities, namely, the dynamic social structure of provincial cities and their countrysides, and the Christian beliefs concerning death. But are these conditions not also shared with the ports of the Levantine coast and the towns of the Anatolian interior? What makes late antique Greek burial particularly Greek?

The hard part of any regional study is finding the limits. They can be vague and porous. Indeed, graves and their contents from northern Epirus up the Illyrian coast, for example, at Butrint and Salona are not dissimilar from contemporary remains found in central to southern Greece;[105] and the building with dense *loculi* and *arcosolia* at the Panayitsa near Pythagoreion on Samos unmistakably resembles the complex of the Seven Sleepers at nearby Ephesus.[106] Expanding the field of view, however, does not necessarily lead to easy answers. In comparing mortuary remains across multiple regions, we should not press for robust results or reliable distribution maps without considering a vast, and

therefore plausibly representative, dataset. A recent survey of 'Early Christian' burials from Greece to the Near East, which is admittedly an introduction to the subject, steps into this interpretive trap.[107]

For now, I resort to general impressions. Beyond the broad popularity of the Christian message of life through death, the available sources do not provide strong evidence for variation in specific rituals and beliefs among the eastern communities. However, even cursory inspection of the archaeological record reveals gross differences in the structural and artefactual components of burial between Greece and other parts of the eastern Mediterranean. The peoples of western and southern Asia Minor, Syria-Palestine, and North Africa continued to use traditional sepulchral design and decoration in Late Antiquity, often in innovative ways, particularly chamber tombs, sculpture, wall-painting, and mosaic.[108] We find few parallels for the monumental scale or artistic ornament of these civic cemeteries in the Greek world, where, with certain exceptions (see below), the remains indicate a preference for burial in plain compartments, even in the case of larger, more prominent chambers attached to churches. While differences in funerary assemblages across large areas are harder to ascertain, the diversity and richness of grave goods at certain eastern sites stands in stark counterpoint to the spare, mundane pitchers and bronze jewellery that typify many Greek cemeteries. As the comparative study of burial across the eastern Mediterranean advances and more evidence is published to a high standard, we will be better equipped to test the hypothesis that, as a wide pattern measured in relative terms, mortuary simplicity in the Greek world contrasted with mortuary elaboration in Asia, the Near East, and Africa during Late Antiquity.

We are on firmer ground to examine regional variability inside south-eastern Europe and the Aegean basin. Within its overarching uniformity, the mortuary record shows degrees of differentiation. The development of certain sepulchral forms can be attributed to regional geology, such as the Melian and Messenian 'catacombs' excavated from thick beds of soft, chalky limestone. Other forms seem to have been innovations by local builders who exploited the natural topography or offered certain benefits, and their designs grew popular among residents who frequented the same cemeteries and markets. So in the Corinthia, a variation on the chamber tomb, shaft-grave, or *arcosolium* appeared from

---

105   E.g. Marin and Buljević (1994); Duval, Marin, and Bonačić Mandinić (2000); Hodges, Bowden, and Lako (2004).

106   Miltner (1937); Laskaris (2000) 479–82.

107   Fox and Tritsaroli (2019).

108   For surveys, see e.g. Brandt *et al.* (2017); Ivison (2017); Eger and Mackensen (2018); Ardeleanu and Cubas Díaz (2019); and chapters in this volume.

the urban periphery to the countryside in Late Antiquity (see above). Presumably this regional form succeeded because it furnished a secure compartment that could be readily cut down into the dense oolitic limestone or at an angle into the friable marl that were exposed on Corinth's natural terraces. The elaborate structures and paintings that distinguish the cemeteries of Thessalonica represent another regional phenomenon. This unusual complexity might be interpreted as a late legacy of the venerable tradition of Macedonian chamber tombs, or as a consequence of social competition during an era of economic prosperity for the city. Furthermore, the manufacture of certain elements in late antique funerary practice was regionally circumscribed. Close comparison of the epitaphs of Athens and Corinth, despite their geographic proximity, shows diverging uses of terminology, formulae, verse, and biblical citations that can be plausibly linked both to prevailing local tastes and to the particular cultural milieu in the two cities.[109] Likewise, the regionalization of ceramic production during the 6th to 7th c. led to the creation of implements in new shapes and styles, including vessels and lamps in Boeotia, Phocis, and the Corinthia.[110] Although the rituals they served might not have varied substantially from place to place, recognizably regional objects could have imparted a sense of local familiarity that consoled mourners who yearned to belong as they suffered from loss. In sum, a range of environmental, commercial and industrial, social and economic, and cultural factors could have generated regional variability in mortuary behaviour across the Greek world during Late Antiquity, if not also across the eastern Mediterranean.

While such variation over large regions and subregions is an important subject for historical study, the most meaningful differences in the experience of many Greeks were undoubtedly intraregional. The host of disparities between urban and rural communities, from the diversity of identities to subsistence and exchange to hygiene and diet, must have influenced the forms, spaces, and rituals of burial in these separate but interconnected contexts. The urban-rural divide is a new horizon for the funerary archaeology of late antique Greece. While few regions have produced enough varied evidence to explore the topic with any depth, one valuable case study is Corinth with its Isthmian hinterland.[111] I have observed elsewhere that the mortuary homogeneity in the agrarian settlement among the ruins of the Panhellenic Sanctuary contrasts with the mortuary

heterogeneity in the sprawling cemeteries of nearby Corinth. The wide variation between elaborate and simple interments that characterized urban burial flattened out in many rural communities, so that graves in small villages appear more regular than do contemporary graves in large cities. This pattern may reflect a lower level of diversity in rural communities that adopted an egalitarian strategy of mixed agriculture, where social coherence and sharing resources, not competition, even in the theatre of death, were crucial for the survival of all.

Burial and Society across Time: The Diachronic View

The particular relationship between burial and society under discussion was not only distinctly Greek but also distinctly late antique. If we survey Greek burial practices from the Roman to Byzantine eras, we are struck by a paradigm shift in Late Antiquity. Indeed, many conventions of observing death and performing burial in Greece today are rooted in forms and rituals that first gained wide acceptance during the 5th to 7th c. Rather than attempting to anatomize the pace and course of this transformation, I will outline broad developments.[112]

Across this whole time span, the simplest forms of interment, which we can reasonably identify as nonelite, do not evolve drastically. However, the preferred monumental context for elite burial during earlier centuries was impressive chambers with prominent façades and decorative features, sometimes pedestals or altars, or plain or sculpted sarcophagi, whereas in later centuries it was a chamber on average smaller and less impressive than before, sometimes merely a built cist. Over the centuries epitaphs changed from large slabs boldly inscribed with the names of the head of a house or lineage, spouse and children, and sometimes references to freed-persons and descendants, to smaller stones over more modest graves that symbolized or alluded to Christianity and identified only one or a few family members with a single name and sometimes an epithet. Mourners throughout the Roman and into the Byzantine eras used longstanding burial grounds or chose convenient places for interment out of opportunity. But the distribution of elite burial shifted over time from conspicuous locales oriented to the old urban and suburban topography, outside city gates and along extramural traffic routes over land and sea, to accessible areas

109   Sironen (1997), (1999), (2018) 201–11; Rife (2022c).
110   Petridis (2000), (2007), (2010a), (2010b); Morison and Rife (2022); Rife (2022b).
111   Rife (2012) 206–32.
112   For surveys of the Early to Middle Roman era, see Rife (1999) and Flämig (2007). For representative sites, see e.g. Brock and Mackworth Young (1949) 80–92; Dusenbery (1998); Parlama and Stampolidis (2000); Rife et al. (2007); and Slane (2017).

of settlement, sometimes ruined, and often around or at churches.

Two of the most striking diachronic developments in Greek burial practice were in the handling of the dead body and the choice of funerary objects. Close interaction between the living and the dead, including physical contact through grasping, kissing, and smelling, was a common experience in ancient Mediterranean communities. Moreover, many examples of accumulated bodies inside not only Late Roman to Early Byzantine cists but also Early to Middle Roman compartments or sarcophagi are documented across the Greek world. During Late Antiquity, however, mourners conscientiously applied a consistent model for the placement of the head and limbs of the corpse, and they moved skeletal remains, whether for redeposition or extraction, in an orderly and selective manner. Furthermore, mourners over time used ritual tools that were increasingly restricted in appearance and function. Earlier graves and chamber tombs could contain a wide range of personal possessions, such as cosmetic accoutrement, coffers, mirrors, toys, and even pets, a variety of storage and serving vessels in terracotta and glass, and unguentaria, sometimes in large groups. In contrast, the late antique funerary assemblage, which does not even appear in many burials, typically included small numbers of plain pouring and drinking vessels and few accessories, especially crosses.

This dramatic evolution in the materials, spaces, and behaviours of Greek burial surely resulted from a complicated nexus of factors. At the risk of oversimplification, I propose that paradigmatic changes in mortuary practices reflect two large-scale processes that culminated in Late Antiquity. First, the widespread establishment of Christianity in Greek urban and rural communities propagated a new concept of life after death through divine salvation and promoted a heightened awareness of the timeless sanctity of the body. Second, the old bouleutic class declined as a dominant force in civic life and supralocal authorities emerged, while the Church as an institutional presence and an interactive space gained central importance in many communities. These transformations in Greek society can be traced in the shifting topography of burial as well as in the new contents of epitaphs and new ways of handling the dead. They are also evident in the altered modalities of self-presentation. The grand monuments showcased on hills and along highways outside cities gradually disappeared with the old aristocratic families. Diverse mourners in later centuries who belonged to the wide-reaching family of Christ sought foremost protection and hope in the face of death, whether through powerful symbols

and pious rituals or through association with Christian sanctuaries.

Looking Forward to Death: Future Directions in a Field

As we look at the current state of the discipline, we find many bright paths ahead for research on burial and society in late antique Greece. The absorption of current approaches and themes within the international field of funerary archaeology into the scholarly discourse on the Greek world has begun to accelerate in the 21st c. As I hope that my general discussion has shown, there are interesting questions to explore that focus on broad trends in the evolution and variability of mortuary practices across space and time. The intensive study of regions can elucidate the dynamic interaction between urban and rural, central and peripheral communities. One particularly rich context is the Panhellenic Sanctuaries at Olympia, Delphi, Isthmia, and Nemea, all of which survived into the 7th c. as small towns or farming villages. The late phases at these sites have been variously examined, but the potential for concerted synoptic study is great.[113] The well-documented remains of settlement and burial at these 4 sites across central and southern Greece can improve our understanding of rural social structure, local production and regional exchange, the encounter between Christianity and traditional polytheism, cultural memory and the transformation of the classical landscape, and vulnerability and resilience in the countryside.

The impact of any new interpretation derives in no small part from the solidity of its sources and the skill of its analysis. Arguably, the primary mandate for funerary archaeology in late antique Greece should be the collection and presentation of good data – prompt, full, accurate. Researchers can bring new perspectives to old discoveries by returning to the troves of bones, artifacts, notebooks, and photographs still lying unseen in storerooms, or they can design new projects that integrate field expertise and interpretive goals in burial and biology. One basic challenge that funerary archaeologists often face, the vast scale and complexity of their data and the practical and budgetary impediments to full reporting, could be addressed more effectively through electronic publication. Open-access digital archives allow researchers to share objective evidence for endless manipulation and reference by others, which catalyses

---

113 Laurent (1899); Gregory (1993); Petridis (1997), (2010a); Miller (2004); Rife (2012); Völling (2018).

scholarly exchange without precluding any authorial right to unique interpretation. The growing number of publications on burial and bioarchaeology in late antique Greece is a promising sign for the development of a wider and stronger evidentiary base in the coming years. It remains to be seen whether the Greek field will at some point drive methodological and theoretical innovations and contribute significant historical models for other Mediterranean regions, or it will continue catching up and responding to them.

Bibliography

Aigrain E. (1913) *Manuel d'épigraphie chrétienne 2: Inscriptions grecques* (Paris 1913).

Alexiou M. (1978) "Modern Greek folklore and its relation to the past: the evolution of Charos in Greek tradition," in *The "Past" in Medieval and Modern Greek Culture*, ed. S. Vryonis (Malibu 1978) 221–36.

Alexiou M. (2002) *The Ritual Lament in Greek Tradition*, 2nd ed., rev. D. Yatromanolakis and P. Roilos (Lanham Maryland 2002).

Antonaras A. (2010) "Glassware in Late Antique Thessalonikē (third to seventh centuries C.E.)," in *From Roman to Early Christian Thessalonikē: Studies in Religion and Archaeology* (Harvard Theological Studies 54), edd. L. Nasrallah, C. Bakirtzis, and S. Friesen (Cambridge Mass. 2010) 299–331.

Antonaras A. (2017) *Glassware and Glassworking in Thessaloniki (1st Century BC–6th Century AD)* (Oxford 2017).

Ardeleanu S. and Cubas Díaz J. (2019) "Funerary landscapes of the Late Antiquity oecumene – conference report", https://sfb933.hypotheses.org/1391.

Athanasoulis D. (2014) "Makri," *Chronique des Fouilles* 4511, https://chronique.efa.gr/?kroute=report&id=4511.

Avramea A. (1997) *Le Péloponnèse du IVe au VIIIe siècle: Changements et persistances* (Byzantina Sorbonensia 15) (Paris 1997).

Baldini I. (2014) "Atene: la città cristiana," in *Gli Ateniensi e il loro Modello di Città*, edd. L. M. Caliò, E. Lippolis and V. Parisi (Rome 2014) 309–321.

Bandy A. (1970) *The Greek Christian Inscriptions from Crete* (Athens 1970).

Bayet C. (1878a) *De tituli atticae christianis antiquissimis* (Paris 1878).

Bayet C. (1878b) "La nécropole chrétienne de Milo", *BCH* 2 (1878) 347–59.

Beck L. (ed.) (1995) *Regional Approaches to Mortuary Analysis* (New York and London 1995).

Bees N. (ed.) ([1941] 1978) *Inscriptiones graecae christianae veteres et byzantinae 1: Peloponnesus, Isthmos, Korinthos* (Athens 1941; Chicago repr. 1978).

Blegen C. (1928) *Zygouries: A Prehistoric Settlement in the Valley of Cleonae* (Cambridge Mass. 1928).

Bookidis N. and Stroud R. (1997) *Corinth XVIII.3: The Sanctuary of Demeter and Kore: Topography and Architecture* (Princeton 1997).

Bourbou C. (2004) *The People of Early Byzantine Eleftherna and Messene (6th–7th Centuries A.D.): A Bioarchaeological Approach* (Athens 2004).

Bourbou C. (2016) *Health and Disease in Byzantine Crete (7th–12th Centuries AD)* (Abingdon 2016).

Bourbou C., Fuller B., Garvie-Lok S., and Richards M. (2011) "Reconstructing the diets of Greek Byzantine populations (6th–15th centuries AD) using carbon and nitrogen stable isotope ratios," *American Journal of Physical Anthropology* 146 (2011) 569–81.

Brandt J. R., Hegelberg E., Bjørnstad G., and Ahrens S. (2017) (edd.) *Life and Death in Asia Minor in Hellenistic, Roman, and Byzantine Times* (Oxford and Philadelphia 2017).

Brélaz C. (2018) "The authority of Paul's memory and Early Christian identity at Philippi," in *Authority and Identity in Emerging Christianities in Greece and Asia Minor* (Ancient Judaism and Early Christianity 103), edd. C. Breytenbach and J. Ogereau (Leiden and Boston 2018) 240–66.

Brock J. and Mackworth Young G. (1949) "Excavations in Siphnos," *BSA* 44 (1949) 1–92.

Broneer, O. (1954) *Corinth I.4: The South Stoa and its Successors* (Princeton 1954).

Buchet J.-L. and Sodini J.-P. (1984) "Les tombes," in *Aliki II: La basilique double* (Études thasiennes 10), edd. J.-P. Sodini and K. Kolokotsas (Athens and Paris 1984) 211–42.

Buikstra J. and Beck L. (edd.) (2006) *Bioarchaeology: The Contextual Analysis of Human Remains* (London 2006).

Carpenter R. (1929) "Researches in the topography of Ancient Corinth – I," *AJA* 33 (1929) 345–60.

Carpenter R. and Bon A. (1936) *Corinth III.2: The Defenses of Acrocorinth and the Lower Town* (Cambridge Mass. 1936).

Catling H., Smyth D., Musgrave J., and Jones G. (1976) "An Early Christian osteotheke at Knossos," *BSA* 71 (1976) 25–47.

Charanis P. (1952) "On the capture of Corinth by the Onogurs and its recapture by the Byzantines," *Speculum* 27 (1952) 343–50.

Chatzioti, E.-M. (1988) "Γ´ Εφορεία Προϊστορικών και Κλασικών Αρχαιοτήτων. Ανασκαφικές εργασίες. Αθήνα 1–4," *ArchDelt* 36.2.1 (1988) 10–17.

Coleman J. (1986) *Excavations at Pylos in Elis* (Hesperia suppl. 21) (Princeton 1986).

Creaghan J. and Raubitschek A. (1947) "Early Christian epitaphs from Athens," *Hesperia* 16 (1947) 1–54.

Curta F. (2005) "Female dress and 'Slavic' bow fibulae in Greece," *Hesperia* 74 (2005) 101–46.

Dandis S. (1983) Ἀπειλεκτικαὶ Ἐκφράσεις εἰς τὰς Ἑλληνικὰς Ἐπιτυμβίους Παλαιοχριστινικὰς Ἐπιγραφάς (Athens 1983).

Danforth L. (1982) *The Death Rituals of Rural Greece* (Princeton 1982).

Davidson G. (1937) "The Avar invasion of Corinth," *Hesperia* 6 (1937) 227–40.

Davidson G. (1952) *Corinth* XII: *The Minor Objects* (Princeton 1952).

Davidson Weinberg G. (1974) "A wandering soldier's grave at Corinth," *Hesperia* 43 (1974) 512–21.

Diamandis N. (2004) "Το παλαιοχριστιανικό νεκροταφείο της Κισάμου," in *Creta romana e protobizantina. Atti del Congresso internationale (Iraklion, 23–30 settembre 2000)* 2, edd. M. Livadiotti and I. Simiakaki (Padua 2004) 383–96.

Deligiannakis G (2016) *The Dodecanese and the Eastern Aegean Islands in Late Antiquity, A.D. 300–700* (Oxford 2016).

Di Vita A. (ed.) (1988) *Gortina I* (Rome 1988).

Dinsmoor W. ([1941] 1975) *Observations on the Hephaisteion* (*Hesperia* suppl. 5) (Princeton 1941; Amsterdam repr. 1975).

Drandakis N. and Gioles N. (1980) "Ἀνασκαφὴ στὸ Τηγάνι τῆς Μάνης", *Prakt* (1980) 247–58.

Duday H. (2009) *Archaeology of the Dead* (Oxford 2009).

Duday H., Le Mort F., and Tillier A.-M. (2014) "Archaeothanatology and funeral archaeology. Application to the study of primary single burials", *Anthropologie* 52.3 (2014) 235–46.

Dusenbery E. (1998) *Samothrace* 11: *The Nekropoleis and Catalogues of Burials* (Princeton 1998).

Eger C. and Mackensen M. (edd.) (2018) *Death and Burial in the Near East from Roman to Islamic Times: Research in Syria, Lebanon, Jordan and Egypt* (Münchner Beiträge zur provinzialrömischen Archäologie 7) (Wiesbaden 2018).

Elderkin G. (1945) *Golgotha, Kraneion, and the Holy Sepulchre* (Springfield Mass. 1945).

Emmanouelides N. (1989) *Το Δίκαιο της Ταφής στο Βυζάντιο* (Athens 1989).

Engels J. (1998) *Funerum sepulcrorumque magnificentia: Begräbnis- und Grabluxusgesetze in der griechisch-römischen Welt mit einigen Ausblicken auf Einschränkungen des funeralen und sepulkralen Luxus im Mittelalter und in der Neuzeit* (Hermes Einselschriften 78) (Stuttgart 1998).

Fedwick P. (1976) "Death and dying in Byzantine liturgical traditions," *Eastern Churches Review* 8 (1976) 152–61.

Feissel D. (1983) *Recueil des inscriptions chrétiennes de Macédoine du IIIe et VIe siècle* (*BCH* suppl. 8) (Paris 1983).

Feissel D. and Philippidis-Braat A. (1985) "Inventaires en vue d'un recueil des inscriptions historiques de Byzance. III. Inscriptions du Péloponnèse (à l'exception de Mistra)," *TravMém* 9 (1985) 267–395.

Février P.-A. (1987) "La mort chrétienne," in *Segni e riti nella chiesa altomedievale occidentale: 11–17 aprile 1985* (Settimane di studio del Centro italiano di studi sull'alto Medioevo 33) (Spoleto 1987) 881–952.

Flämig C. (2007) *Grabarchitektur der römischen Kaiserzeit in Griechenland* (Internationale Archäologie 97) (Rahden 2007).

Fowler H. and Stillwell R. (1932) *Corinth* I: *Architecture and Topography* (Cambridge Mass. 1932).

Frantz A. (1965) "From paganism to Christianity in the temples of Athens", *DOP* 19 (1965) 187–205.

Frantz A. (1988) *Agora* XXIV: *Late Antiquity: A.D. 267–700* (Princeton 1988).

Frend W. (1996) *The Archaeology of Early Christianity: A History* (Minneapolis 1996).

Frend W. and Johnston D. (1962) "The Byzantine basilica church at Knossos", *BSA* 57 (1962) 186–238.

Gejvall N.-G. and Henschen F. (1968) "Two Late Roman skeletons with malformation and close family relationship from Ancient Corinth," *OpAth* 8 (1968) 179–201.

Geraskli E. (2004) "Παλαιοχριστιανικό νεκροταφείο στη Βροντή Καρπάθου: Πρώτη παρουσίαση," in *Χάρις Χαῖρε: Μελέτες στη Μνήμη της Χάρης Κάντζια*, ed. D. Damaskos (Athens 2004) 389–402.

Gerousi E. (2014) *Sepulkralkultur auf der Insel Thera (Santorin): Der spätantike Friedhof in Perissa und seine Ausgrabungsfunde unter besonderer Berücksichtigung der Tonlampen* (Marburg 2014).

Gregory T. (1993) *Isthmia V: The Hexamilion and Fortress* (Princeton 1993).

Grinsell L. (1961) "The breaking of objects as a funerary rite," *Folklore* 72 (1961) 475–91.

Guarducci M. (1978) *Epigrafia greca 4: Epigrafi sacre pagane e cristiane* (Rome 1978).

Haldon J. (1997) *Byzantium in the Seventh Century: The Transformation of a Culture*, rev. ed. (Cambridge 1997).

Hamilaki K. (2009) "Το νεκροταφείο στο λόφο Αγριλέζα στο Δήλεσι Βοιωτίας," in *Αρχαιολογικό έργο Θεσσαλίας και Στερεάς Ελλάδας 2006: Πρακτικά επιστημονικής συναντήσης, Βόλος 16.3–19.3.2006 2: Στερεά Ελλάδα*, ed. A. Ainian (Volos 2009) 1167–86.

Herzfeld M. (1986) *Ours Once More: Folklore, Ideology, and the Making of Modern Greece* (New York 1986).

ICG = Breytenbach C. and Zimmermann C. (edd.), *Inscriptiones Christianae Graecae: A Database of Early Christian Inscriptions*, https://icg.uni-kiel.de.

Ivison E. (1996) "Burial and urbanism at late antique and Early Byzantine Corinth (c. A.D. 400–700)", in *Towns in Transition: Urban Evolution in Late Antiquity and the Early Middle Ages*, edd. N. Christie and S. Loseby (Brookfield 1996) 99–125.

Ivison E. (2017) "Funerary archaeology," in *The Archaeology of Byzantine Anatolia from the End of Antiquity to the Coming of the Turks*, ed. P. Niehwohner (Oxford and New York 2017) 160–75.

Jalabert L. and Mouterde R. (1926) "Inscriptions grecques chrétiennes," *DACL* 7 (1926) coll. 623–94.

Karamanoli-Siganidou M. (1973–1974) "Ἀρχαιότητες και Μνημεία Δυτικής Μακεδονίας: 1973, 1974," *ArchDelt* 29.3.3 (1973–1974) 706–14.

Kent J. (1966) *Corinth* VIII.3: *The Inscriptions 1926–1950* (Princeton 1966).

Keramopoullos A. (1917) "Θηβαϊκά, Α´ μέρος — Ἀνασκαφαὶ ἐν Θήβαις," *ArchDelt* 3 (1917) 2–252.

Keramopoullos A. (1929) "Παλαιαὶ χριστιανικαὶ καὶ βυζαντιναὶ ταφαὶ ἐν Θήβαις", *ArchDelt* 10, 1926 (1929) 124–36.

Kilian K. (1980) "Zu einigen früh- und hochmittelalterlichen Funden aus der Burg von Tiryns", *ArchKorrBl* 10 (1980) 281–90.

Koch G. (2000) *Frühchristliche Skarophage* (Munich 2000).

Konstantinidis P. (1881) "Σαρκοφάγος Κληματίου ἐπισκόπου Ἀθηνῶν", *Parnassios* 5 (1881) 822–25.

Korka E. and Rife J. (edd.) (2022) *On the Edge of a Roman Port: The Excavations at Koutsongila, Kenchreai, 2007–2014* (Hesperia suppl. 52) (Princeton 2022).

Kormazopoulou L. and Chatzilazarou D. (2010) "Τα αγγεία του σπηλαιοβαράθρου Ανδρίτσας Αργολίδας: Προκαταρκτική παρουσιάση ενός κλειστού συνόλου του τέλους της ύστερης αρχαιότητας και κάποιες απόπειρες ερμηνείας," in *Κεραμική της ύστερης αρχαιότητας από τον Ελλαδικό χώρο (3ος–7ος αι. μ.Χ.). Επιστημονική συνάντηση*, edd. D. Papanikola-Bakirtzi and D. Kousoulakou (Thessaloniki 2010) 169–84.

Koukoules P. (1940) "Βυζαντινῶν νεκρικὰ ἔθιμα", *EpetByz* 16 (1940) 3–80.

Koukoules P. (1951) *Βυζαντινῶν βίος καὶ πολιτισμός* 4 (Athens 1951).

Kyriakakis J. (1974) "Byzantine burial customs: care of the deceased from death to the *prothesis*," *Greek Orthodox Theological Review* 19 (1974) 37–72.

Lampakis G. (1907) "Περὶ τῶν ἐν Μήλῳ χριστιανικῶν κατακομβῶν, τοῦ ἐν αὐτῇ βαπτιστηρίου καὶ ἑτέρων χριστιανικῶν ἀρχαιοτήτων," *Deltion tes Christianikes Archaiologikes Hetaireias* 1.7 (1907) 29–37.

Larsen C. (1997) *Bioarchaeology: Interpreting Behavior from the Human Skeleton* (Cambridge 1997).

Laskaris N. (1996) "Παλαιοχριστιανικὰ καὶ Βυζαντινὰ ταφικὰ μνημεῖα τῆς Ἑλλάδος", *Byzantiaka* 16 (1996) 295–350.

Laskaris N. (2000) *Monuments funéraires paléochrétiens (et byzantins) de Grèce* (Athens 2000).

Laurent J. (1899) "Delphes chrétien", *BCH* 23 (1899) 206–89.

Leontsini M. and Panopoulou A. (2013) "'Μαγικά' και αποτροπαϊκά τεκμήρια από τη βυζαντινή Κόρινθο: Συμβολικές χρήσεις και συλλογικές συμπεριφορές", in *Αντικήνσωρ. Τιμητικός τόμος Σπύρου Ν. Τρωιάνου για τα ογδοήκοστα γενέθλια του/Antecessor: Festschrift für Spyros N. Troianos zum 80. Geburtstag* 1, edd. V. Leontaritou, K. Bourdara, and E. Papagianni (Athens 2013) 855–80.

Lindenlauf A. (2001) "Thrown away like rubbish – disposal of the dead in Ancient Greece," *Papers from the Institute of Archaeology* 12 (2001) 86–99.

Loukatos D. (1940) "Λαογραφικαὶ περὶ τελευτῆς εἰδήσεις παρὰ Ἰωάννῃ Χρυσοστόμῳ", *Epeteris tou Laografikou Archeiou* 2 (1940) 30–117.

Loukatos D. (1978) *Εἰσαγωγὴ στὴν ἑλληνικὴ λαογραφία*, 2nd ed. (Athens 1978).

Loverdou-Tsigarida K. (1985) "Ἀρχαιολογικές έρευνες στην χριστιανική Βεργίνα", in *Πεμπτό Συμποσίο Βυζαντινῆς και Μεταβυζαντινῆς Αρχαιολογίας και Τέχνης. Πρόγραμμα και Περίλειψεις Εισηγεσέων και Ανακοινοσέων (Αθήνα 7, 8, και 9 Ιουνίου 1985)* (Athens 1985) 44–45.

Makropoulou D. (2001) "Ταφικά ευρήματα, νομίσματα και νομισματικοί θησαυροί στα παλαιοχριστιανικά κοιμητήρια της Θεσσαλονίκης", in *Αφιέρωμα στη μνήμη του Σωτήρη Κίσσα*, edd. A. Kalamartzi-Katsarou and S. Tampaki (Thessaloniki 2001) 263–72.

Makropoulou D. (2007) *Τάφοι και ταφές από το Λυτικό Νεκροταφείο της Θεσσαλονίκης (β´ μισό 3ου αι.–6ος αι. μ. Χ.)* (Ph.D. diss., Univ. of Athens 2007).

Mallegni F. (1988) "Settore L: Analisi dei resti schletrici umani", in *Gortina I*, ed. A. Di Vita (Rome 1988) 339–401.

Marin E. and Buljević Z. (1994) *Salona christiana: Arheološki Muzej-Split, 25.9.–31.10.1994* (Split 1994).

Marki E. (1987) "Ἀνίχνευση παλαιοτέρων ἐπιδράσεων στὴν παλαιοχριστιανικὴ ταφικὴ ἀρχιτεκτονικὴ καὶ τὴ νεκρικὴ λατρεία", in *Ἡ Καθημερινὴ Ζωὴ στὸ Βυζάντιο. Τομὲς καὶ Συνέχειες στὴν Ἑλληνιστικὴ καὶ Ῥωμαϊκὴ Παράδοση. Πρακτικὰ τοῦ Α´ Διεθνοὺς Συμποσίου, 15–17 σεπτεμβρίου 1988*, edd. C. Angelidi and C. Maltezou (Athens 1987).

Marki E. (2006) *Η Νεκρόπολη της Θεσσαλονίκης στους Υστερορωμαϊκούς και Παλαιοχριστιανικούς Χρόνους (μέσα του 3ου έως μέσα του 8ου αι. μ.Χ.)* (Athens 2006).

Mays S. (1998) *The Archaeology of Human Bones* (London and New York 1998).

McCormick M. (2016) "Tracking mass death during the fall of Rome's empire (II): a first inventory," *JRA* 29 (2016) 1008–46.

Megas G. (1940) "Ζητήματα ἑλληνικῆς λαογραφίας. 6. Τὰ κατὰ τὴν τελευτήν", *Epeteris tou Laografikou Archeiou* 2 (1940) 166–205.

Meleti P. (2013) "Παλαιοχριστιανικό νεκροταφείο στην Αρχαία Κόρινθου," in *The Corinthia and the Northeast Peloponnese: Topography and History from Prehistoric Times until the End of Antiquity. Proceedings of the International Conference Organized by the Directorate of Prehistoric and Classical Antiquities, the ΛΖ´ Ephorate of Prehistoric and Classical Antiquities, and the German Archaeological Institute, Athens, Held at Koutraki, March 26–29, 2009 (Athenaia 4)*, edd. K. Kissas and W.-D. Niemeier (Munich 2013) 161–68.

Miller S. (1979) "Excavations at Nemea, 1978", *Hesperia* 48 (1979) 73–103.

Miller S. (1981) "Excavations at Nemea, 1980", *Hesperia* 50 (1983) 45–67.

Miller S. (1983) "Excavations at Nemea, 1982", *Hesperia* 52 (1983) 70–95.

Miller S. (1988) "Excavations at Nemea, 1984–1986", *Hesperia* 57 (1988) 1–20.

Miller S. (2001) *Nemea* II: *The Stadium* (Berkeley and Los Angeles 2001).

Miller S. (2004) *Nemea: A Guide to the Site and Museum*, 2nd ed. (Athens 2004).

Miltner F. (1937) *Forschungen in Ephesos* IV.2: *Das Cömeterium der sieben Schläfer* (Vienna 1938).

Mitchell S. (1993) *Anatolia* 1–2: *Land, Men, and Gods in Asia Minor* (Oxford 1993).

Morison M. and Rife J. (2022) "Roman and late antique pottery," in *On the Edge of a Roman Port: The Excavations at Koutsongila, Kenchreai, 2007–2014* (Hesperia suppl. 52), edd. E. Korka and J. Rife (Princeton 2022) 583–736.

Morris I. (1987) *Burial and Ancient Society: The Rise of the Greek City-State* (Cambridge 1987).

Morris I. (1992). *Death-Ritual and Social Structure in Classical Antiquity* (Cambridge 1992).

Moxnes H. (1997) *Constructing Early Christian Families: Family as Social Reality and Metaphor* (London 1997).

Nalpandis D. (ed.) (2002) "Κοιμητήρια, ταφές και ταφικά έθιμα", in *Καθημερινή Ζωή στο Βυζάντιο. Ώρες Βυζαντίου*, ed. D. Papanikolaou-Bakirtzi (Athens 2002) 533–87.

Oikonomou A. (1988) "Lampes paléochrétiennes d'Argos," *BCH* 112 (1988) 481–502.

Oikonomou-Laniado A. (1998) "Les cimetières paléochrétiens d'Argos", in *Recherches franco-hélleniques* 3: *Argos et l'Argolide, topographie et urbanisme*, edd. A. Pariente and G. Touchais (Athens and Paris 1998) 405–16.

Oikonomou-Laniado A. (2003) *Argos paléochrétienne: Contribution à l'étude du Péloponnèse byzantin* (*BAR-IS* 1173) (Oxford 2003).

Orlandos A. (1952–1954) *Ἡ ξυλόστεγος παλαιοχριστιανικὴ βασιλικὴ τῆς Μεσογειακῆς Λεκάνης* 1–2 (Athens 1952–1954).

Osbourne R. and Alcock S. (2012) "Introduction", in *Classical Archaeology*, 2nd ed., edd. S. Alcock and R. Osbourne (Malden Mass., Oxford, and Chichester 2012) 1–10.

Pallas D. (1951) "Σαλαμινιακά (συνέχεια)", *ArchEph* 1950–1951 (1951) 163–81.

Pallas D. (1954) "Αἱ 'βαρβαρικαὶ' πόρπαι τῆς Κορίνθου", *Hellenika* suppl. 7 (1954) 340–96.

Pallas D. (1961) "Ἀνασκαφὴ βασιλικῆς ἐν Λεχαίῳ", *Prakt* 1956 (1961) 164–78.

Pallas D. (1968) "Ὁ Ἅγιος Ὀνούφριος Μεθώνης: Παλαιοχριστιανικὸν κοιμητήριον, βυζαντινὸν ἀσκητήριον", *ArchEph* (1968) 118–73.

Pallas D. (1972) "Ἀνασκαφικὴ ἔρευνα εἰς τὴν βασιλικὴν τοῦ Κρανείου ἐν Κορίνθῳ", *Prakt* 1970 (1972) 98–117.

Pallas D. (1974) "Ἀνασκαφῆς τῆς βασιλικῆς τοῦ Κρανείου", *Prakt* 1972 (1974) 205–50.

Pallas D. (1975) "Investigations sur les monuments chrétiens de Grèce avant Constantin", *CahArch* 24 (1975) 1–19.

Pallas D. (1977) *Les monuments paléochrétiens de Grèce découverts de 1959 à 1973* (Rome 1977).

Pallas, D. (1989) "Ἡ Ἀθήνα στὰ χρόνια τῆς μετάβασης ἀπὸ τὴν ἀρχαία λατρεία στὴ Χριστιανική", *Epistemonike Epeteris tes Theologikes Scholes en Athenais* 28 (1989) 851–930.

Pallas D. and Dandis S. (1979) "Ἐπιγραφὲς ἀπὸ τὴν Κορίνθο," *ArchEph* 1977 (1979) 61–83.

Panelas G. (2022) "The metal finds," in *On the Edge of a Roman Port: The Excavations at Koutsongila, Kenchreai, 2007–2014* (Hesperia suppl. 52), edd. E. Korka and J. Rife (Princeton 2022) 1051–1114.

Papadopoulos J. (1989) "Roman amphorae from the excavations at Torone," *ArchEph* (1989) 67–103.

Papadopoulos J. (2000) "Skeletons in wells: towards an archaeology of social exclusion in the Ancient Greek world", in *Madness, Disability, and Social Exclusion: The Archaeology and Anthropology of "Difference"*, ed. J. Hubert (London 2000) 96–118.

Papanikola-Bakirtzi D. and Kousoulakou D. (edd.) (2010) *Κεραμική της υστέρης αρχαιότητας από τον Ελλαδικό χώρο (3ος–7ος αι. μ.Χ.). Επιστημονική συνάντηση* (Thessaloniki 2010).

Parker Pearson M. (1999) *The Archaeology of Death and Burial* (College Station Tex. 1999).

Parlama L. and Stampolidis N. (2000) edd. *Athens: The City Beneath the City. Antiquities from the Metropolitan Railway Excavations* (Athens and New York 2000).

Pazaras T. (ed.) (2009) *Ανασκαφικές έρευνες στην περιοχή Επανομής Θεσσαλονίκης. Το Νεκροταφείο στο Λιμόρι και η Βασιλική στο Μπγιαδούδι* (Thessaloniki 2009).

Pearce J. (2013) *Contextual Archaeology of Burial Practice: Case Studies from Roman Britain* (Oxford 2013).

Pearce J. and Weekes J. (edd.) (2017) *Death as a Process: The Archaeology of the Roman Funeral* (Oxford 2017).

Pelekanides S. (1955) "Ἡ ἐκτὸς τῶν τειχῶν παλιοχριστιανικὴ βασιλικὴ τῶν Φιλίππων", *ArchEph* (1955) 114–79.

Pelekanides S. (1963) "Gli affreschi paleocristiani ed i più antichi mosaici parietali di Salonico", *Collana di quaderni di antichità ravennati, cristiane e bizantine*, Ravenna 2 (1963) 7–29.

Pelekanides S. (1969) "Die Malerei der konstantinischen Zeit", in *Akten des* VII. *Internationalen Kongresses für christliche Archäologie: Trier, 5.–11. September 1965* (Vatican and Berlin 1969) 215–35.

Pelekanides S. (1978) "Kultprobleme im Apostel-Paulus-Octagon von Philippi in Zusammenhang mit einem älteren Heroenkult", in *Atti degli 9th Congresso internazionale di archeologia cristiana* 2 (Vatican and Rome 1978) 339–97.

Pelekanides S. and Mentzos A. (1990) "Οκτάγωνο Φιλίππων. Πρωτα συμπερασματα μετα τις νεοτέρες έρευνες", in *Μνήμη Δ. Λαζαρίδη: Πόλις και Χώρα στην Αρχαία Μακεδονία και Θράκη. Πρακτικά Αρχαιολογικού Συνεδρίου, Καβάλα 9–11 Μαϊού 1986* (Thessaloniki and Athens 1990) 597–606.

Perdrizet P. (1905) "Inscriptions de Salonique", *MÉFR* 25 (1905) 81–96.

Petrakakos D. ([1905] 1971) *Die Toten im Recht nach der Lehre und den Normen des orthodoxen morgenländischen Kirchenrechts und der Gesetzgebung Griechenlands* (Leipzig 1905; Aalen repr. 1971).

Petrakos P. (1977) "Ἀρχαιότητες καὶ μνημεῖα Φθιώτιδος καὶ Φωκίδος. Κάλλιον", *ArchDelt* 22.2.2, 1972 (1977) 375–84.

Petridis P. (1997) "Delphes dans l'Antiquité tardive: Première approche topographique et céramologique", *BCH* 121 (1997) 681–95.

Petridis P. (2000) "Échanges et imitations dans la production des lampes romaines et paléochrétiennes en Grèce centrale", in *L'artisanat en Grèce ancienne: Les productions, les diffusions*, edd. F. Blondé and A. Muller (Lille 2000) 241–50.

Petridis P. (2007) "Relations between pottery workshops in the Greek mainland during the Byzantine period," in *Çanak: Late Antique and Medieval Pottery and Tiles in Mediterranean Archaeological Contexts. Proceedings of the First International Symposium on Late Antique, Byzantine, Seljuk, and Ottoman Pottery and Tiles in Archaeological Context (Çanakkale, 1–3 June 2005)* (Byzas 7), edd. B. Böhlendorf-Arslan, A. Osman Uysal and J. Witte-Orr (Istanbul 2007) 43–54.

Petridis P. (2010a) *Fouilles de Delphes* V.4: *La céramique protobyzantine de Delphes. Une production et son contexte* (Paris 2010).

Petridis P. (2010b) "Ρωμαϊκά και πρωτοβυζαντινά εργαστήρια κεραμικής στον ελλαδικόο χώρο", in Papanikola-Bakirtzi and Kousoulakou (2010) 81–96.

Polites N. ([1931] 1975) "Τὰ κατὰ τὴν τελευτήν", in *Λαογραφικὰ Σύμμεικτα* 3, 2nd ed. (Athens 1931; repr. 1975) 323–62.

Poulou-Papadimitriou N., Tzavella E., and Ott J. (2012) "Burial practices in Byzantine Greece: archaeological evidence and methodological problems for its interpretation," in *Rome, Constantinople and Newly-Converted Europe: Archaeological and Historical Evidence* 1, edd. M. Salamon, M. Wołoszyn, A. Musin, P. Špehar, M. Hardt, M. Kruk, and A. Sulikowska-Gąska (Krakow and Leipzig 2012) 377–428.

Psarologaki N. (2010) "Η μαγεία της αρχαιολογίας και η αρχαιολογία της μαγείας. Αντικείμενα μαγικού χαρακτήρα με χριστιανικό περίβλημα", in *Βάσκανος Οφθαλμός. Σύμβολα Μαγείας από Ιδιωτικές Συλλογές*, ed. C. Merkouri (Athens 2010) 87–99.

Rakita G., Buikstra J., Beck L., and Williams S. (edd.) (2005) *Interacting with the Dead: Perspectives on Mortuary Archaeology for the New Millenium* (Gainesville 2005).

Rebillard É. (1993) "Κοιμητήριον et *coemetrium*: Tombe, tombe santé, nécropole", *MÉFRA* 105 (1993) 975–1001.

Rebillard É. (1999) "Les formes de l'assistance funéraire dan l'Empire romain et leur évolution dan l'antiquité tardive", *AnTard* 7 (1999) 280–82.

Rebillard É. (2009) *The Care of the Dead in Late Antiquity* (Ithaca and London 2009).

Rife J. (1999) *Death, Ritual, and Memory in the Greek World during the Early to Middle Roman Periods* (Ph.D. diss., Univ. of Michigan 1999).

Rife J. (2004–2009) "An Early Christian epitaph from the Panathenaic Stadium in context", *Horos* 17–21 (2004–2009) 267–78.

Rife J. (2012) *Isthmia* IX: *The Roman and Byzantine Graves and Human Remains* (Princeton 2012).

Rife J. (2022a) "Catalogue of burials", in *On the Edge of a Roman Port: The Excavations at Koutsongila, Kenchreai, 2007–2014* (Hesperia suppl. 52), edd. E. Korka and J. Rife (Princeton 2022) 359–494.

Rife J. (2022b). "Lamps", in *On the Edge of a Roman Port: The Excavations at Koutsongila, Kenchreai, 2007–2014* (Hesperia suppl. 52), edd. E. Korka and J. Rife (Princeton 2022) 749–904.

Rife J. (2022c). "Inscriptions", in *On the Edge of a Roman Port: The Excavations at Koutsongila, Kenchreai, 2007–2014* (Hesperia suppl. 52), edd. E. Korka and J. Rife (Princeton 2022) 1195–214.

Rife J. and D. Andrikou (2022). "Architecture and activity", in *On the Edge of a Roman Port: The Excavations at Koutsongila, Kenchreai, 2007–2014* (Hesperia suppl. 52), edd. E. Korka and J. Rife (Princeton 2022) 185–239.

Rife J., Morison M., Barbet A., Dunn R., Ubelaker D., and Monier F. (2007) "Life and death at a port in Roman Greece: the Kenchreai Cemetery project 2002–2006", *Hesperia* 76 (2007) 143–81.

Robert L. (1960) "Épitaphes et acclamations byzantines à Corinthe", *Hellenica* 11–12 (Paris 1960) 21–52.

Roebuck C. (1951) *Corinth* XIV: *The Asklepieion and Lerna* (Princeton 1951).

Rowell G. (1977) *The Liturgy of Christian Burial: An Introductory Survey of the Historical Development of Christian Burial Rites* (London 1977).

Rush A. (1941) *Death and Burial in Christian Antiquity* (Washington, D.C. 1941).

Rudolph W. (1979) "Excavations at Porto Cheli and Vicinity, Preliminary Report V: The Early Byzantine Remains", *Hesperia* 48 (1979) 294–320.

Saïd S. (2005) "The mirage of Greek continuity: on the uses and abuses of analogy in some travel narratives from the seventeenth to the eighteenth century," in *Rethinking the Mediterranean*, ed. W. Harris (Oxford 2005) 268–93.

Samellas A. (2002) *Death in the Eastern Mediterranean (50–600 A.D.). The Christianization of the East: An Interpretation* (Tübingen 2002).

Sanders G. (2002) "Corinth", in *The Economic History of Byzantium: From the Seventh through the Fifteenth Centuries*, ed. A. Laiou (Washington, D.C. 2002) 647–54.

Sanders G. (2004) "Problems in interpreting urban and rural settlement in Southern Greece, A.D. 365–700", in *Landscapes of Change: The Evolution of the Countryside from Late Antiquity to the Early Middle Ages*, ed. N. Christie (Aldershot 2004) 163–93.

Sanders G. (2005a) "Urban Corinth: an introduction," in *Urban Religion in Roman Corinth: Interdisciplinary Approaches* (Harvard Theological Studies 53), edd. D. Schowalter and S. Friesen (Cambridge Mass. 2005) 11–14.

Sanders G. (2005b) "Archaeological evidence for Early Christianity and the end of Hellenic religion at Corinth," in *Urban Religion in Roman Corinth: Interdisciplinary Approaches* (Harvard Theological Studies 53), edd. D. Schowalter and S. Friesen (Cambridge Mass. 2005) 419–44.

Scheid J. (ed.) (2008) *Pour une archéologie du rite. Nouvelles perspectives sur l'archéologie funéraire* (Rome 2008).

Scheid J. and Rüpke J. (edd.) (2010) *Bestattungsrituale und Totenkult in der römischen Kaiserzeit* (Stuttgart 2010).

Schell D. (1989) *Griechische Totenbräuche. Ein quellenkritischer Beitrag zur Brauchforschung im modernen Griechenland* (Bonn 1989).

Schiffer M. (1987) *Formation Processes of the Archaeological Record* (Albuquerque 1987).

Schmidt B. (1926) "Totengebräuche under Gräberkult im heutigen Griechenland", *ArchRW* 24 (1926) 281–318.

Scranton R. (1951) *Corinth 1.3: Monuments in the Lower Agora and North of the Archaic Temple* (Princeton 1951).

Scranton R. (1957) *Corinth* XVI: *Medieval Architecture in the Central Area of Corinth* (Princeton 1957).

Setton K. (1950) "The Bulgars in the Balkans and the occupation of Corinth in the seventh century", *Speculum* 25 (1950) 502–43.

Setton K. (1952) "The Emperor Constans II and the capture of Corinth by the Onogur Bulgars", *Speculum* 27 (1952) 351–62.

Shay T. (1985) "Differentiated treatment of deviancy in death as revealed in anthropological and archaeological material", *JAnthArch* 4 (1985) 221–41.

Shelley J. (1943) "The Christian basilica near the Cenchrean Gate at Corinth", *Hesperia* 12 (1943) 166–89.

Sironen E. (1997) *The Late Roman and Early Byzantine Inscriptions of Athens and Attica: An Edition with Appendices on Scripts, Sepulchral Formulae, and Occupations* (Helsinki 1997).

Sironen E. (1999) "Formulae in Early Christian Epitaphs of Corinthia", in *XI Congresso Internazionale di Epigrafia Greca e Latina. Roma, 18–24 settembre 1997: Preatti* (Rome 1999) 741–45.

Sironen E. (ed.) (2008) *Inscriptiones graecae* II/III²: *Inscriptiones Atticae aetatis quae est inter Herulorum incursionem et Imp. Mauricii tempora* (Berlin 2008).

Sironen E. (ed.) (2016) *Inscriptiones graecae* IV³: *Inscriptiones Corinthiae saeculorum IV, V, VI* (Berlin 2016).

Sironen E. (2018) "Early Christian inscriptions from the Corinthian and the Peloponnese", in *Authority and Identity in the Christianities of Asia Minor and Greece* (Ancient Judaism and Early Christianity 103), edd. C. Breytenbach and J. Ogereau (Leiden and Boston 2018) 201–16.

Slane K. (2017) *Corinth* XXI: *Tombs, Burials, and Commemoration in Corinth's Northern Cemetery* (Princeton 2017).

Snively C. (1984) "Cemetery churches of the Early Byzantine period in Eastern Illyricum: location and martyrs", *Greek Orthodox Theological Review* 29 (1984) 117–24.

Snively C. (1998) "Intramural burial in the cities of the late antique diocese of Macedonia," in *Acta* XIII *Congressus internationalis archaeologiae christianae* 2, edd. N. Cambi and E. Marin (Vatican City 1998) 491–98.

Snodgrass A. (1987) *The Archaeology of Greece: The Present State and Future Scope of a Discipline* (Berkeley and Los Angeles 1987).

Snodgrass A. (2006) *Archaeology and the Emergence of Greece* (Ithaca 2006).

Sodini J.-P. (1977) "Témoignages archéologiques sur la persistance à l'époque paléochrétienne et byzantine de rites funéraires païens", in *La Mort au Moyen Âge: Colloque de l'Association des historiens médiévistes français réunis à Strasbourg* (Strasbourg 1977) 11–21.

Sodini J.-P. (1986) "Les 'tombes privilégiées' dans l'Orient chrétien (à la exception du diocèse d'Egypte)", in *L'Inhumation privilégiée du IVe au VIIIe siècle en Occident*, edd. Y. Duval and J.-C. Picard (Paris 1986) 233–43.

Sodini J.-P. (2007) "Transformation of cities in Late Antiquity within the provinces of Macedonia and Epirus", in *The Transition to Late Antiquity: On the Danube and Beyond*, ed. A. Poulter (Oxford 2007) 311–36.

Soteriou G. (1917) "Τὰ ἐρείπια τοῦ παρὰ τὸν Ἄρειον Πάγον βυζαντινοῦ ναοῦ", *ArchDelt* 2, 1916 (1917) 118–46.

Soteriou G. (1919) "Παλαιὰ χριστιανικὴ βασιλικὴ Ἰλίσου", *ArchEph* (1919) 1–31.

Soteriou G. (1927) *Εὑρητήριον τῶν Μεσαιωνικῶν Μνημείων τῆς Ἑλλάδος* 1: *Μεσαιωνικὰ Μνημεῖα Ἀττικῆς* 1 (Athens 1927).

Soteriou G. (1928) "Ἡ χριστιανικὴ κατακόμβη τῆς νήσου Μήλου", *PraktAktAth* (1928) 33–46.

Soteriou G. (1929) "Αἱ χριστιανικαὶ Θῆβαι τῆς Θεσσαλίας", *ArchEph* (1929) 1–158.

Soteriou G. (1935) "Ἀνασκαφαὶ Νέας Ἀγχιάλου", *Prakt* (1955) 52–69.

Soteriou G. ([1942] 1962) *Χριστιανικὴ καὶ Βυζαντινὴ Ἀρχαιολογία* 1 (Athens 1942; repr. 1962).

Soteriou G. (1955) "Ἀνασκαφὴ Νέας Ἀγχιάλου", *Prakt* (1955) 132–9.

Soteriou G. (1956) "Ἀνασκαφαὶ ἐν Νέᾳ Ἀγχιάλῳ", *Prakt* (1956) 110–18.

Spieser J.-M. (1976) "La christianization des sanctuaires païens en Grèce", in *Neue Forschungen in griechischen Heiligtümern*, ed. U. Jantzen (Tübingen 1976) 309–20.

Spyridakis G. (1950) "Τὰ κατὰ τὴν τελευτὴν ἔθιμα τῶν Βυζαντινῶν ἐκ τῶν ἁγιολογικῶν πηγῶν", *EpetByz* 20 (1950) 75–171.

Stikas E. (1955) "Συνέχισις τῆς ἀνασκαφῆς τῆς παρὰ τὴν Βραυρῶνα παλαιοχριστιανικῆς βασιλικῆς", *Prakt* 1952 (1955) 53–76.

Stikas E. (1964) "Κοιμητηριακή βασιλική Παλαιᾶς Κορίνθου", *Prakt* 1961 (1964) 129–36.

Stikas E. (1966) "Ἀνασκαφή κοιμητηριακῆς Βασιλικῆς Παλαιᾶς Κορίνθου", *Prakt* 1962 (1966) 129–36.

Stone D. and Stirling L. (edd.) (2007) *Mortuary Landscapes of North Africa* (*Phoenix* Suppl. 43) (Toronto 2007).

Stillwell R., Scranton R., and Freeman S. (1941) *Corinth 1.2: Architecture* (Cambridge Mass. 1941).

Sweetman R. and Becker M. (2005) "Knossos medical faculty site: late antique graves and other remains," *BSA* 100 (2005) 331–86.

Travlos J. and Frantz A. (1965) "The church of St. Dionysius the Areopagite and the palace of the Archbishop of Athens in the 16th Century", *Hesperia* 34 (1965) 157–202.

Tritsaroli P. (2006) *Pratiques funéraires en Grèce centrale à la période byzantine: Analyse à partir des données archéologiques et biologiques* (Ph.D. diss., Muséum national d'histoire naturelle, Paris 2006).

Tritsaroli P. (2017) "Life and death at Early Byzantine Akraiphnio, Greece: a biocultural approach", *Anthropologie* 55 (2017) 243–63.

Tritsaroli P. and Kardima C. (2017) "The people of Early Byzantine Maroneia," *Bioarchaeology of the Near East* 11 (2017) 29–62.

Trombley F. (2001) *Hellenic Religion and Christianization, c. 370–529* 1–2 (Leiden 2001).

Tsigaridas E. (1977) "Βυζαντινὰ καὶ μεσαιωνικὰ μνημεῖα Μακεδονίας-Θράκης. Α΄ Κεντρικὴ καὶ δυτικὴ Μακεδονία", *ArchDelt* 28.2.2, 1973 (1977) 477–501.

Tzavella E. (2008) "Burial and urbanism in Athens (4th–9th c. A.D.)", *JRA* 21 (2008) 353–68.

Tzavella E. (2010) "Κεραμική από αθηναϊκούς τάφους του τέλους της αρχαιότητας και οι μαρτυρίες της για τον 7ο αι. στην Αττική", in *Κεραμική της υστέρης αρχαιότητας από τον Ελλαδικό χώρο (3ος–7ος αι. μ.Χ.). Επιστημονική συνάντηση*, edd. D. Papanikola-Bakirtzi and D. Kousoulakou (Thessaloniki 2010) 649–70.

Vaes J. (1984–1986) "Christliche Wiederverwendung antiker Bauten: Ein Forschungsbericht", *Ancient Society* 15–17 (1984–1986) 305–443.

van Nijf O. (1997) *The Civic World of Professional Associations in the Roman East* (Amsterdam 1997).

Velkovska E. (2001) "Funeral rites according to the Byzantine liturgical sources," *DOP* 55 (2001) 21–51.

Vida T. and Völling T. (2000) *Das slawische Brandgräberfeld von Olympia* (Archäologie in Eurasien 9) (Rahden 2000).

Vikatou O. (2002) "Το χριστιανικό νεκροταφείο στην Αγία Τριάδα Ηλίας. Συμβολή στη μελέτη της χειροποίητης κεραμικής," in *Πρωτοβυζαντινή Μεσσήνη και Ολυμπία. Αστικός και Αγροτικός Χώρος στη Δυτική Πελοπόννησο. Πρακτικά του Διέθνους*

Συμποσίου, edd. P. Themelis and V. Kondi (Athens 2002) 238–70.

Völling T. (2001) "The last Christian Greeks and the first pagan Slavs in Olympia," in *Οι Σκοτεινοί Αιώνες του Βυζαντίου*, ed. E. Kountoura-Galaki (Athens 2001) 303–323.

Völling T. (2018) *Olympia in frühbyzantinischer Zeit. Siedlung – Landwirtschaftliches Gerät – Grabfunde – Spolienmauer* (*OlForsch* 34) (Berlin 2018).

Walbank M. E. H. (2005) "Unquiet graves: burial practices of the Roman Corinthians," in *Urban Religion in Roman Corinth: Interdisciplinary Approaches* (Harvard Theological Studies 53), edd. D. Schowalter and S. Friesen (Cambridge, Mass. 2005) 249–80.

Walbank M. E. H. and Walbank M. (2006) "The grave of Maria, wife of Euplous: a Christian epitaph reconsidered", *Hesperia* 75 (2006) 267–88.

Walbank M. E. H. and Walbank M. (2015) "A Roman Corinthian family tomb and its afterlife", *Hesperia* 84 (2015) 149–206.

Walbank M. (2010) "Where have all the names gone? The Christian community in Corinth in the Late Roman and Early Byzantine eras," in *Corinth in Context: Comparative Studies on Religion and Society*, edd. S. Friesen, D. Schowalter, and J. Walters (Leiden 2010) 257–323.

Walter C. (1976) "Death in Byzantine iconography", *Eastern Churches Review* 8 (1976) 113–27.

Werner W. (1955) "Byzantinische Gürtelschnallen des 6. und 7. Jahrhunderts aus der Sammlung Diergardt", *KölnJb* 1 (1955) 36–48.

Werner W. (1956) Review of Davidson, *Corinth* XII, *ByzZeit* 49 (1956) 140–42.

Williams C., MacIntosh J., and Fisher J. (1974) "Excavations at Corinth, 1973", *Hesperia* 43 (1974) 1–76.

Williams C., Snyder L., Barnes E., and Zervos O. (1998) "Frankish Corinth: 1997", *Hesperia* 67 (1998) 223–64.

Williams C. and Zervos O. (1992) "Frankish Corinth: 1991", *Hesperia* 61 (1992) 133–91.

Wiseman J. (1967a) "Excavations at Corinth, the gymnasium area, 1965", *Hesperia* 36 (1967) 13–41.

Wiseman J. (1967b) "Excavations at Corinth, the gymnasium area, 1966", *Hesperia* 36 (1967) 402–428.

Wiseman J. (1969) "Excavations in Corinth, the gymnasium area, 1967–1968", *Hesperia* 38 (1969) 64–106.

Wiseman J. (1972) "The gymnasium area at Corinth, 1969–1970", *Hesperia* 41 (1972) 1–42.

Yangaki A. (2004) "Οι τάφοι", in *Πρωτοβυζαντινή Ελεύθερνα. Τομέας I* 1, ed. P. Themelis (Rethymno 2004) 115–86.

Zeiss H. (1940) "Avarenfunde aus Korinth", in *Serta Hoffileriana: Commentationes gratulatorias Victori Hoffiler sexagenario* (Zagreb 1940) 95–99.

From Necropoleis to Koimētēria: Burial Practices in Late Antique (late 3rd–7th c. AD) Sagalassos, South-West Turkey

Sam Cleymans and Peter Talloen

Abstract

This paper brings an overview of the changing traditions and beliefs towards death, interment and afterlife in late antique (late 3rd–7th c.) Sagalassos (south-west Turkey). Late Antiquity is often regarded as a transitional phase from pagan to Christian practices. To understand this gradual shift, this paper looks into several aspects of burial culture, ranging from the treatment of the body, over grave design to grave good assemblages, as evidenced by the excavated, late antique graves and skeletal assemblages from Sagalassos. As such, the continuity and change can be traced from Roman Imperial (1st–3rd c.) to Late Roman (late 3rd–5th c.) and eventually Early Byzantine (6th–7th c.) times. Altogether, the evidence from Sagalassos shows that many of the practices that are considered typically Christian, such as a modest grave design, were a continuation of pre-existing Roman Imperial or Late Roman practices of which the meaning and intention altered with the advent of Christendom. Moreover, funerary practices appear to have mirrored broader trends of urban development that are equally observed in the monumental centre of Sagalassos.

Sagalassos, City of the Living (and the Dead)

Late antique funerary culture remains an understudied phenomenon for much of Asia Minor, mostly because the quite simple graves characteristic for this period are only accidentally encountered in excavations. The limited indications at the surface, such as the lack of aboveground tomb architecture, make that Early Byzantine cemeteries are seldom identified and thus targeted in archaeological research. At Sagalassos, an ancient city in the historical region of Pisidia (south-west Asia Minor), so far 42 late antique (late 3rd–7th c.) graves, containing the skeletal remains of at least 46 individuals, have been unearthed. Here too, it took until 2011 before the first late antique burials were unearthed. In contrast, by 2011, already more than 500 Late Hellenistic and Roman Imperial (1st c. BC–3rd c.) burial containers and monumental tombs had been documented,[1] and two tombs had been excavated.[2]

Detailed research on the stratigraphy, material culture, chronology, and skeletal remains have allowed the reconstruction of the funerary culture at late antique Sagalassos. This paper focusses on the changing burial rites by contrasting various (bio)archaeological and historical sources to come to a better understanding of the practices, beliefs and emotions towards death, afterlife, and interment at late antique Sagalassos.

This study revolves around 6 aspects that are inherent to burial customs: 1) the treatment of the body, 2) the location and positioning of burial plots, 3) the grave design, 4) body position and orientation, 5) family or other group-related practices, and 6) the deposition of grave goods. By bringing changes observed for these aspects into synthesis, we aim to shed more light on the overall evolution of mortuary culture at Sagalassos, and how it correlated with other social phenomena within this town and its hinterland. With this case study, we hope to contribute to broader discussions on burial practices elsewhere in late antique Anatolia, and on the role of Christianity and paganism.

The city of Sagalassos, located some 100 km north of Antalya, has been excavated and studied by an international and interdisciplinary research team under the direction of KU Leuven (Belgium) for the past 30 years (Fig. 1). Sagalassos was inhabited from Late Achaemenid/Early Hellenistic times (5th–3rd c. BC) until the Middle Byzantine period (10th–13th c.). After its heyday in Roman Imperial times (1st-first half 3rd c.), the Late Roman period (second half 3rd-first half 5th c.) was marked by the absence of new monumental construction. Nevertheless, the existing infrastructure was not only preserved, but minor and major modifications took place, adjusting the existing infrastructure to the changing needs of the community, and thus maintaining the overall monumental character of the city.[3] Artisanal production continued[4] and agricultural production specialized and adapted to the changing climatic and environmental conditions.[5] The introduction of Christianity in Pisidia constituted the start of a new phase in the evolution of religious life in the region, but it does not seem to have had any profound impact on the religious

---

1 Köse (2005).
2 Waelkens *et al.* (1989–1990); Waelkens *et al.* (1991).

3 Waelkens *et al.* (2006) 226–27; Poblome *et al.* (2017) 302–303.
4 Poblome and Fırat (2011).
5 Kaptijn *et al.* (2013); Poblome (2015); Talloen and Poblome (2019).

Alexandra Dolea and Luke Lavan (eds) *Burial and Memorial in Late Antiquity*
(Late Antique Archaeology 13) (Leiden 2024), pp. 811–831

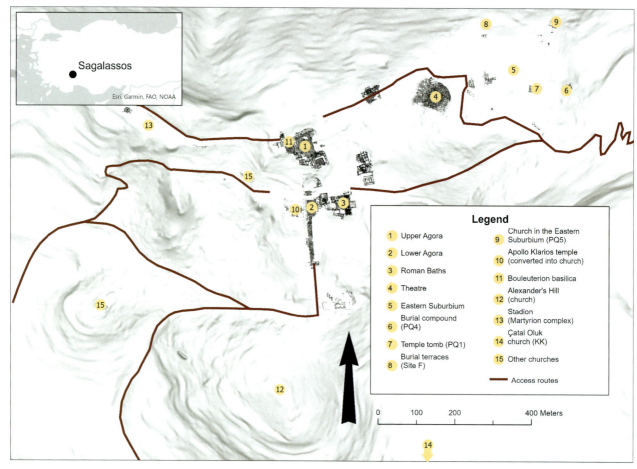

FIGURE 1   Map of Sagalassos showing the main archaeological features discussed in the paper.

practices in Sagalassos until the end of the 4th c. when all traditional sanctuaries were suddenly closed and official forms of polytheistic ritual came to an end, signalling drastic changes within a short period of time.[6] Between the end of the 5th and the middle of the 6th c., at least 9 churches were constructed at Sagalassos, resulting in a Christianization of the cityscape.[7] Towards the end of the 6th c., pottery production in the Eastern *Suburbium* came to a halt and was relocated.[8] Although certain areas in the monumental centre were well-maintained or rebuilt, Sagalassos acquired a different urban character from the middle of the 6th c. onwards due to processes of encroachment and increasing neglect of several public buildings.[9] Around the middle of the 7th c., the city was struck by an earthquake of more than 5.5 Ms, destroying many of the public buildings,[10]

some of which had already been put (partly) out of use.[11] At around the same time, Arab incursions into central Anatolia saw the repeated ransacking of the nearby provincial centre of Pisidian Antioch.[12] Sagalassos remained a Byzantine centre until the early 13th c., when it was abandoned around the time Seljuk tribes took over the region. Archaeological data for community life in this period are less abundant.[13]

The Burial Practices of the Roman Imperial Period

In order to identify changes and continuity of burial practices in Late Antiquity, we will first introduce the burial practices of the preceding Roman Imperial period (1st–first half 3rd c.) at Sagalassos. Although during the (Late) Hellenistic period only cremation appeared to have been practiced, inhumation began from the 1st c. as attested in two chamber tombs with multiple

---

6   Talloen (2019).
7   Waelkens *et al.* (2006); to the 8 churches *intra* and *extra muros* mentioned by Talloen (2019) also the church situated at Çatal Oluk, in the southern periphery of Sagalassos should be added since it too was part of the Southern Necropolis (Claeys and Poblome (2013)).
8   Poblome *et al.* (2017) 304.
9   Waelkens *et al.* (2006) 231–35; Poblome (2014) 630–33.
10   Sintubin *et al.* (2003) 359–74; Similox-Tohon *et al.* (2005).

11   Poblome *et al.* (2010).
12   Belke and Mersich (1990) give an overview of the sources.
13   Vionis *et al.* (2009); Vanhaverbeke *et al.* (2009); Poblome (2014); Poblome *et al.* (2017).

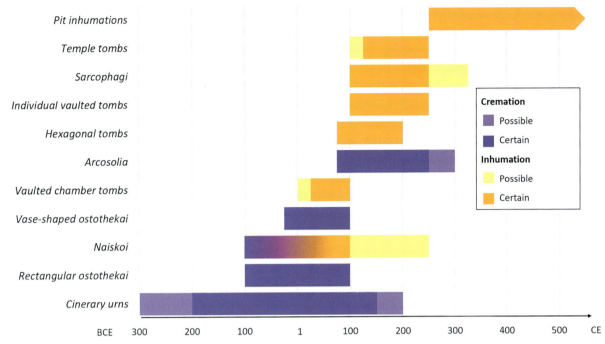

FIGURE 2   A chronological visualisation of cremation and/or inhumation per grave type at Sagalassos.

interments.[14] Cremation continued until the 3rd c. as evidenced by the *arcosolia* – arched niches carved into the rock face housing cremains or cinerary urns – in the Northern Necropolis.[15] The gradual replacement of cremation by inhumation is highlighted by the evolution in number and variety of grave types and burial containers, such as *sarcophagi* (Fig. 2).

As was common practice in antiquity, and even enacted into law, the dead were not allowed to be buried within the town.[16] At Sagalassos too, the Roman *necropoleis* surrounded the city. Sepulchral architecture and burial containers were mostly located on vantage points and along the entranceways to town. As such, these tombs would attract the attention of passers-by and thus ensure the commemoration of the dead, a phenomenon commonly documented for Roman *necropoleis* in Asia Minor and beyond.[17] This trend had already begun in the Late Hellenistic period, with the introduction of rectangular *osteothekai*[18] – stone cinerary urns – and peaked during the Roman Imperial period when elaborate structures, such as temple tombs and walled burial compounds, flanked the main roads, or were erected on slopes or hilltops (Fig. 3).[19]

As indicated by Fig. 2, the inhabitants of Roman Sagalassos used a broad variety of grave types. Especially in the 2nd c., the coexistence of cremation and inhumation resulted in the broadest variation. One striking aspect is that all Roman Imperial inhumation graves are arranged in stone and/or brick masonry. The burial containers (e.g., *sarcophagi*, *osteothekai*) and most of the cremation graves (e.g., *arcosolia*) too, were carved out of stone. Plain pit burials have so far not been attested for the Roman Imperial period. The presence of nails and post-depositional movement of skeletal remains indicate that inhumations took place either in a shroud, in a wooden coffin, or – as documented for a single skeleton – on a wooden platform, depending on the burial plot they were found in. As such the choice for the one or the other may have been that of the family or group responsible for the entombment. The orientation of the graves, in turn, did not systematically adhere to any of the cardinal points. Rather it followed (or was perpendicular to) the contour lines of the natural relief or the walls of the sepulchral enclosures, or the grave's façade faced the nearest entrance road to enhance visibility.

As discussed elsewhere, the dead entombed within the same burial plot or tomb most likely belonged to the same family, based on similarities in grave good assemblages and the chronology of the construction and use of the grave.[20] Moreover, epigraphic evidence from *sarcophagi* indicates family relations.[21] For the Roman

14   Cleymans and Beaujean (2020) 50–52; Cleymans and Beaujean (2022).
15   Köse (2005) 145–47.
16   Cic., *Leg.* 2.23.58.
17   For Asia Minor, see Spanu (2000) 173; elsewhere: von Hesberg (1992) 19–26.
18   Köse (2005) 76–77.
19   Cleymans *et al.* (2018); Cleymans and Beaujean (2022).

20   Cleymans and Beaujean (2020) 52–55; cf. Cleymans *et al.* (2018) 140–43.
21   Köse (2005) 105–07, 129–30 and 143–45.

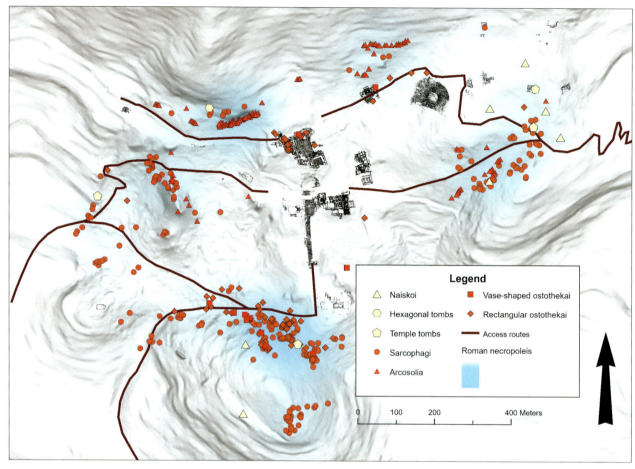

FIGURE 3   The Roman Imperial *necropoleis* of Sagalassos.

Imperial period, the only skeletal remains of non-adults originated from two 1st c. chamber tombs with multiple inhumations.[22] For the 2nd c., none of the excavated graves contained non-adult skeletal remains. Given that pre-industrial societies experienced high levels of non-adult mortality (30–70% under the age of 15),[23] their absence at Sagalassos indicates that children were barred from being interred inside the normal burial plots – a common practice in the Roman Empire.[24]

Grave good assemblages at Roman Sagalassos were generally relatively rich and varied, especially in female graves. The objects donated to the deceased were often of high-quality materials and making, as indicated by two pairs of golden earrings with pearl inlays, a gilded and silver ring, and golden *epistomia* – small sheets placed on the mouth of the departed.[25] Several of the grave goods even appear to be specially crafted or adjusted for funerary use, as these did not show any

traces of use-wear or were purposely broken.[26] Finally, the assemblages donated to men and those given with women were quite distinct. An example of such gender practices was that in Roman Imperial Sagalassos every male received a coin, placed in the mouth as fare to pay the ferrymen Charon for taking the soul of the deceased over the river Styx, whereas none of the females did.[27]

Late Antique Burial Practices

In Late Antiquity, burials continued within the extent of the existing Roman *necropoleis* that encircled the monumental centre and residential quarters of Sagalassos (Fig. 4). For the Late Roman period (second half of the 3rd–5th c.), all 38 excavated graves are located in the Eastern Necropolis: in the *hyposoria* of a Roman Imperial period temple tomb (PQ1),[28] on the terraces of the steep northern slopes (Site F),[29] and inside a walled burial

22   Charlier (1995) 210.
23   Lewis (2007) 22.
24   Cleymans *et al.* (forthcoming). For instances elsewhere in the
       Roman Empire, see Scott (1999); Pearce (2001).
25   Cleymans *et al.* (2018) 132–33.

26   Poblome *et al.* (2012) 8–9.
27   Stroobants *et al.* (2019) 486.
28   Claeys and Poblome (2014).
29   Cleymans *et al.* (2021) 185–88.

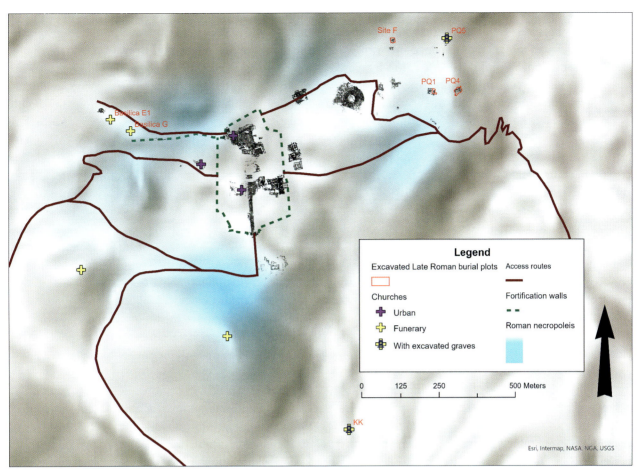

FIGURE 4   The late antique excavated and surveyed burial sites around Sagalassos. The excavated Late Roman burial plots are marked in red, and the churches with a cross.

compound originating in the 2nd c. (PQ4).[30] The 4 documented Early Byzantine (6th–7th c.) burials, in turn, still took place in the former Roman *necropoleis*, but were now arranged within cemeteries close to or around churches: three graves immediately south of a basilica in the Southern Necropolis in a small valley with the name Çatal Oluk (κκ),[31] and one in the foundation trench of a church built on a promontory in the north-east of the Eastern Necropolis (PQ5).[32] Although the preliminary results of geophysical surveying (resistivity) mentioned the identification of at least 8 possible graves around a basilica (Basilica G) in the former Stadion,[33] GPR survey conducted in the summer of 2021 indicated that the anomalies are present at 10 m below the surface and therefore certainly cannot be burials. Therefore, we decided not to build on this evidence.

Body Treatment

The archaeologically most visible difference in body treatment during Late Antiquity is the constant choice for inhumation, whereas in Roman Imperial times cremation continued at Sagalassos, although gradually growing less important. It thus seems that the evolution that started around the turn of the millennium had come to an end by the later 3rd c. The (re)introduction of inhumation in the Roman Empire has been explained in a number of ways. Although the role of mystery cults and of the Judaic and Christian belief systems[34] have been emphasized before, these hypotheses were quickly rejected as the turn to inhumation started too early and was too widespread to be merely the result of foreign cults.[35] More recently, Emma-Jayne Graham proposed a more convincing explanation by stressing the agency of the dead body itself.[36] For Roman Italy, she documented an intensification of care for the body around the same time that *libitinarii* (undertakers) started to take over burial organization in the 1st c. AD. As the preparation

30   Cleymans *et al.* (2018) 144–54.
31   Claeys and Poblome (2013).
32   Talloen and Beaujean (2015).
33   De Giorgi and Leucci (2018) 755–58.

34   Cumont (1949) 387–90; De Visscher (1963) 40–41.
35   Toynbee (1971) 40.
36   Graham (2015).

of the deceased was no longer the duty of the family, the relatives became distanced from the bodily aspects of death, such as the stench of the decaying corpse. To reconnect emotionally with the deceased, an increased care for the body through inhumation became preferred over the violent destruction of the body by fire.

For Sagalassos, the burial data seem to corroborate the latter hypothesis, although there is no evidence for local burial associations or professional undertakers so far.[37] Throughout the Roman Imperial period, a gradual intensification in shielding off the body can be observed. While Early Roman Imperial chamber tombs were designed for multiple inhumations – every new interment requiring the reopening of the grave and shoving aside (partly) decomposed human remains of previous inhumations – 2nd c. entombments primarily took place in individual vaulted tombs that provided space for a single corpse and could not be reopened. More monumental tombs, however, continued to provide space for several corpses, as indicated by the *hyposoria* underneath the excavated temple tomb (PQ1),[38] or by the epitaphs on *sarcophagi* mentioning that the stone casket was intended for two or three family members.[39] These epitaphs on *sarcophagi* further evidence for the reuse of these containers in the Middle Roman Imperial period.[40] Conversely, the Late Roman pit inhumations contained in all but one case – an adult female with neonate[41] – the skeletal remains of a single individual and all consisted of coffin burials (see further). As such, the dead body was fully withdrawn from sight. Also, the Late Roman end of cremation did not result from the growing importance of Christianity. Only from the second half of the 4th c., traditional religious practices, as embodied in pagan shrines and iconography, started disappearing, while Christianity would only gradually leave its mark from the beginning of the 5th c. onwards;[42] by that time, cremation had already ceased for almost a century.

In Byzantine Sagalassos, the rite of inhumation continued without exception. The reasons to do so, however, became more explicitly grounded in the Christian belief system. Although cremation is not formally prohibited by the Holy Script, the reasons to opt for inhumation are found in the Bible. According to Christian theology, not only the soul lives on after death, but during the Second

Coming, the body itself resurrects.[43] To allow this, the body should remain intact and thus inhumation became the only acceptable option.[44] Byzantine written sources inform us that with these changing believes, also the relation with the dead body altered. Whereas Roman families gradually became distanced from the bodily aspects of death and decay by hiding away corpses in closed containers, Christian authors called for contact and care.[45] The 3rd c. Christian treatise *Didascalia et Constitutiones Apostolorum*, for example, proclaimed: 'On this account you are to approach without restraint those who rest and you shall not declare them unclean'.[46] Hereby, the Roman distancing from the deceased should not be considered as a fear for "death pollution", as is often proclaimed.[47] A recent re-evaluation of literary sources on this phenomenon in Rome concluded that the first mentions of death pollution only appeared in Late Antiquity.[48] So far, the limited evidence from Early Byzantine Sagalassos does not permit us to make further inferences on changes in the care of the deceased body.

Location of Burial

Late Roman inhumations continued in the Roman *necropoleis* that surrounded Sagalassos. Instead of arranging new sepulchral enclosures or architectural tombs, older burial plots and tomb structures were reused. So far, 34 simple pit inhumations, cut in the underlying soil substrate and/or bedrock, have been unearthed: 29 in the PQ4-burial compound, and 5 on the burial terraces in the northern part of the Eastern Necropolis (Site F).[49] Moreover, at several places throughout the excavated grave sites, already existing mortuary architecture was usurped. For example, in the *hyposoria* underneath the 2nd c. temple tomb (PQ1) at least 6 new interments took place.[50] At the burial terraces (Site F) and the compound (PQ4)[51] as well, an individual vaulted grave was opened, the previous remains shoved aside, and a new coffin burial added. As such, little changed in the positioning of the burials compared to the Roman Imperial period; the *necropoleis* continued to form transitional zones encircling Sagalassos.[52]

37   Cleymans and Beaujean (2020) 56.
38   Claeys and Poblome (2014).
39   E.g. Köse (2005) 105–106.
40   E.g. Cleymans and Uytterhoeven (2022).
41   Cleymans *et al.* (2018) 146–47.
42   Talloen (2019) 173–80.

43   John 11:25; Luke 20:34–38; 1 Corinthians 15:12–58; Revelation 20:4–5.
44   Paxton (1990) 24–25; Volp (2002) 189.
45   Paxton (1990) 25; Davies (1999) 198–99.
46   *Didascalia et Constitutiones Apostolorum* 1.376.
47   E.g., Lindsay (2000).
48   Emmerson (2020).
49   Cleymans *et al.* (2021) 185–87.
50   Claeys and Poblome (2014).
51   Cleymans *et al.* (2018) 152–53; Cleymans *et al.* (2021) 187–88.
52   Cleymans and Beaujean (2022).

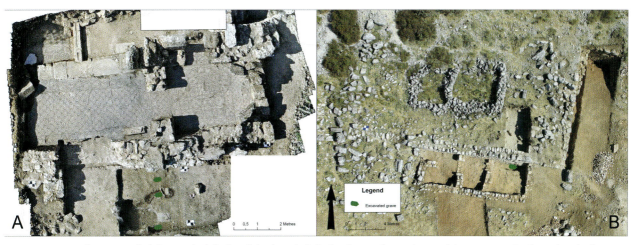

FIGURE 5   Aerial pictures of A) the Çatal Oluk church (KK), and B) the basilica in the northeast of the Eastern Suburbium (PQ5). The location of excavated graves is indicated with a green arrow with the same orientation as the head of the deceased.

Somewhere around AD 500, burials at Sagalassos shifted from the *necropoleis* to church cemeteries. The oldest known inhumation in association with a church took place in the first half of the 6th c., as was attested in the foundation trench of a basilica (PQ5) in the north-east of the Eastern *Suburbium*.[53] In the southern suburb of Sagalassos too, three 7th c. graves were uncovered south of the church in the Çatal Oluk valley (KK) (Fig. 5).[54] These Early Byzantine inhumations took place in association with extramural churches (Fig. 4), often erected within the extent of the former *necropoleis*. Although the church became the new point of attraction for mortuary practices, none of the excavations of intramural basilicas yielded evidence for graves. The ban on burials within town thus seems to have continued. Just as in Roman law, the Byzantine *Corpus Iuris Civilis* (529–534) and several subsequent legal texts prohibited burials *intra muros*.[55] Throughout the Byzantine Empire, this resulted in the construction of extramural churches around which inhumations took place.[56]

A special form of extramural churches were the *martyria*, churches built over the graves of martyrs or at places they had frequented. These churches exerted a large attraction for interments, since the proximity of holy relics was sanctified and thus was considered to protect the deceased – a practice denoted as *depositio ad sanctos*.[57] The two basilicas in the Stadion of Sagalassos – a large transept basilica and a smaller tripartite basilica – have been tentatively identified as

part of such a *martyrion* complex (Fig. 6).[58] Christian martyrology informs us that *stadia* were often used for the public execution of condemned criminals, such as early Christians, who then became regarded as saints or martyrs.[59] Graves in the former Stadion of Sagalassos, therefore, cannot be fully excluded. Although the GPR did not identify any graves, the simple pit inhumations which are typical for late antique Sagalassos (see *infra*) would not show up on the GPR-signal. The wish to be buried near a church was originally not a religious obligation. The principle of being laid to rest in the proximity of a saint, and *in extensis* near church sites – or a *locus sanctus* in Latin – gave people the hope for a better chance of reaching heaven.[60] It was this principle that originally attracted families to bury their kin near churches. To meet with this wish of the urban Christian populations in the Byzantine Empire, more and more extramural churches with a clear sepulchral purpose were constructed to allow people to be buried near a *locus sanctus* and at the same time retain the ban on extramural interments.[61]

This trend was not uncontested in Byzantine times, especially when taking place around intramural churches or within the basilica itself. St. Augustine of Hippo (354–430), for example, wrote that it was not the location of interment, but the state of the soul that merits the dead.[62] A law from 361, incorporated in the *Codex Theodosianus*,[63] in turn, forbade inhumations within church buildings, and St. Gregory the Great

53   Talloen and Beaujean (2015).
54   Claeys and Poblome (2013).
55   *Dig.* 47.12; *Cod. Theod.* 9.17.6; *Cod. Iust.* 3.44.12; *Epitome Legum* 11.39.43. See also Saradi (2006) 432–34.
56   Yasin (2005) 433; Achim (2015).
57   Ivison (1993) 26; Brandenburg (1995); Saradi (2006) 434–35.

58   Waelkens *et al.* (2006) 241; Talloen (2019) 193.
59   Thompson (2002).
60   Paxton (1990) 25–26; Effros (1997).
61   Ivison (2017) 165–66.
62   August. *De sepultura animarum* 100.1.
63   *Cod. Theod* 9.17.6.

FIGURE 6   Left: Plan of the former *Stadion* with the two churches of the possible *Martyrion* complex (Basilica E1 and Basilica G).
            Right: A view of the narthex and main entrance of Basilica E1 in the former Stadion. Part of the wall of the apse is still standing
            in the back.

(540–604) stated that only a pure soul could reside inside a church.[64] In Byzantine Anatolia, ideas about intramural burials gradually changed between the 6th and 9th c. Leo VI (886–912) finally officialised intramural inhumation with a decree stating that interments had to happen in or near churches, regardless of whether the church itself was located *intra* or *extra muros*.[65] At Sagalassos, the first attested burials within town only appeared in the Middle Byzantine graveyard (11th–first half 13th c.), when a cemetery was arranged around a funerary chapel on the location of the converted temple for Apollo Klarios.[66] Even here, there is some doubt on whether this area still belonged to the Middle Byzantine extent of Sagalassos. In none of the excavated basilicas at Sagalassos were intra-church interments encountered.

Grave Design

Whereas the so far documented Roman tombs were all erected in stone and/or brick masonry, all late antique graves consisted of simple pit inhumations (Fig. 7). Notwithstanding this basic design – a pit cut in the underlying soil substrate and/or bedrock – some variation was present. Among the 36 excavated Late Roman plain pit inhumations, 21 were (partly) aligned with rubble stones (58%) but none were protected with a durable cover. Yet, in some cases where the pit was partly cut out of bedrock, middle-sized rubble stones – probably refuse from trenching – were part of the grave

fill. These simple pit inhumations formed the most common grave type throughout Byzantine Anatolia[67] and Early Byzantine Greece.[68] The early 6th c. grave at the church in the Eastern Necropolis (PQ5) was stone-lined too, whereas all three 7th c. inhumations in the Çatal Oluk valley (KK), in turn, belonged to the *alla cappuccina* type (Fig. 8). Inhumations covered with such gabled roofs consisting of large tiles were quite common in late antique Anatolia, as indicated by examples from Ilıpınar near Proussa (Bithynia) and Oymaağaç Höyük (Paphlagonia).[69]

Simple pit graves are often interpreted as the burial rite for the urban poor.[70] At Sagalassos, however, the clear chronological distinction between Roman Imperial tombs in stone and brick masonry and late antique simple pit inhumations points to a diachronic shift in funerary rites, rather than to a distinction between social strata. This transition from stone and/or brick grave architecture to simpler, less visible burial types is not restricted to Sagalassos. Various surveys in the *necropoleis* of ancient towns documented the end of monumental tombs and stone burial containers somewhere in the 3rd c. For example, at Elaiussa Sebaste[71] and Pergamon[72] the construction of aboveground funerary architecture

64   Greg. *Dial.* 4.52.2.
65   Leo VI, *Novels* 53.
66   Cleymans and Talloen (2018).
67   Ivison (2017) 164.
68   Poulou-Papadimitriou *et al.* (2012) 379 ; absent at Isthmia: Rife (2012) 180.
69   Ilıpınar: Roodenberg (2009) 155; Oymaağaç Höyük: Hnila (2015).
70   Toynbee (1971) 101; Hopkins (1983) 207–211.
71   Machatschek (1967) 119–20.
72   Radt (1999) 272–73.

FIGURE 7   Example of a Late Roman coffin inhumation of a probable male older than 40 at death in a
simple pit cut into the underlaying soil substrate and bedrock of the burial compound (PQ4).

FIGURE 8   The three excavated *tombe alla cappuccina* south of the Çatal Oluk church (KK).

FIGURE 9   Example of a pit burial of a Late Roman probable male of 18–23 years old at death with the
location of the nails being indicative for the use of a wooden coffin.

ceased shortly after the 2nd c. At Ephesos, this process was more gradual and seems to have started earlier, as already by Middle Roman Imperial times funerary monuments became less elaborate.[73] Just as at Sagalassos, late antique graves at Pergamon consisted mostly of pit inhumations carved into the bedrock.[74]

This rather sudden shift away from conspicuous tomb design, so characteristic at Roman Imperial Sagalassos, can possibly be explained by a combination of a lack of suitable space and a transition to archaeologically less visible burial practices.[75] Indeed, the Roman Imperial *necropoleis* at Sagalassos gradually became filled up, forcing families to buy and prepare less suitable areas from the 2nd c. onwards. Especially in the Eastern Necropolis that partly overlapped with the artisanal quarter, burial plots and monumental tombs were often reused or dismantled for the construction of a pottery workshop or to be used as dump sites, and vice versa.[76] Heedful of the possibility that their investments in new funerary architecture might be trifling, efforts possibly shifted to other conspicuous practices, such as elaborate funerary processions (*pompa funebris*) or communal dinners in honour of the departed. Nevertheless, by usurping highly visible Roman structures, such as a temple tomb or walled compound, the Late Roman

inhabitants of Sagalassos recycled the aspect of visibility, still attracting attention to the burial plots.

In Early Byzantine Sagalassos, conspicuous design was guided away from the tombs themselves to the edifice they surrounded. Churches in the Early Byzantine East were often positioned along access roads, on vantage points on hills or promontories, or at the location of previous derelict sanctuaries.[77] This was also the case at Sagalassos, as shown on Fig. 4, where the churches were either located near the access roads (the possible *martyrion*), on top of hills (all but the *martyrion*), or on the location of a former sanctuary (e.g., the Apollo Klarios temple transformed into a basilica).[78] Although the cemeteries and graves were not designed to stand out in the landscape, there was a clear association with these churches that became highly apparent features in the landscape.

Deducting whether the deceased was buried in a shroud or coffin is hindered by the disappearance of the perishable materials these were made of. Nails found spread around the skeleton, both underneath and above the human remains, can generally serve as positive evidence for the use of wooden coffins (Fig. 9). This identification can be corroborated by the movement of skeletal elements in the grave: footbones that fell open or a skull that tilted backward, for example, show that during decomposition the body lay in an open space,

73   Steskal (2017) 234.

74   Radt (1999) 272–73.

75   Cleymans and Beaujean (2022).

76   Claeys (2013); Claeys and Poblome (2019).

77   Gauthier (1999); Wataghin (2003); Severin (2003).

78   Talloen and Vercauteren (2011).

such as a casket.[79] Based on this combined evidence, wooden coffins were the most common container type in Late Roman Sagalassos. For 31 of 38 (82%) Late Roman inhumations coffin-use was clearly attested. The PQ5-burial seems to have happened in a coffin too, as indicated by the 20 nails found around the skeleton, but the three *tombe alla cappuccina* from Çatal Oluk did not contain any nails. Keeping in mind that coffins could have been made with wooden pegs instead of with nails, the position of the human remains from those inhumations also did not provide a decisive answer. In any case, Byzantine iconography indicates that shrouding became standard practice in Asia Minor, probably from the 6th c. onwards.[80]

As all Late Roman inhumations were subterranean, the lack of interferences or disturbances by other pit graves, despite the high burial density, indicates that some sort of grave markers must have been present. Yet, only for one Late Roman inhumation of a small child (two-three years at death) in the burial compound (PQ4), a grave marker was preserved. The small coffin in which this non-adult was buried was covered with 4 upstanding elongated stones, which supported a fragment of a vase-shaped *osteothēkē* that remained visible at the surface.[81] Likely, non-durable grave markers indicated the location of the dead. Of the Early Byzantine graves, two of the *tombe alla cappuccina* were disturbed when two large storage vessels or *dolia* were dug into the ground. This suggests that soil probably covered the gabled tiles and thus the graves remained invisible at the surface, or that the preservation of these burials was deemed less important than the arrangement of the *dolia*.

Orientation and Positioning of the Body

The orientation of the grave and body is often used as an argument in the identification of (non-)Christian burials. The reasons to opt for the one or other orientation, however, are numerous.[82] When considering the Late Roman inhumations, 31 of 38 (82%) are laid out in a more or less east – west direction with an almost equal distribution between those with the head pointing east (n = 16) and west (n = 15). That the vast majority was buried in an east – west orientation mostly resulted from the fact that the two excavated burial plots – the burial compound (PQ4) and terraces (Site F) – are arranged in this same direction. The burials thus seem to have followed the orientation of the main enclosure or retaining

walls nearby. Those buried in a north – south direction either consisted of reused Roman tomb structures which already had a north – south orientation or were child graves of which this divergent orientation permitted the smaller pit to fit in spaces too small for an east – west burial.

The Early Byzantine graves, in turn, all followed the orientation of the church they were associated with. Although these basilicas were intended to have an east – west orientation, many slightly differed due to the contour lines of the relief. The three bodies next to the Çatal Oluk basilica (κκ) were inhumed with the head at the west end of the grave. As such, these adopted the preferred Christian orientation, meant to let the deceased face east, the direction from which Christ would appear during the time of his Second Coming.[83] The person next to the church in the Eastern Necropolis (PQ5), in contrast, was buried with the head pointing east.

Except for one Late Roman child (3–5 years at death) that lay on its left side, all inhumations were inhumed in a supine position. Of the 29 Late Roman individuals for which the preservation of the skeleton allowed to deduct the position of the limbs, 18 (62%) had their hands folded over the abdomen, and the other 11 (38%) the arms extended lateral to the body. All 4 Early Byzantine inhumations were interred in supine position. The two skeletons with the arms preserved had their hands folded over the abdomen. This position was recorded as customary by several Byzantine authors.[84]

Group-Related Practices

Whereas children seemed excluded from the Middle Roman Imperial burial plots, they reappeared in Late Antiquity. Of the 42 excavated Late Roman individuals, 9 (21%) were younger than 15 years at death. With mortality in this age class normally ranging 30–70% in pre-industrial societies (see above), this number is still too low to assume that all children have a place in the normal burial plots. A Late Roman increase of child inhumations in skeletal assemblages has been documented in Britain too but remains a point of discussion.[85]

Both on the burial terraces (Site F) and in the compound (PQ4), the newly arranged Late Roman pit inhumations formed clusters or pairs. This suggests some sort of relation among the individuals interred there. While at Site F, apart from their close proximity to each other, there is no further evidence pointing to kinship or other in-group relations, mtDNA-haplotypes combined with clusters of similar grave good assemblages at the burial

79   Duday (2009); Blaizot (2014).
80   Moore (2016).
81   Cleymans *et al.* (2018) 152.
82   Rahtz (1978).
83   Matthew 24:27.
84   For a list of the sources, Rife (2012) 185 n. 119.
85   Watts (1989); *pro*: Scott (1999); *contra*: Pearce (2001).

FIGURE 10   Genetic and archaeological evidence for family clusters in the eastern half of the burial compound (PQ4). Blue cluster: three
individuals of haplogroup X2b and all deceased had received a ceramic object; Brown cluster: two individuals of haplogroup
T1a1'3 and all received a coin and at least one glass *unguentarium*; Purple cluster: five individuals of haplogroup K1a.

compound (PQ4) strongly suggest family-related burial practices (Fig. 10).[86] West of a partition wall within this burial plot, for example, a row of 4 individuals was buried. All 4 had received two glass *unguentaria* and a coin, and two of the 4 shared the same haplotype (haplogroup T1a1'3). Similarly, of a cluster of 6 along the east wall of the compound 4 had a ceramic object deposited in their tomb, and three out of 4 successfully analysed individuals belonged to haplogroup X2b. Finally, within a third cluster of 6 graves in the south-east part of the compound, 4 individuals shared the same haplotype (haplogroup K1a). It thus seems that several families decided

to reuse this Roman Imperial burial plot to inhume their departed relatives.

As insufficient Roman Imperial skeletal remains have been analysed for mtDNA, it remains unclear whether or not these Late Roman families were related to the Roman Imperial family that originally built, owned, and used the burial compound in the 2nd and early 3rd c. Having said that, the reuse of the burial plot by several families rather argues against real or imagined kinship relations. When considering the chronology of the compound, usurpations of Roman Imperial plots or tombs only happened at least 60 to 80 years after the last entombment by the original owners.[87] This may indicate that a burial site was only reused two to three

---

86   Discussed in detail in Cleymans *et al.* (2018) 154–55; Cleymans and Beaujean (2020) 55–56. The mtDNA-haplotypes were published in Ottoni *et al.* (2016).

87   Cleymans *et al.* (2018) 144; Cleymans *et al.* (2021) 189.

generations later, when the family had possibly died out or had forgotten the existence of the plot. So far, no looting activities can be attributed to the Late Roman period. During the reuse of existing tombs, as identified at Site F[88] and possibly at PQ4[89] where each time a single vaulted tomb was opened for a new interment, the skull of the Roman Imperial deceased was placed on top of the new coffin, possibly as some sign of respect. It thus seems that the Roman Imperial tombs and skeletal remains were, notwithstanding the usurpations of burial plots and the reuse of existing tomb structures, maintained and treated as sepulchral spaces, not as loci for self-enrichment or looting.

For Early Byzantine Sagalassos, the very small excavated skeletal assemblage does not allow for further interpretations on family or other in-group practices. In the Byzantine Empire no segregation between adults and non-adults after death was present,[90] as was also attested at the Middle Byzantine graveyard of Sagalassos.[91] Nevertheless, examples at Anemurium, Alanahan[92] and Amorium[93] show that infants that probably died before being baptised, where buried around the *baptisterion*. Although separated from the rest of the community, these small children were still allowed an interment in the communal cemeteries. Unfortunately, the presence of a single non-adult in the Early Byzantine skeletal assemblage of 4 is insufficient for further evaluation. The small dataset also hampers inferences on the in-group logic of burial. In general, Christian burial grounds are considered as moving away from the Roman family logic to serve as places for the (baptized) community to be interred indiscriminately.[94]

The respect paid to older graves by Late Roman families did not continue in Early Byzantine times. Almost all datable examples of grave looting, spoliation of sepulchral architecture, and dumping of stone and pottery refuse in burial plots took place between the end of the 5th and the end of the 6th c. A *sarcophagus* that once stood in a niche in the north wall of the burial compound (PQ4), for example, was moved, opened, and emptied in the 6th c.[95] Almost all ashlar stones were removed from within and in front of the same niche. Underneath the floor slabs of the niche, a small, vaulted chamber that housed a cremation urn and some ceramic grave goods, was opened and looted. Finally, at least 4 large pottery

dumps were discovered within the compound, all containing 6th c. pottery, after which the entire area was covered with refuse from stone quarrying higher up the mountain flank, sealing it off permanently.[96] At around the same time, the superstructure of the excavated temple tomb (PQ1) was dismantled, leaving only its podium in place. Later, a large pottery dump was deposited within the enclosure, covering the podium. The ceramics from the stratigraphic layers related to the dismantling and pottery refuse both dated to the 6th c.[97] Evidence for looting is present at Site F too, but its chronology is not clear.[98] Altogether, this suggests that the Early Byzantine inhabitants of Sagalassos felt insufficiently connected to their ancestors to respect their graves or reuse the burial places.

Grave Good Assemblages

In Late Roman Sagalassos, the tradition of depositing funerary gifts continued and grave goods were still quite varied. Common objects, found in 10 graves, were glass *unguentaria*, while the ceramic variant was only found in a single burial. In grave contexts, these objects are assumed to have been either containers for cosmetics or ointments which were used by the deceased during life, or were part of the funerary ritual for pouring fragrant oils or balms over the corps, after which they were placed in the grave.[99] The *unguentaria* were often deposited next to the skull. Ceramic vessels, such as jugs (n = 9), bowls (n = 2), oil lamps (n = 2), and cups (n = 2), were quite common as well, though only present in small numbers, usually one or two in a grave. Generally, these too were placed next to the head. Whether these objects served as a grave good or as container for food offerings or liquids remains unclear. This is also the case for two spherical glass vessels, each found next to the head of a deceased (Fig. 11).

Jewellery was represented by 4 copper-alloy or iron rings, 4 copper-alloy or iron bracelets, and a single golden earring.[100] Glass bead necklaces became more popular in this period and were given to 9 individuals. Although beads are mostly associated with adult females and children,[101] these also ended up in two male graves. Two individuals wore an amulet around the neck, of which one was identified as a *phylakterion*, a metal sheet engraved with a spell rolled-up and put in a tube-shaped

88   Cleymans *et al.* (2021) 187.
89   Cleymans *et al.* (2018) 152–53.
90   Talbot (2009) 283–85 and 306.
91   Cleymans *et al.* (forthcoming).
92   Moore (2013) 83–84.
93   Demirel (2017).
94   Yasin (2005).
95   Cleymans and Uytterhoeven (2022).

96   Cleymans *et al.* (2018) 155–58.
97   Claeys and Poblome (2014).
98   Cleymans *et al.* (2021) 190.
99   Anderson-Stojanović (1987).
100   The second earring was never found despite the grave's fill being sieved.
101   Swift (2003) 337.

FIGURE 11   The grave good assemblage of a Late Roman 3–5 year old child in the burial compound (PQ4)
who received a Cu-alloy bracelet, two glass unguentaria, a ceramic cup and a necklace or
bracelet (?) in glass beads.

FIGURE 12   The chalcedony cameo of Medusa from the Late
Roman grave of a 10–12 year old child in the burial
compound (PQ4).

amulet.[102] The other example was a chalcedony cameo
depicting the head of Medusa, a common apotropaic
device in antiquity (Fig. 12).[103] Dress accessories became
more common: 4 metal (clothing) pins, two buckles, and
a crossbow fibula were unearthed. Worked bone hairpins, most of which were found underneath the skull
suggesting that they were still in place, were retrieved
in 4 graves. In contrast to the Roman Imperial burials
where a single individual could receive up to 7 pins, only
one per grave was found in Late Roman times. Another
worked bone pin was interpreted as a cosmetics applica-
tor as it was placed in a ceramic jug.

In contrast to the high-quality grave goods in Roman
Imperial tombs, Late Roman burial gifts swere generally
of a lesser quality. Only one object was made of precious metal – the golden earring – and another of semi-
precious stone – the chalcedony cameo. Most of the
objects showed traces of use during life, such as the hairpins with weathered shafts. Nevertheless, some selection
had clearly taken place. Several of the objects were not
functional (anymore) in daily life as they showed production errors or were too worn for further use. An excellent example is an early 5th c. bowl (type 1B130) from the
central *hyposorium* in the podium of the excavated temple tomb (PQ1), as shown on Fig. 13. This ceramic object
showed *peri-cocturam* cracks in the base, which would

102   For a similar Early Byzantine *phylakterion* from Sagalassos, see
Eich and Eich (2012).
103   Karoglou (2018) 22.

FIGURE 13   The Late Roman grave good assemblage from the central *hypogaeum* underneath the podium of the temple tomb (PQ1). The two oil lamps were used, as indicated by the fire clouding around the nozzle. Their decoration is of poor quality and the pouring hole of the one on the left was made *post-cocturam*. The bowl showed *peri-cocturam* cracks on its base, making it unsuitable for holding liquids.

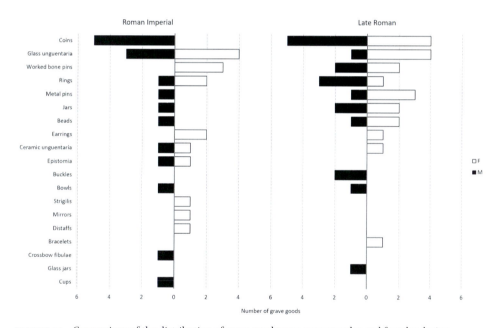

FIGURE 14   Comparison of the distribution of grave good types among males and females during the Roman Imperial and Late Roman periods (includes only those grave goods found in association with a skeleton for which the sex was attested during the physical anthropological study).

make the bowl useless for holding liquids. Two oil lamps from the same context displayed production errors too, making these unsuitable for market sale. Finally, some sort of age and gender differentiation took place, albeit to a lesser extent than in Roman Imperial Sagalassos. This is particularly true for jewellery and dress accessories. Hairpins and bracelets, for example, exclusively belonged to women, while crossbow brooches were typical for male burials.[104] Non-adults under the age of 10, in turn, formed the only group that received cups. All other grave goods are more-or-less evenly distributed between men, women, and children (Fig. 14).

A category of funerary gifts not discussed so far but illustrating the same patterns as the other grave

---

104   Cf. Soupault (2003); Müller and Steuer (2011) 108.

goods, are coins.[105] The interpretation of coins as a
fare for Charon is based on the writings of several
ancient authors,[106] mentioning the tradition of placing
an obol in the mouth of the deceased at the moment
of death or during burial. In the Late Roman graves at
Sagalassos, coins were the most common grave goods:
13 out of 42 individuals (31%) were given one (or two in
two cases). These were evenly distributed among men
(n = 5), women (n = 4), and non-adults (n = 4), whereas
in the Roman Imperial period only men received these.
Moreover, the denominations (small bronze coins and
BI nummi/Antoniani), as well as the quality of the coin,
were lower in Late Roman times. Based on the clustering of the graves containing a coin and the assumed
kinship relations these may display, it seems that some
Late Roman families clung to the tradition of paying the
ferryman, while others did not. The family obviously
played a central role in Late Roman funerary rituals.

Given the small sample of only 4 excavated Early
Byzantine graves and the disturbance of two of these,
the following observations on grave goods during the
Early Byzantine period should be considered tentative.
Objects were only found associated with two individuals.
The adult male buried next to the church in the Eastern
Necropolis (PQ5) wore a rectangular copper-alloy belt
buckle with glass inlays around a Latin cross (Fig. 15).

This badge of religious identity, together with the find
location beside the church, clearly indicates that this
person was Christian. Similar belt buckles with glass
inlays have been encountered throughout the Byzantine
Empire and mainly dated to the second half of the 5th
and 6th c.[107] A glass *unguentarium* and 9 glass beads
were found in the only undisturbed non-adult inhumation of 7th c. Çatal Oluk. These beads were either blue
or green in colour, and 4 were tubular in shape while
the other 5 were globular. As indicated by examples
from Early Byzantine Northern Greece and Late Roman
Europe,[108] both the colour combination and alternating
tubular and globular shapes were quite common. Based
on this very limited excavated evidence, it remains difficult to say whether only non-adults received grave
goods, a common practice in the Byzantine Empire also
attested at Middle Byzantine Sagalassos.[109]

From *Necropoleis* to *Koimētēria*

So far, the discussion on late antique burial practices –
different from the preceding Roman Imperial period and
the subsequent post-earthquake Byzantine period at
Sagalassos – treated the Late Roman and Early Byzantine
periods separately, as two distinct temporal blocks. This
division corresponds with the general descriptions on
how burial practices developed in the Roman East from
the *necropoleis* to *koimētēria*. Indeed, from the 3rd c.
onwards, the word *koimētērion* appears in Christian
contexts in the Roman East and gradually replaced the
concept of "necropolis".[110] The latter literally means "city
of the dead" and was the most frequently used term in
Roman Imperial times to designate burial grounds.[111]
This reference to a city evokes images of liveliness and
a range of activities taking place. The well-documented
Eastern Necropolis of Sagalassos was such a place where
funerary practices partly overlapped with artisanal
activities. As aboveground tombs were often placed next
to the main access roads of the city, there was constant
passage through these burial grounds. In Byzantine
times, the terminology shifted to *koimētērion*, literally
'sleeping place'. Although the word was already used
in the 4th c. BC,[112] it did not appear in Roman 'pagan'
contexts. In the Roman Empire, *koimētērion* made its

105   Discussed in detail in Stroobants *et al.* (2019).

106   Ar., *Ran.* 140–141; Lucian, *Charon* 11; Lucian, *Luct.* 10; Prop.
        4.11.7–8; Juv. 3.265–268; Apul., *Met.* 6.18.4–5. For a complete
        overview of all literary references, see Thüry (2016) *Tabelle 7*
        and *Tabelle 9*.

107   For various parallels, see Schulze-Dörrlamm (2002).

108   Northern Greece: Antonaras (2003) 331; Europe: Swift
        (2003) 337.

109   Pitarakis (2009) 153; Talbot (2009) 300–301; On Sagalassos:
        Cleymans and Talloen (2018) 292–93.

110   Brandenburg (1994); Rebillard (1993).

111   Hope (2009) 155.

112   Diosadas, *apud* Ath., *Deipnosophistes* IV.143c.

advent at the end of the 2nd c., already in a Christian text.[113] In contrast to the lively *necropoleis*, this new term hints at a more peaceful resting place, referring to the Christian belief that death is not the end, but that body and soul will resurrect.[114] At Sagalassos, burials indeed moved away from the busy *necropoleis* towards cemeteries surrounding churches. These churches, although still within the extent of the former *necropoleis*, were often farther removed from the entranceways or busy suburban activities. The basilica in the Eastern Necropolis, for example, is located on a more remote promontory in the north-east and build around the time artisanal production was moving away from the nearby Eastern *Suburbium*. Similarly, the church at Çatal Oluk is situated in a quiet valley shielded from busy city-life.

At Sagalassos too, such (relatively sudden) demarcations in funerary culture have been observed, the first situated around the middle of the 3rd c. when the construction of monumental tomb architecture halted and was replaced by coffin inhumations in simple pits and the second with the onset of Christian graves near churches from around AD 500 onwards. These shifts stand out because of their distinctive character, but in fact entail only a small aspect of the overall mortuary culture. Most of the Late Roman practices were a continuation of already existing Roman Imperial customs, such as the deposition of coins, body orientation following the direction of contour lines and nearby walls, the family being responsible for organizing several aspects of burial, and a continued use of the *necropoleis*. Similarly, Late Roman grave goods often consisted of recycled objects, personal ornaments, or dress accessories from daily life that ended up in the grave. Conversely, the documented practices from the Early Byzantine period conform largely with Christian funerary culture and corresponding beliefs on the afterlife, resulting in change in terms of grave orientation, exclusively inhumation rites, deposition near churches, limited number of grave goods (as far as can be reconstructed from the limited skeletal assemblage), and modest grave design.

Yet, some elements indicate that this transition was not as abrupt as it would seem at first, but comprised some slower, more gradual processes as well. First, the oldest known Christian interment at Sagalassos, being the early 6th c. burial next to the basilica in the Eastern Necropolis, faced west – instead of the expected eastward-facing position – and was inhumed in a coffin and not shrouded. Whereas certain aspects of the burial point to Christian practices (the belt-buckle with cross, the location next to a church), some older

traditions appear to have continued as well. Or perhaps not all Christian customs may have been introduced yet. Moreover, although the Early Byzantines clearly distanced themselves from the older, 'pagan' burial plots and architecture by regarding these as sites for spoliation, dumping, and looting, the general area of the *necropoleis* remained in use for funerary practices, albeit now only in close proximity to the newly erected extra-urban churches.

The differences with the previous periods mirror broader social phenomena taking place at late antique Sagalassos. In the Late Roman *necropoleis*, for example, no new tomb structures were built, and the overall quality of the grave goods decreased. Yet, at the same time the existing graves and burial plots were treated with respect, reused, and well-maintained. This correlates with the Late Roman way the inhabitants of Sagalassos treated public architecture in town: no new large-scale building projects were launched before the middle of the 5th c., but continued use and maintenance of the existing infrastructure, combined with minor and major modifications speak to the vitality of the community. The disappearance of monumental tomb architecture was earlier in this paper explained as a combination of competition for space and a shift in investments from grave design to communal practices. On a higher level, this new way of dealing with death and interment, revolving around reuse and maintenance, cannot be unlinked from the Late Roman way of life. The specialization and diversification patterns documented for the artisanal and agricultural production at Late Roman Sagalassos have elsewhere been associated with rural population growth as well as the partial decrease in economic connectivity and exchange throughout the Roman Empire following from the crisis of the 3rd c.[115] By opting for new and more sustainable production strategies, the inhabitants of Sagalassos intended to find an equilibrium to sustain its population. The move away from public and private building projects and focus on more sustainable processes of reuse, upkeeping, and the preservation of Roman funerary customs, can thus be regarded in the same vein. By keeping and recycling already existing burial plots, grave architecture, and objects to be used as grave goods, the funerary practices at Sagalassos mirrored the developments within the urban centre.[116]

The rise of Christianity during the Early Byzantine period affected many aspects of life at Sagalassos, including death. Yet as pointed out above, several elements of continuity could be ascertained in funerary practices of

---

113   Tert., *De anim.* 51.7.
114   Rebillard (1993) 976.

115   Poblome (2015).
116   Cleymans and Beaujean (2022).

this period, albeit now with a Christian touch. The afore-mentioned sustainability of Late Antiquity, reflected by modest grave design and few grave goods, became combined with the Early Christian ideals of modesty and poverty.[117] As a result, funerary gifts and personal possessions, including markers of religious beliefs, disappeared almost completely. Having said that, there was not yet a standard Christian funerary liturgy at this time and the family generally remained the principal player in funerals.[118] While monumental grave architecture may have become something of the past, major investments were now made in the form of several (at least 6) funerary churches surrounding Sagalassos. These provided new topographical foci within the traditional burial grounds of the city and introduced monumental sacred architecture in the extra-urban area on an unprecedented scale. The beliefs of the Christians that the end of the world was near and that the righteous dead would be raised, made the cemeteries foci of worship.[119] These focal points were monumentalised through the construction of opulent basilicas which became the visual markers of the transformation of the *necropoleis* into *koimētēria*. Social status would from now on be expressed by prominent burial locales in close proximity to the sanctuary.

Acknowledgements

This research was supported by the Research Fund of KU Leuven and the Research Foundation – Flanders (FWO). We would like to thank the Ministry of Culture and Tourism of the Republic of Turkey, its General Directorate of Culture and Museums (Kültür Varlıkları ve Müzeler Genel Müdürlüğü), and its annual representatives for permission to excavate, for support, and much-appreciated help during the fieldwork campaigns. A word of gratitude is devoted to Prof. Jeroen Poblome (KU Leuven), for reading and commenting upon an earlier draft and supporting this research. Furthermore, we would wish to thank all archaeologists, workmen, and team members who made this research possible. Copyrights of all illustrations belong to the Sagalassos Archaeological Research Project.

---

117   Rhee (2017).
118   Rebillard (2009) 139.
119   See Yasin (2009).

Bibliography

Primary Sources

Apul. *Met.* = J. Arthur Hanson ed. and transl., *Apuleius. Metamorphoses* (*The Golden Ass*), 2 volumes (Loeb Classical Library 44) (Cambridge Mass. 1996).

Ar. *Ran.* = J. Henderson ed. and transl. *Aristophanes, Frogs, Assemblywomen and Wealth* (Loeb Classical Library 180) (Cambridge Mass. 2002).

August. *De sepultura animarum* = Augustine of Hippo, *De sepultura animarum*

Cic. *Leg.* = C. W. Keyes transl. *Cicero, On the Republic, On the Laws* (Loeb Classical Library 213) (Cambridge Mass. 1928).

Cod. Iust. = P. Krüger ed. *Corpus Iuris Civilis 2: Codex Iustinianus* (Berlin 1906).

Cod. Theod. = C. Pharr ed. and transl., *The Theodosian code and novels, and the Sirmondian constitutions* (New York 1952–1969; rev. 2001).

Didascalia et Constitutiones Apostolorum = J. Davies transl. *Didascalia et Constitutiones Apostolorum*, J. Davies, *Death, Burial, and Rebirth in the Religions of Antiquity* (London 1999).

Dig. = J. E. Spruit, R. Feenstra, and F. Wubbe ed. and transl., *Corpus iuris civilis: tekst en vertaling*, 6 volumes (Zutphen 1994–2001).

Diosadas, *apud* Ath., *Deipnosophistes* = C. B. Gulick ed. and transl. *Athenaeus, Deipnosophistae*, 7 volumes (Loeb Classical Library) (Cambridge Mass. 1927–1941).

Epitome Legum = C. E. Z. von Lingenthal ed. *Liber juridicus alphabeticus sive synopsis minor et Ecloga Legum in epitome expositarum* (Lipsiae 1856).

Greg. *Dial.* = Greg. *Dial.* = PL 77. 149–430.

Juv. = S. Morton Braund ed. and transl. *Juvenal and Persius* (Loeb Classical Library 91) (Cambridge Mass. 2004)

Leo VI, *Novels* = P. Noailles and A. Dain transl. *Les novelles de Léon VI le sage* (Paris 1944).

Lucian, *Charon* = A. H. Harmon transl. *Lucian Volume II, The Downward Journey or The Tyrant. Zeus Catechized. Zeus Rants. The Dream or The Cock. Prometheus. Icaromenippus or The Sky-man. Timon or The Misanthrope. Charon or The Inspectors. Philosophies for Sale* (Loeb Classical Library 54) (Cambridge Mass. 1915).

Lucian, *Luct.* = A.H. Harmon transl. *Lucian Volume IV, Anacharsis or Athletics. Menippus or The Descent into Hades. On Funerals. A Professor of Public Speaking. Alexander the False Prophet. Essays in Portraiture. Essays in Portraiture Defended. The Goddesse of Surrye* (Loeb Classical Library 162) (Cambridge Mass. 1925).

Prop. = G. P. Goold ed. and transl. *Propertius, Elegies* (Loeb Classical Library 18) (Cambridge Mass. 1990).

Tert. *De anim.* = E. A. Quain transl. *Tertullian, On the Soul*, Fathers of the Church 10 (1950) 179–309.

Secondary Sources

Achim I. A. (2015) "Churches and graves of the early Byzantine period in Scythia Minor and Moesia Secunda. The development of a Christian topography at the periphery of the Roman Empire", in *Death and Changing Rituals: Function and Meaning in Ancient Funerary Practices*, edd. R. Brandt, M. Prusac, and H. Roland (Oxford 2015) 287–342.

Anderson-Stojanović V. R. (1987) "The chronology and function of ceramic unguentaria", *AJA* 91 (1987) 105–122.

Antonaras A. (2003) "The use of glass in Byzantine jewellery – the evidence from Northern Greece (fourth-sixteenth centuries)", *Annales du 16e Congrès AIHV* (2003) 331–35.

Belke K. and Mersich N. (1990) *Phrygien und Pisidien* (Tabula Imperii Byzantini 7) (Vienna 1990).

Blaizot F. (2014) "From the skeleton to the funerary architecture: a logic of the plausible", *Anthropologie* 52.3 (2014) 263–84.

Brandenburg H. (1994) "Coemeterium. Der Wandel des Bestattungswesens als Zeichen des Kulturumbruchs der Spätantike", *Laverna* 5 (1994) 206–233.

Brandenburg H. (1995) "Altar und Grab. Zu einem Problem des Märtyrerkultes im 4. und 5. Jh.", in *Martyrium in multidisciplinary perspective: Memorial Louis Reekmans*, edd. M. Lamberigts, L. Reekmans, and P. Van Deun (Leuven 1995) 71–98.

Charlier C. (1995) "Les crânes d'époque romaine de Sagalassos. Épaisseur des parois", in *Sagalassos III. Report on the Fourth Excavation Campaign of 1993*, edd. M. Waelkens and J. Poblome (Leuven 1995) 357–66.

Claeys J. (2013) "Marginale archeologie? De Oostelijke Voorstad van Sagalassos (Zuidwest-Turkije)", *TMA* 50 (2013) 23–29.

Claeys J. and Poblome J. (2013) "Sagalassos' un Güneyi: Çatal Oluk 2 Bizans Kilise Alanının Kazı Çalışmaları", in *Sagalassos 2011 kazı ve restorasyon sezonu* (*KST* 34.3), edd. M. Waelkens *et al.* (2013) 146.

Claeys J. and Poblome J. (2014) "Alan PQ1: Naiskos Mezarı", in *Sagalassos'ta 2012 yili kazı ve restorasyon çalışmaları* (*KST* 35.2), edd M. Waelkens, R. Rens, J. Richard *et al.* (2014) 249.

Claeys J. and Poblome J. (2019) "Meanwhile in suburbia", in *Sagalassos. Meanwhile in the Mountains*, edd. J. Poblome, E. Torun, P. Talloen, and M. Waelkens (Istanbul 2019) 135–47.

Cleymans S. and Talloen P. (2018) "Protection in life and death: pendant crosses from the cemetery of Apollo Klarios at Sagalassos, Turkey", *EJA* 21.2 (2018) 280–98.

Cleymans S., Talloen P., Beaujean B., Van de Vijver K., and Poblome J. (2018) "From burial plot to dump site: the history of the PQ4 compound at Sagalassos (southwest Anatolia)", *Anatolica* 44 (2018) 123–63.

Cleymans S. and Beaujean B. (2020) "Het bloed spreekt. Familiebegravingen in Romeins (eerste tot vijfde eeuw na Christus) Sagalassos, Zuidwest-Turkije", *TMA* 62 (2020) 50–58.

Cleymans S. and Uytterhoeven I. (2022) "From cradle to casket: the biography of a sarcophagus at Sagalassos, SW Anatolia", *IstMitt* 71 (2022) 89–120.

Cleymans S. and Beaujean B. (2022) "Where to put them? Burial location in Middle Hellenistic to Late Roman (second century BC–fifth century AD) Sagalassos, southwest Anatolia", *AnatSt* 72 (2022) 167–94.

Cleymans S., Van de Vijver K. and Matsuo H. (forthcoming) "Who did the Moriai favour most? Life expectancy at Roman and Middle Byzantine Sagalassos".

Cleymans S., Claeys J., Van de Vijver K. and Poblome J. (2021) "Burial Terraces in the Eastern Necropolis. The excavations of Site F at Sagalassos (SW Anatolia)", *Anatolica* 47 (2012) 147–98.

Cumont F. V. M. (1949) *Lux Perpetua* (Paris 1949).

Davies J. (1999) *Death, Burial, and Rebirth in the Religions of Antiquity* (London 1999).

De Giorgi L. and Leucci G. (2018) "The archaeological site of Sagalassos (Turkey): exploring the mysteries of the invisible layers using geophysical methods", *Exploration Geophysics* 49.5 (2018) 751–61.

de Visscher F. (1963) *Le droit des tombeaux romains* (Milan 1963).

Demirel F. A. (2017) "Infant and child skeletons from the Lower City Church at Byzantine Amorium", in *Life & Death in Asia Minor in Hellenistic, Roman, and Byzantine times: Studies in Archaeology and Bioarchaeology*, edd. J. R. Brandt, E. Hagelberg, G. Bjørnstad, and S. Ahrens (Oxford 2017) 306–317.

Duday H. (2009) *The Archaeology of the Dead: Lectures in Archaeothanatology* (Oxford 2009).

Effros B. (1997) "Beyond cemetery walls: early medieval funerary topography and Christian salvation", *Early Medieval Europe* 6.1 (1997) 1–23.

Eich A. and Eich P. (2012) "Ein neues Silberamulett aus Sagalassos", *Rivista di filología e di istruzione classica* 140.1 (2012) 5–19.

Emmerson A. L. (2020) "Re-examining Roman death pollution", *JRS* 110 (2020) 5–27.

Gauthier N. (1999) "La topographie chrétienne entre idéologie et pragmatisme", in *The Idea and Ideal of the Town between Late Antiquity and the Early Middle Ages*, edd. G. P. Brogiolo and B. Ward Perkins (Leiden 1999) 195–209.

Graham E.-J. (2015) "Corporeal concerns: the role of the body in the transformation of Roman mortuary practices", in *Death Embodied: Archaeological approaches to the treatment of the corpse*, edd Z. Devlin and E.-J. Graham (Oxford 2015) 41–62.

Hnila P. (2015) "Rural necropoleis and settlement dynamics. Thoughts on Roman and Byzantine graves at Oymaağaç Höyük, Samsun province", in *Landscape dynamics and settlement patterns in Northern Anatolia during the Roman*

The Archaeology of Late Antique Mortuary Practices in the Near East

Ádám Bollók

Abstract

The present paper offers a concise overview of the main trends in late antique mortuary archaeology in Near Eastern countries (Israel, Jordan, Lebanon, Syria, the Palestinian Authority, and the adjacent south-western and northern territories). The first part covers the general characteristics of the mortuary remains and reviews the major challenges to late antique funerary archaeology, with a special emphasis on the consequences of ancient and modern looting. The second part presents some of the major findings by local specialists and foreign missions and explores the chief concerns of burial communities when sending off and interring their dead.

Introduction: General Considerations

As the German classical archaeologist Hans Lohmann wryly noted in a recent publication reviewing the results of his team's intensive field surveys in and around the western Anatolian town of Mykale, "as it is well known, graves and necropolises constitute a group of monuments which were deliberately dug deep in the earth [... and thus] they largely escape notice during field surveys."[1] Although this assertion certainly holds true for several regions and periods, the late antique Near East is hardly one of them. Accordingly, the mortuary archaeology of these territories is bedevilled by the consequences of this unfortunate situation.

When speaking about the archaeology of late antique mortuary practices in the Near East, the study area covers the territory of 7 modern political entities, namely Egypt with her north-eastern territories on the Sinai Peninsula,[2] Israel, the Palestinian Authority, Jordan, Lebanon, Syria, and the south-eastern part of Turkey. Similarly to the archaeological excavations carried out in the wider region in general, the exploration of late antique mortuary remains is likewise highly uneven in terms of geographical coverage. As far as I am aware, a visual tool comparable to the recently published distribution map created by the 'Invisible Dead' Project of Durham University for mortuary sites of the Chalcolithic to Roman periods[3] has not been generated

for Late Antiquity until 2018. However, the abundance of findspots in the southern Levant and their scarcity in the northern part of our study area reveal very similar patterns. The single major difference is that in the wake of the field surveys undertaken in the region, and not least because of the exceptionally well-preserved architectural remains and the period's high settlement density, the late antique burial sites of the north Syrian Limestone Massif[4] and the Euphrates Valley[5] are far better documented than those of several previous periods. Unfortunately, in the overwhelming majority of cases, virtually nothing else than tomb architecture and the surviving portions of their decoration are recorded.

Chronologically speaking, the 'Late Antiquity' of western scholarship – that is, the 3rd to 7th/8th c. – is generally divided into Late Roman, Early and Late Byzantine as well as Umayyad periods in the Levantine region. 'Late Roman' can cover the 3rd and early 4th c., 'Early and Late Byzantine' roughly the 4th to 5th and 6th to earlier 7th c., respectively, and Umayyad the later 7th and earlier 8th c.[6] In contrast, in Turkish archaeology, the 4th and (earlier) 5th c. are often referred to as Late Antiquity, while the later 5th/6th and 7th c. are considered as Early Byzantine, although in more recent studies, Early Byzantine may be reserved for the later 7th to earlier 9th c.[7] It must also be borne in mind that due to many regional traits in the material record, the necropolis areas of the Roman and Byzantine periods, especially the severely looted ones, cannot always be properly separated from each other and, thus, these sites are often designated as 'Roman-Byzantine'.

Owing to the enormous geographical and chronological coverage of the topic, the following discussion makes no pretence at comprehensiveness, let alone at completeness. While in the following an attempt will be made to touch upon the key themes, general problems,

---

1 Lohmann (2017) 268.
2 Not surprisingly, the mortuary remains of the Sinai have strong ties with their Egyptian cultural milieu, cf. Tudor (2011) 114–115.
3 Cf. Bradbury and Philip (2015) 332, fig. 1.

4 For a general survey of late antique tombs in northern Syria, see Greisheimer (1997). For fields surveys made in single *wadis*, see Peña, Castellana and Fernández (1987); Peña, Castellana and Fernández (1990); Peña, Castellana and Fernández (1999); Peña, Castellana and Fernández (2003).
5 Séiquer and Carrillo (1998); Egea Vivancos (2004); Egea Vivancos (2005). For two major sites, Halabiya-Zénobia and Tell al-Sin, each with an impressive number of tombs, see Lauffray (1991) 207–224; Blétry (2012); Montero Fenollós and al-Shbib (2008).
6 For this traditional periodisation, see e.g. Parker (1999) 139. For alternative approaches, see Holumn (2003) 352–53; Magnes (1993) 346.
7 Cf. Vroom (2011).

© KONINKLIJKE BRILL BV, LEIDEN, 2024 | DOI:10.1163/9789004687974_015
Alexandra Dolea and Luke Lavan (eds) *Burial and Memorial in Late Antiquity*
(Late Antique Archaeology 13) (Leiden 2024), pp. 832–855

and main achievements of the mortuary archaeology of the late antique Near East, the perspective of the present paper will inevitably reflect the author's own focus to a certain extent.[8] In view of the region's immense geological, geographical, ethnic, and cultural diversity, it cannot come as a genuine surprise that several grave and tomb forms were used for burying the dead during the late antique centuries. Rock-cut hypogea and rock-cut tombs[9] might be the most frequently documented types, but there are also aboveground and underground built tombs, aboveground tomb edifices erected over underground rock-cut burial spaces, free-standing sarcophagi, simple cist graves dug into the ground/bedrock or built from stones or tiles, *alla cappuccina* graves, cist graves covered with sarcophagus lids, built cist graves dug into the floors of churches, and, occasionally, amphora burials.[10]

The appearance and frequencies of given types are heavily influenced by the geological conditions of different regions, while the representation of particular types is in itself dependent on research agendas and strategies. It may be also noted that while family tombs and hypogea can be easily recognised and recorded during field surveys, certain forms of stone-lined cist graves are more likely to be discovered in the course of excavations. Moreover, owing to the latter's often fairly simple and common forms, their dating on typological grounds can run into serious difficulties. And since these graves elicited little scholarly attention for decades, their exploration and evaluation remained underdeveloped in the region.[11] Yet, some of the above-listed grave and tomb types, such as rock-cut hypogea, built tombs, and cist graves are often discovered side-by-side in the same necropolis area.[12] It is not always easy to establish whether or not the different types had been used simultaneously, especially if the given necropolis was re-used for burials and/or was affected by looting.

The majority of the above-mentioned burial installations were erected with the intention of accommodating more than one individual. Accordingly, multiple burials appear across much of the region throughout Late Antiquity. In comparatively rare cases, closed assemblages containing a single burial have also been recorded, but most of them fall into the 3rd and earlier 4th c.[13] and the Early Islamic era (often extending beyond the period discussed here).[14] However, in some regions, where geological and geographical conditions permitted the opening of 'flat cemeteries' extending over larger areas, single interment graves or small number burial plots are also recorded from the 'Byzantine centuries'. Among them, the Khirbat al-Samrā cemetery, whose burials span Late Antiquity, deserves special attention. Its ongoing archaeological exploration not only provides closed burial assemblages, so rare in the entire region, but sometimes also preserves unusual funerary artefacts and mortuary practices which offer unique glimpses into the mortuary behaviour of the local population.[15] It is, therefore, especially regrettable that the funerary stelae, some of which are inscribed with the name and age at death of the departed, were often removed from their original place, and so cannot be linked to particular assemblages.[16]

Similarly, stone-lined cist graves, funerary stelae, and closed mortuary assemblages of Late Roman and Byzantine date were documented at Khirbat al-Dharih

---

8   For previous overviews of the mortuary archaeology of late antique Palestine, see Kuhnen (1990) 278–82, 345–50; Parker (1999) 168–69. For Jordan, the best available starting points are Watson (2001) and Krug (1998), although the latter's main focus of interest is tomb architecture. For Syria, Sartre (1989) offers a still useful brief summary of the late antique centuries, although with a clear focus on the Roman period. For the Hauran, Sartre-Fauriat (2001) offers a comprehensive treatment, while for the Roman age, including the Late Roman era, the recent monograph by de Jong (2017) provides a new synthesis.

9   For the difference between rock-cut hypogea and rock-cut tombs, see Newson (2015) 350.

10   For typological overviews, see the literature cited in nn.49–57 below.

11   Cf. Avni, Dahari and Kloner (2008a) 103–104.

12   See e.g. the necropolises of Hama (Ploug (1986)) and Serǧilla (Charpentier (2013)) in Syria, of Gadara in Jordan (Smith (1992) 216–17), and of Bet Guvrin, Jerusalem (Avni, Dahari and Kloner (2008b) for the latter two), Nesher-Ramla (Kol-Ya'akov

(2010) esp. 118) and Tell en-Naṣbeh (McCown (1947) esp. 121–23, figs. 19–20) in Israel.

13   A group of Late Roman burial sites largely made up of single interments, partly in cist graves and partly in family tombs, is associated with the Phoenician population in north-western Israel (north-western Galilee); for a typical example, see Peleg 1991, and for an overview with further literature, see Stern and Getzov (2006). Further groups of single interments are known from Late Roman Aelia Capitolina/Jerusalem (Winter (2015) with further literature), from the Late Roman and Byzantine Negev (e.g. Govrin (2003); Nagar and Sonntag (2008) with further literature), from among the mortuary assemblages in Transjordan associated with the region's nomadic and semi-nomadic population (Ibrahim and Gordon (1987); al-Salameen and Falahat (2009)), and from different parts of Syria (Badre *et al.* (1994) 285–93; Sakal (2010)).

14   Kuhnen (1990) 351, n.70; Toombs (1985), Sonntag and Zelin (2002); Fischer (2012) with further literature.

15   Humbert (1998), Nabulsi (1998); Nabulsi *et al.* (2007); Nabulsi *et al.* (2008); Nabulsi *et al.* (2009); Nabulsi (2010); Eger, Nabulsi and Ahrens (2011); Nabulsi *et al.* (2011); Nabulsi, Husan and Schönrock-Nabulsi (2013).

16   For the stelae and their inscriptions, see Desreumaux and Couson (1998), Gatier (1998) 367–80, Desreumaux (1998); Nabulsi and MacDonald (2014); Bader *et al.* (2017).

in central Transjordan.[17] The abundance of late antique inscribed tombstones in the wider region, in al-Karak and its broader area, and further south at Faynan (the latter with *ca.* 1,000 tombstones, of which only less than one percent bear inscriptions) point to the existence of similar burial grounds. Unfortunately, at the latter sites, with the exception of a research excavation as part of the Wadi Faynan project and a salvage excavation at the severely looted site at Ghawr al-Ṣāfī, only minimal or no excavation has taken place.[18] Closer to the coastal area, in the Negev, similar cemeteries also predominated, as attested by the high number of late antique stone-lined cist graves documented at Beʾer-Shevaʿ, Tell Malḥata, Reḥovot-in-the-Negev and others. Reḥovot also produced countless inscribed tombstones, including ones carved in the form of very schematic human busts, parallels of which surface in the Negev, farther to the west, and at al-Felusiyat in northern Sinai (ancient Ostrakine, Egypt).[19] In the coastal area, but farther to the north near Gaza, another necropolis with stone-lined cist graves was documented.[20] The chain of sites characterised by cist graves and funerary stelae continues in a northerly direction from central Transjordan, too, as demonstrated by a few excavated necropolises and the inscribed tombstones of the Golan and the southern Hauran; however, the majority of the currently known inscriptions and funerary assemblages at these sites date from the Late Roman period.[21]

It is perhaps clear from the above brief overview that the pre-eminent problem of late antique Near Eastern mortuary archaeology is closely connected to the highly visible nature of its subject matter. Across the region, tombs, necropolises, and cemeteries were designed to be visited, seen, and admired in order to maintain family relations, preserve of the deceased's memory, and convey the owners' and their families' wealth and status. Conforming to Roman custom, urban necropolises often flanked both sides of the main roads leading into the major cities,[22] as the best-preserved and partially excavated al-Bass necropolis of Tyre shows.[23] In rural areas, however, they tend to surround settlements, often forming smaller or larger tomb groups. The same spatial arrangement is encountered in several urban areas too,[24] where geographical conditions and available space did not favour the emergence of Roman-style 'necropolis roads' or the local population preferred to use their old necropolis areas with pre-Roman antecedents. Even if funerary sculpture appears to have gone out of fashion after the early 4th c.,[25] the habit of commemorating the dead in epitaphs, as we have seen in above, declined less rapidly in several regions of the Near East than in other parts of the Roman Empire. This is clearly shown by the extensive numbers of grave and tomb inscriptions from Syria and Palestine published in epigraphic corpora and individual studies, a process aided by the erection of grave markers. However, this otherwise fortunate state of affairs turns out to be a mixed blessing as these grave markers not only attract archaeologists but also looters, for whom heavy stone covers and doors[26] proved little deterrence to entering graves, tombs, necropolises and cemeteries dug deep into the ground.

Limitations of the Evidence

Built and rock-cut family tombs were even more likely to fall prey to the greed of contemporaries and later generations, as well as to practices devoid of harmful intentions, but nonetheless destructive in their ultimate outcome. The price paid for the maintaining family relations in death, a habit harking back to ancient times in the Near East, and for unabashed social display was the ever-present threat of grave looting. On the other hand, built tombs and those hewn into the rock

17   Lenoble *et al.* (2001).

18   Inscriptions from the al-Karak region: Canova (1954); Ghawr al-Ṣāfī: Politis (1998) 630–31; Faynan: Knauf (1986); Findlater *et al.* (1998). A small-scale excavation producing 15 yet unpublished graves in Mʾuta: Al-Samadi (2001).

19   Beʾer Shevaʿ: Abadi-Reiss and Eisenberg-Degen (2013) with the previous literature. Tell Malḥata: Eldar and Nahlieli (1982) 68. Reḥovot-in-the-Negev: Tsafrir and Holum (1987/1988) 91; Tsafrir and Holum (1988) 124–26. al-Felusiyat: Dahari and Di Segni (2009) with further literature.

20   Nabulsi *et al.* (2010).

21   Pagan and Christian inscribed stelae from the Golan: Gregg and Urman (1996). Hauran: Sartre-Fauriat and Sartre (2016). Built graves from Banias: Hartal *et al.* (2009). Tall Damiyah: Petit (2013) 242–43.

22   Sever. *De fide et lege naturae*; *Pseudo-Chrysostomica, De morte*.

23   Excavated tombs and a selection of their contents: Chéhab (1984), Chéhab (1985), Chéhab (1986). The first analysis of the cemetery: de Jong (2010). For further examples, mainly of Roman date, see de Jong (2017) 21–28.

24   As a typical example, see the well-documented Bet Guvrin necropolis: Avni, Dahari and Kloner (2008b).

25   Skupinska-Løvset (1983); Sartre-Fauriat (2001) 1, 241–91; Altheeb (2015).

26   A survey of basalt doors from Syria with further literature: Falcioni and Severini (2006). Besides these well-known pieces often sold for a good price on the antiquities market, undecorated doors carved from local stones (an *in situ* find from Beth Sheʾan: e.g. Avshalom-Gorni (2000) 51*, figs. 3–4, another from al-Thawra, Syria: Badawi (2010) 268, fig. 4), small-scale rectangular stone blocks pushed in the door-recesses and circular 'rolling-stone' doors were also frequently used.

offered excellent opportunities for recycling as building materials,[27] shelter,[28] and conversion into makeshift dwellings, barns, hiding complexes, cisterns etc.[29] Contemporaries were well aware of these dangers, especially of the undesirable consequences of excessive mortuary display. By emphasising the inescapable danger of tomb-robbing, the Church Fathers repeatedly urged their flock to abandon the old custom of interring their dead relatives enshrouded in luxurious garments, accompanied by an array of expensive articles. Their admonitions went unheeded.[30] Almost a millennium later, Ibn Khaldun, the 14th c. Arab historian, fully aware that "graves afforded opportunities for treasure hunting", rebuked his contemporaries in vain by stressing that "trying to make money from buried and other treasures is not a natural way of making a living".[31]

Modern heritage management and legal systems have also proven virtually powerless to stop the illicit antiquities trade. Therefore, it is hardly surprising that the 19th c. travellers and the early archaeological missions first documenting the well-preserved funerary monuments of the north Syrian Limestone Massif, the south Syrian Hauran region, and the rock-cut tombs and hypogea of Palestine found that the easily accessible monuments had since long been emptied by successive generations of local residents.[32] These early explorers complained about the enormous amount of information that had been lost due to the large-scale destruction

wreaked by the ignorance and greed of the locals.[33] Yet, their own work did not always produce significantly better documentation of late antique remains. The widespread and systematic nature of tomb-looting was likewise noted by western scholars based in the region during the last decades of Ottoman rule.[34] Later, public and private collections spending huge sums of money, accompanied by the ever-growing public interest in Biblical times, created a massive demand for artefacts originating from the Levant. This saw instances of grave robbery skyrocket. In Judaean Shephelah alone, "thousands of illegal excavations to locate ancient tombs were carried out in and around tells from the biblical period; *ca.* 6,200 burial caves have been violated."[35]

Even if these issues appear to have little relevance for mortuary practices, this phenomenon has a profound impact on our research methodologies and strategies as well as on the very questions we can and cannot address. To illustrate this point, let me refer to some statistics. In the region of Mount Carmel in north-western Israel, roughly 800 ancient graves and tombs were documented by excavations and surveys by the 1980s. Among these, *ca.* 260 could be securely dated from the Hellenistic to late antique period on typological grounds, but not a single one of late antique date was found undisturbed.[36] During their survey of 6 late antique sites in northern Jordan, J. C. Rose and D. L. Burke of Arkansas University recorded 570 looted tombs, ranging from 15 to 200 tombs per site. None of the visible burial locations escaped disturbance.[37] A recent survey by Paul Newson in the Beka' Valley in northern Lebanon produced similar results. He emphasised that despite the "surprisingly large quantity of evidence collected over the years … only the relatively recent excavations of the sarcophagus burials at Douris and Kamid el-Loz as well as the tombs at Hammara provided complete and undisturbed assemblages of grave goods and human remains".[38] Of these, only the latter is late antique in date, but its material remains unpublished.[39] The excavators of Abila of the Decapolis likewise noted that "the looting and destruction of necropolises is proceeding at an alarming rate"[40] and their project, which was one of the few placing due emphasis on mortuary remains in the region, was substantially impeded by grave robbers.[41] A similar

---

27 In 4th c. Anatolia, where the situation was quite similar to the one in the Near East, Gregory of Nyssa, while discouraging the practice itself, considered it pardonable to dismantle built tombs in order to re-use their building material for "something more important and of common benefit". At the same time, harming the dead body and looting its belongings were "condemned with the same sentence as simple fornication". Greg. Nyss., *Ep.* 31.7.

28 See e.g. Smith (1992) 219–21.

29 Smith (1992) 222–26. Late antique tombs partially destroyed and converted into cisterns during the Ottoman period: Zilberbod and Amit (1999) 81–83, 56*–57*. A Roman tomb reused in Late Antiquity for burial purposes, then reused as a makeshift dwelling: Syon (1995). Bedouins living in Roman period and late antique tombs in early 20th c. Arsuf (ancient Apollonia), Israel: Tal (1995) 110. Modern burial: Macalister (1912) 1, 352. Tombs used as makeshift 'bunkers' and ammunition storages in the mid-20th c. and later: Kuhnen (1989) 48; Rose *at al.* (2004a) 47. Tombs currently utilised as barns and makeshift dwellings: Egea Vivancos (2005) 154, fig. 52, 175 fig. 73; Russo (2015).

30 See e.g. the evidence collected from John Chrysostom: Stander (2009) esp. 77–78. More references on mortuary display and grave looting are gathered: Kyriakakis (1974) 49–51; Bollók (forthcoming).

31 Ibn Khaldun, *Muqaddimah* 5.4.

32 de Vogüe (1865–1877); Clermont-Ganneau (1896–1899); Butler (1919–1920).

33 Cf. Renan (1864) 155–56.

34 Vincent (1910) 576–77.

35 Ganor (2003) 69*.

36 Cf. Kuhnen (1987) 172; Kuhnen (1989) 48.

37 Rose and Burke (2004).

38 Newson (2015) 368–69.

39 Ghadban (1985) 396–403.

40 Wineland (2001) 46.

41 Wineland (2001) 40–46.

image can be drawn from a survey published 20 years ago of the available evidence on the mortuary landscape of Roman and late antique Apollonia-Arsuf. Despite the efforts of archaeologists working on the site since the earlier 20th c., often no more could be done than to record the previous destructions, document the tomb architecture, and collect the remaining finds.[42]

The number of examples can be easily multiplied. But it is probably more instructive to quote the recently published results of a field survey undertaken by Salah Hussein al-Houdalieh, archaeologist of the al-Quds University of Jerusalem and a native of Saffa, a village located 16 km west of Ramallah. Besides conducting field surveys, he interviewed local tomb looters active in the region since the 1970s as part of his research, and to visit the sites they had previously looted. In his study area, the previous archaeological surveys had documented 11 archaeological sites, while he was able to double this number. He concentrated on 14 of the known sites and catalogued 119 robbed tombs, whose majority, as far as it can be established on the basis of tomb typologies, are late antique in date.[43] According to the information gathered from the looters, they had found approximately 6,000 artefacts in these 119 tombs, which included *ca.* 2,720 ceramic oil lamps, 2,290 coins, 320 glass beads, 280 metal earrings, 110 metal finger-rings, 105 pottery vessels, 70 metal arm-rings, 50 metal necklaces, and 100 other objects.[44]

Even if these numbers appear very high at first glance, there is no reason to doubt them. The lack of glass vessels is rather striking, since normally they are abundantly represented in other assemblages, and as Rose and Burke's above-quoted survey shows, these pieces can be sold for a very good price on the antiquities market.[45] However, the few undisturbed grave assemblages published from the broader region seem to confirm the relative abundance of ceramic lamps and jewellery pieces.[46] And, bearing in mind that lamps, coins, and metal jewellery are typically highly sought-after artefacts on the antiquities market,[47] we may safely assume that less valued or more fragile pieces were simply neglected or discarded. Yet, the re-excavation of a number of tombs in the Saffa region also demonstrated that where 'professional' looting gangs were active, their members worked 'carefully'

and thus no more than a handful of finds made of durable material escaped their attention or were broken. These investigations also revealed that besides being used as rubbish dumps by locals, the looted and partly emptied tombs sometimes served as repositories for the looters' leftover materials, including human bones, from other disturbed burials. This removal of remains and materials from their original resting places represents a further loss of archaeological information.[48]

This brief overview hopefully illustrates one of the major challenges in the interpretation of late antique Near Eastern mortuary remains. Although thousands or rather tens of thousands of graves and tombs used for burial in Late Antiquity have been recorded, the overwhelming majority can merely be used for constructing tomb typologies. Accordingly, fairly elaborate, but sometimes slightly inconsistent, typologies were established for southern Commagene,[49] northern Syria,[50] the northern Euphrates valley,[51] Halabiya,[52] the Hauran in southern Syria,[53] the Carmel region in Israel,[54] the Bet Guvrin necropolis,[55] and, based on the exemplary excavations carried out at Tell Hesban, for the Roman- and Byzantine-period sites of modern-day Jordan.[56] The latter was subsequently complemented with new typologies constructed for three sites in northern Jordan, namely Yasileh, Ya'mun, and Sa'ad.[57] However, the typological approach, although necessary, has its own limitations. First of all, the forms of the graves and tombs offer fairly limited evidence on actual mortuary rituals. The options for constructing chronological sequences are in many cases even more restricted, especially because in the late antique Near East, land was at a premium and, consequently, the custom of reusing earlier burial installations for funerary purposes was widespread. Therefore, it is often practically impossible to determine whether a looted tomb constructed in the Iron Age, the Hellenistic or the Roman period and located in the same funerary precinct as the late antique tombs had been re-opened and re-used subsequently.[58] Moreover, if a late antique

42   Tal (1995). Excavations conducted at the site in the past decades yielded closed tomb assemblages: Rudin *et al.* (2018).

43   Al-Houdalieh (2014) 224.

44   Al-Houdalieh (2014) 230, Table 1.

45   Rose and Burke (2004) 7.

46   Cf. the 195 oil lamps, 14 glass vessels, 7 jewellery pieces, and 7 beads of the tomb found at Atara, located 15 km north of Ramallah and *ca.* 15 km north-east of Saffa: Taha (2003).

47   Rose and Burke (2004).

48   Al-Houdalieh, Bernbeck and Pollock (2017).

49   Ergeç (2003).

50   Greisheimer (1997).

51   Egea Vivancos (2004).

52   Lauffray (1991) 207–224; Blétry (2012).

53   Sartre-Fauriat (2001) 2, 39–80; Fischer and Oenbrink (2010).

54   Kuhnen (1987) 49–61; Kuhnen (1989) 172–74.

55   Avni, Dahari and Kloner (2008a).

56   Hesban: Waterhouse (1994); Waterhouse (1998). Jordan: Krug (1998).

57   Rose, Burke and Johnson (2004); Johnson (2004); Al-Muheisen (2008).

58   For a typical example, see the results of the Tell en-Naṣbeh excavations (McCown (1947), where "objects from the Late Roman and Byzantine periods were discovered in at least

tomb was later also re-used as a hiding complex, an agricultural installation, a barn or a dwelling, excavations may bring to light artefacts deposited there during this later phase of use, whose separation from the mortuary offerings is not always an easy task.[59]

Multiple burials, the high percentage of looted monuments, and recurring tomb re-use are an unattractive combination, not least because both our chronological systems and our understanding of several components of funerary rituals heavily depend on the analysis of closed assemblages. In the case of multiple burials, refined fieldwork techniques and meticulous osteoarchaeological investigations are also necessary for gaining a proper understanding of the formation process of the archaeological record, without which it is difficult or downright impossible to offer a detailed reconstruction of mortuary rituals. However, such is the poorly developed research interest in osteoarchaeology, human skeletal remains are often discarded by looters and sometimes even by excavators. In Israel, where the archaeological heritage management system is highly developed and there is a keen scholarly interest in physical anthropology, religious opposition as well as the legislation acknowledging and incorporating these objections do not support bioarchaeological research. Human skeletal remains are often studied on site and have to be re-buried after excavation; from time to time, the excavations of graves and tombs have to be suspended in the face of ultra-orthodox opposition.[60] However, the evaluation of graves and tombs sometimes filled with 100 or more individuals[61] cannot move beyond a certain level without osteoarchaeological studies.

It is hardly surprising then that our knowledge of several aspects of late antique Near Eastern mortuary archaeology is fairly limited. One of our most important tools for establishing chronology, the compilation of an up-to-date list of closed burial assemblages containing single interments, remains incomplete.[62] Consequently, very little is known about the artefact combinations characteristic for age and sex groups, and it is not particularly easy to visualise the deceased on their biers. Neither do we have a list of the graves and tombs found in an undisturbed condition during excavation. Therefore, in the overwhelming majority of cases, little more can be done than attempt to establish the overall use-life of a tomb based on the chronological sequence of the objects found in it.

Major Results and Tasks

By placing an all too strong emphasis on the difficulties bedevilling research into late antique Near Eastern mortuary archaeology, I do not intend to suggest that no advances have been made or that significant results cannot be achieved in this field. A detailed classification and chronology are available for several ceramic lamp types,[63] glass vessels,[64] jewellery pieces and costume accessories,[65] even if several readily accessible, but older and outdated publications sometimes misdate certain objects by a century or so. An important step has also been taken towards creating a regional chronological framework for the mortuary finds of the Roman and late antique centuries in Palestine by applying the German *Kombinationsstatistik* method;[66] unfortunately, as it was published in German, it has not gained general currency in Near Eastern archaeology dominated by English and French publications. Our understanding of monastic funerals, and to a certain extent of church burials, has been significantly improved by several new discoveries and analyses.[67] The same holds true for the victims of military violence and epidemics, whose final resting places stand in the forefront of current research interest.[68] Extraordinary burial assemblages and sites, like the 4th c. interment of a physician (in all likelihood

---

18 tombs around the site [...] and in addition tombs at Khirbet 'Aṭṭara [...]. Only four of these tombs [...] had plans typical of the Late Roman and Byzantine periods. Others were cut in earlier times and were reused during the Late Roman and Byzantine periods." Zissu and Klein (2014) 206. Late antique burials in Iron Age tombs at Lachish (Tomb 106, Grave 4021; Cave 504): Tufnell (1953) 187, 243, 251–52, pl. 40.2, pl. 54, pl. 57.47–48, pl. 82.134–35. A case study on the re-use of Roman period tombs: Avni (1993).

59 Cf. n.29 above. For a tomb hewn in the Roman period, used for mortuary purposes in Late Antiquity and then as a dwelling in the subsequent era, see Sussman (1976).

60 Parker (1999) 168; Reich (1996); Shiloh (1997); Barkay (1997); cf. also Peterson-Solimani, Soliman, and Weiss (2001); Zilberbod and Amit (2001); Bar'el (2002).

61 Cf. Kuhnen (1989) 48.

62 As emphasised by Fischer (2010) 498 n.5; Fischer and Oenbrink (2010) 216, n.105. An important step was made in this direction in the 1980s by Kuhnen (1989) 49–72, to whom, however, mainly tombs with multiple interments were available.

63 The majority of late antique lamp classes manufactured in present-day Israel are covered by Sussman 2017. Jerash lamps: da Costa (2001) 246.

64 The basic framework was created by Barag (1970), which offers a still useful summary. Since then, the new findings are scattered throughout a huge number of individual reports. For a brief summary, see e.g. Gorin-Rosen and Winter (2010).

65 E.g. Schulze-Dörrlamm (2002).

66 Kuhnen (1989) 49–72.

67 Sodini (1986); Hirschfeld (1992) 130–43; Goldfus (1997); Kogan-Zehavi (1998); Zelinger and Barbé (2017) 58–66.

68 Avni (2010); McCormick (2015); McCormick (2016).

a dentist) at Gadara[69] and the famous Bet She'arim catacombs,[70] likewise attract special attention.

Yet, the bulk of the evidence is still scattered throughout individual reports, whose primary goal is rarely more ambitious than the publication of the excavated material. Theoretically informed approaches are few and far between.[71] And while archaeologists can rarely do better than to draw from the material evidence published in excavation reports when painting images of the funerary cultures of given periods and societies, those interested in the mortuary archaeology of the late antique Near East need to be aware that an enormous portion of the material evidence originating from mortuary contexts is kept in private and public collections, displayed in exhibitions, and published in museum and exhibition catalogues.[72] The most obvious examples are the thousands of intact glass vessels of Roman and late antique date. Needless to say, we will never be in the position of proving their mortuary origin beyond doubt, but a strong case can be made. Even a cursory comparison of the limited metal jewellery, dress accessories and even rarer intact glass vessels from settlement excavations with the same classes of artefacts discovered in undisturbed funerary contexts offers an idea of the enormous data loss caused by looting. This holds particularly true for the final resting places of the rich and the well-to-do, whose graves and tombs were the most exposed to looting, leaving the mortuary behaviour of their social class to be studied largely through late antique texts and tomb architecture.[73]

Thus, in order to gain a better understanding of late antique Near Eastern mortuary practices, three major goals need to be met: to explore the limitations of the available evidence, to systematise the accumulated material, and to analyse select issues against a theoretical background. There are two other equally pressing tasks: to (properly) publish the large body of evidence discovered and rescued during past decades in all countries and to launch new excavations at key sites – an enterprise also complicated by recent political developments. Returning to the first three points, I have already touched on the limitations, not least because of the need to establish a proper methodology for exploring the formation process of the archaeological record in a field where the usual conventional approaches of European mortuary archaeology cannot always be readily applied.[74] Next, we need to review and assess closed assemblages of single interments and undisturbed mortuary contexts and their contents.

Let me illustrate the above points by a few characteristic examples. Sealed graves with single interments and fully articulated skeletons are comparatively rare. However, several graves of the Be'er Sheva',[75] the Emar,[76] and the Khirbat al-Samrā[77] necropolises and a few graves preserved in churches, like Grave C101/2, the burial of a child under 12 found in one of the Humayma churches,[78] may provide informative and sometimes even surprisingly rich assemblages. Sealed graves with multiple burials are often more problematic to evaluate on account of the intermingling of both the human bones and the associated artefacts. Still, under fortunate circumstances, the superimposed layers of interments can be separated by employing rigorous field techniques, as clearly demonstrated, for instance, by the excavators of the Khirbat al-Dharih cemetery[79] (Figs. 1–2) and the work of the American team in the North Cemetery of Beit She'an in the 1920s and 1930s.[80] Unfortunately, nothing was published of the latter's findings except for a few photos and very laconic descriptions. A few old preliminary and a recent brief report on the excavation and the finds kept in the University of Pennsylvania Museum of Archaeology and Anthropology hardly fills this gap.[81]

Yet, even less well-preserved contexts have something to offer. For example, the fairly detailed fieldwork report on a rock-cut hypogeum (Fig. 3.5) excavated at Emmaus shows that a meaningful chronological sequence could be constructed (Fig. 3). Large candlestick (Fig. 3.9) as well as wheel-made (Fig. 3.7) and early channel-nozzle lamps (Fig. 3.8) found on the stairs leading to the funeral chamber (Fig. 3A) date the last sealing of the tomb to the late 7th c. or slightly later.[82] At the other end of the timeline, a belt buckle of the Syracuse class (Fig. 3.6), discovered in one of the lower layers of Arcosolium 1 (Fig. 3B), indicates that the cave was used for funerary purposes already in the late 6th or earlier 7th c.[83] A glass vessel (Fig. 3.4) originating from an upper layer of the

69   Künzl and Weber (1991).

70   Mazar (1973); Schwabe and Lifschitz (1974); Avigad (1976).

71   Bradbury and Philip (2015) 310.

72   Already noted by Vincent (1910) 577; Barkay (1997) 57; Fischer (2010) 503; Fischer and Oenbrink (2010) 217–18.

73   Bollók (forthcoming).

74   For the possibilities and limitations, see Kuhnen (1989) 50–52.

75   Govrin (2003).

76   Sakal (2010).

77   See n.15 above.

78   Shumka, Olsen, and Ramsay (2013).

79   Lenoble et al. (2001).

80   See the photos published by Rowe (1930) pl. 6.

81   E.g. Rowe (1927a); Rowe (1927b); Rowe (1930) 52–53, pl. 5–6; FitzGerald (1932); Fleck (n.d.).

82   Fleckenstein and Fleckenstein (2005) 304, 306, 321, 323–24. For the dates, see Magness (1993) 251, 255–56.

83   Fleckenstein and Fleckenstein (2005) 305, 308, 338, pl. 5. For the date, see Schulze-Dörrlamm (2002) 179.

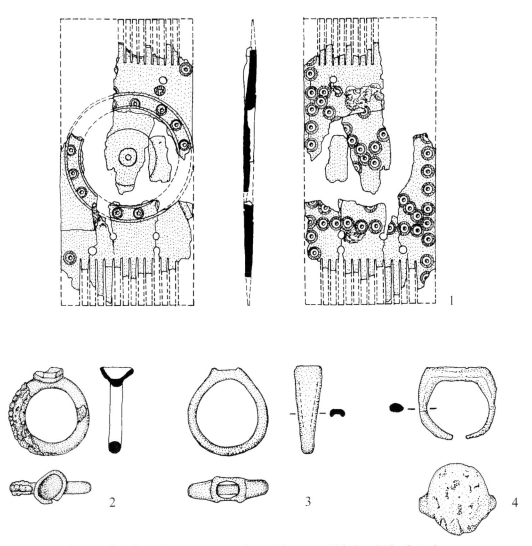

FIGURE 1   Associated artefacts of Inhumation 2 in Grave C, Cemetery C, Khirbat al-Dharih, Jordan
(drawing: Magda Éber, after Lenoble *at al.* (2001) fig. 22.6–8, fig. 23.1).

arcosolium does not contradict this date.[84] According to anthropological analyses, the arcosolium housed the bones of at least 3 adults and 5 children.[85] The cave's longer use is further indicated by the successive layers of interments in the central chamber (Fig. 3C), where *ca.* 7 individuals lay in and under a 1 m thick accumulation of earth.[86] The presence of a late example of a small candlestick lamp in one of the lower layers is roughly consistent with the buckle's suggested late 6th/early 7th c. date.[87] The glass vessels (Fig. 3.3) of the upper and lower

layers[88] indicate that depositions were made roughly simultaneously in the arcosolium and in the central chamber for a certain period of time. However, at some point, the earth accumulating in the central chamber blocked access to the arcosolium and the last interments were confined to the central space. Here, most lamps from the upper layers are of the large candlestick types (Fig. 3.1–2),[89] which also appear among the lamps discovered on the steps.

While the above analysis does not call for special skills, the nature of the published evidence rarely enables a detailed reconstruction of chronological sequences or the formation processes of the archaeological record. Thus, publications of mortuary remains often have to limit themselves to evaluating the available evidence

84   Fleckenstein and Fleckenstein (2005) 305, 308, 351, pl. 8. For the date, see Jackson-Tal (2015) 182.

85   Grossschmidt and Tutschek (2005) 427.

86   Fleckenstein and Fleckenstein (2005) 304, Grossschmidt and Tutschek (2005) 427.

87   Fleckenstein and Fleckenstein (2005) 305, 307, 329. For the date, see Magness (1993) 250. Sussman's (2017, 92, 118) suggestion to restrict the type's date mainly to the later 4th and early 5th c. does not seem entirely convincing and requires further research.

88   Fleckenstein and Fleckenstein (2005) 205, 307, 344–48, pls. 1–5.

89   Fleckenstein and Fleckenstein (2005) 304, 307, 317, 320, 322. For the date, see Magness (1993) 251.

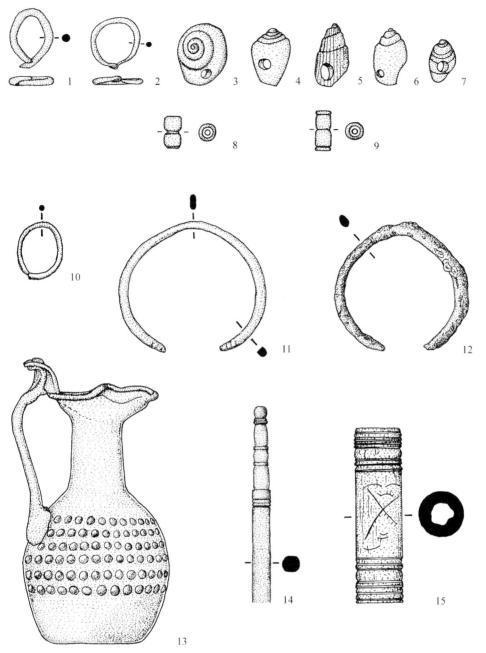

FIGURE 2   Associated artefacts belonging to three individuals found in Grave F, Cemetery C, Khirbat al-Dharih: 1–2: Inhumation F6 (adult); 3–9: Inhumation F5 (child); 10–15: Inhumation F3 (child) (drawing: Magda Éber, after Lenoble *et al.* (2011) fig. 25.4–8, fig. 26.1–4).

from a chronological perspective, thereby establishing the beginning and the end of the time of use of graves and tombs. Because of this, there is good reason to look forward to the final publication of burial sites such as the one excavated at Ḥorbat Castra on Mount Carmel, where 46 sealed tombs, including ones of the Roman and Byzantine periods, have been discovered.[90]

The cataloguing, classification, dating, and structural analysis of the artefact types recovered from mortuary contexts provide many intriguing insights into the major

concerns of late antique people burying their dead relatives. Although, more often than not, only a cumulative evaluation of the accessible evidence can be made, some interesting patterns do emerge. Perhaps the most surprising feature is the strong concentration of amuletic devices in late antique burials, even if it is a continuation of Roman period and more ancient practices, which were only moderately affected by Christianisation. Small bells, circular glass pendants, mirrors, old scarabs and Persian period seals, pierced coins, cylindrical bullae, inscribed leaf-shaped pendants, amuletic finger-rings and armbands, pectoral crosses, and pilgrim eulogiae

90   Yeivin and Finkielsztejn (1999) 37, 26*; Zemer (1999).

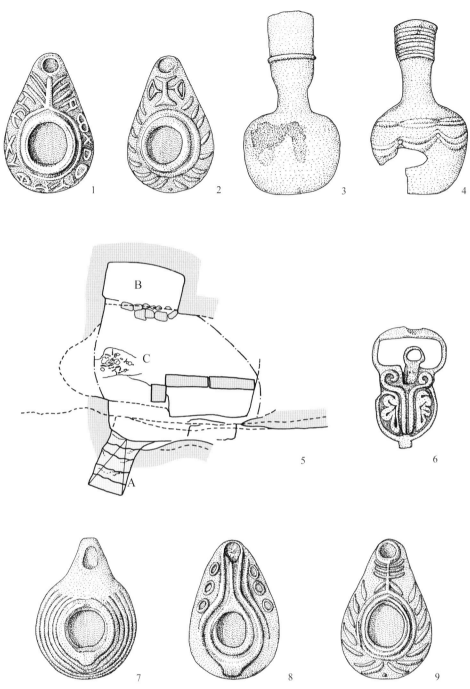

FIGURE 3   Belt buckle, glass vessels, and ceramic lamps from a 6th to 7th c. tomb at Emmaus, Israel
(drawing: Magda Éber, after Fleckenstein and Fleckenstein (2005) 314, plan 7, 318, 'lamp 2',
320, 'lamp 4', 322–324, 'lamps 6–8', 345, pl. 2, 351, pl. 8).

(Fig. 4) provided protection for the dead, and, most probably, for the surviving relatives of the possibly malcontent dead as well.[91] In the rare instances when we can associate them with particular skeletons, they frequently, but hardly exclusively, accompany children.

Furthermore, as far as it can be established on the strength of the material evidence, Christians, Jews, Samaritans, and polytheists shared a common interest in protecting their deceased as well as themselves from the dead by using these devices, even if it is difficult to tell to what extent they shared similar or identical underlying beliefs.[92] Yet, in all likelihood, for Christians, the presence of amuletic devices can hardly be dissociated from the demons believed to dwell in or near tombs,[93] or from the demons vying for the soul of the deceased

---

91   Bollók (2013); Bollók (2016); Bollók (2018).

92   For the Samaritan case, see the recent analysis of Tal and Taxel (2015).

93   T. Sal. 17 (71); Joh. Chrys. De S. Droside martyre 6.

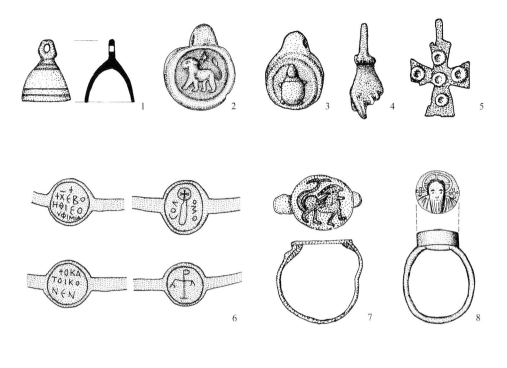

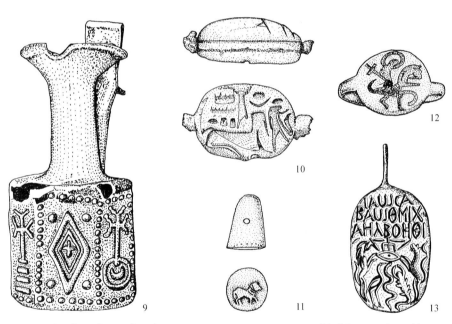

FIGURE 4   Amuletic devices from late antique mortuary contexts: 1. small bell from Ḥorbet Zikhrin,
             Israel; 2–3. stamped glass amuletic pendants from Nazareth and Tarsiha, Israel;
             4. *manu fica* amulet from Khirbat al-Shubaika, Israel; 5. pectoral cross from Tell en-Naṣbeh,
             Israel; 6. armband with Psalm 90 from al-Thawra, Syria; 7–8, 12. amuletic finger-rings from
             Sajur, Gezer, and Shilet al-Dhahr, Israel; 9. glass eulogia container from Ma'in, Jordan; 10.
             scarab from Umm al-Rasas, Jordan; 11. Persian-period seal from Ḥorbet Zikhrin, Israel; 12.
             leaf-shaped amuletic pendant from Gush Halav, Israel (drawing: Magda Éber, after 1. Haddad
             (2007) 51, fig. 8.4; 2. Richmond (1932) pl. xxxiii.4; 3. Iliffe (1934) pl. viii.3; 4. Tatcher, Nagar
             and Avshalom-Gorni (2002) 268, fig. 11.12; 5. McCown (1947) pl. iii.44; 6. Aliquot (2010) 279,
             figs. 2–5; 7. Braun, Dauphin and Hadas (1994) 112, fig. 5.9; 8. Macalister (1912) 1, 374, fig. 193; 9.
             Barag (1985); 10. Niccacci (1994) 275; 11. Jackson-Tal (2007) 62, fig. 3;
             12. Sellers and Baramki (1953) 23, fig. 24.1; 13. Makhouly (1939) pl. xxxii.h1).

populating late antique literary narratives.[94] It is hardly a coincidence that in the Armenian liturgical tradition, as an act of sealing the grave at the burial, the sign of the cross was made over the corpse by the priest performing the funeral service. The apotropaic significance of this polysemantic gesture is highlighted in the prayer recited by the priest while making the sign of the cross once more over the grave during the memorial service held at the site on the first day after burial, which includes a supplication to God to protect the dead from "impure demons".[95] Unsurprisingly, the liminal state between physical, earthly death and the judgement to come was regarded as a particularly dangerous condition by most late antique people. The services offered by the Church for Christians in the form of prayers for the departed soul and liturgical commemoration were but one means of helping the soul of the departed, even though this apparently did not satisfy all needs.[96]

Another important concern was the preservation of one's memory and the consolation of mourning relatives. Besides funerary monuments and inscriptions ensuring long-term memorialisation, the conservation of a pleasant memory of the dead relative for the short- and middle-term was promoted by constructing an ideal image of them during the brief period while they were laid in state.[97] In the views of the contemporaries, elegant garments and a pleasing appearance were believed to impart dignity to their wearers.[98] The performance of proper preparation of the dead for their burial offered consolation to the surviving relatives.[99]

Due to the prevalence of multiple burials and the high incidence of subsequent disturbances, it is difficult to associate the preserved personal adornments, mainly jewellery items and costume accessories, with single individuals or to analyse them according to age and sex groups. Still, the contents of the comparatively rare closed assemblages and the consistent appearance of the same artefact types – earrings, necklaces, beads, finger-rings, armbands, and belt buckles – in mortuary contexts shows that no fundamental changes had occurred since Roman times.[100] Nevertheless, this broad assertion should be refined in several respects in order

to avoid over-generalisation. To cite but two examples, the number of belt buckles in mortuary contexts significantly increased from the later 5th c. onward, and the apparent reluctance of Jewish communities to excessively beautify their deceased with several jewellery items seems to have continued into Late Antiquity.

After washing and anointing, the deceased were dressed in their garments. Belts and footwear were also included. Females were beautified with make-up and jewellery, their hairstyle was fixed with hairpins, combs, and hair-nets. It is difficult to say how elaborate these hairstyles generally were, but the majority of the known assemblages dated between the 4th and the 7th c. contain no more than one or two hairpins, and the presence of several pins is not particularly widespread.[101] However, before concluding too hastily, it should be emphasised that since hairnets made of textile as well as combs and hairpins manufactured of wood are preserved only under favourable climatic (micro)conditions, their presence was in all likelihood much more common than what can be gleaned from the archaeological record.[102] Besides these beautifying objects, females were accompanied with a few household items such as spindle whorls,[103] which praised female virtuousness and the dutiful life they lived for the good of their household.[104]

Reasonable objections against drawing such a general 'ideal image' of the 'beautiful dead' can be easily raised. The most immediate concerns the disproportionate distribution of associated artefacts among members of the burial populations of particular cemeteries. First, it seems quite clear that children and females in general were accorded different jewelleries, costume elements, and other artefacts much more frequently than males. Furthermore, the currently known single internments clearly show – and this is something that would have been otherwise expected with good reason – that the number of associated artefacts varied significantly from individual to individual: many were interred without any objects made of imperishable materials, others were furnished with but a few pieces, while a fairly small number of the deceased were bestowed with a

94   Cf. Kyriakakis (1974) 39–40; Dirkse (2014).

95   Schmidt (1994) 44–46, 93, 264.

96   Rebillard (2009) 153–75.

97   For this period, see Kyriakakis (1974) 49–59; Volp (2002) 176–85.

98   Joh. Chrys. *De inani gloria et de educandis liberis* 14–15.

99   *Pseudo-Chrysostomica, In Iob sermo 1.*; cf. also the discussion in Bollók (2020) 477–79.

100   For associated objects in Roman period Syria, see de Jong (2017) 77–101. For Palestine, see the patterns emerging from Kuhnen (1989) 49–72.

101   Tomb 2 at Ḥorbat Zikhrin with 20 bone hairpins: Haddad (2007) 53–54, fig. 11.

102   For hairnets, see the Near Eastern material introduced into her discussion of Egyptian hairnets and headgears by Linscheid (2010). Wooden combs: Doumar (Damascus): Al-Maqdissi and Hussami (1990) 466, fig. 7. Khirbat al-Dharih: Lenoble *et al.* (2001) 135–36, fig. 22.8. Migdal Ha-'Emeq: Tatcher and Gal (2009) 30*, fig. 20.9. Tall al-Sin: Montero Fenollós and al-Shbib (2008) pl. XLIV.3.

103   E.g. Waterhouse (1994) 298; Tal and Taxel (2015) 184, 186 fig. 3.6.

104   Cf. Taylor (2018) 178, 183.

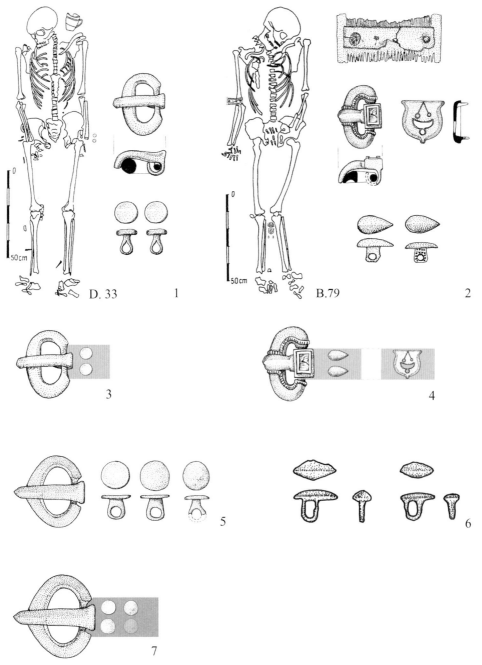

FIGURE 5   1–2. Graves D.33 and B.79 of the Piatra Frecăţei necropolis, Romania; 3–4. possible
reconstruction of the association of buckles and rivets of Graves D-33 and B.79; 5, 7. belt
buckle and flat rivets from 'Tomb B' of the Ḥorvat Karkur 'Illit church, Israel, and the possible
reconstruction of their association; 6. two lentil-shaped rivets from Sajur, Israel (drawing:
Magda Éber, after 1–4. Petre (1987) pl. 120–121; 5, 7. Nikolsky *et al.* (2004) 239, fig. 53.5, 244,
fig. 54.8; 6. Braun, Dauphin and Hadas (1994) fig. 5.6–7).

disproportionately large number of objects.[105] Since
the latter are often children, social display alone does
not explain their parents' behaviour, whose underlying reasons may be in the role ascribed to children, or
to these particular children, in these communities.
While the presence of associated artefacts provides the

clearest information on the care ancient people lavished
on their dead, we need to remember the ritual acts that
leave minimal or no traces in the material record and
the textile parts of the deceased's attire which, in the
majority of the cases, likewise disappear from mortuary contexts. These were invested with immense significance and, thus, the lack of associated artefacts should
by no means be interpreted as the burial community's

_____

105   Cf. Rose *et al.* (2004b) 129; Nabulsi *et al.* (2009) 170.

lack of concern for their departed loved ones or a lack of effort to present their 'ideal image' during the entire funeral process.

Another difficulty arises from the fact that the bulk of the excavated material originates from secondary contexts. Let me illustrate this point with a few eloquent examples. Flat, circular head rivets and lentil-shaped rivets, so-called *Gürtelhaften*, are frequent finds in south-western, western, and central European barbarian burial assemblages of the later 5th and 6th c.[106] Habitually, they were buried with the dead as belt accessories, used for securing the buckles worn by the deceased on the funeral bier. Thus, it would be tempting to assign the same function to the two lentil-shaped rivets from Loculus (Hebr. *kokh*) 2 of the Sajur tomb (Fig. 5.6). Doubly so, because a similar rivet was associated with a belt buckle in Tomb 2 at the nearby Khirbat al-Shubaika site.[107] However, cautionary remarks can also be made regarding this assumption. First, the majority of the cave's other finds date from the Roman period, even if objects assigned to the 5th or 6th c. were also found,[108] and thus the date of our rivets, described as 'buttons'[109] by the publishers, can only be established on typological grounds and based on the chronologies of faraway provinces.[110] Second, rivets with lentil-shaped and those with flat, circular heads were also discovered in Graves A83, B68, B79, and D33 as well as in 'Ritual Deposit' E277 of the Piatra Fracăței necropolis in the Lower Danube region (Fig. 5.1–4).[111] Their positions,

and those of the accompanying belt buckles, in general between the knees[112] suggest that either the belts were put into the grave as grave goods rather than as part of the funerary attire, or that the legs had been bound together by the belt in a ritual act.

But what conclusion can be drawn from the Sajur rivets, whose original position remains unknown, as does whether or not they were originally associated with a buckle? The situation is slightly better in the case of the 4 rivets with flat, circular heads (Fig. 5.5) discovered in 'Tomb B' of the Ḥorvat Karkur 'Illit church,[113] which were also accompanied by a buckle of Schulze-Dörrlamm's Class A9 (Fig. 5.5).[114] While neither the publication of the burials nor that of the finds provide any useful information on the position of the rivets and the buckle in the grave,[115] the anthropologists noted that all 5 were found "on the woman",[116] suggesting that they may indeed have been parts of a belt. One may also speculate that the two small copper-alloy rings "found partly covered with a fine tissue",[117] "near [the female's] right leg",[118] could perhaps also be associated with the woman's belt. Further sites, including Khirbat al-Samrā in Jordan, with its three rivets of the circular, flat head type accompanying

106 Cf. Martin (1989); Schulze-Dörrlamm (1990) 261–63.

107 Sajur: Braun, Dauphin and Hadas (1994) 112, fig. 5.6–7; Khirbat al-Shubaika: Tatcher, Nagar and Avshalom-Gorni (2002) 285, fig. 10.8.

108 E.g., Braun, Dauphin and Hadas (1994) 112 fig. 5.3, 5, 9. For a similar situation at Kisra, situated *ca.* 5 km from Sajur: Stern (1997) 122–24, figs. 12.47, 13.59, 17*.

109 Another type of 'button' known from a 3rd–4th c. tomb: Harding (1950) 88, no. 247, pl. XXVII. 247. For a further type of possibly later date, see Iliffe (1934) 15, pl. VIII.6. Yet, it may be noted that late antique 'buttons' constitute a problematic category of objects. Before the emergence of cast globular buttons with small attachment loops (cf. Badawi (2010) 272, fig. 10.4) sometime in the 6th–7th c., the majority of artefacts originating from late antique mortuary contexts described as 'buttons' are objects whose function cannot be easily established either on the strength of their form or of their position in the burial, and they are identified as 'buttons' mainly because it seems to be the best guess as to their function in a mortuary context, cf. Macalister (1912) 1, 316, pl. LXXVII.6; Figueras, Areal Guerra and Metz (2004) 233, nos. 3–4, fig. 52.3–4, 235, 239–40.

110 On the limitations of this approach, see the cautionary remarks of Fischer and Oenbrink (2010) 218.

111 Rivets with flat, circular head: Grave A83: Petre (1987) 63, pl. 112.167b; Grave D33: Petre (1987) 66, pl. 120.184f; 'Ritual Deposit' E277: Petre (1987) 62, pl. 111.166h. Rivets with lentil-shaped head: Grave B68: Petre (1987) 67, pl. 121.186c;

Grave B79: Petre (1987) 67, pl. 121.185d. The former class seems to be slightly earlier than the latter, since Grave A83 and 'Ritual Deposit' E277 can be dated to the last decades of the 5th and the first decades of the 6th c. on the basis of a buckle of Schulze-Dörrlamm's Class A11 in the former (Petre (1987) pl. 112.167c; Schulze-Dörrlamm (2002) 26) and another one of Class A9 in the latter (Petre (1987) pl. 111, 166g; Schulze-Dörrlamm (2002) 20), while Grave B79 can be assigned to the middle third/second half of the 6th c. on the strength of the buckle and the belt ornament of the assemblage (Petre (1987) pl. 121.185b–c). Circular- and lentil-shaped rivets made of precious metals and set with garnets, which served as models of our pieces, date from the later 5th c., cf. Schulze-Dörrlamm (1990) 261.

112 See Petre (1987) 63, 66–67, pl. 112.167a, 168a, pl. 121.185a.

113 The reports of the excavator (Figueras (2004) 60) and the anthropologists (Zias and Spigelman (2004) 308, 315) speak about 4 rivets discovered in the tomb, while the final publication of the finds mentions only three (Nikolsky *et al.* (2004) 241, no. 1, 239, fig. 53.5, 243, phot. 250). There are further apparent contradictions between the three reports, indicating the lack of final editing work on the contributions. The excavator knows of only two deceased buried in 'Tomb B' (Figueras (2004) 60), while the anthropologists speak about three adult males and an adult female laid to rest in the wooden coffin (Zias and Spigelman (2004) 308), even if another part of their paper lists only a male in his forties and a female in her twenties (Zias and Spigelman (2004) 313, table 1).

114 Nikolsky *et al.* (2004) 245, no. 29, 244, fig. 54.8, 240, 247.6.

115 Figueras (2004) 60; Nikolsky *et al.* (2004).

116 Zias and Spigelman (2004) 308.

117 Nikolsky *et al.* (2004) 239–41, no. 5, fig. 53.9, phot. 249.

118 Zias and Spigelman (2004) 308.

a belt buckle in Grave 498,[119] Darayya near Damascus in southern Syria, with its flat, hexagonal-shaped head rivet,[120] and Palmyra with its combination of circular head and lentil-shaped rivets associated with a later 6th c. buckle[121] also testify to the custom of fastening the leather straps of the belts with such rivets in Near Eastern contexts. Thus, they provide a context into which the Ḥorvat Karkur ʿIllit pieces (Fig. 5.5, 7), and perhaps the Sajur ones, can be fitted.

To be sure, circular and lentil-shaped rivets are exceptional cases due to their comparative rarity among Near Eastern mortuary finds and their possible use for more than one purpose. It may be rightly argued that the role of jewellery pieces and costume accessories can be more easily established, and, in the majority of cases, no serious objections can be raised as to the functions of these artefacts. Yet, we can easily miss the point if we do not take into account that mortuary contexts were created through a set of ritual actions, with even the most trivial objects potentially deposited for more than one reason. Wooden combs, for instance, could be worn by the deceased as an integral part of their coiffures, but they could likewise accompany the dead as grave goods.[122] The same holds true for jewellery pieces, although in the majority of instances when their positions in the excavated burials are recorded and known, they were indeed worn by the deceased. In a few instances, the metal attachments of wooden caskets also originate from mortuary contexts,[123] suggesting that certain objects found in the tombs may have accompanied the dead as grave goods rather than as items worn by the deceased laid on the bier. Of course, caskets could contain different sorts of artefacts and if their contents cannot be documented in the course of the excavation or their decoration does not provide clues as to their function, like that of a toilet casket discovered in one of the Khisfin graves does,[124] their purpose in the grave remains a matter of speculation.

It would also be instructive to know how long the carefully dressed and adorned dead were visible. We can be fairly certain that the most common approach was to bury the dead within a day after the onset of death, and if for one reason or another the body had to be kept

unburied for a longer period of time, a special conservation treatment was necessary.[125] However, the particulars of the deceased's appearance were not always visible to the wider community during the entire period between lying in state and the final internment. Literary texts,[126] lead coffins,[127] and the recurrent presence of wooden coffin fragments[128] and iron nails in graves and tombs seem to attest to the frequent use of coffins, which may or may not have concealed the dead from sight. Iron nails may have served different purposes: they could originate from wooden biers[129] or served apotropaic purposes in mortuary contexts.[130] Yet, the high percentage of multiple and looted burials again forms a serious obstacle to gaining a more nuanced understanding of their role in mortuary contexts. Additionally, mention must also be made of the written[131] and artistic records, which suggest that corpses were often wrapped in several layers of textile shrouds. As shown by a number of scenes illustrating the lament over the dead bodies of Deborah, Isaac, and Jacob by their families and the internments of Jacob and Rachel in the *Vienna Genesis*, a 6th-c. Syrian-Palestinian manuscript, possibly from Antioch itself,[132] the body was wrapped in textile shrouds fastened by bandages at some point after lying in state and lamentation, but before the funeral procession. This procedure resulted in bodies that resemble the late antique Egyptian 'mummies', whose wrapping methods can be studied in detail through the material record.[133] Still, as in Egypt, we have every reason to assume that the custom of wrapping the dead and of burying them in their funeral attire without additional wrapping were practiced simultaneously.

119   Nabulsi *et al.* (2011) 28–29, fig. 3.

120   Eger and Hamoud (2011) 73, fig. 6b–c, 75–76.

121   Assaʾd and Ruprechtsberger (1987) 142, fig. 9.

122   See the carved bone comb discovered among the ribs of the deceased in Grave D of Cemetery C2 at Khirbat al-Dharih: Lenoble *et al.* (2001) 135–36, fig. 22.8.

123   Kol-Yaʾakov and Farhi (2012) fig. 10.

124   Carved ivory plaques of a fairly large (30 cm × 10 cm) toilet casket decorated with images of the three Graces and a Nereid riding on a hippocampus: Sartre-Fauriat (2001) 83, fig. 114, 86.

125   As emphasised in one of the narratives preserved in the hagiographic texts relating to Daniel of Sketis, after Mark the Fool's death in Alexandria, his 'corpse was not buried for five days and they were forced to embalm blessed Mark's remains'. *V. Dan. Scet.* 3.

126   Joh. Chrys. *Hom. 27 in Matth.* 7.

127   Cf. Rahmani (1999).

128   Sakal (2010) 5.

129   Glimpses into the construction method of biers made of organic materials and their fate after the burial can only be gained from the archaeological evidence known from Egypt, where organic materials are far better preserved. For 'funerary beds' of late antique date (constructed without iron nails), which were used for carrying the deceased to the cemetery and were then buried with the dead, see Huber (2009).

130   As argued by Tal and Taxel (2015) 107, in the case of the Tel Barukh tombs, each of which yielded no more than one to three iron nails discovered in different locations and thus do not necessarily suggest the nails' utilitarian purpose.

131   Joh. Chrys. *Hom. 63. in Joh.* 2., *Hom. 85 in Joh.* 4, *Hom. 27 in Matth.* 7.

132   Österreichische Nationalbibliothek, *Cod. theol, gr.* 31, fol. 13v (Deborah and Rachel), fol. 14r (Isaac), fol. 24v (Jacob).

133   See Horak (1995) and Elisabeth O'Connell's paper in the present volume.

It is sometimes difficult to decide whether certain objects accompanied the dead as utensils used in mortuary rituals or as funerary offerings. Kohl and perfume containers are apparent cases in point since their general use continued even after the disappearance of several other glass vessel types. Other typical elements of 3rd to 4th c. assemblages such as glass plates, ewers, shallow and deep bowls, beakers, and cups containing food and drink offerings appear fairly rarely in mortuary contexts from the 5th, and even more from the 6th c. onwards, but the regular inclusion of jugs, jars, spherical flasks, and kohl tubes persists. A somewhat similar tendency was observed in other regions of the eastern and central Mediterranean, where the deposition of a single jar became the norm from the 6th c. This has been interpreted as a reflection of the Christian practice of pouring holy oil, water or wine over the dead body during the funeral liturgy and the subsequent placement of these vessels next to the dead.[134] Be that as it may, in the Near East, several glass vessels, including small jugs, jars, and flasks, were most probably filled with perfumed oils and creams,[135] which may have been employed for anointing the dead. However, anointing was chiefly performed at home. Since several glass vessels of this later date – like incense burners[136] – have sometimes been recovered from the central chambers of hypogea and rock-cut tombs,[137] it is tempting to presume that they were left there to mask the odour of decomposition. Still, this does not exclude the possibility that the ones placed beside the dead served multiple purposes.

While the contents of some of them veiled the smell of decay, they may also have been meant to serve the needs of the dead, together with other cosmetic containers (like kohl containers), while others could have been used for libations.[138] Finally, it cannot be entirely excluded that the ancient belief in the ritual pollution of everything that came into physical contact with the dead persisted during Late Antiquity. In the case of Jewish and Samaritan communities, the literary evidence seems to confirm the observance of this pollution taboo,[139] and there is no reason to assume that polytheist communities would have abandoned their old ways in this respect. Furthermore, even if Christianity's new anthropology is generally believed to have repudiated concerns about the polluting nature of death and dead

bodies,[140] we cannot be certain how deeply and universally the new teaching penetrated the wider circles of contemporary society and how long old habits persisted among less educated, ordinary Christians.

Multiple functions can also be ascribed to oil lamps, which are abundantly represented in the funerary record, even if the number of pieces placed directly next to the dead, on lamp-stands carved into the wall or in small niches[141] is not particularly high in most cases. Where dozens or even hundreds of lamps survive, the majority was found in the central chambers of rock-cut tombs and hypogea, and they are mostly of the same date and sometimes even of the same class.[142] Therefore, these pieces seem to have been left behind by the mourners sealing the tomb after the last interment or by family members who returned to perform certain post-funeral duties. Their practical function aside, it remains a matter of conjecture whether the lamps used during the funeral were considered as objects threatened with ritual pollution, whether they were seen as a means of warding off demons and providing the deceased with the light of eternal life,[143] or whether they perhaps combined all of these and other qualities.[144]

Conclusions

While this brief survey is doubtless too general, it is my hope that it illustrates the main lines of research[145] and the major limitations inherent in the nature of the material record. It most probably also conveys the monotony of a field without a sufficient number of stratified sites and the lack of involvement of osteoarchaeologists on a daily basis. Of course, specialists of physical anthropology and isotope analysis have made significant contributions, but these comparatively rare instances cannot

134   Vroom (2003) 139–41.
135   Cf. the evidence collected by de Jong (2017) 86.
136   Rahmani (1980); Taxel and Iserlis (2014).
137   Cf. Kogan-Zehavi (2006).
138   Cf. Rife (2012) 195–96.
139   Reich (1996) 33; but cf. Tal and Taxel (2015) 200.

140   Cf. Volp (2002) 240–63; Volp (2016/2017) 182.
141   Husseini (1935) pl. LXXXIV.4; Tal and Taxel (2015) 11, fig. 1.14.
142   E.g. Atara: Taha (2003) 90–97, Tab. 2. Gezer, Tombs 18, 99, 160, 193, 196 and 199: Macalister (1912) 1, 310, 338–39, 366–67, 375–77 3, pls. 72, 92–94, 110–12, 117–19; Hama, Tomb G 15: Ploug (1986) 10–103, 111–13. Jerusalem: Kogan-Zehavi (2006). Shilet al-Dhahr: Sellers and Baramki (1953); Tel Barukh, Tomb 2: Tal and Taxel (2015) 15, table 2. Tell en-Nasbeh, Tombs 19 and 22: McCown (1947) 116–22.
143   Menzel (1953); Seidel (2009) 90.
144   See also Tal and Taxel (2015) 198–99.
145   Disregarding a few notes and references, I deliberately refrained from entering into details regarding the ethnic interpretation of the mortuary record, an issue standing in the forefront in Levantine research, and attempted to concentrate on more general questions, mainly related to mortuary rituals. For the former research direction, see the methodologically sound attempts in Getzov and Stern (2006); Tal and Taxel (2015).

fill the gap left by the lack of routine in-depth analytical investigations. The habit of concentrating on the city of the living and leaving the dead to the dead, as Luke and Matthew's Jesus suggested to the young man aspiring to discipleship,[146] is not entirely unknown in other regions of the Mediterranean either. It would be pointless to deny that western academic interest creates demand in the eastern Mediterranean and that comparatively few Western European and North American archaeological projects focus their attention on late antique mortuary remains.[147] Those that do are often initiated and led by osteoarchaeologists and their results frequently remain inaccessible in their entirety to archaeologists. Since late antique monastic and church life and the material evidence related to them stand in the forefront of current academic interest, it is not surprising that one of the most developed fields is the analysis of monastic and church burials, while our knowledge of urban and rural necropolises largely rests on the results of field surveys, rescue excavations, and accidental discoveries made during urban excavations.

To be sure, by relying on the former class of evidence, several intriguing aspects of the changes in mortuary behaviour in the wake of Christianisation have indeed been detected. Yet, these results are sometimes also fraught with the danger of overshadowing other equally important traits. To mention but a single one, we may refer to the marked scarcity of cemetery churches from our region.[148] Although several factors could contribute to this state of affairs, such as the apparent concentration of mortuary sites in the southern Levant where, for quite understandable reasons, local Jewish and Samaritan populations did not erect such edifices, none of them explains their general scarcity. There is also surprisingly little unambiguous archaeological evidence for funerary and commemorative meals consumed at the actual burial sites, especially in the light of similar installations from more westerly provinces. A *stibadium* erected in the Tyros necropolis[149] is an apparent case in point, and while the bulk of the evidence provided by the regular presence of pottery sherds in graves and tombs could theoretically support an interpretation along these lines, their archaeological contexts are

very often less than certain. Unfortunately, due to the above-described high incidence of ancient and modern disturbance, it can rarely be established definitively how these ceramic sherds ended up in their places of discovery.[150] However, knowing that intact ceramic vessels are regularly encountered in better-preserved tomb assemblages, an in-depth evaluation of these finds scattered through individual publications will certainly contribute to a better understanding of this phenomenon.[151]

In spite of all these and other shortcomings inherent in the nature of the available material record, I am nevertheless inclined to conclude the present overview on a positive note. While it may seem as if I have placed an all too strong emphasis on the difficulties bedevilling late antique Near Eastern mortuary archaeology, the above discussion has hopefully highlighted some of the tasks and perspectives of future research, which can contribute to a deeper understanding of both the actual mortuary rituals and their changes over the *longue durée*. It is my belief that several patterns of late antique mortuary behaviour can be fairly accurately reconstructed if our analysis is based on a larger body of evidence and due emphasis is put on approaching it from a comparative perspective.

Bibliography

Primary Sources

Greg. Nyss., *Ep.* = A. Silvas transl. *Gregory of Nyssa: The Letters. Introduction, Translation and Commentary* (Supplements to VigChr 83) (Leiden and Boston 2007).

Ibn Khaldun, *Muqaddimah* = F. Rosenthal transl. Ibn Khaldûn: *The Muqaddimah. An Introduction to History*, vol. 2 (Bollingen Series 43) (New York 1958).

Joh. Chrys. De S. Droside martyre = PG. 50, 629–40. W. Mayer transl. *St John Chrysostom: The Cult of the Saints. Select Homilies and Letters* (Crestwood 2006) 158–76.

Joh. Chrys. Hom. in Joh. = PG 59. C. Marriott transl. John Chrysostom: *Homilies on the Gospel of St. John.* NPNF Ser. I, vol. 14 (New York 1890) 1–334.

Joh. Chrys. Hom. in Matth. = PG 57–58. G. Prevost transl. John Chrysostom: *Homilies on the Gospel of St. Matthew.* NPNF Ser. I, vol. 10 (New York 1888).

Joh. Chrys. De inani gloria et de educandis liberis = A.-M. Malingrey ed. and transl. Jean Chrysostome: *Sur la vaine gloire et l'éducation des enfants* (SC 188) (Paris 1972).

Pseudo-Chrysostomica, De morte = PG 63, 801–812.

---

146 Luke 9.60; Matthew 8.22.
147 To single out a few positive examples, see the excavations at Abila (Wineland (2001) 40–46), Faynan (Findlater *et al.* (1998)), Khirbat al-Samrā (n.15), and Yasilah, Ya'amun, and Sa'ad (see n.57; summaries of the anthropological work: Al-Muheisen and El-Najjar (1994); Rose, el-Najjar and Burke (2004); Rose, el-Najjar and Burke (2007)).
148 Cf., however, the discussion in Avni, Dahari and Kloner (2008b) 201–216.
149 Duval (1997) 149, fig. 9.

150 Cf. Tal and Taxel (2015) 201; Rife (2012) 196.
151 For a brief overview of previous arguments with the earlier literature, see Avshalom-Gorni (2000) 58*–60*.

Pseudo-Chrysostomica, In Iob sermo 1 = J. Oosterhuis-den Otter ed. and transl. *Four Pseudo-Chrysostomian Homilies on Job* (CPG 4564, BHG 939d–g). *Transmission, Critical Edition, and Translation* (Ph.D. diss., VU Univ., Amsterdam 2015) 212–25.

Sever. *De fide et lege naturae* = PG 48, 1081–88.

T. Sal. = D. C. Duling transl. Testament of Solomon, in *The Old Testament Pseudoepigrapha, vol. 1: Apocalyptic Literature and Testaments*, ed. J. H. Charlesworth (London 1983) 935–87.

V. Dan. Scet. = R. Greer transl. "The Greek accounts", in T. Vivian *et al.* (2008) *Witness to Holiness: Abba Daniel of Scetis: Translations of the Greek, Coptic, Ethiopic, Syriac, Armenian, Latin, Old Church Slavonic, and Arabic Accounts* (Cistercian Publications 219) (Kalamazoo 2008) 43–96.

Secondary Sources

Abadi-Reiss Y. and Eisenberg-Degen D. (2013) "Be'er Sheva', Balfour Street", ESI 125 (2013) http://www.hadashot-esi.org.il/Report_Detail_Eng.aspx?id=4375&mag_id=120.

Al-Houdalieh S. H. (2014) "Vandalised and looted, rock-cut tombs of the Roman and Byzantine periods: a case study from Saffa village, Ramallah province", PEQ 146 (2014) 224–40.

Al-Houdalieh S. H., Bernbeck R., Pollock S. (2017) "Palestinian looted tombs and their archaeological investigation", *Journal of Eastern Mediterranean Archaeology and Heritage Studies* 5 (2017) 198–239.

Aliquot J. (2010) "Une nouvelle citation du psaume 90 sur un bracelet de la region de Gabala (Jablé)", *Syria* 87 (2010) 277–79.

Al-Maqdissi M. and Hussami S. (1990) "Deux hypogées de l'époque byzantine (IVᵉ–Vᵉ s. après J.-C.) dans la region de Doumar", *Syria* 67 (1990) 465–66.

Al-Muheisen Z. (2008) "Archaeological excavations at the Yasileh site in Northern Jordan: the necropolis", *Syria* 85 (2008) 315–37.

Al-Muheisen Z. and El-Najjar M. (1994) "An anthropological study of the human remains from Yasileh: a classical site in Northern Jordan", *Mu'tah: Journal for Research and Studies* 9 (1994) 5–27.

Al-Salameen Z. and Falahat H. (2009) "Burials from Wadi Mudayfa'at and Wadi Abu Khasharif, Southern Jordan – results of a survey and salvage excavations", *Mediterranean Archaeology and Archaeometry* 9 (2009) 85–108.

Al-Samadi T. (2001) "Findings of the archaeological salvage excavations at Byzantine M'uta graveyard", *Newsletter of the Institute of Archaeology and Anthropology, Yarmouk University* 23 (2001) 24–26.

Altheeb D. (2015) "Funerary sculptures in the Tomb of Abedrapsas at Frikya", *ZOrA* 8 (2015) 236–49.

Assa'd K. and Ruprechtsberger E. M. (1987) "Palmyra in spätantiker, oströmischer (byzantinischer) und frühislamischer Zeit", in *Palmyra: Geschichte, Kunst und Kultur der syrischen Oasenstadt*, ed. E. M. Ruprechtsberger (Linz 1987) 137–48.

Avigad N. (1976) *Beth She'arim, vol. 3: Catacombs 12–23* (Jerusalem 1976).

Avni G. (1993) "Christian secondary use of Jewish burial caves in Jerusalem in the light of new excavations at the Aceldama tombs", in *Early Christianity in Context: Monuments and Documents* (Studium Biblicum Franciscanum, Collectio Maior 38), edd. F. Manns and E. Alliata (Jerusalem 1993) 265–76.

Avni G. (2010) "The Persian conquest of Jerusalem (614 C.E.) – an archaeological assessment", BASOR 357 (2010) 35–48.

Avni G., Dahari U., and Kloner A. (2008a) "The architecture and typology", in *The Necropolis of Bet Guvrin – Eleutheropolis* (Israel Antiquities Authority Reports 36), Avni G., Dahari U., and Kloner A. (Jerusalem 2008) 103–117.

Avni G., Dahari U., and Kloner A. (2008b) *The Necropolis of Bet Guvrin – Eleutheropolis* (Israel Antiquities Authority Reports 36) (Jerusalem 2008).

Avshalom-Gorni D. (2000) "A burial cave of the Byzantine period at Bet She'an", *'Atiqot* 39 (2000) 49*–60*, 198–200 (in Hebrew with English summary).

Badawi M. (2010) "La tombe protobyzantine d'al-Thawra dans l'arrière-pays de Gabala (Jablé, Syrie)", *Syria* 87 (2010) 265–75.

Bader N. *et al.* (2017) "New Greek inscriptions from Ḥirbet es-Samrā cemetery in north Jordan", ZDMG 133 (2017) 176–85.

Badre L. *et al.* (1994) "Rapport préliminaire sur les 4ᵉ–8ᵉ campagnes de fouilles (1988–1992)", *Syria* 71 (1994) 259–346.

Barag D. (1970) *Glass Vessels of the Roman and Byzantine Periods in Palestine* (Ph.D. diss., Hebrew Univ. of Jerusalem 1970) (in Hebrew).

Barag D. (1985) "Finds from a Tomb of the Byzantine Period at Ma'in", *Liber Annuus* 35 (1985) 367–74.

Bar'el A. (2002) "Ḥorbat Ma'aravim", HA/ESI 114 (2002) 121–22, 98*–99*.

Barkay G. (1997) "Politics – not religious law – rules ultra-Orthodox demonstrators", *BARev* 23 (1997) 56–57, 77.

Blétry S. (2012) "Les nécropoles de Halabiya-Zénobia. Premier résultats (2009 et 2010)", *Syria* 89 (2012) 305–330.

Bollók Á. (2013) "Apotropaion and burial in early Byzantium: some preliminary considerations", in *Byzanz und das Abendland: Begegnungen zwischen Ost und West*, ed. E. Juhász (Budapest 2013) 227–41.

Bollók Á. (2016) "The 'phylactery of the cross' and late antique/early Medieval mortuary practices in the eastern Mediterranean and on its fringes", in *GrenzÜbergänge: Spätrömisch, frühchristlich, frühbyzantinisch als Kategorien der historisch-archäologischen Forschung an der mittleren Donau* (Forschungen zu Spätantike und Mittelalter 4), edd. I. Bugarski, O. Heinrich-Tamáska, V. Ivanišević, and D. Syrbe (Remshalden 2016) 215–30.

Bollók Á. (2018) "Portable sanctity brought to the afterlife. Pilgrim eulogia as grave good in the late antique Eastern Mediterranean", in *Across the Mediterranean – Along the Nile. Studies in Egyptology, Nubiology and Late Antiquity dedicated to László Török on the Occasion of His 75th Birthday*, edd. T. A. Bács, Á. Bollók, and T. Vida (Budapest 2018) 763–803.

Bollók Á. (2020) "The Christianisation of the mortuary realm in the late antique Levant as seen through the written and the archaeological record", *ARAM* 32 (2020) 471–99.

Bollók Á. (forthcoming) "Mortuary display and the burial of the rich in the late antique eastern Mediterranean" (forthcoming).

Bradbury J. and Philip G. (2015) "The Invisible Dead Project: a methodology for 'coping' with the dead", in *How to Cope with the Dead: Mourning and Funerary Practices in the Ancient Near East* (Ricerchi di Archeologia de Vicino Oriente 5), ed. C. Felli (Florence 2015) 309–336.

Braun E., Dauphin C., and Hadas G. (1994) "A rock-cut tomb at Sajur", *'Atiqot* 24 (1994) 103–115.

Butler H. C. (1919–1920) *Syria: Publications of the Princeton University Archaeological Expeditions to Syria in 1904–5 and 1909, Division II: Architecture, Section A: Southern Syria; Section B: Northern Syria* (Leyden 1919–1920).

Canova R. (1954) *Iscrizioni e monumenti protocristiani del paese di Moab* (Sussidi allo studio delle antichità cristiane 4) (Vatican City 1954).

Charpentier G. (2013) "L'architecture funéraire", in *Serğilla. Village d'Apamène* 1: *Une architecture de pierre*, 3 vols (*BAHBeyrouth* 203), edd. G. Tate *et al.* (Beirut and Damascus 2013) 451–73.

Chéhab M. (1984) *Fouille de Tyr. La nécropole II: description des fouilles, premiére part: au sud de la route: complexes I–XXII* (BMusBeyr 34) (Paris 1984).

Chéhab M. (1985) *Fouille de Tyr, la nécropole III: description des fouilles, deuxiéme part: au nord de la route: complexe XXIII–XL* (BMusBeyr 35) (Paris 1985).

Chéhab M. (1986) *Fouille de Tyr, la nécropole IV: description des fouilles* (BMusBeyr 36) (Paris 1986).

Clermont-Ganneau C. (1896–1899) *Archaeological Researches in Palestine during the Years 1873–1874*, 2 vols (London 1896–1899).

da Costa K. (2001) "Byzantine and early Islamic lamps: typology and distribution", in *La céramique byzantine et proto-islamique en Syrie-Joradanie (IVe–VIIIe siècles apr. J.-C.)* (BAHBeyrouth 159), edd. E. Villeneuve and P. M. Watson (Beirut 2001) 241–57.

Dahari U. and Di Segni L. "More early Christian inscribed tombstones from el-Huweinat in northern Sinai", in *Man Near a Roman Arch. Studies Presented to Prof. Yoram Tsafrir*, edd. L. Di Segni, Y. Hirschfeld, J. Patrich, and R. Talgam (Jerusalem 2009) 125–41.

de Jong L. (2010) "Performing death in Tyre: the life and afterlife of a Roman cemetery in the province of Syria", *AJA* 114 (2010) 597–630.

de Jong L. (2017) *The Archaeology of Death in Roman Syria. Burial, Commemoration, and Empire* (Cambridge 2017).

de Vogüe C. (1865–1877) *Syrie centrale. Architecture civile et religieuse du Ier au VIIe siècle*, 2 vols (Paris 1895–1877).

Desreumaux A. (1998) "Les inscriptions funéraires araméennes de Samra", in *Khirbet es-Samra en Jordanie 1: La voie romaine, le cimitière, les documents épigraphiques* (Bibliothèque de l'Antiquité Tardive 1), edd. J.-B. Humbert and A. Desreumaux (Turnhout 1998) 435–509.

Desreumaux A. and Couson D. (1998) "Catalogue des stèles funéraires", in *Khirbet es-Samra en Jordanie 1: La voie romaine, le cimitière, les documents épigraphiques* (Bibliothèque de l'Antiquité Tardive 1), edd. J.-B. Humbert and A. Desreumaux (Turnhout 1998) 281–316.

Dirkse S. (2014) "Τελωνεῖα: the tollgates of the air as an Egyptian motif in patristic sources and early Byzantine hagiography", in *Medieval Greek Storytelling: Fictionality and Narrative in Byzantium* (Mainzer Veröffentlichungen zur Byzantinistik 12), ed. P. Roilis (Wiesbaden 2014) 41–53.

Duval N. (1997) "Le lit semi-circulaire de repas: une invention d'Hélagabale (Hel. 25, 1.2–3)", in *Historiae Augustae Colloquium Bonnense* (Bistoriae Augustae Colloquia 5), edd. G. Bonamente and K. Rosen (Bari 1997) 129–52.

Egea Vivancos A. (2004) "Costumbres funerarias en el Alto Éufrates sirio durante época romana y bizantina", *HuelvaArq* 20 (2004) 89–114.

Egea Vivancos A. (2005) *Eufratense et Osrhoene: problemiento romano en el Alto Éufrates sirio* (Antigüedad y Christianismo 22) (Murcia 2005).

Eger C. and Hamoud M. (2011) "Spätrömisch-frühbyzantinischer Grabbrauch in Syrien. Die Nekropole von Darayya bei Damaskus", *Antike Welt* 42 (2011) 70–76.

Eger C., Nabulsi A., and Ahrens A. (2011) "Ein spätrömisches Grab mit einem Glasbecher E. 216 und einem Skarabäus aus Jordan – Khirbet es-Shamra, Grab 310", *KölnJb* 44 (2011) 215–31.

Ergeç R. (2003) *Nekropolen und Gräber in der südlichen Kommagene* (Asia Minor Studien 47) (Bonn 2003).

Eldar I. and Nahlieli D. (1982) "Tel Malḥata", *ESI* 1 (1982) 67–69.

Falcioni P. and Severini F. (2006) "In margine alla ricerca sulle porte basaltiche siriane", *Temporis Signa* 1 (2006) 353–74.

Figueras P. (2004) "The tombs", in *Ḥorvat Karkur 'Illit: A Byzantine Cemetery Church in the Northern Negev* (Final Report of the Excavations 1989–1995) (Beer-Sheva Archaeological Monographs 1), ed. P. Figueras (Beer-Sheva 2004) 55–68.

Figueras P., Areal Guerra R., and Metz V. (2004) "Bone, leather and other materials mostly found in tombs", in *Ḥorvat Karkur 'Illit: A Byzantine Cemetery Church in the Northern Negev* (Final Report of the Excavations 1989–1995)

(Beer-Sheva Archaeological Monographs 1), ed. P. Figueras (Beer-Sheva 2004) 232–36.

Findlater G. *et al.* (1998) "The Wadi Faynan project: the south cemetery excavation, Jordan, 1996: a preliminary report", *Levant* 30 (1998) 69–83.

Fisher T. (2010) "Zu spätantik-frühbyzantinischen Grabbeigaben aus Qrayya/Hauran", in *Hauran V: la Syrie du Sud du néolithique à l'antiquité tardive* (BAHBeyrouth 191), edd. M. al-Maqdissi, F. Braemer, and J.-M. Denzter (Beirut 2010) 497–504.

Fisher M. (2012) "The early Islamic cemetery", in *Ḥorvat Meṣad: A Way-station on the Jaffa-Jerusalem Road* (*Tel Aviv University Sonia and Marco Nadler Institute of Archaeology Monograph Series* 30), ed. M. Fisher (Tel Aviv 2012) 56–60.

Fischer T. and Oenbrink W. (2010) "Spätantik-byzantinische Grabfunde aus al-Qrayya im Hauran/Südsyrien", *KölnJb* 43 (2010) 197–243.

FitzGerald G. M. (1932) "Excavations at Beth-Shan in 1931", *Palestine Exploration Fund Quarterly Statement for 1932* [64] (1932) 138–48.

Fleck V. (n.d.) "The Late Antique Tombs of the Northern Cemetery at Beth Shean", https://static1.squarespace.com/static/534849e8e4b0dd67a1620643/t/5370f2cfe4b02080 8025ebc3/1399911119974/Northern+Cemetery+fleck.pdf.

Fleckenstein K. H. and Fleckenstein L. (2005) *Emmaus-Nicopolis: Ausgrabungen 2001–2005* (Neckenmarkt 2005).

Ganor A. (2003) "Antiquities robbery in Israel", *HA/ESI* 115 (2003) 93–94, 68*–70*.

Gatier P.-L. (1998) "Les inscriptions grecques et latines de Samra et de Rihab", in *Khirbet es-Samra en Jordanie 1: La voie romaine, le cimitière, les documents épigraphiques* (Bibliothèque de l'Antiquité Tardive 1), edd. J.-B. Humbert and A. Desreumaux (Turnhout 1998) 359–431.

Ghadban C. (1985) "Monuments de Hammara (Béqa'-Sud, Liban). *Nova et vetera*", *Ktema* 10 (1985) 287–309.

Goldfus H. (1997) *Tombs and Burials in Churches and Monasteries of Byzantine Palestine (324–628 A.D.)* (Ph.D. diss., Princeton 1997).

Gorin-Rosen Y. and Winter T. (2010) "Selected insights into Byzantine glass in the Holy Land", in *Glass in Byzantium: Production, Usage, Analysis*, edd. J. Drauschke and D. Keller (Mainz 2010) 165–81.

Govrin Y. (2003) "Be'er Sheva'", *HA/ESI* 115 (2003) 88–89, 65*–66*.

Gregg R. C. and Urman D. (1996) *Jews, Pagans, and Christians in the Golan Heights. Greek and Other Inscriptions of the Roman and Byzantine Eras* (*South Florida Studies in the History of Judaism* 140) (Atlanta 1996).

Greisheimer M. (1997) "Cimetières et tombeaux des villages de la Syrie du nord", *Syria* 74 (1997) 165–211.

Grossschmidt K. and Tutschek H. (2005) "Anthropologische Aussagen und ein mikroradiographischer Nachweis von Brandspuren", in *Emmaus-Nicopolis: Ausgrabungen 2001–*

2005, K. H. Fleckenstein and L. Fleckenstein (Neckenmarkt 2005) 404–435.

Haddad E. (2007) "A burial cave from the first–second centuries CE and double-arcosolia tombs from the fourth–fifth centuries CE on the fringes of Ḥorbat Zikhrin", *'Atiqot* 56 (2007) 25–57, 74*–75* (in Hebrew with English summary).

Harding G. L. (1950) "A Roman family vault on Jebel Jofeh, 'Amman", *QDAP* 14 (1950) 81–94.

Hartal M. *et al.* (2009) "The northern cemeteries", in *Panias IV: The Aqueduct and the Northern Suburbs* (Israel Antiquities Authority Reports 40), ed. M. Hartal (Jerusalem 2009) 111–42.

Hirschfeld Y. (1992) *The Judean Desert Monasteries in the Byzantine Period* (New Haven and London 1992).

Holumn K. (2003) "Constructing the past in cities of Byzantine Palestine", in *One Hundred Years of American Archaeology in the Middle East*, edd. D. R. Clark and W. H. Matthews (Boston 2003) 351–64.

Horak U. (1995) "Kopische Mumien. Die koptische Tote in Grabungsberichten, Funden und literarischen Nachrichten", *Biblos* 44 (1995) 39–71.

Huber B. (2009) "The funerary beds from the monastic cemetery at el-Ghalida (el-Kom el-Ah. mar/Šaruna)", in *Clothing the House. Furnishing Textiles of the 1st Millennium AD from Egypt and Neighbouring Countries*, edd. A. De Moor and C. Fluck (Tielt 2009) 57–72.

Humbert J.-B. (1998) "Le cimitière de Samra. Présentation historique et archéologique", in *Khirbet es-Samra en Jordanie 1: La voie romaine, le cimitière, les documents épigraphiques* (Bibliothèque de l'Antiquité Tardive 1), edd. J.-B. Humbert and A. Desreumaux (Turnhout 1998) 259–70.

Husseini S. A. (1935) "A fourth-century A.D. tomb at Beit Fajjār", *QDAP* 4 (1935) 175–77.

Ibrahim M. M. and Gordon R. L. (1987) *A Cemetery at Queen Alia International Airport* (Yarmouk University Publications, Institute of Archaeology and Anthropology Series 1) (Wiesbaden 1987).

Iliffe J. H. (1934) "Rock-cut tomb at Tarshīhā", *QDAP* 3 (1934) 9–16.

Jackson-Tal R. (2007) "Early Roman and early Byzantine glass vessel from T2 and T4 near Ḥorbat Zikhrin", *'Atiqot* 56 (2007) 59–63, 76*.

Jackson-Tal R. (2015) "Glass vessels", in Tal and Taxel (2015) 182–84.

Johnson K. L. (2004) "Sa'ad tomb types", in *Sa'ad: A Late Roman/Byzantine Site in Northern Jordan*, edd. J. C. Rose and D. L. Burke (Irbid 2004) 109–111.

Knauf E. A. (1986) "Three new tombstones from Feinan", *Newsletter of the Institute of Archaeology and Anthropology, Yarmouk University* 2 (1986) 16–17.

Kogan-Zehavi E. (1998) "The tomb and memorial of a chain-wearing anchorite at Kh. Tabaliya, near Jerusalem", *'Atiqot* 35 (1998) 135–49.

Kogan-Zehavi E. (2006) "A burial cave of the Byzantine period in the Naḥalat Aḥim Quarter, Jerusalem", 'Atiqot 54 (2006) 61*–86*, 160–161 (Hebrew with English summary).

Kol-Ya'akov S. (2010) "The cemetery", in Salvage Excavations at Neshar – Ramla Query, vol. 1, ed. S. Kol-Ya'akov (Haifa 2010) 103–119.

Kol-Ya'akov S. and Farhi Y. (2012) "Asqelon (al-Nabi Ḥussein): evidence for the burial of Jews, Christians and pagans in a late Roman-period burial ground", 'Atiqot 70 (2012) 87–111, 88 (in Hebrew with English summary).

Krug H. P. (1998) "Comparative Roman-Byzantine tombs in Transjordan", in The Necropolis of Hesban: A Typology of Tombs (Hesban 10), D. Waterhouse (Berrien Springs 1998) 133–71.

Kuhnen H.-P. (1987) Nordwest-Palästina in hellenistisch-römischer Zeit. Bauten und Gräber in Karmelgebiet (Quellen und Forschungen zur prähistorischen und provinzialrömischen Archaäologie 1) (Weinheim 1989).

Kuhnen H.-P. (1989) Studien zur Chronologie und Siedlungsarchäologie des Karmel (Israel) zwischen Hellenismus und Spätantike, 3 vols (Beihefte zum Tübingener Atlas des Vorderen Orients B.72) (Wiesbaden 1989).

Kuhnen H.-P. (1990) Palästina in griechisch-römischer Zeit (Handbuch der Archäologie, Vorderasien II.2) (Munich 1990).

Künzl E. and Weber T. M. (1991) "Das spätantike Grab eines Zahnarztes zu Gadar in der Dekapolis", DamMitt 5 (1991) 81–118.

Kyriakakis J. (1974) "Byzantine burial customs: care of the deceased from death to the prosthesis", Greek Orthodox Theological Review 19 (1974) 37–72.

Lauffray J. (1991) Ḥalabiyya-Zenobia. Place forte du limes oriental et la Haute-Mésopotamie au VIᵉ siècle, vol. 2 (BAHBeyrouth 138) (Paris 1991).

Lenoble P. et al. (2001) "Fouilles de Khirbet Edh-Dharih (Jordanie), I : le cimetière au sud du Wadi Sharheh", Syria 78 (2001) 89–151.

Linscheid P. (2010) Frühbyzantinische textile Kopfbedeckungen: Typologie, Verbreitung, Chronologie und soziologischer Kontext nach Originalfunden (Spätantike – frühes Christentum – Byzanz B.30) (Wisebaden 2010).

Lohmann H. (2017) "Die Mykale in Kaiserzeit, Spätantike und frühbyzantinischer Zeit", in Forschungen in der Mykale, vol. 1.1: Survey in der Mykale (Dilek Daglan/Aydin) 2001–2009: Landeskunde eines westkleinasiatischen Gebirgszuges vom Chalkolithikum bis in spätosmanische Zeit, vol. 1, edd. H. Lohmann, G. Kalaitzoglou, and G. Lüdorf (Asia Minor Studien 77.1) (Bonn 2017) 237–74.

Macalister R. A. S. (1912) The Excavation of Gezer, 1902–1905 and 1907–1909, 3 vols (London 1912).

Magness J. (1993) Jerusalem Ceramic Chronology, Circa 200–800 CE (Sheffield 1993).

Magness J. (2003) "The Byzantine and Islamic periods – the fourth century through modern times", in One Hundred Years of American Archaeology in the Middle East, edd. D. R. Clark and W. H. Matthews (Boston 2003) 345–49.

Makhouly N. (1939) "Rock-cut tombs at el Jīsh", QDAP 8 (1939) 45–50.

Martin M. (1989) "Bemerkungen zur chronologischen Gliederung der fürhen Merowingerzeit", Germania 67 (1989) 121–41.

Mazar B. (1973) Beth She'arim, vol. 1: Catacombs 1–4 (Jerusalem 1973).

McCown C. (1947) Tell en-Naṣbeh, vol 1: Archaeological and Historical Results (Berkeley and New Haven 1947).

McCormick M. (2015) "Tracking mass death during the fall of Rome's empire I", JRA 28 (2015) 325–57.

McCormick M. (2016) "Tracking mass death during the fall of Rome's empire (II): a first inventory of mass graves", JRA 29 (2016) 1004–1046.

Menzel H. (1953) "Lampen im römischen Totenkult", in Festschrift des Römisch-Germanischen Zentralmuseums in Mainz zur Feier seines hundertjährigen Bestehens 1952, vol. 3, ed. H. Klumbach (Mainz 1953) 131–38.

Montero Fenollós J. L. and al-Shbib S. edd. (2008) La necrópolis bizantina de Tall as-Sin (Deir ez-Zor, Siria). (Memorias del Proyecto Arqueológico Medio Éufrates Sirio 1) (Madrid 2008).

Nabulsi A. (1998) "The Byzantine cemetery in Samra", in Khirbet es-Samra en Jordanie 1: La voie romaine, le cimitière, les documents épigraphiques (Bibliothèque de l'Antiquité Tardive 1), edd. J.-B. Humbert and A. Desreumaux (Turnhout 1998) 271–79.

Nabulsi A. (2010) "Khirbat as-Samrā cemetery: Site E, season 2009", ADAJ 54 (2010) 217–19.

Nabulsi A., Husan A., and Schönrock-Nabulsi P. (2013) "The 2012 seasons of excavations in the ancient Khirbat as-Samrā cemetery", ADAJ 57 (2013) 551–57.

Nabulsi A. and Macdonald M. C. A. (2014) "Epigraphic diversity in the cemetery at Khirbet es-Samrāʾ, Jordan", PEQ 146 (2014) 149–61.

Nabulsi A. et al. (2007) "The ancient cemetery in Khirbat as-Samrā after the sixth season of excavation (2006)", ADAJ 51 (2007) 273–81.

Nabulsi A. et al. (2008) "The 2007 season of excavations at Khirbat as-Samrā ancient cemetery", ADAJ 52 (2008) 203–207.

Nabulsi A. et al. (2009) "Khirbat as-Samrā ancient cemetery: preliminary discussion of Site C", ADAJ 53 (2009) 167–72.

Nabulsi A. et al. (2010) "Excavation at the Blakhiya Byzantine cemetery in Gaza, 1996", RBibl 117 (2010) 602–613.

Nabulsi A. et al. (2011) "The ancient cemetery of Khirbat as-Samrā: 2010 excavations at site A2", ADAJ 5 (2011) 25–31.

Newson P. (2015) "Greco-Roman burial practices in the Bekaa Valley, Lebanon, and its adjacent uplands", Journal of

Eastern Mediterranean Archaeology and Heritage Studies 3 (2015) 349–71.

Niccacci A. (1994) "Un scarabeo in una tomba bizantina", in *Umm al-Rasas – Mayha'ah*, vol. 1: *Gli scavi del complesso di Santo Stefano*, M. Piccirillo and E. Alliata (*Studium Biblicum Franciscanum, Collectio Maior* 28) (Jerusalem 1994) 275–76.

Nikolsky V. *et al.* (2004) "Metal objects", in *Ḥorvat Karkur 'Illit: A Byzantine Cemetery Church in the Northern Negev* (*Final Report of the Excavations 1989–1995*) (Beer-Sheva Archaeological Monographs 1), ed. P. Figueras (Beer-Sheva 2004) 237–64.

Nagar Y. and Sonntag F. (2008) "Byzantine period burials in the Negev: anthropological descriptions and summary", *IEJ* 58 (2008) 79–93.

Parker T. S. (1999) "An empire's new Holy Land: the Byzantine period", *NEA* 62 (1999) 134–80.

Peña I., Castellana F., and Fernández R. (1987) *Inventaire du Jébel Baricha. Recherches archéologiques dans la region des Villes Mortes de la Syrie du Nord* (*Studium Biblicum Franciscanum, Collectio Minor* 33) (Jerusalem 1987)

Peña I., Castellana F., and Fernández R. (1990) *Inventaire du Jébel al-A'la. Recherches archéologiques dans la region des Villes Mortes de la Syrie du Nord* (*Studium Biblicum Franciscanum, Collectio Minor* 31) (Jerusalem 1990)

Peña I., Castellana F., and Fernández R. (1999) *Inventaire du Jébel Wastani. Recherches archéologiques dans la region des Villes Mortes de la Syrie du Nord* (*Studium Biblicum Franciscanum, Collectio Minor* 36) (Jerusalem 1999).

Peña I., Castellana F., and Fernández R. (2003) *Inventaire du Jébel Doueili. Recherches archéologiques dans la region des Villes Mortes de la Syrie du Nord* (*Studium Biblicum Franciscanum, Collectio Minor* 43) (Jerusalem 2003).

Peleg M. (1991) "Persian, Hellenistic and Roman burials at Loḥamei HaGeta'ot", *'Atiqot* 20 (1991) 131–52.

Peterson-Solimani M., Soliman G., and Weiss D. (2001) "Ḥorbat Gader", *HA/ESI* 113 (2001) 110–113, 73*–74*.

Petit L. (2013) "Recycling the valley: preliminary reports of the 2012 excavations at Tall Dāmiyah", *ADAJ* 57 (2013) 239–46.

Petre A. (1987) *La romanité en Scythie Mineure (IIᵉ–VIIᵉ siècles de notre ère). Recherches archéologiques* (Bucharest 1987).

Ploug G. (1986) "The Graeco-Roman necropolis", in *Hama. Fouilles et recherches 1931–1938*, vol. III.3: *The Graeco-Roman Objects of Clay, the Coins and the Necropolis*, A. Papanicolaou Christensen, R. Thomsen, and G. Ploug (Copenhagen 1986) 70–113.

Politis K. (1998) "Survey and rescue collections in the Ghawr al-Ṣāfī", *ADAJ* 42 (1998) 627–33.

Rahmani L. Y. (1980) "Palestinian incense burners of the sixth to eighth centuries C.E.", *IEJ* 30 (1980) 116–22.

Rahmani L. Y. (1999) *A Catalogue of Roman and Byzantine Lead Coffins from Israel* (Jerusalem 1999).

Rebillard É. (2009) *The Care of the Dead in Late Antiquity*, transl. E. Trapnell Rawlings and J. Routier-Pucci (*Cornell Studies in Classical Philology* 59) (Ithaca and London 2009).

Reich R. (1996) "'God knows their names'. Mass Christian grave revealed in Jerusalem", *BARev* 22 (1996) 26–33.

Renan E. (1864) *Mission de Phénicie*, 2 vols (Paris 1864).

Richmond E. T. (1932) "A rock-cut tomb at Nazareth", *QDAP* 1 (1932) 53–54.

Rife J. (2012) *The Roman and Byzantine Graves and Human Remains* (*Isthmia* 9) (Princeton 2012).

Rose J. C. and Burke D. L. (2004) "Making money from buried treasures", *Culture Without Context* 14 (2004) 4–8.

Rose J. C., Burke D. L., and Johnson K. L. (2004) "Tombs", in *Sa'ad: A Late Roman/Byzantine Site in Northern Jordan*, edd. J. C. Rose and D. L. Burke (Irbid 2004) 99–108.

Rose J. C., el-Najjar M., and Burke D. L. (2004) "Trade and the acquisition of wealth in rural late antique north Jordan", *Studies in the History and Archaeology of Jordan* 9 (2004) 61–70.

Rose J. C. *et al.* (2004a) "Cemeteries and Contents", in *Sa'ad: A Late Roman/Byzantine Site in Northern Jordan*, edd. J. C. Rose and D. L. Burke (Irbid 2004) 43–98.

Rose J. C. *et al.* (2004b) "Artifacts", in *Sa'ad: A Late Roman/Byzantine Site in Northern Jordan*, edd. J. C. Rose and D. L. Burke (Irbid 2004) 115–48.

Rose J. C., el-Najjar M., and Burke D. L. (2007) "Bioarchaeology of Northern Jordan. A decade of cooperative American and Jordanian student research", in *Crossing Jordan. Northern American Contributions to the Archaeology of Jordan*, edd. T. E. Levy *et al.* (London and Oakville 2007) 419–26.

Rowe A. (1927a) "The discoveries at Beth-Shan during the 1926 season", *The Museum Journal* 18 (1927) 9–45.

Rowe A. (1927b) "Excavations in Palestine. The new discoveries at Beth-Shan", *Palestine Exploration Fund Quarterly Statement for 1927* [59] (1927) 67–84.

Rowe A. (1930) *The Topography and History of Beth-Shean* (*Publications of the Palestine Section of the Museum of the University of Pennsylvania* 1) (Philadelphia 1930).

Rudin T. *et al.* (2018) "Two burial caves at Kefar Shemaryahu: More on Samaritan and Christian interactions in the Byzantine-period Central Coastal Plain", *Liber Annuus* 68 (2018) 269–302.

Russo J. D. (2015) "Tomb tracking: a new burial survey of Roman Galilee (1st–6th cent. CE)", *The Ancient Near East Today: Current News About the Ancient Past* 3 (2015) 1–6.

Sakal F. (2010) "Graves and grave goods of the late Roman and medieval cemeteries", in *Emar after the Enclosure of the Tabqa Dam: The Syrian-German Excavations 1996–2002*, vol. 1: *Late Roman and Medieval Cemeteries and Environmental Studies* (Subartu 25), edd. U. Finkbeiner and F. Sakal (Turnhout 2010) 3–52.

Sartre A. (1989) "Architecture funéraire de la Syrie", in *Archeologie et histoire de la Syrie*, vol. 2: *La Syrie de l'époque achéménide à l'avènement de l'Islam* (Schriften zur vorderasiatischen Archäologie 1), edd. J.-M. Dentzer and W. Orthmann (Saarbrücken 1989) 423–46.

Sartre-Fauriat A. (2001) *Des tombeaux et des morts: monuments funéraires, société et culture en Syrie du Sud du Ier s. av. J.-C. au VIIe s. apr. J.-C*, 2 vols (*BAHBeyrouth* 158) (Beirut 2001).

Sartre-Fauriat A. and Sartre M. (2016) *Inscriptions grecques et latines de la Syrie*, vol. 14: *Le Batanée et le Jawlān oriental*, 2 vols (*BAHBeyrouth* 207) (Beirut 2016).

Schmidt A. (1994) *Kanon der Entschlafenen. Das Begräbnisrituale der Armenier. Der altarmenische Bastattungsritus für die Laien* (*Orientalia Biblica et Christiana* 5) (Wiesbaden 1994).

Schulze-Dörrlamm M. (1990) *Die spätrömischen und frühmittelalterlichen Gräberfelder von Gondorf, Gem. Kobern-Gondorf, Kr. Mayen-Koblenz*, 2 vols (*Germanische Denkmäler der Völkerwanderungszeit* B.14) (Stuttgart 1990).

Schulze-Dörrlamm M. (2002) *Byzantinische Gürtelschnallen und Gürtelbeschläge im Römisch-Germanischen Zentralmuseum*, vol. 1: *Die Schnallen ohne Beschläge, mit Laschenbeschläge und mit festem Beschläg des 5. bis 7. Jahrhunderts* (*Katalog vor- und frühgeschichtlicher Altertümer* 30) (Mainz 2002).

Schwabe M. and Lifschitz B. (1974) *Beth She'arim, vol. 2: The Greek Inscriptions* (Jerusalem 1974).

Shiloh D. (1997) "Fierce protest over bones threatens to halt archaeology in Israel", *BARev* 23 (1997) 54–55, 76–77.

Seidel Y. (2009) *Künstliches Licht im individuellen, familiären und öffentlichen Lebensbereich* (Vienna 2009).

Séiquer G. M. and Carrillo J. G. (1998) "Urbanismo: ciudades y necrópolis", in *Romanización y christianismo en la Síria mesopotamica*, edd. G. M. Séiquer and J. G. Carrillo (Antigüedad y Christianismo 15) (Murcia 1998) 247–98.

Sellers O. R. and Baramki D. C. (1953) "A Roman-Byzantine burial cave in Northern Palestine", *BASOR Supplementary Studies* 15–16 (1953) 1–5, 7–55.

Shumka L., Olsen J. P., and Ramsay J. (2013) "Tomb groups", in *Humayma Excavation Project*, vol. 2: *Nabatean Campground and Necropolis, Byzantine Churches, and Early Islamic Domestic Structures* (American School of Oriental Research Archaeological Reports 18), edd. J. P. Olsen and R. Schick (Boston 2013) 381–401.

Skupinska-Løvset I. (1983) *Funerary Portraiture of Roman Palestine. An Analysis of the Production in its Culture-Historical Context* (*Studies in Mediterranean Archaeology, Pocket Book* 21) (Gothenburg 1983).

Smith R. W. (1992) "Secondary use of the necropoleis of the Decapolis", *Aram* 4 (1992) 215–28.

Sodini J.-P. (1986) "Les tombes privilégiées dans l'orient chrétien (à l'exception du diocèse d'Égypte)", in *L'inhumation privilégiée du IVe au VIIIe siècle en Occident: actes du colloque tenu à Créteil les 16–18 mars 1984*, edd. Y. Duval and J.-Ch. Picard (Paris 1986) 233–43.

Sonntag F. and Zelin A. (2002) "Ḥorbat Liqit", *HA/ESI* 114 (2002) 120–121, 97*–98*.

Stander H. F. (2009) "Theft and robbery in Chrysostom's time", *Acta Theologica* 29 (2009) 74–85.

Stern E. J. (1997) "Burial caves at Kisra", *'Atiqot* 33 (1997) 103–135, 17 (in Hebrew, with English summary).

Stern E. J. and Getzov N. (2006) "Aspects of Phoenician burial customs in the Roman period in light of an excavation near el-Kabri (Kabri)", *'Atiqot* 51 (2006) 91–123.

Sussman V. (1976) "A burial cave at Kefar 'Ara", *'Atiqot* 11 (1976) 92–101.

Sussman V. (2017) *Late Roman to Late Byzantine/Early Islamic Period Lamps in the Holy Land: The Collection of the Israel Antiquities Authority* (Oxford 2017).

Syon D. 1995 "Nuris", *ESI* 14 (1995) 73.

Taha H. (2003) "A Byzantine tomb at Atara", in *One Land – Many Cultures: Archaeological Studies in Honour of Stanislao Loffreda OFM* (*Studium Biblicum Franciscanum, Collectio Maior* 41), edd. G. C. Bottini, L. Di Segni, and L. D. Chrupcała (Jerusalem 2003) 87–110.

Tal O. (1995) "Roman-Byzantine cemeteries and tombs around Apollonia", *Tel Aviv* 22 (1995) 107–120.

Tal O. and Taxel I. (2015) *Samaritan Cemeteries and Tombs in the Central Coastal Plain. History and Archaeology of the Samaritan Settlement Outside Samaria (ca. 300–700 CE)* (*Ägypten und Altes Testament* 82) (Münster 2015).

Tatcher A. and Gal Z. (2009) "Ancient cemetery at Migdal Ha-'Emeq (el-Mujeidil)", *'Atiqot* 61 (2009) 131–32, 1*–47*.

Tatcher A., Nagar Y., and Avshalom-Gorni D. (2002) "Excavations at Khirbet el-Shubeika: the burial caves", in *Eretz Zafon: Studies in Galilean Archaeology*, ed. Z. Gal (Jerusalem 2002), 263–88 (in Hebrew, with English Summary).

Taxel I. and Iserlis M. (2014) "Two-part ceramic incense burners in late Roman and Byzantine Palestine: technological, regional and ethno-religious aspects", in *Roman Pottery in the Near East. Local Production and Regional Trade (Roman and Late Antique Mediterranean Pottery* 3), edd. B. Fischer-Genz, Y. Gerber, and H. Hamel (Oxford 2014) 159–69.

Taylor C. G. (2018) *Late Antique Images of the Virgin Annunciate Spinning. Allotting the Scarlet and the Purple (Texts and Studies in Eastern Christianity* 11) (Leiden and Boston 2018).

Tsafrir Y. and Holum K. G. (1987/1988) "Reḥovot – 1986", *ESI* 6 (1987/1988) 89–91.

Toombs L. E. (1985) *The Joint Archaeological Expedition to Tell el-Hesi 2: Tell el-Hesi. Modern Military Trenching and Muslim Cemetery in Field I, Strata I–II* (American Schools of Oriental Research Excavation Reports) (Waterloo 1985).

Tsafrir Y. and Holum K. G. (1988) "Reḥovot in the Negev: preliminary report, 1986", *IEJ* 38 (1988) 117–27.

Tudor B. (2011) *Christian Funerary Stelae of the Byzantine and Arab Periods from Egypt* (Marburg 2011).

Tufnell O. (1953) *Lachish III (Tell ed-Duweir): The Iron Age* (London and New York 1953).

Yeivin Z. and Finkielsztejn G. (1999) "Ḥorbat Castra – 1993–1997" *HA/ESI* 109 (1999) 23*–27*, 32–38.

Vincent H. (1910) "Le pillage des tombes dans la vallée du Jordain", *RBibl* 7 (1910) 576–78.

Volp U. (2002) *Tod und Ritual in den christlichen Gemeinden der Antike* (Supplements to *VigChr* 65) (Leiden and Boston 2002).

Volp U. (2016/2017) "Sacra privata, family duties, and the dead: insights from the fathers and cultural anthropology", *ArchRel* 18/19 (2016/2017) 171–85.

Vroom J. (2003) *After Antiquity. Ceramics and Society in the Aegean from the 7th to the 20th Century A.C. A Case Study from Boeotia, Central Greece (Archaeological Studies Leiden University* 10) (Leiden 2003).

Vroom J. (2011) "The other Dark Ages: early Medieval pottery finds in the Aegean as an archaeological challenge", in *When Did Antiquity End? Archaeological Case Studies in Three Continents* (BAR-IS 2268), ed. R. Attoui (Oxford 2011) 137–58.

Waterhouse D. (1994) "Tomb types in the Roman and Byzantine cemeteries of Hesban", in *Hesban: After 25 Years*, edd. D. Merling and L. T. Geraty (Berrien Springs 1994) 283–99.

Waterhouse D. (1998) *The Necropolis of Hesban: A Typology of Tombs* (Hesban 10) (Berrien Springs 1998).

Watson P. (2001) "The Byzantine period", in *The Archaeology of Jordan (Levantine Archaeology* 1), edd. B. MacDonald, R. Adams, and P. Bienkowski (Sheffield 2001) 461–502.

Wineland J. (2001) *Ancient Abila: An Archaeological History* (BAR-IS 989) (Oxford 2001).

Winter T. (2015) "Late Roman funerary customs in light of the grave goods from the cemetery on Ṣallaḥ ed-Din street, Jerusalem", *'Atiqot* 80 (2015) 81–123.

Zelinger Y. and Barbé H. (2017) "A Byzantine Monastery in Naḥal Qidron, Jerusalem", *'Atiqot* 89 (2017) 49–82.

Zemer A. (1999) ed. *Castra at the Foot of Mount Carmel: The City and Its Secrets* (Haifa 1999).

Zias J. and Spigelman M. (2004) "Report on burials and osteoarchaeological analysis", in *Ḥorvat Karkur 'Illit: A Byzantine Cemetery Church in the Northern Negev (Final Report of the Excavations 1989–1995)* (Beer-Sheva Archaeological Monographs 1), ed. P. Figueras (Beer-Sheva 2004) 307–315.

Zilberbod I. and Amit D. (1999) "Mazor (El'ad), Area H8, Area P", *HA/ESI* 109 (1999) 79–83, 55*–57*.

Zilberbod I. and Amit D. (2001) "Mazor (El'ad), Area H7 (B)", *HA/ESI* 113 (2001) 67–68, 48*–49*.

Zissu B. and Klein E. (2014) "On the use and reuse of rock-cut tombs and a ritual bath at Tell en-Naṣbeh: new perspectives on the Roman and Byzantine necropoleis", in *"As for Me, I Will Dwell at Mizpah …": The Tell en-Naṣbeh Excavations after 85 Years* (Georgias Studies in the Ancient Near East 9), edd. J. R. Zorn and A. J. Brody (Piscataway 2014) 199–224.

The Archaeology of Death, Burial and Commemoration in Late Antique Egypt

Elisabeth R. O'Connell

Abstract

This contribution will argue that the richness of Egypt's archaeological, including papyrological, record is uniquely poised to demonstrate the successive stages of death, burial and commemoration for individuals and communities in Late Antiquity. While Egypt was a constituent part of the larger Roman Empire by the 4th c., the body of evidence is rarely exploited by archaeologists of the period. This material can provide rare insight into various identity markers such as status, gender, language, religion and even 'ethnicity' (i.e., real or perceived descent). This chapter seeks to introduce the nature and limits of the evidence (i), the history of the subject, in particular its foundation in the discovery of 'Coptic' textiles (ii) and the current state of fieldwork at sites in different regions of Egypt (iii). Such a regional survey is a first step toward identifying what is distinctive about Egypt, and what is shared with other parts of the late antique world.

Introduction

Around AD 600, Abraham, bishop of Hermonthis dictated his last will and testament in Coptic to a notary who translated it for him into Greek. Measuring over a metre in length, the surviving portion of the papyrus document stipulates the property to be inherited by his successor as abbot of the monastery of the holy martyr Phoibammon. It also sets out his expectations for his burial and commemoration.

> I wish and order that, after my exit from this life, the wrapping of my body (*soma*) and my holy pro-sphora offerings (*tas hagias mo(u) prosphoras*) and meals (*agapas*) [in my memory] and the designated days of my death [period] (*tas tou thanato(u) episêmous hêmeras*) be filled by your care according to the custom of the country and according to my intention and plan (*P.Mon. Phoib. Test.* I 77.57–59).[1]

Abraham's wishes do not reflect his ecclesiastical status, but demonstrate the concerns of contemporary men and women from the region of Memnoneia/Jeme in Upper Egypt, also known as Western Thebes (Figs. 1–2).[2] About a dozen other wills from the area survive. Written in Coptic, sometimes with an Arabic protocol, they date to the years following the Muslim conquest of Egypt (*ca.* 641) and thus show shifts in the cultural milieu, in which Greek was replaced by Coptic in legal texts at a local level, and Arabic introduced.

Each of Abraham's expectations for his burial is paralleled in other partially extant wills preserving different combinations of the same concerns: 1) preparation of the body 2) burial 3) the administration of prosphora donations (defined below) and 4) commemoration, at a meal for the poor and annually thereafter. Since it is mainly the burial (2) which is visible in the archaeology, such texts enhance our knowledge of the rituals and other actions attending death. The evidence from these wills is supported by both contemporary burials found in the very same region and documents concerning their production, which show that the dead were wrapped in shrouds (*hbos*) and bound with distinctive tapestry-woven bands (*keira*).[3]

Among the legal texts from the region, those belonging to three women (Elisabeth, Anna and Susanna) show the same concerns as Abraham's. In her will, composed in Coptic in 723, Elisabeth bequeathed all of her property to her second husband, and tasked him with the clothing of her body and the administration of her prosphora donation.

> And when I shall depart from the body (*soma*), first you are to take care for the clothing (*hobs*, var. *hbos*) of my body (*soma*) and my holy prosphora offering, as for every Christian woman (*P.KRU* 68.64–6).[4]

---

[1] English translation, MacCoull (2000) 56; image of papyrus in Fluck, Helmecke and O'Connell (2015) 95, no. 101.

[2] The "ritualization of mortuary practice" in Abraham's will does not "reflect the author's ecclesiastical status", *contra* Frankfurter (2018) 179. For an up-to-date list of wills from the Theban region, see Garel (2015) 38; *P.Mon. Phoib. Test.*

[3] Winlock and Crum (1926) 45–50; O'Connell (Forthcoming a).

[4] MacCoull (2009) 88.

© KONINKLIJKE BRILL BV, LEIDEN, 2024 | DOI:10.1163/9789004687974_016
Alexandra Dolea and Luke Lavan (eds) *Burial and Memorial in Late Antiquity*
(Late Antique Archaeology 13) (Leiden 2024), pp. 856–889

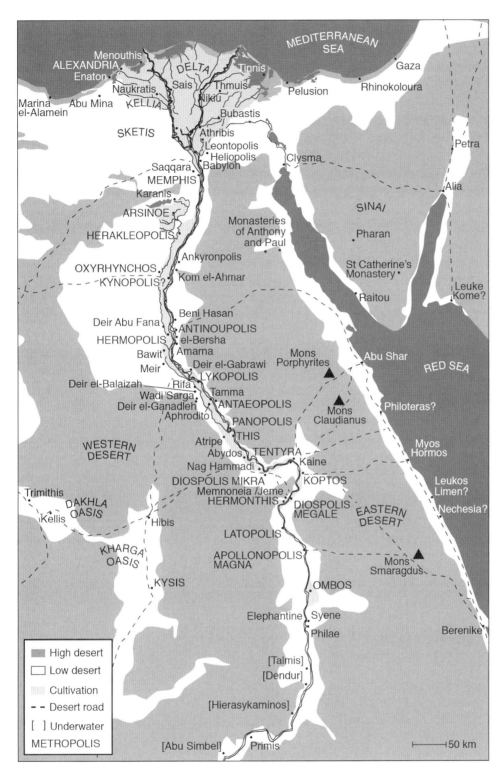

FIGURE 1   Map of Egypt.
MAP M. WACHTAL; COPYRIGHT E. R. O'CONNELL

Prosphora donations were given in the form of real property, goods, or cash.[5] In this context, the donations were made in order to provision *agapai,* which were either communal meals for the poor or food supplied to the poor at a local monastery.[6] In return, the deceased received intercessory prayers commending him or her to the saint and thenceforth to God, as Anna makes clear in a document that functions as a will dated 734.[7]

5   J. P. Thomas (1987) 78; Wipszycka (1972) 69–70.

6   Wipszycka (1972) 9–70; Papaconstantinou (2001) 320–22; O'Connell (Forthcoming a).

7   Wipszycka (2007) 336.

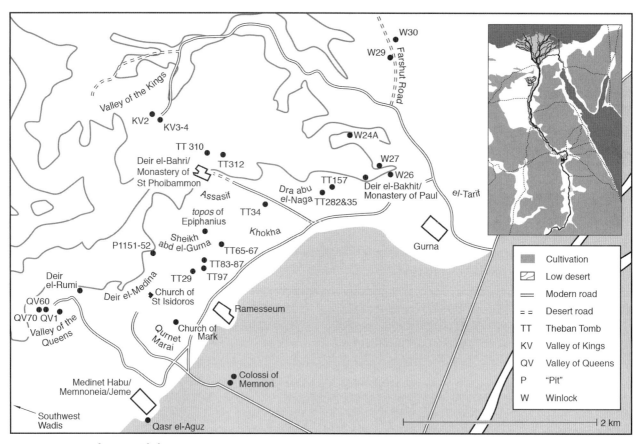

FIGURE 2   Map of Western Thebes.
MAP M. WACHTAL; COPYRIGHT E. R. O'CONNELL

So God put it into my heart that I should make a donation of this little memorial to the holy monastery ... [of]..., the holy Apa Paul's Kolol, the great anchorite: first of all so that his supplications and his holy intercessions may obtain favour for me before the true Judge, and so that my little memorial may remain concerning the great *agape* now practiced towards the poor who come to the holy monastery, ... (*P.KRU* 106. 65–74).[8]

Commemoration on the 'designated days of death' (*P.Lond.* I 77.58) took place on the 3rd, 7th and 13th days after death and annually thereafter. In one of two copies of Susanna's will written, before 722, she instructs her grandchildren concerning her annual commemoration.

And concerning my death: my male (grand)children are to bury (*kôs*) me, according to the custom (*ethos*) of the village (*time*), and my 5 (grand)children are to give the 5 years' worth of offerings on my behalf, once a year (*P.KRU* 76.52–54; cf. another copy of her will, *P.KRU* 66.42–43).[9]

It is probable that Anna's commemoration was performed at the Monastery of Apa Paul at Dra abu el-Naga, and Susanna's and Elisabeth's in Bishop Abraham's own Monastery of St. Phoibammon, which stood upon the remains of the temple of Hatshepsut at Deir el-Bahri (Fig. 3). Late antique burials discovered at both these and other sites in Western Thebes illustrate the clothing of the body that the testators had in mind (Fig. 4).[10] Thus, we gain unprecedented access to the steps taken in the process of death, burial and commemoration in this single region.

Egypt's combination of archaeology and texts provides a privileged vantage point for examining the processes of death and burial in Late Antiquity, and exploring the intersection of family and status, as well as gender, linguistic, religious and even 'ethnic' identity. Conversely, the abundance of evidence has been challenging for scholars to synthesize, partly because its study falls between the disciplines of Egyptology, Classical Archaeology, Ancient History and Art History. This contribution seeks to: (i) introduce the nature and limits of evidence from late antique Egypt, (ii) the history of the subject, in particular its foundation in the

8   MacCoull (2009) 168.
9   MacCoull (2009) 75.

10   The archaeological evidence for the monastery is compiled in Godlewski (1986).

FIGURE 3   Western Thebes, Deir el-Bahri. View of the remains of the tower of the Monastery of
Phoibammon, *ca.* 1890.
COURTESY OF THE EGYPT EXPLORATION SOCIETY

discovery of 'Coptic' textiles, and (iii) the current state of fieldwork with a region-by-region survey of fieldwork at sites in Egypt. By doing so, I hope to introduce the archaeological, including papyrological, evidence in a way in which it can be better compared and contrasted both within Egypt and with other parts of the Roman and post-Roman Empire, especially as represented within this volume.

First, definitions are required. 'Late Antiquity' in Egypt describes the period *ca.* 200–800, which witnessed the spread of Christianity and the arrival of Islam.[11] After the 2nd and early 3rd c., we can begin to detect shifts in the material culture of Egypt and again in the 8th c., although in some areas significant change really begins in the 10th c. with the Fatimid period (969–1171). For this reason, in material culture studies in particular, 'Egypt in the First Millennium' is sometimes invoked to best capture continuity and change.[12] 'Coptic' is often used indiscriminately to describe a period, culture, language and religion. Here, more precise terms are favoured, and 'Coptic' is mainly reserved for the last stage of the

ancient Egyptian language, written in a modified Greek script. Similarly, 'Medieval' is preferred to 'Early Islamic', and used to describe the period *ca.* 800–1500. 'Egypt' is defined by the traditional boundary at the first cataract, as it was under Diocletian *ca.* 298, and, therefore, toward the beginning of our late antique chronology. Nevertheless, the borders of Egypt were moveable, to the south with Nubia, to the west with Cyrenaica and to the east with Sinai. 'Upper Egypt' for the purposes of this contribution refers to the length of the Nile from Syene/Aswan to Memphis, near modern Cairo, and 'Lower Egypt' to the Delta.[13]

Nature and Limitations of the Evidence

The Egyptian landscape is a palimpsest. In antiquity, the agriculture of the Nile Valley, the Delta, Fayum and the oases of the Western Desert supported populations that were large by ancient standards. The Eastern and Western Deserts were more sparsely inhabited, but dotted with mines, stone quarries and forts, and criss-crossed with roads connecting the Nile Valley to the Red Sea coast to the east, and the oases and beyond to Saharan and sub-Saharan Africa to the west and south. Owing to the

---

11   For a useful survey of periodization in Egypt, see Bagnall (2003).

12   The 'First Millennium A.D.' has been used in material culture studies in the past decade, e.g. O'Connell (2014a), especially concerning textiles from Egypt, see De Moor and Fluck (2007), (2009), (2011); De Moor, Fluck and Linscheid (2013), (2015).

13   Egypt is sometimes instead divided into Upper, Middle and Lower Egypt.

FIGURE 4
Western Thebes, Deir el-Bahri. Two mummiform
bundles from the Monastery of the holy martyr
Phoibammon, *ca.* 1890.
COURTESY OF THE EGYPT EXPLORATION
SOCIETY

limited amount of arable land, settlements and cemeteries are usually multi-phase.

Egypt's dry climate preserves an extraordinary range
of material culture. The sheer abundance of evidence,
however, has made it difficult for scholars to recognize what is distinctive about Egypt in Late Antiquity
and what is shared with the wider contemporary
Mediterranean world. Egypt's assumed distinctiveness
has led to the isolation of 'Coptic' studies, whereas, at
least from the 4th c., Egypt may be better studied as a
constituent part of the late antique world.[14] By this time,
several features of earlier practice, including elite Roman
period funerary traditions, are no longer discernible in
the archaeological record (foremost mummification
by embalming). Alongside the mortuary topography,
structures, markers and burials (themselves described
below),[15] well-preserved texts survive on papyrus and
other media that demonstrate aspects of death and

burial, the funerary industry, and other activities such as
the deposition of curses in cemeteries.

Pharaonic Egypt's Long Shadow: 'Coptic' Archaeology and Disciplinary Divides

The archaeology of late antique Egypt, together with
other 'late' phases of occupation, has traditionally been
neglected in favour of pharaonic Egypt, or rather, its
stone temples and tombs.[16] Even a few decades ago, the
mudbrick remains of later habitation were removed
as 'overburden', and 'intrusive burials' discarded and
ignored. Only in order to retrieve 'Coptic' textiles were
late antique cemeteries targeted for excavation/plunder,
beginning from the 1880s (below). The archaeology of
the period has largely been undertaken by Egyptologists
or by Biblical and, later, Coptic scholars often working out of Religious Studies departments. Many early
archaeologists such as W. M. F. Petrie and G. A. Reisner,
nevertheless, made detailed records, and it is thus possible to reconstruct excavations and finds on the basis of
their archives today.

---

14   Bagnall (1993) 321–22.
15   For recent brief surveys of death and burial in Egypt, see Horak
      (1995); Dunand (2007); Fluck and Helmecke (2015); O'Connell
      (2018).

16   For the development of late antique archaeology as a disci-
      pline in Egypt, see O'Connell (2014b).

The development of 'Coptic studies' as a discipline in the 20th c. has provided the structure for research and publication, even if it has hindered the integration of Egypt in larger studies of the late antique Mediterranean. From the beginning, the discipline had strong ties to the Coptic Orthodox Church. In 1907, the Coptic Museum was founded with support from the Church, and later, from 1931, it was administered by the Egyptian Antiquities Service. The *Société d'archéologie copte* (SAC), today headquartered within the St. Mark's Cathedral complex in Cairo, published the first volume of its journal in 1934. In 1976, the International Association of Coptic Studies was founded, and congresses now take place every 4 years with a plenary lecture and sessions dedicated to archaeology. Since the late 1960s, the most systematic work at late antique sites – mainly churches, but also funerary monuments – has been undertaken by the architect Peter Grossmann and published in his indispensable 'black book'.[17]

In Egypt, antiquities inspectorates are separated between pharaonic (including Graeco-Roman) and Coptic/Islamic, divisions that are reproduced in museum displays and the school curriculum.[18] Increasingly, with the professionalization of archaeology, Egyptologists can no longer avoid adopting its tools so that later phases are documented, even if they are more rarely published. Today, survey and urban rescue archaeology, together with planned excavation of late antique sites, are improving on what has been, until recently, a haphazard discipline. Projects with research-driven agendas promise diachronic studies of single sites up to the present, and are attracting funding partly on this basis (e.g. at Dra abu-Naga and Umm el-Qa'ab, below). Reflection on the social history of archaeology in Egypt and, in particular, the contribution of Egyptian labour, has been a particularly fruitful avenue for modern historians in recent years.[19]

Outside of Egypt, archaeologists and art historians have long struggled to incorporate evidence from Egypt into larger studies of the late antique world, hindered by limitless corpora (especially of organic material such as textiles and papyri), vast bibliographies (including especially field reports and catalogues), and even whole disciplines that have developed to study categories of objects (papyrology). Divisions by language (Greek, Coptic, Arabic, but also Latin, Aramaic, Hebrew), material (papyri, ostraca, stone stelae) and genre (literary and documentary papyri, funerary and other inscriptions) have often meant that texts from the same findspot

are studied by different specialists, further alienating non-specialists seeking to gain an overview. Since the 19th c., art historians have sometimes sought to distinguish especially between 'Byzantine' and 'Coptic' stone sculpture and textiles, sometimes elevating the former and dismissing the latter.[20] Finally, until recently 'Coptic' archaeology has been practically synonymous with church and monastery architecture in Egypt, to the detriment of other settlement studies. As a result, monasteries are over-represented in the archaeological record and it is particularly monastic cemeteries that have been studied systematically.[21]

Continuity or Change?: Evidence of Funerary Practice in Roman Egypt

Roman period painted wooden portraits (so-called 'Fayum portraits'), plaster masks and linen shrouds have been relatively well studied by art historians in Classics and Egyptology, especially since the mid-1990s following several international exhibitions.[22] Such elite burials combine the quintessential Egyptian funerary practice of mummification with the Roman tradition of naturalistic commemorative portraiture.[23] The combination of styles and iconographies can be arresting for the modern viewer, such as when the deceased is shown in naturalistic style wearing Roman costume and holding a glass patera (offering dish) containing wine, flanked by ancient Egyptian deities in traditional style, all within a jewelled frame (Fig. 5). The dates of the latest portraits are disputed but probably end in the early 4th c., when mummification by embalming probably also ceased. Recent work, above all by Christina Riggs, has contextualized such finds within their archaeological and social contexts.[24] Scientific analysis is increasingly extended to Roman period mummies.[25] While the emphasis has been on the Hellenized Fayum and sites like Antinoopolis, individual shrouds and fragmentary wooden portraits are also now known from the Mediterranean coast at Marina Alamein, and in Upper Egypt, in Western Thebes. The vast majority of Roman period mummies do not bear painted shrouds or masks but are sometimes dated by their distinctive wrappings.[26] In general, they are found in reused tombs,

17 Grossmann (2002), esp. 315–47 for funerary monuments.
18 Reid (2002) and (2015).
19 Doyen (2018) with bibliography.

20 Thomas (2007) 142–53.
21 Dunand (2007).
22 For a recent survey see Borg (2012).
23 For surveys of Roman period funerary practice in Egypt, see Dunand (1995) and Riggs (2005).
24 Riggs (2005); Picton, Quirke and Roberts (2007).
25 3 of 8 investigated mummies are Roman period in Taylor and Antoine (2014) 134–69.
26 Gessler-Löhr (2012).

FIGURE 5   Provenance unknown. Painted linen shroud,
            ca. AD 150–200.
            EA 68509, COURTESY OF THE TRUSTEES OF THE
            BRITISH MUSEUM

in loculi, on mudbrick benches in purpose-built structures, in pottery and wooden coffins and in pit graves.[27]

So-called mummy-labels belong especially to the Roman period.[28] Bearing the name of the deceased, they are understood by modern scholars as a substitution for a funerary stela or as identification for the dead (Fig. 6). Some bear instructions for transport, e.g. 'Remains of Apollonia (to be shipped) to Panopolis. Deliver to Panechates the embalmer'.[29] Some are bilingual with the name and occasionally the date of death given in demotic Egyptian on one side and Greek on the other.

The last labels bearing a date belong to the early 4th c.[30] Greek labels with Christian formulae and Coptic labels have been dated to the 5th–6th c. but the limits of the mummy-label corpus, and how they might form a category distinct from grave stelae, require further scrutiny.[31]

Roman funerary stelae in collections today have rarely been studied in the context of their findspot, either because they were reused in antiquity, or because they were collected/plundered from their mudbrick monuments without recording. Where they have been discovered *in situ*, they are found in barrel-vaulted mudbrick tombs with stelae emplacements at one end,[32] or atop rectangular mudbrick tombs (e.g., Antinoopolis, Fig. 7). In some representational stelae, naturalistic figures of the deceased stand or are seated in symposium settings comparable to other Eastern Mediterranean contexts, or, in Upper Egyptian contexts, in traditional Egyptian scenes in which they offer to Osiris.[33]

Animal mummification was an industry parallel to human mummification, often located in the same necropolises and exhibiting comparable bandaging techniques. Since it was one of Egypt's most distinctive practices, the date of its cessation would be desirable to establish as another metric for the end of traditional religious practice in Egypt. A select few animals were considered the living manifestations of individual gods (such as the Apis bull of Memphis or Buchis bull of Hermonthis) and buried with appropriate provision. Millions more were deposited in vast catacombs or buried in the open ground, often in pots, as votives dedicated to gods (e.g., baboons, cats, ibises, hawks, snakes, shrews and other animals).[34] The practice flourished with state sponsorship from the Late Period, declining in the Early Roman period with the apparent withdrawal of state financial support.[35] The stela of the last known burial of a Buchis bull at Hermonthis is dated to year 57 of Diocletian, i.e., AD 340, in the reign of Constantius II.[36] The votive animal cemeteries at Saqqara near Memphis, Tuna al-Gebel near Hermopolis and Abydos near This/Girga are also

27   Cartron (2012).
28   For introduction, major corpora with bibliography, see Vleeming (2011) (including some dated to the Late Ptolemaic period).
29   Sherwood Fox (1913) no. 1, 438–40.

30   For 4th c. mummy-labels from Medinet Habu, see Wilfong (1995).
31   For Christian mummy-labels, see Torallas Tover (2013). For a Coptic label, see Delattre (2005).
32   Hooper (1961).
33   E.g. Edgar (1903) pls. 19–24; Abdalla (1992).
34   Animal mummies are very occasionally pets buried with their owners, and joints of meat are sometimes wrapped for consumption in the afterlife, but these practices do not seem to extend into the Roman period.
35   Driesch *et al.* (2005).
36   Grenier (1983).

FIGURE 6   Western Thebes, Deir el-Bahri. Three *ca.* AD 220–250 mummies. The Greek text on the
            wooden label attached to the mummy on the left identifies him as 'Pachons, son of
            Psesarmese [and of] Seneponychos from the village of Ternouthe'.
            COURTESY OF THE EGYPT EXPLORATION SOCIETY

said to date up to the 4th c., but without any convincing proof.[37]

Among the vast numbers of papyri and ostraca (broken pot sherds, limestone flakes and other objects used as writing substrates) that survive from Egypt, a small number evidence aspects of death and burial.[38] So-called literary papyri, such as copies of the text called by Egyptologists the *Book of Breathing*, describe funerary rituals to help the deceased to navigate the Egyptian afterlife, up through the Roman period (mainly *ca.* 1st–2nd c.).[39] Other documents, however, provide evidence for the everyday lives of funerary workers. The archives of funerary priests and necropolis workers in particular demonstrate aspects of how the work was organized. For the Ptolemaic period, the archives of families of funerary priests and other funerary workers are known from Thebes (*P.Choach.Survey, P.Tor.Choach*), Hawara (*P. Hawara; P. Hawara 01, P.Ashm*) and Memphis

---

37   Ikram (2015). Future radiocarbon dating and work on pottery
       vessels in which animal mummies are found may illuminate
       the chronological span of animal cemeteries.

38   Montserrat (1997).

39   Smith (2009).

FIGURE 7   Antinoopolis, North Necropolis. Roman period tombs with stelae *in situ*.
COPYRIGHT DELLA MISSIONE ARCHEOLOGICA IN EGITTO DELL'ISTITUTO
PAPIROLOGICO 'G. VITELLI', UNIVERSITÀ DEGLI STUDI DI FIRENZE – ITALIA

FIGURE 8A–B   Set of curtains or room dividers reused as shrouds.
EA 29771, COURTESY OF THE TRUSTEES OF THE BRITISH MUSEUM

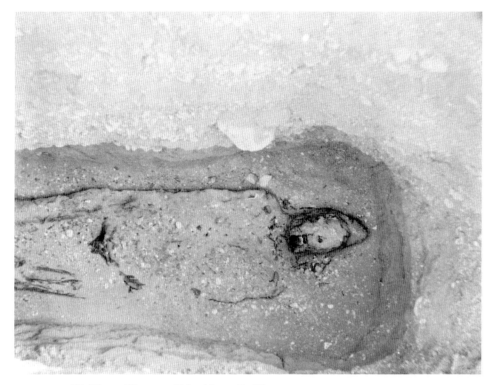

FIGURE 9   Wadi Sarga. Pit grave with burial, *ca.* 7th–8th c.

(*P.Dem.Memphis*). At Thebes, for example, they record the process of buying, selling, and inheriting ancient tombs and the rights to carry out the funerary cults of the dead (*P.Choach.Survey*). A Late Roman archive of another family of funerary workers from Kysis/Dush in the Kharga Oasis dates AD 247–314. Exceptionally, it contains a letter about funeral expenses, which amount to 520 drachmas (*P.Nekr.* 18, *ca.* 260–275),[40] and a Christian letter about a body (*P.Nekr.* 28, late 3rd c.). A general survey of titles of funerary workers in Greek documents *ca.* 3rd c. BC to 6th c. AD shows the diminishing role of specialists, and the simultaneous simplification and wider dissemination of burial rites, whereby from the 3rd c., every member of the funerary industry might be called *exopylitês* ('he who lives outside the gate').[41] Physicians (*iatroi*) supervised funerary workers in the Roman period, and whether or not they continued to do so in Late Antiquity, when they are closely associated with monks and clerics, is not clear.[42] In the 7th and 8th c., the archives of monks and clerics living in Western Thebes (see introduction above) demonstrate

that they were responsible for weaving shrouds (*hboos*) and bands (*keiria*). But whether or not this was solely their responsibility, to the exclusion of weavers in towns or families, is unclear.[43]

Whether one chooses to concentrate on continuity or change, there is a discernible shift between the 2nd and the 4th/5th c. Features such as the representation of vignettes from ancient Egyptian mythology and animal cemeteries illustrate Egypt's distinctiveness in the first centuries under Roman rule. By the 4th c., these practices apparently ended, and artificial mummification probably also ceased, but this remains to be confirmed by future systematic scientific analysis. Egypt's documents are particularly helpful in tracing continuity and change, but large numbers of papyri are lacking for precisely the 4th/5th c., the period during which most of Egypt's population became Christian.[44]

Late Antique Mortuary Topography, Structures, Markers, Burials and Rituals

The location of extant late antique cemeteries generally depends on regional topography. Especially in the Nile Valley, the desert escarpment rising above the cultivation was the traditional location of ancient Egyptian burials and the usual place for late antique cemeteries as well. In the Delta, Fayum, oases, deserts and on the

---

40   A camel purchased some years later in 302 AD cost 700 drachmas (*P.Nekr.* 32).
41   Derda (1991) 35–36.
42   For a close association between physicians, monks and clerics in Late Antiquity, see Derda and van der Vliet (2006) 32. Some scholars have suggested that monks took over the roles of earlier funerary workers in general, on the etiological character of the story of Pathermouthis, see Gascou (1992).

43   Cromwell (2017).
44   Bagnall (1995) 85–89.

FIGURE 10   Karara. Two mummiform bundles, *ca.* 4th–8th c.
COURTESY OF ÄGYPTOLOGISCHES INSTITUT, RUPRECHT-KARLS-UNIVERSITÄT
HEIDELBERG

coasts, cemeteries were generally just beyond the cities, towns, fortresses and monasteries they served. Organic remains are preserved beyond the cultivation in most of these regions, but they are poorly preserved in the Delta, which is historically Egypt's most populous region.

Structures

In general, across the period *ca.* AD 200–800, there is a range of monumental and non-monumental types of burial. The dead were placed in or under purpose-built funerary monuments, in reused tombs of all periods, or inhumed in lined or unlined pits indicated by funerary stelae or other markers (below). Toward the end of this chronology, pit burials were the norm. The head-west orientation of burials is often assumed to indicate they are Christian, but a systematic approach to the data alongside other criteria is desirable. Evidence for coffins and funerary beds has been documented especially at sites in Middle Egypt.[45] Recorded coffins are usually makeshift, but an elaborately painted wooden coffin, the so-called 'peacock coffin' from Karara in Middle Egypt (5th–7th c.), is exceptional for its quality and completeness (see Fig. 11).[46]

Markers

Greek and Coptic funerary stelae are the best recorded group of grave markers (for the pottery and wooden markers, see Bawit and North Saqqara below). They have rarely been documented *in situ*. When they are, they were mounted in mudbrick superstructures covering graves (e.g., Antinoopolis below) or placed directly over burials (e.g., Antaeopolis/Qaw el-Kebir below). At some sites, near-contemporary stelae were reused in public spaces (e.g., Saqqara, Aswan below). Beginning in the mid-1800s, large numbers were collected, with catalogues appearing at the end of the 19th and beginning of the 20th c., and individual sites represented especially in articles and fieldwork reports, rather than monographs.[47] Corpora of Greek funerary stelae have been attributed to the regions of Latopolis/Esna, Hermonthis/Armant, Panopolis/Akhmim, Antinoopolis, Tenis/Hakoris, and towns in the Fayum and in or near Alexandria. They have been dated mainly to the *ca.* 5th–7th/8th c. By comparison, Coptic stelae have been found at most of these locations as well as in the region of Apollonopolis Magna/Edfu and in monasteries near

45   Huber (2009), (2013a).
46   Huber and Nauerth (2018).

47   The most up-to-date bibliography is 'Coptic funerary stelae and inscriptions bibliography', Department of Ancient History, Macquarie University, Sydney. https://www.mq.edu.au /about_us/faculties_and_departments/faculty_of_arts/depart ment_of_ancient_history/coptic/coptic_bibliographies/cop tic_funerary_stelae_bibliography/.

FIGURE 11   Karara. Peacock coffin, *ca.* 7th–8th c.
COURTESY OF ÄGYPTOLOGISCHES INSTITUT, RUPRECHT-KARLS-UNIVERSITÄT HEIDELBERG

Syene/Aswan, This/Girga, Antaeopolis/Qaw el-Kebir, Lykopolis/Asyut, Hermopolis/Ashmunein and Saqqara, mainly *ca.* 7th–10th c.[48] Arabic stelae belonging to the first centuries of Muslim rule cluster at Alexandria, Fustat/Cairo and Syene/Aswan.[49]

Burials

People were typically buried in (or with) their clothes. In many of the cases surveyed below (3), individuals wearing their clothes were also wrapped in multiple shrouds (or reused soft furnishings, Fig. 8), and bound by cord, strips of linen or distinctive woollen tapestry-woven bands. Rags or otherwise disused clothing were often used as packing around the neck to stabilize the head and protect the face, resulting in a 'mummiform bundle'.[50] Only recently have late antique individuals received the same types of scientific analysis long accorded to ancient Egyptian mummies. Both types of burial from Karara and now in Heidelberg were CT-scanned and radiocarbon dated. Both styles of burial were concurrent, rather than strictly successive. Female mummiform bundles were found to wear multiple necklaces and bangles, with personal and household items,

such as wooden spindles and combs, metal ladles, baskets, pins and needles contained within their wrappings (Karara,[51] Mostagedda and Matmar, below).

The publication of biological data is relatively rare and presented in specialist publications rather than as part of fieldwork reports.[52] Presentations are still limited to ageing, sexing, and forensics (below) because relatively little laboratory work is possible in Egypt, and samples may not be removed from the country. Dating burials is difficult in the absence of systematic recording and radiocarbon dating. Only in the Dakhla Oasis has isotope analysis been performed.[53] The ethics of presentation and display are topics which extend to late antique burials.[54]

Social data has been retrieved from mummy-labels and grave stelae, with the death dates used to map seasonal mortality.[55] Other social information, such as the organization of the funerary industry and commemorative practices, can be gleaned (but unfortunately not defined) by everyday documents surviving on papyri and ostraca (above).

48   Tudor (2011) 172, 215.
49   Hawari (2015) with bibliography in n.4.
50   Especially at excavated cemeteries in the region of Antaeopolis and the corridor to the Fayum (Naqlun, Deir el-Banat). For a detailed description, see Huber (2007).

51   Gessler-Löhr *et al.* (2007), (2010).
52   A useful exception is a monograph on child burial, Nenna (2012).
53   Dupras *et al.* (2016).
54   Fletcher, Antoine and Hill (2014); Calament and Durand (2013).
55   Scheidel (2001) with bibliography.

Ritual Associated with Burial and the Ritual Use of the Dead and their Graves

Physical evidence for funerary ritual beyond interment is rarely mentioned explicitly in publications, although it is beginning to appear more often. Pottery and glass dishes and vessels associated with burials were used during the funeral or in (annual) post-interment commemorative practices (Medinet Habu, Gebel el-Tuna, Antinoopolis and Alexandria, below).

From the content of ritual (or 'magical') texts, it is clear that the Hellenistic and Roman practice of depositing curses with the dead in cemeteries continued. Handbooks and spells indicate that the dead are to undertake action against the target or appeal to powers beyond to do so.[56] Careful excavation and recording of cemeteries in the future may reveal such textual finds *in situ* as a curse written on a human bone, probably found in a cemetery.[57] Some of the spells found in handbooks would leave little material trace, if such rituals indeed were ever carried out. The *ca.* 100–300 demotic and Greek London-Leiden handbook prescribes an erotic spell to be written in the blood of a hoopoe bird on a leaf with some of the victim's hair enclosed and placed in the mouth of a corpse (PDM XIV.1070–77).[58] A spell to be written with a corpse finger is prescribed by a *ca.* 550–650 Coptic handbook now in Cairo.[59]

History of Excavation and Study: 'Coptic' Textiles

Unwrapping the dead was an early and regular response in the European encounter with mummies starting from the 1600s.[60] Ancient Egyptian mummies were wrapped in linen. In the Roman period, dyed wool decorative elements became popular on tunics, other elements of everyday dress, and soft furnishings. Since people were usually buried in their clothes in Late Antiquity (in contrast to earlier periods), this is what excavators found when they unwrapped the dead. Beginning in the 1870s and especially the 1880s, the first late antique cemeteries were probed by excavators located at sites such as Panopolis/Akhmim, Antinoopolis, Saqqara and others in the Fayum.[61] Whereas scholars working on different regions have focused on monuments (largely in the Roman East) or burials (in the Roman West), the early

focus on textiles in Egypt shaped the approach to the excavation, selection, study and publication of burials. A residue of this approach continues to the present. Two case studies are given here in order to demonstrate continuity and change in scholarship, as well as some of the challenges specific to Egypt.

The Excavation of Panopolis/Akhmim

Systematic exploration of the Roman and late antique cemeteries of Panopolis/Akhmim was spearheaded by the Director of the Antiquities Service, Gaston Maspero, beginning in 1884.[62] Over the course of 4 seasons, thousands of mummiform bundles were uncovered and the bodies unwrapped. By the late 1880s, 'Akhmim' textiles had become shorthand for richly coloured saleable items, and the site became the focus of official and unofficial excavations.[63] In a letter from Robert Forrer dated 1895, he describes the plundered cemeteries.

> Everywhere, as far as the eye could see, one notices black holes in the hills, other black points can be identified as corpses of opened and unwrapped mummies, which have carelessly been put down, decomposing very slowly ... often a complete corpse with skin and hair; a cadaver without a head.[64]

Forrer and others set the agenda for digging cemeteries. His first volumes on textiles from the site distinguish between those regionally-produced, tapestry-woven wool and linen fabrics (what came to be known as 'Coptic' textiles) and what he identified as international, elite 'Byzantine' textiles, such as silks.[65] The focus was on unwrapping bodies to retrieve textiles, or, more precisely the colourful woollen and other decorative elements that were cut out from garments and reused soft furnishings. The bodies of the people they clothed were discarded.

Until recently, textiles were mainly studied by art historians interested in style and iconography. Specialists have begun to focus on the function of the original textiles, identifying elements of dress such as tunics and mantles, accessories such as hair-nets and socks, and soft furnishings such as wall-hangings, curtains, and mattress and cushion covers.[66] Radiocarbon dating and dye-analysis of historic collections have become

---

56   E.g., Meyer and Smith (1994) no. 89, 188–90.
57   Meyer and Smith (1994) no. 97, 203–204.
58   Betz (1986) 246.
59   Meyer and Smith (1994) no. 128, 270–73.
60   For a concise history of unwrapping mummies, as well as a trenchant critique of Egyptology, see Riggs (2014) 44–76.
61   Müller (2005); Thomas (2007); Fluck (2006).

62   Maspero (1887) 210–23.
63   Fluck (2008).
64   Forrer (1895), 31; Engl. transl. in Fluck (2008).
65   Forrer (1891a), (1891b); Thomas (2007) 141–42.
66   Schrenk (2004).

common.[67] Rarely has it been possible to reconstruct burials. In an exceptional case, fragments of a silk tunic with scenes from the apocryphal *Life of the Virgin Mary* adhered to a Dionysian wall-hanging reused as a shroud, raising questions concerning the religious identity of the individual.[68]

Based on the descriptions of Maspero, Forrer and others, the cemeteries can be only generally located and types of tomb structures reconstructed.[69] Renewed study of the late antique cemetery of Panopolis/Akhmim is complicated by the fact that three modern monasteries occupy the area.[70] The field of debris containing bones and textiles described by Forrer is just as apparent today, and the ravaged bodies have been understood by some modern-day Coptic Christians as early Christian martyrs. Some of the more complete ancient dead are dressed in white satin garments and on display in the Monastery of the Martyrs.[71]

The Excavation of Antinoopolis

From the 1890s, another large late antique cemetery was excavated at Antinoopolis, the city founded by Hadrian where Antinoos famously drowned in the Nile. Albert Gayet worked at the site from 1896 to 1910, exhibiting the finds (including burials) after each campaign and before the collections were dispersed to French and other international museums. As a result, tens of thousands of Antinoopolis textiles, or fragments thereof, are now in collections and the subject of numerous catalogues. Recent research, above all by Florence Calament, has sought to re-associate burial assemblages.[72] Since 1935, an Italian mission has periodically worked at Antinoopolis.[73] The north and south cemeteries contain several funerary churches, including the cult site of St. Collouthos in the North Necropolis, surrounded by monumental tomb complexes, tomb superstructures and pit burials.[74] The most famous tomb complex in the North Necropolis is built of mudbrick, and its interior is decorated with wall-paintings including one depicting the deceased, Theodosia, flanked by St. Collouthos and the Virgin Mary.[75] Later work has revealed a mass grave

of 120 corpses wrapped in shrouds and covered with thick layers of salt.[76] Systematic bioarchaeological analysis at the site was initiated following the discovery of an intact burial in an area of the so-called peristyle in the North Necropolis, with burials said to date *ca.* 3rd–7th c. A Coptic grave stelae belonging to a woman named Tgol, who went to her rest the first of the month of Athyr in the first indiction (28/29 October), surmounted a mudbrick superstructure, with a female burial below with an infant at her feet.[77] The deceased was buried in her clothes, with her saffron-coloured mantle covering her face, and laid in a makeshift wooden coffin.[78] Other burials, some also intact, were discovered in the same area, and included several children, shrouded and bound, most wearing the clothes they would have worn in life.[79]

Panopolis/Akhmim and Antinoopolis were two important late antique capitals demonstrating a range of burial types, but, as yet, we are poorly equipped to speculate concerning chronology. The characteristic mummiform bundles seem to be largely contemporary with people buried in their clothes. With the compiling of radiocarbon dates in historic collections or renewed archaeological investigation, it may be possible to say more. Both sites have been heavily looted following the 21 January 2011 Revolution.

Current State of Fieldwork in Egypt

Owing to the history of discovery in Egypt, evidence of late antique settlement and cemetery sites in the Nile Valley has often been removed or destroyed in favour of the ancient Egyptian remains they cover. New research requires knowledge of past Egyptologists' excavations, priorities and archives. The following is a survey of regions in which fieldwork has taken place in recent decades. The evidence is not always directly comparable because projects have undertaken different methods (survey, excavation and rescue archaeology) and therefore produced variable results. I have nevertheless sought to provide here each project's dating and their stated rationale for dating, if reported (pottery, radiocarbon samples, etc.);[80] number of burials identified; tomb or grave type; and distinctive features. In order to cover so many locations in a brief chapter, this section functions as a kind of gazeteer and my summaries, out

---

67 See especially the proceedings of the Textiles of the Nile Valley Study Group, De Moor and Fluck (2007), (2011) and De Moor, Fluck and Linscheid (2013), (2015), (2017).

68 Schrenk (2004) 185–89, 26–34, nos. 1 and 62.

69 Kuhlmann (1983), figs. 14 and 17.

70 Kuhlmann (1983) 52; McNally and Schrunk (1993) 10–11; Timm (1984–1992) 1: 87–88.

71 Visited March 2006.

72 Calament (2005); Calament, Eichmann and Vendries (2012); Calament and Durand (2013).

73 Pintaudi (2008a).

74 Pintaudi (2008b), (2014).

75 Manfredi (1998) 24, 29.

76 Grilleto (1981) 119–23.

77 Mintouli (2008).

78 Fluck (2014).

79 Fluck (2015).

80 In many cases, these may prove controversial.

of necessity, will be selective, demonstrating my own interests and concerns.[81]

By clustering sites by region, some patterns emerge. Regions traditionally neglected by Egyptologists have been more productive for work in the past few decades, especially in the oases, and on the Mediterranean and Red Sea coasts. Herein, the regions are defined by their late antique capitals and are organized from south to north along the Nile to the Fayum and Delta, and thereafter, to the coasts, Eastern Desert and Western Desert oases. This is done in recognition of environmental and topographical factors, which influence the location of cemeteries, orientation of burials, and types of superstructure, if any, but also to signal the relationship of cemeteries to their nearby settlements. Future regional studies may provide more systematic coverage.[82]

In the following, the place names given are those most commonly used in the discipline, rather than systematically Greek, Coptic or modern Arabic;[83] however, to make the map (see Fig. 1) more legible, I have preferred Greek place names usually paired with the modern cities or villages at or near those sites. In cases in which edited contemporary inscriptions or papyri and ostraca are abundant, I provide the sigla of the edition(s), so that evidence therein, if it exists, can be more readily accessed.

Syene/Aswan Region

At the traditional southern border of Egypt, at the first cataract at Syene/Aswan, are the standing remains of a large Medieval fortress, where, after the Muslim conquest of Egypt, the *ca.* 652 Baqt treaty between Muslim Egypt and the successive Christian Kingdoms of Nubia may have been agreed.[84] Recent work on the earlier 6th–7th c. fortress has revealed evidence for its violent destruction, including an apparent mass grave of soldiers killed in battle.[85]

At the city of Syene/Aswan itself, on-going rescue archaeology is providing keyhole glimpses of the late antique city, including now a central cathedral with a baptistry and vaulted burial chamber, perhaps dating as early as the 5th c.[86] Lining the ancient road beyond the south wall of the city is a cemetery containing thousands of mudbrick superstructures with Arabic inscriptions dating as early as the 8th c.[87] Now stored on site or in Egyptian and international collections, their contents include demographic data of particular interest since Aswan was Egypt's second city to Fustat/Cairo and stood on one of the regular Hajj routes. Since the cemetery has been subsequently reused in modern times, there has been no attempt at documenting burials.[88]

Across the river, on the west bank, at the Monastery of Hadra, the earliest remains of the monastery itself date to the 7th c., and it continued to be in use until the 12th–13th c.[89] Two large cemeteries were located to the south and east of the monastery, the former containing barrel-vaulted chambers and the latter simple pit graves; both were associated with grave stelae when they were first described.[90] Within the monastery, the partially rock-cut church contained a barrel-vaulted burial chamber, and some 200 fragments of funerary stelae dating to the 8th c. were apparently reused for paving in a 10th or 11th c. restoration.[91] Now in the Coptic Museum in Cairo, *ca.* 140 of the fragments are the subject of renewed study.[92]

Hermonthis/Armant Region

At the northern limit of the district of Hermonthis/Armant, opposite Diospolis megale/Luxor, the village of Memnoneia/Jeme stood in and around the earlier temple of Rameses III at Medinet Habu.[93] Beyond its walls to the north, east and west were extensive cemeteries, heavily plundered by the early 20th c.[94] Some superstructures were partially recorded in the early 20th c. and 1991.[95] To the north and east, mudbrick domed superstructures, square in plan, were sunken into the earth so that only the domes were visible. Accessible down

---

81   Other surveys are restricted by different research questions; e.g., the presence of Greek or Coptic funerary stelae governs the parameters of Tudor (2011) and Dunand (2007) does not seek to be comprehensive.

82   For a model approach in Egypt, see Stevens (2018).

83   The key resources are Timm (1984–1992), now supplemented with an index; Brune (2007); Atiya (1992); Bagnall and Rathbone (2004). The bibliography for burial sites is usefully compiled in Tudor (2011) 19–136, but the information in the summaries must be used with caution.

84   Gascoigne and Rose (2012); Rose and Gascoigne (2013); van der Vliet (2013).

85   Österreichisches Archäologisches Institut, *Fortification Hisn al-Bab: Border Relations of Egypt and Nubia in Late Antiquity and the Early Middle Ages*, in https://www.oeaw.ac.at/en/oeai /research/military-infrastructure-and-transport-routes/hisn -al-bab-late-antique-border/ (last accessed Sept. 2018).

86   W. Müller (2014) 67.

87   Björnesjö (2013); Speiser *et al.* (2013); Hawari (2015).

88   Speiser *et al.* (2013), 222.

89   Richter (2015).

90   Monneret de Villard (1927), 117–20; Maspero (1887) 225.

91   Monneret de Villard (1927) 76, 155.

92   Krastel (2017).

93   For an overview of the site, see Wilfong (2002); for the history of discovery and publication of late antique sites in this region, see O'Connell (2014a); for the best maps of the region, see Pimpaud and Lecuyot (2013).

94   Winlock and Crum (1926) 5, pl. 1. For Ptolemaic and Roman cemeteries in the region, see also Strudwick (2003).

95   Hölscher (1954); el-Bialy (1992).

a few steps, the entrance in some cases was blocked by empty amphorae probably associated with a funerary meal.[96] In rare instances in which tombs were undisturbed, mummies lay on low, white-washed beds with small pottery vessels as grave goods. These and burials with or without ceramic coffins were thought to be contemporary and date to the second half of the 3rd c.[97] Mummy-labels associated with this cemetery dated up to the early 4th c.[98] To the south of these tomb structures are the remains of a funerary church containing pit graves, with at least two lined with bricks and including internal head-supports.[99] To the west of the town, a heavily plundered cemetery was probably the main burial ground for residents in the 7th–8th c. heyday of the town. Dated by pottery, it consisted of oblong graves cut into the rock to a depth of 1 m or pits with small side chambers at 2 m depth.[100]

On the desert escarpment rising above the town are the remains of 1) two monasteries, the Monastery of St. Phoibammon founded by Apa Abraham and the Monastery of Apa Paul (introduction, above), 2) three churches and 3) several clusters of monastic dwellings, some of which have their own cemeteries. It is unfortunate that contemporary burials to the west of the town have not been recorded for comparison. Where organic remains survive, bodies in the burials on the desert escarpment are treated uniformly as mummiform bundles, wrapped in shrouds and bound by tapestry-woven bands, with organics such as juniper berries and salt distributed between the wrappings.

At the Monastery of St. Phoibammon, excavators reported burials discovered in what appeared to be benches in the antechamber of what was originally the chapel of Hatshepsut and probably functioned as a church in Late Antiquity.[101] Their location suggests that these would have been elite burials, perhaps even those of Abraham and his successors. At the Monastery of Apa Paul at Dra abu el-Naga, the cemetery may have originally contained up to 400 burials, most robbed today.[102] Older burials were cut into the rock. Later, they were covered with sand and rubble serving as a foundation

for secondary burials enclosed in rectangular graves. Rows of side-by-side graves are separated by footpaths. Some remains are skeletal, but others are well-preserved mummiform bundles. Where the sex has been determinable (for 22 of the 26 extant burials contemporary with the monastery), all were male, suggesting they were associated with the monastery.[103]

Small cemeteries were also present at three churches in the region. The mudbrick church dedicated to St. Mark the Evangelist at the top of the hill of Qurnet Marai (*O.Marc*) originally had 5 or 6 graves located on an artificial terrace east of the building complex, just along the east wall (and apse) of the church. Three mummiform bundles were discovered intact, lying in simple pits.[104] In the valley to the north, at the temple of Hathor/Church of St. Isidoros at Deir el-Medina, two rows of graves, 12 in all, were found along the eastern exterior walls.[105] The founder of the church and 12 other men, some known to be his successors, are commemorated with their dates of death in a long inscription on the south exterior wall of the church, and this may name the men buried there.[106] Along the cultivation, at the Ramesseum, a small church therein had 10 burials in and around it.[107] Due to the conditions of preservation near the cultivation, the Ramesseum burials are skeletal with limited textile remains. It is not clear if the church and its cemetery are related to a monastic or other settlement. Among the 10 bodies studied, 2 are female.[108] A Coptic funerary stela belonging to the hegoumene Maria and dated 891 is said to come from the Ramesseum and may have belonged to this cemetery.[109]

At least three monastic dwelling complexes on the desert escarpment also have their own small cemeteries. To the south of the Theban promontory at the putative first *topos* of Phoebammon (*O.Phoeb.*), two intact burials, wrapped in shrouds and bands, were located in pits dug into the plateau above the settlement in a bay of cliffs.[110] At Sheikh abd el-Gurna, outside the boundary wall of the *topos* of Epiphanius built in and around a cluster of tomb-dwellings, 10 or 11 burials were localized under and around a mudbrick superstructure (*P.Mon.Epiph.*).

96   Hölscher (1934), pl. 34; (1954) 42–44, fig. 50, pls. 27–28; el-Bialy (1992).
97   Hölscher (1954) 43.
98   Wilfong (1995).
99   Hölscher (1954) 56–57, fig. 61.
100 Winlock and Crum (1926) 5.
101 Godlewski (1986) 47–48.
102 For an introduction to the cemetery, see Burkard and Eichner (2007). For the identification of the site and overviews, see Beckh *et al.* (2011); Polz *et al.* (2012); so far, only textiles from the settlement site, and not the cemetery, have been published, Tatz (2017).

103 Lösch, Hower-Tilmann and Zink (2012).
104 Castel (1979); Grossmann (2013).
105 Baraize (1914).
106 Heurtel and Daumas (2004).
107 Lecuyot (2000).
108 Macke (2012).
109 Wilfong (2002) 106–107, 154. The 9th c. date is about 100 years later than other documented communities in the region.
110 Bachatly *et al.* (1961) pls. 113–15. The modern transliteration Phoebammon is maintained here as a convention to readily distinguish it from the Monastery of Phoibammon at Deir el-Bahri.

These were all male, and identified as monastic on the basis of the characteristic leather girdles and aprons.[111] At the nearby so-called *topos* of Kyriakos (*O.Cyriakos*), a double grave was found in the courtyard of a tomb dwelling (TT 65).[112]

There are only up to 5 funerary stelae from Western Thebes, none discovered *in situ*. This small number is in marked contrast with the capital to the south, Hermonthis/Armant, where *ca.* 70 funerary stelae were purchased by excavators.[113] We may, therefore, wonder if funerary inscriptions on walls were common in Western Thebes, as at the Church of Isidorus at Deir el-Medina.

This/Girga Region

As at Western Thebes, extensive late antique remains of habitation are recorded at nearly every ancient cemetery within the monumental ancient Egyptian necropolis at Abydos near the ancient capital This, at or near Girga. The exact location of the Monastery of Moses, so well-known from both literary and epigraphic sources, within this region has not been established, but indeed most of the sites recorded so far appear to be monastic.[114] Evidence of 'Coptic' burials appears in earlier excavation reports, and about a dozen grave stelae are known in collections today.[115] Recent work at the site of an earlier pre-dynastic cemetery, south of the Seti I temple, has uncovered at least a dozen burials in simple pit graves, each wrapped in linen secured by bands and dated by their textiles to the Late Roman/Byzantine period.[116]

On the east bank opposite This/Girga, at Naga ed-Deir, there are rock-cut tombs on the desert escarpment and pre-dynastic cemeteries at its base. In and around the latter, over 265 'Coptic' burials were recorded in the early 20th c., and revisited more recently as part of a synthetic study on the late antique phase of the region.[117] Where gender could be determined in the early 20th c. study, the corpus included 43 males, 38 females and 40 'immature' bodies, suggesting a civic rather than monastic population. In general, bodies were dressed in one to three tunics, and placed on wooden or palm supports; salt and organics were distributed over the bodies. Each was wrapped in 1 to 6 shrouds, with excess folds and other textile or plant fibre covering the face to protect it, and the resulting bundle was bound by bands. Jewellery,

including crucifix pendants, was worn by the deceased, and glass vessels and weaving implements sometimes accompanied burials. A pierced coin from the third year of the reign of Justinian I (AD 529) was worn as a pendant by a child.[118] Three grave stelae are attributed to the site.

Panopolis/Akhmim Region

There are monastic cemeteries on the west bank in addition to the large civic cemetery excavated at Panopolis/Akhmim from the 1880s onward (above). Near Atripe stands the famous Church of Shenoute or the 'White Monastery'.[119] An extraordinary triconch tomb chapel with barrel-vaulted substructures is now thought to be the tomb of Shenoute himself (d. 465). The painted programme includes typical funerary motifs, including a jewelled cross, peacocks and gazelles, as well as a figure with a square halo thought to be Shenoute.[120] Shenoute's own *Rules* give instructions for funerals (*Rules* 216–26, 229), including a limit to the number of shrouds (*hboos*, var. *hbos*) and bands (*keiria*) in which bodies may be wrapped (i.e., three shrouds and two sets of bands each), and the direction that children shall not receive them at all (*Rule* 216).[121]

Antaeopolis/Qaw El-Kebir Region

On the east bank, at and north of Antaeopolis/Qaw el-Kebir, running along the desert escarpment, are a series of cemeteries excavated under Petrie between 1922–1927, and by Guy and Winifred Brunton in 1927– 1931. Best known for their pre-dynastic remains are Qaw, Hemamieh, Badari, Mostagedda, and Matmar, all of which also yielded burials dated from Roman to Medieval times.[122] At Qaw, Hemamieh and Badari, buildings identified as churches or chapels, some with evidence of wall-paintings, contained burials *in situ*.[123] Numerous Coptic funerary stelae were collected and, at Badari, they were found *in situ* running along the interior walls of one of these structures.[124] Coptic grave stelae were also collected from Matmar, with only a small proportion found *in situ*,[125] but no stelae were apparently collected from Mostagedda.[126] New work reconstructing the history of excavation and distribution of objects from both late antique Mostagedda and Matmar

---

111   Winlock and Crum (1926) 45, 50.

112   Bács (2009).

113   Mond and Myers (1937) 259–66 (most are said to have been reburied), 2: pls. 72–73; (1940) 1:195–96, 2: pl. 14.

114   O'Connell (2020).

115   Peet (1914); O'Connell (2020); van der Vliet (2020).

116   Hossein (2011); Gabr (2011) 282–84, burials 1–8, 10–11, and 13.

117   O'Connell (2001) 16–22, 34–35, 66–76; see now also, O'Connell (2020) 5–9.

118   O'Connell (2001) pl. 9.

119   Brooks Hedstrom and Bolman (2011).

120   Bolman, Davies and Pyke (2010); Bolman *et al.* (2014).

121   Layton (2014) 177–83.

122   Brunton (1927–1930), (1937), (1948).

123   Brunton (1927–1930) 3: 26–29, 30–32, 33–34, pls. 49–57.

124   Brunton (1930) 31, pl. 56.

125   Brunton (1948) pl. 68.

126   Brunton (1937) 139–46, pl. 83.

shows that the dead were shrouded, usually in or with their clothes, and more rarely shoes, and wrapped in tapestry-woven bands, sometimes with wooden (or perhaps palm?) supports, and deposited in unlined graves.[127] Jewellery was worn or deposited with females. Other grave goods included pottery and glass vessels, dishes and other objects, baskets and, probably, mirrors. On the basis of radiocarbon-dated textiles from the sites, the burials at Matmar were largely *ca.* 4th–7th c., with a peak in the 5th/6th c., and those at Mostagedda were *ca.* 4th–8th/9th c.[128]

Lykopolis/Asyut Region

On the desert escarpment overlooking the regional capital of Lykopolis/Asyut, monastic settlements and dwellings were installed in and around earlier pharaonic tombs.[129] At the turn of the 20th c., Christian burials were described in pits hewn into the rock, sometimes side-by-side, separated only by a thin wall. Some bodies were buried in wooden coffins or covered by reed or palm-fibre mats.[130] Today, new work synthesizing old records and new excavations has documented three largely plundered Christian cemeteries. On top of the mountain plateau at Deir el-Azam, above the rock-cut tombs inhabited in Late Antiquity, lay a complex of buildings with a church and surrounded by a wall.[131] Burials were found inside the church, and surrounding the complex were *ca.* 1,400 graves.[132] While the complex may have been built as early as the 5th c. AD,[133] the cemetery contains men, women and children with combs bearing Arabic inscriptions and imitation tiraz textiles, suggesting they belong to a non-monastic, Medieval Christian community. The pottery dates mainly to the 8th–10th c., with glazed wares dating to the 12th–13th c. 6 other Christian burials were recently found in an area called Kom el-Shuqafa, also on the plateau, where pottery suggests a date before the 6th c. AD.[134] Below the plateau, at Deir el-Meitin, burials were mentioned in *ca.* 1900, but the area is entirely plundered today. Coptic funerary stelae found in nearby tombs may relate to this cemetery.[135]

On the desert escarpment south of Lykopolis/Asyut are several monastic settlements occupying pharaonic rock-cut tombs and gallery quarries at Deir el-Rifa, Deir el-Balayza, Wadi Sarga and Deir el-Ganadlah.[136] The sites were investigated by Petrie in the same seasons and conflated so that the findspots of grave stelae are sometimes uncertain. Characteristically of the time, it was only the inscribed material that was published, e.g., at Deir el-Balayza (*P.Bal.*) and Wadi Sarga (*P.Sarga*). From archival sources and objects in collections today, however, it is possible to reconstruct and study these sites.[137] The excavator R. Campbell Thompson was specifically tasked by the Byzantine Research Fund to find cemeteries at or near the monastery located at Wadi Sarga in order to secure 'Coptic textiles' for the British Museum collection. Among the 'many graves opened' in Cemetery 1 at the mouth of Wadi Sarga, he numbered just 8, 2 of which contained 2 bodies. He summarized that they were 'poor burials', wrapped in shrouds, with head to the west, and he further commented on the excellent preservation of their beards (Fig. 9).[138]

Hermopolis/El-Ashmunein Region

On the east side of the river is Antinoopolis (*P.Ant.*), founded *ca.* 138 (above), when its district (nome) was carved out of the already existing Hermopolite district. On the west bank is the more ancient capital Hermopolis/el-Ashmunein (*BGU* XVII, *P.Herm.*, *P.Lond.Herm. P.Sorb.*II, *P.Mon.Apollo*).[139] At some distance to the west, across the Bahr Yusuf, is one of its cemeteries, Tuna al-Gebel, with extensive catacombs containing millions of ibis and other animal burials as well as funerary monuments of the Ptolemaic and Roman periods. Tomb 'houses' are arranged in streets, many with relief sculpture and elaborate wall-paintings.[140] Recent work has concentrated on secondary burials within these complexes, for which *in situ* ceramics have been interpreted as grave goods or as evidence for food preparation or dining as part of feasting. Material has been dated up to the 4th/5th c.[141] Roman tombs along the earlier processional route to the ibis catacombs likewise demonstrate evidence of funerary ritual up to the 4th c.[142]

127 Pleşa (2017a), (2017b).
128 Pleşa (2017a), (2017b).
129 It has been argued to be the location of the dwelling of the famous Apa John of Lycopolis known to us through 5th c. literary sources: Kahl (2014), with bibliography.
130 Maspero (1900) 113–14; De Bock (1901) 88–91.
131 Maspero (1900); Kahl (2014) 130.
132 Maspero (1900) 110, 115.
133 Kahl *et al.* (2010), 207; Kahl (2014) 130.
134 Kahl *et al.* (2010) 207–208; Kahl (2014) 130.
135 Maspero (1900) 111; Kahl (2014) 130.

136 Petrie (1907) 2, 39–43.
137 O'Connell (2014c).
138 Among the textiles preserved from the Wadi Sarga excavation, most are furnishing textiles and cannot be localized in the cemeteries on the basis of the excavation notebooks, see Pritchard (2017).
139 Bailey (1991).
140 Lembke (2012).
141 Mamedow (2017).
142 Flossmann-Schütze (2017).

To the south of Hermopolis, the Monastery of Apollo at Bawit was one of the largest and most important monasteries in Egypt (*P.Bawit, P.Bawit Clackson, P.Brux.Bawit, P.Louvre Bawit, O.BawitIFAO*). While it appears in the literature from *ca.* AD 400, the earliest archaeological remains date to the 6th, but especially 7th–8th, c. When it was first excavated by Jean Clédat at the turn of the 20th c., it took him some time to identify what he was excavating, and whether they were painted funerary chapels or monastic dwellings with oratories.[143] Indeed, they were the latter, but scholars have remarked on the architectural and decorative similarity between the two. From the settlement site, in three directions stretch cemeteries with different combinations of super- and substructures and pits covered by stones or marked with poles. Two cemeteries seem to be comprised of monastery residents, while a third contains men, women, and children and remained in use up until modern times.[144]

Oxyrhynchus/El-Bahnasa Region

Oxyrhynchus, located along the Bahr Yusuf, is most famous for its papyri-producing rubbish heaps (*P.Oxy.*). The remains of its town and its cemeteries were investigated by Petrie, with building sculpture from funerary monuments now distributed in museum collections.[145] Recent work has documented one Christian funerary complex in use between the late 4th and early 7th c.[146] It consists of a decorated chapel with access to several 'crypts' (i.e. reused Roman period tombs). Wall-paintings in the chapel depict a range of subjects (e.g. Jonah and the whale), in more and less formal styles, and dipinti consisting of crosses, wreaths and texts within tabula ansata.[147] Bioarchaeology has been conducted on the largely skeletonized human remains from the site: e.g. one crypt contained 110 individuals, including 78 children, and another contained 21 individuals, 7 of them children.[148]

Ankyronpolis/El-Hibeh Region

To the north, on the other side of the river, is Ankyronpolis/el-Hibeh and a series of sites to its south at and between Karara and Sharuna/Kom el-Ahmar. At Ankyronpolis/el-Hibeh, recent work has included the analyses of several late antique graves carved into the top of the first millennium BC tell. These were revealed

following the plundering of the site. To date, publications on the typical mummiform bundle pit burials have focused on bioarchaeological and textile analysis.[149]

At Karara in 1913/1914, Hermann Ranke excavated a heavily plundered cemetery of *ca.* 750 burials. Mudbrick superstructures and pit burials contained shrouded and bound mummiform bundles with particularly large, triangular structures protecting the head (Fig. 10).[150] The famous peacock coffin (above), with a triangular head-piece, is now in Heidelberg (Fig. 11).[151] Several of the late antique mummiform bundles have been CT-scanned and radiocarbon dated to the 7th–9th c. (above).[152] At Sharuna/Kom el-Ahmar, 10 km south of Karara, about 200 graves containing about 1,000 men and women have been uncovered in and around a funerary church.[153] The burials therein have been dated between the 4th/5th and 8th c.[154] At a nearby monastic complex of Deir el-Qarabin, one documented, unlooted burial belonged to a man aged 40–60, with radiocarbon analysis of the bones yielding a *ca.* 380–460 date. The documented unwrapping of the body enabled excavators to reconstruct the process of wrapping and shrouding.[155] At nearby el-Ghalida, a monastic cemetery in front of a series of monastic dwellings was the subject of a rescue archaeology mission in 1996. Remains of 25–30 males, aged *ca.* 10–60, were identified. In addition to the bioarchaeological remains, the site yielded evidence of so-called funerary beds or biers used to transport the bodies. These beds were studied in great detail. Sometimes the palm struts are found in burials, as at Karara; here, the textile covers are extant too, enabling reconstruction. Radiocarbon dates from bones from one burial yielded a date of 890–1020.[156]

Fayum

The Fayum is a depression irrigated by the Bahr Yusuf, and thus not officially an 'oasis', as it is sometimes termed. Periodically, and especially in the Ptolemaic and Roman periods, cultivation was extended with irrigation networks making it especially productive agriculturally. The topography is different from the Nile Valley with cemeteries found on rises or on the open ground beyond settlements, rather than on the steep desert escarpment. The capital, Arsinoe/Medinet al-Fayum, has long

143   Clédat (1904–1999).
144   The bibliography on Bawit is extensive, see Bénazeth (2015) and Hadji-Minaglou (2015).
145   Petrie (1925) 16–18; Krumeich (2003).
146   For dates according to pottery, see Subías Pascual (2011) 113.
147   Subías Pascual (2003).
148   Subías Pascual (2008) 145; Codina Reina (2016).

149   Yohe, Gardner and Heikkinen (2012); Yohe *et al.* (2012).
150   Ranke (1926); Nauerth (1996).
151   Huber and Nauerth (2018).
152   Gessler-Löhr *et al.* (2007), (2010).
153   Huber (1998), (2004).
154   Huber (2009).
155   Huber (2007).
156   Huber (2009).

FIGURE 12   Naqlun. Mummiform bundle, *ca.* 7th c.
COURTESY OF W. GODLEWSKI, PAM ARCHIVES

been a source for textiles on the antiquities market.[157] Furthermore, new work at Hawara, at the mouth of the Fayum, has indicated that the famous Roman period cemetery also contained later 4th–6th c. burials.[158]

At Naqlun, the earliest monastic dwellings (*ca.* 450–500) are located on the rise above the cultivation (*P.Naqlun*), with a Medieval monastery below.[159] In the 6th–7th c. non-monastic cemetery of *ca.* 200 men, women, and children (of which 16 have been studied in some detail), bodies are shrouded and bound (Fig. 12).[160] A later, Medieval cemetery comprised of *ca.* 500 burials, most in wooden coffins, more rarely with mud-brick vaults, dating from the 11th–14th c. is likewise a lay Christian population.[161] Lying head-west, many had funerary biers similar to those from the Sharuna region in their graves, while their clothes and shrouds with funerary inscriptions in Arabic are identical to contemporary Muslim burials.[162] One man was buried with a Coptic codex containing the Gospel of John, dated by its colophon to AD 1100.[163]

About 1.5 km north-west of Naqlun is Deir el-Banat. Despite its name, it does not include a monastic cemetery, but designates a necropolis spanning from the Late Ptolemaic to the Early Medieval period. Excavators have uncovered 271 graves containing a total of 345 burials, in the 'Graeco-Roman' Southern Necropolis and 'Coptic' Northern Necropolis.[164] Burials characterized as Christian comprise simple pit graves with bodies wearing tunics or 'torn-up' garments, wrapped in shrouds and bound, with a head-west orientation.[165]

Along the eastern edge of the Fayum at Fag el-Gamus, since 1982, excavation has focused on the identification of 'pagan' or 'Christian' practice among 1st–7th c. burials.[166] Over 1,000 burials at Fag al-Gamus have been counted and are identified by excavators as Christian on the basis of the direction of the head, with the oldest head-east burials radiocarbon dated to AD 79–230 and oldest head-west dated AD 128–284. With the head-west burials, amphorae fragments and drinking cups suggested grave-side rituals to the excavators.[167] To date, publication has focused on textiles.[168]

Along the southern edge of the Fayum, Tebtunis, best known for its Ptolemaic temple and Roman period town

157   Fluck (2006).
158   Uytterhoeven (2009) 468, 475.
159   Godlewski (2015).
160   Dzierzbicka and Ożarek (2012); Godlewski (2006).
161   Godlewski (2015); Zych (2008).
162   Fluck and Helmecke (2015) 236–37.
163   Godlewski (2005) 79.

164   Voytenko (2016); Tolmacheva (2017).
165   Tolmacheva (2017) 33–34.
166   Griggs (2005).
167   Griggs (2005) 192.
168   South and Muhlestein (2013); South (2017) with bibliography.

(*P.Tebt.*), has also revealed late antique and Medieval settlement.[169] An 8th–9th c. cemetery, the limits of which were not reached, contained *ca.* 830 burials, *ca.* 93% of which were newborns and children. Whereas newborns were found either wrapped in textile and deposited in the sand, or in amphorae or cooking pots, children were found wrapped in textile, sometimes on a board or in a coffin, itself sometimes wrapped in bands. Cooking pots found throughout the necropolis evidence funerary ritual.[170]

Memphis/Saqqara Region

At South Saqqara, the Monastery of Jeremias and its cemetery was excavated by James Quibell in 1906 to 1910, with later work by Peter Grossmann.[171] Building material for the monastery itself was largely reused from pharaonic monuments and near-contemporary late antique tombs, including a mausoleum with benches. As in the church of the Monastery of Hadra at Aswan (above), dozens of 7th–8th c. Coptic funerary stelae were later reused as paving in the refectory and other public spaces.[172] At North Saqqara, the Monastery of Apa Antinos (*P.Bingen* 123) occupied the remains of the Central Temple of the Sacred Animal Necropolis.[173] To the south of the complex, a cemetery comprised pits, many with mudbrick superstructures, some with grave stelae or pot sherds bearing funerary texts *in situ*.[174] Within, the head-west burials were shrouded and bound, sometimes on a board (including reused planks from earlier coffins), or wrapped in (palm?) fibre mats.[175] Of 166 graves opened, 138 contained 159 individuals. The presence of only 3 children and 28 females suggested to the excavators that the population was monastic and/or the females were interred at a later point.[176]

At Dashur, a few km south of Saqqara, there are extensive cemeteries containing burials dating from the Ptolemaic to late antique periods. Excavators at the site do not unwrap burials as a matter of policy. Instead, conservators have designed a 'mummy-kit' in order to safely remove, transport, study, and store mummies and late antique mummiform bundles. The latter have been dated from the 3rd to the 7th c.[177]

The Roman fortress at Babylon was besieged by the Muslim general 'Amr ibn al'As in *ca.* 640, and his camp became the new capital of Fustat.[178] When the Fatimids moved their capital nearby to al-Qahira in the 10th c., the road between the two became a massive cemetery.[179] A funerary complex therein is one of the few Muslim burial sites to be systematically documented.[180] As attested at 8th–12th c. Muslim cemeteries at Syene/Aswan (above) and at Kom al-Dikka in Alexandria (below), there was a great variety of tomb-types. As at Kom al-Dikka, bodies at Fustat were placed on their sides, with the head facing Mecca, and some evidence for wooden coffins is likewise recorded.

The Delta

The Egyptian Delta comprises a third of the governorates of modern Egypt (9/27), suggesting the importance of its agricultural yield. Despite its importance, the Delta is one of the least known regions of Egypt in Late Antiquity. All of this is changing fast with several archaeological surveys, especially in the Western Delta, showing an abundance of activity.[181] But evidence of burial is sparse because the region does not preserve organic remains like other areas of Egypt.

Alexandria Region and the Mediterranean Coast

To the west, at Alexandria, the Lake Mareotis region has also been subject to survey.[182] The extensive necropolis at Gabbari, located south-west of the ancient city, contains rock-cut hypogea, with burials therein spanning the 3rd c. BC to the 7th c. AD.[183] Christian painted funerary inscriptions are abundant in one area of the earlier necropolis, signalling reuse of earlier loculi.[184] The contents of one loculus of one chamber of a hypogeum was dated to Late Antiquity and contained 35 children under 5 years of age. They were wrapped in textiles, and sometimes plastered, so that they looked like mummies to the excavators.[185] Keyhole excavations elsewhere in the city are allowing further sites to be located and studied as a result of rescue archaeology. To the east of the ancient city, a site on Khalil el-Khayat Street was excavated in 2011 and revealed two (Hellenistic?) tomb structures with *ca.* 30 4th–5th c. graves containing *ca.* 9 adults buried in pits and *ca.* 21 children, 20 of which were buried

169   Gallazzi (2010).
170   Gallazzi and Hadji-Minaglou (2012).
171   Quibell, Thompson, and Spiegelberg (1909); Quibell and Thompson (1912); Grossmann (1971–2009).
172   For inscriptions, see Wietheger (1992).
173   Smith, Davies and Frazer (2005) 141–66, fig. 4.
174   Martin (1974) fig. 10, pls. 4–5.
175   Martin (1974), 21.
176   Jeffreys and Strouhal (1980) 29, 33.
177   Cortés (2009).

178   Sheehan (2010) 79–96.
179   Gayraud (1999).
180   Gayraud (1999).
181   O'Connell (Forthcoming b).
182   Blue and Khalil (2011).
183   Empereur and Nenna (2001–2003); Alix *et al.* (2012).
184   Heinen (2002).
185   Blaizot (2012).

in Late Roman amphorae.[186] The burials were generally south-west to north-east in orientation; the direction of the head was inconsistent.

At Kom al-Dikka, the location of a Roman theatre and auditoria, which were used until the beginning of the 7th c., the western area began to be used for rubbish and burial from the 8th c.[187] Renewed excavation of a Muslim cemetery has documented burials as early as the 8th c., and otherwise 10th–11th/12th c.[188] Marble grave stelae inscribed in Arabic with verses from the Qur'an and commemoration of individuals has been found, dated as early as the 9th c.[189] There is considerable variation in the 60 recently excavated graves, which were pits with or without slab coverings, and stone boxes made up of limestone slabs, also apparently with or without coverings. They are oriented north-west to south-east, with skeletonized remains indicating that bodies were placed on their sides, facing Mecca.[190] Some showed evidence of reuse, with earlier remains pushed to the west to make room for additional burials.[191] As at Fustat/Cairo, wooden coffins have also been found.[192] Glass, glazed-ware vessels, game counters and complete lamps have been assessed as evidence of gifts from visitors.[193]

To the south of Alexandria at Marea, from where pilgrims probably departed for the enormous pilgrimage centre at Abu Mina, recent work has revealed near the lake harbour a large 5th/6th c. Christian basilica with two crypts below the altar. At Abu Mina itself, there were burial crypts in the many churches in the complex[194] and associated cemeteries, only some of the tombs of which were described 100 years ago.[195]

Along the Mediterranean coast, the port town at Marina el-Alamein was active until the 4th/5th c. The south-western necropolis contains 1st c. BC–1st c. AD monumental stone tombs over hypogea either hewn into the rock or built with stone slabs underground. Wooden painted panel portraits were associated with

a few mummies, and burial in the same complexes is thought to have continued into the 2nd or even 3rd c.[196] Among over 900 people assessed, 233 were sub-adult, with 100 under 4 years of age.[197] To the east of this necropolis, located near a later 5th c. church, were found 3rd–4th c. burials in amphorae covered by sand and lined with stones.[198]

Eastern Desert and Red Sea Coast
Many Late Roman cemeteries associated with quarry settlements, forts and praesidia in the Eastern Desert and port sites on the Red Sea coast have been surveyed.[199] The cemetery at Mons Claudianus was largely plundered, while Christian burials are known from funerary stelae from Mons Porphyrites.[200] At the port site of Berenike, cult sites represent Egyptian, Greek and Roman hybrid deities as well as Christian, Palmyrene, South Arabian and Zoroastrian religious activities.[201] A 4th–5th c. cemetery located along the road linking the town to the Nile Valley comprised mausolea and pit burials. The former were built of the local material of choice at the town, coral heads, and contained evidence of coffins (i.e. the nails and corner pieces from wooden coffins). About 640 ring-cairn burials lay to the west and south-west of the town and these are also 4th–5th c., leading excavators to wonder if status, age, religion or ethnicity may have been factors in the decision to bury in one or the other location and in the choice of monument type.[202]

Western Desert Oases
Due especially to their relative inaccessibility, sites in the Western Desert oases are much better preserved than elsewhere in Egypt. Kharga and Dakhla oases are home to the earliest known churches and Christian burials in Egypt. Planned and targeted excavation of cemeteries is the norm, as is the application of bioarchaeological and other scientific analyses.

In the Dakhla Oasis, the Late Ptolemaic and Roman town of Kellis/Ismant el-Kharab has been systematically excavated since 1986, with several cemeteries located around the town and in the hinterland.[203] A mid-4th c. church at the town's western limit contained two burials

186 Sabah (2012) 256–57.
187 For the late antique site prior to its use as a cemetery, see Derda, Markiewicz and Wipszycka (2007); for the Muslim cemetery, see Promińska (1972).
188 The sectors are dated as follows: in area U (north-western part of the site) are tombs from the Upper (11th and 12th c.) and Middle (9th/10th c.) phases of the cemetery, and in area CW are tombs from the Upper and Lower (8th/9th c.) phases: Kulicka (2015), 62.
189 Kulicka (2010) 485–87.
190 Kulicka (2016) 56–57.
191 Kulicka (2010) 493.
192 Zych (2003).
193 Kulicka (2010) 496.
194 Grossmann (1989) 189–231.
195 Kaufmann (1918) 169–73, pls 130–42.

196 Daszewski and Zych (2012) 283–85, 289.
197 Kaczmarek (2012) 298.
198 Daszewski and Zych (2012) 283–85, 289.
199 Sidebotham, Hense and Nouwens (2008), 197–212; Sidebotham (2011) 276.
200 Peacock and Maxfield (1997) 137–38; Sidebotham, Hense and Nouwens (2008) 210.
201 Sidebotham (2014).
202 Sidebotham (2011) 264.
203 For an overview of sites and bibliography, see Bowen (2003).

before the sanctuary and 9 within the complex, all completely undisturbed, head-west, in pits with or without mudbrick covers. The *ca.* 4th c. Kellis 2 Cemetery comprises an estimated 4,000 burials in over 700 graves excavated to date.[204] Pit graves, some with mudbrick linings or covers to protect the body, are oriented head-west, with the bodies shrouded and bound with linen bands. In some instances, bodies were treated with "pine, acacia and caster oils mixed with clay and placed on the body", myrrh or covered in rosemary and other botanics.[205] Multiple methods of scientific analysis have been undertaken on the Kellis 2 Cemetery, making its population the best studied in Egypt.[206] The remarkable uniformity of burials at both Kellis 2 and the church contrasts with practices at the town's other cemeteries, suggesting to excavators that they contain a Christian population.[207] At nearby Trimithis/Amheida, a town which peaked in the Roman period, a 4th c. church excavated in 2012 has likewise proven to contain undisturbed burials, with 8 in or alongside the church and 3 within a sealed crypt.[208] Isotopic analysis has been undertaken at both Kellis and Trimithis.[209] Comparison between cemeteries at Kellis has suggested that the 4th c. cemeteries' inhabitants had a markedly different diet from the earlier populations, and may have been from elsewhere.[210]

Kharga Oasis, or the 'Great Oasis', flourished in the Roman period. A cemetery at Bagawat, to the west of its capital Hibis/el-Kharga, is often said to have been in use from the *ca.* 3rd–7th c., and to have contained both 'pagan' and Christian burials. But datable evidence suggests a 4th–7th c. date and probable Christian character.[211] The cemetery comprises *ca.* 260 chapels, some with extant wall-paintings, e.g. a depiction from Exodus and scenes of Paul and Thecla.[212] Graves were pits sometimes surmounted by mudbrick or stone superstructures, or instead comprised hypogea. Excavated from 1908, the architecture and textiles are planned for full publication.[213] In general, the deceased was shrouded and bound with linen bands, with salt distributed over the bundle.[214]

To the north is el-Deir, the location of a Roman period fort (the departure point through the desert to This/Girga), and numerous necropoleis of all periods.[215] In one cemetery said to be Christian, *ca.* 150 tombs (some empty) containing *ca.* 120 people were discovered.[216] Pottery associated with burials is said to date to the 4th c.[217] Most of the dead were deposited in pit graves, with only 4 more elaborate tombs containing multiple burials.[218] Burials at the north end of the cemetery are head-west in orientation, while those to the south are oriented north-west to south-east.[219] Shrouded bodies were bound by linen or cotton bands, or other fibre cords.[220] They were buried with jewellery and vegetal remains, sometimes within the wrappings.

To the south lies Kysis/Dush, at a desert crossroads connecting Kharga to the Nile Valley at Apollonopolis Magna/Edfu. Its investigated cemeteries date from the 1st–5th c. Among the 95 published tombs are some with one or more chambers entered via descents with or without stairs, and pits with one or two chambers.[221] They contain *ca.* 700 people. While no evidence has been found for Christianity in Kysis/Dush, the excavators have suggested that traditional mummification for one family group up to *ca.* AD 315 indicated they were 'pagan', but shrouded and wrapped burials said to date *ca.* 380 are identified as Christian, apparently because they were treated differently, with desiccation achieved by including slabs of salt in their wrappings.[222] An embroidered tunic found as packing material within the shrouds of a young girl, thought to have been buried in the 4th c., has elicited excitement due to the clavi decoration depicting nude winged figures holding wreaths and variously interpreted as victories, 'cupids' or dancers.[223]

Conclusions

When the Bishop Abraham and the property owners Elisabeth, Anna and Susanna drew up their wills, they instructed their families, be they spiritual or biological, to carry out their wishes. The corpus of wills from Western Thebes shows that both men and women sought the same burial rites, provided they had some status. These wills show the shift from Greek to Coptic

204   Bowen (2012).
205   Bowen (2012) 357.
206   Dupras *et al.* (2016) with bibliography.
207   Bowen (2012).
208   Bagnall *et al.* (2015) 128, 130.
209   Dupras *et al.* (2016).
210   Dupras *et al.* (2008) 121–25.
211   Bagnall and Rathbone (2004) 253.
212   Fakhry (1951); Cipriano (2016).
213   Kajitani (2006); P. Grossmann pers. comm. For objects, see The Metropolitan Museum of Art, https://www.metmuseum.org/exhibitions/listings/2012/kharga-oasis (last accessed 15 Oct 2018).
214   Kajitani (2006), 100, 104.

215   Dunand *et al.* (2010–2015).
216   Coudert (2012) 457–58.
217   Coudert (2012) 457–58.
218   Coudert (2012) 453.
219   Coudert (2012) 242.
220   Coudert (2012) 457.
221   Dunand *et al.* (1992–2005).
222   Dunand (2007) 169–71.
223   Letellier-Willemin (2013).

in legal documents that occurred fairly quickly following the Muslim conquest of Egypt *ca.* 641. Abraham had dictated his will in Coptic to be recorded in Greek in compliance with Roman law. Thereafter, notaries were free to use Coptic.[224] There is no question of their religious affiliation: Abraham was a bishop, and Elisabeth explicitly wishes to be buried as befits 'every Christian woman' (*P.KRU* 68.66). Some wills also stipulate that they be buried 'according to the custom of the country (*kata ton epichôrion nomon*)' and 'according to the character (*ethos*) of the village', respectively (see introduction). While the former in particular has been used to suggest that Abraham preferred to be 'mummified' in an Egyptian fashion,[225] I suggest that we should take a more local approach as implied by the vocabulary each testator employs.

Continuity and Change in Egypt

Egyptologists have long assumed, on the model of 'eternal Egypt', that later burial practice was a poor ('Coptic') version of earlier tradition. Coptic literary texts have been mined for evidence to support continuity of the Egyptian ideology that sought to preserve the body for the afterlife, and the tension between this and ascetic Christian renunciation of the body has been explored.[226] The question of continuity and change is a fundamental one, but, as the above survey (3), makes clear, we do not always have solid dates gained either through stratigraphic excavation or scientific methods, such as radiocarbon dating, that would clarify chronology. Certainly, there has been little emphasis on the interred people themselves. The variation in the layout of cemeteries, tomb architecture and decoration, patterns of reuse of earlier structures, orientation of burial and the treatment of the body suggest that these features cannot furnish a reliable chronology.

By adopting a regional approach to the archaeology of death, burial, and commemoration in Egypt, patterns may better emerge. So too differences between cemeteries belonging to capitals, the countryside and monasteries may become more distinct.[227] Some differences between regions are apparent in the survey above – e.g. linen bands were used in the oases, whereas bands incorporating wool are typical in the Nile Valley – and this is probably based on the ready availability of materials. The region of Ankyronpolis/el-Hibeh and the entrance to the Fayum are distinctive for the size of the mummiform bundles built up to protect the body and especially the head. Even as we adopt a more nuanced approach to sites and regions within Egypt, there are also some advantages to generalizing in order to better appreciate what Egypt may have had in common with the contemporary late antique world.

Egypt in the Late Antique World

In general, we can find commonalities with burial practices in other parts of the empire and former empire in the expression of family, gender, linguistic, religious, and 'ethnic' identity, as well as status. The defining unit for burial groups undoubtedly continued to be the family.[228] In monasteries, the biological family was replaced by the spiritual family, and these families too were buried together in their cemeteries.[229] In some instances, monasteries also became the locus of burial for lay populations (e.g. Deir Anba Hadra at Syene/Aswan, Deir el-Azzam at Lykopolis/Asyut, Bawit and Naqlun near the Hermopolis). This may be due to the perceived holiness of the place, or because monasteries were often themselves located in earlier cemeteries which presented themselves as ideal locations for burial, or both. Gender is signalled through grave goods, especially jewellery, but also kitchen utensils and weaving implements as at Mostagedda and Matmar. Unique to Egypt is the excellent preservation of textiles, which further signal gender, but especially status. Elite status could be further marked through elaborate tomb monuments, funerary stelae, and coffins, as well as grave goods. Only in a few instances are the origins of a population by descent ('ethnicity') considered by current projects, either as a result of differing contemporary tomb styles, as at Berenike, or isotope analysis, as at Kellis.

Whether or not populations were 'pagan' or Christian is the defining question for some research projects. Evidence for Christian burial includes the location of burials in churches and monasteries, the subjects of wall-paintings and other tomb decoration, funerary stelae or other epigraphic evidence, and the iconography of decoration on textiles and jewellery. If such markers are missing, head-west orientation of pit burials is common in what are otherwise clearly Christian cemeteries (e.g. associated with monasteries), but there is enough variation to suggest that it should not be the only criterion

---

224   For the introduction of Arabic, and its registers of use in the first centuries of Muslim rule, see Sijpesteijn (2013); for Arabic replacing Coptic in everyday communication among Christian communities in the Fatimid period, when the Arabic language gained cultural prestige beyond Muslim communities, see Papaconstantinou (2007).

225   Krause (1991), 1697.

226   Krause (1983); Fischhaber (1997).

227   The regions of the capitals of Antaeopolis and Lykopolis particularly may furnish a nice data set in this regard.

228   Rebillard (2009).

229   For biological and spiritual families, see O'Connell (Forthcoming a).

to be deployed.[230] The absence of children from some cemeteries, and their inclusion in others, has led to some discussion of whether the latter may be a Christian feature.[231] Muslim burials are apparently distinctive, with the body on its side, and the face oriented toward Mecca. Nevertheless, only a handful of Muslim cemeteries have been investigated owing to the Egyptian government's prohibition, and we might wonder if the burials of people who adopted Islam would be recognizable in the archaeological record without other markers.

It is true that what I have termed 'mummiform bundles' visually resemble earlier Egyptian mummies. But such bundles are also more simply shrouded and bound bodies, albeit with regional characteristics. Recent documentation of 4th c. burials in Trier employing microscopy and other scientific techniques, for example, has demonstrated that the elite were dressed, shrouded and bound, deposited in stone sarcophagi and embedded and covered in soft gypsum or fir wood shavings.[232] Like the salt distributed with Egyptian burial shrouds and over the body, gypsum and wood shavings would likewise have had a drying and absorptive effect.[233] Depictions of the dead, foremost, a shrouded and bound Lazarus, appear on a wide-range of media such as stone sarcophagi, ivories and gold glass. Were shrouded and bound bodies the norm, or at least one common option throughout the late antique world, for which Egypt simply offers the best levels of preservation? Continuity with ancient Egyptian practice may be more superficial, than actual.

Bibliography

All papyrological abbreviations are cited throughout the chapter in accordance with the conventions established in J. F. Oates *et al.*, *Checklist of Greek, Latin, Demotic and Coptic Papyri, Ostraca and Tablets,* http://papyri.info/docs/checklist (last accessed Sept. 2018) and P. M. Sijpesteijn, J. F. Oates, A. Kaplony, E. M. Youssef-Grob, and D. Potthast, *Checklist of Arabic Documents.* http://www.naher-osten.lmu.de/isapchecklist (last accessed Sept. 2018).

Abdalla A. (1992) *Graeco-Roman Funerary Stelae from Upper Egypt* (Liverpool 1992).

Alix G., Boës É., Georges P., and Nenna M.-D. (2012) "Les enfants dans la nécropole gréco-romaine du Pont de Gabbari à Alexandrie: Problématiques et études de cas", in *L'enfant et la mort dans l'Antiquité II: Types de tombes et traitement du corps des enfants dans l'Antiquité gréco-romaine. Actes de la table ronde internationale organisée à Alexandrie, Centre d'Études Alexandrines, 12–14 novembre 2009* (Études Alexandrines 26), ed. M.-D. Nenna (Alexandria 2012) 79–137.

Atiya A. S. (1991) *The Coptic Encyclopedia*, 6 vols (New York and Toronto 1991).

Bachatly C. *et al.* (1961) *Le monastère de Phoebammon dans la Thébaïde I* (Publications de la Société d'Archéologie Copte) (Cairo 1961).

Bács T. A. (2009) "The late antique period on Sheikh abd el-Gurna: the monastery of Cyriacus", in *Hungarian Excavations in the Theban Necropolis: A Celebration of 102 Years of Fieldwork in Egypt. Catalogue for the Temporary Exhibition in the Egyptian Museum, Cairo, November 6, 2009–January 15, 2010*, edd. T. A. Bács *et al.* (Budapest 2009).

Bagnall R. S. (1993) *Egypt in Late Antiquity* (Princeton 1993).

Bagnall R. S. (1995) *Reading Papyri, Writing Ancient History* (London 1995).

Bagnall R. S. (2003) "Periodizing when you don't have to: the concept of Late Antiquity in Egypt", in *Gab es eine Spätantike?*, ed. B. Sirks (Frankfurt 2003) 39–49.

Bagnall R. S. *et al.* (2015) *An Oasis City* (New York 2015).

Bagnall R. S. and Rathbone D. edd. (2004) *Egypt from Alexander to the Copts: An Archaeological and Historical Guide* (Cairo and New York 2004).

Bailey D. M. (1991) *Excavations at El-Ashmunein IV: Hermopolis Magna. Buildings of the Roman Period* (London 1991).

Baraize M. É. (1914) "Compte rendu des travaux exécutés à Déîr-el-Médinéh", *ASA* 13 (1914) 19–24.

Beckh T., Eichner I., and Hodak S. (2011) "Briefe aus der koptischen Vergangenheit: Zur Indentifikation der Klosteranlage Deir el-Bachît in Theben-West", *Mitteilungen des Deutschen Archäologischen Instituts, Kairo* 67 (2011) 15–30.

Bénazeth D. (2015) "Bawit in the twenty-first century: Bibliography 1997–2014", in *Christianity and Monasticism in Middle Egypt: Al-Minya and Asyut*, edd. G. Gabra and H. N. Takla (Cairo 2015) 199–214.

Betz H.-D. (1986) *The Greek Magical Papyri in Translation* (Chicago and London 1986).

el-Bialy M. A. (1992) "Découverte d'une nécropole tardive aux environs de Gurnet Murrai", *Memnonia* 3 (1992) 83–87.

Björnesjö S. (2013) "The history of Aswan and its cemetery in the Middle Ages", in *The First Cataract of the Nile: One Region – Diverse Perspectives* (Sonderschriften des Deutschen Archäologischen Instituts, Kairo 36), edd. D. Raue, S. J. Seidlmayer, and P. Speiser (Berlin 2013) 9–14.

Blaizot F. (2012) "Le loculus A1 de la salle B28.3, nécropole du Pont de Gabbari, Alexandrie: Une sépulture collective réservée aux très jeunes enfants", in *L'enfant et la mort dans l'Antiquité II: Types de tombes et traitement du corps des enfants dans l'Antiquité gréco-romaine. Actes de*

---

230   Dunand (2007) 174.
231   Bowen (2012).
232   Reifarth (2013), esp. 425; and Reifarth *et al.* (Forthcoming).
233   Reifarth (2013) 146–47.

la table ronde internationale organisée à Alexandrie, Centre d'Études Alexandrines, 12–14 novembre 2009 (Études Alexandrines 26), ed. M.-D. Nenna (Alexandria 2012) 151–208.

Blue L. K. and Khalil E. (2011) *The Lake Mareotis Research Project: A Multidisciplinary Approach to Alexandria's Economic Past* (BAR-IS 2285) (Oxford 2011).

Bolman E. S., Davis S. J., and Pyke G. (2010) "Shenoute and a recently discovered tomb chapel at the White Monastery", *Journal of Early Christian Studies* 18 (2010) 453–62.

Bolman E. S. *et al.* (2014) "The tomb of St. Shenoute at the White Monastery: final conservation and documentation", *Bulletin of the American Research Center in Egypt* 204 (2014) 21–24.

Borg B. (2012) "Portraits", in *Oxford Handbook of Roman Egypt*, ed. C. Riggs (Oxford 2012) 613–29.

Bowen G. E. (2003) "Some observations on Christian burial practices at Kellis", in *The Oasis Papers 3: Proceedings of the Third International Conference of the Dakhleh Oasis* (Dakhleh Oasis Project 14), edd. G. E. Bowen and C. A. Hope (Oxford 2003) 167–79.

Bowen G. E. (2012) "Child, infant and foetal burials of the Late Roman period at Ismant el-Kharab, ancient Kellis, Dakhleh Oasis", in *L'enfant et la mort dans l'Antiquité II: Types de tombes et traitement du corps des enfants dans l'Antiquité gréco-romaine. Actes de la table ronde internationale organisée à Alexandrie, Centre d'Études Alexandrines, 12–14 novembre 2009* (Études Alexandrines 26), ed. M.-D. Nenna (Alexandria 2012) 351–72.

Brooks Hedstrom D. and Bolman E. S. (2011) "The White Monastery Federation Project: survey and mapping at the monastery of Apa Shenoute (Dayr al-Anba Shinūda), Sohag, 2005–2007", *DOP* 65/66 (2001) 333–64.

Brune K.-H. (2007) *Index zu Das christlich-koptische Ägypten in arabischer Zeit (Stefan Timm)* (Beihefte zum Tübinger Atlas des Vorderen Orients; Reihe B. Geisteswissenschaften 41.7) (Wiesbaden 2007).

Brunton G. (1927–1930) *Qau and Badari*, 3 vols. (British School of Archaeology in Egypt and Egyptian Research Account 45, 46, 50) (London 1927–1930).

Brunton G. (1937) *Mostagedda and the Tasian Culture* (British Museum Expedition to Middle Egypt) (London 1937).

Brunton G. (1948) *Matmar* (British Museum Expedition to Middle Egypt) (London 1948).

Burkard G. and Eichner I. (2007) "Zwischen pharaonischen Gräbern und Ruinen: Das Kloster Deir el-Bachit in Theben-West", in *Begegnung mit der Vergangenheit: 100 Jahre in Ägypten: Deutsches Archäologisches Institut Kairo 1907–2007*, edd. G. Dreyer and D. A. Polz (Mainz 2007) 270–74.

Calament F. (2005) *La révélation d'Antinoé par Albert Gayet: Histoire, archéologie, muséographie* (2 vols) (Bibliothèque d'Études Coptes 18) (Cairo 2005).

Calament F. and Durand M. edd. (2013) *Antinoé à la vie, à la mode: Visions d'élégance dans les solitudes* (Lyons 2013).

Calament F., Eichmann R., and Vendries C. edd. (2012) *Le luth dans l'Égypte byzantine: La tombe de la "Prophétesse" d'Antinoé au Musée de Grenoble* (Orient Archäologie 26) (Berlin 2012).

Cartron G. (2012) *L'architecture et les pratiques funéraires dans l'Égypte romaine* (BAR-IS 2398) (Oxford 2012).

Castel G. (1979) "Étude d'une momie copte", in *Hommages à la mémoire de Serge Sauneron, 1927–1976* (Bibliothêque d'Étude 81) (Cairo 1979) 121–43.

Cipriano G. (2016) "Ritual equipments in the cemetery of el-Bagawat (Kharga Oasis): some remarks", in *Coptic Society, Literature and Religion from Late Antiquity to Modern Times. Proceedings of the Tenth International Congress of Coptic Studies, Rome, September 17th–22nd, 2012, and Plenary Reports of the Ninth International Congress of Coptic Studies, Cairo, September 15th–19th, 2008* (Orientalia Lovaniensia Analecta 247), edd. P. Buzi, A. Camplani, and F. Contardi (Leuven 2016) 1447–62.

Clédat J. *et al.* (1904–99) *Le monastère et la nécropole de Baouît* (3 vols) (Cairo 1904–1999).

Codina Reina D. (2016) "Le monde funéraire byzantin du Ve au VIIe siècles sur le site d'Oxyrhinchus, el-Bahnasa, Égypte", in *Coptic Society, Literature and Religion from Late Antiquity to Modern Times. Proceedings of the Tenth International Congress of Coptic Studies, Rome, September 17th–22nd, 2012, and Plenary Reports of the Ninth International Congress of Coptic Studies, Cairo, September 15th–19th, 2008* (Orientalia Lovaniensia Analecta 247), edd. P. Buzi, A. Camplani, and F. Contardi (Leuven 2016) 1397–1412.

Cortés E. (2009) "Long-term preservation of Ptolemaic to late antique period burials at the Metropolitan Museum of Art Excavation in Dahshur, Egypt", in *Conservation of Three-Dimensional Textiles: 7th North American Textile Conservation Conference Pre-prints* (Québec City 2009) 219–38.

Coudert M. (2012) "The Christian necropolis of el-Deir in the North of Kharga Oasis", in *The Oasis Papers 6: Proceedings of the Sixth International Conference of the Dakhleh Oasis* (Dakhleh Oasis Project 15), edd. R. S. Bagnall *et al.* (Oxford 2012) 451–58.

Cromwell J. (2017) "The threads that bind us: Aspects of textile production in late antique Thebes", in *The Cultural Manifestations of Religious Experience: Studies in Honour of Boyo G. Ockinga* (Ägypten und Altes Testament 85), edd. C. Di Biase-Dyson, and L. Donovan (Münster 2017) 213–24.

Daszewski W. A. and Zych I. (2012) "Child burials of the Roman period in the necropolis of Marina El-Alamein, Egypt", in *L'enfant et la mort dans l'antiquité II: Types de tombes et traitement du corps des enfants dans l'antiquité Gréco-Romaine. Actes de la table ronde internationale organisée à Alexandrie, Centre d'Études Alexandrines, 12–14 Novembre 2009* (Études

Alexandrines 26), edd. M.-D. Nenna (Alexandria 2012) 283–92.

De Bock W. (1901) *Matériaux pour servir à l'archéologie de l'Égypte chrétienne* (St Petersberg 1901).

De Moor A. and Fluck C. edd. (2007) *Methods of Dating Ancient Textiles of the 1st Millenium AD from Egypt and Neighbouring Countries: Proceedings of the 4th Meeting of the Study Group 'Textiles from the Nile Valley', Antwerp, 16–17 April 2005* (Tielt 2007).

De Moor A. and Fluck C. edd. (2009) *Clothing the House: Furnishing Textiles of the 1st Millenium AD from Egypt and Neighbouring Countries. Proceedings of the 5th Conference of the Research Group 'Textiles from the Nile Valley', Antwerp, 6–7 October 2007* (Tielt 2009).

De Moor A. and Fluck C. edd. (2011) *Dress Accessories of the 1st Millenium AD from Egypt: Proceedings of the 6th Conference of the Research Group 'Textiles from the Nile Valley', Antwerp, 2–3 October 2009* (Tielt 2011).

De Moor A., Fluck C., and Linscheid P. edd. (2013) *Drawing the Threads Together: Textiles and Footwear of the 1st Millennium AD from Egypt. Proceedings of the 7th Conference of the Research Group 'Textiles from the Nile Valley', Antwerp 7–9 October 2011* (Tielt 2013).

De Moor A., Fluck C., and Linscheid P. edd. (2015) *Textiles, Tools and Techniques of the 1st Millennium AD from Egypt and Neighbouring Countries: Proceedings of the 8th Conference of the Research Group 'Textiles from the Nile Valley', Antwerp, 4–6 October 2013* (Tielt 2015).

De Moor A., Fluck C., and Linscheid P. edd. (2017) *Excavating, Analysing, Reconstructing: Textiles of the 1st Millennium AD from Egypt and Neighbouring Countries. Proceedings of the 9th Conference of the Research Group 'Textiles from the Nile Valley', Antwerp, 27–29 November 2015* (Tielt 2017).

Delattre A. (2005) "Une etiquette de momie copte de l'ancien Collection G. A. Michaelides", *Chronique d'Égypte* 80 (2005) 373–74.

Derda T. (1992) "Necropolis workers in Graeco-Roman Egypt in the light of Greek papyri", *JJurP* 21 (1992) 13–36.

Derda T., Markiewicz T., and Wipszycka, E. edd. (2007) *Alexandria: Auditoria of Kom El-Dikka and Late Antique Education* (Journal of Juristic Papyrology Supplement 8) (Warsaw 2007).

Derda T. and van der Vliet J. (2006) "I.Deir El-'Azab 1–4," *JJurP* 36 (2006) 21–33.

Doyen W. (2018) "The history of archaeology through the eyes of Egyptians", in *Unmasking Ideology in Imperial and Colonial Archaeology: Vocabulary, Symbols and Legacy*, edd. B. Effros and G. Lai (Los Angeles 2018) 173–200.

Driesch A. von den *et al.* (2005) "Mummified, deified and buried at Hermopolis Magna: the sacred birds from Tuna el-Gebel, Middle Egypt", *Ägypten und Levante/Egypt and the Levant* 15 (2005) 203–44.

Dunand F. (1995) "Practique et croyances funéraires en Égypte romaine," in *Aufstieg und Niedergang der römischen Welt (ANRW): Rise and Decline of the Roman World 2. Principat 18/5*, ed. W. Haase (Berlin and New York 1995) 3216–315.

Dunand F. (2007) "Between tradition and innovation: Egyptian funerary practices in Late Antiquity", in *Egypt in the Byzantine World, 300–700*, ed. R. S. Bagnall (Cambridge 2007) 163–84.

Dunand F., Heim J.-L., and Lichtenberg R. (2010–2015) *El-Deir nécropoles*, 3 vols. (Paris 2010–2015).

Dunand F. and Lichtenberg R. (2012) "L'inhumation des enfants dans les nécropoles de l'oasis de Kharga, désert libyque", in *L'enfant et la mort dans l'Antiquité II: Types de tombes et traitement du corps des enfants dans l'Antiquité gréco-romaine: Actes de la table ronde internationale organisée à Alexandrie, Centre d'Études Alexandrines, 12–14 novembre 2009* (Études Alexandrines 26), ed. M.-D. Nenna (Alexandria 2012) 331–49.

Dunand F. *et al.* (1992–2005) *La nécropole de Douch I–II: Exploration archéologique* (Documents de Fouilles Institut Francais d'Archeologie Orientale du Caire 26 and 45; Douch 1 and 5) (Cairo 1992–2005).

Dupras T., Schwarcz H. P., and Fairgrieve S. I. (2008) "Dining in the Dakhla Oasis: determining diet from stable isotopes", in *The Oasis Papers 2: Proceedings of the Second International Conference of the Dakhleh Oasis Project* (Dakhleh Oasis Project 12), ed. M. F. Wiseman (Oxford and Oakville 2008) 119–27.

Dupras T. L., Williams L. J., Wheeler S. M., and Sheldrick P. G. (2016) "Life and death in the desert: a bioarchaeological study of human remains from the Dakhleh Oasis, Egypt", in *Mummies, Magic and Medicine in Ancient Egypt: Multidisciplinary Essays for Rosalie David*, edd. C. Price, R. Forshaw, A. Chamberlain, and P. Nicholson (Manchester 2016) 286–304.

Dzierzbicka D. and Ożarek M. (2012) "Two burials from cemetery A in Naqlun: archaeological and anthropological remarks", *Polish Archaeology in the Mediterranean (Research 2009)* 21 (2012) 233–43.

Edgar C. C. (1903) *Greek Sculpture* (Cairo 1903).

Empereur J.-Y. and Nenna M.-D. edd. (2001–2003) *Nécropolis* (Etudes alexandrines 5, 7) (Cairo 2001–2003).

Fakhry A. (1951) *The Necropolis of el-Bagawåat in Kharga Oasis* (Cairo 1951).

Fischhaber G. (1997) *Mumifizierung im koptischen Ägypten: Eine Untersuchung zur Körperlichkeit im 1. Jahrtausend n. Chr.* (Ägypten und Altes Testament 39) (Wiesbaden 1997).

Fletcher A., Antoine D., and Hill J. D. edd. (2014) *Regarding the Dead: Human Remains in the British Museum* (Research Publication 197) (London 2014).

Flossmann-Schütze M. C. (2017) "Spätzeitliche und griechisch-römische Menschenbestattungen am Ibiotapheion von

Tuna el-Gebel", in *Burial and Mortuary Practices in Late Period and Graeco-Roman Egypt: Proceedings of the International Conference held at Museum of Fine Arts, Budapest, 17–19 July 2014*, ed. K. A. Kóthay (Budapest 2017) 131–42.

Fluck C. (2006) "Textiles from Arsinoe/Madient al-Fayyum reconsidered: Greg Schweinfurth's finds from 1886", in *Textiles in Situ: Their Find Spots in Egypt and Neighbouring Countries in the First Millennium CE*, ed. S. Schrenk (Riggisberg 2006) 17–31.

Fluck C. (2008) "Akhmim as a source of textiles", in *Christianity and Monasticism in Upper Egypt 1: Akhmim and Sohag*, edd. G. Gabra and H. N. Takla (Cairo 2008) 211–24.

Fluck C. (2014) "Textiles from the so-called 'tomb of Tgol' in Antinoupolis", in *Egypt in the First Millennium AD: Perspectives from New Fieldwork* (British Museum Publications on Egypt and Sudan 2), ed. E. R. O'Connell (Leuven 2014) 115–23.

Fluck C. (2015) "Children's burials from Antinoopolis: discoveries from recent excavations", in *Christianity and Monasticism in Middle Egypt: Al-Minya and Asyut*, edd. G. Gabra and H. N. Takla (Cairo 2015) 215–27.

Fluck C. and Helmecke G. edd. (2015) "Burial practice", in *Egypt: Faith after the Pharaohs* (London 2015) 232–41.

Fluck C., Helmecke G., and O'Connell E. R. edd. (2015) *Egypt: Faith after the Pharaohs* (London 2015).

Forrer R. (1891a) *Die Gräber- und Textilfunde von Achmim-Panopolis* (Strassburg 1891).

Forrer R. (1891b) *Römische und byzantinische Seiden-textilien aus dem Gräber-felde von Achmim-Panopolis* (Strassburg 1891).

Forrer R. (1895) *Mein Besuch in El-Achmim: Reisebriefe aus Aegypten* (Strassburg 1895).

Frankfurter D. (2018) *Christianizing Egypt: Syncretism and Local Worlds in Late Antiquity* (Princeton and Oxford 2018).

Gabr A. M. (2011) "A new Archaic period cemetery at Abydos: Osteological report", in *Egypt at its Origins 3: Proceedings of the Third International Conference, Origin of the State. Predynastic and Early Dynastic Egypt, London, 27th July–1st August 2008* (Orientalia Lovaniensia Analecta 205), edd. R. F. Friedman and P. N. Fiske (Leuven 2011) 281–91.

Gallazzi C. (2010) "Umm-el-Breigât (Tebtynis) 2004–2008: Gli scavi nel settore bizantino", *Rendiconti dell'Istituto Lombardo di Scienze e lettere. Classe di Lettere e Scienze Morali e Storiche* 144 (2010) 183–208.

Gallazzi C. and Hadji-Minaglou G. (2012) "Sépultures de nouveau-nés et d'enfants dans une nécropole de la fin du VIIIe et du IXe siècles apr. J.-C. à Umm-el-Breigât, Tebtynis", in *L'enfant et la mort dans l'Antiquité II: Types de tombes et traitement du corps des enfants dans l'Antiquité gréco-romain. Actes de la table ronde internationale organisée à Alexandrie, Centre d'Études Alexandrines, 12–14 novembre 2009* (Études

Alexandrines 26), ed. M.-D. Nenna (Alexandria 2012) 389–406.

Garel E. (2015) *Les testaments des supérieurs du monastère de Saint-Phoibammôn à Thèbes (VIIe siècle): Édition, traduction, commentaire* (Ph.D. diss., École Pratique des Hautes Études 2015).

Gascoigne A. L. and Rose P. J. (2012) "The forts of Hisn al-Bab and the First Cataract frontier from the 5th to 12th centuries AD", *Sudan & Nubia* 16 (2012) 88–95.

Gascou J. (1992) "La Vie de Pathermouthios: Moine et fossoyeur (Historia Monachorum X)", in *Itinéraires d'Égypte: Mélanges offerts au Père Maurice Martin S.J.* (Bibliothèque d'Étude 107) (Cairo 1992).

Gayraud R.-P. (1999) "Le Qarafa al-Kabra, derniére demeure des Fatimides", in *L'Égypte fatimide – son art et son histoire: Actes du colloque organisé à Paris les 28, 29 et 30 mai 1998*, ed. M. Barrucand (Paris 1999) 443–64.

Gessler-Löhr B. (2010) "Two child mummies and some grave goods of the Byzantine period from the Egyptian collection at Heidelberg University, Germany", in *Mummies of the World*, edd. A. Wieczorek and W. Rosendahl (Munich 2010) 310–15.

Gessler-Löhr B. (2012) "Mummies and mummification", in *The Oxford Handbook of Roman Egypt*, ed. C. Riggs (Oxford 2012) 664–83.

Gessler-Löhr B. et al. (2007) "Ausklang: Eine koptische Mumie aus christlicher Zeit", in *Ägyptische Mumien: Unsterblichkeit im Land der Pharaonen* (Mainz 2007) 255–77.

Godlewski W. (1986) *Deir el-Bahari V: Le monastére de St. Phoibammon* (Warsaw 1986).

Godlewski W. "The medieval Coptic cemetery at Naqlun", in *Christianity and Monasticism in the Fayoum Oasis*, ed. G. Gabra (Cairo and New York 2005) 173–83.

Godlewski W. (2006) "Al-Naqlun: links between archaeology and textiles", in *Textiles in Situ: Their Find Spots in Egypt and Neighbouring Countries in the First Millennium CE* (Riggisberger Berichte 13), ed. S. Schrenk (Riggisberg 2006) 33–42.

Godlewski W. (2015) "Monastery of the Archangel Gabriel, Naqlun", in *Egypt: Faith after the Pharaohs*, edd. C. Fluck, G. Helmecke, and E. R. O'Connell (London 2015) 128–30.

Grenier J. C. (1983) "La stèle funéraire du dernier taureau Bouchis (Caire JE 31901=Stèle Bucheum 20): Ermant – 4 novembre 340", *BIFAO* 83 (1983) 197–208.

Griggs C. W. (2005) "Early Christian burials in the Fayoum", in *Christianity and Monasticism in the Fayoum Oasis*, ed. G. Gabra (Cairo and New York 2005) 185–95.

Grilleto R. (1981) "I copti e la mummificazione, note agliscavi della necropolis di Antinoe", in *Corso di cultura sull'arte ravennate e bizantina* (Ravenna 1981) 119–23.

Grossmann P. (1971–2009) "Reinigungsarbeiten im Jeremiaskloster von Saqqara, I–IV", *Mitteilungen des Deutschen*

Archäologischen Instituts, Kairo 27 (1971) 173–80; 28 (1972) 145–52; 36 (1980) 193–202, 38 (1982) 155–72; 65 (2009) 49–81.

Grossmann P. (1989) *Abū Mīnā I: Die Gruftkirche und die Gruft* (Archäologische Veröffentlichungen 44) (Mainz 1989).

Grossmann P. (2002) *Christliche Architektur in Ägypten* (Handbuch der Orientalistik 62) (Leiden-Boston-Cologne 2002).

Grossmann P. (2013) "Neue Beobachtungen in der Kirche von Qurnat Mar'ī in Theban West", *JCS* 15 (2013) 253–60.

Hadji-Minaglou G. (2015) "Recent excavations at Bawit", in *Christianity and Monasticism in Middle Egypt: Al-Minya and Asyut*, edd. G. Gabra and H. N. Takla (Cairo 2015) 229–40.

Hawari M. (2015) "Early Islamic tombstones from Aswan", in *Egypt: Faith after the Pharaohs*, edd. C. Fluck, G. Helmecke, and E. R. O'Connell (London 2015) 244–45.

Heidel J. B. (2012) *The Antinoupolis Oracle: Newsletter of the Antinoupolis Foundation*, vol. 2–3 (2012).

Heinen H. (2002) "Dipinti aus der West-Necropole Alexandrias Gabbari", in *Nécropolis II* (Études Alexandrines 7), edd. J.-Y. Empereur and M.-D. Nenna (Cairo 2002) 639–52.

Heurtel C. and Daumas F. (2004) *Les inscriptions coptes et grecques du temple d'Hathor à Deir al-Médîna: Suivies de la publication des notes manuscrites de François Daumas, 1946–1947* (Bibliotheque d'Études Coptes 16) (Cairo 2004).

Hölscher U. (1934) *The Excavation of Medinet Habu I: General Plans and Views* (University of Chicago, Oriental Institute Publications 21) (Chicago 1934).

Hölscher U. (1954) *The Excavation of Medinet Habu V: Post-Ramesside Remains* (University of Chicago, Oriental Institute Publications 66) (Chicago 1954).

Hooper F. A. (1961) *Funerary Stelae from Kom Abou Billou* (Ann Arbor 1961).

Horak U. (1995) "Koptische Mumien: Der koptische Tote in Grabungsberichten, Funden und literarischen Nachrichten", *Biblos* 44 (1995) 39–71.

Hossein Y. M. (2011) "A new Archaic period cemetery at Abydos", in *Egypt at its Origins 3: Proceedings of the Third International Conference, Origin of the State. Predynastic and Early Dynastic Egypt, London, 27th July–1st August 2008* (Orientalia Lovaniensia Analecta 205), edd. R. F. Friedman and P. N. Fiske (Leuven 2011) 269–80.

Huber B. (1998) "Al-Ahmar / Šaruna: Découverte d'une ville de province", in *Proceedings of the Seventh International Congress of Egyptologists, Cambridge 3–9 September 1995* (Oriental Institute Publications 82), ed. C. J. Eyre (Leuven 1998) 575–82.

Huber B. (2004) "Die Grabkirche von Kom el-Ahmar/Šaruna (Mittelägypten): Archäeologie und Baugeschichte", in *Coptic Studies on the Threshold of a New Millennium: Proceedings of the Seventh International Congress of Coptic Studies, Leyden 2000* (Orientalia Lovaniensia Analecta 133), edd. M. Immerzeel and J. van der Vliet (Leuven 2004) 1081–1103.

Huber B. (2007) "The textiles of an early Christian burial from el-Kom el-Ahmar/Šaruna (Middle Egypt)", in *Methods of Dating Ancient Textiles of the 1st Millennium AD from Egypt and Neighbouring Countries: Proceedings of the 4th Meeting of the Study Group 'Textiles from the Nile Valley', Antwerp, 16–17 April 2005*, edd. A. Moor and C. Fluck (Tielt 2007) 36–66.

Huber B. (2009) "The funerary beds from the monastic cemetery at el-Ghalida (el-Kom el-Ahmar / Šaruna)", in *"Clothing the House": Furnishing Textiles of the 1st Millenium AD from Egypt and Neighbouring Countries. Proceedings of the 5th Conference of the Research Group 'Textiles from the Nile Valley', Antwerp, 6–7 October 2007* (Tielt, 2009) 57–72.

Huber B. (2013) "Ein koptischer Sarg: Zwischen Tradition und Innovation", *Bulletin de la Société d'Archéologie Copte* 52 (2013) 77–98.

Huber B. and Nauerth C. (2018) "Coptic coffins from Qarara: the Pfauensarg – the peacock coffin – in context", in *Ancient Egyptian Coffins: Craft Traditions and Functionality* (British Museum Publications on Egypt and Sudan 4), edd. J. H. Taylor and M. Vandenbeusch (Leuven 2018).

Ikram S. (2015) *Divine Creatures: Animal Mummies in Ancient Egypt*, rev. ed. (Cairo 2015).

Jeffreys D. G. and Strouhal E. (1982) "North Saqqara 1978–9: The Coptic cemetery site at the Sacred Animal Necropolis. Preliminary report", *JEA* 66 (1980) 28–35.

Kaczmarek M. (2012) "Anthropological studies on juvenile skeletal remains from the necropolis at Marina el-Alamein, Egypt", in *L'enfant et la mort dans l'Antiquité II: Types de tombes et traitement du corps des enfants dans l'Antiquité gréco-romaine. Actes de la table ronde internationale organisée à Alexandrie, Centre d'Études Alexandrines, 12–14 novembre 2009* (Études Alexandrines 26), ed. M.-D. Nenna (Alexandria 2012) 293–313.

Kahl J. (2007) *Ancient Asyut: The First Synthesis After 300 Years of Research* (Asyut Project 1) (Wiesbaden 2007).

Kahl J. (2014) "Gebel Asyut al-gharbi in the First Millennium AD", in *Egypt in the First Millennium AD: Perspectives from New Fieldwork* (British Museum Publications on Egypt and Sudan 2), ed. E. R. O'Connell (Leuven 2014) 127–38.

Kahl J., El-Khadragy M., Verhoeven U., Prell S., Eichner I., and Beckh T. (2010) "The Asyut Project: Seventh season of fieldwork (2009)", *Studien zur Altägyptischen Kultur* 39 (2010) 191–210.

Kajitani N. (2006) "Textiles and their context in the third to fourth century CE cemetery of al-Bagawat, Khargah Oasis, Egypt, from the 1907–1931 excavations by The Metropolitan Museum of Art", in *Textiles in Situ: Their Find Spots in Egypt and Neighbouring Countries in the First Millennium CE* (Riggisberger Berichte 13), ed. S. Schrenk (Riggisberg 2006) 95–115.

Kaufmann C. M. (1918) *Die heilige Stadt der Wüste: Unsere Entdeckungen Grabungen und Funde in der altchristlichen Menasstadt weiteren Kreisen in Wort und Bild geschildert* (Kempten-Munich 1918).

Krastel L. (2017) "Die koptischen Stelen des Deir Anba Hadra im Koptischen Museum: Die Arbeiten des Jahres 2017", *iDAI.publications* (2017) 35–38 (https://www.topoi.org/project/b-4-6-1/ [accessed 08/09/2018]).

Krause M. (1983) "Das Weiterleben ägyptischer Vorstellungen und Bräuche im koptischen Totenwesen", in *Das römisch-byzantinische Ägypten: Akten des internationalen Symposions 26.-30. September 1978 in Trier*, edd. G. Grimm, H. Heinen, and E. Winter (Mainz 1983) 85–92.

Krause M. (1991) "Mummification", in *The Coptic Encyclopedia*, ed. A. S. Attiya (New York and Toronto 1991) 1696–98.

Krumeich K. (2003) *Spätantike Bauskulptur aus Oxyrhynchos: Lokale Produktion, äussere Einflüsse* (Wiesbaden 2003).

Kuhlmann K. (1983) *Materialien zur Archäologie und Geschichte des Raumes von Achmim* (Sonderschriften des Deutschen Archäologischen Instituts, Kairo 11) (Mainz 1983).

Kulicka E. (2010) "Remarks on the typology of Islamic graves from the cemeteries on Kom el-Dikka in Alexandria", *Polish Archaeology in the Mediterranean* 20 (2010) 483–98.

Kulicka E. (2015) "Islamic necropolis at Kom el-Dikka in Alexandria: Research in the 2010–2013 seasons", *Polish Archaeology in the Mediterranean* 24 (2015) 62–72.

Kulicka E. (2016) "Appendix: Islamic cemetery at Kom el-Dikka in Alexandria: Research in 2014 and 2015", *Polish Archaeology in the Mediterranean* 25 (2016) 51–63.

Layton B. (2014) *The Canons of Our Fathers: Monastic Rules of Shenoute* (Oxford 2014)

Lecuyot G. (2000) "Le Ramesseum à l'époque copte: A propos des traces chrétiennes au Ramesseum", in *Études Coptes VI: Huitième journée d'Études, Colmar 29–31 mai 1997* (Cahiers de la Bibliothèque Copte 11), ed. A. Boud'hors (Paris-Louvain 2000) 121–34.

Lembke K. (2012) "City of the dead: Tuna el-Gebel", in *The Oxford Handbook of Roman Egypt*, ed. C. Riggs (Oxford 2012) 205–222.

Letellier-Willemin F. (2012) "Contribution of textiles as archaeological artefacts to the study of the Christian cemetery of el-Deir", in *The Oasis Papers 6: Proceedings of the Sixth International Conference of the Dakhleh Oasis Project* (Dakhleh Oasis Project 15), edd. R. S. Bagnall *et al.* (Oxford and Oakville 2012) 491–99.

Letellier-Willemin F. (2013) "The embroidered tunic of Dush: a new approach", in *Drawing the Threads Together: Textiles and Footwear of the 1st Millennium AD from Egypt. Proceedings of the 7th Conference of the Research Group 'Textiles from the Nile Valley', Antwerp 7–9 October 2011*, edd. A. De Moor, C. Fluck, and P. Linscheid (Tielt 2013) 22–33.

Lösch S., Hower-Tilmann E., and Zink A. (2012) "Mummies and skeletons from the Coptic monastery complex Deir el-Bachit in Thebes-West, Egypt", *Anthropologischer Anzeiger* 70 (2012) 27–41.

MacCoull L. S. B. (2000) "Apa Abraham: Testament of Apa Abraham, Bishop of Hermonthis, for the Monastery of St. Phoibammon near Thebes, Egypt," in *Byzantine Monastic Foundation Documents* (Dumbarton Oaks Studies 35), ed. J. P. Thomas (Washington D.C. 2000) 51–58.

MacCoull L. S. B. (2009) *Coptic Legal Documents: Law as Vernacular Text and Experience in Late Antique Egypt* (Medieval & Renaissance Texts & Studies 377; Arizona Studies in the Middle Ages and the Renaissance 32) (Tempe 2009).

Macke A. (2012) "Une nécropole copto-byzantine découverte sur le bas-côté nord (BCN) du Ramesseum", *Memnonia* 23 (2012) 165–79.

Mamedow M. (2017) "Die Rekonstruktion ritueller Handlungen: Funktionale Analyse und Kontextualisierung von Keramik aus einem ptolemäisch-römischen Gräberfeld in Mittelägypten", in *Burial and Mortuary Practices in Late Period and Graeco-Roman Egypt: Proceedings of the International Conference held at Museum of Fine Arts, Budapest, 17–19 July 2014*, ed. K. A. Kóthay (Budapest 2017) 61–70.

Manfredi M. (1998) "Gli scavi italiani ad Antino", in *Antinoe cent'anni dopo: Catalogo della Mostra. Firenze, Palazzo Medici Riccardi, 10 novembre 1998*, ed. L. Del Francia Barocas (Florence 1998) 23–28.

Martin G. T. (1974) "Excavations in the Sacred Animal Necropolis at North Saqqara, 1972–3: Preliminary report", *JEA* 60 (1974) 15–29.

Maspero G. (1887) "Rapport à l'Institut Égyptien sur les fouilles et travaux exécutés en Égypte pendant l'hiver de 1885–1886", *Bulletin de l'Institut Égyptien* 7 (1887) 196–251.

Maspero G. (1900) "Les fouilles de Deir el Aizam (Septembre 1897)", *ASAE* 1 (1900) 109–119.

McNally S. and Schrunk I. D. (1993) *Excavations in Akhmim, Egypt: Continuity and Change in City Life from Late Antiquity to the Present: First Report* (BAR 590) (Oxford 1993).

Meyer M. and Smith R. (1994) *Ancient Christian Magic: Coptic Texts of Ritual Power* (San Francisco 1994)

Mintouli D. (2008) "Antinoe, necropoli nord 2007: La tomba di Tgol. Prime informazioni", in *Antinoupolis 1: Scavi e materiali*, ed. R. Pintaudi (Florence 2008) 61–73.

Mond R. and Myers O. H. (1937) *Cemeteries of Armant 1–2* (Egypt Exploration Society Memoirs 42) (London 1937).

Mond R. and Myers O. H. (1940) *Temples of Armant 1–2* (Egypt Exploration Society Memoirs 43) (London 1940).

Monneret de Villard U. (1927) *Il monastero di S. Simeone presso Aswân*, 3 vols. (Milan 1927).

Montserrat D. (1997) "Death and funerals in the Roman Fayum", in *Portraits and Masks: Burial Customs in Roman Egypt* (London 1997).

Müller M. (2005) "From the history of archaeology: the destruction of Late Antiquity necropolises in Egypt reconsidered", in *Modern Trends in European Egyptology: Papers from a Session Held at the European Association of Archaeologists Ninth Annual Meeting in St. Petersburg 2003* (BAR-IS 1448), ed. A.-A. Maravelia (Oxford 2005) 43–48.

Müller W. (2014) "Syene (ancient Aswan) in the first millennium AD", in *Egypt in the First Millennium AD: Perspectives from New Fieldwork* (British Museum Publications on Egypt and Sudan 2), ed. E. R. O'Connell (Leuven 2014) 59–69.

Nauerth C. (1996) *Karara und El-Hibe: Die spätantiken ('koptischen') Funde aus den badischen Grabungen 1913–1914* (Heidelberg 1996).

Nenna M.-D. (ed.) (2012) *L'enfant et la mort dans l'Antiquité II: Types de tombes et traitement du corps des enfants dans l'Antiquité gréco-romaine: Actes de la table ronde internationale organisée à Alexandrie, Centre d'Études Alexandrines, 12–14 novembre 2009* (Études Alexandrines 26), ed. M.-D. Nenna (Alexandria 2012).

O'Connell E. R. (2001) *Naga ed-Deir: A Late Antique Monastery in Upper Egypt* (MA thesis, Univ. of California, Berkeley 2001).

O'Connell E. R. (2010) "Excavating Late Antique Western Thebes: A history", in *Christianity and Monasticism in Upper Egypt II: Nag Hammadi – Esna*, edd. G. Gabra and H. N. Takla (Cairo 2010) 253–70.

O'Connell E. R. ed. (2014a) *Egypt in the First Millennium AD: Perspectives from New Fieldwork* (British Museum Publications on Egypt and Sudan 2) (Leuven 2014).

O'Connell E. R. (2014b) "The discovery of Christian Egypt: from manuscript hunters toward an archaeology of Late Antiquity", in *Coptic Civilization: Two Thousand Years of Christianity in Egypt*, ed. G. Gabra (Cairo 2014) 143–56.

O'Connell E. R. (2014c) "R. Campbell Thompson's 1913/14 excavation of Wadi Sarga and other sites", *British Museum Studies in Ancient Egypt and Sudan* 21 (2014) 121–92.

O'Connell E. R. (2018) "Egypt; dead, disposal of, Egypt", in *Oxford Dictionary of Late Antiquity*, ed. O. Nicholson (Oxford 2018).

O'Connell E. R. ed. (2020) *Abydos in the First Millennium AD* (British Museum Publications on Egypt and Sudan 11) (Leuven 2020).

O'Connell E. R. (2020) "Abydos and the Thinite region in the First Millennium AD," *Abydos in the First Millennium AD* (British Museum Publications on Egypt and Sudan 11), ed. E. R. O'Connell (Leuven 2020) 1–31.

O'Connell E. R. (Forthcoming a) "Family matters: Care for the dead in late antique Western Thebes", in *New Perspectives on Religion, Education and Culture at Christian Western Thebes (VI–VIII)* (Society of American Papyrologists Suppl. Series), edd. A. Maravela and A. Mihálykó Tothne (Ann Arbor forthcoming).

O'Connell E. R. (Forthcoming b) "Archaeology 2012–2016", in *Proceedings of the 11th International Congress of Coptic Studies, Claremont, California, USA, 25–30 July* (OLA), edd. H. K. Takla, E. Agaidy, and T. Vivian (Leuven forthcoming).

Österreichisches Archäologisches Institut, *Fortification Hisn al-Bab: Border Relations of Egypt and Nubia in Late Antiquity and the Early Middle Ages*, in https://www.oeaw.ac.at/en/oeai/research/military-infrastructure-and-transport-routes/hisn-al-bab-late-antique-border/ (last accessed Sept 2018).

Papaconstantinou A. (2001) *Le culte des saints en Égypte: Des Byzantins aux Abbassides. L'apport des inscriptions et des papyrus grecs et coptes* (Paris 2001).

Papaconstantinou A. (2007) "'They shall speak the Arabic language and take pride in it': reconsidering the fate of Coptic after the Arab conquest", *Le Muséon* 120 (2007) 273–99.

Peacock D. and Maxfield V. (1997) *Mons Claudianus 1987–1993: Survey and excavation I. Topography and quarries.* (Fouilles de l'Institut Français d'Archéologie Orientale du Caire 37) (Cairo 1997).

Peet, T. E. (1914) *The Cemeteries of Abydos* 2 (Memoirs of the Egypt Exploration Fund 34) (London 1914).

Petrie W. M. F. (1905) *Roman Ehnasya (Herakleopolis Magna)* (Memoir of the Egypt Exploration Fund 26) (London 1905).

Petrie W. M. F. (1907) *Gizeh and Rifeh* (British School of Archaeology in Egypt 13) (Warminster 1907).

Petrie W. M. F. (1925) *Tombs of the Courtiers and Oxyrhynkhos* (British School of Archaeology in Egypt 37) (London 1925).

Picton J., Quirke S., and Roberts P. C. edd. (2007) *Living Images: Egyptian Funerary Portraits in the Petrie Museum* (London 2007).

Pimpaud A.-B. and Lecuyot G. (2013) "Cartes pour l'étude de la rive gauche de Thèbes aux époques romaines et byzantines", *Memnonia* 24 (2013) 147–54.

Pintaudi R. ed. (2008a) *Antinoupolis I* (Scavi e materiali 1) (Florence 2008).

Pintaudi R. (2008b) "Gli scavi dell'Istituto Papirologico 'G. Vitelli' di Firenze ad Antinoe (2000–2007): Prime notizie", in *Antinoupolis I*, ed. R. Pintaudi (Scavi e materiali 1) (Florence 2008) 1–40; 539–52.

Pintaudi R. ed. (2014) *Antinoupolis II* (Scavi e materiali 3) (Florence 2014).

Pleşa A. D. (2017a) "The late antique and early Islamic necropolises at Matmar and Mostagedda, Middle Egypt: a reassessment of the excavation and present state of the collection", in *Excavating, Analysing, Reconstructing: Textiles of the 1st Millennium AD from Egypt and Neighbouring Countries. Proceedings of the 9th Conference of the Research Group 'Textiles from the Nile Valley', Antwerp, 27–29 November 2015*, edd. A. De Moor, C. Fluck, and P. Linscheid (Tielt 2017) 72–87.

Pleşa A. D. (2017b) "Religious belief in burial: Funerary dress and practice in the late antique and early Islamic cemeteries at Matmar and Mostagedda, Egypt (late fourth–early ninth century CE)", *Ars Orientalis* 47 (2017) 18–42.

Polz D. A. *et al.* (2012) "Topographical archaeology in Dra'Abu el-Naga: three thousand years of cultural history", *Mitteilungen des Deutschen Archäologischen Instituts, Kairo* 68 (2012) 115–34.

Pritchard F. (2017) "Textiles from Wadi Sarga, a 6th to 8th-century monastic site in Middle Egypt excavated in 1913/1914", in *Excavating, Analysing, Reconstructing: Textiles of the 1st Millennium AD from Egypt and Neighbouring Countries. Proceedings of the 9th Conference of the Research Group 'Textiles from the Nile Valley', Antwerp, 27–29 November 2015*, edd. A. De Moor, C. Fluck, and P. Linscheid (Tielt 2017) 60–71.

Promińska E. (1972) *Investigations on the Population of Muslim Alexandria: Anthropological-Demographic Study* (Travaux du Centre d'archéologie méditerranéenne de l'Académie polonaise des sciences 12) (Warsaw 1972).

Quibell J. E., Thompson H. S., and Spiegelberg W. (1909) *Excavations at Saqqara (1907–1908)* (Cairo 1909).

Quibell J. E. and Thompson H. S. (1912) *Excavations at Saqqara (1908–9, 1909–10): The Monastery of Apa Jeremias* (Cairo 1912).

Ranke H. (1926) *Koptische Friedhöfe bei Karâra und der Amontempel Scheschonks I bei el Hibe: Bericht über die badischen Grabungen in Ägypten in den Wintern 1913 und 1914* (Berlin and Leipzig 1926).

Raue D., Seidlmayer S. J., and Speiser P. (edd.) (2013) *The First Cataract of the Nile: One region – Diverse Perspectives* (Sonderschriften des Deutschen Archäologischen Instituts, Kairo 36) (Berlin 2013).

Rebillard É. (2009) *The Care of the Dead in Late Antiquity*. Engl. trans. (Cornell Studies in Classical Philology 59) (Ithaca 2009).

Reid D. M. (2002) *Whose Pharaohs? Archeology, Museums and Egyptian National Identity from Napoleon to World War I* (Berkeley 2002).

Reid D. M. (2015) *Contesting Antiquity in Egypt: Archaeologies, Museums and the Struggle for Identities from World War I to Nasser* (Cairo 2015).

Reifarth N. (2013) *Zur Ausstattung spätantiker Elitegräber aus St. Maximin in Trier: Purpur, Seide, Gold und Harze* (Internationale Archäeologie 124) (Rahden 2013).

Reifarth N., Merten H., Teegen W.-R., Amendt J., Vanden Berghe I., Heron C., Wiethold J., Drewello U., Drewello R., and Clemens L. (Forthcoming) "On the threshold of a new era: Early Christian elite burials from St. Maximin, Trier (Germany)," in *Burial and Memorial 2: Regional Perspectives* edd. A. Dolea and L. Lavan (LAA 13.2).

Richter T. S. (2015) "The Monastery Deir Anba Hadra: epigraphy, art and architectural studies on Aswan's western bank." *Archaeology in Egypt: Magazine of the German Archaeological Institute Cairo* 3 (2015) 20–25.

Riggs C. (2005) *The Beautiful Burial in Roman Egypt: Art, Identity and Funerary Religion* (Oxford 2005).

Riggs C. ed. (2012) *Oxford Handbook of Roman Egypt* (Oxford 2012).

Riggs C. (2014) *Unwrapping Ancient Egypt* (London 2014).

Rose P. J. and Gascoigne A. L. (2013) "Hisn al-Bab: more symbol than substance", in *The Power of Walls: Fortifications in Ancient Northeastern Africa. Proceedings of the International Workshop Held at the University of Cologne, 4th–7th August 2011* (Colloquium Africanum 5), edd. F. Jesse and C. Vogel (Cologne 2013) 251–68.

Sabah A. (2012) "Burials of the Kahlil el-Khayat site, Kafr Abdou District, East Alexandria", in *L'enfant et la mort dans l'Antiquité II: Types de tombes et traitement du corps des enfants dans l'Antiquité gréco-romaine. Actes de la table ronde internationale organisée à Alexandrie, Centre d'Études Alexandrines, 12–14 novembre 2009* (Études Alexandrines 26), ed. M.-D. Nenna (Alexandria 2012) 253–74.

Scheidel W. (2001) *Death on the Nile: Disease and the Demography of Roman Egypt* (Mnemosyne supplements 228) (Leiden and Boston 2001).

Schrenk S. (2004) *Textilien des Mittelmeerraumes aus spätantiker bis frühislamischer Zeit* (Abegg-Stiftung. Textilsammlung der Abegg-Stiftung 4) (Riggisberg 2004).

Sheehan P. (2010) *Babylon of Egypt: The Archaeology of Old Cairo and the Origins of the City* (Cairo 2010).

Sherwood Fox W. (1913) "Mummy-labels in the Royal Ontario Museum", *AJP* 34 (1913) 437–50.

Sidebotham S. E. (2011) *Berenike and the Ancient Maritime Spice Route* (Berkeley-London 2011).

Sidebotham S. E. (2014) "Religion and burial at the Ptolemaic-Roman Red Sea emporium of Berenike, Egypt", *African Archaeological Review* 31.4 (2014) 599–635.

Sidebotham S. E., Hense M., and Nouwens H. M. (2008) *The Red Land: The Illustrated Archaeology of Egypt's Eastern Desert* (Cairo and New York 2008)

Sijpesteijn, P. M. (2013) *Shaping a Muslim State: The World of a Mid-Eighth-Century Egyptian Official* (Oxford 2013).

Smith H. S., Davies S., and Frazer K. J. (2005) *The Sacred Animal Necropolis at North Saqqara.* (Egypt Exploration Society Excavation Memoir 75) (London 2005).

Smith M. (2009) *Traversing Eternity: Texts for the Afterlife from Ptolemaic and Roman Egypt* (Oxford 2009).

South K. (2017) "The use of basket-weave linen in burials of the necropolis of Fag el-Gamus, Egypt", in *Excavating, Analysing, Reconstructing: Textiles of the 1st Millennium AD from Egypt and Neighbouring Countries. Proceedings of the 9th Conference of the Research Group 'Textiles from the*

Nile Valley', Antwerp, 27–29 November 2015, edd. A. De Moor, C. Fluck, and P. Linscheid (Tielt 2017) 88–107.

South K. and Muhlestein K. M. (2013) "Regarding ribbons: the spread and use of narrow purpose-woven bands in Late Roman Egyptian burials", in *Drawing the Threads Together: Textiles and Footwear of the 1st Millennium AD from Egypt. Proceedings of the 7th Conference of the Research Group 'Textiles from the Nile Valley', Antwerp 7–9 October 2011*, edd. A. De Moor, C. Fluck, and P. Linscheid (Tielt 2013) 56–73.

Speiser P. *et al.* (2013) "Umayyad, Tulunid and Fatimid tombs at Aswan", in *The First Cataract of the Nile: One Region – Diverse Perspectives* (Sonderschriften des Deutschen Archäologischen Instituts, Kairo 36), edd. D. Raue, S. J. Seidlmayer, and P. Speiser (Berlin 2013) 211–22.

Stevens A. (2018) "Death and the city: the cemeteries of Amarna and their urban context", *CAJ* 28 (2018) 103–126.

Strudwick N. (2003) "Some aspects of the archaeology of the Theban Necropolis in the Ptolemaic and Roman periods," in *The Theban Necropolis: Past, Present and Future* (London 2003) 167–88.

Subías Pascual E. (2003) *La corona immarcescible: Pintures de l'antiguitat tardana de la Necròpolis Alta d'Oxirinc (Mínia, Egipte)* (Institut Català d'Arqueologia Clàssica 1) (Barcelona 2003).

Subías Pascual E. (2008) *La maison funéraire de la nécropole haute à Oxyrynchos (el Minyâ, Égypte): Du tombeau à la diaconie* (Barcelona 2008).

Tatz S. (2017) "The textile finds from the monastery of Deir el-Bachît/Paulos monastery (6th–10th century) in Western Thebes", in *Excavating, Analysing, Reconstructing: Textiles of the 1st Millennium AD from Egypt and Neighbouring Countries. Proceedings of the 9th Conference of the Research Group 'Textiles from the Nile Valley', Antwerp, 27–29 November 2015*, edd. A. De Moor, C. Fluck, and P. Linscheid (Tielt 2017) 108–124.

Taylor J. H. and Antoine D. (2014) *Ancient Lives, New Discoveries: Eight Mummies, Eight Stories* (London 2014).

Thomas J. P. (1987) *Private Religious Foundations in the Byzantine Empire* (Dumbarton Oaks Studies 24) (Washington, D.C. 1987).

Thomas T. K. (2007) "Coptic and Byzantine textiles found in Egypt: corpora, collections and scholarly perspectives", in *Egypt in the Byzantine World, 300–700*, ed. R. S. Bagnall (Cambridge 2007) 137–62.

Timm S. ed. (1984–1992) *Das christlich-koptische Ägypten in arabischer Zeit: Eine Sammlung christlicher Stätten in Ägypten in arabischer Zeit, unter Ausschluss von Alexandria, Kairo, des Apa-Mena-Klosters* (6 vols) (Beihefte zum Tübinger Atlas des Vorderen Orients; Reihe B. Geisteswissenschaften 41.1–6) (Wiesbaden 1984–1992).

Tolmacheva E. (2017) "Archaeological textiles at the Deir el-Banat site (Fayyum): parallels, study, conservation and general description", in *Excavating, Analysing, Reconstructing: Textiles of the 1st Millennium AD from Egypt and Neighbouring Countries. Proceedings of the 9th Conference of the Research Group 'Textiles from the Nile Valley', Antwerp, 27–29 November 2015*, edd. A. De Moor, C. Fluck, and P. Linscheid (Tielt 2017) 32–59.

Toralles Tovar S. (2013) "Egyptian burial practices in Late Antiquity: the case of Christian mummy labels", in *Cultures in Contact: Transfer of Knowledge in the Mediterranean Context*, edd. S. Torallas Tovar and J. P. Monferrer (Córdoba 2013) 13–24.

Tudor B. (2011) *Christian Funerury Stelue of the Byzantine and Arab Periods from Egypt* (Marburg 2011).

Uytterhoeven I. (2009) *Hawara in the Graeco-Roman Period: Life and Death in a Fayum Village* (Orientalia Lovaniensia Analecta 174) (Leuven 2009).

van der Vliet J. (2013) "Contested frontiers: Southern Egypt and northern Nubia, AD 300–1500: the evidence of the inscriptions", in *Christianity and Monasticism in Aswan and Nubia*, edd. G. Gabra and H. N. Takla (Cairo 2013) 63–77.

van der Vliet J. (2020) "Coptic epitaphs from Abydos", *JCS* 22 (2020) 205–228.

Vleeming S. (2011) *Demotic and Greek-Demotic Mummy Labels and Other Short Texts Gathered from Many Publications (Short Texts II 278–1200)* (Studia Demotica 9) (Leuven 2011).

Voytenko A. (2012) "Preliminary report on Coptic burial customs at the necropolis of Deir el-Banat", in *Achievements and Problems of Modern Egyptology: Proceedings of the International Conference Held in Moscow on September 29–October 2, 2009*, edd. G. A. Belova and S. V. Ivanov (Moscow 2012) 402–411.

Voytenko A. (2016) "Grave 249/2 at Deir el-Banat: a typical example of Coptic ordinary burial custom", in *Coptic Society, Literature and Religion from Late Antiquity to Modern Times: Proceedings of the Tenth International Congress of Coptic Studies, Rome, September 17th–22nd, 2012, and Plenary Reports of the Ninth International Congress of Coptic Studies, Cairo, September 15th–19th, 2008* (Orientalia Lovaniensia Analecta 247), edd. P. Buzi, A. Camplani, and F. Contardi (Leuven 2016) 1421–32.

Wietheger C. (1992) *Dar Jeremias-Kloster zu Saqqara unter besonderer Berücksichtigung der Inschriften* (Arbeiten zum Spätantiken und Koptischen Ägypten 1) (Altenberge 1992).

Wilfong T. G. (1995) "Mummy labels from the Oriental Institute's excavations at Medinet Habu", *BASP* 32 (1995) 157–81.

Wilfong T. G. (2002) *Women of Jeme: Lives in a Coptic Town in Late Antique Egypt* (Ann Arbor 2002).

Winlock H. E. and Crum W. E. (1926) *The Monastery of Epiphanius at Thebes I* (Publications of the Metropolitan Museum of Art Egyptian Expedition 3) (New York 1926).

Wipszycka E. (1972) *Les ressources et les activités économiques des églises en Égypte du IVᵉ au VIIIᵉ siècle* (Papyrologica Bruxellensia 10) (Brussels, 1972).

Wipszycka E. (2007) "The institutional church", in *Egypt in the Byzantine World, 300–700*, ed. R. S. Bagnall (Cambridge 2007) 331–49.

Yohe R. M. *et al.* (2012) "The evolution of Byzantine burial practices between the third and seventh centuries CE in Middle Egypt", *Coptica* 11 (2012) 59–87.

Yohe R. M., Gardner J. K., and Heikkinen D. (2012) "An initial report on bioarchaeological investigations at the Tell El-Hibeh site, Middle Egypt", in *Evolving Egypt: Innovation, Appropriation and Reinterpretation in Ancient Egypt* (BAR-IS 2397), ed. K. Muhlestein (Oxford 2012) 105–124.

Zych I. (2003) "Wooden coffins from the Moslem cemetery at Kom el-Dikka", *Polish Archaeology in the Mediterranean* 14 (2003) 32–37.

Zych I. (2008) "Cemetery C in Naqlun: preliminary report on the excavation in 2006", *Polish Archaeology in the Mediterranean* 18 (2008) 230–46.

Abstracts in French

Aspects de la pratique funéraire tardo-antique dans le sud de la Grande-Bretagne

Paul Booth

Ce résumé tente de présenter une vue d'ensemble des principales caractéristiques des pratiques funéraires romaines tardives dans le centre et le sud de la Grande-Bretagne, en mettant l'accent sur les résultats de fouilles et d'analyses récentes. Ceux-ci incluent quelques exemples urbains, mais l'article se concentre principalement sur les inhumations dans des contextes ruraux, y compris dans les soi-disant 'petites villes'. Cela va des sépultures individuelles aux cimetières, dont l'organisation et l'orientation sont variables. Le rite principal était l'inhumation en position allongée, mais l'article passe également en revue des variantes, d'autres formes d'inhumation, différents types de construction de tombes et de mobilier funéraire. Il souligne l'importance des données ostéologiques pour comprendre à la fois l'individu enterré et des questions plus larges telles que les origines et la santé des communautés. Les variations régionales sont considérées comme importantes et partiellement liées à des facteurs socio-économiques. Les interactions avec les premières pratiques anglo-saxonnes et l'influence du christianisme dans les sépultures tardives et 'post-romaines' sont également prises en compte.

L'enterrement dans l'Antiquité tardive : témoignages récents de Londinium

Victoria Ridgeway et Sadie Watson

Cet article détaille les avancées dans l'étude des sépultures de l'Antiquité tardive à Londres au cours des deux dernières décennies, en mettant l'accent sur des exemples non publiés. Il souligne l'investissement dans les techniques bioarchéologiques et leur importance pour les études démographiques. Les données suggèrent que la population de Londres était très diversifiée et qu'il y avait une mobilité à travers l'Empire tout au long de la période romaine tardive. Des exemples spécifiques sont discutés, notamment avec l'analyse de deux sites fouillés à Southwark, sur la rive sud de la Tamise, illustrant le caractère extensif et la grande diversité des pratiques en jeu dans le Londres romain tardif. Cela constitue une étude de cas qui pourrait servir de modèle pour l'examen du reste des cimetières de Londres.

Témoignage récent du cimetière tardo-antique de Cantorbéry : le site de l'ancien Garage de Hallet en contexte

Elizabeth Duffy, Adrian Gollop et Jake Weekes

Cet article étudie un cimetière romain tardif fouillé dans l'ancien Garage Hallet, à Cantorbéry, en 2010 et 2011, du côté nord-ouest de la ville romaine tardo-antique. Au total, 140 sépultures ont été étudiées, le plus grand nombre à avoir été fouillé à Cantorbéry à l'époque. L'article présente les résultats d'une étude plus récente des sites de cimetières de la même période situés dans le sud-est de la ville, mais extra-muros, respectivement à Rhodaus Town et à l'ancien Garage Peugeot. Les premiers résultats d'une étude bioarchéologique du site du Garage Hallet sont ensuite présentés, un projet qui s'étendra avec le temps aux nombreux nouveaux *comparanda* des cimetières du sud de Cantorbéry, et à d'autres centres urbains de la Grande-Bretagne romaine tardive. Suivent une note méthodologique concernant la reconstruction archéologique du processus funéraire, ainsi que quelques considérations initiales sur le processus funéraire à Hallet et sa comparaison avec les autres nouveaux sites de Cantorbéry.

Levis aesto terra – sépultures de l'élite paléochrétienne de Saint-Maximin, Trèves (Allemagne)

Nicole Reifarth, Hiltrud Merten, Wolf-Rüdiger Teegen, Jens Amendt, Ina Vanden Berghe, Carl Heron, Julian Wiethold, Ursula Drewello, Rainer Drewello et Lukas Clemens

La communauté paléochrétienne de Trèves a laissé derrière elle un large éventail de témoignages fascinants qui nous permettent de faire la lumière sur ses origines, ses antécédents sociaux, ses rites funéraires et ses destins individuels à une époque de changement politique et culturel radical entre le IVe et le VIIIe s. J.-C. Les découvertes discutées ici concernent des sépultures d'une basilique de cimetière du IVe s. découverte sous l'église de l'ancienne abbaye bénédictine de Saint-Maximin. La salle funéraire tardo-antique exceptionnellement grande et la qualité particulière de ses inscriptions, des textiles et d'autres matériaux trouvés là, s'expliquent par le patronage de la cour impériale de Trèves et soulignent sa position par rapport aux autres centres paléochrétiens dans la région.

Modèles funéraires dans les villes tardo-antiques (IIIe–VIIe s.) : examen des données archéologiques en Italie du Nord

Alexandra Chavarría Arnau

L'une des principales transformations soulignées par les chercheurs analysant le paysage urbain au cours de l'Antiquité tardive concerne l'évolution des modes funéraires et le développement progressif des sépultures intra-muros. C'est un phénomène traditionnellement lié aux processus de christianisation, à la construction d'églises à l'intérieur des villes et surtout à une modification du rapport entre les personnes et les corps des morts, en particulier ceux des martyrs et des saints. Dans cet article, j'essaierai de démontrer qu'entre le IVe et le VIe s., les sépultures à l'intérieur des murs des villes sont rares et presque jamais liées à des édifices chrétiens. Au moins dans le nord de l'Italie, les populations romaines et ostrogothiques ont continué à respecter les traditions romaines, enterrant leurs morts dans des cimetières existants situés dans des zones péri-urbaines à l'extérieur des murs de la ville. Certaines de ces zones funéraires existaient depuis l'époque républicaine et impériale et contenaient des sépultures païennes et chrétiennes. D'autres semblent avoir été créés, toujours dans les faubourgs, au IIIe s. et se sont développées un siècle plus tard en de vastes zones funéraires chrétiennes. Les véritables changements dans les pratiques funéraires à l'intérieur des villes ne commenceront qu'à partir de la fin du VIe s. avec la multiplication des sépultures dispersées et, plus tard encore, le développement des cimetières intra-muros liés aux chapelles privées et, plus rarement, aux églises épiscopales.

Pratiques funéraires dans la Sardaigne de l'Antiquité tardive : aperçu et potentiel

Mauro Puddu

Cet article offre un aperçu de l'état des recherches de l'archéologie funéraire dans la Sardaigne de l'Antiquité tardive. Il expose les problèmes les plus récurrents rencontrés par les archéologues travaillant dans ce domaine. Pour ce faire, cet article met en évidence certaines études clés renommées et les résultats récents provenant de fouilles majeures dans le sud et le centre de la Sardaigne, telles que Cornus et Pill'e Matta. Tout en fournissant une synthèse du travail effectué jusqu'à présent, cet article met en évidence un élément souvent négligé qui a récemment attiré davantage l'attention à l'échelle internationale : la manipulation des sépultures. Il s'agit d'une réutilisation structurée, souvent respectueuse, des tombes. En observant les interactions entre les communautés tardo-antiques et leur passé plus ou moins récent, cet article met en évidence le potentiel des études de manipulation funéraire pour répondre à certaines questions clés sur la Sardaigne de l'Antiquité tardive.

Rites funéraires en Sicile byzantine : nouvelles approches et découvertes

Valentina Caminneci, Maria Serena Rizzo et Martin Carver

Les premiers siècles de la Sicile byzantine présentent un répertoire complet des pratiques mortuaires méditerranéennes pour la période : tombes creusées dans la roche et creusées dans la terre (*formae*), tombes en pierre et à couvercle, niches voûtées (*arcosoli*), catacombes et chambres souterraines (*ipogei*), inhumations dans des sarcophages et des amphores (*enchytrismòs*), tombes creusées au niveau du sol (*sub divo*) et au-dessus du sol (*subdiali*). Les archéologues siciliens, depuis Paolo Orsi au XIXe s., ont apprécié et exploré cet héritage, s'interrogeant sur la signification de sa diversité, qu'elle

soit régionale, temporelle, sociale ou religieuse. Ce chapitre se concentre sur deux campagnes récentes d'un intérêt particulier: d'abord, celle d'Agrigente, qui parmi tous les lieux de sépulture byzantins en Sicile a été étudié de la manière la plus complète et la plus scientifique ; et deuxièmement, la contribution d'un projet du Conseil Européen de la Recherche intitulé *La Sicile en Transition* (SICTRANSIT) qui examine les pratiques mortuaires et les propriétés biomoléculaires de 253 individus dans 22 cimetières, dont 13 sont principalement byzantins. L'article discute des sépultures des périodes paléo-byzantine (du Ve au VIIIe s.) et médio-byzantine (IXe au XIIIe s.).

Sépultures romaines tardives en Slovénie

Kaja Stemberger

Ce chapitre examine l'état de la recherche sur les cimetières romains tardifs en Slovénie. Datée entre la fin du IIIe et le VIe siècle, et le VIe siècle, l'Antiquité tardive slovène coïncide avec le mouvement des langobardes de la Pannonie vers l'Italie et avec l'installation des Slaves sur le territoire slovène moderne. En conséquence, la période de l'Antiquité tardive généralement étudiée en même temps que le haut Moyen Âge dans les études slovènes, c'est-à-dire séparément de l'archéologie romaine et classique. Ce chapitre résume les recherches sur les sépultures de l'Antiquité tardive en Slovénie publiées jusqu'en 2018, et discute de certaines questions théoriques.

Mourir aux confins de l'Empire : pratiques funéraires dans la province de Scythie (IVe–VIIe s. apr. J.-C.)

Ciprian Crețu et Andrei D. Soficaru

Malgré le nombre important de sépultures découvertes en Scythie Mineure et datées entre le IVe et le VIIe s., une approche systématique des données mortuaires fait encore défaut. Cet article vise à combler ce manque. Après un bref historique, il discute des archives archéologiques disponibles et de l'état actuel des recherches, ainsi que des sujets majeurs tels que le paysage mortuaire et les diverses pratiques funéraires documentées dans la province du Bas-Danube à la fin de la période romaine et au début de la période byzantine.

Sépulture et société dans le monde grec pendant l'Antiquité tardive

Joseph F. Rife

L'étude de l'inhumation dans le monde grec de l'Antiquité tardive est confrontée à un grand nombre de données et à d'importantes questions historiques. Ce domaine, qui évolue lentement, a longtemps été influencé par des modes venues de l'archéologie classique, l'archéologie paléochrétienne et les études folkloriques. Les vestiges physiques des rituels funéraires, inégalement étudiés et publiés, nous informent sur les formes d'inhumation, les pierres tombales, le traitement des corps et des objets, et les cadres topographiques des sépultures. Les variations dans ces vestiges reflètent l'expression de différentes identités, y compris le statut, la famille, la profession, l'ethnicité et la nouvelle perspective chrétienne sur la mort. La variabilité des pratiques mortuaires peut être retracée dans l'espace, à la fois entre et surtout au sein des régions, ainsi qu'au fil du temps, de l'époque romaine à l'époque byzantine, ce qui révèle un changement de paradigme dans les concepts et les usages de l'inhumation dans l'Antiquité tardive.

Des nécropoles aux cimetières : pratiques funéraires dans l'Antiquité tardive (fin IIIe–VIIe s.) Sagalassos, Turquie du Sud-Ouest

Sam Cleymans et Peter Talloen

Cet article donne un aperçu de l'évolution des traditions et des croyances concernant la mort, l'inhumation et l'au-delà à la fin de l'Antiquité (fin du IIIe–VIIe s.) à Sagalassos (sud-ouest de la Turquie). L'Antiquité tardive est souvent considérée comme une phase de transition entre les pratiques païennes et chrétiennes. Pour comprendre ce changement progressif, cet article examine plusieurs aspects de la culture funéraire, allant du traitement des corps à la conception des tombes, en passant par les assemblages de biens funéraires, comme en témoignent les tombes tardo-antiques et les assemblages squelettiques fouillés à Sagalassos. Ainsi la continuité et le changement peuvent-ils être retracés de l'époque impériale (Ier–IIIe s.) à la fin de l'époque romaine (fin IIIe–Ve s.) et finalement au début de l'époque byzantine (VIe–VIIe s.). Dans l'ensemble, les données de Sagalassos montrent que de nombreuses pratiques considérées comme typiquement chrétiennes, telles qu'une conception de tombe modeste, se situaient dans la continuité de pratiques romaines impériales préexistantes ou romaines tardives dont le sens et l'intention changèrent avec l'avènement du Christianisme. De plus, les pratiques funéraires semblent avoir reflété des tendances plus larges de développement urbain qui sont également observées dans le centre monumental de Sagalassos.

L'archéologie des pratiques mortuaires de l'Antiquité tardive au Proche-Orient

Adam Bollók

Cet article offre un aperçu concis des principales tendances de l'archéologie mortuaire de l'Antiquité tardive dans les pays du Proche-Orient (Israël, Jordanie, Liban, Syrie et les territoires adjacents du sud-ouest et du nord). La première partie présente les caractéristiques générales des vestiges mortuaires et passe en revue les grands enjeux de l'archéologie funéraire de l'Antiquité tardive, avec un accent particulier sur les conséquences des pillages anciens et modernes. La deuxième partie présente quelques-unes des principales découvertes faites par les spécialistes locaux et les missions étrangères, et explore les principales préoccupations des communautés au moment de quitter et d'inhumer leurs morts.

L'archéologie de la mort et de la sépulture dans l'Égypte de l'Antiquité tardive

Elisabeth O'Connell

Le présent article soutient que la richesse des archives archéologiques de l'Egypte, y compris papyrologiques, est particulièrement pertinente pour démontrer les étapes successives de la mort, de l'inhumation et de la commémoration des individus et des communautés dans l'Antiquité tardive. Alors que l'Égypte faisait partie intégrante de l'Empire romain au IVe s., les archéologues de la période exploitent rarement son corpus de données. Or, ce matériel peut fournir un aperçu rare de divers marqueurs d'identité tels que le statut, le sexe, la langue, la religion et même 'l'origine ethnique' (c'est-à-dire l'ascendance réelle ou perçue). Cet article vise à introduire la nature et les limites de ces données (I), l'histoire du sujet, en particulier son fondement lors de la découverte des textiles 'coptes' (II), et l'état actuel du travail de terrain dans des sites de différentes régions d'Égypte (III). Une enquête régionale de ce genre constitue une première étape vers l'identification de ce qui est propre à l'Égypte et de ce qu'elle a en commun avec d'autres parties du monde tardo-antique.

Indices

Objects

Science

Places

LATE ANTIQUE
ARCHAEOLOGY

Series Editor
LUKE LAVAN

Late Antique Archaeology is published annually by Brill, based on papers given at the conference series of the same title, which meets annually in London. Contributions generally aim to present broad syntheses on topics relating to the year's theme, discussions of key issues, or try to provide summaries of relevant new fieldwork. Although papers from the conference meetings form the core of each volume, relevant articles, especially syntheses, are welcome from other scholars. All papers are subject to satisfying the comments of two anonymous referees, managed by the discretion of the editors. The editorial committee includes Albrecht Berger, Will Bowden, Kimberly Bowes, Averil Cameron, Beatrice Caseau, James Crow, Jitse Dijkstra, Sauro Gelichi, Jean-Pierre Sodini, Bryan Ward-Perkins, Emanuele Vaccaro and Enrico Zanini. The next volume, based on papers given at meetings in 2018–2019, will concern *Imperial and Royal Archaeologies of Late Antiquity*. Journal abbreviations follow those used by the *American Journal of Archaeology*, whilst literary sources are abbreviated according to the *Oxford Classical Dictionary* (3rd edn. Oxford 1999) xxix–liv and when not given here, following A. H. M. Jones *The Later Roman Empire* (Oxford 1964) vol. 2, 1462–76, then G. W. H. Lampe *A Patristic Greek Lexicon* (Oxford 1961).

For programme information and notes for contributors, with contact details, visit:
www.lateantiquearchaeology.wordpress.com

For submissions and ordering information visit:
www.brill.com/publications/journals/late-antique-archaeology